TORTS AND PERSONAL INJURY LAW

TORTS AND PERSONAL INJURY LAW

William Buckley

Lawyers Cooperative Publishing

Delmar
Publishers Inc.

Cover design by John Orozco
Cover image by NU-TECH Animation

Delmar Staff
Administrative Editor: Jay Whitney
Editing Supervisor: Judith Boyd Nelson
Production Supervisor: Larry Main
Design Coordinator: Karen Kunz Kemp

For information, address:

Delmar Publishers Inc.
3 Columbia Circle
Albany, New York 12212

Printed in the United States of America

   2 3 4 5 6 7 8 9 10 XXX 99 98 97 96 95 94 93

Library of Congress Cataloging-in-Publication Data

Buckley, William, 1958-
   Torts and personal injury law / William Buckley.
     p. cm.
   ISBN 0-8273-5056-2 (textbook)
   1. Torts—United States. 2. Personal injuries—United States.
3. Legal assistants—United States—Handbooks, manuals, etc.
I. Title.
KF1250.Z9B83   1993
346.7303′23—dc20
[347.306323]   92-23761
                                             CIP

CONTENTS

DEDICATION

This book is dedicated to Janet and our children, Daniel and Samantha, who also appear periodically throughout the book's hypotheticals. Without their support and encouragement, I would never have attempted or completed this project.

DELMAR PUBLISHERS INC.

 AND

LAWYERS COOPERATIVE PUBLISHING

ARE PLEASED TO ANNOUNCE THEIR PARTNERSHIP
TO CO-PUBLISH COLLEGE TEXTBOOKS FOR
PARALEGAL EDUCATION.

DELMAR, WITH OFFICES AT ALBANY, NEW YORK, IS A PROFESSIONAL EDUCATION PUBLISHER. DELMAR PUBLISHES QUALITY EDUCATIONAL TEXTBOOKS TO PREPARE AND SUPPORT INDIVIDUALS FOR LIFE SKILLS AND SPECIFIC OCCUPATIONS.

LAWYERS COOPERATIVE PUBLISHING (LCP), WITH OFFICES AT ROCHESTER, NEW YORK, HAS BEEN THE LEADING PUBLISHER OF ANALYTICAL LEGAL INFORMATION FOR OVER 100 YEARS. IT IS THE PUBLISHER OF SUCH RE-KNOWNED LEGAL ENCYCLOPEDIAS AS **AMERICAN LAW REPORTS, AMERICAN JURISPRUDENCE, UNITED STATES CODE SERVICE, LAWYERS EDITION,** AS WELL AS OTHER MATERIAL, AND FEDERAL- AND STATE-SPECIFIC PUBLICATIONS. THESE PUBLICATIONS HAVE BEEN DE-SIGNED TO WORK TOGETHER IN THE DAY-TO-DAY PRACTICE OF LAW AS AN INTEGRATED SYSTEM IN WHAT IS CALLED THE "TOTAL CLIENT-SERVICE LI-BRARY®" (TCSL®). EACH LCP PUBLICATION IS COMPLETE WITHIN ITSELF AS TO SUBJECT COVERAGE, YET ALL HAVE COMMON FEATURES AND EXTEN-SIVE CROSS-REFERENCING TO PROVIDE LINKAGE FOR HIGHLY EFFICIENT LEGAL RESEARCH INTO VIRTUALLY ANY MATTER AN ATTORNEY MIGHT BE CALLED UPON TO HANDLE.

INFORMATION IN ALL PUBLICATIONS IS CAREFULLY AND CONSTANTLY MON-ITORED TO KEEP PACE WITH AND REFLECT EVENTS IN THE LAW AND IN SOCIETY. UPDATING AND SUPPLEMENTAL INFORMATION IS TIMELY AND PROVIDED CONVENIENTLY.

FOR FURTHER REFERENCE, SEE:

AMERICAN JURISPRUDENCE 2D: AN ENCYCLOPEDIC TEXT COVERAGE OF THE COMPLETE BODY OF STATE AND FEDERAL LAW.

AM JUR LEGAL FORMS 2D: A COMPILATION OF BUSINESS AND LEGAL FORMS DEALING WITH A VARIETY OF SUBJECT MATTERS.

AM JUR PLEADING AND PRACTICE FORMS, REV:MODEL PRACTICE FORMS FOR EVERY STAGE OF A LEGAL PROCEEDING.

AM JUR PROOF OF FACTS: A SERIES OF ARTICLES THAT GUIDE THE READER IN DETERMINING WHICH FACTS ARE ESSENTIAL TO A CASE AND HOW TO PROVE THEM.

AM JUR TRIALS: A SERIES OF ARTICLES DISCUSSING EVERY ASPECT OF PARTICULAR SETTLEMENTS AND TRIALS WRITTEN BY 180 CONSULTING SPECIALISTS.

UNITED STATES CODE SERVICE: A COMPLETE AND AUTHORITATIVE ANNOTATED FEDERAL CODE THAT FOLLOWS THE EXACT LANGUAGE OF THE STATUTES AT LARGE AND DIRECTS YOU TO THE COURT AND AGENCY DECISIONS CONSTRUING EACH PROVISION.

ALR AND ALR FEDERAL: SERIES OF ANNOTATIONS PROVIDING IN-DEPTH ANALYSES OF ALL THE CASE LAW ON PARTICULAR LEGAL ISSUES.

U.S. SUPREME COURT REPORTS, L ED 2D: EVERY REPORTED U. S. SUPREME COURT DECISION PLUS IN-DEPTH DISCUSSIONS OF LEADING ISSUES.

FEDERAL PROCEDURE, L ED: A COMPREHENSIVE, A–Z TREATISE ON FEDERAL PROCEDURE—CIVIL, CRIMINAL, AND ADMINISTRATIVE.

FEDERAL PROCEDURAL FORMS, L ED: STEP-BY-STEP GUIDANCE FOR DRAFTING FORMS FOR FEDERAL COURT OR FEDERAL AGENCY PROCEEDINGS.

FEDERAL RULES SERVICE, 2D AND 3D: REPORTS DECISIONS FROM ALL LEVELS OF THE FEDERAL SYSTEM INTERPRETING THE FEDERAL RULES OF CIVIL PROCEDURE AND THE FEDERAL RULES OF APPELLATE PROCEDURE.

FEDERAL RULES DIGEST, 3D:ORGANIZES HEADNOTES FOR THE DECISIONS REPORTED IN FEDERAL RULES SERVICE ACCORDING TO THE NUMBERING SYSTEMS OF THE FEDERAL RULES OF CIVIL PROCEDURE AND THE FEDERAL RULES OF APPELLATE PROCEDURE.

FEDERAL RULES OF EVIDENCE SERVICE:REPORTS DECISIONS FROM ALL LEVELS OF THE FEDERAL SYSTEM INTERPRETING THE FEDERAL RULES OF EVIDENCE.

FEDERAL RULES OF EVIDENCE NEWS

FEDERAL PROCEDURE RULES SERVICE

FEDERAL TRIAL HANDBOOK, 2D

FORM DRAFTING CHECKLISTS: AM JUR PRACTICE GUIDE

GOVERNMENT CONTRACTS: PROCEDURES AND FORMS

HOW TO GO DIRECTLY INTO YOUR OWN COMPUTERIZED SOLO PRACTICE WITHOUT MISSING A MEAL (OR A BYTE)

JONES ON EVIDENCE, CIVIL AND CRIMINAL, 7TH

LITIGATION CHECKISTS: AM JUR PRACTICE GUIDE

MEDICAL LIBRARY, LAWYERS EDITION

MEDICAL MALPRACTICE — ALR CASES AND ANNOTATIONS

MODERN APPELLATE PRACTICE: FEDERAL AND STATE CIVIL APPEALS

MODERN CONSTITUTIONAL LAW

NEGOTIATION AND SETTLEMENT

PATTERN DEPOSITION CHECKLISTS, 2D

QUALITY OF LIFE DAMAGES: CRITICAL ISSUES AND PROOFS

SHEPARD'S CITATIONS FOR ALR

SUCCESSFUL TECHNIQUES FOR CIVIL TRIALS, 2D

STORIES ET CETERA — A COUNTRY LAWYER LOOKS AT LIFE AND THE LAW

SUMMARY OF AMERICAN LAW

THE TRIAL LAWYER'S BOOK: PREPARING AND WINNING CASES

TRIAL PRACTICE CHECKLISTS

2000 CLASSIC LEGAL QUOTATIONS

WILLISTON ON CONTRACTS, 3D AND 4TH

FEDERAL RULES OF EVIDENCE DIGEST: ORGANIZES HEADNOTES FOR THE DECISIONS REPORTED IN FEDERAL RULES OF EVIDENCE SERVICE ACCORDING TO THE NUMBERING SYSTEM OF THE FEDERAL RULES OF EVIDENCE.

ADMINISTRATIVE LAW: PRACTICE AND PROCEDURE

AGE DISCRIMINATION: CRITICAL ISSUES AND PROOFS

ALR CRITICAL ISSUES: DRUNK DRIVING PROSECU-
TIONS

ALR CRITICAL ISSUES: FREEDOM OF INFORMATION
ACTS

ALR CRITICAL ISSUES: TRADEMARKS

ALR CRITICAL ISSUES: WRONGFUL DEATH

AMERICANS WITH DISABILITIES: PRACTICE AND COM-
PLIANCE MANUAL

ATTORNEYS' FEES

BALLENTINE'S LAW DICTIONARY

CONSTITUTIONAL LAW DESKBOOK

CONSUMER AND BORROWER PROTECTION: AM JUR
PRACTICE GUIDE

CONSUMER CREDIT: ALR ANNOTATIONS

DAMAGES: ALR ANNOTATIONS

EMPLOYEE DISMISSAL: CRITICAL ISSUES AND
PROOFS

ENVIRONMENTAL LAW: ALR ANNOTATIONS

EXPERT WITNESS CHECKLISTS

EXPERT WITNESSES IN CIVIL TRIALS

FORFEITURES: ALR ANNOTATIONS

FEDERAL LOCAL COURT RULES

FEDERAL LOCAL COURT FORMS

FEDERAL CRIMINAL LAW AND PROCEDURE: ALR AN-
NOTATIONS

FEDERAL EVIDENCE

FEDERAL LITIGATION DESK SET: FORMS AND ANAL-
YSIS

PREFACE

Assembling the Torts Puzzle

Tort law can be puzzling to the beginning student, so this book applies the analogy of a puzzle to the study of the subject. With each chapter, the reader assembles additional pieces until the big picture becomes clearly visible, giving tort law a predictable pattern and approach.

The Plan Behind Torts and Personal Injury Law

This text attempts a complete overview of tort law. Chapter 1 introduces the reader to the American legal system. Chapter 2 summarizes tort legal analysis. Chapter 3 discusses intentional torts to persons. Chapter 4 focuses upon intentional torts to property. Chapter 5 considers intentional tort defenses. Chapter 6 is devoted to negligence. Chapter 7 penetrates special negligence actions, such as premises liability, vicarious liability, bailments, and negligent infliction of emotional distress. Chapter 8 addresses negligence defenses. Chapter 9 begins strict, or absolute, liability, a subject that is completed in Chapter 10, dealing with products liability. Chapter 11 touches on several special tort actions, such as nuisance, negligence per se, wrongful death, and wrongful life. Chapter 12 pertains to tort immunities. Chapter 13 discusses paralegal ethics.

Chapter Features

Chapters begin with an outline summary. Chapters 2 through 12 feature data-graphic torts to accompany the computer graphic videotape (discussed below). Each chapter ends with a summary, review questions, projects, and hypothetical problems and answers (except for chapter 1, which has no hypotheticals). Chapters 1 through 12 offer a running margin glossary identifying key terms throughout the text.

The text combines theoretical and practical applications. Accompanying each tort topic are hypothetical examples to illustrate how the abstract rules pertain to real life. Illustrative cases are included to portray the actual application of legal principles in appellate court opinions, legal encyclopedia summaries, and the *Restatement (Second) of Torts.*

Ancillary Materials

Several ancillary materials accompany the text. These include an instructional computer-animation videotape, an instructor's manual, a computerized test bank, and state-specific pocket-part supplements.

Data-Graphic Torts: A Unique Feature

One unique feature of this text are its accompanying computer-animation video "stills." The stills are geared to the data-graphic torts that begin chapters 2 through 12. As an instructional tool, it intertwines factual summaries from the hypotheticals with the computer-graphic images used as demonstrative evidence in such cases. The stills put this text on a technological cutting edge unique among comparable publications. No other paralegal text currently available includes this feature.

The Instructor's Manual

The instructor's manual provides a proposed lecture outline, summarizes chapter objectives, answers reprint case questions and project questions, suggests lecture hints, and supplies suggested readings for students.

The Computerized Test Bank

Most college textbooks include an accompanying test bank. Usually the bank is relegated to a bulging, soft-cover edition that is cumbersome to use and requires incessant retyping of questions. *Torts and Personal Injury Law* avoids this hassle by computerizing the test bank. The computer test bank furnishes an adaptable cache of examination questions and answers. Multiple choice and true/false questions are used for each chapter. These questions (and answers) also appear in the Instructor's Manual.

Acknowledgements

Torts and Personal Injury Law could not have been produced without the planning, insights, suggestions, and imaginations of many people. For their tireless efforts to create an interesting and challenging work, I thank my editors at Delmar (in particular, Jay Whitney), Graphics West, and Brooke Graves of Graves Editorial Service; Steven D. Nelson of the College of Great Falls, Great Falls, Montana, for his penetrating recommendations, especially in the areas of negligence and legal ethics; Deborah J. Kottel of the College of Great Falls, who introduced me to paralegal education; the American Law Institute, the National Law Journal, and the *Rutgers Computer & Technology Law Journal,* for graciously allowing use of reprinted portions of their scholarly materials; and all my legal assistant students, who taught me to teach. Most of the names used throughout the hypotheticals are variations of actual students' first names, although none are identifiable.

Additionally, I would like to acknowledge the excellent contributions of the following reviewers, whose insights have vastly improved the text:

Gordon Brown
North Shore Community College
Beverly, Massachusetts

Lisa Kivett Gilbreath
Southeastern Paralegal Institute
Dallas, Texas

Dennis J. Krystek
University of Southern Mississippi
Long Beach, Mississippi

Ellen O'Donnel
North Shore Community College
Beverly, Massachusetts

Cathy Okrent
Schenectady County Community College
Schenectady, New York

William Ott
Goldy Beacom College
Wilmington, Delaware

CHAPTER 1
Introduction to the American Legal System

DATA-GRAPHIC TORTS

Tort litigation enjoys the benefit of many state-of-the-art innovations that provide the parties with the most technologically advanced illustrations available. In tort lawsuits and criminal prosecutions, photography made its first appearance in the courtroom at the end of the nineteenth century. Gradually, black-and-white (and later color) photographs were accepted as demonstrative evidence and eventually became commonplace. Tort litigators took visual evidence further, using motion pictures into the 1960s and then moving to videotape in the late 1960s and early 1970s, to help prove their own, or disprove opponents', allegations.

Visual evidence has now taken the next giant step in the tort arena. *Computer-generated graphics* have become the newest evidentiary vehicle in tort lawsuits. Computers are used to simulate many tort situations: automobile accidents, injuries caused by defective products, toxic chemical seepage, body functions or medical procedures, the effects of physical injuries, the causes of and effects from harmful activities, and many other applications. What the jury could not have seen when it actually happened can, from other available evidence, be reconstructed and visually presented through the computer. These simulations, increasingly used in civil litigation during the early 1990s, offer advantages that photographs, audio recordings, and videotape lack—namely, the ability to present various possible sequences of events at the flick of a keyboard.

To keep pace with this new technology, this textbook offers "Data-Graphic Torts," a series of tort actions with accompanying videotape employing computer-animated tort simulations, provided courtesy of the NU-TECH™ CORPORATION, which produces computerized evidence for civil and criminal lawsuits. Chapter 2's Data-Graphic Torts section explains this new technology. In chapters 3 through 12, each Data-Graphic opener features a computer-graphic tort illustration from a NU-TECH™ video still. The videotape shows how these computer animations can be used to document or explain the factual issues in each problem, just as they would be used to amplify expert testimony in tort actions.

INTRODUCTION

The study of law resembles a jigsaw puzzle. There are hundreds of seemingly unrelated parts that appear totally different at first glance. These pieces may be classified by general legal concept (torts, contracts, property, civil procedure, evidence, etc.), but the distinctive vocabulary and unique orientation of each subject can be confusing at the beginning. With patience and careful study, these diverse segments begin to fit together into patterns. Finally, the complete legal picture appears, a composite of all the individual portions of the law. All are interconnected to complete a logical, comprehensible image.

Assembling the legal puzzle requires patience and commitment. The shape of each piece—the specific field of law, the special vocabulary, the analytical focus, the rules underlying the law—must be carefully examined. Soon it becomes clear that one has developed a new skill, *legal problem solving,* and connecting the pieces suddenly becomes much easier.

This text investigates one aspect of legal study, *tort law.* To begin this difficult but challenging endeavor, it may be most helpful to begin the puzzle at the edges, since the flat-sided pieces are easiest to find. These include the basic framework of legal study: the structure of federal and state legal systems, the sources of law, and the participants in the legal process.

The pieces to be identified and assembled in this chapter include:

- The federal and state court systems in the United States.
- The functions and structures of trial and appellate courts.

- Courts' jurisdiction to hear particular lawsuits or appeals.
- The relationship among constitutions, statutes, administrative rules and regulations, and common law as sources of American legal concepts.
- The types of precedent in court decisions.
- The uniformity and stability of the common law through precedent and stare decisis.
- The relationships between parties involved in a lawsuit.
- The differences between civil and criminal litigation.

1.1 FEDERAL AND STATE LEGAL SYSTEMS

When examining American governmental systems and, in particular, their judicial components, political scientists employ several approaches. These include examining the various levels of government and discussing court structures and jurisdiction. This section explores these topics.

Levels of Government

One method of analyzing the American legal system is to profile the different governmental bodies involved. There are three levels of government in the United States: federal, state, and local. Each level has three components: executive, legislative, and judicial.

Federal System

In the federal system, there are three branches of government: the executive, the legislative, and the judicial. The **executive branch** is directed by the president and enforces statutes enacted by the **legislative branch**, which is Congress. The executive branch also contains the president's *Cabinet,* which is composed of several *administrative agencies,* such as the Department of the Treasury and the Department of Health and Human Services. Somewhat between the executive and legislative branches is the so-called "fourth branch," the *independent regulatory agencies* such as the Securities and Exchange Commission and the Federal Trade Commission. These agencies derive their powers from Congress and key positions are appointed by the president. The **judicial branch** consists of the United States Supreme Court and the lower federal courts. Figure 1-1 illustrates the federal system.

State Systems

State governmental systems are also organized into executive, legislative, and judicial branches. At the state level, the governor heads the executive branch, enforcing the statutes passed by the state legislature, which is the legislative branch. The judicial branch is composed of the state supreme

---

LEGAL TERMS

executive branch
One of three branches of government at the federal, state, and local levels. The executive branch enforces and administers statutes enacted by the legislative branch. Examples include the president and the cabinet, governors, mayors, and administrative agencies.

legislative branch
One of three branches of government at the federal, state, and local levels. The legislative branch enacts statutes or ordinances that are subordinate only to constitutions in the hierarchy of law. Examples include Congress, state legislatures, city councils, and county commissions.

judicial branch
One of three branches of government at the federal, state, and local levels. The judicial branch conducts civil and criminal trials and resolves legal disputes between litigants. It also interprets legislation and examines the actions of the executive and legislative branches to determine if they are constitutional. Examples include the federal courts, state appellate courts, and local trial courts.

Executive Branch	Legislative Branch	Judicial Branch
President Cabinet agencies	Congress	United States Supreme Court United States Circuit Courts of Appeals United States District Courts United States Magistrates
	Independent regulatory agencies (so-called "fourth branch")	

FIGURE 1-1
Federal Governmental
System

court and, in many states, intermediate appellate courts, an arrangement that is explained in the next section.

Local Systems

City and county governments also use the three-branch system. At the local level, the executive branch is usually the office of the mayor or city manager. The legislative branch consists of the city or county council, which may be called by a variety of names, such as the Board of Commissioners. In some localities, these councils also perform executive functions in place of a mayor or city manager. This is especially true at the county level. The judicial branch consists of city and county courts. Figure 1-2 portrays a typical state and local governmental arrangement.

Types of Courts

When studying law, the judicial branch perhaps becomes most important, since so much is determined by prior court decisions. There are essentially two types of courts: trial and appellate.

Branch	Executive	Legislative	Judicial
State	Governor Administrative agencies	General Assembly	State supreme court Intermediate appellate courts
Local	Mayor or city manager City/County administrative agencies	City council County commissioners	City and county courts

FIGURE 1-2
Typical State and Local
Governmental Systems

Trial Courts

Trial courts decide particular lawsuits between litigants. They hear testimony, take evidence, and determine who wins or loses at trial.

Local trial courts may be called district courts, circuit courts, superior courts, municipal courts, city courts, county courts, magistrate courts, small claims courts, courts of common pleas, or justices of the peace. In the state of New York, trial courts are (surprisingly) called supreme courts, while the top court is called the New York Court of Appeals. Local trial courts are usually organized geographically by city, county, or district.

At the federal level, trial courts are called *United States District Courts.* There is at least one United States District Court in every state, United States Territory, and the District of Columbia. Populous states, such as Texas or California, have several districts defined by geographical description (Western District, Northern District, etc.). United States District Courts try cases involving federal statutes or treaties, admiralty and maritime law disputes, and questions of United States constitutional law. They also review decisions of federal administrative agencies. United States District Courts may also hear cases concerning state law when the parties are residents of different states or countries (called *diversity of citizenship*) and the claims being litigated exceed $50,000. *United States Magistrates* are the federal equivalent of county justices of the peace. Overburdened United States District Courts often "boot down" cases to magistrates who will conduct the trials subject to district court review.

Judges and Juries

Trials may be conducted with or without a jury. Those with juries are, not surprisingly, called **jury trials**, while those without juries are called **bench trials**. In a jury trial, the jury decides factual issues, such as the speed of the vehicles involved in a collision, the condition of the pavement at the accident site, and which witnesses have presented the most credible description of events. Thus, the jury is called the **trier-of-fact**, because it weighs the evidence to decide what actually occurred in the case. The judge, on the other hand, acts as the **arbiter-of-law**, which means that he or she decides any legal questions, such as admissibility of certain evidence or whether to grant certain procedural motions by the litigants' attorneys. In a bench trial, the judge must serve as both the trier-of-fact and the arbiter-of-law, as no jury is involved.

Appellate Courts

Appellate courts review the decisions of trial courts to determine if the trial judge made the correct rulings to apply the law to the facts of the case. Appellate courts examine the trial transcripts to determine if the trial judge committed any legal errors that prejudiced the outcome of the case.

State supreme court
State intermediate courts of appeals
Local trial courts District, circuit, superior, common pleas, county, city, small claims, magistrate, justices of the peace

FIGURE 1-3
Typical State and Local Court Systems

Such errors are called *reversible* because they require the appellate court to reverse the lower court's decision and **remand**, or send back, the case to the trial court with instructions on how to resolve the pertinent issues. It is extremely rare for an appellate court to reconsider the factual findings of the jury or judge, since the appellate judges were not present at the trial and would not be in as good a position as were the jury or judge to make factual conclusions.

Several states have intermediate courts of appeals to evaluate trial appeals, and all states have supreme courts that may in turn review the decisions of the intermediate appellate courts (or hear appeals directly from the trial courts, if there are no intermediate courts in a state). The highest or "supreme court" of a few states may be called something different, such as New York's Court of Appeals. Figure 1-3 provides an example of a state and local judicial arrangement, with the state supreme and intermediate appellate courts above the local trial courts. Recall that the local trial courts are called by different names in different cities or counties. The illustration lists many of the most common terms used, although no single locality uses all of them.

In the federal system, the United States Circuit Courts of Appeals review United States District Court decisions and the United States Supreme Court may ultimately examine these circuit court findings. The United States Supreme Court may also elect to consider decisions of state supreme courts that involve constitutional questions. There are 13 federal circuits: one through eleven, the District of Columbia, and a special Federal Circuit that hears trade-oriented appeals. The numbered circuits cover specific geographic regions of the country and review decisions from United States District Courts within the same geographic area. The special Federal Circuit court hears appeals from the Court of International Trade (a special federal trial court formerly known as the United States Customs Court), the United States Claims Court (another special federal trial court formerly known as the Court of Claims), the International Trade Commission, and other United States District Courts. Figure 1-4 details the federal court system.

Jurisdiction

Whether a lawsuit may be filed and heard in a particular court depends upon the court's jurisdiction. Generally, **jurisdiction** is the court's

arbiter-of-law
The role of the judge in a trial. As arbiter-of-law, the judge decides all issues of law in the lawsuit, including admissibility of evidence and granting or denial of the litigants' motions.

appellate courts
Courts that review the decisions of trial courts to determine if the trial judge made the correct rulings to apply the law to the facts of the case. Appellate courts examine the trial transcripts to determine if the trial judge committed any legal errors that prejudiced the outcome of the case. Examples of appellate courts include the United States Supreme Court, United States Circuit Courts of Appeals, and state supreme courts.

remand
The decision of an appellate court to send a case back to the trial court with instructions as to how certain legal issues should be correctly decided. This term is often used with *reversed*, which means that the appellate court overturned the trial court's decision in a case.

United States Supreme Court
13 United States Circuit Courts of Appeals
United States District Courts (including specialty Bankruptcy and Tax Courts) United States Claims Court United States Court of International Trade
United States Magistrates

FIGURE 1-4
Federal Court System

authority (1) to try certain types of cases, and (2) to bind the parties involved in the lawsuit by its decisions. These two aspects of jurisdiction are different and thus must be explained in detail.

Subject Matter Jurisdiction

Courts are given the power to try certain types of cases by constitutions or statutes; this is called **subject matter jurisdiction**. Juridiction may be further subdivided into six categories: original, exclusive, concurrent, general, limited, and appellate.

A court with **original jurisdiction** has been given the authority to decide the outcomes of trials. This is the court in which the lawsuit is first filed. This would be a United States District Court at the federal level, or one of the trial courts at the local level (which were discussed previously).

A court with **exclusive jurisdiction** is the only court in which certain types of lawsuits may be filed. For instance, United States Bankruptcy Courts handle all bankruptcy lawsuits.

Many courts have **concurrent jurisdiction**, which enables them to try the same types of lawsuits. For example, a justice of the peace may be able to hear the same lawsuit as a small claims court. United States District Courts may try cases involving a state's laws when there is diversity of citizenship and $50,000-plus claims in dispute, but such lawsuits could also be tried by that state's courts.

A court with **general jurisdiction** has the right to try a lawsuit involving any type of law, except for special restricted types such as bankruptcy. For example, a county superior court has general jurisdiction to hear any civil or criminal lawsuits involving that state's laws.

A court with **limited jurisdiction** may only try cases involving that court's specialty. For instance, in the local arena, probate courts may hear only probate cases; small claims courts may try only cases in which the amount in dispute is less than a certain dollar amount (often $5,000 or less); municipal courts may hear only cases involving violations of city ordinances.

A court with **appellate jurisdiction** has the authority to review the decisions of lower trial and appellate courts. For example, the United States

Supreme Court has appellate jurisdiction over all the federal circuit and district courts. The Michigan Supreme Court has appellate jurisdiction over the Michigan Court of Appeals and all trial courts in Michigan.

Jurisdiction over Parties

As previously indicated, subject matter jurisdiction may be geographical or categorical. In addition to subject matter jurisdiction, courts also must have jurisdiction over the participants or the claims disputed in the lawsuit. There are two situations in which this type of jurisdiction occurs: first, jurisdiction over the parties themselves and second, jurisdiction over the object itself in dispute. These are called **in personam** (personal) and **in rem** (object) **jurisdiction**, respectively. **Quasi in rem jurisdiction** exists when courts must decide the ownership rights to a specific piece of property between litigants.

In Personam Jurisdiction In personam jurisdiction exists when the trial court has authority over the actual persons involved in a lawsuit. A state court has in personam jurisdiction over residents of that state. Thus, trial courts in Ohio have personal jurisdiction over Ohio residents. If a Pennsylvania citizen conducts business in Ohio, then Ohio courts would have personal jurisdiction over him or her.

In Rem & Quasi In Rem Jurisdiction In rem jurisdiction exists when the trial court has authority over the object (or "thing," which is what *rem* means) involved in the lawsuit. This normally involves property rights that are being disputed. For instance, in a probate case, a probate court in Texas has in rem jurisdiction to supervise the estate's administration if some of the property of the estate is situated in Texas. Most cases, however, involve a combination of personal and object jurisdiction. To illustrate, consider a Nevada resident who owns land in Connecticut. He wishes to sell the property to a Connecticut resident, so he travels to Connecticut to complete the sale. A dispute arises as to whether the Nevada resident has marketable title to the real estate. The Connecticut courts would have personal jurisdiction over at least the Connecticut resident and, under the civil procedural theory of minimum contacts, also over the Nevada resident. The Connecticut courts would also have quasi in rem jurisdiction, because the Connecticut courts would be called upon to decide the litigants' rights to the Connecticut property.

Knowing the structure of the American legal system is simply the first piece of the tort law puzzle. Learning the sources of American law is a connecting piece.

concurrent jurisdiction
Several courts that have the authority to try the same types of cases. For instance, a county small claims court often may hear the same civil cases as a municipal court. Justices of the peace and state district courts often hear the same types of criminal cases.

general jurisdiction
A court having the right to try a lawsuit involving any type of law. In the state systems, most counties have courts that may try all civil or criminal cases. These are often called district, superior, or circuit courts.

limited jurisdiction
A court's authority to try only certain types of lawsuits. For example, small claims courts often hear only civil cases involving claims under a certain dollar amount, such as $5,000 or less.

appellate jurisdiction
An appellate court's authority to hear appeals from trial or lower appellate court decisions. Examples include the United States Supreme Court, the United States Circuit Courts of Appeals, and the state supreme and intermediate appellate courts.

in personam jurisdiction
Personal jurisdiction. The trial court's authority to make binding decisions over the actual persons involved in the lawsuit. For example, state courts have in personam jurisdiction over state residents.

1.2 SOURCES OF LAW

The American legal system derives its law essentially from four sources: constitutions, statutory law, administrative rules and regulations, and common law.

Constitutions

Constitutions are the highest form of law in this country. The United States Constitution is the supreme law of the land. Each state has its own constitution, which is the ultimate source of law within that state but is subordinate to the federal constitution. Constitutions are primarily designed to limit governmental power against the public and to protect fundamental liberties such as free speech or due process of law. When the original United States Constitution was drafted in 1787, it established the organization and powers of the federal government, along with certain civil liberties which the federal government could not violate. These civil liberties are guaranteed in the *Bill of Rights*, which consists of the first 10 amendments to the United States Constitution. These freedoms are made mostly applicable to state and local governments by the Fourteenth Amendment. The United States Constitution has been amended 26 times, often expanding but sometimes restricting our freedom as citizens against the authority of government.

Statutory Law

Statutory law is the next lower rung on the legal ladder. Statutes are enacted by legislatures, which include Congress on the federal level, state legislatures on the state level, and city or county councils on the municipal level (which enact statutes commonly called *ordinances*). Statutory law must comply with broad constitutional restrictions. All legislative acts at every stage of government must obey the United States Constitution and state and local legislation must also comply with that state's constitution.

Administrative Rules and Regulations

The next lower rung on the legal ladder is **administrative rules and regulations**, which are issued (or *promulgated*) by administrative agencies to enforce or clarify statutes or ordinances. At the federal level, Congress passes a statute authorizing an administrative agency to provide rules to regulate a particular type of activity. Statutes of this sort are called *enabling acts*, because they enable the agency to regulate. Thus, for example, Congress has given the Department of the Interior the power to regulate and manage federal public lands. Congress has also given the Federal Communications Commission authority to regulate television and radio broadcast

LEGAL TERMS

in rem jurisdiction
Object jurisdiction. The trial court's authority to make binding decisions over the object, or thing, in dispute in a lawsuit. This usually involves disputed property rights. *Rem* is Latin for "thing."

licensing. At the state level, the legislature gives state administrative agencies regulatory power just as Congress does at the federal tier.

Administrative rules and regulations cannot exceed or contradict what legislatures have provided for in their statutes. Still, in practice rules and regulations carry as much weight as statutes.

Common Law

The lowest rung on the legal ladder is **common law**, or *judge-made law*. Common law is comprised of court decisions, issued primarily by state appellate courts reviewing the judgments of trial courts that have been appealed by one or more of the parties involved in the lawsuit. Appellate court opinions collectively constitute the common law. Centuries of judicial decrees in England became part of the American common law during colonial times. One exception is Louisiana, which derived its law from French civil law (and does not use the term "common law") and the Napoleonic Code (statutory law). After the United States secured its independence, American courts further expanded and developed the common law through their own decrees.

Varieties of Common Law

The common law often differs among the states, since each state's appellate courts issue their own opinions on a case-by-case basis. Thus, the common law in California may differ substantially from the common law of Idaho, although there are probably similarities in general legal concepts. For example, every state uses comparable legal theories to define broad concepts, such as what makes a contract or what constitutes products liability. The fine points of common law, however, will almost certainly vary between states. One should become aware of the common law in one's own state to be certain what "the law" may be there. Recall, too, that each state has its own legislature that enacts its own statutes. These also vary widely from state to state.

Hierarchy of Sources of Law

Common law decisions cannot contradict statutes, administrative rules and regulations, or constitutions. There is a clear hierarchy among these sources of law. Constitutions reign supreme, followed by statutes and ordinances, followed by administrative rules and regulations, followed by the common law. Figure 1-5 outlines this structure.

Common Law Precedents

What makes common law useful is its predictability and uniformity. The legal rules expressed in previous appellate court decisions are valuable

quasi in rem jurisdiction
Exists when courts must decide the ownership rights to a specific piece of property between litigants. Occurs most often when the rights to property located in one state are disputed in a lawsuit in that state's courts.

constitutions
The highest form of law in the United States. The United States Constitution is the supreme law of the land. Each state has its own constitution which is the supreme law of that state, subordinate only to the federal constitution.

statutory law
Statutes and ordinances enacted by legislatures. Statutory law is subordinate only to constitutions in the hierarchy of law.

administrative rules and regulations
Rules issued or promulgated by administrative agencies to enforce or interpret statutes and ordinances. These agencies are granted authority to make regulations by enabling acts passed by legislatures.

common law
Judge-made law. Common law is composed of court decisions issued primarily by state appellate courts. Each state has its own common law, which may vary considerably between states. American common law is based upon English common law and is centuries old.

Federal Hierarchy	State Hierarchy
United States Constitution	State constitution
Federal statutes	State statutes
Federal administrative rules and regulations	State administrative rules and regulations
	Common law

FIGURE 1-5
Hierarchy of Sources
of Law

guides to how cases should be decided today and tomorrow. This enables citizens to predict how courts will rule, and this predictability enables people to anticipate legal problems by knowing the general legal rules that courts will follow. Common law also permits uniformity in decision making. Courts in a town follow the same state common law as courts in other communities in that state. For these reasons, common law decisions are called **precedents**, which means that they direct today's courts in resolving legal questions based on the rules of law as defined in previous appellate opinions.

Mandatory precedents are those which must be followed in a particular court system. For example, decisions by a state supreme court must be followed by lower appellate and trial courts in that state.

Persuasive precedents are decrees that come from courts outside a particular state or federal jurisdiction. For example, a decision of the Montana Supreme Court is binding as mandatory precedent on Montana trial courts, but it would be persuasive precedent to the Iowa Supreme Court. It is called persuasive because the court hearing an appeal may adopt or reject the precedent's ruling, depending upon whether the appellate court is persuaded by the precedent. Consider another example on the federal level. Decisions by the United States Court of Appeals for the Fifth Circuit are mandatory precedent for the Fifth Circuit court itself (since its own decisions bind it) and on all United States District Courts within the Fifth Circuit. Such decisions, however, would be merely persuasive to United States District Courts in other circuits, as well as to the other United States Circuit Courts of Appeals and any state courts.

Stare Decisis

Appellate courts are reluctant to change precedents, because stability and predictability are enhanced when the law remains relatively constant over the decades. This hesitancy to modify precedents is called **stare decisis**, which translates from the Latin as, "Let the decision stand." This doctrine acts as a restraint on appellate judges not to discard long-standing legal principles that have been handed down through the generations as the common law.

LEGAL TERMS

precedent
Common law decisions made by courts in the past, which direct today's courts in deciding legal issues in litigation. There are two types of precedent: mandatory and persuasive. *Mandatory precedents* must be followed by the courts of a particular system. *Persuasive precedents* are nonbinding decisions originating from outside a particular court system. Precedents may be changed by the courts that issued them or by higher appellate courts within the same system.

Changing Precedents

Stare decisis does not mean that common law is unalterable, however. A court issuing an opinion may later change the precedent it established. For example, the United States Supreme Court declared in 1896 that it was constitutional to permit "separate but equal" public facilities for different races. In 1954, the Court overruled this precedent and declared that governmental discrimination on the basis of race or color is unconstitutional. No court beneath the United States Supreme Court could have accomplished this, however. Precedents may be changed or discarded only by the courts making them or by courts with superior appellate powers. For instance, the United States Supreme Court may overrule any United States Circuit or District Court or even state supreme courts on constitutional law matters. The California Supreme Court may overrule the California intermediate appellate courts. But the Indiana Court of Appeals may not overrule the Indiana Supreme Court, because the court of appeals is a subordinate appellate court. The Florida Supreme Court cannot overrule the Arkansas Supreme Court, because they are not in the same jurisdiction.

Sources of Tort Law

Tort law is derived both from common and statutory law. Legislatures often enact statutes to supplement, modify, or supersede common law tort principles. For example, under the common law, the government was exempt from tort liability under the doctrine of sovereign immunity. Today, many state legislatures have passed statutes to abolish sovereign immunity for most tort claims against the government. Courts may turn the tables on the legislatures by issuing new common law rulings interpreting the meaning of statutes. In this way "the law" matures, with both courts and legislatures adjusting the law to meet the changing needs of society.

1.3 PARTICIPANTS IN THE LEGAL PROCESS

The vocabulary surrounding lawsuits provides several important pieces of the torts puzzle. This section examines who is involved in litigation.

Civil versus Criminal Lawsuits

Litigation is simply another term for a *lawsuit*, which is a dispute between two or more parties regarding civil or criminal law issues. **Civil law** involves disputes between private parties and defines legal rights and obligations between them. Torts are part of civil law. **Criminal law** defines conduct prohibited by legislative bodies, which also prescribe punishments for violations.

stare decisis
Latin for "Let the decision stand." A legal doctrine that restricts appellate courts from changing common law precedents frequently. The concept adds stability to the law by honoring long-standing, accepted legal concepts affirmed through generations of court decisions.

litigation
Another term for lawsuit. A dispute between two parties regarding civil or criminal law, in which the parties ask the courts to resolve legal conflicts.

civil law
Law that pertains to disputes between private parties and defines legal rights and obligations between parties. Tort law is an example.

criminal law
Law that defines conduct prohibited by legislative bodies, for which penalties, including fines and imprisonment, are prescribed.

Parties in Civil Litigation

The parties to a civil lawsuit include the plaintiff, the defendant, and possibly third parties. The **plaintiff** is the party that has allegedly suffered some legal wrong at the hands of the **defendant**, the party responsible for infringing upon the plaintiff's legal rights. The plaintiff files a lawsuit against the defendant, using the courts as the forum to argue that the defendant should be held responsible for the plaintiff's injuries and should accordingly compensate the plaintiff for its losses. The plaintiff's legal claim is called a **cause of action**. The plaintiff may have several causes of action against the defendant. For instance, if Audrey bought a diseased horse from the Happy Horse Stables and was led to believe that the horse was healthy when, in fact, it was not, she would probably claim fraud and breach of warranty in her lawsuit. She would thus have two causes of action. If the plaintiff wins against the defendant in the lawsuit, the plaintiff is said to have received a **judgment** against the defendant. The judgment will likely order the defendant to pay the plaintiff money damages as compensation.

Third-Party Joinder

Third parties may be brought (or *joined*) into the litigation if they may have caused or contributed to the losses alleged. For example, if Wilbur pulls his automobile in front of Tom, causing Tom to swerve his truck and collide with Jane (a pedestrian), then Jane (the plaintiff) might sue Tom (the defendant), who in turn would bring Wilbur into the lawsuit as a third-party defendant, since Wilbur was actually responsible for the sequence of events that caused Jane's injuries. This process of bringing in third parties is called **joinder**.

Multiple Parties

A lawsuit may involve multiple plaintiffs or multiple defendants, depending upon the number of parties participating in the activities that led to the lawsuit. If Julia purchased a defective lawn mower that exploded and injured her, she (as the plaintiff) might sue the hardware store at which she bought the mower, as well as the wholesale distributor and manufacturer. All these parties would be multiple defendants in the same lawsuit. If Julia and her next-door neighbor, Sidney, were both maimed in the mower blast, they might join in a single lawsuit as multiple plaintiffs, although each would be pursuing his or her own cause of action.

Parties in Criminal Litigation

The parties in a criminal lawsuit are different from those in a civil action. In criminal cases, the public, through the authority of the state (or, if federal, the United States), brings the accused criminal, the defendant, to

---

LEGAL TERMS

plaintiff
   The party filing a lawsuit. The plaintiff is the party whose legal rights have allegedly been infringed by the defendant.

defendant
   The party against whom a lawsuit is filed. The defendant allegedly infringed upon the legal rights of the plaintiff, who filed the lawsuit. In tort law, the *tortfeasor* is normally the defendant. In criminal proceedings, the defendant is alleged to have violated the criminal law.

cause of action
   The plaintiff's legal claim(s) against the defendant. Frequently, the plaintiff has more than one cause of action in a lawsuit.

judgment
   A court's decision in favor of one of the litigants. At the trial court level, judgment is given either to the plaintiff or the defendant.

joinder
   The process of bringing third parties into a lawsuit. Most often, a third-party defendant is joined into a lawsuit because of his or her liability to the plaintiff.

court to determine his or her guilt or innocence. Of course, masses of citizens do not actually haul defendants bodily into the courtroom. Instead, the government provides a special officer, called the prosecutor or district attorney in many localities, who files the criminal charges against the defendant on the public's behalf. At the state level, this official might be called the attorney general; at the federal tier, he or she would be the United States Attorney serving in the Department of Justice under the United States Attorney General. Criminal lawsuits differ from their civil counterparts in that criminal prosecutions are intended to convict and punish the criminal offender, while civil lawsuits are designed to settle disputes between private parties. In criminal actions, the convicted defendant may be punished by imprisonment or fined by the government. In civil suits, however, the defendant who loses judgment to the plaintiff must compensate the plaintiff directly.

Burdens of Proof in Civil and Criminal Litigation

Civil and criminal law may be further distinguished in terms of burdens of proof.

Civil Actions

In a civil lawsuit, the plaintiff must prove her case by a **preponderance of the evidence**, meaning that she must convince the judge or jury that her version of the facts is correct and that she is entitled to judgment. This degree of proof is sometimes called presenting a **prima facie case**, or "crossing the 51 percent line," since the plaintiff must "out-prove" the defendant by over half the evidence. In certain cases, such as those involving fraud, misrepresentation, intentional infliction of emotional distress, and probate contests, the plaintiff must prove her case by **clear and convincing evidence**, which is more difficult than a mere preponderance.

Criminal Actions

By contrast, in a criminal lawsuit the prosecutor must prove the case **beyond a reasonable doubt**. This means that the judge or jury must believe the defendant's guilt without significant reservations. This burden of proof is much more difficult than either of the proof levels required in civil cases. This heavier burden on the government exists to protect defendants from overzealous prosecutors who might succeed in convicting innocent individuals with less evidence if the proof requirements were easier to satisfy.

Shifting the Burden of Proof

Once the plaintiff (or prosecutor) has satisfied his burden of proof, the burden shifts to the defendant, who must now disprove the plaintiff's or

preponderance of the evidence
In civil litigation, the burden of proof that the plaintiff must satisfy to convince the judge or jury that he or she is entitled to judgment. This is sometimes called "crossing the 51 percent line," since the plaintiff must "out-prove" the defendant by over half the evidence. More often, it is referred to as making a prima facie case.

prima facie case
The plaintiff's burden of proof in civil cases. Normally this is equivalent to the preponderance of the evidence.

clear and convincing evidence
In particular civil cases, usually involving certain intentional torts, the plaintiff's burden of proof to convince the judge or jury to award judgment in his or her favor.

beyond a reasonable doubt
The prosecutor's burden of proof in a criminal case. The defendant must be proven guilty of having violated the criminal law beyond a reasonable doubt by the judge or jury. This is the most difficult burden of proof to meet.

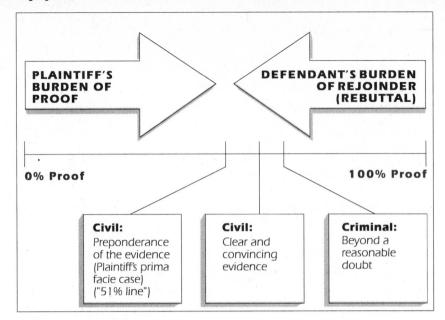

FIGURE 1-6

Battle of the Burdens of Proof in Civil and Criminal Cases

LEGAL TERMS

burden of rejoinder (or rebuttal)
The defendant's burden of proof to disprove the plaintiff's evidence in a lawsuit.

appellant
The party that lost at trial is called the appellant or *petitioner* on an appeal. The appellant argues that the trial court erred in its decisions in the case and that the appellate court should reverse the trial court's decisions.

petitioner
The party that lost at trial is called the petitioner or *appellant* on an appeal. The petitioner argues that the trial court erred in its decisions in the case and that the appellate court should reverse the trial court's decisions.

prosecutor's case. Thus, the defendant must persuade the judge or jury that her version of the facts entitles her to judgment or dismissal of the plaintiff's or prosecutor's complaint. This is called the defendant's **burden of rejoinder** or **burden of rebuttal**. Figuratively, the defendant must "push" the plaintiff's proof backwards across the plaintiff's proof lines. Figure 1-6 illustrates this process of battling burdens of proof.

Parties in Appellate Cases

After the trial judge or jury returns a decision, the case may be appealed to an appellate court. The party appealing the case is called the **appellant** or the **petitioner**, and is normally the party that lost at trial. The party that won at trial is called the **appellee** or the **respondent**.

SUMMARY

1.1. The American legal system is comprised of separate executive, legislative, and judicial branches at the federal and state levels. There are two types of courts in the judiciary: trial and appellate. Trial courts decide the outcomes of lawsuits. Appellate courts review the decisions of trial courts and issue decrees that become part of the common law. When issuing opinions, appellate courts look to past decisions to see what rules of law best apply to the cases before them. These previously resolved cases are called precedents. Stare decisis discourages hasty changes in common law. Trial and appellate courts have different jurisdictions, depending upon their power to hear the subject matter of the case and to make decisions binding upon the litigants.

1.2. American law comes from constitutions, statutes, ordinances, administrative rules and regulations, and common law. All sources of law in the United States must comply with constitutions, with the United States Constitution being the supreme law of the land, and with each state's constitution being supreme in that particular state, subordinate only to the United States Constitution. Statutes and regulations are also superior to common law.

1.3. In a civil lawsuit, the plaintiff sues the defendant to recover legal remedies for violations of legal rights. In a criminal lawsuit, the public, through a governmental prosecutor, files criminal charges against the defendant. Civil litigation resolves disputes between private parties, while criminal litigation attempts to punish and deter violators of criminal statutes. The burdens of proof in civil cases (preponderance of the evidence or clear and convincing evidence) are easier to achieve than in criminal cases (beyond a reasonable doubt).

appellee
The party that won at trial is called the appellee or *respondent* on an appeal. The appellee argues that the trial court was correct in its decisions in the case and that the appellate court should affirm the trial court's decisions.

respondent
The party that won at trial is called the respondent or *appellee* on an appeal. The respondent argues that the trial court was correct in its decisions in the case and that the appellate court should affirm the trial court's decisions.

REVIEW QUESTIONS

1. Briefly outline the federal and state court systems. Indicate which courts are trial and which are appellate. How does your state's court structure compare with the generic state system discussed in this chapter? With the federal system?

2. Distinguish between jury and bench trials. How do they differ? How do their activities differ from those of appellate courts?

3. What are the specific types of subject matter jurisdiction? How are these different from the court's authority over the parties or the claims disputed in the litigation?

4. List the sources of law, beginning with the most powerful and ending with the least authoritative. Why should these sources be ordered in this way?

5. What are precedents? Are some more authoritative than others? Why should this be so?

6. Explain the process through which precedents are modified. Would you describe this mechanism as stable or dynamic? How might you explain the reasons for this stability or continual change?

7. List the different litigants in a civil and a criminal lawsuit. Compare how these parties are distinguishable. Might you explain this variation in terms of the separate goals sought in civil or criminal actions?

8. Explain how civil and criminal litigation differ. Who is the injured party and who is the injuring party in each? What are the separate goals of each? How does each party prove its case in each?

PROJECTS

1. How do statutes and ordinances become law in your state and city? What legislative bodies are responsible for enacting statutory law? Where might you obtain copies of your city's ordinances? Of your state's statutes?

2. How does the appeals process operate in your state's judicial system? Are there intermediate appellate courts between the trial courts and the state supreme court?

3. Is there more than one trial court in your city? If so, what are their different names? How do they correspond to the terms used in this chapter to describe local trial courts?

CHAPTER 2
Introduction to Torts and Legal Analysis

DATA-GRAPHIC TORTS

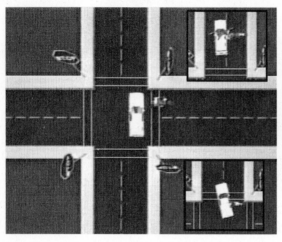

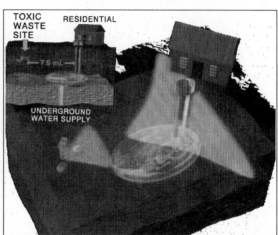

One of the special features of this textbook is its accompanying computer-animated videotape, which demonstrates a variety of computer-generated animations of various torts. The excellent simulation work is courtesy of the Nu-Tech Corporation™, a firm specializing in computer-generated graphics for litigation support.

Computer graphics have become an innovative complement to the tort litigator's evidentiary arsenal. The following excerpt from Sherman, "Moving Graphics," 14 *National Law Journal* 1, 32-33 (Apr. 6, 1992), discusses the importance of this new technological tool. Reprinted with the permission of *The National Law Journal,* Copyright, 1992. The New York Law Publishing Company.

[Trials are undergoing] a technological revolution that will allow lawyers to transform experts' dry, verbal testimony into dynamic, TV-like shows that can [. . .] play out for [jurors] an advocate's version of events. [. . .]

[Computer-generated a]nimation "will be used more and more in all trial arenas," says plaintiffs' attorney Frank L. Branson of Dallas' Law Offices of Frank L. Branson P.C., a pioneer in use of computer animation

in civil trials, where such high-tech visual aids in the past five years have become almost commonplace. [. . .]

Others agree. John M. Dedman, lawyer and director of training at the Houston-based National College of District Attorneys, says: "You are going to see a lot of it [in criminal trials], particularly in environmental prosecutions because you can show seepage and contamination a lot easier" with computer graphics. And Peter D. Barnett, a criminologist with the Richmond, Calif., consulting firm Forensic Science Associates, calls such animation "the wave of the future."

There is a lot of excitement about these technologies among the lawyers, forensic scientists and, not surprisingly, companies that produce them and are discovering a new market. [. . .]

Computer animation was first used in a 1979 airplane crash case, says Mr. [Alan] Treibitz [senior vice president at Englewood, Colo.'s Z-Axis Corp., one of the larger established companies offering computer animation to civil litigators]. The high price tag kept the use of such an aid confined largely to plane crash cases, partly because of the potentially huge liability.

But the overall cost of computers has been dropping dramatically, and the market for computer animations has been growing steadily—particularly in the last five years, he says. "Roughly speaking . . . the same sort of computer animation that five years ago would have cost $25,000 to $30,000 would now cost about $5,000." [. . .]

The price depends on how long an animation lasts, the number of characters involved and the amount of movement they make, says Mr. [Alexander] Jason [an investigative technologist in Pinole, Calif.] [. . .]

[According to Mr. Barry Krischer, a Florida defense counsellor,] "This [computer-generated graphics] is just an extension with new technology of a posed photograph."

INTRODUCTION

The first part of the torts puzzle, the American legal system, has been pieced together. This chapter begins assembling another section of the puzzle—namely, the definition of a tort, the three broad categories of torts, the history of tort law, the public policy objectives behind tort law, and analytical processes used to understand appellate court opinions and to solve hypothetical problems. Once these pieces are assembled, the first clear images of the "big picture" will begin to appear.

The puzzle pieces to be identified and assembled in this chapter include:

- Definitions of torts.
- An outline of intentional torts.
- The initial shape of negligence.
- The first shapes of strict (absolute) liability.
- The historical roots of tort law.
- The public policy objectives of tort law in terms of compensating injured parties, holding wrongdoers liable, and allocating losses across society.
- Development of an analytical framework to understand appellate court opinions.
- Construction of an analytical formula to solve hypothetical problems by applying the legal principles to the facts of the case.
- Assembly of an analytical formula that allows any tort law problem or question to be continuously narrowed to reveal the answer.
- Demonstration of how tort law analysis goes from the general to the specific.

2.1 TORTS DEFINED

A **tort** is a wrongful injury to a person or his or her property. The person inflicting the harm is called the **tortfeasor** (*feasor* meaning "doer"). The word *tort* is French, taken from the Latin *torquere* (meaning "to twist") to characterize behavior that warps or bends society's rules about avoiding harm to others. The French phrase *de son tort demesne* (meaning "in his

LEGAL TERMS

tort
A wrongful injury to a person or a person's property. There are three broad categories of torts: intentional torts, negligence, and strict (absolute) liability. Other torts include nuisance and wrongful death.

tortfeasor
The person who commits a tort. Translated from the Latin, the tortfeasor is the "doer" of the tort.

own wrong") was used to describe grievous misconduct between individuals and to assign blame to the responsible party.

Broad Categories of Tort Law

Tort law considers the rights and remedies available to persons injured through other people's carelessness or intentional misconduct. Tort law also holds persons in certain circumstances responsible for other people's injuries regardless of blame. Torts are commonly subdivided into three broad categories: intentional torts, negligence, and strict (or absolute) liability.

Intentional Torts

Intentional torts consist of actions that are designed to injure another person or that person's property. The tortfeasor intends a particular harm to result from the misconduct. There are several specific types of intentional torts: battery, assault, false imprisonment, infliction of emotional distress, fraud, misrepresentation, malicious prosecution, abuse of process, invasion of privacy, defamation (libel and slander), trespass, conversion, slander of title, disparagement of goods, and defamation by computer. Each of these is discussed in detail in later chapters. For now, a brief summary will provide a road map for later chapters.

Specific Intentional Torts: Brief Definitions **Battery** occurs when a tortfeasor touches another person without consent. **Assault** is an attempted battery. **False imprisonment** happens when an individual is intentionally confined against his or her will. **Infliction of emotional distress** results from someone's outrageous conduct that is designed to cause another to suffer anxiety, fright, or anguish. **Fraud** occurs when the tortfeasor intentionally makes false statements to entice someone to give up something of value to the tortfeasor. **Misrepresentation** exists when one person makes a false statement (or behaves so as) to deceive another individual. **Malicious prosecution** happens when a prosecutor purposefully and in bad faith files groundless criminal charges against a defendant. **Abuse of process** exists when a plaintiff maliciously uses the court system against a defendant to achieve some unlawful objective. **Invasion of privacy** occurs when someone publicly exploits another's private affairs in an unreasonably intrusive manner. **Defamation** is an injury to one's reputation in the community and may be inflicted by *libel,* which is written defamation, or *slander,* which is oral defamation. **Trespass** is unlawful or unreasonable interference with the use of someone's property. **Conversion** is wrongfully taking personal property from its rightful owner, either permanently or for an indefinite period of time. **Slander of title** happens when someone falsely and maliciously disparages the ownership rights that a legal owner has in his or

LEGAL TERMS

intentional torts
Torts in which the conduct is intended to harm another person or a person's property. All intentional torts include two elements: intent and injurious behavior.

battery
When a tortfeasor touches another person without consent.

assault
An attempted battery.

false imprisonment
When an individual is intentionally confined against his or her will.

infliction of emotional distress
Results from someone's outrageous conduct which is designed to cause another to suffer anxiety, fright, or anguish.

fraud
When the tortfeasor intentionally makes false statements to entice someone to give up something of value to the tortfeasor.

misrepresentation
When one person makes a false statement (or behaves so as) to deceive another individual.

malicious prosecution
When a prosecutor purposefully and in bad faith files groundless criminal charges against a defendant.

abuse of process
When a plaintiff maliciously uses the court system against a defendant to achieve some unlawful objective.

her property. **Commercial disparagement** occurs when one makes a false or misleading statement about a business to discourage the public from patronizing that business. **Defamation by computer** exists when personal information about an individual that is kept in a computer system is misused or is incorrect and results in injury to that person's reputation or ability to obtain credit.

Negligence

Negligence is the failure to exercise reasonable care to avoid injuring others. It is distinguishable from intentional torts in that negligence does not require the *intent* to commit a wrongful action; instead, the wrongful action itself is sufficient to constitute negligence. Intentional torts, as the name indicates, require the tortfeasor to intend to commit the wrongful act. What makes misconduct negligent is that the behavior was not reasonably careful and someone was injured as a result of this unreasonable carelessness.

Strict, or Absolute, Liability

Strict (or **absolute**) **liability** is the tortfeasor's responsibility for injuring another regardless of intent, negligence, or fault. The most important type of strict liability is *products liability,* a theory under which the manufacturer or other seller of an unreasonably dangerous or defective product is held liable for injuries the product causes. Strict liability is different from intentional torts in that intent to commit an absolute liability tort is irrelevant. Likewise, strict liability is distinguishable from negligence, because the tortfeasor is responsible under absolute liability regardless of how careful he or she might have been.

For the moment, these concepts are presented here to establish basic terminology and minimal definitions. Subsequent chapters explore each of these topics in greater detail.

The Unique Elements of Each Tort

Each type of tort contains its own unique elements. For instance, battery may be readily distinguished from defamation because it carries its own definition and rules that separate it from other intentional torts. Likewise, the elements of negligence are different from strict liability's components, and so on. The key to understanding tort law is to identify the type of broad tort category involved in the case. Ask whether the problem contains intentional torts [and, if so, which particular one(s)], negligence, or strict liability. Next, apply the appropriate rules of law to the specific facts of the case.

Like all forms of law, torts have undergone a long and interesting period of growth and development. Section 2.2 briefly examines the history of tort law.

invasion of privacy
When someone publicly exploits another's private affairs in an unreasonably intrusive manner.

defamation
Injury to one's reputation in the community; *libel* (written defamation) and *slander* (oral defamation).

trespass
Unlawful or unreasonable interference with the use of someone's property.

conversion
Wrongfully taking personal property from its rightful owner, either permanently or for an indefinite period of time.

slander of title
When someone falsely and maliciously disparages the ownership rights that a legal owner has in his or her property.

commercial disparagement
When one makes a false or misleading statement about a business to discourage the public from patronizing the business.

defamation by computer
When personal information about an individual that is kept in a computer system is misused or is incorrect and results in injury to that person's reputation or ability to obtain credit.

2.2 HISTORY OF TORT LAW

Tort law, like all American law, traces its origins to English and Western European history. After the Norman conquest of England in 1066, William the Conqueror brought Norman law (which itself was heavily influenced by Roman law) to intermingle with Anglo-Saxon and Celtic legal traditions. The result was the common law, which at the time was the underlying legal principles and social attitudes gleaned from generations of judicial decisions by local tribunals. Even today, the bulk of tort law has been derived from our common law heritage, as discussed in chapter 1.

The King's Writs

During the Middle Ages, much of this common law was passed on orally, although substantial portions were written down by scriveners, who were mostly monks or church clerics. Thus, common law often varied widely among localities, even those separated by only a few miles. To unify these divergent legal ideas, the king eventually established formal procedures by which crown subjects could petition the king's courts for redress. These formal processes were called the king's writs. Two writs were originally available for tortious conduct: the writ for trespass and the writ for trespass on the case.

Medieval Trespass

In medieval times, trespass was different from the modern offense that goes by the same name, which today involves wrongful interference with another person's use of his or her property. Beginning in the thirteenth century, *trespass* was defined as a serious breach of the king's peace. This breach included any acts that, directly and by use of force, caused injuries to other persons or their property. For example, if Tom punched Harry in the face, this was a battery and would be considered trespass under the king's writs; Tom's offense was direct and forcible. The king's courts punished trespassers in much the same way modern courts often punish criminal offenders, through monetary fines.

Trespass on the Case

Trespass on the case was intended to remedy breaches of the peace that were not direct or forceful. For instance, if Tom cut down a tree and thereby frightened Harry's horse, from which Harry was thrown and injured as a result, this would be an indirect (although easily connected) sequence of events. Although Tom's cutting the tree was not aimed toward Harry, Harry still was hurt as a result. Thus, Tom's conduct would be viewed as a trespass on the case under medieval English law.

Evolution from Medieval Trespass Writs to Modern Tort Law

The king's trespass writs were sufficient during the Middle Ages, when life was rural and essentially uncomplicated. However, as society urbanized and the population increased, these writs proved unable to remedy a variety of conflicts, especially those associated with technological developments such as machines and new forms of power and transportation. Tort law had to expand to permit wrongfully injured persons to seek relief in court. During the eighteenth and nineteenth centuries, English tort law began to shift from the old trespass writs to torts involving intent and fault, which are known today as intentional torts and negligence. This evolution was copied in the United States. Gradually, the common law grew to include the modern torts discussed throughout this text. Today's tort law is a combination of English and American common law plus statutory law.

What does tort law seek to accomplish? Section 2.3 examines the social and economic purposes that influence, and are influenced by, tort law.

2.3 PUBLIC POLICY OBJECTIVES IN TORT LAW

Like every aspect of our legal system, there are several purposes underlying tort principles. These include (1) protecting persons and property from unjust injury by providing legally enforceable rights; (2) compensating victims by holding accountable those persons responsible for causing such harms; (3) encouraging minimum standards of social conduct among society's members; (4) deterring violations of those standards of conduct; and (5) allocating losses among different participants in the social arena.

Protecting Persons and Property: Accountability

Like the king's writs, modern tort law strives to prevent unjustified harm to innocent victims. Tort law enables private citizens to use the legal system to resolve disputes in which one party claims that the other has acted improperly, resulting in harm. The system compels the tortfeasor to compensate the injured party for his or her losses. This *accountability* (or *culpability*) factor is crucial to our legal sense of fair play and equity. People should be held responsible for their actions, especially when they wreak havoc on others. Redress should be available for innocent victims of carelessness, recklessness, or intentional injury.

Minimum Standards of Social Conduct: Deterrence

To function meaningfully in American society, citizens must understand society's norms and values. One extremely important norm encourages the public to behave so as to avoid hurting others or their belongings. Tort law is largely composed of *minimum standards of conduct,* and persons functioning below such thresholds are defined as tortfeasors, while

LEGAL TERMS

negligence
   Broadly defined as the failure to exercise reasonable care to avoid injuring others or their property. This includes both actions and failures to act (omissions). Its elements include a duty of reasonable care and scope of duty, breach of duty by the tortfeasor, causation of injury, proximate cause, and damages.
strict (absolute) liability
   When the defendant is liable to the plaintiff regardless of fault.

individuals acting at or above such criteria are acceptable to the community. However, the intention is not to ensure conformity; rather, the ideal is to inspire people to respect the dignity and integrity each individual possesses. We should not infringe heedlessly upon another's activities unless we are willing to accept such interference with our own lives. Tort law discourages abuses by establishing a clear system of legal rights and remedies enforceable in court proceedings. We know that we can go to court when someone strikes us, invades our privacy, creates a nuisance, or acts negligently toward us. Likewise, we know that we might be hauled into court if we do these things to others. By establishing minimum standards of conduct, tort law sets the rules for living—those "rules of thumb" by which we try to get along with other people.

Allocating Losses among Different Individuals or Groups

It is easy to grasp the idea that an individual tortfeasor should compensate the victim for the tortfeasor's wrongdoing. However, in modern society there are often many different participants in virtually any activity, and it is less clear who should be labeled as tortfeasor or victim. For example, at the time of the American Revolution, most Americans were fairly self-sufficient and dealt directly with other individuals for goods or services. If a colonist bought a broken plow or a poorly shod horse from the local blacksmith, he or she knew who to take to task. However, as the United States became more industrialized, commercial transactions ceased to be one-on-one interactions. Today, people buy canned fruit from a local grocery that bought it from a wholesaler that bought it from a manufacturer. If the fruit is spoiled, perhaps the purchaser's spouse or child, rather than the purchaser, will suffer the injury. The culpability lines become less clear as the producer of the defective item becomes more removed from the ultimate user. Tort law has evolved *products liability* to determine who is in the best position to bear the costs of defective products—the innocent user or the sellers and manufacturers. It is an economic decision that courts and legislatures have made in stating that industry can best afford the costs of injuries caused by dangerously made goods. In other words, the burden of shouldering the economic loss is placed upon commercial business instead of the individual suffering the harm. This illustrates how tort law can be used to assign the expenses associated with misfortune, even when fault is hazy at best. More commonly, though, a single tortfeasor can be identified and saddled with the financial obligation.

2.4 UNDERSTANDING APPELLATE COURT OPINIONS

In the torts puzzle, there appear to be gaps between the basic definitions and how they can be used to solve tort problems. Connecting pieces must be found. These pieces involve legal analysis and are the most important parts of the puzzle, since legal analysis is the critical aspect of law study. The puzzle literally cannot be completed without it. Legal analysis consists of understanding appellate court opinions and applying rules of law to different factual situations. This section considers these missing pieces.

Briefing Cases

Many of the chapters of this book include reprinted portions of appellate court opinions to illustrate various tort principles. At first glance, court decisions may appear garbled or unfocused. A structured formula applied to each case helps organize the ideas that the courts express. There are several such methods, but the most popular is explained here.

Structured Analysis

A structured analysis breaks an opinion into several components: facts, procedural history, issues on appeal, rulings, and rationale. This approach represents the standard analytical framework used by law school and paralegal students.

Facts   From the court opinion, the reader gleans the *facts* that underlie or are necessary to the appellate court's final determination of the case. These are sometimes called the *legally significant facts*. Many facts in the case provide mere background information; these are called *background facts*. Although background facts are not critical to the court's decision, they must be noted to comprehend the complete circumstances involved in the litigation. Sometimes appellate opinions include irrelevant facts that have no real bearing on the outcome of the appeal.

Procedural History   The *procedural history,* or *judicial history* as it is sometimes called, is the appellate court's summary of the previous events in the lawsuit: who sued whom, what legal claims were involved, and (most importantly) how the trial court decided the case (if a bench trial) or in whose favor the jury returned its verdict. Procedural history may include a summary of a lower appellate court's decision rendered before the case was appealed to the court that wrote the opinion being studied. Procedural information is critical to grasp the importance of the appellate court's ruling.

Issues   The *issues* include the questions appealed from the trial court's judgment. Every appeal has at least one issue being reviewed by the appellate court, although more often several issues are involved. Issues are normally phrased in terms of a question: Did the trial court err in admitting certain evidence? Given the facts proven during trial, did the defendant commit a certain tort against the plaintiff?

Ruling   The *ruling* is the appellate court's decision in the case. This decree is directed toward the trial (or lower appellate) court's ruling. If the appellate court agrees that the trial court was correct in deciding the issue on appeal, then the appellate court *affirms* the trial court's judgment. If the appellate court disagrees with the trial court's determination of the appealed issue, then the appellate court *reverses* or *vacates* the trial court's decree. Often reversal or vacation is accompanied by a *remand,* or return, of the case to the trial court with instructions from the appellate court. These instructions may be simply that judgment should be entered for the plaintiff or the defendant (depending, of course, upon which side the appellate court thinks should prevail), or they may include directions that certain factual questions be retried by the trial court.

Rationale   The *rationale* is the appellate court's reasoning to explain its ruling. It is the process through which the court applies the rules of law to the facts of the case. This application is accomplished by linking a series of arguments that appear to lead inexorably to a single logical conclusion (which, conveniently, happens to be the court's decision). Consider the following example. Suppose a state statute requires owners of agricultural vehicles used to haul grain to obtain a special commercial license. Charles sells his old twin-axle grain truck to Donny, who plans to use it in a furniture delivery business. Donny purchases ordinary truck license plates. Has Donny violated the statute? In its rationale, an appellate court would first explain the statutory language (i.e., rule of law) and then apply it to the facts of the case. Thus, although Donny bought a vehicle formerly used to haul grain, its present function is entirely nonagricultural (i.e., conveying furniture). Because the truck is not being used to carry grain, Donny would not be required to purchase the special licenses and thus has not violated the statute.

Briefing an Appellate Court Opinion

As mentioned previously, law school and paralegal students most often use this briefing formula to analyze appellate court opinions. To illustrate how this is done in practice, an actual appellate court opinion has been reproduced here, followed by a suggested case brief that summarizes the elements of the opinion using the briefing formula. To assist in reading opinions reprinted in this book, certain tangential matters and terminology are summarized or explained in brackets: "[ ]." Any parts of the original opinion that have been omitted are indicated in bracketed messages or by bracketed ellipses: "[. . .]."

Edwards v. Terryville Meat Co.
577 N.Y.S.2d 477 (N.Y. App. Div. 1991).
(N.Y. Supreme Court, Appellate Division)
December 23, 1991

Before MANGANO, P.J., and KUNZEMAN, EIBER and BALLETTA, JJ.

MEMORANDUM BY THE COURT.

In a negligence action to recover damages for personal injuries, the plaintiffs appeal [. . .] from [. . .] an order and judgment [. . .] of the Supreme Court, Suffolk County (Cannavo, J.), entered September 11, 1989, as granted the defendant's motion for summary judgment dismissing the complaint [. . .].

ORDERED that the order and judgment entered September 11, 1989, is affirmed [. . .].

In this slip-and-fall case, it was incumbent upon the plaintiffs to come forth with evidence showing that the defendant had either created the allegedly dangerous condition or that it had actual or constructive notice of the condition (*see, Eddy v. Tops Friendly Markets,* 91 A.D.2d 1203, 459 N.Y.S.2d 196, *aff'd,* 59 N.Y.2d 692, 463 N.Y.S.2d 437, 450 N.E.2d 243[1983]). "To constitute constructive notice, a defect must be visible and apparent and it must exist for a sufficient length of time prior to the accident to permit defendant's employees to discover and remedy it" (*Gordon v. American Museum of Natural History,* 67 N.Y.2d 836, 837, 501 N.Y.S.2d 646, 492 N.E.2d 774 [1986]). The injured plaintiff was in the defendant's store for only about 10 minutes before she allegedly slipped and fell on an unknown milky-colored substance which she concededly did not see until after she fell. There is no evidence that the defendant caused the substance to be on the floor, nor is there sufficient evidence to establish that the defendant had either actual or constructive notice of the substance [citations omitted]. Accordingly, the Supreme Court properly granted the defendant's motion for summary judgment.

A Suggested Case Brief

Citation: *Edwards v. Terryville Meat Co.,* 577 N.Y.S.2d 477 (N.Y. App. Div. 1991).

Facts: Injured plaintiff was in defendant's store 10 minutes when she slipped and fell on unknown milky substance on floor. Plaintiff did not see substance until after falling. No evidence that defendant caused substance to be on floor.

Proc.: Injured plaintiff and spouse sued defendant for negligence. Supreme Court of Suffolk County granted defendant's motion for summary judgment dismissing plaintiffs' complaint.

Issue: Did trial court err in granting defendant's motion for summary judgment?

(*Implied Issue*) Did plaintiffs present sufficient evidence to establish defendant's liability for negligently causing plaintiff's injuries?

Ruling: Appellate Division affirmed supreme court's decision.

Rationale: This is a slip-and-fall negligence case. To establish defendant's negligence, plaintiffs must prove either that (1) defendant caused slippery substance to be on floor, or (2) defendant knew (or had constructive notice) that substance was on floor. Constructive notice requires that substance be present on floor for sufficient length of time prior to accident to permit defendant's employees to discover and remedy it. In this case, there was no evidence that defendant had created the hazard that befell plaintiff. Further, there was insufficient evidence that defendant had actual or constructive notice of the substance, given the short time (10 minutes) that plaintiff was in store until she slipped and fell. Thus, trial court correctly granted defendant's motion for summary judgment.

2.5 ANALYZING HYPOTHETICAL PROBLEMS

Briefing cases is simply one step toward understanding legal concepts. The rules of law discussed in these cases must then be applied to various factual situations. This book poses many hypothetical fact problems (or, simply, hypotheticals) to help develop these analytical talents. Perhaps the most popular analytical framework for hypotheticals is discussed here.

Analytical Framework for Hypotheticals

This framework sequentially investigates four general elements of a problem: issue, rules of law, application of the rules to the facts, and conclusions. With this approach, legal principles are applied to specific factual scenarios. When analyzing a hypothetical, first decide which *issues* are presented. To accomplish this, one must identify the general area of law involved in the problem. For instance, if John takes Peter's bicycle without permission, then John has committed some type of tort. This identifies the broad area of law (torts). Next, the different parts of the general legal area must be explored to see which specific tort applies. As discussed earlier in this chapter, the particular tort John appears to have engaged in is called conversion. So the issue would be whether or not John converted Peter's property. This question can be answered by referring to the appropriate *rule of law*. To generalize, the rule of law for conversion defines it as the wrongful deprivation of another's property without consent. This rule must now be *applied* to the facts. John took Peter's property without permission. This means John wrongfully deprived Peter of the use and enjoyment of his property. This constitutes conversion. The *conclusion* would be that Peter may successfully sue John to recover possession of the bicycle, plus damages, since these legal remedies would be appropriate for conversion (as an upcoming chapter explains).

This analytical formula is a useful tool in applying abstract legal principles to different fact situations. The following hypothetical applies the legal concepts of *Edwards* to the given facts.

HYPOTHETICAL

Delroy Magnus visited the Gym Dandy Fitness Center to use its weight and steam rooms. As he walked from the locker room into the weight room, he slipped and fell on a puddle of water on the floor. The puddle was caused by leaking water pipes along the wall leading to the steam room. Delroy broke his left arm as a result of the fall. Mary Perrington, another patron, mentioned that she had seen the puddle when she first arrived at the center approximately two hours before Delroy's accident.

Legal Analysis in Action

Would Delroy's negligence lawsuit against Gym Dandy Fitness Center succeed? Applying the rules of law from the *Edwards* case, Delroy (the plaintiff) must prove that Gym Dandy (the defendant) either created the hazardous condition or had actual or constructive notice of the danger. The puddle was caused by Gym Dandy's leaking water pipes, so Gym Dandy created the danger that hurt Delroy. Further, Mary testified that the puddle had been visible on the floor for two hours. That was sufficient time for Gym Dandy's employees to observe and correct the problem. Thus, Gym Dandy had constructive notice of the puddle and the danger it posed to customers. The conclusion: Gym Dandy was negligent in creating the puddle upon which Delroy fell and was injured. Accordingly, Delroy's negligence lawsuit against Gym Dandy should be successful.

Factual Distinctions Result in Different Conclusions

The facts in the Delroy hypothetical are clearly distinguishable from those in the *Edwards* case. As a result, a different conclusion was reached in Delroy's case than in *Edwards*. This illustrates how a rule of law may be applied to various factual situations to reach different results. This is exactly what appellate courts do when deciding cases dealing with similar legal issues. It is also what attorneys and paralegals do when applying rules of law to the particular facts of a client's case.

2.6 SOLVING TORT PROBLEMS: NESTED ANALYTICAL BOXES

Another approach to tort problem solving is moving from broad subject areas to specific types of torts. This method identifies the exact issues, rules of law, and conclusions in a problem by helping the reader to narrow the analytical focus.

Tort Analysis: From General to Specific

Tort analysis should go from the general to the specific. For example, how can one tell if infliction of emotional distress has occurred unless one is aware that some type of tort law was involved in the problem? Experienced paralegals may appear to strike the analytical nail directly on the head, such as the legal assistant who immediately recognizes assumption of risk in a negligence case. In reality, that paralegal has streamlined the analytical process, but still has moved from the general to the specific. Implicitly, that paralegal recognized a general negligence problem and then narrowed it to a specific defense—assumption of risk—necessary to excuse the negligent conduct. It is best to learn each step of the approach so as to avoid stumbling.

The Analogy of Nested Analytical Boxes

Tort analysis may be likened to nested boxes. *Nested boxes* are ones that may be placed inside each other, with the smaller boxes "nested" inside the larger ones. The largest box corresponds to the *general areas of tort law,* which are intentional torts, negligence, and strict liability. Inside is a slightly smaller box, which corresponds to the *specific subtopic* of the general area of torts. Knowing an intentional tort has occurred, one must then ask: Which one? Inside this second box is a smaller third box, which represents the *facts* of the case that may be used to frame the issues involved in the problem. This third box holds a smaller fourth box, which corresponds to the *elements* of the particular tort. These elements comprise the rules of law that must be applied to the facts, and this *application* could be likened to a smaller fifth box. The *conclusion* to the problem would be the smallest box of all, nested inside the others. Figure 2-1 illustrates the nested-box analogy for tort analysis.

Nesting Hypotheticals

Two hypotheticals should more clearly illustrate the nesting process.

HYPOTHETICAL 1: FRAUD AND MISREPRESENTATION

In an effort to sell his 1966 Ford automobile to Della, Roger claims that the vehicle's total mileage is 20,000 miles when, in reality, it is 520,000 miles. This sounds like an intentional tort, which opens the first analytical box. Inside is the next box: Which type of intentional tort might apply? When one person misinforms another, as Roger has done to Della, it is most likely fraud or misrepresentation. Having opened this second box, one must now construct the issues in terms of the facts (box three): When Roger sold Della

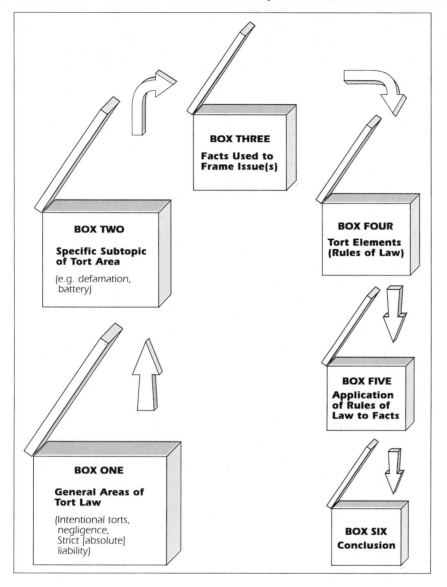

FIGURE 2-1
Nested Analytical Boxes

a 1966 Ford and told her it had been driven only 20,000 miles when, in fact, it had been driven 520,000 miles, has Roger committed fraud or misrepresentation? The fourth box contains the elements of fraud and misrepresentation, which respectively are (broadly) intentionally making a false statement to entice someone to give up something of value to the defrauder, and making a false statement to deceive another. Inside the fifth box, one applies the rules to the facts. Roger intentionally distorted the truth about his automobile's mileage to encourage Della to give up something valuable to him (namely, her money to buy it). Roger's false statement about the mileage also deceived Della. Now the sixth box, the conclusion, is clear: Roger has committed fraud and misrepresentation against Della, who may now sue Roger to recover damages.

HYPOTHETICAL 2: TRESPASS

Jerry lives next to a vacant lot owned by Steven. Jerry dumps his grass clippings onto Steven's lot after mowing his lawn. Eventually, these grass clippings begin to smell and attract rats. Steven never gave Jerry permission to dump grass (or anything else) on Steven's lot. What legal rights does Steven have, if any?

The first box is easily opened. Jerry's actions appear to fall within the intentional torts category, since Jerry is deliberately discarding his grass clippings onto Steven's lot. The second box presents a momentary riddle, but a quick glance among the summarized definitions in § 2.1 of this chapter reveals that Jerry may have committed trespass against Steven. Box three contains the framed issue: Did Jerry trespass against Steven by dumping grass on Steven's lot without permission? In box four, the elements of trespass are described; generally, trespass is unlawful interference with another person's use of his or her property. Applying this rule to the facts, in box five, Jerry's actions (1) were unlawful, in that he did not have Steven's permission to dump grass onto Steven's lot, and (2) interfered with Steven's use of his property, since Steven could not use his lot freely without having to contend with the grass and vermin. The conclusion springs forth from box six: Jerry is liable to Steven for the intentional tort of trespass.

SUMMARY

2.1. Tort law involves the study of wrongful conduct. Torts are wrongful injury to another's person or property. The wrongdoer is called the tortfeasor, and tort law provides the injured party with legal rights and remedies that may be enforced in a court of law. Torts may be divided into three general categories: intentional torts, negligence, and strict (absolute) liability. Intentional torts consist of misconduct designed to injure another person or that person's property. Negligence is the failure to exercise reasonable care to avoid injuring others. Strict (absolute) liability holds the tortfeasor liable for injuring another regardless of intent, negligence, or fault.

2.2. Much of tort law comes from ancient English and early American court decisions. In medieval England, there were primarily two torts, which were called trespass and trespass on the case. These were breaches of the king's peace. Today, there are many more tort actions, since society is much more complicated today than during the Middle Ages, and tort law has become more sophisticated to deal with modern legal problems.

2.3. Tort law seeks to accomplish several goals. First, it serves to protect innocent persons and their property from careless or intentional injury at the hands of tortfeasors. It also attempts to hold tortfeasors responsible for their misconduct. Second, tort law encourages minimum standards of conduct among the public to avoid injuring others through heedless, reckless, or intentional behavior. It also deters persons from injuring other people and their property by holding tortfeasors liable for such mischief. Third, tort law allocates losses among different groups or individuals, based upon society's decision (as expressed through its legislatures and courts) as to who is best able to bear such misfortunes.

2.4. The study of law often involves reading appellate court opinions. These cases contain the rules of common law that are applied to the facts of different cases. One approach that helps to clarify appellate court opinions isolates the facts, procedural history, issues, rulings, and rationale of an appellate court's opinion. It is commonly used to brief cases.

2.5. To apply the rules of law to different hypothetical problems, one method breaks down the factual scenario in terms of the issues, rules of law that must then be applied to each case's specific facts, and the conclusions regarding the probable outcome of the hypothetical case.

2.6. When analyzing tort law problems, the analogy of nested boxes may prove useful. The largest box consists of the general tort topic area. Inside are smaller boxes, each taking the reader closer to answering the question. The second box contains the specific tort involved; the third box contains the issues framed by the facts; the fourth box contains the rules of law for the particular tort involved; the fifth box applies the rules of law to the facts; and the sixth (and smallest) box contains the conclusions to the hypothetical.

REVIEW QUESTIONS

1. How is a tort best defined? What are the three broad categories of torts? How might you define each variety?

2. What are intentional torts? What are the specific types of intentional torts? How might you broadly define them?

3. What is negligence? How might you distinguish it from intentional torts? From strict (absolute) liability?

4. How might you define strict, or absolute, liability? How might you distinguish it from intentional torts? From negligence?

5. Discuss the historical roots of tort law. From what country or countries did torts originate? How have torts changed since their inception?

6. What are the purposes that tort law attempts to accomplish? Do these objectives sometimes conflict? Do they sometimes complement one another?

7. Suggest an analytical framework you might use to dissect an appellate court opinion. Indicate how each step takes you closer to determining what the appellate court's decision is and how it reached its conclusions.

8. Suggest an analytical formula you might use to answer a hypothetical fact problem. In what order are these steps taken? Why do you think this order is appropriate? Is each step of the technique necessary to reach the next phase?

9. What method might you use to analyze tort problems? How does this approach help you reach your answers? Do you see any similarities between this method and those discussed in the text? Any differences?

10. Does tort analysis move from the specific to the general, or vice versa? Why is the correct approach best suited to answering tort hypotheticals?

PROBLEMS

Using the definitions of specific torts discussed in §2.1 of this chapter, answer the following hypotheticals, using the analytical approaches discussed earlier.

1. Thomas Casterman is a 12-year-old boy who enjoys climbing trees. The Casterman family just moved into a new house. The electric wires to Thomas's house run from an electric pole through the high branches of an oak tree in his back yard. While the rest of the family was moving into the home, Thomas ran to the back yard to climb the tree. As he neared the top, he grabbed the electric wires with his right hand. The wires were not insulated and Thomas was severely burned from the resulting electric shock. He also broke both his legs when he fell, unconscious, from the tree. Thomas's father wishes to know if he might successfully sue the utility company for negligence.

2. Shady Acres is a subdivision being developed by Bartholomew Real Estate Management, Inc. (BREM). While bulldozing the lots and streets, BREM's crews created huge piles of dirt. BREM did not erect any barriers to keep these dirt piles in place. Pamela Jovanco owns a house at the bottom of a hill upon which BREM placed several earth piles. During heavy rains, mud would slide down the hill and cover Pamela's entire yard. Some mud even seeped through her basement windows, damaging her basement carpet and furniture. Pamela wonders if trespass has occurred.

3. Samantha Billingsly stood outside her downtown hotel hailing a cab. The driver screeched to a halt alongside the curb. Samantha opened the rear door of the automobile and began to climb inside. In doing so, she placed her right hand on the roof of the car where the top of the door would close. Suddenly, the cab driver accelerated the automobile, causing the rear door to slam shut onto Samantha's hand. Samantha suffered lacerations and several broken bones in her right hand and wrist. She also suffered a neck injury as she was thrown against the back seat as the taxi lurched forward. The cab driver later explained that he had accelerated suddenly to avoid being struck by a shuttle bus, which he thought was about to collide with his taxi when he saw it approaching very rapidly in his rear-view mirror. Using negligence theory, Samantha would like to sue the Blue Cab Company, which owns the taxi.

4. Eddie Peterson owned a coyote, which he captured while hunting last summer in the mountains. The coyote had become quite tame and at parties, to entertain guests, Eddie would routinely allow the animal to eat out of his hand. One day, Eddie's next-door neighbor, Angela Starlight, a seven-year-old girl, visited Eddie's back yard to play with the coyote. Angela's parents had warned her several times to avoid approaching the coyote, although neither they nor Angela had ever seen the animal bite or growl at anyone. When Angela reached out to pet the coyote, it bared its teeth and snapped at her hand, biting and cutting her severely. Angela's parents sued Eddie under the theory of absolute liability. Under most states' common law, owners are strictly liable for injuries caused by their wild animals.

PROBLEM ANSWERS

1. *Issue:* Was the utility company negligent in running uninsulated electric wires through a tree, which injured Thomas Casterman while he was climbing the tree?

   Rule of Law: Negligence is the failure to exercise reasonable care to avoid injuring others.

   Application of Rule to Facts: Uninsulated electric wires are extremely dangerous to anyone who might come into contact with them. A utility company is expected to use reasonable care to protect bystanders from electric shock from its wires. Insulating the wires would have prevented the injury to Thomas. It was reasonably foreseeable that adventurous children like Thomas would climb trees and come into contact with electric wires. The utility violated its duty of care to protect against injuries to children climbing trees, such as the harm that befell Thomas Casterman.

   Conclusion: The utility is liable to the Castermans for causing Thomas's injuries.

2. *Issue:* Did BREM commit trespass against Pamela Jovanco?

Rule of Law: Trespass is unlawful or unreasonable interference with the use of someone's property.

Application of Rule to Facts: By allowing piles of dirt and mud, carried by rainfall, to flow down a hill onto Pamela's property, damaging her land and house, BREM's actions would be considered an unreasonable use that injured another's land. Therefore . . .

Conclusion: BREM has committed trespass against Pamela.

3. *Issue:* Is the cab company liable for negligence when one of its drivers, through sudden and unexpected acceleration, injures a passenger attempting to enter the vehicle?

Rule of Law: Negligence is the failure to exercise reasonable care to avoid injuring others.

Application of Rule to Facts: The cab driver failed to exercise reasonable care in safeguarding Samantha Billingsly. The driver should have anticipated that his sudden, unexpected acceleration would cause the door to slam shut on Samantha's hand and force her into the back seat.

Conclusion: Because the cab driver failed to use reasonable care in safeguarding Samantha, the driver was negligent in causing her injuries and the cab company would be liable.

4. *Issue:* Is a coyote owner absolutely liable for injuries caused by the animal if it bites a seven-year-old girl?

Rule of Law: Strict (or absolute) liability is the tortfeasor's responsibility for injuring another, regardless of intent, negligence, or fault. As noted in the facts, most states' common law applies strict liability to wild animal cases.

Application of Rule to Facts: By their very nature, wild animals are not tame, like dogs or cats. Because the coyote is a wild animal, the owner would be absolutely liable for the injury it inflicts upon others. So . . .

Conclusion: Eddie Peterson is strictly liable for Angela Starlight's injuries caused by his coyote.

PROJECTS

1. Brief *Zink v. Owens-Corning Fiberglass Corp.,* 65 Ohio App. 3d 637, 584 N.E.2d 1303 (1989). Focus upon the Ohio Court of Appeals' discussion of whether the defendant landowner breached its duty of care to its employee.

2. Brief *Suckenik v. Levitt,* 177 A.D.2d 416, 576 N.Y.S.2d 258 (1991). Did the plaintiff prove that he was injured as a result of the defendant's defamatory letter? What did the appellate division consider the key element in this appeal?

CHAPTER 3

Intentional Torts: Injuries to Persons

OUTLINE

DATA-GRAPHIC TORTS

Goode v. Tormare

Thomas Goode visited his physician, Dr. Morley Tormare, complaining of abdominal pain. Dr. Tormare diagnosed the ailment as gall bladder valve dysfunction, aggravated by high saturated fats in the bloodstream. Dr. Tormare advised Goode to reduce his dietary fat intake. Goode adjusted his diet, but the symptoms persisted. Instead of prescribing a new medicine recommended in the medical literature for gall bladder cases, Dr. Tormare advised an operation to repair the damaged valve. Goode was frightened at the prospect of surgery, but reluctantly agreed. After undergoing the procedure, Goode heard about the new "wonder drug" from another physician. After a battery of hospital tests, gall bladder specialists discovered that Dr. Tormare's operation had reduced Goode's gall bladder response efficiency to dietary fat by nearly 50 percent.

Aside from the medical malpractice issues, Goode might sue Dr. Tormare for battery. A physician commits battery against a patient for conducting an unconsented surgical procedure. The key in this hypothetical is informed consent. Did Goode knowingly consent to Dr. Tormare's

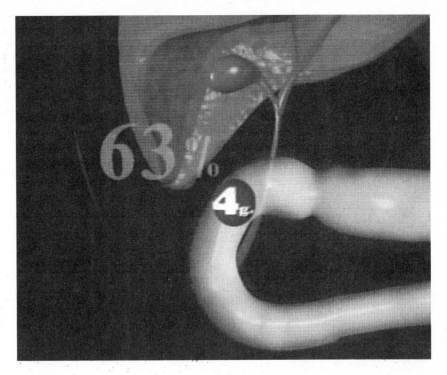

surgical procedure? Dr. Tormare did not discuss alternative treatment with Goode, such as the new, more effective medicine that was available. This information was crucial to Goode's decision as to whether to allow surgery. Thus, Goode did not give informed consent to Dr. Tormare's surgery and Dr. Tormare would be liable to Goode for battery.

INTRODUCTION

Intentional torts are relatively simple pieces to assemble in the torts puzzle, because they reflect actions that are familiar to everyday life. Understanding intentional torts is an important first venture into the heart of the puzzle, where fitting the pieces becomes more challenging.

The puzzle pieces to be assembled in this chapter have a common shape—they are all intentional torts causing injuries to persons. Search for these pieces:

- Assault and battery.
- False imprisonment.
- Intentional and reckless infliction of emotional distress.
- Fraud and misrepresentation.
- Malicious prosecution and abuse of process.
- Invasion of privacy.
- Defamation (libel and slander).

3.1 INTENTIONAL TORTS IN GENERAL

Intentional torts consist of conduct that is fashioned to harm another person or his or her property. The mischief is directed with the purpose of inflicting injury. All intentional torts include two elements: intent and injurious behavior. **Intent** may be broadly defined as the desire to achieve a particular result. Specifically, the tortfeasor must intend to accomplish the harmful consequences of his or her actions. This does not require malice or ill will, however; the tortfeasor must simply intend to cause the consequences that give rise to the tort. Commonly, though, those consequences include some type of harm. Then these acts must actually conclude in the injury that was intended.

For certain peculiar intentional torts, intent, strictly speaking, is not required. For example, for reckless infliction of emotional distress, intent is not essential. The tortfeasor need only know (or reasonably should know) that his or her outlandish actions will produce emotional injury. This knowledge element acts as a substitute for intent.

Intent and Action Together

Intent reflects the tortfeasor's state of mind and must occur simultaneously with the misconduct. For example, assume that David and Steven are carpenters. Steven tosses a piece of wood across a room into a pile, but before it lands the wood strikes David in the throat. Steven would not be liable for battery, because, although the board struck David, Steven did not intend this to happen. Suppose David thought about throwing the board back at Steven, but did nothing and walked away. David would not be liable for assault because no action accompanied his desire.

Intentional torts present a relatively black-and-white image of the law, in which it is fairly easy to distinguish the "good" person from the "bad." The victim seems truly exploited, and the tortfeasor is clearly responsible and to blame (from a moral or ethical point of view) for having purposefully injured the victim. Our sense of fair play is rewarded when intentional tortfeasors are held accountable for their mischief.

LEGAL TERMS

intentional torts
Torts in which the conduct is intended to harm another person or that person's property. All intentional torts include two elements: intent and injurious behavior.

intent
In tort law, the desire to achieve a harmful result which the law defines as tortious.

3.2 ASSAULT AND BATTERY

The preceding example of the careless carpenters depicts two of the most common intentional torts: assault and battery. Of all torts, these are perhaps the most straightforward.

Assault Defined

Assault is an attempt by one person to make harmful or offensive contact with another individual without consent. Actual physical contact is not necessary; in fact, contact converts an assault to a battery. Assault is distinguishable from battery in that no touching is required.

Freedom from Apprehension

The rights being protected by recognition of this tort involve each person's right to control what touches his or her person. Assault is also intended to protect individuals from the fear or apprehension that unconsented contact will take place. **Apprehension** means that a person reasonably fears for his or her physical safety in anticipation of being struck by the unconsented harmful or distasteful contact. This apprehension must be *reasonable,* meaning that the anxiety must be rational given the perceived threat of contact. For example, if a four-year-old warns that she is going to punch her father's head off, her father probably would not be overly concerned, as it would be unreasonable for an adult to fear a child's threatened battery under such circumstances. Threats at a distance also do not present sufficient reason for alarm, because it is physically impossible for the threatening party to fulfill the threat. This states the next legal requirement for assault: immediate threat of contact.

Imminent Threat of Contact

Assault involves the imminent or immediate threat that unconsented contact is about to occur. The fear arises from the likelihood that someone or something unwanted is about to strike. For instance, Michelle's threat to hit George while talking to him on the telephone does not present an immediate risk, since the task cannot be completed at the time the threat was made. Therefore, no assault has taken place.

assault
The tortfeasor's attempt to make harmful or offensive contact with another person without consent. Assault is an attempted battery and is an intentional tort. Its elements include the tortfeasor's placing the intended victim in reasonable apprehension for his or her physical safety, and an imminent threat of contact as a result of the tortfeasor's conduct.

apprehension
An element of assault. An assault occurs if the intended victim reasonably fears for his or her physical safety as a consequence of the tortfeasor's actions. This fear is called *apprehension.*

THE CASE OF THE CRAZY TRUCKER

Assault involves more than just an errant punch or kick. The imminent threat of battery can occur through an object that the tortfeasor directs at the victim. An example is a thrown rock that misses the victim. An assault occurred if the victim was placed in reasonable apprehension of being struck by the approaching stone.

In the following case, note how the "insane" truck driver commits assault against the plaintiffs through his reckless driving.

Rosenberg v. Packerland Packing Co.
55 Ill. App. 3d 959, 370 N.E.2d 1235
(1977)
(Appellate Court of Illinois)
December 13, 1977

PUSATERI, Justice:
In this consolidated appeal, we are concerned with whether each count of

plaintiffs' [. . .] complaint states a cause of action. [. . .] [P]laintiffs-appellants appeal from the dismissal of Counts I and III of their complaint for failure to state a cause of action. [. . .] [P]laintiffs [. . .] alleged that an agent, servant, or lessee of defendant Packerland Packing Co. controlled its tractor and trailer, which defendant owned and operated as an interstate common carrier, in such a manner as to come within two feet of plaintiffs' vehicle at speeds of seventy to eighty miles per hour, and even after signalling by the plaintiffs that said truck should pass them, the unknown operator of defendant's truck continued to make feints at the rear of plaintiffs' vehicle as if he were going to strike the plaintiffs' vehicle, all of this occurring over a "long span of time." It was alleged that the date of the occurrence was March 9, 1975, that the place of occurrence was I-94 in Lake County, Illinois, and that both vehicles were proceeding in a southerly direction. [. . .] [Plaintiffs alleged that the truck driver] was probably insane.

Count II alleged that the truck driver's conduct constituted the intentional infliction of emotional distress and an intentional assault, and that defendant Packerland was liable [. . .].

[W]e believe the conduct alleged in Count II may constitute the intentional tort of assault. An assault is a reasonable apprehension of an imminent battery. [Citation omitted.]

[. . .]

We affirm the trial court's ruling that Count II of the complaint states a valid cause of action and reverse the dismissal of Count III. The cause is remanded for further proceedings.

Affirmed in part, reversed in part, and remanded.

CASE QUESTIONS

1. What specific actions did the defendant's truck driver engage in that constituted assault?
2. What if the driver's truck had touched the plaintiffs' vehicle? What additional intentional tort would then have occurred?
3. The court's discussion of the intentional infliction of emotional distress claim was omitted here. You may wish to look up the full opinion and compare the Illinois common law elements with those discussed in § 3.4.

Examples should illustrate these elements. Although assault is a fairly straightforward tort, its elements may best be explored hypothetically.

HYPOTHETICALS

Palmer and Davis begin arguing in a bar. Palmer balls up his fists and pulls his arm backward as if to swing at Davis. Davis ducks in anticipation of a punch. Has Palmer committed assault?

Applying the legal elements of assault, as previously discussed (which are (1) the tortfeasor's attempt to make unconsented harmful or offensive contact, which (2) makes the victim apprehensive for his or her physical safety, and (3) the threat of contact is imminent), it is clear that Palmer has assaulted Davis. Palmer attempted to touch Davis in a harmful or offensive manner when he drew his arm back to swing. Davis did not consent to this action and feared for his safety, as is obvious since he ducked, expecting to be pelted with Palmer's fist. The danger of contact was immediate, as Palmer could complete his swing and punch within a matter of seconds.

□ □ □

Consider another example. Morrison and Fleetly are playing basketball in a gymnasium. Fleetly yells that Morrison stepped out of bounds as he dribbled the ball upcourt. Morrison smiles and fakes a forceful pass to Fleetly's head, causing Fleetly to flinch in anticipation that the ball will hit him in the face. Has Morrison committed assault?

Consent is the key to this hypothetical. Morrison and Fleetly had agreed to play basketball together. It is well known that sports activities such as this involve a certain degree of incidental contact to which participants consent. This could involve being struck by the ball as it is deliberately passed from one player to another. Because Fleetly implicitly agreed in advance to such types of contact while playing the game, Morrison did not assault him.

All elements must exist for assault to occur. If any one feature is absent, then there is no assault. For instance, suppose in the first illustration that Davis had not reacted at all to Palmer's arm gesture. Perhaps Palmer and Davis often indulged in horseplay, such as by pantomiming fist fights, and so Davis assumed that it was just another joking episode. That would remove the apprehension element and thus there would be no assault. Suppose in the second example that Morrison simply threw the ball down and shouted at Fleetly, "Next time you call me a liar, I'll plant this right upside your head!" In that case, the threatened contact would not be imminent, since Morrison warned only of behavior at some unspecified future time, which might in fact never take place. Accordingly, no assault would have happened.

Battery Defined

A completed assault is called a battery. Strictly defined, a **battery** is the intentional, unconsented touching of another person in an offensive or injurious manner. There are three basic elements to this tort:

1. Unconsented physical contact
2. Offensive or harmful contact
3. The tortfeasor's intent to touch another person in an offensive or injurious manner.

Physical Contact Required

Actual touching is necessary for a battery to occur. However, contact need not be made with a person's body. It is sufficient for the tortfeasor to touch the victim's clothing, or an object that the victim is carrying, such as

LEGAL TERMS

battery
   The tortfeasor's intentional, unconsented touching of another person in an offensive or harmful manner. Battery is a completed assault and is an intentional tort.

a purse, or an object in which the victim is sitting, such as a chair or automobile. These items are said to become *extensions* of the person which, if touched, translates into touching the person himself or herself.

Lack of Consent

Battery occurs only if the victim did not consent to the physical contact. Consent can be *expressed* or *implied*. Expressed consent is relatively easy to identify. For example, participants in sporting events readily consent to physical contact routinely associated with the activity. Implied consent arises out of particular situations, in which individuals, by being involved, implicitly agree to some types of minor contact. For instance, people walking in crowds impliedly consent to incidental contact as they accidentally bump into passersby. It is reasonable and normal to expect that this will occur in crowded places, and those involved are (or should be) willing to tolerate some minor jostles.

Harmful or Offensive Contact

Battery requires touching that is harmful or offensive. Although harmful contact should be relatively simple to perceive, offensive touching may present some surprises. Often, offensive contact may be intended as positive or complimentary, such as a pat on the back or kiss on the cheek from a co-worker. The recipient, however, may find these actions distasteful. This addresses the consent issue. People do not usually consent to touching that repulses them.

Whether or not the physical contact is offensive is judged by a **reasonable person standard**. Would a reasonable person have been insulted by the contact, given the same or similar circumstances? Reasonableness is often based upon the victim's actions in conjunction with the tortfeasor's. For example, if two co-workers are accustomed to "goofing around" by jokingly touching one another (pats on the back, fake punches, tickling, etc.), then such behavior would not be reasonably offensive. In effect, the participants consented to the activity. On the other hand, a male supervisor touching a female employee in a sexually explicit fashion could reasonably be perceived as degrading and offensive.

Intent

Battery, like all intentional torts, includes an element of intent. The tortfeasor must have intended to make contact with another individual in a harmful or offensive manner. Thus, accidentally bumping into someone in an elevator as it jerked into motion would not be a battery, because the contact was unintentional. But pinching that person while leaving the elevator would be battery, as the act was purposefully designed to make offensive contact.

LEGAL TERMS

reasonable person standard
An imaginary individual used to define reasonable care in negligence cases. The reasonable person is expected to behave reasonably under a given set of circumstances to avoid harming others. The tortfeasor's conduct is compared to the reasonable person's to determine if the tortfeasor violated the duty of reasonable care. The trier-of-fact decides the reasonable person standard in a particular case.

Transferred Intent

Sometimes the tortfeasor tries to strike someone but ends up hitting someone else. For instance, if Robert threw a stone at Stuart but struck Mark instead, then Robert has committed battery against Mark. Although Robert intended to strike Stuart, his intent is said to be carried along by the object he set into motion—the stone—and his intent is thus transferred with the stone onto whomever it reaches—in this case, Mark. Note, too, that Robert has assaulted Stuart by throwing the stone and missing, provided that Stuart was placed in reasonable apprehension, etc.

Transferred intent is an effective tool for protecting persons from misdirected physical contacts. It holds the tortfeasor accountable for the consequences of his or her actions even though, strictly speaking, he or she did not desire to hit the third person involved.

transferred intent
In battery cases, the tortfeasor's intention to strike another person through some object, such as a thrown stone. Also occurs when the tortfeasor intends to strike one victim but inadvertently hits another individual instead.

THE CASE OF THE "NUKED" PLAINTIFF

Transferred intent is not restricted to objects one can hold in one's hand. Battery can occur if the tortfeasor contacts the victim with any offensive or harmful substance, such as liquids (acids) or toxic gases.

The following case demonstrates how radioactive gases caused a battery. The facts are supplied in great detail so that the reader may fully appreciate the horror of the defendant's alleged behavior and the apparent subsequent cover-up. In this case, the alleged conduct was deliberate, which makes the facts even more chilling.

Field v. Philadelphia Electric Co.
388 Pa. Super. 400, 565 A.2d
1170 (1989)
(Superior Court of Pennsylvania)
September 12, 1989

HESTER, Judge:
This is an appeal from an April 29, 1988 order which granted appellees' demurrer to five counts of appellants' eight-count complaint. George and Dawn Field (appellants) instituted this action against Philadelphia Electric Co., Bartlett Nuclear, Inc.,[. . .] (appellees) to recover for injuries resulting from an alleged intentional exposure to high levels of radiation [. . .]. [T]he trial court dismissed the counts of appellants' complaint which

sought damages for intentional exposure to radiation [. . .] and intentional infliction of emotional distress [. . .].

The trial court determined that: [. . .] there was no common law cause of action for intentional exposure to radiation [. . .]. We reverse and remand for proceedings consistent with this opinion.

Initially, we examine the facts upon which we base this adjudication. [. . .]

Accordingly, for purposes of this appeal, we accept as true the following allegations, which are contained in appellants' complaint. George Field was employed by Bartlett Nuclear, Inc. ("Bartlett") and hired as an independent contractor by the Philadelphia Electric Co. ("PECO") to work at its Peach

Bottom Nuclear Plant as a health physics technician. Bartlett is a corporation which provides personnel to manage operational problems at utilities which own and operate nuclear power plants. [. . .]

On February 6, 1985, as a result of a plant shutdown, George Field was directed by PECO personnel to enter an off-gas pipe tunnel in unit three of Peach Bottom. He observed standing water on the floor of the tunnel and radioed to PECO personnel that he thought it unsafe to remain in the water. In response, he was ordered to test for radiation, which he did. After performing the tests, he returned from the tunnel and advised PECO personnel that the standing-water problem should not be resolved while the plant was being operated since it would be dangerous to work in the tunnel while the plant was operational.

Despite these warnings from Field, who was trained and hired in the area of safety control and cleanup, on March 1, 1985, while Peach Bottom was operating, PECO ordered Field and other personnel into the tunnel to resolve the standing-water situation. While Field was in the tunnel, PECO personnel deliberately vented radioactive gases into the tunnel where they knew Field was working. This action was taken in order to keep the reactor operating. The highly radioactive steam triggered a survey meter, a device in Field's possession that measures radiation levels. Field's survey meter went off-scale in the tunnel. As this indicates levels of radiation in excess of that permitted by the Nuclear Regulatory Commission ("NRC"), [. . .] Field immediately directed all personnel to leave the tunnel. He was not aware why the radiation level increased at that time. Two radiation detectors, one located at the tunnel entrance and another located at the control point to the tunnel, both

alarmed when Field passed through them. This also indicated radiation exposure in excess of that permitted by NRC regulations. Field then analyzed air samples at the tunnel entrance with his survey meter, and the meter once again indicated radiation levels in excess of levels permitted by NRC regulations.

Field posted warning signs to the entrances to the contaminated areas, but PECO ordered the signs removed. Later that day, Field asked that his internal exposure to radiation be determined by equipment that was unavailable to him, but PECO refused the request and refused to answer his questions regarding the incident. [. . .]

On March 4, 1985, Field discovered that the reactor operators on March 1, 1985, had deliberately ordered the radioactive steam to be bypassed from the regular system and vented into the tunnel where the operators knew Field was working. This action was taken solely to keep the reactor operational. Field asked three other PECO personnel about the level of his exposure; he was assured that the matter was being investigated, and he was ordered not to discuss the incident with anyone. [. . .] In late July, Field was told by his supervisor that the investigation was complete and documentation regarding the event had been discarded. Field then told his supervisor that he was going to report the incident to the NRC. [. . .]

At one point during Field's inquiries about the incident, PECO personnel made two false statements to Field. They told Field that his field badge indicated that he had not been exposed to radiation on March 1, 1985. They also told him that on March 1, 1985, his survey meter had given an incorrect reading regarding the level of radiation due to moisture in the instrument.

On August 8, 1985, Field again was ordered into the off-gas tunnel at unit three to perform work. He performed tests on the standing water which established that it contained such high levels of radiation that Field believed that he had been misinformed by PECO about the level of his exposure to radiation on March 1st. Later that day, Field demanded that water be retrieved from the tunnel for analysis.

In the meantime, on August 6 and 7, 1985, the NRC conducted an unannounced investigation [. . .]. On September 25, 1985, Field was terminated for alleged absenteeism. A subsequent NRC investigation of Field's termination led it to conclude that Field had been terminated because he had reported his overexposure to radiation to the NRC. [. . .]

The next issue before us is whether count one of appellants' complaint, entitled tort of intentional exposure to radiation, states a cognizable cause of action. We conclude that it does. In the count, appellants allege that PECO deliberately exposed Field to radiation by operating the reactor knowing that Field would be exposed to dangerous levels of radiation and by deliberately venting radioactive steam on Field knowing his location. We believe this states a cause of action in battery. See Restatement (Second) of Torts § 18 comment c (intent to contact someone with offensive foreign substance constitutes contact for purposes of battery).

Barber v. Pittsburgh Corning Corp, 365 Pa. Super. 247, 529 A.2d 491 (1987), *rev'd on other grounds,* 521 Pa. 29, 555 A.2d 766 (1989), provides a dispositive analysis on whether an "intent" to cause harmful contact is present based on the allegations in appellants' complaint. [. . .] We noted that intent in the context of tort litigation is defined to include the desire to bring about the likely consequences of an intentional act. [. . .]

Instantly, the intent to contact is established by the deliberate venting of steam on Field, with knowledge of his whereabouts. Under *Barber,* the fact that PECO did not intend to harm Field is immaterial. If there is intentional contact, the consequences substantially certain to follow from such contact are within the scope of the tort. [. . .] Accordingly, we conclude that count one states a cause of action in battery under Pennsylvania law.

[. . .]

In accordance with the foregoing, the order is reversed and the case is remanded for proceedings consistent with this opinion. [. . .]

CASE QUESTIONS

1. Although the court did not discuss the point, how does transferred intent apply in *Field?*
2. Did the court determine the defendant's intent to commit battery by exposing Field to radioactive steam? What was the court's rationale?
3. The court's discussion of the plaintiffs' intentional infliction of emotional distress claims was omitted here. You may wish to read the full opinion to compare Pennsylvania common law with the elements discussed in § 3.4.

Battery lends itself to a variety of boisterous hypotheticals. Consider the following examples.

HYPOTHETICALS

Helen is a production analyst for a local investment firm. She is one of only three women in the operation. Another analyst, Calvin, regularly flirts with her. Helen responds politely but coolly to these episodes. One day Calvin, while standing behind Helen, takes hold of her upper arms and leans over her shoulder as if to inspect the file she has before her on her desk. Calvin wisecracks about the "nice view," to which Helen responded by grimacing. Has Calvin committed battery against Helen?

The three basic elements of battery have been satisfied. Helen did not consent to Calvin's touching. Her previous encounters with Calvin did not establish a playful relationship in which she might have encouraged such actions; in fact, she expressly discouraged Calvin's flirting. A reasonable person would have found Calvin's behavior offensive. Helen was insulted by the contact, as evidenced by her expression. Calvin intended to touch Helen in the way she found distasteful. Accordingly, Calvin is liable to Helen for battery.

□ □ □

Consider another illustration. Shelley is a clerk at a hotdog stand in a football stadium. Phillip, a customer, purchased lunch from another clerk. Shelley thought Phillip unusually rude, so, as Phillip turned to walk away, Shelley threw Phillip a plastic catsup bottle, shouting that he had forgotten his condiments. The bottle brushed Phillip's jacket sleeve and caused him to spill his beverage onto his pants. The bottle then struck Iris in the head, covering her with catsup. Has Shelley committed battery against Phillip and Iris?

Again, the elements unfold clearly. Phillip did not consent to being touched. Shelley's intent to make contact transferred to the catsup bottle that struck Phillip's clothing, which was an extension of his person. Shelley's contact was harmful because it caused Phillip to spill his drink onto himself. Shelley purposefully touched Phillip in a fashion that injured him. Furthermore, Shelley's intent to strike Phillip was transferred with the bottle, so that in hitting Iris, transferred intent applied. Shelley is liable to both Phillip and Iris for battery.

What if Shelley had been merely another spectator at the football game and, instead of throwing anything, had simply jostled Phillip, causing the spillage onto both Phillip and Iris, as they all were walking down the stairway to their seats? This would be considered incidental contact to which Shelley, Iris, and Phillip impliedly consented. Thus, no battery would have happened.

Figure 3-1 summarizes the elements of assault and battery.

Assault	Battery
Attempt to make harmful or offensive contact with another person without consent	Unconsented physical contact
Placing the victim in reasonable apprehension for physical safety	Offensive or harmful contact
Threat of imminent contact	Intent to touch another person in offensive or injurious manner

FIGURE 3-1

Elements of Assault and Battery

Other intentional torts are less straightforward than assault and battery. False imprisonment poses particular wrinkles and is discussed in the next section.

3.3 FALSE IMPRISONMENT

False imprisonment occurs when the tortfeasor intentionally confines someone without his or her consent. This tort is meant to protect each individual's right to control his or her own freedom of movement. Essentially, there are four elements to false imprisonment:

1. Confinement without captive's consent
2. Tortfeasor's intent to confine victim
3. Confinement for an appreciable length of time
4. No reasonable means of escape.

Confinement

All methods of confinement include (1) a restriction of the victim's freedom of movement, (2) the captive's awareness or fear of the restriction, and (3) the victim's nonconsent to the restriction. The second element prevents the victim from escaping, either because no routes of escape are available, or the victim is afraid to attempt escape for fear of the tortfeasor's reprisals.

There are several ways in which the tortfeasor may confine his or her captive. These include physical barriers and express or implied threats of force.

Physical Barriers Restricting Movement

Physical barriers are the most common method of falsely imprisoning someone. Placing the captive in a locked room or a moving automobile (while refusing to stop) are common examples. However, the physical barriers need not be so small as a single room or vehicle. A captive may be restricted to the grounds of a series of adjacent buildings. It is even possible for the victim to be penned in by such unexpected blockades as an automobile

LEGAL TERMS

false imprisonment Occurs when a tortfeasor confines a victim without consent. Elements of this intentional tort are: confinement without captive's consent, tortfeasor's intent to confine victim, confinement for an appreciable (meaning unreasonable) length of time, and no reasonable means of escape available to the captive.

blocking the victim's access from a driveway to a street. The physical barrier need only restrict the captive's freedom of movement. This essentially traps the victim, either by some actual physical obstruction, such as a locked door, fence, or wall, or by an object which the tortfeasor is using to restrain the captive, such as the automobile blocking the driveway or even the tortfeasor's own body obstructing a doorway.

Express or Implied Threats of Force

Sometimes no locked door or wall is necessary to confine a person. Threats of physical or emotional violence can be quite effective. In this way, confinement is achieved by expressed intimidation. The victim is afraid to escape for fear of physical or emotional injury. For example, when the tortfeasor warns, "If you leave this room, I will break your legs," the captive is likely to remain as instructed. Similarly, the tortfeasor could threaten, "If you leave this house, I will tell Joe that you wrecked his new car." In this situation, the victim is restrained by the threat of emotional injury, if certain information is revealed that would incriminate the captive.

These types of threats need not be explicit, however. Implied threats also work effectively. For instance, if a store manager tells a shoplifting suspect to wait in a room for questioning "so that nobody has to telephone the police," the threat of arrest and criminal prosecution is clearly implied, and the suspect will probably comply out of fear.

Captive's Consent to Confinement

The intentional tort of false imprisonment cannot occur if the victim consents to the captivity. **Consent** includes awareness and acceptance of the confinement. Thus, if a shoplifting suspect agrees to remain in a room pending questioning by store security, this would constitute consent, because the patron knows and accepts the restriction to the room.

Intent to Confine

The tortfeasor must intend to confine the victim for false imprisonment to happen. Consider the example of an accidental lock-in at a department store, where a customer is inadvertently locked in the store after closing hours. There would be no false imprisonment, because the store management had no desire to confine the patron.

Intent may be expressed or implied by conduct. The tortfeasor who states his or her intention to confine another person is easiest to identify. Often, however, intent is indicated by conduct. Again, the shoplifting illustration presents a good example. A shoplifting suspect is stopped by store security and is asked to accompany the guard. Without any word of explanation, the guard takes the suspect to a back room, has the suspect enter, closes the door, and departs. There have been no explicit indications of confinement—the door was not locked—but implicitly it is understood, based on the behavior of the guard, that the suspect is to remain in the room. Accordingly, the intent to restrain may be implied.

Confinement for Appreciable Time Period

Although no definite time period is required, false imprisonment occurs only if the confinement has existed for an appreciable length of time. This depends upon the specific facts of each case. Usually, *appreciable confinement* is defined as unreasonable under the circumstances. That could be a matter of seconds, if someone is restrained in an extremely hazardous situation, such as in a burning building; or it could be a question of an hour or two, such as during a shoplifting investigation.

No Reasonable Means of Escape

False imprisonment cannot happen if the captive has a reasonable avenue of escape. In other words, the confinement must be complete. If the victim could simply walk away from the situation, then no false imprisonment transpired. Reasonable means of escape depend upon the facts of each case, but usually they include any route that a reasonable person would use under the circumstances to flee. For example, if Roger makes improper advances upon Betty in his automobile, and Betty has only to open the door to leave, then she has a reasonable avenue of escape, and no false imprisonment has happened. However, if Roger made the same advances on Betty in a fourth-floor apartment, in which the only exits were one door (which Roger blocked) and the windows, then false imprisonment would have occurred. Betty could hardly be expected to escape by leaping from a fourth-story window.

LEGAL TERMS

consent
 A victim's voluntary acceptance of the tortfeasor's actions, provided that the victim understood (or reasonably should have understood) the consequences of the tortfeasor's behavior. Consent is a defense to every intentional tort.

THE CASE OF THE OVERZEALOUS STORE SECURITY OFFICER

Many false imprisonment cases involve shoplifting. All too often, store employees, anxious to curb theft of merchandise, become overzealous in their efforts. Suspected shoplifters, on the flimsiest circumstantial evidence, are occasionally subjected to unreasonable searches, confinements, interrogations, and the accompanying stresses and embarrassment. When the evidence against such suspects is extremely speculative, as in the case reprinted here, the result is often tort litigation. The suspect becomes the plaintiff. The store, as the defendant, suddenly finds itself attempting to justify its employees' outrageous conduct. Depending upon the facts, possible causes of action may include false imprisonment, infliction of emotional distress, assault, battery, invasion of privacy, or defamation. In the following case, false imprisonment and intentional infliction of emotional distress were successfully claimed, although only the issue of punitive damages was being considered on appeal.

Rogers v. T.J.X. Cos.
329 N.C. 226, 404 S.E.2d 664 (1991)
(Supreme Court of North Carolina)
June 12, 1991

MARTIN, Justice.

This action was filed on 12 August 1988 by the plaintiff for compensatory and punitive damages for false imprisonment and intentional infliction of emotional distress. Summary judgment for defendants was granted by Judge Henry W. Hight, Jr., on 3 October 1989. The Court of Appeals reversed the trial court on all claims except the punitive damages issue. [. . .] The only issue before this Court is whether there is a genuine issue of material fact on the plaintiff's claim for punitive damages. We hold that the trial court erred in granting summary judgment for the defendants on that issue and therefore reverse the Court of Appeals.

The action arose out of events occurring on 17 July 1988 at the T.J. Maxx department store in Cary, North Carolina, owned by defendant T.J.X. Companies, Inc. Taken in the light most favorable to the plaintiff, as we must for summary judgment purposes, the evidence tends to show the following. Plaintiff entered T.J. Maxx, hereinafter "the store," about 4:30 P.M. shopping for linens. She wore bermuda shorts and a T-shirt and carried a pocketbook, approximately twelve inches by twelve inches. The purse contained two cosmetic bags, a wallet, two pens, a glasses' case, and a ziploc bag containing material and wallpaper samples. Plaintiff went first to the cosmetics area and then to the linens department. After leaving the linens department, she walked around a counter containing dishes and crystal and then left the store without making a purchase. Plaintiff never entered the lingerie department and never examined any items of lingerie.

As plaintiff exited the store, Michael Nourse stopped her, identified himself as a store security officer, and asked her to return to the store because he wished to talk with her about some merchandise. Nourse carried a badge of his own design and an identification card issued by the company; he showed these items to plaintiff. Plaintiff told him that he was making a mistake, but complied with his request and accompanied Nourse to his office at the back of the store. Plaintiff testified that she did not feel that she had a choice about accompanying Nourse because "he was the law of the store" and she had to obey him. On the way to the office, Nourse asked another store employee, Sheri Steffens, to join them and act as a witness.

Once inside the small office, plaintiff immediately dumped the contents of her purse onto the desk. Nourse told plaintiff to take a seat, but she refused, saying that this would not take long because she was a good customer and had not stolen anything. Nourse responded, "Good customers will steal," and again directed her to have a seat. Telling her he would soon return, he then left the office for five to fifteen minutes. Plaintiff testified that she believed that he might have gone to call the police, and she stepped out of the office to look for them. Seeing no one, she gathered up her belongings, but did not feel free to leave because Nourse had told her he would return. Steffens paged Nourse, who returned momentarily. He said to plaintiff, "Ma'am, all we want is our merchandise. What did you do with it? You were in our lingerie department." Plaintiff denied wrongdoing, again dumped her purse on the desk, and told him that he must have seen her putting the packet of material samples into her purse. As she reached to gather her belongings, Nourse instructed her not to touch anything.

Nourse pulled down a clipboard hanging on the wall and showed her a card which said that the store employees had the right to detain her if they had reason to believe she had been shoplifting. Nourse repeatedly questioned plaintiff about the location of the missing merchandise as she tried to read the card. Plaintiff told him to "shut up" so that she could concentrate. Nourse remarked to Steffens, "Usually the dog that barks the loudest is guilty." Nourse then told plaintiff that he could call the police if she wanted them to settle it; that he could handcuff her to a chair; and that he would call the police and have them put her in jail. Plaintiff continued to deny the allegations and asked if he wanted her to take her clothes off to prove that she had not done anything, even though she was a very modest person. Steffens testified that plaintiff was very upset throughout the incident and that Nourse's attitude and demeanor toward plaintiff was sarcastic.

Nourse instructed plaintiff to sign two forms, one of which was a waiver of Miranda rights. The other form released T.J. Maxx from liability for any claims arising out of the incident. Neither of the papers had been filled out when plaintiff signed. Plaintiff testified that she signed the release form only because she believed that she would not be allowed to leave the store and go home if she did not sign it. Nourse refused to give plaintiff copies of the forms, because it was not company policy. After signing the papers, plaintiff left the store and drove home. She had been in the security office approximately 35 minutes. About one-half hour after plaintiff left the store, Nourse announced to Steffens that he had found the missing merchandise, a beige brassiere.

Plaintiff's evidence showed that she became sick, nervous and upset as a result of the incident. She had difficulty sleeping and took sleeping pills for two weeks as prescribed by her doctor. In addition, she testified that she no longer went shopping, because she felt as if someone was always looking over her shoulder.

False imprisonment is the illegal restraint of the person of any one against his or her will. [Citation omitted.] The tort may be committed by words or acts; therefore, actual force is not required. Restraint of the person is essential, whether by threats, express or implied, or by conduct. [Citation omitted.] The Court of Appeals held that plaintiff had established facts sufficient to support her claim for false imprisonment [. . .].

[The Court's discussion of punitive damages and intentional infliction of emotional distress is omitted.]

Taken in the light most favorable to the plaintiff, the evidence tends to show that (1) defendant Nourse impersonated a police officer by using a badge of his own design; (2) plaintiff was restrained against her will in the store security office for approximately one-half hour; (3) plaintiff was badgered, insulted and pressured to confess by defendant Nourse despite her efforts to prove her innocence; (4) plaintiff was frightened and upset and asked if she could leave; (5) defendant unlawfully detained plaintiff after [a] determination that no offense had been committed [citation omitted]; (6) plaintiff was made to give up personal information including her driver's license number, telephone number, and social security number; and (7) plaintiff was forced to sign a release of liability as a condition to her release from Nourse's custody. [. . .]

We hold that there was sufficient evidence of outrageous conduct, in addition to that conduct constituting the false imprisonment, to survive defendants' motion for summary judgment.

[. . .] Accordingly, we reverse in part the decision of the Court of Appeals and remand the case to them for further proceedings not inconsistent with this opinion.

REVERSED IN PART AND REMANDED.

CASE QUESTIONS

1. Given the facts in *Rogers,* did the plaintiff satisfy the elements (as discussed in this chapter) for assault, battery, intentional infliction of emotional distress?
2. You might wish to read the complete *Rogers* opinion to compare North Carolina's common law regarding intentional infliction of emotional distress with the elements discussed in § 3.4, as well as in some of the other cases partially reprinted in this chapter.

Many false imprisonment cases involve shoplifting or alleged shoplifting, as did *Rogers.* The difficulty in these cases stems from the conflicting interests involved: the patron's freedom to move about freely versus the business's right to protect its property from theft. Notice that there are competing tort interests here. The customer seeks protection from false imprisonment, while the store owner wishes to prevent conversion and trespass to chattel (two intentional torts discussed in chapter 4).

HYPOTHETICALS

Consider Sophie's predicament. A cashier thought he spotted Sophie taking some merchandise and placing it in her purse without paying for it. As Sophie walked out the exit, store security grabbed her. She violently protested, but the guards, without explanation, bodily forced her into a small, unlit room in the rear of the store. They then locked the door, and Sophie sat for three hours until the store manager, who had been on a delivery errand, returned to question her. She was, in fact, innocent of any wrongdoing. Was there false imprisonment?

The confinement was without Sophie's consent, as evidenced by Sophie's protests of the guards' physical handling of her. The restraint was obvious because the door was locked. The store security guards intended to confine Sophie by locking her in the room. She was restrained there for three hours, which would probably be considered unreasonable, particularly because the room was small and unlit. She had no reasonable means of escape, again because the only door to the room was locked. Therefore, the store would be liable to Sophie for false imprisonment.

□ □ □

Consider also the case of Murphy. Murphy drove his automobile into a restricted area of a manufacturing plant. Plant security instructed him to remain parked in his vehicle pending the arrival of the supervisor. Murphy said he had no reason to hang around, since he had done nothing wrong. The security officers then left. There were no barriers preventing Murphy from simply driving off the premises, through an open gate, to the highway. Was there false imprisonment?

The critical element in this hypothetical is the reasonable route of escape. Murphy could easily have slipped away, and the guards made no implied or expressed threats (such as arrest and criminal prosecution if he attempted to leave). Accordingly, no false imprisonment took place.

Figure 3-2 illustrates the elements of false imprisonment.

3.4 INFLICTION OF EMOTIONAL DISTRESS

We have all encountered episodes in our lives in which other persons have intentionally caused us emotional upset. Anyone with a sibling can relate to misconduct designed to annoy and distress. In the law of intentional torts, infliction of emotional distress has developed as a separate cause of action to protect injured parties from other people's efforts to cause shock, fright, or other psychological trauma.

Emotional distress may be broadly defined as mental anguish caused by a tortfeasor. Synonyms such as fright, anxiety, shock, grief, mental suffering, or emotional disturbance are commonly used by the courts to describe this tort. The condition can include shame or embarrassment as well.

The critical aspect of infliction of emotional distress is that the victim suffers from mental anguish rather than from some physical injury caused by the tortfeasor. It is the psychological harm that this tort intends to remedy.

Not just any insult or offensive behavior will result in this tort, however. The misdeed must be so *outrageous* that a reasonable person would suffer severe emotional injury as a consequence. This is the key element to all infliction of emotional distress cases. Minor annoyances or indignities are part of everyday life, and these are not included in this tort. If it were otherwise, the courts would overflow with lawsuits, based upon the irritations we all encounter from other people almost daily. Obviously, the law cannot reshape the world into the loving, peaceful utopia we might prefer, but it can discourage flagrant actions tailored to cause mental suffering.

In the field of intentional torts, there are two varieties of infliction of emotional distress: intentional and reckless. A third version, negligent infliction, is discussed in chapter 7.

LEGAL TERMS

emotional distress
Mental anguish. In the intentional torts called intentional and reckless infliction of emotional distress, the mental anguish is caused by the tortfeasor's outrageous conduct.

Confinement without captive's consent
Intent to confine
Confinement for appreciable length of time
No reasonable means of escape

FIGURE 3-2
Elements of False Imprisonment

Intentional Infliction

Intentional infliction of emotional distress contains three elements:

1. Outrageous conduct by the tortfeasor
2. Conduct intended to cause severe mental anguish in the victim
3. The victim's suffering severe mental anguish as a consequence of the tortfeasor's behavior.

Outrageous Conduct

As noted earlier, the tortfeasor's behavior must be sufficiently outrageous. The common test for outrageous conduct is one of reasonableness. Would a reasonable person suffer substantial emotional distress as a result of the tortfeasor's actions? Were these activities so outlandish as to *shock the conscience* of a reasonable person? Or, put another way, would a person of *ordinary sensibilities* suffer mental pain as a consequence? This generally excludes all but the most extreme types of egregious conduct.

Examples of outrageous conduct abound in the legal literature. Tasteless practical jokes often provide fodder for emotional distress litigation. Consider the person who places a dead mouse inside a soda pop bottle from which someone is drinking and then tells the drinker about the mouse. Or the heartless prankster who tells a parent that his or her child has just been struck and killed by an automobile when, in fact, this never occurred, as the joker knew perfectly well. Or the person who places revealing photographs of a nude sunbather all around the sunbather's place of employment for fellow workers to see. Or the individual who repeatedly telephones another at all hours of the day and night over several weeks. These are clear instances of outrageous conduct that most people would agree are highly offensive and would cause intense emotional dismay to the victims.

Intentional Acts

Obviously, intentional infliction cases must include the element of intent. The tortfeasor must purposefully behave so as to create mental anguish in the victim; the tortfeasor desires to cause anguish. This separates intentional infliction from reckless infliction, which does not require that the tortfeasor tailor his or her acts to cause mental suffering, as is discussed later in this section.

Actual Emotional Distress

Naturally, the victim must actually suffer emotionally as a result of the tortfeasor's antics. Again, the test for anguish revolves around the way a reasonable person of ordinary sensibilities would react to the tortfeasor's actions. Courts have often complained that determining genuine emotional suffering from faked distress is extremely difficult, because anyone can pretend to be

LEGAL TERMS

intentional infliction of emotional distress
An intentional tort that occurs when the tortfeasor's outrageous conduct, which is intended to cause severe mental anguish in the victim, actually causes the victim such emotional suffering as a result of the tortfeasor's actions.

reckless infliction of emotional distress
An intentional tort that occurs when the tortfeasor's outrageous conduct causes the victim to suffer severe mental anguish. Intent to produce the emotional suffering is not necessary. Instead, it is sufficient that the tortfeasor knew, or reasonably should have known, that his or her misbehavior would produce emotional distress. Often even with this tort, the tortfeasor's conduct is wanton, with no apparent regard for the victim's suffering.

upset by something. However, physical symptoms usually accompany mental distress, such as loss of sleep, weight, appetite, or vigor; illnesses brought on after the mental shock; or other signs of effect, such as tremors, twitches, or sensitivity to loud or sudden noises. It is important to note, though, that modern courts do *not* require physical manifestations in intentional infliction cases. Mental suffering alone, unaccompanied by physical effects, is sufficient, provided that the trier-of-fact is convinced of the authenticity of the distress.

Reckless Infliction

The elements of **reckless infliction of emotional distress** are the same as for intentional infliction, except that intent is not necessary. Instead, it is adequate that the tortfeasor knew or reasonably should have known that his or her deeds would cause severe emotional distress to the victim. The behavior must still be outrageous, but it is enough that the tortfeasor carelessly or wantonly acted so as to emotionally disturb the victim.

Many reckless infliction cases include the mishandling of the remains of deceased persons. Consider a common fact pattern: A funeral home cremates the deceased instead of following the family's clear and explicit instructions regarding burial. Even though the funeral home did not intend this error, the conduct could be construed as so reckless as to fall within this tort.

Another type of fact situation involves the unanticipated effect of a practical joke. Consider the pranksters who vandalized someone's automobile by smearing it with manure, knowing that the vehicle owner took enormous pride in the car's appearance. The jokers knew that the owner had a weak heart, but were only expecting to shake up the owner. When the owner saw his prize automobile, he collapsed from a heart attack. This illustrates wanton misconduct. Although the pranksters did not intend the victim to suffer heart failure as a consequence of their deed, the tortfeasors' behavior revealed utter disregard for the health and well-being of the victim, and accordingly they would be liable for reckless infliction of emotional distress.

SIDEBAR

In *Rosenberg, Field,* and *Rogers,* all partially reprinted earlier in this chapter, the courts addressed emotional distress issues. Do you believe that the facts in these cases support claims for intentional infliction of emotional distress? Why or why not?

THE CASE OF THE DAY CARE TANTRUMS

Many intentional tort cases involve multiple causes of action. Intentional torts sometimes cascade, like falling dominoes in a chain reaction, once the participants lose self-control. Tempers flare wildly and the pushing and shoving starts. This may lead to even more disgraceful behavior. The facts in the following case demonstrate this escalation effect. The tortfeasor begins with assault and battery, adds false imprisonment as anger heightens, and finishes the "tantrum" with intentional infliction of emotional distress (which, in Kansas, is characterized as the tort of *outrage*). As with the *Field* case, reprinted in § 3.2, the facts are presented in some detail to illustrate how the defendant's actions became increasingly atrocious.

Sidebar: Do the facts in the *Taiwo* case support additional claims for assault, battery, and false imprisonment?

After reading § 3.6, consider whether the facts in *Taiwo* would support additional claims for abuse of process or malicious prosecution.

Taiwo v. Vu

249 Kan. 585, 822 P.2d 1024 (1991)
(Supreme Court of Kansas)
December 6, 1991

ABBOTT, Justice:

Sherry and Obafemi Taiwo filed a civil suit against Kim Phan Thi Vu alleging assault, battery, false imprisonment, and intentional infliction of emotional distress (the tort of outrage). The jury awarded $20,000 to the Taiwos, and the trial judge assessed $3,000 in punitive damages. Ms. Vu appealed to the Court of Appeals. The Court of Appeals set aside the judgment and remanded for a new trial [. . .]. We granted the Taiwos' petition for review.

The underlying facts [. . .] are as follows:

In August 1988, Ms. Vu hired Sherry Taiwo, a certified school-teacher, to bring Ms. Vu's day-care center, Peppermint Patty's Daycare Center in Overland Park, Kansas, into compliance with state laws. Mrs. Taiwo soon resigned because Ms. Vu would not agree to follow state laws.

About three o'clock in the afternoon on August 31, 1988, Mrs. Taiwo and her husband, a Nigerian national, went to Peppermint Patty's to pick up Mrs. Taiwo's final paycheck. Ms. Vu repeatedly refused to give the check to either Mrs. Taiwo or Mr. Taiwo. A disagreement ensued, and Ms. Vu called the police. Ms. Vu told Officer Dennis R. Baldwin that Mrs. Taiwo's check would not be ready until around 6 p.m. Mrs. Taiwo agreed to come back later. When the Taiwos returned to the day-care center at the appointed hour and Mrs. Taiwo went inside to pick up her check, Ms. Vu initially refused to give Mrs. Taiwo her paycheck. Ms. Vu eventually prepared a check; however, the rate of pay had been reduced from $4.50 to $3.35 an hour, and the number of hours had been cut. Mrs. Taiwo and Ms. Vu argued about the check. Then, Ms. Vu shoved Mrs. Taiwo in the chest and told her to take the check or leave it. Mrs. Taiwo asked, "Why are you doing this?" Ms. Vu replied, "Because you quit I'm going to inconvenience you." Ms. Vu then left the building, locking Mrs. Taiwo inside the day-care center. After Mrs. Taiwo discovered she was locked inside, she attempted unsuccessfully to attract her husband's attention through a window. As she was looking through the window, Mrs. Taiwo saw Ms. Vu walk behind the Taiwos' car and write something down. Ms. Vu then came back inside the day-care center, called the police, and reported that "a black man [is] sitting out in my parking lot vandalizing my car." Officer Baldwin arrived 10 to 20 minutes later and talked with the Taiwos outside of the day-care center. Mrs. Taiwo explained the problem with the check. Baldwin suggested to the Taiwos that they contact an attorney because the difference in Mrs. Taiwo's pay was not subject to criminal law. After the Taiwos accepted the check and left, Ms. Vu then came outside to talk with the officer. Ms. Vu reported that Mr. Taiwo broke the rear window of her van. Baldwin regularly patrolled the parking lot. He previously had noticed the same damage to the rear window while on routine patrol and thus knew the accusation was false.

The next morning Ms. Vu went to the Overland Park Police Department. Ms. Vu reported that Sally Matthies, who worked at the Town and Country Store (which is across the street from Peppermint Patty's), had seen a black male damaging Ms. Vu's Cadillac (a different vehicle than the van) and had taken down the suspect's license plate number. Ms. Vu told the police she thought a former employee had done the damage. Ms. Vu then signed a police report. [. . .]

A check on the license plate number referred the police to the Taiwos. Detective Jesse Rollwagen sent Mr. Taiwo a letter, stating that a vandalism report had been filed with the Overland Park Police and that Mr. Taiwo's license plate number had been given as belonging to the suspect.

Upon receipt of the letter, the Taiwos immediately called Rollwagen and repeatedly asserted their innocence. The Taiwos agreed to and did take polygraph tests [. . .].

After the police received the results of the polygraph tests, Rollwagen again contacted Sally Matthies. She quickly recanted her story. She told Rollwagen she did not work at Town & Country, but was actually employed by Ms. Vu and Ms. Vu had instructed her to lie to the police.

Rollwagen contacted Ms. Vu again. After she reiterated the same story, Rollwagen told her Sally Matthies had recanted her story and he knew Sally was one of Ms. Vu's employees. In response, Ms. Vu claimed the name of the witness was Sally Matty, then Sally Martin, and finally Mary Ann Martin. Ms. Vu challenged the detective to prove the Taiwos had not damaged her vehicle.

Rollwagen informed the Taiwos they would not be prosecuted. [. . .]

This court has defined the tort of outrage as follows:

"One who by extreme and outrageous conduct intentionally or recklessly causes severe emotional distress to another is subject to liability for such emotional distress. [Citations omitted.] Proof of four elements is required to establish the cause of action: (1) The conduct of defendant must be intentional or in reckless disregard of plaintiff; (2) the conduct must be extreme and outrageous; (3) there must be a causal connection between defendant's conduct and laintiff's mental distress; and (4) plaintiff's mental distress must be extreme and severe.

"Liability for extreme emotional distress has two threshold requirements which must be met and which the court must, in the first instance, determine: (1) Whether the defendant's conduct may reasonably be regarded as so extreme and outrageous as to permit recovery; and (2) whether the emotional distress suffered by plaintiff is in such extreme degree the law must intervene because the distress inflicted is so severe that no reasonable person should be expected to endure it." [Citation omitted.]

Ms. Vu claims that the Taiwos failed to prove the extreme and outrageous conduct requirement. [. . .] The uncontested evidence reflects that [Ms. Vu's] behavior was intentional and malicious: she assaulted, battered, and falsely imprisoned Mrs. Taiwo; she first lied to a law enforcement officer when she called the police and then she lied to Officer Baldwin, both times claiming Mr. Taiwo had vandalized her van; she filed a false police report against the Taiwos concerning her Cadillac; Ms. Vu then induced an employee to lie to the police about the Taiwos' involvement in vandalism [. . .].

[Ms. Vu] abused the criminal justice process to her own ends. Even when the police gave her the opportunity to correct her story, she refused. Reasonable people could regard her behavior as atrocious and utterly intolerable in a civilized society. [. . .] [T]he question should be submitted to the jury.

Ms. Vu also contends that the Taiwos failed to show they suffered extreme and severe mental distress. [. . .]

"Emotional distress passes under various names such as mental suffering, mental anguish, nervous shock, and includes all highly unpleasant mental reactions, such as fright, horror, grief, shame, embarrassment, anger, chagrin, disappointment, and worry. However, it is only when emotional distress is extreme that possible liability arises.["]

[. . .]

Mrs. Taiwo testified she was fearful and very upset when Ms. Vu pushed her; she did not know what Ms. Vu would do next. Mrs. Taiwo was afraid when Ms. Vu locked her inside the day-care center that she would leave her there. Mrs. Taiwo was upset, scared, and felt taken advantage of when the Taiwos received the letter from Detective Rollwagen and when it appeared the police did not believe the Taiwos were innocent of the charges. [. . .] Until the police notified the Taiwos that all charges against them were being dismissed, Mrs. Taiwo was worried they might be arrested. [. . .]

Mr. Taiwo testified that he was scared when he received the letter from Rollwagen. [. . .] Being from Nigeria, he did not know how the police or criminal justice system in this country works. He was scared he was going to go to jail even though he had not committed a crime. [. . .]

In our opinion, the enormity of the outrage created by Ms. Vu's conduct is sufficient to satisfy the second threshold requirement of severe and extreme mental distress. Thus, the trial court did not err in submitting the case to the jury.

[. . .]

The judgment of the Court of Appeals reversing the district court and remanding for new trial is reversed. The judgment of the district court is affirmed.

CASE QUESTIONS

1. How do the elements to Kansas's common law outrage tort differ from those for infliction of emotional distress as discussed in this chapter?
2. Which of Ms. Vu's actions were sufficiently outrageous to satisfy the tort's elements?

It should not be very difficult to imagine other emotional damage infliction scenarios like those previously mentioned. However, there are many instances in which the egregious behavior is more subtle.

HYPOTHETICALS

Phyllis could offer an example. She owed money on a charge account at a local appliance store. Unfortunately, she missed several payments because of financial difficulties. Susan, the store sales manager, began repeatedly telephoning Phyllis at work and late in the evenings at home, demanding that Phyllis pay the balance due. The calls continued over several weeks. Phyllis's supervisor became angry that Phyllis was wasting company time taking these phone calls. The calls at night woke Phyllis several times and agitated her enough to keep her awake. As a result, Phyllis's job performance slumped. Phyllis lost weight and became irritable because of lack of sleep. Has Susan intentionally inflicted emotional distress upon Phyllis?

Susan's actions were designed to upset Phyllis greatly to coerce Phyllis to pay the overdue debt. Susan acted in an outrageous manner—reasonable persons would find repeated telephone calls late at night and on the job to be highly offensive. Phyllis suffered substantial mental anguish (with physical manifestations) as a result of Susan's conduct. Accordingly, Susan would be liable to Phyllis for intentional infliction of emotional distress.

□ □ □

Consider another illustration. Baker and Mortimer are accountants with the same firm. Baker planted a fake letter of termination on Mortimer's desk, in which the office manager accused Mortimer of misappropriation of client funds. Upon reading the letter, Mortimer became distraught, shaking and sweating violently and feeling nauseous. Mortimer burst into the manager's office to deny the allegations, at which time Baker disclosed his gag. Has Baker inflicted emotional distress upon Mortimer?

All the elements are present in this hypothetical, including intent to cause mental anguish. Baker should tally his own personal accounts, since he will be liable to Mortimer for intentional infliction of emotional distress.

Figure 3-3 summarizes the elements of infliction of emotional distress.

3.5 FRAUD AND MISREPRESENTATION

Fraud occurs when a tortfeasor makes false statements to entice the victim to give up something of value to the tortfeasor. **Misrepresentation** exists when the tortfeasor knowingly makes false statements or purposefully behaves in such a way as to deceive the victim. The two torts are quite similar. Both involve false statements or actions. Both include deception as the tortfeasor's objective. Yet fraud features the element of underhanded economic gain: the victim surrenders something valuable to the tortfeasor as a result of the spurious comments. As a practical matter, however, a

LEGAL TERMS

fraud
An intentional tort that occurs when the tortfeasor makes false statements to entice the victim to give up something of value to the tortfeasor. Similar to the intentional tort of misrepresentation.

misrepresentation
An intentional tort that occurs when the tortfeasor knowingly makes false statements or purposefully behaves in such a way as to deceive the victim. Comparable to the intentional tort of fraud.

Intentional Infliction	Reckless Infliction
Outrageous conduct	Outrageous conduct
Conduct intended to cause severe mental anguish	Conduct known (or reasonably should be known) to cause severe mental anguish
Victim suffers severe mental anguish as result	Victim suffers severe mental anguish as result

FIGURE 3-3
Elements of Infliction of Emotional Distress

tortfeasor who commits fraud also commits misrepresentation, although they technically are not the same tort. Still, many courts view them as synonymous.

Definitions and Distinctions

The elements of each tort are practically interchangeable. For fraud, the following must exist:

1. The defrauder must intend to deceive by making false statements
2. The defrauder must know that the statements made are false
3. The purpose of the false statements must be to entice the victim into giving the tortfeasor something of value.

For misrepresentation, the first two elements of fraud must occur. Some courts, however, also add the third element to misrepresentation, making it identical to fraud. In such jurisdictions, the two concepts are thus redundant.

False Statements Intended to Deceive

A tortfeasor commits fraud or misrepresentation by making false statements designed to delude the victim. For example, if Aaron tells Stephanie that he can repair her broken dishwasher for $100, when Aaron knows that he lacks the requisite skill and knowledge to do so, then Aaron has made false statements intended to mislead Stephanie into paying him the money for work he cannot perform.

Knowledge of Falsity of Information

The tortfeasor must know that the information given to the victim is false for fraud or misrepresentation to happen. For instance, if Henry sells Michelle a new computer with a defective floppy disk drive of which Henry was totally unaware, then Henry has not engaged in either fraud or misrepresentation, because he did not know about the product defect when he made the sale.

Tortfeasor's Profit from Deception

For fraud, the defrauder must make false statements tailored to encourage the victim to surrender something of value to the tortfeasor. In the preceding example, Aaron duped Stephanie in order to receive her money. This constitutes fraud.

THE CASE OF THE FAKED FINANCING

Fraud and misrepresentation often involve money matters. For a variety of reasons, funds may be promised but not delivered. Sometimes, deceit is the root of the evil. In the following case, a lending institution fails in its loan obligation and commits misrepresentation into the bargain. In Arkansas, this tort is called *deceit.*

*Fidelity Mortgage Company of
Texas v. Cook*
307 Ark. 496, 821 S.W.2d 39 (1991)
(Supreme Court of Arkansas)
December 23, 1991

BROWN, Justice.

The appellant, Fidelity Mortgage Company of Texas, appeals from a judgment for deceit in favor of the appellee, James Martin Cook, d/b/a Cook Construction Company, in the amount of $35,538.29. The salient issue on appeal is whether the circuit judge, who tried the case without a jury, clearly erred in finding that the elements of deceit existed in this case.

We hold that the circuit judge did not err in his findings, and we affirm his decision.

The facts involve the building of a hunting lodge instigated by two men who had formed a partnership—James Cunningham and John Staggers. The partners had agreed between themselves that Cunningham would put up the land for the lodge and Staggers would arrange the financing for the construction. The original contractor for the job quit, apparently due to a problem in getting paid. Staggers then approached a second contractor, James Cook. Cook was agreeable to doing the job for $250,000 but only if he could receive assurances that he would be paid.

Staggers had had a previous business relationship with W.R. Parker, a principal with Fidelity Mortgage Company. They discussed the need for financing to build a hunting lodge, and Parker put Staggers in touch with James Trimble, a vice-president of Fidelity. Trimble

faxed Staggers a letter on September 23, 1988, which stated that Fidelity "hereby agrees . . . to loan up to $250,000 (new loan) at a rate of 12% per annum." A commitment fee of $2,500 was required from Staggers. There was no statement in the letter that Fidelity would act as a broker for the loan or seek participation from other financial institutions. Staggers in turn faxed a copy of the letter to Cook's attorney that same day.

On the following day, September 24, 1988, Cook entered into a construction contract with Staggers and Cunningham to build the hunting lodge. Under that contract, Staggers and Cunningham were to pay Cook $150,000 after a certain part of the project had been completed. Cook began construction on September 26, 1988. During the first week of construction, Cook's attorney called Fidelity and talked to Trimble and was assured that Fidelity would pay the money to Cook in accordance with the construction contract. Trimble also testified that during the last week in September Staggers asked him to write a letter stating that the Fidelity loan was to be used to build a hunting lodge and that payments would be made to Cook pursuant to the construction contract.

On October 11, 1988, Cook submitted a bill for $150,000 to Staggers after completing the requisite part of the project. Payment was not made on that date, and Cook's attorney advised him to stop work. Due to assurances from Trimble that payment would be forthcoming, Cook continued work on the project.

Three days later, on October 14, Trimble, on behalf of Fidelity, wrote the letter that

Staggers had requested in which he specifically stated that the loan was for the hunting lodge property and that payments would be made to Cook in accordance with the construction contract. By letter dated October 18, Trimble wrote Staggers that payment would be delayed because one of the trustees (later identified as W.R. Parker) was needed to approve the check, and he was out of the country.

At some point between October 17 and October 21, 1988, Cook stopped work on the project. The amount of work performed by Cook and the fact that Cook was not paid are not in dispute. Fidelity, through Trimble, finally severed its business relationship with Staggers in November or December. At that time Trimble advised Cook's attorney that Staggers had never paid the $2,500 loan commitment fee.

Cook first sued Staggers and Cunningham for $150,000. He obtained judgment and foreclosed his lien against the hunting lodge property, thereby realizing $50,000. [. . .]

Cook next sued Fidelity for deceit on the basis that Fidelity misrepresented its capacity to make the loan and to pay him and further that it intentionally induced him to rely on these false representations. After the bench trial, the circuit judge found for Cook and assessed damages against Fidelity in the amount of $35,538.29, which represented Cook's out-of-pocket expenses for the job, less the amounts received by garnishment and foreclosure.

Fidelity urges on appeal that the elements of deceit were not proven in this case and that the circuit judge clearly erred in finding that they were. We have had occasion recently to discuss the five elements of deceit, which are:

1. The defendant makes a false representation—ordinarily, one of fact;

2. The defendant knows that the representation is false or he does not have a sufficient basis of information to make it; that is, scienter;
3. The defendant intends to induce the plaintiff to act or to refrain from acting in reliance upon the misrepresentation;
4. The plaintiff justifiably relies upon the representation;
5. The plaintiff suffers damage as a result of the reliance.

[Citations omitted.] Each element must be proven by a preponderance of the evidence in order to prove deceit. [Citation omitted.]

a. False Representation

We have no trouble in sustaining the circuit judge's finding of misrepresentation. Simply stated, Fidelity agreed to loan $250,000 to Staggers when its net worth totalled less than $50,000. Had there been any hint that Fidelity would act as the broker for the loan or would ask for institutions to participate in the loan, our conclusion would be different. But there was no such intimation in the loan commitment letter signed by Trimble on behalf of Fidelity on September 23. There, he stated clearly and unequivocally under a heading entitled "Commitment:"

> Fidelity Mortgage Company of Texas hereby agrees to loan up to $250,000 (new loan) at a rate of 12% per annum.

This Fidelity simply did not have the capability to do.

We have noted recently that many courts now construe false representation to include "(1) Concealment of material information and (2) Non-disclosure of certain pertinent information." [Citation omitted.] If Fidelity did not have sufficient assets of its own as of September 23 to make the loan, Trimble should have arranged for independent financing from other institutions before writing the loan commitment letter. But he did not do this. Rather, he obligated Fidelity to make the loan while concealing insufficient net worth and knowing full well that Fidelity did not have the capability to make good on its promise.

Fidelity argues that it was not obligated to make payments because it never received the $2,500 loan fee from Staggers. In the numerous conversations and letters between Fidelity and Cook during September and October 1988, there was no mention that the fee had not been paid. Yet all during this period Trimble made verbal and written assurances on behalf of Fidelity that Cook would be paid for his work. The trial judge correctly found that this conduct constituted a false representation.

b. Scienter

Nor do we agree that Fidelity lacked the intent to misrepresent. Trimble and Parker did not reveal the net worth of Fidelity to Cook or his attorney during the critical period of construction. Nor did they indicate that the loan fee had not been paid. On the contrary, the statements of Trimble were in the nature of assurances that all was well and that the delay in payment was only due to Parker's temporary unavailability. Only much later did the true circumstances concerning Fidelity and its relationship to Staggers come to light.

[. . .]

d. Justifiable Reliance

There is no question that Cook relied on the loan commitment. Equally as clear is the fact that Fidelity, through Trimble, knew about the construction contract and gave assurances to Cook and his lawyer that it would be paid. Neither Cook nor his attorney were alerted to the fact that anything was amiss. The trial judge's finding of justifiable reliance is not in error.

[. . .]

The decision of the trial judge is affirmed.

CASE QUESTIONS

1. What is *scienter?* What is its importance to misrepresentation?
2. Why did the court say that its decision would have been different if Fidelity had arranged independent financing from other institutions? Would this have negated the first two elements of deceit?

Classic illustrations of fraud or misrepresentation seem to utilize used car sales situations, which have become the brunt of many jokes. Still, the examples profile the elements quite well.

HYPOTHETICALS

Ask Mayfield, for instance, who purchased an automobile from Honest Eddy's Used Car Palace. Honest Eddy himself assured Mayfield that the chosen vehicle had been driven only 5,000 miles by a driving instructor from Ontario, that the brakes had just been replaced, and that the engine had been re-tuned. Honest Eddy knew that none of this was true and merely wanted to make the sale at all costs. Mayfield bought the car and drove away. Much to Mayfield's horror and embarrassment, within a week the automobile began to emit huge plumes of blue smoke from its exhaust. It also shook violently upon acceleration and made grinding noises. Has Honest Eddy committed fraud and misrepresentation against Mayfield?

The elements piece together. Honest Eddy knew that the automobile was defective, but lied about its condition to induce Mayfield to buy it. Mayfield surrendered to Honest Eddy something of value (namely, money— the car's purchase price). Because there was deception, misrepresentation exists. Honest Eddy is liable to Mayfield for fraud and misrepresentation.

□ □ □

Richard could supply another illustration. He purchased a home from Quality Construction Company (QCC). QCC's sales director assured Richard that the house had been treated for termites when, in fact, it had not. QCC had paid an exterminator to inspect the house, and the exterminator's report advised of the need for termite treatment. After living in the house for a few months, Richard discovered a serious termite infestation. Did QCC engage in fraud or misrepresentation?

The critical elements here are intent and knowledge. Did QCC's sales director know that no termite treatment had been done? QCC had received the exterminator's report recommending treatment. Thus, the sales director should have known that treatment was necessary and should have known that QCC had not performed this task. Thus, knowledge may be *imputed* under the circumstances. Intent, however, is more difficult to ascertain. Did the sales director purposefully mislead Richard? Since the director should have known that no treatment had been applied, his contrary statement to Richard demonstrated his desire to delude Richard. This equals intentional deception. Thus, misrepresentation can be proven. Also, because QCC's objective was to entice Richard to buy the house, the third element of fraud exists.

Figure 3-4 outlines the elements of fraud and misrepresentation.

3.6. MALICIOUS PROSECUTION AND ABUSE OF PROCESS

Usually the common law distinguishes malicious prosecution from abuse of process in this way: Malicious prosecution occurs in criminal prosecutions, while abuse of process happens in civil litigation. They are similar intentional torts.

Fraud	Misrepresentation
False statements intended to deceive	False statements intended to deceive
Knowledge of falsity of statements	Knowledge of falsity of statements
Statements designed to entice victim into surrendering something of value	

FIGURE 3-4
Elements of Fraud and Misrepresentation

Malicious Prosecution

Malicious prosecution arises when a private citizen files with the prosecutor a groundless criminal complaint against another person (who is named as the defendant in the subsequent criminal proceeding). The following elements comprise this tort:

1. Groundless criminal prosecution against the accused
2. The complainant's malice in filing the spurious charges
3. The accused's acquittal from, or dismissal of, the criminal charges
4. Injury to the accused as a result of the prosecution.

Groundless Criminal Prosecution

The individual registering a criminal complaint with the police or prosecutor is sometimes called the **complainant**. The complainant's actions are considered bogus if he or she preferred criminal charges without probable cause that the accused was guilty of the crime. **Probable cause** is routinely defined as the reasonable belief that the accused is guilty of the alleged crime. This belief need exist only at the time the criminal charges are initiated for probable cause to exist. However, if it later becomes obvious through investigation that the accused did not commit the alleged crime, then the complainant's insistence on continuing prosecution would be malicious prosecution.

Malice

Malice in filing spurious criminal charges may be inferred from the circumstances surrounding the case. If the complainant knew (or reasonably should have known) that the accused did not commit the alleged crime, then malice is implied. Also, if the complainant is using the criminal prosecution to obtain some improper objective, such as intimidating the accused into settling a disputed civil claim or to extort money from the accused, then this likewise implies malice.

LEGAL TERMS

malicious prosecution
An intentional tort that happens when a private citizen maliciously files with the prosecutor a groundless criminal complaint against another person who is acquitted from, or has dismissed, the criminal charges against him or her. The victim must prove some injury as a result of the malicious prosecution, and this is often shown by harm to the victim's reputation.

complainant
Person filing a criminal complaint with the police or prosecutor.

probable cause
In malicious prosecution cases, the reasonable belief that the accused is guilty of the alleged crime.

malice
In malicious prosecution cases, the complainant's intent to file spurious criminal charges against the victim.

Accused's Acquittal from, or Dismissal of, the Criminal Charges

To recover successfully for malicious prosecution, the accused must have been acquitted of the groundless criminal charges initiated by the complainant, or the prosecution must have been otherwise disposed of in the accused's favor (dismissal of charges, for instance).

Injury to the Accused

Like all torts, the accused must prove actual injury as a consequence of the wrongful prosecution. This is most often accomplished by showing damage to the accused's reputation in the community or financial standing, mental anguish, or legal expenses associated with defending the criminal charges.

Abuse of Process

Abuse of process is the civil equivalent of malicious prosecution. It occurs when the tortfeasor misuses a legal proceeding against another person to achieve an unlawful objective. The elements of abuse of process are:

1. Misuse of a legal proceeding, or threat of such misuse
2. Misuse to achieve unlawful objectives
3. Injury to the victim as a result of the misuse.

Misuse of Legal Proceedings to Achieve Unlawful Goals

The tortfeasor must intentionally misuse (or threaten to misuse) a legal proceeding against another person to accomplish an objective to which the process abuser is not legally entitled. The tortfeasor normally threatens frivolous civil litigation in an attempt to frighten the victim into paying a disputed claim. For example, the process abuser might file a groundless lawsuit against an innocent defendant in an attempt to "scare up some quick money." This occasionally occurs in personal injury litigation when fault is difficult to assign and prove; the personal injury plaintiff abuses process by suing a convenient (but innocent) defendant (who usually has assets or insurance but seems unlikely to defend a frivolous lawsuit).

Litigation is not the only legal process that may be misapplied, however. Creditors filing improper mechanic's liens against debtors to collect on disputed debts, or debtors threatening to file bankruptcy to avoid creditors, would also be guilty of abuse of process.

The pivotal aspect of abuse of process is the tortfeasor's misuse of a legal proceeding to gain some indirect benefit to which he or she is not legally entitled. The tortfeasor has an ulterior motive for manipulating the legal proceeding. The following hypotheticals illustrate how legal process may be exploited in this way.

LEGAL TERMS

abuse of process
  An intentional tort that occurs when the tortfeasor misuses a civil legal proceeding against another person to achieve an unlawful objective, and the victim is harmed as a result. Misuse can include the threat to misuse legal process.

THE CASE OF BULLDOZING LEGAL PROCESS

Anger causes people to act irrationally. Persons wishing to attack others may, out of exasperation, turn to the legal system to exact revenge, even though no legal rights have been violated. Many abuse of process and malicious prosecution cases arise in this fashion, as the following case illustrates.

Pote v. Jarrell
412 S.E.2d 770 (W. Va. 1991)
(Supreme Court of West Virginia)
December 17, 1991

PER CURIAM:

The appellants, Richard Jarrell and Hollis Jarrell, appeal from a jury verdict entered in the Circuit Court of Lewis County, awarding damages to the appellee, Kenneth Pote [. . .]. Appellee Pote filed a civil action against the appellants primarily on the theories of malicious prosecution and abuse of process [. . .]. The appellants' principal argument on appeal is that the trial court erred in denying their motions for a directed verdict on the grounds that they relied on the advice of counsel in initiating criminal charges against appellee Pote and that they did not willfully or maliciously misuse lawfully issued process. This Court is of the opinion that there is no reversible error, and accordingly, the judgment of the circuit court is affirmed.

[. . .]

The incident [. . .] occurred in October of 1987. Because of the nature of this case, it is necessary to recite the facts at some length.

Pote, in his capacity as manager of Interstate Drilling, Inc., arranged to have the appellants, Richard and Hollis Jarrell, who, were partners in an independent contracting business known as Rick's Dozer Service, provide a TD-15 bulldozer on Interstate Drilling's site to rework a road to a well location and to assist in moving pipe and equipment to the well site. The appellants provided Pote with a bulldozer and a bulldozer operator, Doyle James. Mr. James operated the bulldozer on the day of the incident for approximately three to four hours. Upon completing his work, Mr. James drove the bulldozer to the bottom of the hill near the well location [. . .] and left for the day. Pote and some other workers, however, continued to work on the well in an effort to remove a "packer." At approximately 5:30 p.m., the well had a sudden release of pressure which caused oil and water to surge to the top of the well rig and spill onto the ground. Pote and the other workers attempted to control the flow with shovels. When their attempts to control the flow were unsuccessful, two of the workers [. . .] suggested to Pote that they go to the bottom of the hill to get the bulldozer and use it to dig a ditch to contain the flow. [. . .] Pote, who asserted he was faced with an emergency situation, authorized [the two workers] [. . .] to use the bulldozer. With the use of the bulldozer, they were successful in digging a ditch to contain the flow and in keeping it from going over the hill onto the landowner's property.

[. . .]

Pote and Richard Jarrell eventually had a heated confrontation over Pote's use of the bulldozer without authorization. After their argument, however, Pote telephoned Richard Jarrell to apologize and assured him that Interstate Drilling would pay for any damage done to the bulldozer.

[. . .]

Richard Jarrell followed the recommendation of his attorney and went to the office of the magistrate to inquire about a warrant for

Pote's arrest. Upon hearing the facts involved in the incident, the magistrate informed Richard Jarrell that he believed it was a civil matter. He did not issue a warrant. Richard Jarrell then went to the office of the prosecuting attorney [. . . and] filed a complaint for a warrant charging the appellee with the offense of feloniously and willfully injuring and tampering with a vehicle in violation of [state statutes for felonious or willful vehicular damage; citation omitted].

Pote received an invoice from appellants [. . .] requesting payment in the sum of $3,560.21 for damages to the bulldozer and for lost time and income. [. . .] Pote then met with Hollis Jarrell and advised him that he would only reimburse [Jarrell] for the actual damage to the bulldozer and not for the lost time and income. Pote gave Hollis Jarrell a check for [the bulldozer damage]. Hollis Jarrell advised Pote that if he did not pay the entire amount of the invoice, he would have him arrested. [. . .] Pote [later] mailed the appellants a check covering the amount of lost income and time.

The magistrate sent Pote a summons to appear which was received by Pote the day after he mailed the check to the appellants. Pote did not appear and a warrant was then issued for his arrest. Pote was arrested, photographed and fingerprinted, and then released on his own recognizance.

[. . .] At trial, the circuit court directed a verdict of acquittal on the felony charge in favor of Pote and the case was submitted to the jury on the misdemeanor offense. Within minutes, the jury found that Pote was not guilty. [. . .]

It is well established in West Virginia that a cause of action may lie for malicious prosecution or abuse of process. At the outset of our resolution of the issues before us, we shall distinguish between malicious prosecution and abuse of process.

[. . .] "In an action for malicious prosecution, plaintiff must show: (1) that the prosecution was set on foot and conducted to its termination, resulting in plaintiff's discharge; (2) that it was caused or procured by defendant; (3) that it was without probable cause; and (4) that it was malicious. If plaintiff fails to prove any of these, he cannot recover." [Citation omitted.]

[. . .] "Generally, abuse of process consists of the willful or malicious misuse or misapplication of lawfully issued process to accomplish some purpose not intended or warranted by that process." [Citations omitted.]

It appears from the record before us that Pote presented sufficient evidence from which a jury could find that he established all of the elements of his causes of action. The evidence presented to the jury showed that the appellants procured a felony warrant against Pote and caused him to be prosecuted [. . .]. [T]he case against Pote was prosecuted to its termination, resulting in Pote's discharge. [. . .] With respect to the issue of whether there was probable cause to instigate a criminal prosecution against Pote, there was no evidence presented to the jury indicating that Pote feloniously and willfully damaged the bulldozer. Furthermore, the jury heard testimony from the magistrate that the appellants were informed that this was a civil matter rather than a criminal matter. Moreover, the appellees introduced evidence to the jury attempting to show that the appellants misused the criminal process by initiating criminal proceedings against Pote for the sole purpose of obtaining payment for damages to the bulldozer. Thus, we find that Pote established the elements [. . .] and presented sufficient evidence from which the jury could conclude that they proved those elements by a preponderance of the evidence.

[. . .]

Thus, for the reasons stated herein, we conclude that the judgment of the Circuit Court of Lewis County should be affirmed. Affirmed.

CASE QUESTIONS

1. Did the court find that the Jarrells had committed *both* malicious prosecution and abuse of process? Explain.
2. If the Jarrells had filed a civil action against Pote to recover the bulldozer damages, would that have been abuse of process? Why or why not?

When tortfeasors engage in malicious prosecution and abuse of process, their victims are often left with an unpleasant taste from the experience. The victims develop a cynical bitterness toward the apparent ease with which the legal system was manipulated against them. But tort law strives to restore the balance (and the victims' faith in the system) by affording remedies against these intentional torts. The following examples demonstrate how the legal system bites back when misused in this fashion.

HYPOTHETICALS

Martin was offended when a bookstore that sold provocative literature opened in his neighborhood. He registered with the prosecutor a criminal complaint for pornography against the bookstore in the hope that it would shut down or move away. Nothing that the bookstore sold violated the city's pornography ordinance, as the prosecutor informed Martin. Nonetheless, Martin exerted pressure on the prosecutor (through a contact in the mayor's office) to proceed, and subsequently the court dismissed the charges upon the bookstore's attorney's motion. The bookstore lost substantial business as a result of adverse publicity in the newspapers surrounding the case. Has Martin maliciously prosecuted?

Martin's criminal complaint against the bookstore was frivolous, because its merchandise did not violate any criminal ordinance. Since the prosecutor had told Martin that the bookstore was not acting illegally, Martin lacked probable cause to believe in the bookstore's guilt. Martin's malice could be inferred, because he knew of the bookstore's innocence but insisted on pressing the criminal prosecution to coerce the bookstore into closing or moving. The bookstore successfully dismissed the criminal charges. It also suffered financial injury as a result of Martin's actions. Accordingly, Martin is liable to the bookstore for malicious prosecution.

□ □ □

Felmore's Shipping Company delivered a shipment of desks to Northern Office Supply Corporation. One of Northern's employees, Tony, damaged several desks while moving them into storage with a fork loader truck. The desks were undamaged previously. Northern's president, Gertrude, filed suit against Felmore's, claiming that the desks had been damaged in shipment by Felmore's employees. Has Northern abused process against Felmore's?

Gertrude knew that Felmore's was not responsible for the marred desks. Thus, Northern's lawsuit against Felmore was groundless. Filing frivolous litigation constitutes misuse of legal process. It may be deduced that Gertrude's purpose in filing Northern's lawsuit was to intimidate Felmore's into settling the case out of court through its insurance carrier. Felmore's injury exists in that it must defend against this baseless legal action, incurring attorneys' fees, litigation expenses, and lost time for employees required to testify. The lawsuit could also damage Felmore's reputation if the business community became aware of the action, which could easily occur, as lawsuits are a matter of public record. Northern will therefore be liable to Felmore's for abuse of process.

Figure 3-5 specifies the elements of malicious prosecution and abuse of process.

3.7 INVASION OF PRIVACY

Invasion of privacy is largely a twentieth-century concept. In 1888, Judge Cooley of the Michigan Supreme Court, in his famous torts treatise, analyzed a series of nineteenth-century court decisions on defamation, trespass upon a personal property right (such as lectures or publications), and breach of confidence under implied contract law. Cooley surmised that a broader right was being protected and defined the legal interest in the famous phrase *the right to be let alone* (Cooley, *Torts* 29 [2d ed. 1888]). In 1890, a famous *Harvard Law Review* article co-authored by (later United States Supreme Court Justice) Louis Brandeis substantially expanded Cooley's theory, coining the phrase *right to privacy* (Warren & Brandeis,

Malicious Prosecution	Abuse of Process
Groundless criminal prosecution	Misuse of legal proceeding (or threat of misuse)
Complainant's malice	Misuse to achieve unlawful objectives
Accused's acquittal or dismissal of charges	
Accused's injury	Injury to victim

FIGURE 3-5
Elements of Malicious Prosecution and Abuse of Process

"The Right to Privacy," 4 *Harv. L. Rev.* 193 [1890]). American courts and legislatures throughout the twentieth century have incorporated this tort into their common law and statutes. It may be fairly said that this cause of action arose primarily because of this seminal law review article.

Simply put, **invasion of privacy** exists when someone publicly exploits another person's private affairs in an unreasonably intrusive manner. In tort law, there are four separate types of invasion of privacy:

1. Appropriation

2. Unreasonable intrusion

3. Public disclosure of private facts

4. False light in the public eye.

The United States Supreme Court also recognizes a fifth type of invasion of privacy protected under the United States Constitution. This includes actions by governmental agencies that infringe upon a citizen's life, liberty, or property interests safeguarded by the Constitution. However, this type is not covered by tort law.

Appropriation

Appropriation occurs when the tortfeasor uses a person's name or likeness without permission to gain some benefit. For example, if an advertising company uses a person's photograph to sell a product without that person's consent, then the firm would be liable to the person for invasion of privacy by appropriation. Most cases involving this variety of invasion of privacy consist of unauthorized use of photographs, artist's sketches, or quotations associated with names to sell someone else's goods or services.

Unreasonable Intrusion

Unreasonable intrusion involves an excessive and highly offensive assault upon one's seclusion or solitude. Several illustrations should clarify. If store security demands that a suspected shoplifter disrobe, or if they rifle through the suspect's personal belongings in an illegal search, this would be considered unreasonable intrusion. Intentional eavesdropping upon a private conversation is another example. Recall the Phyllis/Susan hypothetical discussed in connection with infliction of emotional distress? Susan's incessant telephone calls would also constitute unreasonable intrusion. Searching another's mail or trash to discover private information, or obtaining unauthorized access to someone's bank account or tax records, are yet other instances. Courts have also found that illegal, compulsory blood tests equal unreasonable intrusion. Simple trespassing onto an individual's land to snoop would also violate this version of privacy.

LEGAL TERMS

invasion of privacy
An intentional tort that includes four separate versions: appropriation, unreasonable intrusion, public disclosure of private facts, and false light in the public eye.

appropriation
One type of the intentional tort of invasion of privacy. Occurs when the tortfeasor uses a person's name or likeness without permission to gain some benefit.

unreasonable intrusion
One type of the intentional tort of invasion of privacy. Occurs when the tortfeasor engages in an excessive and highly offensive invasion upon another person's seclusion or solitude.

Public Disclosure of Private Facts

When a tortfeasor communicates purely private information about a person to the public without permission, and a reasonable person would find this disclosure extremely objectionable, then invasion of privacy by **public disclosure of private facts** has taken place. Truth is *not* a defense against this tort, because it is the unauthorized and offensive public revelation of private facts that is being protected against.

The most common example of such disclosure involves communications by the mass media. For example, if a newspaper article mentions an ordinary citizen by name and discusses in detail his or her drug dependency problems, and the person did not consent, then public disclosure of private facts has occurred. Public figures, however, generally do not succeed in lawsuits against the media when such disclosures are made without malice.

False Light in the Public Eye

Invasion of privacy by placing a person in a **false light in the public eye** happens if the tortfeasor publicly attributes to that individual spurious opinions, statements, or actions. For instance, if a magazine uses without permission someone's photograph and name in an embarrassing fashion, this would place the victim in a false light publicly. One fact pattern repeated in many court cases concerns a plaintiff's photograph and name which appear in a newspaper adjacent to a negative story appearing on the same page, when the story and photograph appear in such a way as to suggest a connection between the two. Another example would be the advertisement mentioned previously regarding appropriation.

LEGAL TERMS

public disclosure of private facts
One type of the intentional tort of invasion of privacy. Occurs when the tortfeasor communicates purely private information about a person to the public without permission, and a reasonable person would find this disclosure extremely objectionable.

false light in the public eye
One type of the intentional tort of invasion of privacy. Occurs when the tortfeasor publicly attributes to another individual spurious opinions, statements, or actions.

THE CASE OF THE DISSATISFIED BOOKKEEPER

Individuals often complain that their privacy is being invaded by minor intrusions. Few people live in total isolation. In daily life, blunders are observed and snickered at, causing some embarrassment for the unfortunate mistake-maker. As the following case illustrates, not every public disclosure of personal deficiencies gives rise to an intentional tort action. Note how the plaintiff "cascades" a multitude of claims from the same factual circumstances.

Loe v. Town of Thomaston
600 A.2d 1090 (Me. 1991)
(Supreme Judicial Court of Maine)
December 23, 1991

GLASSMAN, Justice.

P. Lynn Loe appeals from a summary judgment entered in the Superior Court [. . .] in favor of the defendants, the Town of Thomaston and William H. Judson, the town manager, on her action for [. . .] defamation, invasion of privacy, [and] intentional infliction of emotional distress [. . .]. We find no error in the record and affirm the judgment of the Superior Court.

The Town hired Loe as a secretary and bookkeeper in September 1986. Loe had no bookkeeping experience, and in January 1988, having become increasingly dissatisfied with her expanded bookkeeping responsibilities, she informed Judson that the job was not working out and that she would be seeking other employment. After examining the Town's books, Judson requested that Loe submit a letter of resignation. Loe refused [. . .].

During the grievance proceedings, the union representative negotiated a settlement that resulted in a $10,000 payment to Loe by the Town in exchange for her resignation and a signed release of all claims against the Town.

Soon after execution of the settlement agreement, a series of newspaper articles revealed that (1) Loe had resigned for personal reasons, (2) Loe had received a $10,000 settlement from the Town, and (3) the Town's books were in disarray. Loe instituted the instant action against the defendants. [. . .] After a hearing, the [trial] court granted the defendants' motion for a summary judgment, and Loe appeals.

[The court's discussion of the defamation claim is omitted.]

[. . .]

Loe also contends that disclosure of the settlement terms constituted an invasion of her privacy. To withstand a summary judgment on this claim she must present facts tending to show that the newspaper articles (1) intruded upon her physical and mental solitude or seclusion, (2) publicly disclosed private facts, (3) placed her in a false light in the public eye, or (4) appropriated her name or likeness for the Town's benefit. [Citations omitted.] Each of these interests in privacy is distinct and is subject to different kinds of invasion. [Citation omitted.] Loe contends that her interests in the first two types of privacy, solitude and private facts, were invaded by the publication of the settlement terms.

A complaint of intrusion upon physical or mental solitude "should minimally allege a physical intrusion upon premises occupied privately by a plaintiff for purposes of seclusion." [Citation omitted.] Loe presents no evidence that the defendants physically invaded premises that she occupied for purposes of seclusion.

Disclosure of private facts, to be actionable, requires more than a mere exposure to undesired publicity. [Citation omitted.] To be actionable, the publicity must be given to private matters as opposed to the public life of the plaintiff and must also be of a kind that would be highly offensive to a reasonable person. [Citation omitted.] Specifically, the articles in this case disclosed Loe's resignation for personal reasons, the $10,000 settlement reached between her and the Town, and the fact that the Town's books were in disarray. Each of these facts is a matter of public concern to the Town's taxpayers and not private matters in which Loe can properly claim a protectible interest. Such publication is not of a kind that would be highly offensive to a reasonable person.

[The court's discussion of the intentional infliction of emotional distress claim is omitted.]

[. . .]

We hold that because Loe failed to generate a genuine issue of material fact as to any of the issues presented, and the defendants were entitled to a judgment as a matter of law, the trial court properly granted the defendants' motion for a summary judgment.

The entry is:

Judgment affirmed.

CASE QUESTIONS

1. You may wish to read the full *Loe* opinion to compare Maine's elements for defamation and intentional infliction of emotional distress with those of the other cases reprinted in this chapter.
2. How do the elements of invasion of privacy compare in *Loe* and this chapter's discussion?

Perhaps no other intentional tort excites the public indignation more than invasion of privacy. Almost everyone desires a sanctuary from the daily intrusions that dominate our urbanized, highly technological, and mobile society. However, the popular conception of the right to privacy does not always afford legal remedies. The following hypotheticals illustrate how the tort elements must first be satisfied.

HYPOTHETICALS

Mel rents a house from Mickey. After Mel had lived there for six months, Mickey notified Mel to move out of the house within 10 days, because Mickey needed the house for his bedridden mother. Mel refused, pointing out that the lease ran for a full year and that it could not be terminated by either party without 30 days' advance notice. After 10 days, Mickey moved into the house with his mother and her two grandchildren. Mel refused to leave the house, and everyone lived in a state of considerable tension for two weeks before Mel finally could not stand it any longer and left. Did Mickey invade Mel's privacy by unreasonable intrusion?

Mickey's actions interfered with Mel's solitude in an excessive and highly offensive manner. Mel had complied with the lease agreement and had a legal right to occupy the premises. Mickey's invasion with his invalid mother and two grandchildren substantially disrupted Mel's domestic tranquility. The stress among the house occupants became so extreme that Mel was at last compelled to abandon his residence. Accordingly, Mickey would be liable to Mel for invasion of privacy by unreasonable intrusion.

□ □ □

Herman was aghast when he opened the day's newspaper to see an advertisement with his picture, in which he was holding a can of Bartell's Beenie-Weenies. Under the photograph was the caption, "Bartell's Makes the Best Beenie-Weenies!" Herman could not recall ever buying this brand and made no such endorsement to anyone associated with the product. He did not give his permission to use the photograph. Has Bartell's invaded Herman's privacy by appropriation?

LEGAL TERMS

defamation
An intentional tort that includes libel and slander. See *libel* and *slander.*

libel
One type of the intentional tort of defamation. Occurs when the tortfeasor communicates to a third person a false and disparaging written statement about the victim. The communication is called *publication.* The victim's reputation in the community must suffer as a result of the tortfeasor's actions.

Bartell's used Herman's likeness in its photograph without his consent. Bartell's hoped to profit from increased sales as a result of this "customer's" endorsement. Bartell's would thus be liable to Herman for invasion of privacy by appropriation.

Furthermore, Bartell's publicly attributed a spurious opinion to Herman in its photograph caption. This would place Herman in a false light in the public eye. Thus, Bartell's would also be liable to Herman for this type of invasion of privacy.

Figure 3-6 summarizes the elements of the four types of invasion of privacy.

3.8 DEFAMATION: LIBEL AND SLANDER

Defamation consists of two varieties: libel and slander. **Libel** is a written false and disparaging statement about an individual that the tortfeasor communicates to a third person. **Slander** is an oral false and disparaging statement about a person that the tortfeasor communicates to a third party. Courts often refer to this communication element as **publication**. Publication of the defamatory information must injure the victim's reputation in the community. The elements can be outlined as follows:

1. Written (libel) or oral (slander) statement
2. False and defamatory statement about a person
3. Tortfeasor's communication of the statement to a third party
4. Harm to the victim's reputation in the community.

Athough the first element is obvious, the others require some elaboration.

slander
One type of the intentional tort of defamation. Occurs when the tortfeasor communicates to a third person a false and disparaging oral statement about the victim. The communication is called *publication*. The victim's reputation in the community must suffer as a result of the tortfeasor's actions.

publication
A tortfeasor's communication to third parties. Publication is an element of defamation (libel and slander), commercial disparagement, slander of title, and defamation by computer.

Appropriation	Unreasonable Intrusion	Public Disclosure of Private Facts	False Light in the Public Eye
Unconsented use of person's name or likeness for profit	Excessive and highly offensive invasion of one's seclusion or solitude	Public communication of private information about person without permission	Publicly attributing spurious opinions, statements, or actions to a person
		Reasonable person finds disclosure extremely objectionable	

FIGURE 3-6
Elements of Invasion of Privacy

Nature of the Statement

For libel, the statement must generally be written in some fashion. This does not necessarily mean writing, such as handwriting, or printed words, such as those appearing on this page. There are many forms of written expression, including such unusual methods as billboards, skywriting with smoke or banners pulled by an airplane, or placing objects such as stones into the shapes of letters. The critical element of writing is whether the information is communicated visually through means of an alphabet.

For slander, the statement must be orally delivered. But it does not have to be words. Gestures, particularly obscene ones, also qualify, provided that the meaning of the gestures is sufficiently clear to onlookers to be defamatory.

Harm to Reputation in the Community

A statement is considered *defamatory* if it causes the fourth element—namely, injury to the victim's reputation in the community. For purposes of libel and slander, **community** is narrowly defined as a significant number of persons acquainted or familiar with the victim. Although some courts have held that "a community of one" is sufficient under certain circumstances, most courts maintain that larger numbers are required. Nevertheless, certain expressions, such as "a handful," "a closely associated group," and "associates in the neighborhood or workplace," suggest small numbers in most instances.

Many courts define the victim's injury in more emotional terms. For example, it has commonly been held that statements are libelous or slanderous if they ridicule, humiliate, or subject the victim to contempt or hatred from among his or her peers.

Publication

The tortfeasor must communicate the false and derogatory statement to a third party. That means that statements made by the tortfeasor directly to the victim are defamatory only if seen or heard by another or others.

Publication takes place through any means by which the false information is disseminated. This includes anything spoken, either in person or over amplification (megaphone or loudspeaker at a ballpark, for instance), radio, television, or telephone; or anything written, including letters, telegrams, scribbled messages, billboards, or printed and published works (such as a letter to the editor in the local newspaper, for instance).

Truth as Absolute Defense

Truth is considered an absolute defense in defamation cases. If the information the tortfeasor communicates is true, then no libel or slander occurred. To successfully use this defense, the tortfeasor must prove the veracity of the statement.

What is true is often a matter of opinion. It always depends upon the nature of the derogatory comments. For example, to call a person born out of wedlock a "bastard" is technically accurate, but in today's society the term is rarely used as defined in the dictionary. Similarly, to refer to a sexually promiscuous individual as a "harlot" or "gigolo" could be deemed factual by reasonable persons, particularly those who are morally opposed to the conduct described. Courts have struggled with the elasticity of truth, and a variety of formulas for pinpointing truth have been posited in court opinions. The most common states that literal truth in every detail is unnecessary. If the statement is substantially true, so that a reasonable person would decide that the accusations were justified given these facts, then truth will operate as a defense to defamation actions.

LEGAL TERMS

community
  In defamation cases, a significant number of persons acquainted or familiar with the victim who see or hear defamatory statements about the victim.

THE CASE OF THE LIVING DEAD

Imagine one's horror at opening the daily newspaper and, while glancing quickly at the obituaries, spotting one's own name listed recently deceased! Although this may be a shocking revelation, it is the type of mistake that newspapers easily and promptly correct. As the following case illustrates, an erroneous obituary does not always constitute defamation.

Decker v. The Princeton Packet, Inc.
116 N.J. 418, 561 A.2d 1122, 85
A.L.R.4th 797 (1989)
(Supreme Court of New Jersey)
August 8, 1989

HANDLER, J.

This case involves a tort action brought against a newspaper seeking damages for defamation and emotional distress attributable to the publication of a false obituary. The Court is called on to address whether an obituary that reports a death, this being the only false statement, can possibly have a defamatory interpretation. [. . .] The trial court and Appellate Division held that defamation and emotional-harm claims were without merit as a matter of law. Plaintiffs appeal these rulings arguing that defendant's publication of a false obituary without verifying its accuracy caused damage to reputation and emotional harm that should be compensated under our tort law.

I.

On February 15, 1985, the defendant, a newspaper, The Princeton Packet, Inc. ("The Packet"), which publishes on Tuesday and Friday of each week, reported the following obituary for Marcy Goldberg Decker, the plaintiff:

Marcy Goldberg Decker of Princeton died suddenly Feb. 11. She was 31.

Ms. Goldberg was the fiance of Robert J. Feldman of Princeton.

She was a lifelong resident of Princeton and is survived by a son, Jackson T.; her mother, Charlotte Goldberg of Trenton; and a brother, Ronald Goldberg of California.

Funeral arrangements were incomplete at press time.

This obituary is incorrect because Marcy Decker was not dead.

All other information in the obituary—her age, residence, and family relationships—was accurate [. . .]. Plaintiff notified defendant by a telephone call two days after the publication that she was in fact alive. The Packet printed the following retraction on February 19, 1985:

> The Packet erroneously reported in Friday's edition that Marcy Decker of Princeton died Feb. 11. The obituary was false. The Packet regrets the error and any inconvenience this may have caused Ms. Decker or her family.

[. . .]

Plaintiffs deposed three employees of defendant to establish their claims that The Packet was unaware of who had submitted the obituary, [and] that it took no steps to determine the validity of the notice [. . .].

[. . .]

A defamatory statement is one that is false and is " 'injurious to the reputation of another' or exposes another person to 'hatred, contempt or ridicule' or subjects another person to 'a loss of the good will and confidence' in which he or she is held by others." [Citations omitted.] Thus, if the statement of Marcy Decker's death in the false obituary could be interpreted by a reasonable person to expose the plaintiff to "hatred, contempt, ridicule or disgrace or subject . . . [her] to loss of the good will and confidence of the community" [citation omitted], then her action for defamation could proceed to trial.

The principle generally endorsed by most authority throughout the country is that an obituary in which the only false statement concerns the death of the individual, published without malicious intent, is not defamatory *per se*. [Citations omitted.] These cases suggest that publication of a notice of death is usually not defamatory because it does not injure one's reputation. As one court explained, "one is [not] demeaned or belittled by the report of his or her death." [Citation omitted.]

The general rule, however, does have an exception where the false obituary contains additional false information that may be defamatory. [. . .]

This Court finds that the general rule and its limited exception should govern this case and other similar cases. Here, the only false aspect of the obituary was the death of plaintiff Marcy Decker. Therefore, under the general rule, the obituary is not defamatory *per se* because the reported death of an individual when viewed from the perspective of a reasonable person of ordinary intelligence and experience does not impugn reputation. As the trial court observed, the publication of the death notice did not impute to the plaintiff any wrong and did not hold her up to ridicule. Death is a natural state and demeans no one.

[. . .] Moreover, the chance of an obituary being incorrect appears slight, and the newspaper can promptly publish a correction, which occurred in this case. Thus, the plaintiffs did have an adequate remedy to correct any false statement and the published correction should have prevented the false obituary from causing any continuing effects.

[. . .] Therefore, we hold that where a newspaper mistakenly prints an obituary for a person who is still alive and then retracts its mistake, there is no defamation *per se*, since announcing the death of someone is not by itself injurious to one's reputation.

[. . .]

Accordingly, the judgment below is affirmed.

CASE QUESTIONS

1. Do you believe the facts in *Decker* satisfy an action for intentional or reckless infliction of emotional distress? For invasion of privacy? Explain.
2. If the plaintiff could discover who planted the false obituary at the newspaper's offices, could she recover for any intentional torts discussed in this chapter against this unknown person? Why or why not?

Defamation is another intentional tort, like assault and battery, that virtually everyone has experienced, either as victim or tortfeasor (or both). One need only recall a recent imprudent remark to mentally invoke accusations of slander or libel. Nevertheless, the elements determine whether defamations has occurred, as the following illustrations show.

HYPOTHETICALS

Arnold owns an automobile painting service. One of his customers, Ginger, was dissatisfied with Arnold's paint job on her automobile; several spots that had not been polished stood out against the rest of the finish. Rather than complain directly to Arnold, Ginger simply began telling all her friends that Arnold was a "con artist" and that he had swindled many other people with sloppy work. Has Ginger slandered Arnold?

Ginger communicated information about Arnold to third persons, and so publication occurred. The information was false, as Ginger's dissatisfaction with a single paint job hardly documented Arnold's dishonesty. The critical issue is whether Ginger's statements were defamatory. It is likely that Ginger's accusations about Arnold's honesty and integrity will substantially injure Arnold's business reputation in the community. This is particularly true because the allegations suggest criminal conduct by an innocent person. Thus, Ginger has slandered Arnold and is liable to him for damages.

□ □ □

Consider the hypothetical of Helga. She enjoyed writing letters to the editor and her missives regularly appeared in the newspaper. One day Helga turned to the editorial page and read the following response to one of her letters:

Dear Editor:
In response to Helga Goldblatt's letter in last week's edition, I must say that this woman is either incredibly stupid or deranged. How can she make those totally unsubstantiated statements about the city's snow removal policy? She knows nothing about it, obviously. I happen to

work for the city street department, and I know that we regularly clear side streets after handling the main streets. It usually only takes a few extra days to get to the side streets, not weeks as she said. Why doesn't she check her facts before bleating about things she is ignorant of?

Jackson Winderson

Has Jackson libeled Helga? Jackson's written communication was published—literally—by appearing in the newspaper. Many people would have been exposed to the letter. Helga's reputation in the community undoubtedly will suffer from Jackson's accusations that she is "stupid" and "deranged." Although it may be true that Helga was uninformed about the city's snow removal policy, truth as to these matters is irrelevant — the defamatory remarks pertained to Helga's mental capacity. Jackson would be liable to Helga for libel.

Figure 3-7 lists the elements of libel and slander.

SUMMARY

3.1. Intentional torts include actions designed to injure another person or his or her property. All intentional torts embrace intent and injurious conduct. These elements must occur together. Intentional torts harming the individual include assault, battery, false imprisonment, infliction of emotional distress, fraud, misrepresentation, malicious prosecution, abuse of process, invasion of privacy, and defamation.

3.2. Assault is the tortfeasor's attempt to inflict harmful or offensive contact upon another person without consent. Assault places the victim in fear of his or her physical safety, even if the anticipated contact would produce only a distasteful reaction. The threat of contact must be imminent. Battery is a completed assault. It is the intentional, unconsented touching of another person in a harmful or offensive manner. Physical contact is required, although it may be only with the victim's clothing or objects held. Transferred intent means that the contact directed at one person carries over to another individual who was inadvertently struck, so that battery would have occurred to the unintended victim.

Libel	Slander
Written statement	Oral statement
False and defamatory statement	False and defamatory statement
Publication to third party	Publication to third party
Injury to victim's reputation in the community	Injury to victim's reputation in the community

FIGURE 3-7
Elements of Defamation:
Libel and Slander

3.3. False imprisonment is the confinement of someone without his or her consent. Confinement must exist for an appreciable length of time. The victim must have no reasonable means of escape. The tortfeasor must intend to confine the victim and act to accomplish confinement. Confinement may be achieved either by physical barriers or by threat of force which intimidates the victim into remaining in the restricted area.

3.4. Infliction of emotional distress has two versions in the intentional torts field: intentional and reckless. Intentional infliction of emotional distress involves outrageous conduct designed to cause severe mental anguish in the victim. The victim must actually suffer emotional turmoil as a result of the tortfeasor's actions. Reckless infliction of emotional distress includes outrageous conduct that the tortfeasor knew, or reasonably should have known, would produce significant emotional injury to the victim. The conduct is considered outrageous if it shocks the conscience of a reasonable person with normal emotional sensibilities.

3.5. Fraud consists of false statements made to entice the victim to surrender something of value to the defrauder. Misrepresentation includes false statements or behavior designed to deceive the victim. In many jurisdictions, the two intentional torts are considered virtually identical and interchangeable. The tortfeasor must know that the statements made are false and intend to deceive the victim.

3.6. Malicious prosecution happens when a private citizen files a groundless criminal complaint with the prosecutor against an innocent person who is named as the defendant in a criminal prosecution action. To sue the complainant, the innocent defendant must be either acquitted or otherwise victorious in the criminal lawsuit. The complainant must have filed the frivolous criminal charges out of malice for the innocent defendant, and malice may be implied from the circumstances surrounding the case. The innocent defendant must be injured as a consequence of the baseless prosecution. Abuse of process is the misuse (or threat of misuse) of a legal proceeding against another to obtain an unlawful objective. The victim must be harmed by the frivolous legal action. It is the civil equivalent of malicious prosecution.

3.7. Invasion of privacy consists of four independent varieties: appropriation, unreasonable intrusion, public disclosure of private facts, and false light in the public eye. Appropriation is the use of a person's name or likeness, without consent, for profit in some way. Unreasonable intrusion involves excessive and highly offensive interference with an individual's seclusion or solitude. Public disclosure of private facts happens when a tortfeasor publicly communicates purely private information about another person and such a disclosure would offend a reasonable person. False light in the public eye occurs when a tortfeasor publicly attributes to another spurious statements, opinions, or actions.

3.8. Defamation includes libel and slander. Libel is written communication of false and disparaging statements about an individual to third parties. Slander involves oral communication that does the same thing. Communication to third persons is called publication. The misinformation disseminated must injure the victim by harming his or her reputation in the community. Community can be narrowly defined as a small number of persons who know the victim. Even one third party is sufficient in some cases for publication to exist. Truth is an absolute defense in defamation actions.

REVIEW QUESTIONS

1. Define and discuss the specific intentional torts causing injuries to persons. Can you give examples of each? Do all intentional torts share any basic elements?

2. What is assault? What is battery? How are the two distinguishable? Similar? When is apprehension necessary? When is physical contact required? What types of contact are included? Must the threat of contact be imminent? Why are intent and consent important? What is transferred intent?

3. Define false imprisonment. What is confinement? How may it be accomplished? How are intent and consent relevant? Must confinement exist for any length of time? What role does escape play?

4. In the field of intentional torts, what are the two types of infliction of emotional distress? How are they alike? Different? What is mental anguish? Outrageous conduct? When is intent necessary?

5. Define fraud and misrepresentation. How are they similar? Distinguishable? Is intent required? What objectives must the tortfeasor have in giving false information?

6. Describe malicious prosecution and abuse of process. Can you determine why they are separate intentional torts? What makes criminal prosecution groundless? What is malice? Must the victim win in criminal litigation? What injury is required? For abuse of process, how can legal proceedings be misused? To what purpose?

7. What are the four varieties of invasion of privacy in tort law? How is each defined? Do you see any similarities between invasion of privacy and any other intentional torts?

8. What are the two aspects of defamation? How are they comparable? What is publication? What makes a statement false and defamatory? What is the role of truth in defamation?

PROBLEMS

In the following hypotheticals, identify the intentional tort(s) committed, if any, and support your answer.

1. Alicia Teldare was waiting in line outside The Elegant Shop just before the store opened on the day of the shop's annual savings sale. Dozens of customers milled around the entrance in anticipation. Many patrons began to grow impatient. Suddenly, the doors were opened, and Alicia was knocked to the ground by Marie Harrington, another customer. Alicia covered her face with her arms in anticipation of being trampled. In her haste to enter, Marie stepped on Alicia's hand and broke Alicia's ring finger.

2. Malcolm Harberry is the manager of The Soft Touch, a ladies' clothing store. Madge Strident, a customer, was looking at accessory jewelry next to the full-length mirrors. Malcolm glanced at the mirrors and thought he saw Madge place something in her purse. He thought it might be jewelry, but he did not actually see the object. As Madge began to exit the store, Malcolm asked her politely to stop. She did so, whereupon Malcolm identified himself and requested that she accompany him to the back room for questioning. She refused. Malcolm insisted, threatening to telephone the police if she attempted to leave the store. She then agreed and the two went to a small room at the rear of the store. Inside, Malcolm asked Madge to empty her pockets and purse, which she did. No jewelry was found. He asked her a few questions about the jewelry and what he had seen. She explained that she had put a handkerchief into her purse, and there was in fact a kerchief inside it. Malcolm apologized for any inconvenience and Madge then left. The interview in the room lasted five minutes.

3. Eugene Bagley III was an aspiring literature student at the state university. He had submitted several short stories and poems to *Rhapsody,* a college literary magazine. Irving Buchanan lived in Eugene's dormitory and had a reputation for playing pranks on fellow dorm residents. Irving wrote a fake letter of rejection on *Rhapsody* letterhead, which a friend had taken from the magazine's office supplies. The letter was a scathing indictment of Eugene's work as plagiarism and amateurish. The letter threatened to notify the English department and academic dean about the alleged plagiarism. Irving signed the magazine's articles editor's name. When Eugene received the letter, he became physically ill and had to visit the university hospital for medication to sleep and concentrate.

4. Dudley Dooley was a salesperson at a local hardware store. Samuel Feeber was a customer looking to buy exterior paint for his storage shed. When Samuel told Dudley he needed paint that could be used on metal siding, Dudley indicated a wood paint. Samuel inquired about

this, but Dudley said that it was not just for wood but for any surface. In fact, the paint would not adhere to any surface other than wood. Dudley had worked in the store for only a few days and knew nothing about any of the paint supplies. Samuel bought the paint and applied it. Within two weeks, the paint peeled off.

PROBLEM ANSWERS

1. This problem involves assault and battery, and whether Alicia Teldare impliedly consented to incidental contact associated with the crowd milling around The Elegant Shop's entrance. First, the elements of each tort should be discussed.

    When Alicia was knocked to the ground by Marie Harrington, this constituted a battery. The physical contact was unconsented and offensive; by knocking Alicia to the ground, Marie clearly intended to touch Alicia in an offensive or injurious manner. Another battery occurred when Marie stepped on and broke Alicia's finger. These batteries are separate incidents.

    Marie also committed assault against Alicia. When Marie knocked Alicia to the ground, Alicia was exposed to possible (further) harmful or offensive contact to her body without her consent. She suffered reasonable apprehension for her physical safety, and the threat of contact was imminent.

    Did Alicia impliedly consent to incidental contact, by gathering outside the store in a crowd before opening time? Yes. But the actual issue is whether Marie's actions were incidental contact. Arguably, being knocked to the ground by a member of a milling crowd could be incidental contact, although a reasonable person would consider such an incident to be unreasonably offensive or harmful. Most courts would rule that such contact is excessive and not incidental, unlike mere jostling between persons in the crowd. Definitely, when Marie stepped on Alicia's hand, this was not incidental contact. By being in the crowd, Alicia did not consent either to being knocked down or to having her finger broken. Thus, the contact was unconsented and Marie would be liable for both instances of battery.

2. This problem focuses upon false imprisonment and perhaps infliction of emotional distress. Madge Strident refused to accompany Malcolm Harberry to the back room for questioning. Malcolm's intent to confine was both expressed (being in the back room) and implied (police threats). Malcolm's threat to telephone the police unless Madge accompanied him to the room constituted an implied threat of force (i.e., police arrest), which satisfied the confinement element (i.e., restricting

her freedom of movement, of which she was aware and to which she did not consent). Certainly, there was confinement when the two entered the small room at the rear of the store, because this created a physical barrier and an express threat of force (Madge could not leave while Malcolm was present to probably prevent her exit).

The key to this problem is the length of the confinement. Was Madge confined for an appreciable length of time? Was five minutes an unreasonable length of time for Malcolm to inspect Madge's purse and ask questions? Many court decisions have held that short times such as this are reasonable, particularly in light of statutes permitting much longer periods of up to one hour or more. Consequently, one may conclude that Malcolm did not falsely imprison Madge.

Infliction of emotional distress is a red herring in this problem. Malcolm's only conduct that could be considered outrageous and designed to produce mental anguish was his threat to telephone the police if Madge attempted to leave the store before the purse search and questioning. Reasonable persons would agree that Malcolm's statement was reasonably calculated to encourage Madge to comply with a reasonable request, since Malcolm reasonably believed that she had shoplifted. His request was made in good faith to protect the store from theft. Therefore, any emotional distress claims should be quickly dispatched.

3. Eugene's situation involves intentional infliction of emotional distress. By writing the fake rejection letter to Eugene on *Rhapsody* letterhead, and including particularly harsh criticisms, allegations of plagiarism, and threats of exposure to the English department, Irving Buchanan engaged in outrageous behavior intended to cause severe mental anguish. Eugene became physically ill and required medical treatment. This satisfied the definition of severe mental anguish. Accordingly, Irving is liable to Eugene for intentional infliction of emotional distress.

    Irving is also liable to Eugene for reckless infliction of emotional distress, if one decides that Irving's actions were wanton and reckless instead of intentional.

4. This problem involves issues of fraud and misrepresentation. Dudley Dooley made false statements regarding the suitability of wood paint for metal surfaces. Since Dudley knew nothing about any of the paint supplies, his comments to Samuel Feeber that wood paint could be applied to any surface were implicitly intended to deceive. Further, Dudley knew these statements were false, as he knew nothing about the paint's qualities. The statements were designed to entice Samuel into surrendering something of value, namely, payment for the wood paint. All of the elements for both intentional torts were satisfied. Therefore, Dudley committed misrepresentation and fraud against Samuel.

PROJECTS

1. Brief *Frank v. National Broadcasting Co.,* 119 A.D.2d 252, 506 N.Y.S.2d 869, 57 A.L.R.4th 507 (1986), *appeal granted,* 69 N.Y.2d 607, 507 N.E.2d 320, 514 N.Y.S. 2d 1024, *appeal withdrawn,* 70 N.Y.2d 641, 512 N.E.2d 558, 518 N.Y.S. 2d 1032 (1987). The case involves defamation as a result of a comedy routine on the popular television program *Saturday Night Live.*

2. Which intentional torts discussed in this chapter are included in your state's common law? Are any defined by statute? Does your state have any additional intentional torts that deal with harm to persons?

3. Paralegal students often separate into small study groups to discuss cases and problems. You may wish to meet with several classmates to discuss the theories in this and other chapters of the book. You might wish to create your own hypothetical fact situations utilizing the intentional torts discussed in this chapter. Use the analytical methods from chapter 2 to answer your group's questions.

CHAPTER 4
Intentional Torts: Injuries to Property

OUTLINE

INTRODUCTION
4.1 TRESPASS TO LAND
    Elements of Trespass to Land
    Entry Defined
    Unauthorized Entry
    No Actual Harm Required
    Intentional Interference
    Possession: Landowner's Exclusive Right to Use
    Trespass Above and Below Land: Is the Sky the Limit?
4.2 TOXIC TORT ACTIONS
    Nature of the Problem
    Toxic Trespass
    Importance of Environmental Statutes
4.3 TRESPASS TO CHATTEL
    Unauthorized Possession of Another's Chattel
    Unauthorized Interference with Use
    Intent to Deprive or Interfere
4.4 CONVERSION
    History
    Elements of Conversion
    Depriving of Possession
    Extent of Deprivation
    Methods of Depriving
    Intent to Deprive and Convert to Own Use
    Lack of Consent
    Conversion as a Crime
4.5 SLANDER OF TITLE, COMMERCIAL DISPARAGEMENT, AND
    DEFAMATION BY COMPUTER

DATA-GRAPHIC TORTS

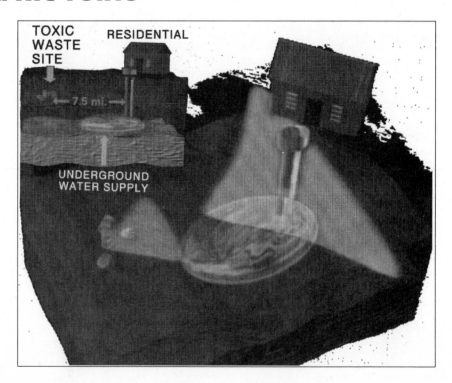

Harrison v. Cascade Chemical Corporation

The Cascade Chemical Corporation (CCC) manufactures a variety of chemicals used in manufacturing telephone and electric pole insulators. Waste chemicals stored in barrels remained highly toxic for over 100 years. In the 1930s, prior to the enactment of federal and state statutory and regulatory requirements for toxic waste disposal, CCC simply buried several hundred barrels on vacant farmland. The barrels were buried 150 feet underground in an abandoned well shaft, which was sealed and filled with dirt and rock. Over time, the barrels slowly leaked into the surrounding ground, contaminating adjacent underground water supplies. Tests indicated that the contamination reached toxic levels within 10 years of initial barrel seepage. The Harrison family lived seven-and-one-half miles from one of CCC's burial sites. The Harrisons built their home in 1975 and drank water from a well 175 feet deep. Unbeknownst to anyone, the well water was contaminated with CCC's toxic runoff. In 1991, the eldest Harrisons, Bob and Ann, both mysteriously suffered liver dysfunction. Tests showed that toxic chemicals in their water supply had gradually destroyed certain liver cell functions, leading to liver failure. The chemicals were directly linked to CCC's buried barrels.

CCC's toxic barrel burials constitute trespass to land. The runoff from the barrels into the Harrisons' well water supply is an unauthorized entry upon their land. By burying the barrels in containers that could leak, CCC's intent to trespass may be implied, because one might reasonably anticipate that such leakage would contaminate underground water supplies such as the Harrisons'. The seepage interferes with the Harrisons' exclusive right to use their land's water supply. Thus, all the elements of trespass to land are satisfied.

INTRODUCTION

The previous chapter examined intentional torts involving injuries to persons. This chapter considers intentional torts that involve harm to property or, more precisely, to property rights. This completes the intentional torts portion of the legal puzzle. About one-third of the puzzle is now complete.

The pieces to be identified and assembled in this chapter include:

- Intentional torts dealing with injuries to property rights.
- Trespass to land.
- Toxic torts.
- Trespass to chattel.
- Conversion.
- Slander of title.
- Commercial disparagement.
- Defamation by computer.

4.1 TRESPASS TO LAND

Trespass is an ancient concept in tort law. In medieval English law, torts originated from trespass and trespass on the case. Under modern American law, trespass has become entrenched in two varieties: trespass to land and trespass to chattel.

Elements of Trespass to Land

Trespass to land occurs when a tortfeasor enters upon a landowner's real estate without consent. The tortfeasor trespasses when he or

LEGAL TERMS

trespass to land
An intentional tort that occurs when the tortfeasor intentionally enters upon a landowner's real estate without consent. This trespass interferes with the landowner's exclusive right of possession.

she intentionally acts in such a way as to violate the landowner's exclusive right to use the land. The elements of trespass to land are threefold:

1. Unauthorized entry upon another person's real estate
2. Tortfeasor's intent to enter without consent
3. Tortfeasor's actions interfering with the landowner's exclusive right to use the land (possession).

Entry Defined

The tortfeasor must enter upon a landowner's real estate without permission. **Entry** occurs when the tortfeasor acts so as to interfere with the landowner's exclusive right to use the property. For example, walking across someone's front lawn constitutes *personal entry,* because the tortfeasor personally entered the land. Also, entry happens if a person throws trash in a neighbor's back yard. This is an example of *physical entry,* because the trash depositor placed an unwanted substance (trash) on the land. Both these examples include the interference element. The front lawn owner cannot utilize his or her property exclusively if someone is walking across it. The neighbor's use of his or her back yard is severely hampered by the accumulation of another's trash. The tortfeasor's conduct in either case has disrupted the landowner's exclusive use of the real estate. This is the foundation of trespass to land.

Unauthorized Entry

The entry must be without consent. This essentially translates as a permission element. For instance, if a farmer allows a person to cross his fields to reach a lake in which to fish, then that person has not committed trespass—the entry was authorized. Similarly, homeowners may invite visitors onto their premises by extending an implied welcome, such as clearing sidewalks of snow up to a house door or placing doorbells outside the doors. This suggests that people may come upon the property to speak with the landowner. Consequently, door-to-door salespersons would not necessarily be trespassing if they had reason to believe that the homeowner welcomed their presence. However, if the yard were fenced in, with a "no soliciting" sign displayed, then the salespersons would know that they did not have permission to enter the property.

Sometimes persons have a lawful right to enter upon another's land. For example, if the landowner gives an easement to a utility company to install utility lines across his or her property, then the utility company has the legal right to enter the premises to install and maintain the lines. Accordingly, no trespass to land could happen. Also, a process server, such as the county sheriff, generally has the legal right to enter the defendant's land to deliver a plaintiff's complaint and summons. No trespass to land would occur in such an instance.

One's lawful right to be upon another's premises may be withdrawn, however. Consider the example of the patron of a store. Customers are invited to come upon the premises to spend money. Suppose one such individual becomes disruptive, annoying other shoppers and employees. The store manager could demand that the agitator leave immediately. At this point, the customer becomes a trespasser, since remaining means that he or she is present upon another's land without consent. Although the provocateur was originally invited into the store as a patron, once he or she was ordered to leave, trespass occurred.

No Actual Harm Required

It is important to note that, under trespass law, the unauthorized entry need not cause any damage to the real estate. It is sufficient that the transgression occurred. Trespass law presumes that injury has happened simply because the tortfeasor has interfered with the landowner's use of the realty. Thus, simply walking across someone's front lawn without permission is trespass to land, although no actual harm arises from the conduct. These types of trespasses to land are often called *technical trespasses*. Courts generally award only nominal damages in such cases. **Damages** are dollar amounts that the defendant must pay the plaintiff if the plaintiff wins judgment against the defendant. In technical trespass cases, courts usually award a paltry sum, such as one dollar, because no actual injury was due to the trespass. The judgment award is ceremonial or symbolic of the technical invasion of the landowner's property rights.

As a practical matter, few lawsuits involve technical trespasses. It is simply too expensive to litigate a trespass action when no injury has resulted. Litigants frequently speak of suing "as a matter of principle," but plaintiffs are rarely sufficiently affluent to afford it.

Intentional Interference

The tortfeasor must have intended to enter the landowner's real estate without consent. Thus, if Twila is forced to cross a neighbor's front yard to escape a pursuing wild animal, she has not committed trespass to land. Twila did not intend to cross her neighbor's property without permission; rather, she was essentially forced across by the chasing animal. However, if she digs a hole in her neighbor's yard while searching for a water pipe, the entry was intentional.

LEGAL TERMS

entry
    Occurs when a tortfeasor interferes with a landowner's exclusive right to use the land. There are two types: personal and physical.

damages
    The injury that a plaintiff suffers as a result of the defendant's actions. The most common types of damages involve compensation for loss of money or value.

Possession: Landowner's Exclusive Right to Use

To comprise trespass to land, the tortfeasor's unauthorized entry must interfere with the landowner's exclusive right to use his or her realty. This is sometimes called the **exclusive right of possession**, which entitles the landowner to use the property without anyone else's meddling. Recall the illustrations from the discussion of entry: the neighbor could not use his or her land exclusively if someone else's trash was being dumped on it. Nor could someone use his or her front lawn exclusively if another person walked across it.

This exclusivity requirement may at first appear overly harsh. One might well ask what wrong has been done just by crossing someone's land. Trespass intends to protect one's real estate in much the same way as assault and battery are intended to protect one's person. The objective is protection from undesired interferences. In this respect, trespass seeks merely to protect one's realty from other people encroaching upon it, just as assault and battery are meant to deter unwanted physical contact.

Trespass Above and Below Land: Is the Sky the Limit?

Trespass to land may occur not only upon the surface of the realty, but also above and below it. In property law, a Latin phrase summarizes the extent of one's ownership of land: *cujus est solum ejus est usque ad coelum* ("he who has the soil owns upward unto heaven and downward to perdition"). Thus, it is possible for trespass to occur in the air above one's land. For instance, if a utility company erects wires across one's land without consent, this would constitute trespass to land, because the landowner owns the air above the soil. This could present insurmountable difficulties for aircraft. Fortunately, modern common law implies an exception for aircraft to fly over private property.

Similarly, one owns the resources under the earth. Although this enters into the complex area of oil, gas, and mineral law (within which special legal theories have evolved), it may be said generally that one owns the mineral resources beneath one's real estate. Accordingly, if someone mines under a person's land without permission, trespass to land has occurred. Cave exploration cases provide an interesting aspect of this theory. In a famous Indiana court case, *Marengo Cave Co. v. Ross,* 212 Ind. 624, 10 N.E.2d 917 (1937), the Supreme Court of Indiana stated that it was a trespass for the cave company to charge admission for tourists to explore caves below the surface of a landowner's property.

LEGAL TERMS

exclusive right of possession
A landowner's right to use his or her property without interference from other persons.

THE CASE OF THE UNHOLY WATERS

Many invasions onto one's realty can result in trespass to land. Persons and manmade objects readily come to mind as examples. But what about natural substances, such as rainwater? This, too, can provide an injured landowner with a cause of action, should the water, as it often does, cause structural damage.

In the following case, displaced rainwater creates a multitude of problems for the property owners. Although the church believes that rain is an act of God, there are times when even the most pious institutions fall victim to poor drainage and even poorer land use planning.

Burt v. Beautiful Savior Lutheran Church of Broomfield
809 P.2d 1064 (Colo. Ct. App. 1990)
(Colorado Court of Appeals)
October 25, 1990

Opinion by Judge DAVIDSON.

Defendant, Beautiful Savior Lutheran Church of Broomfield, appeals a judgment entered on a jury verdict in favor of plaintiffs, Wayne Burt, Donna Draper, and Curtis Draper, for water damage to Burt's real property resulting from defendant's negligence and trespass. We affirm in part, reverse in part, and remand with directions.

Defendant and Burt are adjoining landowners. The Drapers are Burt's daughter and son-in-law, and are tenants in the Burt residence. Defendant's property, which is immediately west of Burt's, is markedly sloped downwards directly toward the Burt property. Both properties have been plagued with water drainage problems for many years.

In 1964, Burt's property was flooded by surface water from a heavy rain. At that time, he installed an underground drain from his backyard to his front yard which emptied into the street. Then, in 1979, defendant converted the area immediately west of Burt's property into a paved parking lot.

Approximately four years later, in August 1983, after another heavy rain caused flooding on his property, Burt dug a ditch, in part of

defendant's property, to drain water into a storm drain on the street. At the same time, in response to flooding on its property, defendant constructed a 15-foot manhole with a sump pump at a corner of its foundation wall and installed a drainpipe underground from the sump pump to the street. This drainpipe extended along the boundary between defendant's and Burt's property emptying into the street just west of the Burt property. According to defendant's evidence, at the time the drainpipe was installed, the church pastor asked Burt if he objected to the removal of certain trees which Burt had planted on defendant's property in 1961. The pastor testified that, although he told Burt there was a danger of roots clogging the new drainpipe, Burt replied he did not want the trees removed.

In 1984, approximately six months after defendant's drainpipe was installed, Burt noticed that water was coming into his basement through cracks in the foundation. Responding to Burt's complaint, defendant constructed a dirt berm on its property to deflect surface water flowing down towards Burt's property. Nevertheless, Burt's foundation continued to crack and deteriorate.

Evidence at trial indicated that defendant had installed a drainpipe which was inadequate in size and had unsealable joints that were virtually certain to leak. The evidence also showed that the drainpipe had been improperly installed and was clogged with tree roots. In

June 1987, defendant replaced the drainpipe and the water flow into Burt's basement stopped.

Burt then brought this action seeking damages for the repair of his basement foundation, alleging theories of negligence and trespass. At the close of the evidence, the court instructed the jury, without objection, on both trespass and negligence. The trial court, however, refused defendant's request to instruct the jury on comparative negligence. In its ruling, the trial court reasoned that comparative negligence was not appropriate because "it's just for the jury to decide whether there is ground water that was there historically or whether it was created by the church's actions." The trial court also refused defendant's requested instruction of plaintiffs' failure to mitigate damages.

The jury returned a verdict for plaintiffs on both trespass and negligence, and defendant appeals, alleging the refusal to so instruct the jury, and other actions by the trial court, constituted reversible error. Plaintiffs cross-appeal on the issues of costs and interests. We affirm the judgment and reverse and remand on the issue of costs and interest.

I

[The Court's discussion of comparative negligence issue is omitted. The Court concluded that the doctrine was inapplicable to trespass actions.]

In early English law, the writ of "trespass" had a basic criminal character and provided a cause of action for all direct and immediate injuries to person or property. "Trespass on the case," a separate writ which developed later, originally allowed remedies for all indirect injuries. [. . .]

In Colorado, liability for trespass requires only an intent to do the act that itself constitutes, or inevitably causes, the intrusion.

[Citation omitted.] Specifically, trespass is the physical intrusion upon property of another without the permission of the person lawfully entitled to the possession of the real estate. [Citation omitted.] "One is subject to liability to another for trespass, irrespective of whether he thereby causes harm to any legally protected interest of the other, if he intentionally . . . enters land in the possession of the other, or causes a thing or a third person to do so. . . ." [Citations omitted.]

Thus, a landowner who sets in motion a force which, in the usual course of events, will damage property of another, is guilty of trespass on such property. [Citations omitted.] Here, defendant's act of constructing the drainpipe in such a way as to cause water leakage into Burt's property amounted to a trespass.

[. . .]

Here, defendant does not dispute that the evidence was sufficient to support the jury's verdict for plaintiffs on their trespass claim. Therefore, because the defense of comparative negligence is inapplicable to trespass, the failure of the court to instruct the jury thereon was not error.

II

[The Court's discussion of the mitigation of damages issue is omitted.]

Compensation for injury resulting from trespass can include (a) the diminution of market value or the costs of restoration, (b) the loss of use of the property, and (c) discomfort and annoyance to the occupant. [Citations omitted.] Since the Drapers were in possession of the property and therefore are entitled to damages for trespass, [citation omitted], defendant is liable to the Drapers for the damage to their possessory interests. These damages include the loss of use of their basement and the discomfort and annoyance caused by the smell in their home.

[The Court's discussion on the remaining, tangential issues is omitted.]

CASE QUESTIONS

1. How does the definition of trespass to land in *Burt* compare with the general description in this chapter?
2. When Burt dug his ditch partially upon the defendant's land in August 1983, was this trespass to land?

The sanctity of one's land is an ancient aspect of the human psyche. For millennia, people have used physical force and, as civilization progressed, force of law to protect against such invasions. Today's trespass to land remains an active intentional tort, as these hypotheticals demonstrate.

HYPOTHETICALS

Burrough Excavating Company was digging a basement for a new home. Burrough's backhoe operator dumped the dirt on a vacant lot next to the construction site. This lot was owned by Mark, who never gave Burrough permission to use his lot. Has Burrough trespassed to land against Mark?

The elements line up nicely. Mark did not consent to Burrough's dirt dumping, and so Burrough engaged in unauthorized entry upon another's realty. Burrough obviously intended this entry, since the backhoe operator dumped the dirt on Mark's lot. This dumping interfered with Mark's exclusive use of his property, because he will now have to contend with the dirt pile if he wishes to use his lot. Therefore, Burrough has committed trespass to land against Mark.

□ □ □

Consider another hypothetical. George owns a house next to Elizabeth. Elizabeth has several oak trees on her property with branches that hang over a fence separating her property from George's. George thought the trees were unsightly and trimmed the limbs that hung over onto his yard. He did not ask Elizabeth for permission to remove the limbs. Has a trespass occurred?

Who has trespassed? By allowing her tree branches to cross over onto George's property, Elizabeth committed unauthorized entry onto another's land without consent. Her trees interfered with George's exclusive right of possession, because the branches obstructed George's use of this part of his property. Recall, too, that George owns to the top of the sky under the *ad coelum* doctrine discussed earlier. Anything encroaching upon his airspace constitutes entry. Intent may be implied, since Elizabeth knew the trees crossed the fence but did nothing to remove the overhanging limbs. Thus, Elizabeth has trespassed upon George's land.

Somewhat more problematic is the inverse inquiry: namely, did George trespass against Elizabeth by pruning the trees? Because the trees grew on Elizabeth's property, George's trimming (without permission) encroached upon Elizabeth's use of her trees. But does this constitute unauthorized entry onto another's land? The branches hung over onto George's property, so he did not actually enter upon Elizabeth's land to cut the limbs. He was simply "defending" his property from the encroaching branches. Accordingly, George did not commit trespass to land against Elizabeth.

Recent trespass actions have involved one of the most complex and dynamic developing areas of tort law—namely, toxic tort litigation. Section 4.2 discusses this type of trespass.

4.2 TOXIC TORT ACTIONS

A significant percentage of modern tort litigation is devoted to actions involving toxic chemicals, pollution, hazardous waste disposal and transportation, and other environmentally sensitive issues. These are sometimes referred to as **toxic tort actions**. These lawsuits cover causes of action from all of the torts puzzle pieces: trespass to land, negligence, absolute liability for ultrahazardous substances, products liability, and nuisance. This chapter focuses on the trespass to land aspects of toxic tort litigation.

Nature of the Problem

For much of this century, toxic waste disposal was considered simple. Manufacturers or chemical processors applied a centuries-old approach: "out of sight, out of mind." Hazardous waste was simply buried, dumped into waterways, or burned. Much toxic waste found its way into public and private landfills, rivers, and smoke-belching incinerators. This did not eliminate the noxious nature of the waste products, however; it simply shifted the problem to another location. As the years passed, barrels buried at the underground sites rusted and leaked, sending lethal seepage through the soil, contaminating underground water supplies, injuring people drinking contaminated well water. Toxic burial leakage also percolated from underground through springs, exposing innocent bystanders to carcinogenic or otherwise lethal substances in surface waters. Rivers and streams simply carried the sludge to haunt downstream landowners, who came into contact with the poisons through irrigation or otherwise working with the polluted waters.

Residents near the incineration plants suffered a variety of lung ailments from the poisonous air pollutants.

Traditionally, all these intrusions fell neatly within the intentional tort of trespass to land. Nuisance, which is discussed in chapter 11, provided neighboring landowners another cause of action with which to litigate against the industrial toxic polluters. Absolute liability, discussed in chapter 9, also applied under the ultrahazardous substances theory. Negligence, the subject of chapter 6, lent further legal aid to plaintiffs seeking relief against injuries from the unwanted and toxic invaders.

Toxic Trespass

Trespass to land occurs when toxic substances enter upon another's property. The trespass elements remain the same:

1. Unauthorized entry upon another person's real estate

2. Tortfeasor's intent to enter without consent

3. Tortfeasor's actions interfering with the landowner's exclusive right to use the land (possession).

In the case of toxic substances, the unauthorized entry is seepage or accumulation of the hazardous material on the victim's land. Few owners consent to having toxins placed over, upon, or under their realty. Most people want such materials to be taken as far away from them as possible.

The tortfeasor's intent to enter without permission may be implied from the disposal method used. For instance, toxic waste buried in metal barrels will, over time, rust through and seep into the underground soil, unless the material is contained in an isolated fashion, such as an underground concrete crypt. If the tortfeasor failed to take sufficient precautions to prevent subterranean seepage, then the intent to trespass may be implied. Another example of implied intent is dumping toxic fluids into waterways. The tortfeasor desired the river or stream to carry the dangerous substances downstream, which would plainly deposit the gunk on the shores of other people's property.

The tortfeasor's interference with the plaintiff's exclusive possession of his or her land is equally clear. The toxic residues are a highly offensive and potent invasion, making some real estate uninhabitable. A more significant illustration of trespass would be difficult to imagine.

When landowners' underground water supplies are contaminated with buried toxic waste seepage, trespass to land occurs. A quick review of the elements shows that they are readily satisfied. Many cases in the court reports tell sad tales of families irreparably harmed through long-term consumption of chemically contaminated well water, poisoned as a result of improper underground waste disposal.

LEGAL TERMS

toxic tort actions
Actions involving toxic chemicals, pollution, hazardous waste disposal and transportation, and other environmentally sensitive issues. This litigation applies many tort theories, including trespass to land, negligence, absolute liability for ultrahazardous substances, products liability, and nuisance.

Importance of Environmental Statutes

Aside from trespass, nuisance, absolute liability, and negligence, there are a plethora of federal, state, and local statutes regulating environmental toxins. One important federal statute is the Toxic Substances Control Act. Another is the Hazardous Materials Transportation Act. Another regulates hazardous waste disposal facilities. These statutes are summarized as follows:

61A AM. JUR. 2D, *Pollution Control* §§ 252-53, 277-89 (1981)

[All footnotes omitted.]

[§ 252]   Transporters of hazardous waste must comply with regulations [promulgated pursuant to the Hazardous Materials Transportation Act of 1975, 49 U.S.C. §§ 1801-12 (1992)] which establish standards [. . .] to protect human health and the environment. Such requirements may include recordkeeping, labeling, compliance with the manifest system, and transportation of all such hazardous waste only to the hazardous waste treatment, storage, or disposal facilities which the shipper designates on the manifest form to be a facility holding a valid permit. [. . .]

The safety aspects of loading, unloading, and handling of materials in transportation are the primary responsibility of the Department of Transportation. [. . .]

For purposes of transportation law, "hazardous material" means a substance or material in a quantity and form which may pose an unreasonable risk to health and safety or property when transported in commerce. Such materials may include, but are not limited to, explosives, radioactive materials, etiologic agents, flammable liquids or solids, combustible liquids or solids, poisons, oxidizing or corrosive materials, and compressed gases. The Secretary of the Department of Transportation designates those materials which he finds may pose an unreasonable risk to health and safety or property when transported in commerce.

The Secretary may issue regulations for safe transportation in commerce of hazardous materials. [. . .]

[§ 253]   The EPA is required to establish standards for the location, design, construction, monitoring, and operation of hazardous waste treatment, storage, and disposal facilities. [. . .]

[§ 277]   Among the many chemical substances and mixtures which are constantly being developed and produced, there are some whose manufacture, processing, distribution in commerce, use, or disposal may present an unreasonable risk of injury to health or the environment. These are regulated under a national program administered by the Environmental Protection Agency [EPA]. [This is the Toxic Substances Control Act, 15 U.S.C. § 2601 *et seq.* (1992)]. In exercising any authority, the [EPA] Administrator shall not be deemed to be exercising statutory authority to prescribe or enforce standards or regulations affecting occupational health and safety [which is subject to the Occupational Safety and Health Act, 29 U.S.C. § 651 *et seq.* (1992)].

The Administrator shall coordinate with other federal agencies for the purpose of achieving maximum enforcement while imposing the least burden of duplicative requirements on those subject to regulation. [. . .]

[§ 278]   Any state or political subdivision of a state retains the authority to regulate chemical substances or mixtures. However, if the [EPA] Administrator promulgates a rule to require testing of a chemical substance or mixture, no state or political subdivision may establish a requirement for testing of such substance or mixture for purposes similar to those for which testing is required under the federal rule. States and political subdivisions are also limited in the extent to which they regulate chemical substances or mixtures affected by premarket testing regulations and regulations controlling the manufacture, processing, distribution in commerce, or use of chemical substances or mixtures. These limitations do not affect the state's authority to regulate disposal of chemical substances or mixtures.

[. . .]

[§ 279]   Adequate data should be developed with respect to the effect of chemical substances and mixtures on health and the environment and the development of such data has been made the responsibility of those who manufacture and those who process such chemical substances and mixtures. The Administrator of the Environmental Protection Agency has authority to promulgate rules which require testing of chemical substances or mixtures which may present an unreasonable risk of injury to health or the environment, and which require testing of chemical substances or mixtures which will be produced in substantial quantities, and which either enter or reasonably may be anticipated to enter the environment in substantial quantities or else there is or may be significant or substantial human exposure to such substance or mixture. Testing shall be conducted on such substance or mixture to develop data with respect to the health and environmental effects for which there is an insufficiency of data and experience. It shall be unlawful for any person to fail or refuse to comply with any rule promulgated or order issued with respect to testing rules.

[. . .]

A committee shall recommend which chemical substances and mixtures should be given priority consideration for testing. The committee's recommendation shall be in the form of a list, and the committee shall give priority attention to those chemical substances and mixtures which are known to cause or contribute to, or which are suspected of causing or contributing to, cancer, gene mutations, or birth defects.

[. . .]

[§ 283]   If the information available to the [EPA] Administrator is insufficient to permit a reasoned evaluation of the health and environmental effects of a chemical substance with respect to which notice [of its manufacture or processing] is required, the Administrator may issue a proposed order to prohibit or limit the manufacture, processing, distribution, use, or disposal of such substance [. . .].

The Administrator may seek an injunction in the appropriate District Court of the United States to prohibit or limit the manufacture, processing, distribution in commerce, use, or disposal of such substance. [. . .]

SIDEBAR

The **Hazardous Materials Transportation Act** regulates the transportation of toxic substances. The statute is administered primarily by the United States Department of Transportation.

□ □ □

The **Toxic Substances Control Act**, administered by the EPA, controls the manufacture, processing, distribution, use, and disposal of hazardous materials. Regulations establish the record keeping, research, and testing procedures for development of new chemical substances that may pose environmental or health hazards.

[§ 284]   By rule the [EPA] Administrator can regulate a chemical substance or mixture if he finds that there is a reasonable basis to conclude that the manufacture, processing, distribution in commerce, use, or disposal of such substance, [. . .] will present an unreasonable risk of injury to health or the environment. [. . .]

Except for the reporting and recordkeeping requirements, regulations shall not apply to any chemical substance or mixture being manufactured, processed, or distributed in commerce for export from the United States, provided the substance or mixture or container bears a stamp or label stating that it is intended for export.

It shall be unlawful for any person to fail or refuse to comply with regulations or orders concerning the manufacture, processing, distribution in commerce, use, or disposal of chemical substances or mixtures. It shall be unlawful for any person to use for commercial purposes a chemical substance or mixture which such person knew or had reason to know was manufactured, processed, or distributed in commerce in violation of a rule or order.

[. . .]

[§ 286]   Except for small manufacturers or processors, each person who manufactures or processes [. . .] shall maintain such records and shall submit such reports as the [EPA] Administrator may reasonably require. [. . .] It shall be unlawful for any person to fail or refuse to submit reports or other information. [. . .]

Any person who manufactures, processes, or distributes in commerce any chemical substance or mixture shall maintain records of significant adverse reactions to health or the environment alleged to have been caused by the substance or mixture. Such records shall include records of consumer allegations of personal injury or harm to health, reports of occupational disease or injury, and reports or complaints of injury to the environment. [. . .]

[§ 287]   The [EPA] Administrator or an authorized representative may inspect any establishment, facility, or other premises in which chemical substances or mixtures are manufactured, processed, stored, or held before or after distribution in commerce. [. . .] It shall be unlawful for any person to fail or refuse to permit entry or inspection as required.

[. . .]

[§ 288]   Any person who commits a prohibited act shall be liable for a civil penalty, each day of continued violation constituting a separate violation. [. . .] In determining the amount of a civil penalty, the [EPA] Administrator shall take into account the nature, circumstances, extent, and gravity of the violation or violations and, with respect to the violator, ability to pay, effect on ability to continue to do business, any history of prior such violations, [and] the degree of culpability [. . .].

Criminal penalties are available against any person who knowingly or willfully commits a prohibited act.

[. . .]

[§ 277]   In 1980, the Congress enacted the Comprehensive Environmental Response, Compensation, and Liability Act which is applicable to imminently hazardous chemical substances and mixtures. [. . .]

[§ 289] The term "imminently hazardous chemical substance or mixture" means a chemical substance or mixture which presents an imminent and unreasonable risk of serious or widespread injury to health or the environment. Such a risk to health or the environment shall be considered imminent if it is shown that the manufacture, processing, distribution in commerce, use, or disposal of the chemical substance or mixture [. . .] is likely to result in injury to health or the environment before a final [EPA] rule can protect against such risk.

The [EPA] Administrator may commence a civil action in an appropriate District Court of the United States for seizure of an imminently hazardous chemical substance or mixture and for relief against any person who manufactures, processes, distributes in commerce or uses or disposes of [such substances] [. . .].

Trespass to land is merely one type of trespass action. Trespass to chattel is the other and is discussed next.

4.3 TRESPASS TO CHATTEL

A tortfeasor commits **trespass to chattel** when he or she possesses someone's personal property without consent. A **chattel** is personal property, as opposed to real property, which is land. An automobile, a textbook, a pet dog or cat, and a desk are examples of chattels. Trespass to chattel has elements similar to those of trespass to land:

1. Unauthorized possession of, or interference with the use of, another individual's personal property
2. Intent to deprive (or interfere with) the owner's possession or exclusive use of his or her chattel.

Unauthorized Possession of Another's Chattel

Suppose Nadene takes a neighbor's textbook during class. Unless Nadene obtained the neighbor's consent before seizing the text, Nadene has engaged in unauthorized possession of another's personal property. The book's owner did not give Nadene permission to possess the chattel. When a tortfeasor takes possession of another's personal property without consent, this is sometimes described as the act of **dispossession**. (See also the discussion of conversion in § 4.4.)

Consent may be implied under certain circumstances. For instance, if Alfred gives his car keys to a friend, the implication is that the friend may use Alfred's motor vehicle. Similarly, hotel guests may presume that the management intended them to use the electricity, water, soap, and tissues supplied to the rooms. However, if a patron takes the hotel's pillows, sheets, and towels, this would be unauthorized possession, as staying in a hotel does not implicitly entitle guests to such items.

SIDEBAR

The **Comprehensive Environmental Response, Compensation, and Liability Act** (CERCLA) is another federal statute affecting imminently hazardous substances. CERCLA gives the EPA authority to file civil lawsuits against persons violating these and other federal statutes.

LEGAL TERMS

trespass to chattel
Occurs when the tortfeasor intentionally deprives or interferes with the chattel owner's possession or exclusive use of personal property. The tortfeasor's possession or interference must be unauthorized, which means that the owner cannot have consented.

chattel
Personal property, such as an automobile, a pet, clothing, appliances, this textbook, or a bicycle.

dispossession
Occurs when a tortfeasor deprives a chattel owner of possession of his or her property without consent. An important element in the intentional torts of trespass to chattel and conversion.

Unauthorized Interference with Use

It is possible to trespass to chattel without actually wrenching possession of the personal property from its rightful owner. Interference with the chattel owner's use of the property is sufficient. For instance, if a tortfeasor purposely fed Reggie's prize hogs a contaminated food, so that the hogs became ill and lost weight, then the tortfeasor engaged in unconsented interference with Reggie's use of the animals. If Cherrie's landlord shuts off the electricity to her apartment without permission, then this would also constitute unauthorized interference with the use of her personal property (provided, of course, that Cherrie had paid her electric bill).

Intent to Deprive or Interfere

To commit trespass to chattel, the tortfeasor must intend to interfere with or deprive the chattel owner of possession or the exclusive use of his or her personal property. Intent may be expressed, as it was when Nadene took her neighbor's book. It may also be implied under the circumstances. For example, assume that Cherrie's landlord changed the locks on her apartment door in order to lock her out, although she had paid her rent and had done nothing to violate her rental agreement. This would imply the landlord's intent to deprive Cherrie of possession of her personal property inside the apartment. Her use of the chattels would definitely be hindered.

Similarly, lack of intent may be implied. For example, assume Bud found his neighbor's cow grazing along a public highway and took the animal to his barn for safekeeping until he could telephone the neighbor. Although Bud took possession of the cow without his neighbor's consent, Bud did not intend to interfere with the neighbor's use of the cow. Nor did he wish to deprive his neighbor of possession. Bud simply wished to protect the animal from harm. This is emphasized by his efforts to contact his neighbor to come claim the cow. Thus, Bud lacked intent to trespass to chattel.

Figure 4-1 summarizes the elements of trespass to land and trespass to chattel.

Trespass to Land	Trespass to Chattel
Unauthorized entry upon another person's real estate	Unauthorized possession of another individual's personal property *or* unauthorized interference with another's use of his or her chattel
Intent to enter without consent (no harm to land required)	Intent to dispossess or interfere with owner's use of his or her personal property
Interference with landowner's exclusive right to use land (possession)	Similar to conversion, which also requires tortfeasor to put dispossessed chattel to own use

FIGURE 4-1
Elements of Trespass
to Land and Trespass
to Chattel

A CASE OF NOT-SO-GUT-WRENCHING CONFLICT

Not every invasion of one's personal property constitutes trespass to chattel. Actual dispossession must occur. A trifling interference, fleeting and momentary, will be tolerated under the law. As the following case demonstrates, the invasion of this plaintiff's chattel was insufficient to give rise to this cause of action.

Koepnick v. Sears, Roebuck & Co.
158 Ariz. 322, 762 P.2d 609 (1988)
(Court of Appeals of Arizona)
June 16, 1988

OPINION

FROEB, Presiding Judge.
[. . .] The issues presented on appeal are: [. . .] whether the trial court erred in granting Sears' motion for judgment notwithstanding the verdict (judgment n.o.v.) on Koepnick's trespass to chattel claim. [. . .]

FACTS

Koepnick was stopped in the Fiesta Mall parking lot by Sears security guards Lessard and Pollack on December 6, 1982, at approximately 6:15 p.m. Lessard and Pollack suspected Koepnick of shoplifting a wrench and therefore detained him for approximately 15 minutes until the Mesa police arrived. Upon arrival of the police, Koepnick and a police officer became involved in an altercation in which Koepnick was injured. The police officer handcuffed Koepnick, placed a call for a backup, and began investigating the shoplifting allegations. Upon investigation it was discovered that Koepnick had receipts for the wrench and for all the Sears merchandise he had been carrying. Additionally, the store clerk who sold the wrench to Koepnick was located. He verified the sale and informed Lessard that he had put the wrench in a small bag, stapled it shut, and then placed that bag into a large bag containing Koepnick's other purchases. The small bag was not among the items in Koepnick's possession in the security room. To determine

whether a second wrench was involved, the police and Lessard searched Koepnick's truck which was in the mall parking lot. No stolen items were found. Having completed their investigation, the police cited Koepnick for disorderly conduct and released him. The entire detention lasted approximately 45 minutes.

Koepnick sued Sears for false arrest, assault, trespass to chattel, invasion of privacy and malicious prosecution. The trial court directed a verdict in favor of Sears on all charges except false arrest and trespass to chattel. After a trial on these claims, a jury awarded Koepnick [. . .] $100 compensatory damages and $25,000 punitive damages for trespass to chattel. Sears timely moved for judgment n.o.v. and alternatively for a new trial. The trial court [. . .] granted Sears' motion for judgment n.o.v. on the trespass to chattel charge. [. . .]

Koepnick appeals, challenging the trial court's order granting Sears [. . .] judgment n.o.v. on his trespass to chattel claim. [. . .]

We find no reversible error and therefore affirm the trial court's order granting [. . .] judgment n.o.v. on the trespass to chattel claim.
[. . .]

TRESPASS TO CHATTEL

Arizona courts follow the Restatement (Second) of Torts absent authority to the contrary. [Citation omitted.] The Restatement provides that the tort of trespass to a chattel may be committed by intentionally dispossessing another of the chattel or using or intermeddling with a chattel in the possession of another. Restatement (Second) of Torts § 217 (1965).

The Restatement (Second) of Torts § 221 (1965) defines dispossession as follows:

A dispossession may be committed by intentionally

(a) taking a chattel from the possession of another without the other's consent, or

. . .

(c) barring the possessor's access to a chattel . . . .

Comment b to § 221 provides that dispossession may occur when someone intentionally assumes physical control over the chattel and deals with the chattel in a way which will be destructive of the possessory interest of the other person. Comment b further provides that "on the other hand, an intermeddling with the chattel is not a dispossession unless the actor intends to exercise a dominion and control over it inconsistent with a possession in any other person other than himself."

The Restatement (Second) of Torts § 218 (1965) provides:

One who commits a trespass to a chattel is subject to liability to the possessor of the chattel if, but only if,

(a) he dispossesses the other of the chattel, or

(b) the chattel is impaired as to its condition, quality, or value, or

(c) the possessor is deprived of the use of the chattel for a substantial time, or

(d) bodily harm is caused to the possessor, or harm is caused to some person or thing in which the possessor has a legally protected interest.

Koepnick argued at trial that Lessard's participation in searching his truck constituted an actionable trespass to the truck. He was awarded $100 damages by the jury which he characterizes as damages for a dispossession pursuant to subsection (a) or deprivation of use pursuant to subsection (c) of § 218.

[. . .]

Sears' actions with respect to the trespass consisted of Steve Lessard accompanying a Mesa police officer out to the parking lot and looking in the truck. There is no evidence in the record of an intent on the part of Sears' employee to claim a possessory interest in the truck contrary to Koepnick's interest. No lien or ownership interest claim of any kind was made. Further, there is no evidence that Sears intentionally denied Koepnick access to his truck.

Koepnick was in the City of Mesa's custody at the time of the search and Sears had no control over how the police department conducted its investigation [. . .]

[. . .] In order that an actor who interferes with another's chattel may be liable, his conduct must affect some other and more important interest of the possessor [than for harmless intermeddlings]. Therefore, one who intentionally intermeddles with another's chattel is subject to liability only if his intermeddling is harmful to the possessor's materially valuable interest in the physical condition, quality, or value of the chattel, or if the possessor is deprived of the use of the chattel for a substantial time [. . .]. Sufficient legal protection of the possessor's interest in the mere inviolability of his chattel is afforded by his privilege to use reasonable force to protect his possession against even harmless interference.

Sidebar: The *Koepnick* court stated that an owner could protect his or her chattel from harmless interference through the defense of property defense, discussed in chapter 5. The court felt this was sufficient legal protection of the chattel owner's interests. But how could Koepnick protect his truck from intrusion by the police officer and Sears' security guard, as the defense would lawfully permit, when he was handcuffed and held elsewhere?

The search in question took approximately two minutes. Neither the truck nor its contents were damaged in any manner by the police or Sears' employee. As a matter of law, Sears' action did not constitute an actionable trespass under § 218(c).

[. . .] For a deprivation of use caused by a trespass to chattel to be actionable, the time must be so substantial that it is possible to estimate the loss that is caused. The record in the present case lacks any evidence to permit a jury to estimate any loss caused to Koepnick [as a result of the police officer and Lessard's search of his truck].

[. . .]

We conclude that there was no dispossession of the vehicle as contemplated under § 218 of the Restatement nor was Koepnick deprived of its use for a substantial period of time. [. . .]

The judgment of the trial court is affirmed [. . .].

CASE QUESTIONS

1. Why do you suppose the jury awarded Koepnick such a large damages award, which prompted the trial court to grant judgment notwithstanding the verdict (judgment n.o.v.)? Do you think the jurors would agree that Koepnick suffered no harm as a result of the defendants' actions? Do you?
2. Do you believe that Koepnick satisfied the elements for assault, invasion of privacy, and malicious prosecution?

4.4 CONVERSION

In the history of tort law, trespass to chattel was frequently involved in litigation, often in cases involving domestic livestock. Court opinions from the nineteenth century abound. More recent cases, however, have tended to focus upon conversion, which is a similar but separate tort.

History

Conversion occurs when a tortfeasor, without consent, deprives an owner of possession of the owner's chattel and puts or *converts* the property to the tortfeasor's own use. It is essentially a broader version of trespass to chattel, but both torts developed separately.

Conversion evolved from the common law action of *trover*, which appeared in England during the fifteenth century as a specific type of trespass on the case action. In trover lawsuits, the court determined that the plaintiff, the chattel owner, had a legal right to possess the personal property (namely, because of ownership), and that the defendant, the tortfeasor, had

LEGAL TERMS

conversion
An intentional tort that occurs when a tortfeasor, without consent, intentionally deprives an owner of possession of his or her chattel. The tortfeasor then *converts* the personal property to his or her own use.

taken possession of the chattel for his or her own use. Gradually, this element (taking for one's own use) was described in the English court opinions as "converting the property for one's own use." Thus, the term *conversion* began to replace *trover,* and the modern tort of conversion emerged.

Elements of Conversion

Under modern tort law, conversion contains three elements:

1. Depriving the owner of possession of a chattel
2. Intent to deprive possession and convert the property to one's own use
3. The owner's nonconsent to the tortfeasor's possession and use of the chattel.

Depriving of Possession

Under conversion, the tortfeasor must actually deprive the owner of possession of personal property. The common law usually employs the phrase *exercising dominion and control over the chattel which is inconsistent with the owner's right to exclusive use.* This means that the tortfeasor controls another's personal property so as to prevent the owner from using it. For example, suppose Nadene took her neighbor's textbook and refused to return it. Nadene's "dominion and control" over the book prevents the neighbor from using his or her chattel.

Extent of Deprivation

Normally, conversion is differentiated from trespass to chattel based upon the scope of the deprivation. With trespass to chattel, many courts have held that the deprivation need only be minor or temporary. With conversion, several courts have ruled that the deprivation must be so extensive as to suggest a desire to deprive the owner of possession permanently. There is considerable disagreement among different jurisdictions as to this issue, however. The majority of courts maintain that conversion has occurred simply because the tortfeasor deprived the owner of dominion and control over the chattel, regardless of length of time or permanent intent.

Methods of Depriving

Deprivation of possession may occur in a variety of ways. *Physical possession* of the chattel is most common, although deprivation may happen through *damage or destruction* of the personal property. For instance, if someone plows under Kathy's garden to plant grass seed, this amounts to deprivation of possession, since Kathy can no longer use her vegetables. Similarly, if someone opens a window during a thunderstorm, and rain floods Sig's stereo, the injury has deprived Sig of the use of his chattel.

Deprivation may also take place simply through use. Some forms of personal property cannot be picked up and carried away. For instance, electricity, free-flowing liquids, and other intangible items are commonly defined as chattels under state commercial codes. One possesses such things by using them. If Morgan, Colleen's neighbor, plugs his garage heater into her electric outlet without permission, and Colleen's electric bill suddenly soars, Morgan has deprived her of dominion and control over her electricity. This translates as deprivation of possession.

Intent to Deprive and Convert to Own Use

First of all, conversion requires that the tortfeasor intend to deprive the owner of possession of his or her chattel. This is comparable to trespass to chattel. However, unlike trespass to chattel, conversion also requires that the tortfeasor convert the personal property to his or her own use. For example, assume Joey and Lisa are acquaintances at school. Then suppose that Joey found Lisa's earrings on a bench at the mall. Joey might keep the earrings until he saw Lisa at school later in the week. But, because Joey did not intend to use the earrings himself, he is not guilty of conversion. However, if Joey wore the earrings to the school dance, he would have converted them to his own use.

It is important to note that the tortfeasor does not have to injure the chattel to convert it. Conversion occurs simply because the owner has been deprived of the use of the personal property without having given permission. Injury occurs to the owner's property rights to exclusively use the chattel.

Lack of Consent

Naturally, the owner must not have granted permission to someone to use or possess the chattel. If Victoria allows a classmate to borrow her text overnight to study, then the classmate has not converted the book. Consent may be expressed, as in the book-borrowing situation, or it may be implied. For example, suppose that when Bob leaves his automobile at a mechanic's for an oil replacement, the mechanic also repairs a broken valve and pipe. The mechanic did not convert Bob's property, because Bob impliedly gave the mechanic permission to possess the vehicle for repair purposes. Of course, Bob did not authorize the additional work, but that is a breach-of-contract question. However, if the mechanic went joy-riding in Bob's car after changing the oil, this would be conversion, because Bob did not implicitly consent to that use of his car.

Even though the chattel owner may have consented to a tortfeasor's possession, this permission may be revoked. This could result in a conversion. For example, Bob complains that he did not authorize the additional work done on his automobile, but he is willing to pay for the oil change, which he did request. The mechanic insists that Bob also pay for the unauthorized repairs and refuses to return Bob's car until he pays the extra amount. Because Bob did not agree to these additional charges, he insists that his vehicle be returned immediately. Thus, Bob has revoked the permission he originally gave the mechanic to possess the chattel. If the mechanic does not comply with Bob's demand, the mechanic will be liable for conversion.

Conversion as a Crime

Many state statutes define conversion as a criminal offense. Some statutes use the term *theft* instead. Simultaneously, conversion is considered an intentional tort under the common law. This means that the chattel owner may sue in a civil action under the tort theory of conversion and may also contact the county prosecutor (or other local law enforcement authority) to file a criminal complaint for conversion. These separate legal actions are commonly pursued simultaneously in most jurisdictions.

THE CASE OF THE PURLOINED PURSE

Money is a cherished chattel. It is never in sufficient abundance for most people. Occasionally, some individuals decide to supplement their cash supplies through somewhat unorthodox and illegal means. The following case appears to fit within this category. Although, as the Alabama Supreme Court notes, money is not usually subject to conversion claims, currency from identifiable sources, if converted, will allow the victim a cause of action against the converter.

Greene County Board of Education
v. Bailey
586 So. 2d 893 (Ala. 1991)
(Supreme Court of Alabama)
August 23, 1991

HOUSTON, Justice.
The plaintiff, Greene County Board of Education, appeals from the dismissal of its complaint alleging conversion on the part of the defendants, Roland S. Bailey [and] Sarah N. Bailey [. . .]. We reverse and remand.
[. . .]

[According to the Plaintiff's complaint, between 1972-84, Paramount High School participated in the U.S.D.A.'s National School Breakfast and Lunch Programs. The school filed monthly claims with the State Department of Education for reimbursement for subsidized meals. Roland S. Bailey, sales manager of Alabama Institutional Foods, Inc. (AIF), was directly involved in food sales to Paramount High School. Between 1972-80, Bailey purchased 84 money orders and cashier's checks drawn on the Paramount lunchroom account. Of these, Bailey negotiated 42 checks through

AIF's account at a bank at which his wife, Sarah Bailey, worked as a teller. Sarah processed these checks. The 84 checks were valued at $407,883.50, and only $263,425.65 went toward payment of Paramount's food purchases. $144,457.85 was never credited to Paramount's account nor used in the feeding programs. Bailey allegedly submitted false invoices to Paramount.]

The defendants moved to dismiss the complaint under Rule 12(b)(6) [. . .]. Specifically, the defendants argued that the plaintiff had failed to allege that specific money capable of identification had been converted. The trial court granted the defendants' motion, stating, in pertinent part, as follows:

"The plaintiff contends that the defendants converted money; however, the money was not any specific money and [the complaint states] a general claim for relief. The plaintiff's theory is that the defendants wrongfully obtained money from the account of the plaintiff through a scheme of false invoices. No particular identifiable earmarked money is alleged to have been taken. Under these circumstances, this Court is of the opinion that a count for conversion is not appropriate."

We disagree.

[. . .]

To constitute conversion, there must be a wrongful taking or wrongful detention or interference, or an illegal assumption of ownership, or an illegal use or misuse of another's property. The gist of the action is the wrongful exercise of dominion over property to the exclusion or in defiance of a plaintiff's rights, where the plaintiff has a general or specific title to the property or the immediate right to possession. [Citation omitted.]

Generally, an action will not lie for the conversion of money. However, if the money at issue is capable of identification, then a claim of conversion may be appropriate. In *Lewis v. Fowler,* [citation omitted], this Court discussed at length the circumstances under which an action for conversion will lie to recover a sum of money:

"[T]rover lies for the conversion of 'earmarked' money or specific money capable of identification [. . .] [citations omitted].

"Money in any form is generally regarded and treated as property, and it is well settled that an action will lie for the conversion thereof, where there is an obligation to keep intact and deliver the specific money in question, and where such money can be identified. [Citations omitted.]

[. . .]

"Now, in conversion cases, the courts are not confronted so much with a particular piece of money, i.e., a coin or a bill, but with identified or segregated from which money has come or types of accounts into which money has been deposited.

[. . .] [M]oney directly traceable to a special account is sufficiently identifiable to support an action for conversion.["] [. . . .]

Applying the applicable standard of review to the present case, we are not persuaded that the plaintiff has failed to state a claim for conversion. The allegations of the complaint suggest that the plaintiff may be able to prove that the defendants, through an intricate scheme involving bogus invoices and checks and money orders, converted to their own use funds that had been specifically deposited in the "[Paramount High School] lunchroom account" to pay for the high school's breakfast and lunch programs. [. . .]

Based on the foregoing, we hold that the plaintiff has stated a claim for conversion and, therefore, that the trial court's order dismissing the plaintiff's complaint is due to be reversed and the case remanded for further proceedings.

REVERSED AND REMANDED.

CASE QUESTIONS

1. Based on the facts, did the plaintiff also state a claim for trespass to chattel? Explain.
2. Should the defendants in this case have also been subjected to criminal prosecution for conversion, under the applicable Alabama statutes? Why or why not?

Conversion, like trespass to chattel, is a mobile tort, as it is easy in most instances to grab and carry away someone else's personal property. If the personal property can be carried away, it may be converted. Hence, there are an infinite variety of fact situations involving conversion. Both torts also fire the victim's blood. While reading the following examples, imagine that your own chattels have been converted; your emotional response may make clear why so many such cases are brought.

HYPOTHETICALS

Buford is painting his wooden fence in his backyard. His neighbor, Starling, needs some paint for his garage door. He notices that Buford has more than enough paint to finish the fence, and so Starling "borrows" two gallons to paint his door. Has Starling converted Buford's paint?

Starling deprived Buford of possession of the paint. Starling clearly intended to deprive possession and convert the paint to his own use, since he applied the paint to his garage door. Buford did not consent to Starling's use of the paint. Starling has committed conversion.

□ □ □

Consider Beatrice, who works at an advertising agency. One of her duties is to telephone clients to discuss accounts. Frequently, however, Beatrice telephones long-distance to relatives to discuss family matters. The company has strict regulations prohibiting use of company phones for personal calls. Has Beatrice engaged in conversion?

Deprivation of possession becomes a perplexing query in this hypothetical. Did Beatrice deprive her employer of possession of the telephone? The actual property right being taken here is the use (and cost) of the telephone for placing long-distance calls. Most courts would agree that this satisfies the deprivation requirement. Beatrice intended to use the company's phones for personal use. The company expressly forbade such activities, and so consent was lacking. Accordingly, Beatrice has converted her employer's rights in the telephone system.

Figure 4-2 outlines the elements of conversion.

Depriving owner of possession of his or her personal property (dispossession)
Intent to dispossess and convert chattel to tortfeasor's own use
Chattel owner did not consent to tortfeasor's possession and use of personal property

FIGURE 4-2
Elements of Conversion

4.5 SLANDER OF TITLE, COMMERCIAL DISPARAGEMENT, AND DEFAMATION BY COMPUTER

The intentional torts of slander of title, commercial disparagement, and defamation by computer involve defamed property interests. The trio has a common ancestry. All arose from the intentional tort of defamation, which concerns personal impugnation.

Slander of Title

Slander of title results when a tortfeasor makes false statements about an individual's ownership of property. The false statements are not designed to defame the owner personally; rather, the purpose of the aspersions is to injure the owner's ability to use the property. Slander of title contains three basic elements:

1. False statements regarding a person's ownership of property
2. Intent to hinder or damage the owner's use of the property
3. Communication (publication) of the falsehoods to third parties.

False Statements Regarding Ownership

A tortfeasor commits slander of title by making false statements about a person's ownership of property. This usually occurs when the tortfeasor falsely impugns the title to another's property. Normally, cases involving this tort include real estate and the filing of spurious liens. Recall the example of improperly filed liens from chapter 3's discussion of abuse of process. Often, businesses that provide services to customers who do not pay will file liens against the customers' real estate. The lien attaches to the title of the land so that the property cannot be leased or sold without the lien. Suppose a business threatens to file a lien against a customer who does not owe the business any money. If the lienholder wrongfully files a lien, then the lien has defamed the integrity of the landowner's title. The improper lien falsely suggests to the world that the landowner has not properly paid his or her debts to the lienholder. Anyone thinking of buying or leasing the property will think twice, because lien property may be sold under certain circumstances to satisfy the debt. Few buyers or tenants would want to become entangled with property that is encumbered by a lien. Thus, a spurious lien could injure the landowner's ability to use the property, even

LEGAL TERMS

slander of title
An intentional tort that results when the tortfeasor makes false statements about an individual's ownership of property. The tortfeasor must intend to hinder or damage the owner's use of the property, and the false statements must be communicated to third parties.

though in actuality the lienholder has no legal right to file the lien against the landowner. This improper lien filing constitutes making false statements about someone's ownership of property.

Intent to Hinder or Damage Owner's Use of Property

By making the false statements about ownership, the tortfeasor must intend to hamper or injure the owner's use of his or her property. This is visibly demonstrated in the preceding lien example. The lienholder filed the lien to prevent the landowner from selling or using his or her realty without first paying the debt supposedly owed to the lienholder. But, in fact, no money was due, so the lien was falsely filed.

Communication (Publication) to Third Parties

The false statements about another's property ownership must be transmitted to third parties in slander of title actions. The slander in the preceding lien example is communicated to the public when the lien is recorded at the county recorder's office. It then becomes a matter of public record for the world to take notice.

THE CASE OF THE ERRANT LOT LINE

Slander of title is usually limited to cases involving improperly filed liens. However, the intentional tort surfaces in other lawsuits, such as the one excerpted here. In *Hossler* the dispute involved an uncertain property line. In addition to slander of title, the case demonstrates why it is vital to obtain correct surveys before purchasing or selling real estate.

Hossler v. Hammel
587 N.E.2d 133 (Ind. Ct. App. 1992)
Court of Appeals of Indiana
February 24, 1992

HOFFMAN, Judge.
This appeal arises from a property dispute between Roger and Sandra Hossler (plaintiffs) and Michael Hammel (defendant), owners of adjoining lots in Austin's Addition to the original plat of the town of Etna, Indiana.

The facts relevant to the appeal disclose that the Kecks and the Wheelers, the original owners of the lots, had surveys made in 1953, after which they agreed upon a common boundary line. When plaintiffs purchased their lot in 1970, they agreed to the established boundary line without a survey, and when defendant purchased his lot in 1977, he, too, agreed to the established boundary line without a survey. Plaintiffs rented their lot for several years and had a survey made in 1988 in order to sell the lot. The survey indicated the Addition was 9 feet longer east to west than shown in the original plat, and the surveyor allocated the extra footage equally among 6 lots. When defendant became aware of the survey, he insisted that the entire 9 feet be allocated to his lot due to his previous purchase of property in the original plat. After numerous threats from defendant to demolish 8 feet of their garage, plaintiffs filed an action to quiet title in the disputed strip of land. Following a bench trial, the court entered findings of fact and conclusions of law establishing the property line as that which the parties had originally agreed upon but denying damages to plaintiffs for slander of title.

The sole issue for our review is whether plaintiffs failed to meet their burden of proving the elements necessary to prevail on their slander of title claim.

To prevail in a slander of title action, the plaintiff must prove that the defendant made false statements regarding the plaintiff's ownership of the land in question, that the defendant made the statements with malice, and that the statements caused the plaintiff pecuniary loss. [Citation omitted.] As plaintiffs note on page 29 of their brief, "[t]he bone of contention in this case is whether the Defendant uttered statements with malice." Malicious statements are those made with knowledge of their falsity or with reckless disregard for whether or not they were false. [Citation omitted.]

In *Freiburger v. Fry,* [citation omitted], this Court found malice where, despite the description in his deed, the Defendant had actual knowledge of an existing fence separating the property and that the owner of the other side refused to move it. [Citation omitted.] The instant case is similar to *Freiburger* in that, while defendant may have been relying on the

results of plaintiffs' survey in making his statements, he had actual knowledge of the boundary line from the realtor who sold him the lot as well as from the survey. [Citation omitted.] Moreover, the evidence was undisputed that the boundary line had been agreed upon for over 30 years, and once a person possesses property for 10 years in a continuous, adverse, notorious and exclusive manner, title vests in that person by operation of law. [Citation omitted.]

As the party with the burden of proof on the slander of title issue, plaintiffs are appealing from a negative judgment. Therefore, to be successful they must establish that the judgment is contrary to law. [Citation omitted.] As both parties note, defendant did not testify at trial, and neither of his two witnesses testified as to any statements he made regarding the boundary line. Plaintiffs, on the other hand, presented evidence that defendant threatened to bulldoze their garage, cut holes in their garage with a chainsaw, and keep livestock in their garage. Because this evidence and the evidence of defendant's actual knowledge of the agreed-upon boundary line was without conflict and led to a conclusion opposite that reached by the trial court, the judgment of the trial court is contrary to law and reversed.

Reversed and remanded for determination of damages.

CASE QUESTIONS

1. Would the defendant's actions, rather than statements, have been sufficient to constitute slander of title? Assume that the defendant did not communicate with the plaintiffs. What if the defendant had parked a bulldozer next to the plaintiffs' garage? What if the defendant had placed livestock on his property adjoining the plaintiffs'? Would these actions satisfy the Indiana common law elements? Would they satisfy the elements discussed in this chapter?

2. Assuming the hypothetical facts from question one, what additional tort(s) would the defendant have committed through his actions?

Commercial Disparagement

Another type of slander focuses directly upon the chattel itself: commercial disparagement. **Commercial disparagement** may be defined as false statements communicated (published) to third parties about a person's goods, services, or business enterprise. The intentional tort of commercial disparagement includes three varieties: disparagement of goods, disparagement of services, and disparagement of business. Like slander of title, *disparagement of goods* impedes the chattel owner's ability to use his or her personal property. *Disparagement of services* interferes with a service provider's ability to engage in provision of services. *Disparagement of business* occurs when the tortfeasor impugns the integrity of another's business venture. Commercial disparagement may be divided into three elements:

1. False statements about an individual's goods, services, or business

2. Intent to injure the victim's ability to use goods, furnish services, or conduct business

3. Communication (publication) to third parties.

False Statements about Goods, Services, or Business

The tortfeasor must express false statements about another's personal property, services, or business reputation (sometimes called *goodwill*). For example, if someone carries a sign in front of a grocery store declaring, "This store sells spoiled fruit!," when in fact the store carries fresh and wholesome fruit, then the sign carrier has made disparaging remarks about the quality of the grocery's foodstuffs. This impugns the integrity of both the goods themselves and the store's reputation. Similarly, if someone tells his or her friends that a particular dentist uses inferior materials to fill cavities when, in reality, the dentist uses professionally acceptable materials, then the dentist's services and reputation have been wrongfully impaired.

Intent to Harm Victim's Ability to Use Goods, Supply Services, or Conduct Business

Disparagement of goods requires that the tortfeasor intend to injure the victim's capability to use chattels, provide services, or engage in business. Normally, cases involving goods relate to sales. In the preceding illustrations, the sign carrier obviously desired to discourage other shoppers from buying fruit at that particular grocery. The person criticizing the dentist wished to dissuade friends from seeking the dentist's services. The clear underlying objective in both examples is to hamper the ability of these enterprises to conduct business.

LEGAL TERMS

commercial disparagement
An intentional tort that happens when a tortfeasor communicates false statements to third parties about a person's goods, services, or business enterprise. The tortfeasor must intend to harm the victim's ability to use goods, furnish services, or conduct business. There are three categories: disparagement of goods, disparagement of services, and disparagement of business.

Communication (Publication) to Third Parties

Like slander of title, commercial disparagement requires that the false statements be communicated to third parties. In the examples, the sign carrier transmitted the false complaints to anyone reading the sign. The friends of the disgruntled patient heard the falsehoods about the dentist. Like the intentional torts of slander and libel (defamation) discussed in chapter 3, publication may occur through oral or written means. The preceding examples illustrate both media.

THE CASE OF THE DISPARAGED DISK JOCKEY

Commercial disparagement most commonly occurs with disgruntled customers attacking businesses. However, businesses can also commit this intentional tort, usually against their employees. In the following case, a radio personality found his livelihood jeopardized allegedly as a result of his former employer's disparagement. Note how the court distinguishes defamation from disparagement.

Menefee v.
Columbia Broadcasting System, Inc.
458 Pa. 46, 329 A.2d 216,
74 A.L.R.3d 290 (1974)
(Supreme Court of Pennsylvania)
October 16, 1974

OPINION OF THE COURT

O'Brien, J.

Robert Menefee, whose executrix is the appellant here, was for twenty years a radio personality in and around Philadelphia. Since 1960, he was employed by radio station WCAU in Philadelphia, which is wholly owned by the Columbia Broadcasting System, Inc. In the summer of 1967, Menefee, who referred to himself as "opinionated but lovable," conducted a one-man talk show from 7:30 p.m. to 10:00 p.m. daily, in which he discussed topics of public interest or controversy. On August 25, 1967, WCAU, through its general manager, John O. Downey, and its Director, Michael Grant, [. . .] exercised a right to terminate Menefee's employment on thirteen weeks' notice, opting to pay him an additional salary rather than continue him in his

position for that period. That same day, Grant informed newsmen that Menefee had been fired "because of poor ratings garnered by his nighttime talk show." Several articles subsequently appeared to the same effect in the Philadelphia magazines and newspapers.

Menefee, on January 16, 1968, filed an action in the Court of Common Pleas of Montgomery County against CBS, Inc., and Grant [. . .]. Menefee died on November 9, 1971, one day before trial was to begin. [. . .]

[Plaintiff alleges] the cause of action for untruthful disparagement. [. . .]

Although an action for untruthful disparagement of a property interest resembles actions for defamation, there are several important differences. As the authors of the Restatement of Torts have explained [. . .]

". . . Liability for disparagement [. . .] differs in several highly important particulars from the liability for the publication of matter which is defamatory to the personal reputation of another. In defamation, truth is a defense required to be proved by the publisher as defendant. In disparagement, the person whose property in goods or the quality of whose goods has been attacked must prove that the disparaging statement of fact is untrue or that the disparaging expression of opinion is incorrect. [. . .] In defamation, the publication of all libelous communications and of many types of slanderous communications subjects the publisher to liability even though no pecuniary loss or other harm results therefrom. In disparagement, the publisher is not liable unless the disparaging matter has caused financial loss. [. . .]

The question before us is, do the appellant's complaints make out a cause of action for untruthful disparagement?

In the first cause of action, [. . .] it is alleged that the defendants "falsely conveyed . . . to the public and the broadcasting industry that plaintiff was unable to draw an adequate listening audience, was incapable of earning satisfactory ratings for his program and was therefore incompetent in the performance of his assigned broadcasting duties."

Section 629 of the Restatement defines "disparagement" to be:

> "Matter which is intended by its publisher to be understood or which is reasonably understood to cast doubt upon the existence or extent of another's property in land, chattels or intangible things, or upon

their quality, is disparaging thereto, if the matter is so understood by its recipient."

Since the complaint also alleges that Robert Menefee was a successful radio personality, it can fairly be said that he had an intangible property interest in his broadcasting personality and that a statement that his program could no longer attract satisfactory ratings would tend to disparage that property interest.

In order to be able to recover for disparagement of such a property interest, the plaintiff must show that he suffered a direct pecuniary loss as the result of the disparagement. [. . .]

Thus, appellant must allege and prove that her husband's estate suffered pecuniary loss as the direct result of the impairment of her husband's value to radio stations in the area caused by the defendant's untrue statements. However, she need not prove that a specific radio station refused to hire him because of reports that his ratings had declined. [. . .]

Order of the Superior Court [. . .] reversed. [. . .] Insofar as it dismisses appellant's cause of action for conspiracy to disparage Robert Menefee's broadcast personality, order reversed and case remanded to the Court of Common Pleas of Montgomery County for further proceedings consistent with this opinion.

CASE QUESTIONS

1. How did the court distinguish between defamation and disparagement?
2. Do you believe that the plaintiff would have been successful in a defamation action? Explain.

Defamation by Computer

Defamation by computer is a relatively recent intentional tort. Because of the proliferation of computerized databases that can store virtually any information about anyone, the likelihood of mistakes has increased. Further, as access to computerized material expands, the dissemination of inaccurate information can become enormously damaging to the victim.

Computerized Credit Reporting

Defamation by computer most frequently involves cases concerning erroneous credit information entered into a readily accessible computer database. A credit company reports to a national credit reporting agency that a particular individual has become delinquent in account payments. This bad credit rating can have alarming negative effects upon the person being reported. If the information reported is false, the injury is especially annoying, since future credit may hang in the balance of good credit reports.

Defamation by computer may be defined as the inclusion of false information about a consumer's credit rating, in a computer recordkeeping system, which harms the consumer's ability to secure credit. The tort includes four elements:

1. False information about a person's credit rating
2. Entering such erroneous data into a computerized recordkeeping system
3. Communication (publication) of the incorrect information to third parties
4. Injuring the victim's ability to obtain credit as a result of the false computerized data.

Creation of a New Tort

Legal commentators occasionally spur the development of tort law through their law review articles and treatises. Perhaps the best example is law professor William L. Prosser's writings, which have had significant and immeasurable influence over courts for decades. Prosser's tort handbook is the bible for legal students and remains the best available dissertation on the subject.

Other commentators have entered onto the tort scene with exciting new ideas that spurred courts and legislatures to change the course of the law. The article excerpted here, first published in 1977, blazed the trail for establishment of the intentional tort of defamation by computer. From G. Stevens & H. Hoffman, "Tort Liability for Defamation by Computer," 6 *Rutgers Journal of Computers & the Law* 91 (1977) (footnotes omitted):

> Protection of the individual from the misuse of computerized personal information has received considerable scholarly attention, but little has been written on the tort liability of the information processor. Eventually, courts will be faced with questions concerning the processor's legal responsibilities for defamation and invasion of privacy. Actions to recover damages for such injuries are possible not only

LEGAL TERMS

defamation by computer
    An intentional tort that occurs when the tortfeasor includes false information about a person's credit rating in a computer database. This false information must be communicated to third parties, and it must injure the victim's ability to obtain credit.

against recipients of computerized reports who make the information public, but also against information processors and suppliers. [. . .]

Defamation

Under common law, a prima facie case for defamation is established if the plaintiff successfully pleads that he was identified in a defamatory matter through a "publication" of the charge by the defendant. The message need only be communicated to one person other than the defamed to be actionable, and any means through which a third party receives it can be considered a publication. While an oral statement may be classified as slander and a written statement as libel, a defamatory message designed for visual perception will be considered libelous. [. . .] Liability could be extended to a key punch operator or a programmer under the theory that without their neglect of duty a defamatory statement might not have appeared.

[. . .]

The States should enact uniform guidelines for those in the computer information processing chain. [. . .]

HYPOTHETICALS

Heather moved from her apartment in the city of Shelbydale to a house in the town of Wellington. Heather had a charge account with The Prime Account, a national credit card company. Heather wrote all of her credit card companies to report her address change. The Prime Account failed to change Heather's address in its computer billing system and continued to send its monthly invoices to Heather's Shelbydale address. After 90 days, The Prime Account reported Heather's account as delinquent to a national credit rating service. The service indicated Heather's delinquency in its computerized records, which were included in various credit reports to banks. When Heather applied at the Wellington State Bank for a mortgage loan, the bank refused her request, based upon the bad credit information. Is The Prime Account liable to Heather for defamation by computer?

The Prime Account reported that Heather's account was delinquent, and this was accurate. However, the delinquency was due to Heather's failure to receive her monthly statements. The mailing mistake was The Prime Account's fault. However, this error does not negate the truth of Heather's delinquency. The information reported in the computerized credit systems was correct, and thus defamation by computer has not occurred.

□ □ □

Sylvia owns a bowling alley. Marshall is a professional bowler who frequents one of Sylvia's competitors but occasionally bowls at Sylvia's establishment. Marshall's scores were repeatedly lower at Sylvia's than at any other bowling alley in town. One day, after a particularly frustrating series, Marshall lay down to "sight" the levelness of the alleys. To his eyes, the lanes looked uneven. Marshall telephoned the American Bowling Federation (ABF) to report that Sylvia's alleys did not comply with their standards. If such a criticism were true, the ABF could revoke its certification of Sylvia's facility. This could result in lost business if bowling leagues relocated to other alleys. In fact, the alleys complied with ABF standards. Has Marshall disparaged Sylvia's business enterprise?

Marshall's comments about Sylvia's alleys were false. The defamed article was the quality of Sylvia's bowling alleys, which would include the integrity of the business itself. Marshall communicated these falsehoods to a third party by telephoning the ABF. Marshall's intent may be implied by his conduct. What purpose could he have furthered by telephoning the ABF? The reasonable response would be that he hoped that the ABF would remove its certification from Sylvia's and thus discourage patronage. This translates as intent to injure another's ability to conduct business. The damage to Sylvia's goodwill would be substantial if the ABF revoked its certification. Therefore, Marshall has committed commercial disparagement.

Figure 4-3 illustrates the requirements for slander of title, commercial disparagement, and defamation by computer.

Slander of Title	Commercial Disparagement	Defamation by Computer
False statements regarding person's property ownership	False statements about person's goods, services, or business	False information about a person's credit rating
Intent to impede or injure owner's use of property	Intent to harm victim's ability to use goods, furnish services, or conduct business	Inputting false information into computerized database
Communication (publication) of falsehoods to third parties	Communication (publication) of falsehoods to third parties	Communication (publication) of falsehoods to third parties
Usually involves filing of spurious liens against real estate	Includes disparagement of goods, disparagement of services, and disparagement of business	Injury to victim's ability to secure credit, as a result of erroneous credit data

FIGURE 4-3
Elements of Slander of Title, Commercial Disparagement, and Defamation by Computer

SUMMARY

4.1. Trespass to land occurs when a tortfeasor enters upon another's real estate without permission. The tortfeasor must intend to invade the premises without consent. Also, the tortfeasor's entry must interfere with the landowner's exclusive right to use the land, which is called possession.

4.2. Toxic tort actions involve toxic chemicals, pollution, hazardous waste disposal and transportation, and other environmentally sensitive issues. This litigation applies many tort theories, including trespass to land, negligence, absolute liability for ultrahazardous substances, products liability, and nuisance. The same formula for trespass to land applies in cases involving toxic substances that invade an innocent landowner's property through underwater seepage or surface or air contamination.

4.3. Trespass to chattel occurs when the tortfeasor possesses or interferes with the use of another's personal property without permission. The tortfeasor must intend to dispossess the owner of his or her chattel, or to interfere with the owner's exclusive use of the chattel.

4.4. Conversion deprives a chattel owner of possession of personal property, which the tortfeasor converts to his or her own use. The tortfeasor must intend to dispossess the owner of the chattel and then use it without consent. Conversion occurs whenever the tortfeasor deprives the owner of dominion and control over the personal property. In many jurisdictions, statutes define conversion as a crime, in addition to the common law intentional tort.

4.5. Slander of title occurs when false statements are made about an individual's ownership of property. The tortfeasor's intentions are to handicap or harm the owner's use of the property. Commercial disparagement includes disparagement of goods, of services, and of business. Commercial disparagement involves false statements about a person's goods, services, or business intended to injure the victim's ability to use the property, supply the services, or conduct business. Defamation by computer concerns false information about a person's credit rating that is entered into a computer database. Communication, or publication, of the false information to third parties is required of all three of these intentional torts.

REVIEW QUESTIONS

1. What are the intentional torts that involve injuries to property rights? How are these distinguishable from intentional torts in which the harm is focused on persons?

2. Define trespass to land and trespass to chattel. How do the two intentional torts differ? How are they similar? What is entry? What is exclusive use? What is possession? Can trespass occur above or below

land? What role does consent play in trespass? Is harm to the property required? Must the trespass be intentional? Why or why not? Must trespass to chattel involve dispossession?

3. What are toxic torts? What causes of action are available for injured persons? What federal statutes exist to regulate hazardous or toxic substances? What are the provisions of these statutes?

4. What is conversion? How is it different from trespass to chattel? How is it similar? To what extent must the chattel owner be deprived of possession? How might such deprivation occur? Must the tortfeasor do more than simply dispossess the chattel owner? What are dominion and control, and why are they important? What are the roles of intent and consent in conversion? Can conversion also be a crime? Why?

5. Explain slander of title. How might false statements be made about one's ownership of property? Provide an example of this intentional tort. What intent is involved? What is publication and why is it necessary?

6. List the different types of commercial disparagement. What are the elements of this category of intentional tort? What intent is involved? Why is communication important?

7. What is defamation by computer? Under what circumstances is this intentional tort most likely to arise? Why is communication significant?

PROBLEMS

In the following hypotheticals, identify the intentional tort(s) committed, if any, and support your answers.

1. Pestro Chemical Corporation manufacturers *Dredroxiphine,* a poison used in insect sprays. A railway line delivers tanker cars full of the chemical to be unloaded into the plant. On breezy days, the fumes from the unloading stations drift across the highway onto Elmer Parsley's farm. The odors are pungent and are especially irritating to the sinuses. When Elmer and his family work outside on windy days, they are constantly besieged by the poison's smells. Their eyes water excessively, their noses run, and they are gripped by sneezing fits. Other farmers in the area have complained of similar symptoms. Visits to the family physician have revealed that Elmer has absorbed minute amounts of the chemical in his lungs and through his skin. Medical studies link exposure to the chemical with several forms of cancer. Elmer has farmed on his property since 1947. Pestro constructed its plant in 1972.

2. Ben Stalwart left the Pick-Em-Up saloon after an evening of heavy drinking. Intoxicated, he stumbled across the street to the Tao, an oriental restaurant, and ordered a hamburger. The waitress, an exchange

student at the local high school, did not understand English well, and because Ben's speech was slurred, she misunderstood him. When she returned with an oriental dish, Ben jumped from his chair and shouted loudly, "I didn't order this stinking slop! Get it outta my face!" Several customers stared at Ben as he yelled at the waitress, "I'll get the health department to shut this dump down, before somebody else gets poisoned!" The manager ran out from the kitchen and demanded that Ben leave the premises immediately. Ben refused to leave.

3. Paula Johannsen operates a day care center for children. Crawford Lawley, a nine-year-old, attended the center after school while his parents worked. Paula discovered that Crawford's parents were delinquent in paying their fees by three months. One day Crawford brought in his father's portable computer for show-and-tell. Paula asked Crawford if he would like her to keep the computer locked up for safekeeping. Crawford agreed. At the end of the day, Crawford asked Paula to return the computer, but she refused, stating that she would keep the computer until Crawford's parents paid their bill.

4. Theresa Ishmarz rented an apartment from Whisperwood Apartments. Under the lease, she was responsible for paying for electricity and gas heat. When she moved into the apartment, she noticed that the electricity and gas were already on; the apartment owners paid for the utilities while apartments were vacant. She did not contact the utility companies to have the accounts transferred into her name, and she did not notify the apartment manager about the situation. Theresa lived in the apartment for three months before the error was discovered. She never paid any money for utilities, although utility bills for the apartment totalled $450 for this time period.

5. Harlow Barley is a mason. He installed a concrete patio at the home of James and Zella Grey. Zella stopped by Barley's house one day and paid his wife (in cash) for the work. Zella did not get a receipt. Barley's wife, however, never told Barley about the money. Barley sent several invoices to the Greys, but they ignored them. Thinking the bill remained unpaid, Barley filed a mechanic's lien against the Grey's real estate. Once the Greys discovered the lien, they angrily telephoned Barley and explained about the cash payment. Barley's wife admitted to receiving the money, so Barley considered the matter settled. However, Barley did not release the lien at the county recorder's office.

6. Homer Diemetry owed his dentist for oral surgery. Homer faithfully made monthly payments to the dentist. The dentist's accountant reported to a local credit rating service that Homer had defaulted on the bill. The service included this information in its computerized credit files. Homer applied for a credit card at a local department store, but was denied as a result of the bad credit rating. The department store was a client of the credit rating service and received monthly credit rating summaries.

PROBLEM ANSWERS

1. Pestro Chemical Corporation is engaged in trespass to land as a toxic tort, and Elmer Parsley would sue for damages to his property caused by Pestro's chemical production. Pestro's method of unloading the tanker cars allowed airborne toxic chemical vapors to be carried onto Elmer's farm. This was an unauthorized entry upon Elmer's land. Through its careless method of unloading, Pestro's intent to enter without consent may be implied, as the airborne contamination could have been easily anticipated. Whenever Elmer and his family worked outdoors on windy days, they suffered severe physical reactions from breathing the chemical-tainted air. This was a substantial interference with Elmer's exclusive right to use his real estate (possession). Elmer's family suffered significant health harms. In particular, Elmer had been exposed to a powerful carcinogen. Thus, Elmer's toxic trespass to land action against Pestro would be successful.

2. Ben Stalwart's statements constitute commercial disparagement: specifically, disparagement of goods ("stinking slop") and disparagement of business ("I'll get the health department to shut this dump down, before somebody else gets poisoned!"). Ben's accusations were false statements about the Tao's goods and business enterprise. Ben intended to hurt the restaurant's ability to sell food to its customers and encourage customers to recommend the establishment. Ben published his statements loudly and plainly, so that almost everyone present could hear. It is reasonably likely that the restaurant's business would suffer from indictments of public health hazards. Thus, Ben is liable to the restaurant owner for commercial disparagement.

    Ben is also liable for trespass to land. Although Ben was implicitly invited into the restaurant as a prospective patron, this consent to be present on the premises was withdrawn when the manager ordered Ben to leave. By refusing to depart, Ben became a trespasser to land.

    One might argue that Ben's intoxication prevented him from intending to disparage or trespass. This is irrelevant—a "red herring"—since Ben's degree of intoxication, given his behavior, was insufficient to affect his ability to commit these intentional torts. Additionally, many recent state appellate court decisions disallow intoxication as a defense to various intentional torts, although these usually involve injuries to persons, such as assault, battery, or false imprisonment.

3. Paula Johannsen has committed trespass to chattel by keeping Crawford Lawley's father's portable computer as security for payment of the Lawley's delinquent day care fees. Paula dispossessed Crawford's father of the computer by refusing to return it to Crawford after show-and-tell. Neither Crawford nor his father consented to Paula's keeping the computer. Paula clearly intended to deprive Crawford's father of possession of the chattel. Thus, she engaged in trespass to chattel.

Arguably, Paula also committed conversion. By keeping the computer to compel the Lawleys to pay their delinquent fees, Paula converted the computer to her own use, as security for a debt. The other elements (which are basically the same as trespass to chattel) are also met. As a practical matter, however, most courts would require that Paula actually use the computer itself, rather than merely storing it, so proving this cause of action would be difficult.

4. Theresa Ishmarz committed conversion and trespass to chattel against the apartment owners. Theresa's use of gas and electricity for three months without paying was unauthorized, since the owners had not consented. She knew (or reasonably should have known) from the lease that she was responsible for paying for these utilities. Her failure to notify the utility companies or apartment management implicitly indicates her intent to deprive the owners of the exclusive use of their utilities (dispossession) and convert the utilities to her own use. Thus, Theresa is liable to the apartment owners for these two intentional torts.

In some states, utilities are not considered personal property, although they are defined as goods under most states' versions of the Uniform Commercial Code. Instead, in such jurisdictions, utilities are defined as services, for purposes of intentional torts.

As an aside, most states' criminal codes include the crime of theft of services. Theresa's actions would also constitute this crime, which is often included within criminal conversion statutes.

5. Harlow Barley filed an improper mechanic's lien against James and Zella Grey's real estate. This constituted slander of title. Harlow made a false statement regarding the Greys' ownership of their home, by suggesting to the world that the Greys had defaulted upon a debt for services rendered. Harlow intended to injure the Greys' use of their property. The lien could prevent the Greys from selling the house or, more realistically, from using the house as collateral to secure a loan or credit. By filing the lien at the county recorder's office, publication is presumed, as such records are available to the public for inspection. Harlow aggravated his tortious conduct by failing to remove the lien once he learned that the Greys had paid the debt in full.

6. The dentist's accountant has committed defamation by computer against Homer Diemetry. The accountant reported to the local credit rating service that Homer had defaulted on his bill, when, in fact, he had made all monthly payments in a timely fashion. The accountant should have known that the report was false, based upon records of the dentist's financial transactions. This information was included in the agency's computerized database, which was published to the local department store. This information hurt Homer's ability to obtain credit, because the department store denied Homer's credit application based on the erroneous computer data. Thus, the accountant is liable to Homer for this intentional tort.

Arguably, the credit rating service would also be liable to Homer, although it is questionable whether the agency could have known that the information was false. At best, it could be said that the service was negligent by including false information in its database which, through the exercise of reasonable care, it could have verified. Some courts would include this negligence within defamation by computer, although such a hybrid distorts the distinctions between these causes of action.

PROJECTS

1. Which intentional torts discussed in this chapter are included in your state's common law? Are any defined by statute? Is conversion considered both an intentional tort and a crime in your state? If so, how are the two types of conversion similar and different?

2. Separate into study groups with several classmates to discuss the theories of intentional torts to property. You might wish to create your own hypothetical fact situations utilizing the intentional torts outlined in this chapter. Use the analytical methods discussed in chapter 2 to answer your group's questions.

3. Slander of title often involves the filing of frivolous or unlawful mechanic's liens. How are mechanic's liens filed in your state? Examine your state's statutes pertaining to mechanic's liens. You might also wish to contact your county recorder's office to discover the procedures used for filing mechanic's liens.

CHAPTER 5
Defenses to Intentional Torts

DATA-GRAPHIC TORTS

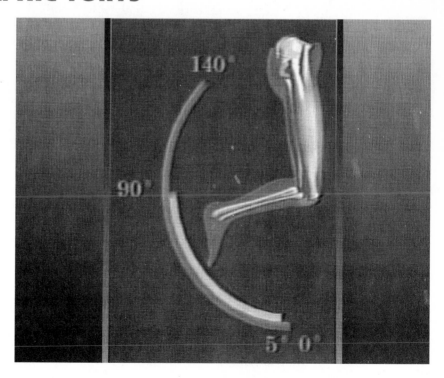

Yang v. Bellows

Alicia Yang played soccer for the local university. Yang stole the ball from an opponent, Claire Bellows, and moved downfield. An angry Bellows charged up behind Yang and, without warning, viciously kicked the back of Yang's right knee, tearing several ligaments. As a result of this injury, Yang lost considerable mobility in her right leg. Before her injury, her range-of-motion was 140 degrees, but afterward she could move the leg backward only to 90 degrees (painfully) and to 20 degrees (comfortably).

Yang sued Bellows for battery, the elements of which are easily satisfied in this scenario. Bellows defended that Yang impliedly consented to incidental contact by voluntarily playing the sport, but this defense will fail. Bellows's deliberate kick to Yang's knee could not reasonably be described as "incidental contact" in the sport of soccer. No player would consent to a deliberate attack from an opponent such as occurred in this hypothetical. Accordingly, Bellows would be liable to Yang for battery. Yang's damages would include, in part, her loss of leg mobility.

INTRODUCTION

Sometimes intentional torts are legally justified, so that the person engaging in the intentional tort is not liable to the victim. These are collectively called *defenses* to intentional torts. Conduct that normally would constitute an intentional tort, such as battery, could be excused under the theory of self-defense, for instance. Defenses are commonly used by the defendant in a civil lawsuit to exonerate the defendant from liability to the plaintiff.

A legal defense arises only when one party responds to another party's allegations in a lawsuit. Usually, the defendant answers the plaintiff's complaint with defenses. However, if the defendant counterclaimed against the plaintiff, it would be the plaintiff who replied with defenses. If third parties were involved in the litigation through cross-complaints, these third parties would answer with defenses. This presumes, of course, that defenses are available with which to respond.

This chapter focuses on the part of the torts puzzle called *justification of tortious conduct through defenses*. When assembling these complex pieces, the following questions may be helpful: (1) May the tortfeasor use a defense to excuse his or her misconduct? (2) Which defenses apply to which intentional torts?

There are several types of legal defenses to intentional torts. This chapter describes and assembles them:

- Self-defense (defense against assault, battery, or false imprisonment).
- Defense of persons or property (defense against assault, battery, or false imprisonment).
- Rightful repossession (defense against trespass to land, trespass to chattel, conversion, assault, and battery).
- Consent (defense to all intentional torts).
- Mistake (defense to most intentional torts).
- Privilege (broad category of defense against intentional torts).

- Necessity (defense to various intentional torts).
- Public officer's immunity for legal process enforcement, and law enforcement and private citizen's defense for warrantless arrest.
- Reasonable discipline by parents and educators over children (defense to assault, battery, false imprisonment, infliction of emotional distress, invasion of privacy).
- Statutes of limitations (defense to all intentional torts).

5.1 SELF-DEFENSE

Self-defense is probably the most familiar legal defense for the average person. It is most commonly applied to the intentional torts of assault and battery, but it may be used in cases involving false imprisonment. **Self-defense** is the exercise of reasonable force to repel an attack upon one's person or to avoid confinement. The nature of the action is simple: the victim of an assault or battery may use that degree of force necessary to prevent bodily injury (or offensive contact) from the attacker. Similarly, the victim of false imprisonment may use the force needed to prevent or escape confinement.

Consider this likely scenario. Walter is angry at Milo and throws a punch at Milo's face. Milo responds by blocking Walter's fist and, grabbing Walter's wrist, Milo twists Walter's arm behind his back until Walter agrees to calm down. This illustrates assault and self-defense: by throwing the punch, Walter placed Milo in reasonable apprehension of an unconsented contact that endangered his physical safety. Under self-defense, Milo was entitled to use whatever force was necessary to repel the attack.

The issue of self-defense would only arise if Walter (as plaintiff) sued Milo (as defendant) for battery. Walter would allege that Milo committed battery by grabbing his wrist and twisting his arm. Milo would reply with the legal defense of self-defense, which justified his actions. Remember that the defendant uses legal defenses to avoid liability to the plaintiff. In our hypothetical, Milo's self-defense argument would defeat Walter's complaint for battery. Bear in mind that Milo would have his own cause of action against Walter for assault, and Walter would not be able to use self-defense as a defense, because he initiated the attack upon Milo.

The elements of self-defense are (1) use of reasonable force (2) to counter an attacking or offensive force and (3) necessary to prevent bodily injury, offensive contact, or confinement.

Reasonable Force

The neutralizing force a person uses in self-defense is limited. The force cannot be greater than what is reasonably necessary to dispel the attacking force. This is called **reasonable force**. In the preceding example, Milo applied only as much force as needed to prevent Walter from striking Milo. Had Milo broken Walter's arm in retaliation, this would clearly have

LEGAL TERMS

self-defense
The exercise of reasonable force to repel an attack upon one's person or to avoid confinement. It is a defense to the intentional torts of assault, battery, and false imprisonment. The reasonable force used to counter an attacking force must be necessary to prevent bodily injury, offensive contact, or confinement.

reasonable force
That degree of force reasonably necessary to dispel an attacking force. It is an element of self-defense and defense of persons or property.

been excessive force, because breaking Walter's arm was unnecessary to stop the assault. Thus, Milo could not use self-defense as a legal justification. Instead, Milo would have become the aggressor and have engaged in battery against Walter. Common law maintains that the victim of an assault or battery may not turn aggressive once the assailant is incapacitated. Thus, if Walter collapsed after Milo twisted his arm, Milo could not kick Walter into unconsciousness and then claim self-defense.

What constitutes reasonable force varies depending upon the circumstances of each case. If Walter attacked Milo with an axe, then deadly force would be involved. Milo would therefore be warranted in responding with deadly force to repulse the onslaught. If Walter threw rocks at Milo, his force would threaten severe bodily harm. Thus, Milo could react with similarly powerful force, such as knocking Walter down with a pole.

The reasonableness issue is difficult to reduce to clearly defined, black-and-white terms. Much depends upon the options available to the victim. Many courts hold that, in the face of deadly force, if a victim might reasonably escape from the attack, then this choice must first be selected before deadly force may be used in self-defense. Several courts apply the same rule to situations involving threats of serious bodily injury. However, the majority of jurisdictions maintain that a person is not required to flee his or her home if threatened by an intruder. This is sometimes called the **castle rule**, in which a dweller is considered "king" or "queen" and may use any amount of force, including deadly force, to resist an intruder, such as a burglar.

Countering an Attacking or Offensive Force

The party exercising self-defense must be opposing an attacking or offensive force. Walter's fist is obviously an attacking force. But suppose Walter spit at Milo. This would be an example of an offensive force, as it is contact by which Milo would probably be offended.

LEGAL TERMS

castle rule
Applies in cases of self-defense or defense of others. This rule permits dwellers to use any amount of force, including deadly force, to repel an intruder.

necessary force
That degree of force reasonably perceived as required to repel an attack or resist confinement. It is an aspect of self-defense.

Necessity to Prevent Injury, Offensive Contact, or Confinement

The force used in self-defense must be necessary to prevent bodily injury, offensive contact, or to avoid confinement. **Necessary force** is that which is reasonably perceived as required to rebuff an attack or confinement. When Milo grabbed Walter's wrist and twisted his arm, Milo felt this action was required to prevent Walter from continuing his assault. The question again becomes one of reasonableness: Did Milo respond with reasonable force necessary to allay Walter's attack? Or was Milo's force unnecessary (and thus excessive) given Walter's actions? Suppose Walter had only tapped Milo on the shoulder with his finger. Milo's wrist-and-arm twist in response would then be considered unreasonable, unneeded, and extreme. Thus, Milo could not avail himself of a self-defense argument against Walter's battery claim.

Say that Walter was attempting to lock Milo in a room against Milo's will. In self-defense, Milo could reply with as much force as required to avoid being confined. This means that Milo could use that degree of force necessary to escape Walter.

THE CASE OF THE VIOLENT VISITATION

When parents divorce, the noncustodial parent normally receives visitation rights as part of the court's decree. Sometimes, however, while exercising these rights, the visiting parent may clash with the ex-spouse or his or her new mate or other family. These conflicts occasionally become turbulent, resulting in physical confrontations. People have an unfortunate tendency not to be able to get along peaceably in certain circumstances.

In most cases, the law protects those who protect themselves. That is the essence of self-defense, and of defense of persons or property. But, as the following case illustrates, self-defense may not preclude liability when it is unclear exactly who is in the wrong.

White v. Massengill
1990 Westlaw 64531
(Tenn. Ct. App. 1990)
(Not Reported in S.W.2d)
(Court of Appeals of Tennessee)
May 18, 1990

CRAWFORD, Judge.

In this assault and battery case, the trial court entered a judgment on a jury verdict for plaintiff, Carl White, against defendant Donald Jerry Massengill, in the amount of $1,392.73. From the trial court's denial of plaintiff's motion for a new trial, plaintiff appeals to this Court.

Plaintiff alleges in his complaint that on September 16, 1988, he went to the house of his ex-wife and her husband, the defendant, Massengill, to pick up his son for weekend visitation. He avers that defendant physically prevented plaintiff's son from leaving the

house and when plaintiff advised defendant that he was going to notify the police, defendant Massengill "suddenly and without warning or provocation, violently attacked plaintiff, striking him in the area of the right eye." Plaintiff alleges that he suffered great pain and suffering, permanent physical injuries, and loss of earnings and earning capacity as a result of the attack.

Defendant's answer [. . .] avers that the conduct of the plaintiff brought on the action of the defendant.

[. . .]

Plaintiff first answers that defendant did not plead provocation as an affirmative defense and therefore the [trial court's jury] charge [which included this defense] was not properly given. [. . .]

Provocation is not considered a defense to an assault and battery action [citation omitted], but may serve to mitigate plaintiff's damages.

[. . .] The testimony is conflicting as to which of the two men threw the first punch. Defendant testified that he struck the plaintiff after plaintiff stepped into the doorway of defendant's house and struck the defendant. [. . .]

There is material evidence that plaintiff's actions brought on the defendant's attack. Whether these actions rose to a level of provocation sufficient to mitigate damages is a matter for jury deliberation. [Citations omitted.]

Appellant's first issue is without merit.

The second issue is whether the trial court erred by allowing defendant to testify about his nonverbalized thoughts at the time of the incident as evidence of his "state of mind."

[. . .]

Plaintiff first argues that defendant's state of mind is not relevant to the issues before the court. We disagree. This is an intentional tort action in which the defendant relies upon provocation in mitigation of damages and self-defense as a bar to recovery. Defendant's beliefs concerning the plaintiff's propensities for violence are pertinent to his motivations in striking the plaintiff.

[. . .]

This issue is without merit.

[. . .]

The record reveals a very sharp conflict in the testimony of the parties concerning the events leading up to and including the altercation between them. Plaintiff said that defendant started the fight, and defendant said that plaintiff started the fight. Clearly, the defendant relied upon provocation and any diminution of damages in an assault and battery case due to provocative conduct by the plaintiff is peculiarly a matter for the jury. [Citation omitted.] Under the proof in this record, there is material evidence to support the verdict of the jury. [. . .]

The judgment of the trial court is affirmed [. . .].

CASE QUESTIONS

1. Did the jury accept the defendant's self-defense argument at trial? How were you able to make this determination?
2. Self-defense was not an issue on appeal. Provocation was disputed as a mitigation of the plaintiff's damages. Why do you suppose the defendant did not cross-appeal on the self-defense issue?
3. Although this was not an issue in the case, do you believe that the trial court should have granted judgment notwithstanding the verdict (j.n.o.v.) for the defendant on the grounds that self-defense barred the plaintiff's recovery? Explain.

Self-defense is perhaps the easiest legal justification to illustrate. Almost any child who has engaged in a playground shoving match can explain the fundamental concept. However, the legal elements require a more discerning eye, as shown in the following example.

HYPOTHETICAL

Toby Nesmith sat alone at a table in a local tavern. He was waiting to meet a friend from work when two men standing nearby got into a shoving match. One of the men (wearing a red shirt) pushed the other (wearing a blue coat) into Toby. In retaliation, Toby shoved "Blue Coat" back into "Red Shirt," knocking them both to the floor.

Red Shirt committed battery against Blue Coat by pushing him. Under the doctrine of transferred intent, when Blue Coat bumped into Toby, Red Shirt transferred his battery onto Toby. By pushing Blue Coat away, Toby used reasonable force to repel an attacking force to prevent injury to himself. Accordingly, Toby could claim self-defense against Red Shirt.

There remains a puzzling question, however. Could Toby claim self-defense against Blue Coat, or did Toby commit battery against Blue Coat? Blue Coat was essentially the instrumentality that Red Shirt put into motion to strike Toby, albeit accidentally. Blue Coat did not intend to contact Toby. Therefore, Blue Coat did not commit battery or assault against Toby.

Toby could still claim self-defense against Blue Coat, however. Toby responded to protect himself against injury from both participants in the shoving match. Thus, self-defense would apply. Further, since Blue Coat was a voluntary participant in the struggle with Red Shirt, Blue Coat consented to physical contact associated with a shoving match. This would include inadvertently bumping into an innocent bystander like Toby. Accordingly, Toby did not commit battery against Blue Coat, since Blue Coat impliedly consented to the incidental contact involved, which would include Toby's return shove.

The elements of self-defense are summarized in Figure 5-1.

Assault and battery may be justifiable in the defense of others or of property, as discussed in § 5.2.

5.2 DEFENSE OF PERSONS OR PROPERTY

As a legal justification for assault or battery, defense of other persons or defense of injury to property is similar to self-defense. A person who

Use of reasonable force
Countering an attacking or offensive force
Actions necessary to prevent bodily injury, offensive contact, or confinement

FIGURE 5-1
Elements of Self-Defense

would otherwise have committed assault or battery may be excused if the action were taken to protect another individual or property from harm. This would include freeing someone subject to false imprisonment.

Defense of Persons: Elements

Defense of persons as a legal justification for assault or battery has the following elements: (1) use of reasonable force (2) to defend or protect a third party from injury (3) when the third party is threatened by an attacking force. For example, if Marie were about to throw a vase at Marjorie, Simon could use reasonable force to subdue Marie before she could complete the throw. Simon would not have committed battery, because he grabbed Marie to prevent her from harming Marjorie. Simon would be entitled to the legal defense of defense of another person to avoid liability for battery.

The same principles used in self-defense to define reasonable force also apply to defense of persons. Thus, Simon could not use excessive force to repel Marie's attack against Marjorie. For instance, if Simon struck Marie sharply in the head with a two-by-four piece of lumber, this would be unnecessarily brutal force to subdue the vase attack.

Also, like self-defense, the repelling force must be used to counter an attacking force. If Marjorie telephoned Simon to complain that Marie had just thrown a vase at her, then Simon could not run over and clobber Marie and then claim defense of another as an excuse.

Defense of Property: Elements

Conduct that otherwise might be assault or battery may be vindicated if the action is taken to defend property from damage or dispossession. A property owner has the right to possess and safeguard his or her property from others. The elements of **defense of property** are (1) use of reasonable force (2) to protect property from damage or dispossession (3) when another person, the *invader,* attempts to injure or wrongfully take possession of the property.

The reasonable force contemplated here is essentially identical to that discussed in regard to self-defense. Many courts, however, restrict the defensive force to the least amount necessary to protect the property from harm or dispossession. This is a narrower definition of reasonableness, suggesting that human well-being is more important than the safety of property. Under this theory, most courts would not allow deadly force or extreme force likely to cause serious bodily injury to be used to defend property under any circumstances.

The property owner or possessor uses reasonable force to repulse an attacking force that is attempting to harm or possess the property. For example, if Frederick is in the process of committing trespass to chattel or conversion, then Helen, who owns the personal property in danger, may use reasonable force to dispel Frederick's efforts at dispossession.

LEGAL TERMS

defense of persons
A defense to the intentional torts of assault, battery, and false imprisonment. Its elements include the use of reasonable force to defend or protect a third party from injury when the third party is threatened by an attacking force.

defense of property
A defense to the intentional torts of assault and battery. Its elements include the use of reasonable force to protect property from damage or dispossession when another person, called the invader, attempts to injure or wrongfully take possession of the property.

The use of reasonable force to expel a trespasser to land is called **ejectment.** Defense of real property cases frequently involve landowners who have placed dangerous traps for trespassers. The trespassers are often seeking to steal personal property and usually violate various criminal statutes involving theft or burglary. Nevertheless, landowners may not set up deadly traps to inflict serious bodily injuries upon such criminals. Spring-loaded guns have been the most common snares litigated. A landowner places a shotgun inside a barn or outbuilding which is triggered by a trip-wire placed across a window or doorway. The thief steps upon the wire while trying to enter and is shot. Courts universally condemn this use of deadly force to defend property.

ejectment
Use of reasonable force to expel a trespasser to land.

THE CASE OF THE DEFIANT TRUCKER

In 1966 the Bobby Fuller Four recorded a popular rock song in which the refrain declared, "I fought the law, and the law won." As the following case demonstrates, this is usually the result. However, note the dissent's approach to defense of property against an arguably unlawful seizure by law enforcement officers. Although this case involved criminal law, the court's discussion of defense of property is relevant to tort law.

Jurco v. State
825 P.2d 909 (Alaska Ct. App. 1992)
(Court of Appeals of Alaska)
February 14, 1992

OPINION

MANNHEIMER, Judge.

David Jurco was convicted, following a jury trial in district court, of disorderly conduct [citation omitted], and resisting arrest [citation omitted]. These offenses resulted from a confrontation between Jurco and members of the State Troopers who had come to Jurco's residence to serve a court order directing them to take possession of Jurco's truck; the Kenai District Court had ordered forfeiture of the vehicle because Jurco had used it in furtherance of a violation of the fish and game laws.

Unbeknown to the troopers, Jurco had recently filed for bankruptcy. The federal bankruptcy court had directed Jurco not to sell or transfer any of his property or allow creditors to take any of his property without court order. Jurco believed that the bankruptcy court's directive obliged him to resist the troopers' attempt to seize his truck. At first, Jurco argued with the troopers. Finding he could not dissuade them, Jurco got into the truck and started it. With Trooper Eugene Kallus trying to hang on to the side of the truck, Jurco drove the truck away to a different location on his property. Jurco then got out of the truck, removed the battery from the vehicle, and began to let the air out of the truck's tires.

At this point, Trooper Kallus informed Jurco that he was placing him under arrest for disorderly conduct. [...]

But even if we assume for purposes of argument that Jurco's interpretation of bankruptcy law is correct, the question remains whether Jurco was entitled to forcibly resist the troopers when they came to execute the Kenai District Court's warrant. We conclude that Jurco was not entitled to forcibly resist the troopers even if he reasonably believed that the seizure of his truck was illegal.

[. . .]

[At common law] a property owner was entitled to use force to resist an unlawful taking of his property. "One whose lawful possession of property is threatened by the unlawful conduct of another, and who has no time to resort to the law for its protection, may take reasonable steps, including the use of force, to prevent or terminate such interference with the property." [Citation omitted.] This [. . .] common-law rule has also been codified in Alaska; AS [Alaska Statutes] 11.81.350-(a) provides:

> Justification: Use of force in defense of property and premises.
>
> (a) A person may use nondeadly force upon another when and to the extent the person reasonably believes it is necessary to terminate what the person reasonably believes to be the commission or attempted commission by the other of an unlawful taking or damaging of property or services.

For purposes of deciding this appeal, we assume that Jurco reasonably believed that the Kenai District Court's order to seize his truck ran afoul of the federal bankruptcy court's order to keep his property together. [Another Alaska statute, Alaska Stat. § 11.81.420, authorized law enforcement officers to use reasonable force, including deadly force, to enforce a court order to seize property, even if the court decree is later determined to have been unlawful.] In such a situation, the joint operation of Alaska Stat. §§ 11.81.420 and 11.81.350(a) would seemingly allow Jurco to use force against the troopers to resist the taking of his truck while at the same time authorizing the troopers to respond with force of their own against Jurco—creating an escalating confrontation that would end only when the troopers resorted to deadly force against Jurco. [. . .]

Sidebar: Is the Alaska Court of Appeals being just a bit melodramatic when characterizing the "escalating confrontation" between Jurco and the troopers as ending only when the police ultimately kill Jurco? The court concludes that the state legislature could not have intended two conflicting statutes—one governing defense of property and the other concerning law officers' enforcement of court orders—to permit members of the public to wrestle with police over chattel possession. Was the court simply exaggerating to justify its rationale?

This could not have been the legislature's intention. With emotions running high on both sides, a property owner who sees that nondeadly force is not enough to make law enforcement officials back down might well begin (unlawfully) to use deadly force on the officers. Or, in the heat of the moment, the officers might mistakenly conclude that the property owner has begun to use deadly force upon them and respond in kind. Both possibilities could easily lead to the infliction of serious injury or death.

Thus, the question presented by Jurco's case is: which of these two statutes did the legislature intend to take precedence when law enforcement officers attempt to execute a court order calling for a seizure of property?

Sidebar: As the Alaska Court of Appeals has framed the issue, which statute will prevail? Are you surprised by this outcome? Or was it predictable from the outset?

We conclude that a person is not entitled to use force to resist the taking of property by law enforcement officers pursuant to a court order.

[. . .]

It follows that Jurco was not entitled to forcibly resist the State Troopers' efforts to seize his truck under the order issued by the Kenai District Court.

[. . .]

The judgment of the district court is AFFIRMED.

BRYNER, Chief Judge, dissenting.

I disagree with the court's decision [. . .]. In my view, Jurco was entitled to [a jury instruction] on his theory of defense [. . .] that he was seeking to protect his property from what he reasonably believed to be an unlawful taking.

[. . .]

The majority of this court effectively amends the defense of property statute by engrafting to it an exception that the legislature evidently chose not to include. The court does so in reliance on its own notions of desirable social policy. It is not this court's prerogative, however, to substitute its political views for those expressed by the legislature in the clear and unrestricted language of [Alaska Stat. §] 11.81.350(a).

CASE QUESTIONS

1. Do you agree with the majority that the legislature intended the law officer enforcement-of-court-orders statute to override the defense-of-property statute? Explain.
2. Do you agree with the dissent that the majority rewrites the two statutes to suit its own vision of preferred social policy?

It should be relatively easy to imagine situations in which reasonable force is used to defend another person from attack. Defense of property, however, may be more difficult to conjure.

HYPOTHETICAL

Consider the case of Isaac, who discovered two teenage hoodlums throwing bricks and stones at his house windows. Isaac crept up behind the duo and leapt from behind some bushes. The delinquents were taken by surprise, and Isaac knocked one to the ground with a kick to the stomach and tackled the other. Although both hoodlums suffered minor abrasions and bruises, neither was injured severely. The two ruffians claim that Isaac has committed battery against them. Does Isaac have a defense?

Isaac used force against the rowdies to prevent damage to his property. The hooligans were attempting to injure Isaac's house. The primary question is whether Isaac used reasonable force to prevent the property damage. Since neither hooligan suffered severe harm as a result of Isaac's actions, the force should be deemed reasonable to neutralize the attackers. Accordingly, Isaac could successfully apply defense of property against the allegation of battery.

The elements of defense of persons or property are listed in Figure 5-2.

Defense of property is often used in situations in which sellers repossess property from defaulting buyers. Rightful repossession as a legal defense is discussed in § 5.3.

5.3 RIGHTFUL REPOSSESSION

An owner of personal property generally has the right to repossess, by force if necessary, a chattel that has been wrongfully taken or withheld. This is the defense of **rightful repossession**. The defense is generally applied to allegations of trespass to land, assault, battery, and sometimes conversion and trespass to chattel. However, the amount of force that may be used is extremely limited. Generally, the elements of rightful repossession include the following: (1) use of reasonable force (2) to retake possession of personal property (3) of which the owner has been wrongfully dispossessed (or to which the owner is denied possession), (4) provided the efforts to retake the chattel are made promptly after the original dispossession or denial of possession occurs. For this defense, reasonable force is defined along the same lines as for defense of property.

Retaking Possession of Personal Property

The chattel owner seeks to repossess personal property to which he or she is entitled. This is the crux of the defense. If someone has wrongfully dispossessed an owner of his or her chattel, then the owner is entitled to enter upon the dispossessor's land to recover the chattel. This provides a defense to trespass to land. Reasonable force may be applied to recover possession of the personal property.

FIGURE 5-2
Elements of Defense
of Persons or
Property

Defense of Persons	Defense of Property
Use of reasonable force	Use of reasonable force
To defend or protect a third party from harm	To protect property from damage or dispossession
Third person is threatened by attacking force	Someone attempts to harm or wrongfully possess property

To illustrate, suppose Raymond took Carl's motorcycle without asking permission and drove the cycle back to his own garage. Carl would be entitled to enter Raymond's garage to recover the cycle. If Raymond attempted to prevent Carl from entering, Carl could use reasonable force to vanquish Raymond and recover the cycle. Carl would not be liable for either trespass to land or battery, because he would have the defense of rightful repossession.

Prompt Repossession Efforts

Older common law cases held that a chattel owner's efforts to repossess personal property must occur soon after the chattel had been wrongfully taken away. Just how promptly this needed to occur, however, was not clearly defined. Many nineteenth-century opinions ruled that hot pursuit was necessary. Hot pursuit is usually defined for purposes of criminal law, but its meaning is the same for this tort defense. **Hot pursuit**, in this context, may be described as a rapid chase as soon as possible after the owner has discovered that his or her chattel is missing. This presumes, of course, that the personal property owner knows who took the chattel.

Wrongful Denial of Possession

The chattel owner need not be dispossessed of the personal property for this defense to apply. Consider the example of someone who originally took possession of the chattel with the owner's consent, but later wrongfully refuses to return it. If the owner then attempted to retake possession and was accused of trespass to land, assault, or battery, the owner could apply rightful repossession as a defense.

Most cases involving denial of possession deal with bailments, in which the owner has delivered possession of the chattel to someone else for a specific purpose, with the explicit understanding that the chattel is to be returned at a certain time or upon demand. When an automobile is taken to a mechanic for repair, for instance, there is a bailment. The mechanic would have lawful possession of the vehicle, because the owner left it for repairs. Suppose, however, that the mechanic made unauthorized repairs and sought to charge the owner. If the owner demanded return of the car and the mechanic refused, then this refusal would constitute wrongful denial of possession. The owner could use reasonable force to enter the mechanic's premises to retake the chattel. The owner would not be liable to the mechanic for trespass to land because of the rightful repossession defense.

Note that this result would be different if there had been a dispute over authorized repairs. Most state statutes provide mechanics with possessory liens, which empower repair persons to keep possession of vehicles until repair charges have been paid. However, some statutes provide that the amounts due must be undisputed.

LEGAL TERMS

rightful repossession
A defense to trespass to land, trespass to chattel, conversion, assault, and battery. Its elements include the use of reasonable force to retake possession of personal property of which the owner has been wrongfully dispossessed, or to which the owner has been wrongfully denied possession. Efforts to retake the chattel must be made promptly after the original dispossession (or denial of possession) occurs.

hot pursuit
In the intentional tort defense of rightful repossession, the property owner's prompt pursuit of the person who wrongfully took the property. The term is also commonly used in criminal law for police pursuit of criminal suspects.

Wrongful Dispossession

For the defense of rightful repossession to apply, the owner's chattel must have been unlawfully dispossessed, or its return have been unlawfully denied. This means that the dispossessor or retainer must not have a legal right to possess (or deny return of) the chattel.

In the preceding bailment example, the mechanic did not possess the automobile unlawfully, because the owner had left it for repairs. However, when the mechanic performed unauthorized work and sought payment, and the owner demanded the car's return, then the mechanic wrongfully possessed the vehicle—specifically, the repair person committed trespass to chattel and possibly conversion. Thus, the owner would be entitled to repossess with reasonable force and could use that defense against the mechanic's lawsuit for trespass to land, assault, or battery.

THE CASE OF THE FREE-ROAMING FELINE

The following case illustrates an unusual application of rightful repossession. Any pet owner, however, will immediately sympathize with the Blanchards. The court discusses self-defense and defense of property, but the case is a classic rightful repossession scenario.

Shehyn v. United States
256 A.2d 404 (D.C. 1969)
(District of Columbia Court
of Appeals)
August 7, 1969

FICKLING, J.

Appellant was convicted by a jury of assault, D.C. Code § 22-504. After the court charged the jury on assault and self-defense, the instruction [on defense of property] . . . was given and objected to on the ground that it did not correctly state the law on the defense of one's property. The objection was well taken. However, we hold it was harmless error in the context of the case as a whole.

Mr. Blanchard, the complainant, and his wife, who were next door neighbors of

appellant, went upon appellant's parking lot to retrieve their pet cat which had escaped from their house and had hidden in appellant's air shaft. Appellant ordered the Blanchards off his property. After they refused, he went inside his house and got a wooden camera tripod about four feet in length and again ordered them to leave. When they refused to leave until they recovered their cat, appellant pushed Mrs. Blanchard aside and struck Mr. Blanchard with the tripod causing injury to his hand, requiring five stitches, and lacerations to his chest. The testimony is conflicting as to why appellant struck Mr. Blanchard. Appellant testified he went into the house to get the tripod because Mr. Blanchard picked up a brick. Blanchard testified he picked up a brick after appellant came out of his house with the tripod, and then he dropped the brick as appellant was advancing upon him because he did not want to strike appellant, who is an elderly man.

It is well settled that a person may use as much force as is reasonably necessary to eject a trespasser from his property, and that if he used more force than is necessary, he is guilty of assault. This is true regardless of any actual or threatened injury to the property by the trespasser, although this would be a factor in determining the reasonableness of the force used. However, in the instant case, Blanchard was not a trespasser. He had a privilege to go peaceably upon appellant's property to retrieve his cat. In *Carter v. Thurston,* 59 N.H. 104 (1877), where logs went upon a riparian owner's property because of a flood, the court stated:

> This right of pursuit and reclamation [of logs] rests upon the same natural right as that which permits the owner of cattle to pursue into an adjoining field and recover his beasts straying from the highway; but in the pursuit and recovery of his cattle or his logs, the owner must do no unnecessary damage, and is responsible for any excess or abuse of his right.

In an assault case where the complainant was injured while recovering his carpenter's plane, the court stated in *Stuyvesant v. Wilcox,* 92 Mich. 233, 52 N.W. 465, 467 (1892):

> But it is a rule well settled that one has such a right in personal property that he may recapture it and take it into his own possession whenever and wherever he may peaceably do so.

This principle was also followed in *Pierce v. Finerty,* 76 N.H. 38, 76 A. 194, 196 (1910), which involved reclamation of trees upon the land of another:

> There is a right of recaption or reclamation of personal property upon another's land without fault of the owner. In such cases, under certain circumstances, the owner of personal property has a right to enter to retake his property, and is not a trespasser if he does so. . . . But the right does not extend to cases where the situation is created by the fault or wrong of such owner.

The applicable rule, which we adopt, is stated in *Restatement (Second) of Torts* § 198 (1965):

> (1) One is privileged to enter land in the possession of another, at a reasonable time and in a reasonable manner, for the purpose of removing a chattel to the immediate possession of which the actor is entitled, and which has come upon the land otherwise than with the actor's consent or by his tortious conduct or contributory negligence.
>
> (2) The actor is subject to liability for any harm done in the exercise of the privilege stated in Subsection (1) to any legally protected interest of the possessor in the land or connected with it, except where the chattel is on the land through the tortious conduct or contributory negligence of the possessor.

[Citations omitted.]

In this case there is no evidence in the record which would indicate that the Blanchards acted in an unreasonable manner or at an unreasonable time when they went upon the parking lot to get their cat. The [jury] instruction, even though erroneous, was actually beneficial to appellant since he had no right to eject the Blanchards while they were exercising a privilege given to them by law, and appellant was not entitled to any defense of property instruction.

Affirmed.

CASE QUESTIONS

1. Although Shehyn, the appellant, was prosecuted under a criminal statute for assault, the defenses used in the case would be identical to those pleaded in a civil lawsuit involving the tort of assault or battery. Did you notice that the Blanchards were alleged to have committed trespass to land? What were their defenses as discussed in *Shehyn*? What portions of the court's opinion alerted you to these defenses?

2. Although the court in *Shehyn* quoted several persuasive precedents from other jurisdictions, it chose to adopt the rule stated in the *Restatement (Second) of Torts* § 198. Why did the *Shehyn* court quote these other state court opinions? Why do you think it adopted the *Restatement* rule, which is considered secondary legal authority, as opposed to the quoted court cases, which are primary authority?

3. Are there any other intentional tort defenses that were not discussed in *Shehyn* but that would apply? What are these? Why do you think they would succeed or fail?

4. Would the decision in *Shehyn* have been different if the Blanchards' cat had entered the appellant's land as a result of the Blanchards' actions? Suppose Mr. Blanchard threw a cat toy too high into the air, causing it to land on top of the appellant's roof, thereby enticing the cat to climb up onto the roof and become trapped there? Would the Blanchards have been legally justified in entering the appellant's real estate under these circumstances?

Rightful repossession seems a noble defense, albeit more difficult to conceptualize than self-defense or defense of others and property. One might express the emotional essence of the doctrine as, "It's mine and I'm taking it back now!" The defense appeals to a sense of entitlement. As you read the following hypothetical, with whom do your sympathies lie?

HYPOTHETICAL

Ann was buying an automobile from Victor. Ann wrote a check to Victor for the final payment and this check bounced (i.e., the bank did not pay it because there were insufficient funds in Ann's account). Victor angrily went over to Ann's house and drove away in the car. As soon as Ann discovered the check problem, she telephoned Victor's apartment and left a message on his answering machine that she would be over directly to pay cash.

The first issue is whether Victor had the right to repossess the automobile once Ann's check bounced. This would depend upon the terms of their agreement or, if the agreement did not address the problem, then upon creditors' rights statutes. For the sake of example, assume that no statutes address the question and that the parties' contract was silent as well.

Although it is true that Ann breached her contract by bouncing her payment check to Victor, she also swiftly corrected the error. Most courts would hold that Victor could not use self-help remedies such as repossession without first contacting Ann to see if she could make good on the check. By repossessing the car without first talking with Ann, and since Ann has paid nearly the entire purchase price (and thus has a substantial equity, meaning property interest, in the vehicle), Victor has committed trespass to chattel. So Ann has been wrongfully dispossessed of her chattel. She could then enter Victor's real estate to recover her automobile without being liable to Victor for trespass to land. Ann would be entitled to the defense of rightful repossession.

It should also be noted that Victor would not be able to claim rightful repossession as a defense to trespass to chattel. Since Victor did not first communicate with Ann regarding the bad check and alternative means of payment, most courts would say that Victor could not defend his retaking of the car on the grounds of rightful repossession. On the other hand, if Victor had telephoned Ann about the check, and she had replied that she could or would not make the final payment, then Victor would be legally entitled to repossess the vehicle. Under this set of circumstances, Victor could use rightful repossession as a defense to trespass to chattel.

A synopsis of rightful repossession appears in Figure 5-3.

5.4 CONSENT

Consent is a broad defense applicable to every intentional tort. **Consent** occurs when the victim of an intentional tort voluntarily agrees to the tortfeasor's actions, provided that the victim understands (or reasonably should understand) the consequences of the tortfeasor's deeds. This knowledge factor is sometimes called **informed consent**.

The consent defense contains the following elements: (1) Voluntary acceptance of an intentionally tortious act (2) with full knowledge or understanding of the consequences. Actually, consent is not a legal defense at all. As shown in the previous two chapters, it is a necessarily missing element

LEGAL TERMS

consent
   A victim's voluntary acceptance of the tortfeasor's actions, provided that the victim understood (or reasonably should have understood) the consequences of the tortfeasor's behavior. It is a defense to every intentional tort.

informed consent
   Occurs when the victim of an intentional tort voluntarily agrees to the tortfeasor's actions, provided that the victim understands (or reasonably should understand) the consequences of the tortfeasor's conduct. This is the knowledge factor of the defense of consent.

Use of reasonable force
To repossess personal property
Owner has been wrongfully dispossessed of the chattel or has been improperly denied possession
Owner's efforts to repossess chattel occur promptly after original dispossession or denial of possession

FIGURE 5-3
Elements of Rightful Repossession

of intentional torts. If consent existed, then the intentional tort could not have occurred. The ancient common law applied the Latin maxim, *volenti non fit injuria,* which translates as, "No wrong may occur to one who is willing." As a practical matter, courts over the centuries have treated consent as a defense to intentional torts.

Informed Consent: Voluntary Acceptance

Consent will be a successful defense to an intentional tort action only if the victim willingly and knowingly agreed to the tortfeasor's conduct. Accordingly, a victim who is coerced into tolerating an intentional tort cannot consent to it, because the victim was compelled to undergo the tort. Further, the victim must comprehend the implications of the tortfeasor's actions to consent to them.

For instance, suppose Randy agrees to wrestle Ralph. Assume that both Randy and Ralph understand the repercussions of wrestling, including possible inadvertent injury. Randy and Ralph will have mutually consented to battery, and so neither could sue the other for this intentional tort if harm did happen. However, assume Randy did not want to wrestle Ralph, but Ralph ridiculed Randy in front of friends, in effect coercing Randy to wrestle. Randy would not have consented because of duress.

Part of the voluntary, or *volition,* factor of consent is the victim's mental capacity to agree. Some persons simply lack sufficient mental abilities to understand the consequences of a tortfeasor's actions. Severely retarded or mentally incapacitated individuals, for example, might not grasp the implications of a tortfeasor's misbehavior. Intoxicated individuals may also have insufficient mental faculties to comprehend the results of an intentional tort. Children, particularly when very young, may lack cognitive development adequate to grasp the ramifications of intentional torts. For such persons, consent could become virtually impossible.

Implied Consent

Consent may be expressed, either orally or in writing, or it may be implied by conduct or circumstances. For instance, public officials or famous persons are assumed to consent to adverse publicity merely by placing themselves in the public limelight. Consent to publicity is therefore implied, and public officials or celebrities cannot recover for libel or slander, unless malice is proven.

The most common example of implied consent involves emergency medical treatment. If a patient is unconscious and is taken to a hospital emergency room, the medical personnel may presume that the patient consents to treatment, at least to the extent of the emergency condition. Thus, if someone is found unconscious on the pavement, suffering from gastrointestinal bleeding, and an ambulance takes her to the hospital, the patient is presumed to agree to treatment of the emergency condition, in this case a "G.I. bleed," which is often life-threatening. Later, if the patient regains consciousness and protests against the treatment (perhaps upon religious grounds), the patient cannot sue for battery for the unauthorized emergency care. However, once conscious and clear-minded, the patient could insist that further treatment be foregone. Failure to stop treatment would then constitute battery. Suppose, instead, that the medical personnel treated beyond the emergency condition, such as removing a portion of diseased skin while treating the intestinal bleeding. Implied consent does not apply to nonemergency treatment, and thus battery would have occurred.

THE CASE OF THE MORE-THAN-TOUCH FOOTBALL GAME

Almost everyone has played contact games. Children delight in games such as "tag," "keep-away," and "hide-and-seek," which usually involve some physical contact. Older children and adults engage in rougher sports in which implied consent accepts incidental contact. Sometimes, however, a player forgets that there are limits to the reasonable force to which participants consent. In the following case, it becomes clear that the plaintiff felt that the defendant went well beyond these acceptable lines. The California Court of Appeal, however, was unimpressed. Perhaps none of the judges had ever played a rough game of touch football.

Knight v. Jewett
232 Cal. App. 3d 1142,
275 Cal. Rptr. 292 (1990)
(California Court of Appeal)
November 27, 1990
Review Granted, 278 Cal. Rptr. 203,
804 P.2d 1300 (Cal. 1991)

TODD, Acting Presiding Justice.

Kendra Knight appeals a summary judgment granted in favor of Michael Jewett in her lawsuit against Jewett for negligence and assault and battery stemming from a touch football game in which she was injured. Knight contends [. . .] it was error to apply the doctrine of assumption of risk to defeat the assault and battery cause of action and [. . .] there were triable issues of fact that should have precluded the granting of summary judgment.

FACTS

On January 25, 1987, Knight and several other individuals, including Jewett, gathered at the Vista home of Ed McDaniels to observe the Super Bowl football game. Knight and Jewett were among those who decided to play a game of co-ed touch football during half-time using a "peewee" football often used by children. Apparently, no explicit rules were written down or discussed before the game, other than the requirement that to stop advancement of the player with the ball it was necessary to touch that player above the waist with two hands. Knight and Jewett were on different teams.

Previously, Knight had played touch football and frequently watched football on television. Knight voluntarily participated in the Super Bowl half-time game. It was her understanding that this game would not involve forceful pushing, hard hitting or hard shoving during the game. She had never observed anyone being injured in a touch football game before this incident.

About five to ten minutes after the game started, Jewett ran into Knight during a play and afterward Knight asked Jewett not to play so rough. Otherwise, she told him, she would stop playing.

On the next play, Knight suffered her injuries, when she was knocked down by Jewett and he stepped on the little finger of her right hand. Kendra had three surgeries on the finger, but they proved unsuccessful. The finger was amputated during a fourth surgery.

According to Jewett, he had jumped up to intercept a pass and as he came down he knocked Knight over. When he landed, he stepped back and onto Knight's hand.

According to Knight's version, her teammate, Andrea Starr had caught the ball and was proceeding up the field. Knight was headed in the same direction, when Jewett, in pursuit of Starr, came from behind Knight and knocked her down. Knight put her arms out to break the fall and Jewett ran over her, stepping on her hand. Jewett continued to pursue Starr for another 10 to 15 feet before catching up with her and tagging her. Starr said the tag was rough enough to cause her to lose her balance and fall and twist her ankle.

Jewett did not intend to step on Knight's hand and did not intend to hurt her.

[. . .]

Knight contends her cause of action for assault and battery is viable and she should be allowed to proceed to trial on it.

[. . .] Jewett argued it must fail because Knight consented to the physical contact.

Consent is a viable defense to the tort of assault and battery. "A person may, by participating in a game, or by other conduct, consent to an act which might otherwise constitute a battery." [Citation omitted.] Here, however, we need not dwell on whether Jewett can successfully interpose a defense of consent to Knight's assault and battery cause of action.

Inasmuch as this case reaches us on appeal from a summary judgment in favor of Jewett, it is only necessary for us to determine whether there is any possibility Knight may be able to establish her case. [Citation omitted.]

A requisite element of assault and battery is intent. [Citation omitted.] Here, however, there is no evidence that Jewett intended to injure Knight or commit a battery on her. Moreover, the record affirmatively shows Knight does not believe Jewett had the intent to step on her hand or injure her. Without the requisite intent, Knight cannot state a cause of action for assault and battery.

A motion for summary judgment is addressed to the sound discretion of the trial court and, absent a clear showing of abuse, the judgment will not be disturbed on appeal. [Citation omitted.] On this record, we discern no abuse of discretion; the granting of summary judgment was proper. [. . .] Affirmed.

CASE QUESTIONS

1. *Knight* demonstrates how the defense of consent cannot be reached unless the elements of intentional torts (in this case, assault and battery), are satisfied. Although the evidence suggested that the defendant lacked the necessary intent to cause injury, could you imply such intent from Jewett's rough conduct during the game?

2. Presume that Knight had proven Jewett's intent to harm her, thus making a prima facie case for assault and battery (the other elements being satisfied under the facts of the case as given in the opinion). Would Jewett's consent defense prevail? Did Knight consent to the harsh play that Jewett was engaging in? If so, did Knight withdraw her consent when she told Jewett to stop playing so roughly?

3. Are there any other intentional tort defenses that were not discussed in *Knight* but that would apply? What are they? Why do you think they would succeed or fail?

Consent is sometimes characterized as the "you asked for it" defense. However, as the following hypothetical demonstrates, there can be doubt as to what the "it" was to which the victim consented.

HYPOTHETICAL

Colleen attended a company banquet in her honor as "sales director of the year." The dinner was a "roast" at which co-workers made humorous remarks about the guest of honor. Several of these comments were loaded with sarcasm and a few were in questionable taste. However, none of the comments was taken seriously by the audience, which understood that it was all in good fun. Under other circumstances, however, some members of the audience might have been offended. Colleen, however, took offense at the more colorful character references. Could she sue her co-employees for slander?

Colleen voluntarily agreed to attend the banquet with a complete understanding that co-workers would use the forum to tease and joke about her. She should have known that some of her fellow employees would push the limits of propriety with a few harsh remarks. Because the audience was not offended (given the "roast" atmosphere), and because Colleen knowingly accepted the potentially slanderous conduct, consent would be a defense to Colleen's slander claim.

The components of consent are listed in Figure 5-4.

Consent is clearly the most pervasive defense to intentional torts. Mistake is also quite extensive, as discussed in the next section.

Voluntary acceptance of intentionally tortious act
Full knowledge or understanding of consequences

FIGURE 5-4
Elements of Consent

5.5 MISTAKE

Sometimes people act based upon inaccurate information or incorrect interpretations of events. The actor intended the result of his or her conduct but behaved under false beliefs. Often, had a person known the true state of affairs, he or she would have behaved differently. Tort law recognizes this tendency toward error, in which everyone has engaged at one time or another. The defense of mistake provides individuals with an escape route from intentional tort liability. As a legal defense, **mistake** is the good faith belief, based upon incorrect information, that one is justified in committing an intentional tort under the circumstances. The elements may be detailed as follows: (1) Good faith conviction that one's actions are justified (2) with the belief based upon faulty information; and (3) the conduct would otherwise be considered tortious but for the erroneous belief.

Good Faith Conviction

The actor must reasonably believe that, under the incorrect facts the actor thinks are true, the actor's conduct will be legally excused. For instance, if Sandra thought Martina was converting her jacket when, in actuality, Martina was merely picking it off the floor, then Sandra would be justified in using reasonable force to recapture her chattel (since she reasonably believed that Martina was attempting to abscond with it). Naturally, the question revolves around the reasonableness of Sandra's perception of events. Was it obvious that Martina was simply picking up the jacket? Did it look as if Martina might have been rifling through the pockets looking for valuables? The good faith conviction, like all elements of mistake, depends heavily upon the specific facts of each case.

Belief Based upon Inaccurate Information

To use mistake as a defense to intentional torts, the actor must base his or her conviction upon erroneous details which, if they had been true, would have justified the conduct. Had Martina actually been trying to take Sandra's jacket (or valuables in its pockets), then Sandra would have been entitled to use reasonable force under the defense of rightful repossession. Assume that Sandra saw Martina looking through the jacket's pockets. Suppose that Martina was simply looking to see if anything had fallen out, but to Sandra it appeared that Martina was searching for valuables. This mistaken perception would be reasonable and would excuse Sandra's repossession efforts (such as grabbing Martina's arm and pulling the jacket out of her hands). Sandra would not be liable to Martina for battery, because of the mistake defense.

Otherwise Tortious Acts

It may seem apparent that the defense of mistake applies only if the actor has engaged in behavior which, except for the defense, would be considered tortious. For example, Sandra would have had to commit an intentional tort against Martina (such as battery) in order to claim the defense of mistake or rightful repossession. Otherwise, Sandra would not need to argue any defenses, since she would not need to justify her actions. This factor is present in all intentional tort defenses.

The Second Restatement of Torts

For decades, the American Law Institute has assembled The Restatements of the Law, which summarize the legal principles discussed in common law decisions. These include the *Restatement of Torts* and its successor, the *Restatement (Second) of Torts*.

In the *Restatement (Second)*'s chapter 45, justification and excuse to tort liability are discussed. The following is an excerpt applicable to the mistake defense.

Restatement (Second) of Torts § 890
Comments a & f
American Law Institute (1979)

In some cases the law creates a privilege [. . .]. [A] privilege is given although it adversely affects the legally protected interests of another. This is ordinarily true when the actor is protected although mistaken (see Comment *f*), as when one acts in self-defense against another whom he reasonably but erroneously believes to be an aggressor. [. . .]

f. Mistake. [. . .]

When the privilege is conditional, a person is sometimes protected by his reasonable belief in the existence of facts that would give rise to a privilege, even though the facts do not exist. Thus one is not liable for using reasonable force in the protection of himself or another against what he reasonably believes to be an aggression of another [citations omitted]; a policeman is not liable for mistakenly arresting one whom he believes to have committed a felony [citation omitted] and a private person is similarly protected if a felony has been committed [citation omitted]; a parent or teacher is not liable for mistakenly but reasonably disciplining a student.

Copyright © 1979 by The American Law Institute. Reprinted with the permission of the American Law Institute.

SIDEBAR

Was the defense of mistake implied in *White v. Massengill,* reprinted in § 5.1? Recall the court's reference to the "Defendant's beliefs concerning the plaintiff's propensities for violence" which prompted him to strike the plaintiff. Did the defendant erroneously believe the plaintiff to be an aggressor, as the *Restatement* Comment discusses?

LEGAL TERMS

mistake
An intentional tort defense. It is a good faith belief, based upon incorrect information, that one is justified in committing an intentional tort under the circumstances.

HYPOTHETICAL

Diedra was shopping at a local convenience store. The manager thought she saw Diedra stick a pack of chewing gum into her purse. When Diedra left the store without stopping at the cashier, the manager asked her to step back inside the store to see the contents of her purse. The manager explained that he thought he had seen her take merchandise without paying. Diedra emptied her purse, but no store items were included. If Diedra claimed that the manager had committed false imprisonment, defamation, or infliction of emotional distress, could the manager use mistake as a defense?

Assume that the manager's acts arguably constituted any one of these intentional torts. Nevertheless, courts would readily rule that, under these circumstances, the manager was justified in detaining Diedra for questioning. So long as the interrogation was conducted reasonably (such as in private for a short time period), then the courts would consider the manager's behavior to be acceptable. The manager had a good faith belief that Diedra had shoplifted (when, in fact, she had not). The manager acted based upon this erroneous conviction, expecting that her conduct would be legally excused under the circumstances.

Mistake is summarized in Figure 5-5.

5.6 PRIVILEGE

As an intentional torts defense, **privilege** is a legal justification to engage in otherwise tortious conduct in order to accomplish a compelling social goal. For example, if a child is drowning in a swimming pool, one might wish to commit trespass to land to save the child's life. Comparatively speaking, the social value of saving a life outweighs the landowner's right to exclude trespassers from his or her property.

Privilege is most commonly a defense to trespass to land, trespass to chattel, conversion, assault, battery, and false imprisonment, although it may be applied against other intentional torts as well. Privilege includes the following considerations:

1. Do the actor's motives for engaging in an intentional tort outweigh the injury to the victim or his or her property?

FIGURE 5-5
Elements of Mistake

Good faith conviction that actor's conduct is justified
Belief based upon erroneous information
Behavior would be tortious except for incorrect belief

2. Was the actor justified in committing the intentional tort to accomplish his or her socially desirable purposes, or could a less damaging action have been taken instead?

This formula shows how courts balance values between the socially acceptable motives of the tortfeasor (actor) and the tort victim's compensation for injury. Privilege presumes that the intentional tort is legally justified because of the higher purposes to be achieved.

Motives and Socially Desirable Goals

Motive describes the goal which a participant wishes to accomplish by taking a particular action. Motive may be discovered by probing the mental state of the actor. This mind-reading occurs in many areas of law. For example, in criminal law, *mens rea* loosely translates from the Latin as "evil thoughts" and suggests a psychological component to criminal conduct. In tort law, motive is synonymous with **intent**, which is broadly defined as the desire to attain a certain result. For purposes of the privilege defense, motive must be socially advantageous to a point which excuses intentionally harming another person or his or her property. The preceding example of trespassing to save a drowning child's life sharply illustrates the clearly superior social objective that would give rise to the defense against the landowner's trespass-to-land lawsuit.

Less Injurious Alternatives

With privilege defenses, courts frequently ask whether the tortfeasor's objectives could have been reached through behavior that would have been less harmful to the victim. Suppose Karen discovers an automobile on fire next to a natural gas storage facility. Given the likelihood that the burning car will ignite the gas tanks, which would explode along with a sizeable portion of the surrounding neighborhood, Karen sprays the flaming vehicle with water, irreparably damaging the engine. The car owner would complain against Karen's conversion or trespass to chattel. Karen would defend by arguing privilege. The court would query: Could Karen have saved the storage facility (and surrounding area) through a less damaging act?

The answer to this question depends upon the extent of the fire. If only a small portion of the automobile were burning, such as something in the trunk, Karen could have isolated the danger by concentrating water only into the trunk compartment. If the interior were also ablaze, Karen would be forced to expose more car to the water to put out the fire. Still, she might have spared the engine compartment. However, if the inferno had engulfed the entire vehicle, she would have no choice other than to inundate it with water.

LEGAL TERMS

privilege
An intentional tort defense. It is the legal justification to engage in otherwise tortious conduct to accomplish a compelling social goal. For example, the defense could apply in a case in which trespass to land was committed to save a drowning person. Similar to the defense of necessity.

motive
The goal that a person wishes to accomplish by taking a particular action. In tort law, motive is similar to intent. It is a factor in the intentional tort defense of privilege.

intent
In tort law, the desire to achieve a harmful result that the law defines as tortious.

Similarity Between Privilege and Other Defenses

Several distinct intentional tort defenses, such as rightful repossession, self-defense, or defense of others or property, are simply particular types of privilege. Each has a social benefits component that justifies otherwise tortious misconduct. Necessity is another form of privilege that has also become a separate defense in its own right. The same is true of public officer's immunity for legal process enforcement, warrantless arrest, and reasonable discipline. These defenses to intentional torts are discussed in the remaining sections of this chapter.

The Restatement (Second) Position

Restatement (Second) of Torts § 890 focuses on privileges, noting that the term is broadly defined to include many of the specific defenses discussed throughout this chapter. The illustrations in the Comments are particularly helpful in understanding the scope of privilege.

Restatement (Second) of Torts § 890 & Comments
American Law Institute (1979)

§ 890. Privileges
One who otherwise would be liable for a tort is not liable if he acts in pursuance of and within the limits of a privilege of his own or of a privilege of another that was properly delegated to him.

Comment:
   a. As stated in § 10, the word "privilege" is used throughout this Restatement to denote the fact that conduct that under ordinary circumstances would subject the actor to liability, under particular circumstances does not subject him to the liability.
   [. . .]
   In some cases the law creates a privilege [. . .] as when the owner of land is given a privilege to eject a trespasser upon his land or to enter the land of another to abate a private nuisance, or when a citizen is given the privilege of arresting a felon [. . .].
   c. *Purpose of privilege—Conditional privileges created by rule of law.* Most of the privileges that are not based on consent are conditioned upon their being performed for the purpose of protecting the interest for which the privilege was given. This is illustrated in cases in which force is used against another; in self-defense or in defense of a third person [citation omitted]; in the defense of the possession of land [citation omitted]; in the recapture of land or chattels [citation omitted]; in an arrest by a private person or a peace officer [citation omitted]; in the prevention of crime [citation omitted] [. . .]; in the disciplining of children [. . .].
   d. *Purpose of privilege—Absolute privileges.* In certain cases in which the interests of the public are overwhelming, the purpose of the actor is immaterial. Thus for some or all statements, complete immunity from civil liability exists as to defamatory statements made during the

course of judicial proceedings [citation omitted], as well as to state-ments by legislators and certain administrative officers while acting in the performance of their functions.

Copyright 1979 by The American Law Institute. Reprinted with the permission of The American Law Institute.

HYPOTHETICAL

Livingston owns a grocery in town. One of his customers notified him that several cans of Buddy Boy's Baked Beans were bulging, which is a symptom of contamination. Livingston opened these cans and discovered that the food had spoiled. He placed an advertisement in the local newspaper warning his customers to return any can of Buddy Boy's, whether bulging or not, because of spoilage. In fact, only four cans of the product were defective. Buddy Boy's manufacturer, E. I. Wilcott & Company, sued Livingston for disparagement of goods. Livingston claimed privilege, arguing that his motive was to protect the public from food poisoning. Would the defense carry the day?

Truth is an absolute defense in any type of defamation action, including commercial disparagement. In our hypothetical, however, the truth was exaggerated. Only a few cans were tainted. Nonetheless, there was no way of determining this without recalling as many cans as possible from Livingston's customers. A court would rule that Livingston was justified in advertising the warning to his customers, and so Livingston would not be liable to E. I. Wilcott & Company for disparagement of goods.

The elements of privilege are abstracted in Figure 5-6.

5.7 NECESSITY

Necessity is another variety of privilege that excuses otherwise tortious misconduct. Under this defense, the tortfeasor is justified in engaging in an intentional tort to prevent more serious injury from an external force. **Necessity** contains three elements: (1) Committing an intentional tort (2) to avert more serious injury (3) caused by a force other than the

Actor's motives in committing intentional tort outweigh injury to victim or property
Actor was justified in engaging in intentional tort to accomplish socially desirable goals
No less damaging alternative action could have been taken

LEGAL TERMS

necessity
An intentional tort defense. Its elements include committing an intentional tort to avert more serious injury caused by some force (other than the tortfeasor), when the tortfeasor's actions were reasonably necessary to avert the greater harm. It is similar to the defense of privilege.

FIGURE 5-6
Elements of Privilege

tortfeasor (4) and the tortfeasor's actions were reasonably necessary to avert the greater harm.

Thwarting a More Substantial Harm

In a necessity situation, the tortfeasor is usually faced with having to choose between the lesser of two evils. On the one hand, the tortfeasor must inflict injury upon a victim or the victim's property. On the other hand, the tortfeasor could do nothing and watch a greater havoc occur. For example, suppose Antonio is aboard a ship that suddenly begins to sink. There are several passengers aboard, including Antonio, as well as valuable cargo. If the cargo were thrown overboard, the boat could stay afloat long enough for help to arrive. So Antonio elects to jettison the cargo and save the passengers' lives. The cargo owner could sue Antonio for trespass to chattel, but the defense of necessity would insulate Antonio from liability. Although Antonio committed an intentional tort, he sought only to prevent greater harm caused by a force beyond his control (namely, the ship's sinking).

External Forces

For necessity to operate as a defense to an intentional tort, the more significant danger being averted must originate from a source other than the tortfeasor. For instance, in the previous illustration, the boat began to sink through no fault of Antonio's. However, suppose he had caused an explosion in the engine room by improper fuel mixing, and thus blew a hole in the hull of the craft. Because Antonio created the greater hazard, he could not claim necessity in discarding the cargo overboard. Had it not been for his misconduct in the engine room, the extreme peril would never have happened. The necessity defense cannot protect a tortfeasor who creates the catastrophic condition and then must engage in an intentional tort to resolve the crisis.

Reasonably Necessary Action

As is generally true with privilege, necessity requires that the tortfeasor's conduct be reasonably necessary to prevent the more substantial danger. Thus, the tortfeasor must use only that degree of force required to avert the greater risk. Using the sinking ship example, suppose that the leak in the ship's hull occurred not because of Antonio's misbehavior but because of faulty sealing techniques. If Antonio could plug the leak rather than abandon ship, it would not be necessary for him to jettison the cargo to save the passengers.

Fires further illustrate this aspect of reasonably required action; many necessity cases involve burning buildings. Several nineteenth-century court opinions discussed "row" structures, which were many discrete buildings attached in long rows down a street. If one were to catch fire, it was likely that the entire block would burn to the ground. To avoid this calamity, the flaming building was often destroyed. There simply was no less damaging alternative when the building was fully ablaze. If the building owner sued for trespass to land, the courts routinely applied the necessity defense to protect the tortfeasor from liability to the building owner.

The Restatement (Second) Position

The *Restatement (Second)* addresses necessity as a defense in emergency situations in which the tortfeasor is compelled to immediate action by a crisis. In such cases, the defense operates to protect the defendant from liability. Note how the *Restatement*'s elements are distinguishable from those previously discussed in the text.

Restatement (Second) of Torts §§ 890, 892D & Comments
American Law Institute (1979)

[**§ 890, Comment a.**] [The emergency defense exists] when the protection of the public is of overriding importance, as when one is privileged to destroy buildings to avert a public disaster. [. . .]

§ 892D. Emergency Action Without Consent
Conduct that injures another does not make the actor liable to the other, even though the other has not consented to it if

(a) **an emergency makes it necessary or apparently necessary, in order to prevent harm to the other, to act before there is opportunity to obtain consent from the other or one empowered to consent for him, and**

(b) **the actor has no reason to believe that the other, if he had the opportunity to consent, would decline.**

Comment:

a. The rule stated in this Section covers a group of exceptional situations in which the actor is privileged to proceed without the consent of another and without any manifested or apparent consent, on the assumption that if the other had the opportunity to decide he would certainly consent. This privilege must necessarily be a limited one and can arise only in situations of emergency, when there is no time to consult the other or one empowered to consent for him, or for reasons such as the unconsciousness of the other his consent cannot be obtained. The mere possibility that the other might consent if he were able to do so is not enough; and the conduct must be so clearly and manifestly to the other's advantage that there is no reason to believe that the consent would not be given. If the actor knows or has reason to know, because of past refusals or other circumstances, that the consent would not be given, he is not privileged to act. [. . .]

Necessity can be a puzzling defense. Its elements compel courts to balance competing interests, employing somewhat more value judgment than usual. This hypothetical illustrates.

HYPOTHETICAL

Kenneth owns an exotic pet store, in which he sells, among other wild animals, several species of snake. One day a customer accidentally knocked a cage containing a python onto the floor, causing the door to spring open. The snake slithered out into the aisles searching for food. An infant was strapped in an automobile safety seat which her mother used as a carrier while shopping. The youngster's mother was several feet away looking at some unusual fish. The snake approached the infant and clearly intended to consume the child. Quickly, another patron, Jeffrey, impaled the python with a hunting knife (which was on display on a nearby shelf). Kenneth sued Jeffrey for trespass to chattel. Could necessity excuse Jeffrey's actions?

Reasonably necessary action is the critical element in this hypothetical. Did Jeffrey have to kill the snake to prevent it from attacking the baby? Could Jeffrey have taken other action to protect the child? Jeffrey could have grabbed the infant seat and carried the child to safety. Then Jeffrey could have summoned Kenneth or another store employee to capture the python. Accordingly, necessity would not be a successful defense, and Jeffrey would be liable to Kenneth for trespass to chattel.

A short review of the elements of necessity is provided in Figure 5-7.

5.8 PUBLIC OFFICER'S IMMUNITY FOR LEGAL PROCESS ENFORCEMENT

Public officials often engage in activity that normally would be considered intentionally tortious. However, because such persons are authorized by law to engage in such conduct, they are protected from liability. Several types of governmental action fall within this protected class. The most

Committing intentional tort
Purpose to avert more harmful injury
Harm threatened by force other than tortfeasor
Tortfeasor's actions were reasonably necessary to prevent danger of greater harm

FIGURE 5-7
Elements of Necessity

common include: (1) process serving; (2) execution sales; (3) attachment or replevin; and (4) arrest by warrant.

Service of Process

Process serving is the method by which a defendant in a lawsuit is notified that a plaintiff has filed suit against the defendant. Service of process is the means used to notify the defendant. Most commonly, the court clerk either mails a copy of the summons and the plaintiff's complaint to the defendant (usually by certified or registered mail), or the sheriff delivers the summons and complaint directly to the defendant. It is the latter case of actual physical delivery that gives rise to litigation. The defendant might sue the sheriff for trespass to land when the sheriff arrived on the defendant's real estate to deliver the summons. However, the sheriff has the power, either by statute or common law, to enter another person's land to serve process. The landowner's lawsuit against the sheriff would fail as a result of this defense.

Execution Sales

When a plaintiff wins judgment against the defendant in a civil action, the defendant usually has a certain period of time, often 30 days, within which to pay the judgment. If the defendant fails to pay, the plaintiff may return to court and file a *writ of execution* requesting the court to order the defendant's property sold to satisfy the judgment. These forced sales are often referred to as **execution sales** or **sheriff's sales**, because the sheriff is frequently the public official responsible for seizing and selling the defendant's property. The defendant might sue the sheriff for trespass to land, trespass to chattel, and conversion after the sheriff comes and gets the defendant's property. However, once again the sheriff is legally protected. Statutes and common law empower law enforcement officials to seize and sell property to satisfy judgments. Therefore, the sheriff would be immune from liability.

Attachment or Replevin

Attachment is a court-ordered remedy in a lawsuit. When a plaintiff is entitled to a remedy against the defendant in a lawsuit, and the defendant is likely to dispose of his or her property to avoid losing it in a subsequent execution action, the plaintiff may ask the court to attach the property on the plaintiff's behalf. The court then orders a law enforcement officer, such as the sheriff, to seize the defendant's property subject to attachment. The defendant might think to sue the sheriff for conversion or trespass to chattel, but the defendant should think again. The sheriff is authorized by statute or common law to take the defendant's property into custody under attachment, and the defendant's cause of action against the sheriff would fail.

LEGAL TERMS

process serving
The method by which a defendant in a lawsuit is notified that a plaintiff has filed suit against the defendant. Also called *service of process.* Governmental officials engaged in process serving are generally immune from intentional tort liability.

execution (sheriff's) sales
Governmental sales of a defendant's property to satisfy a plaintiff's judgment. Governmental officials engaged in execution sales are generally exempt from intentional tort liability.

attachment
Court-ordered remedy in a civil lawsuit, in which the court orders the sheriff to seize the defendant's property on the plaintiff's behalf to prevent the defendant from disposing of the property to avoid paying the plaintiff's judgment. Governmental officials engaged in attachment proceedings are generally immune from intentional tort liability.

Replevin is another court-ordered remedy. A plaintiff sues a defendant who wrongfully possesses the plaintiff's chattel and refuses to return it. The plaintiff asks the court for replevin, which means that the court would order the defendant to return the personal property to the plaintiff. If the defendant still refuses to comply, the court could instruct the sheriff to seize the chattel. The defendant's lawsuit for conversion or trespass to chattel against the sheriff would again be defeated by the law enforcer's defense of legal authority to act.

Arrest by Warrant

Police officers often arrest suspected criminals under the authority of a court-issued warrant for arrest. Suppose the suspect were innocent of any crimes. Could the suspect sue the police department for false imprisonment, assault, battery, and infliction of emotional distress, for having been arrested? If the law enforcement personnel were acting pursuant to an arrest warrant properly ordered by a judge, and if they acted in good faith to apprehend the suspect named in the warrant, then they would not be liable for any intentional torts as a consequence of taking the suspect into custody.

THE CASE OF THE DEFIANT TRUCKER (PART II)

In *Jurco v. State,* partially reprinted in § 5.2, the Alaska Court of Appeals addressed conflicting defenses: namely, defense of property versus law enforcement officers' immunity for legal process enforcement. Reread the case as it applies to this latter defense and as a refresher for the facts. The court also discussed warrantless arrests, which are discussed in a further analysis of this case in § 5.9.

Jurco v. State
825 P.2d 909 (Alaska Ct. App. 1992)
(Court of Appeals of Alaska)
February 14, 1992

MANNHEIMER, Judge.
[. . .]
At common law, a public officer was authorized to use reasonable force against other persons when executing a court order requiring or authorizing the officer to seize another person's property. [Citation omitted.] This common-law rule has been codified in Alaska; [Alaska Statutes §] 11.81.420 provides:

Justification: Performance of public duty.

(a) Unless inconsistent with AS 11.81.320—11.81-410, conduct which would otherwise constitute an offense is justified when it is required or authorized by law or by a judicial decree, judgment, or order.

(b) The justification afforded by this section also applies when . . . the person reasonably believes the conduct to be required or authorized by a decree, judgment, or order of a court of competent jurisdiction or in the lawful execution of legal process, notwithstanding lack of jurisdiction of the court or defect in the legal process[.]

Under this statute, law enforcement officers are empowered to use force to execute court decrees, even if it is later shown that the court had no authority to issue the decree. Thus, in Jurco's case, the State Troopers were authorized to use all reasonable force to execute the Alaska District Court's order to seize Jurco's vehicle, even if Jurco was correct in claiming that the pendency of his bankruptcy petition deprived the state district court of the judicial authority to issue orders affecting his property.

As a practical matter, the public officer immunity defense is not commonly litigated. The power of its protection precludes intentional tort recovery in most cases. The following hypothetical demonstrates why.

HYPOTHETICAL

Dawn sued Debra. The sheriff delivered a copy of the summons and Dawn's complaint to Debra's house. Debra did not appear at trial, and Dawn won a default judgment against Debra. After 30 days, Debra had failed to pay the judgment. Dawn filed a writ of execution with the court, which ordered the sheriff to seize Debra's property. The sheriff again returned to Debra's house to garner the chattels that could be sold at an execution sale. The proceeds from the sale went to satisfy Dawn's judgment. Debra sued the sheriff for trespass to land, trespass to chattel, and conversion. The sheriff applied the defense of legal process enforcement.

This hypothetical is probably the easiest to answer of any in the text. The sheriff was acting under court order to enforce legal processes, and so the defense would succeed. Debra's lawsuit would be promptly dismissed.

The elements of the legal process enforcement defense are listed in Figure 5-8.

5.9 WARRANTLESS ARREST BY LAW ENFORCEMENT OFFICIALS OR CITIZENS

Police officers, and sometimes even ordinary citizens, engage in *warrantless arrests.* Could they be liable for false imprisonment, battery, assault, trespass to land, and infliction of emotional distress?

Statutes and common law authorize law enforcement personnel to arrest criminal suspects even without court-issued warrants under certain

LEGAL TERMS

replevin
  Court-ordered remedy in which the court orders the sheriff to seize property that the defendant has wrongfully taken or withheld from the plaintiff. Governmental officials engaged in replevin proceedings are generally immune from intentional tort liability.

circumstances. For example, when a police officer witnesses a felony, he or she may arrest the suspect immediately. This proper enforcement of a legal process would be a defense against the suspect's intentional torts lawsuit.

Private citizens, too, may take suspected criminals into custody under the theory of *citizen's arrest*. Under the common law, a private citizen may take a suspect into custody if the citizen has witnessed the suspect commit a felony or breach of the peace. This would include situations in which the citizen reasonably thinks that the suspect has committed a felony. Historically, this defense was often used to protect store owners who detained suspected shoplifters from liability for false imprisonment actions.

THE CASE OF THE DEFIANT TRUCKER (PART III)

Jurco v. State, discussed earlier in §§ 5.2 and 5.8, also involved warrantless arrest. As it had done with Jurco's previous issues on appeal, the Alaska Court of Appeals, with "arresting" analysis, ruled against the appellant. Although the court's discussion did not involve tort liability as a result of a warrantless arrest, it is clear that there could be no such liability, because the arrest was lawful.

Jurco v. State
825 P.2d 909 (Alaska Ct. App. 1992)
(Court of Appeals of Alaska)
February 14, 1992

MANNHEIMER, Judge.
[. . .]
Jurco also argues that his arrest was illegal because the troopers did not have an arrest warrant. Jurco acknowledges that [Alaska Stat. §] 12.25.030 authorizes police officers to arrest without a warrant when a

misdemeanor is committed in their presence [. . .].

Finally, even if some additional justification were needed for the troopers' decision to make an arrest instead of issue a citation, that justification was present. It was clear that Jurco was intent on thwarting the troopers' performance of their duty under the court order directing seizure of Jurco's truck; the troopers could reasonably conclude that Jurco would continue to impede their efforts unless he were physically taken into custody.

Modern warrantless arrest normally does not involve private citizen participation to the extent the pre-twentieth-century cases did. However, private police, such as company security, are often involved in today's cases.

HYPOTHETICAL

Carter is a night watchman at a local factory. He noticed someone suspiciously lurking in the shadows near a restricted access building containing company records and other valuables. He turned his flashlight on the suspect, whom he did not recognize. He demanded identification and the reason the stranger was present on factory grounds. The stranger said nothing and attempted to flee. Carter tackled the individual, forcibly returned him to the security office, and telephoned the police. The stranger turned out to be an employee of a competitor to Carter's employer. The stranger sued Carter for battery, false imprisonment, and infliction of emotional distress. Would Carter be entitled to a defense under citizen's arrest theory?

Carter witnessed a simple trespass to land, which is not a felony under either statutory or common law. The stranger had merely trespassed onto the factory's property. Further, the stranger had not breached the peace. However, Carter reasonably believed that the suspect was about to engage in a felony (namely, burglary or theft). In his experience as a security guard, Carter had seen many felons behave just as the stranger had acted. Thus, Carter's reasonable belief that the suspect was about to commit a felony was sufficient to justify his behavior. Carter would not be liable to the stranger for any of the intentional torts.

The warrantless arrest defense, together with the defense of legal process enforcement, are both summarized in Figure 5-8.

5.10 REASONABLE DISCIPLINE

We are all familiar with the concept of discipline. Anyone who has either had or been a parent understands the exercise of authority to maintain order within the household. Students for centuries have exchanged horror stories about strict disciplinary teachers. Such authority figures have used

Legal Process Enforcement	Warrantless Arrest
Process serving	Law enforcement officers' power to arrest pursuant to court-ordered arrest warrant
Execution sales	Citizen's arrest (felonies or breaches of peace)
Attachment or replevin	
Arrest by warrant	

FIGURE 5-8

Types of Legal Process Enforcement Defenses and Elements of Warrantless Arrest Defenses

discipline in both the home and schools, which usually involves inflicting several intentional torts, including assault, battery, false imprisonment, and infliction of emotional distress. The defense of reasonable discipline, however, protects the disciplinarian from tort liability. There are three elements of **reasonable discipline**: (1) Use of reasonable force (2) by a parent, guardian, or authorized individual against a child (3) to maintain order or punish unacceptable misconduct.

Reasonable Force

The force a parent or guardian applies against a child must be reasonable under the circumstances. Naturally, reasonableness depends upon the exact facts of each case, but a general principle may be gleaned from the court decisions. For purposes of this defense, *reasonable force* may be defined as that degree of force required to restore decorum or punish deviant conduct. Force that goes beyond this is deemed excessive.

For example, suppose children are fighting in their home. Their mother or father would have the privilege of applying corporal punishment to stop the conflict, so long as the force was reasonable. The father might physically separate the combatants and spank them. However, if the father hit the children over their heads with a wooden board, this would be excessive force, because order could be restored without such extreme actions.

Parent, Guardian, or Authorized Individual

When a child attends school, the law implies that the teacher assumes the role of parent or guardian while the child is present at the institution. The teacher is referred to as ***in loco parentis***, which translates from Latin as "in place of the parent." This means that the teacher (or school principal) basically enjoys the same right to use reasonable force for discipline as do a child's parents. In recent times, however, courts have become antagonistic to this defense when applied to nonparents or guardians.

In the nineteenth and early twentieth centuries, severe corporal punishment was routine in both public and private schools. The old adage, "spare the rod and spoil the child," was taken rather literally by many firm disciplinarians. Many a student has cringed outside a principal's office awaiting the dreaded paddling or ruler across the knuckles.

In modern education, corporal punishment has been severely discouraged as a disciplinary technique. Teachers and principals today are commonly equipped with psychological and sociological training, and thus school discipline has taken a less physical approach. Occasionally, litigation arises after a child is struck by a teacher as punishment. Educators must be much more careful than in days past when inflicting corporal penalties, because courts are increasingly less tolerant of the discipline defense for nonparents or guardians.

LEGAL TERMS

reasonable discipline
An intentional tort defense. Its elements include the use of reasonable force by a parent, guardian, or authorized individual against a child to maintain order or punish unacceptable misconduct.

Maintaining Order or Punishing Misbehavior

The disciplinarian must be using reasonable force against a child to maintain decorum (such as in a school classroom) or penalize deviant conduct (such as punishing a child who has angrily and intentionally broken a window). However, these motives do not give the disciplinarian a free hand to inflict punishment beyond that which is reasonable. Courts and legislatures are becoming increasingly aware of the significant problem of child abuse, much of which involves parental misconduct that once was judicially protected under the reasonable discipline defense. As social problems become more public and prominent, courts and legislatures become more sensitive to these issues and the search for solutions. As a result, recent court decisions have upheld a child's right to sue parents in tort for using exorbitant force as punishment.

in loco parentis
Latin for "in place of the parent." It is used with the intentional tort defense of reasonable discipline. Parents may authorize other persons, such as teachers or day care personnel, to supervise their children; supervision includes reasonable disciplinary measures.

THE CASE OF THE BRUSH WITH AUTHORITY

In *Authority Song,* Hoosier rock musician John Cougar Mellencamp sang, "I fight authority, authority always wins." Perhaps he was recalling his days in the secondary schools near Seymour, Indiana. Many middle and high school students have felt the full force of the *in loco parentis* doctrine from a teacher or principal. Sometimes the discipline seemed arbitrary, capricious, and excessive. In the case excerpted here, the Michigan Court of Appeals sided with authority against the student.

Willoughby v. Lehrbass
150 Mich. App. 319,
388 N.W.2d 688 (1986)
(Court of Appeals of Michigan)
April 7, 1986

ALLEN, Judge.
[. . .]
On January 23, 1981, plaintiff Frank Dain Willoughby [. . .] was a student in defendant Roger Lehrbass's fifth hour advertising class at Freesoil Community School. On that date, before Lehrbass's class began, the principal asked plaintiff to assist in replacing some doors which had been removed from their hinges. After completing this task, Willoughby walked into the advertising class a few minutes late. According to Lehrbass, another student was

giving an oral presentation for the final examination. Willoughby, nevertheless, walked by Lehrbass's desk and with a sweeping motion of his hand started to brush into the wastebasket a number of folded-up pieces of paper sitting on Lehrbass's desk. Lehrbass was using the slips of paper to select the order in which the students would give their oral preparations.

As Willoughby swept his hand across the desk, Lehrbass grabbed his arm and instructed him not to touch the papers. Willoughby then intentionally or accidentally kicked the wastebasket over, and, according to Lehrbass, mumbled something which sounded disrespectful.

Willoughby then walked to a seat in the front row around where he usually sat.

Although the students did not have assigned seats, they normally sat in the same area each day. Willoughby testified that he tried one seat in the front row but found it broken or too low. He then headed for some empty seats in the back. When he was halfway there, Lehrbass came up from behind, grabbed his left arm and twisted it behind his back in a "half nelson." Lehrbass said, "Come on, Frank, let's go." Lehrbass began marching Willoughby to the principal's office.

Lehrbass pushed Willoughby out of the classroom and up the steps. Willoughby said, "Let go, you're hurting me." On the landing, Willoughby squirmed loose and said he could find the office himself. However, according to Lehrbass, Willoughby started toward the steps going down—away from the office. (Willoughby's version was that he turned around to go *up* the steps.) In any event, Lehrbass then grabbed Willoughby in a "full nelson," with his arms underneath Willoughby's armpits and his palms on the back of Willoughby's neck. Willoughby testified that he heard cracking up and down his back and felt pain and soreness as Lehrbass pushed against his neck and back.

[. . .]

Willoughby testified that he consulted a chiropractor that evening because of continuing soreness in his back, neck, and shoulders. He treated with the chiropractor for some time. Subsequently, he saw an orthopedic surgeon who diagnosed his condition as myofascitis, an inflammation of the back muscles or tissues.

Plaintiffs' complaint, filed July 23, 1981, charged defendants with false imprisonment [. . .] and gross abuse and use of unreasonable force on Willoughby. These latter allegations were apparently based on [Mich. Comp. Laws] § 380.1312, which provides in pertinent part:

"(2) A teacher or superintendent may use reasonable physical force on the person of a pupil necessary for the purpose of maintaining proper discipline over pupils in attendance at school.

"(3) A teacher or superintendent shall not be liable in a civil action for the use of physical force on the person of a pupil for the purposes prescribed in this section, except in case of gross abuse and disregard for the health and safety of the pupil."

[. . .] The case proceeded to trial on the intentional tort count, and the jury returned a verdict of no cause of action in favor of defendants.

[. . .]

On a special verdict form the jury specifically found that Lehrbass had not used anything other than reasonable force in disciplining plaintiff Willoughby. [. . .] [T]he common law rule allowing a teacher to use reasonable force against a student [was codified by Michigan statutes].[. . .]

Plaintiffs next claim error in the jury instructions on battery and the School Code provision concerning corporal punishment. [. . .]

Here, the trial court read the statute to the jury, clearly informing them that (1) a teacher could use reasonable physical force on a pupil *necessary for the purpose of maintaining proper discipline,* and (2) the teacher would not be liable for using physical force on a pupil *for the purpose prescribed in the statute, i.e.,* maintaining proper discipline. (Emphasis added.) The trial court could hardly define the law better than by reading the statute exactly as written. [. . .]

[. . .] The judge found that under [Mich. Comp. Laws] § 380.1312, a teacher has the right to willfully and intentionally touch a pupil under certain circumstances. [. . .]

We find no reversible error.

[. . .]

Although there are no published Michigan opinions dealing with corporal punishment of a student, decisions in other jurisdictions are legion. The general rule is that a teacher is immune from liability for reasonable physical force or punishment used on a pupil to maintain discipline. Factors to consider in assessing the reasonableness of the punishment are the nature of the punishment, the child's age and physical condition, and the teacher's motive in inflicting the punishment. [Citations omitted.]

Courts have held the above principles applicable in actions for assault and battery, where a state statute permits a teacher to use reasonable physical force to maintain order in the classroom. [Citations omitted.] Where punishment is excessive or improper, the teacher may be guilty of assault and battery. [Citations omitted.]

We think that in Michigan, as well, the Legislature intended that a teacher might be guilty of assault and battery when his or her conduct exceeds the parameters of the statute. [Citation omitted.] The statute was [. . .] intended to carve a limited exception into the common-law doctrine in order to provide educators with the necessary means of maintaining discipline in the classroom. Here the trial judge adequately instructed the jury on the tort of battery [. . .] and on the applicable statutory provisions.

[. . .] The testimony is clear and convincing that young Willoughby was creating a classroom disturbance and that defendant Lehrbass felt that it was necessary to take Willoughby to the school office to restore order. While there is conflicting testimony as to just how much force was necessary to apply to Willoughby on the stairway leading to the office, even Willoughby's own witness [. . .] testified that Willoughby was arguing with defendant Lehrbass and struggling to get away all the way up the stairs. Based on our review of the record, we find little evidence that defendant Lehrbass's use of force was unprovoked and unreasonable. Indeed, the weight of the evidence establishes the contrary.

[. . .]

Having found no error mandating reversal, the judgment of the trial court is affirmed. No costs.

CASE QUESTIONS

1. Do you agree with the court that the teacher's use of force was reasonable? Why or why not?
2. Would the outcome of the case have been any different if the plaintiff had suffered permanent physical impairment as a result of the defendant's actions? Explain.
3. When Lehrbass first grabbed Willoughby in the classroom and pushed him through the halls to the stairway, could Willoughby have justified his struggling as a legitimate exercise of self-defense? Would this have made Lehrbass's continued use of force unreasonable? Explain.

The reasonable discipline defense frequently appears in intentional tort cases involving schools or day care facilities. This is logical, as children spend a significant portion of their lives in educational environments.

HYPOTHETICAL

Carol is a 13-year-old student at the Peddleton Middle School. Her history teacher, Mr. Whitewaul, has a reputation as a strict disciplinarian. Eating or drinking anything during his class was absolutely forbidden. Carol suffered from a low-blood-sugar condition and needed to eat a series of special high-energy foods every two hours. One day, Whitewaul discovered Carol eating what looked like a candy bar. He grabbed the food violently out of Carol's hand and threw it in the general direction of the wastebasket. Then, screaming at the top of his voice about six inches from Carol's face, Whitewaul chastised Carol for eating in class. Carol felt humiliated in front of her fellow students and was considerably upset by Whitewaul's yelling. Whitewaul insisted that Carol stand in the corner at the back of the room for the remainder of the period, much to her chagrin. Because of the stress and embarrassment, Carol's blood sugar plummeted, causing her to pass out and fall to the floor. Carol's parents sued Whitewaul for intentional infliction of emotional distress, battery, assault, and false imprisonment. Whitewaul insisted that he was exercising reasonable discipline.

Does Carol, through her parents, have causes of action for each of the intentional torts mentioned? If so, then the discipline defense becomes relevant. As a teacher, Whitewaul stands *in loco parentis* with regard to Carol. Using the formula previously discussed, were Whitewaul's actions reasonably necessary to maintain order or punish misconduct? The force that Whitewaul exerted to wrench the food out of Carol's hand was excessive. He simply could have demanded that she hand him the food, which would have been more reasonable. Whitewaul's thunderous shouting directly into Carol's face was also excessive force. He could have chastised her in a normal tone of voice and accomplished the same objective—namely, alerting Carol and the class that his rule against eating would be strictly enforced. Compelling Carol to stand in the corner (a false imprisonment claim) is also extreme, since Whitewaul had already taken steps to assure that his rule against eating would be in the forefront of each student's mind. Whitewaul's defense of reasonable discipline would fail, and Carol's parents would recover for all of the intentional torts pleaded.

The defense of reasonable discipline is outlined in Figure 5-9.

5.11 STATUTES OF LIMITATIONS

Statutes of limitations are statutes restricting the time within which a plaintiff may file his or her lawsuit for particular causes of action against a defendant. All states have statutes of limitations for almost all tort actions, including intentional torts. The most common tort statutes of limitations are

Use of reasonable force
Force by parents, guardians, or authorized individuals (e.g., educators)
Force used to discipline children or maintain order in groups of children

FIGURE 5-9

Elements of Reasonable Discipline

two years. This means that the plaintiff has two years from the date that an intentional tort occurred to file his or her lawsuit against the defendant. If the plaintiff fails to file within this statutory time period, then his or her cause of action against the defendant is barred forever.

Although two years is a common statute of limitations period for many torts, the exact time period varies among states and between different types of torts. One should always research the specific statute of limitations for each cause of action, whether in tort or in other areas of law. This is a vital piece of information for both the plaintiff and the defendant. If the statute of limitations has expired, the defendant may respond with this defense and have the plaintiff's case dismissed or otherwise disposed of (usually by summary judgment). The plaintiff must be aware of the statute of limitations in order to file the lawsuit in a timely manner. Figure 5-10 shows two typical intentional tort statutes of limitations.

SUMMARY

5.1. Self-defense is the exercise of reasonable force to repel an attack upon one's person or to avoid confinement. Self-defense counters an offensive force that threatens bodily injury, repugnant contact, or sequestration. The amount of force a person may use in self-defense is limited to that amount necessary to repel the attacking force. Any greater resistance is excessive and the defense would be ineffective. The defense is used against allegations of assault, battery, or false imprisonment.

Two-Year Statute of Limitations (for most intentional torts)	Six-Year Statute of Limitations (for fraud)
Indiana Code § 34-1-2-2 (1992):	Indiana Code § 34-1-2-1 (1992):
The following actions shall be commenced within the periods herein prescribed after the cause of action has accrued, and not afterwards:	The following actions shall be commenced within six [6] years after the cause of action has accrued, and not afterwards:
(1) For injuries to person or character, for injuries to personal property, [. . .] within two [2] years.	[. . .] Fourth. For relief against frauds.

FIGURE 5-10

Examples of Intentional Tort Statutes of Limitations

5.2. Defense of persons or property is another legal justification for assault or battery. Defense of persons involves the use of reasonable force to defend or protect a third party from injury when the third person is threatened by an attacking force. Here, reasonable force is defined identically as for self-defense. Defense of property allows reasonable force to protect property from damage or dispossession when an invader attempts to injure or wrongfully take custody of the property. Reasonable force to protect property is usually defined as less force than would ordinarily be allowed to protect persons. Courts generally do not permit deadly force to be used to protect property, although one may apply deadly force in defense of one's home against intruders, under the castle rule.

5.3. Rightful repossession empowers a chattel owner to enter upon another's real estate to legally repossess personal property that has been wrongfully taken or withheld. The chattel owner would not be liable for trespass to land, trespass to chattel, or conversion, because he or she was justified in retaking control of the property. The defense also may protect against claims of assault or battery. Reasonable force may be used to repossess the chattel. Reasonable force is defined along the same lines as for defense of property. The efforts to regain possession must occur promptly after the property is first taken from the owner, or from the time the possessor wrongfully refuses to return the property to the owner. For the defense to succeed, the chattel owner must have been wrongfully dispossessed, or return of the property must have been improperly refused.

5.4. Consent may be a defense to all intentional torts. Consent occurs when a victim of an intentional tort voluntarily agrees to endure the tortious actions. Voluntary agreement involves the victim understanding the consequences of the tortfeasor's conduct. This is called informed consent. Consent may be expressed or implied based upon the behavior of the parties.

5.5. As a defense to intentional torts, mistake is a good faith belief, based upon incorrect information, that a person is justified in committing an intentional tort under the circumstances. This belief must be reasonable, and reasonableness is determined on a case-by-case basis. This belief must be based on erroneous details which, if they had been true, would have excused the intentional torts committed.

5.6. Privilege is sometimes considered a broad category embracing all the other defenses discussed in this chapter. To use the defense, one must ask if the actor's motives for engaging in the intentional tort outweigh the injury to the victim or property. Further, one must ask if the actor was justified in committing the intentional tort to achieve socially desirable goals (which outweigh the injury factor). Could these goals have been accomplished without inflicting the harm to the victim?

5.7. The necessity defense allows a tortfeasor to commit an intentional tort to prevent more serious injury from an external force. The tortfeasor's actions must be reasonably necessary to avert the more substantial danger. Necessity is basically a choice between the lesser of two evils. The tortfeasor cannot cause the greater threat of harm, if the necessity defense is to insulate him or her from liability.

5.8. Public officials are immune from intentional tort liability for the proper enforcement of legal processes, such as service of process, execution sales, attachment, replevin, or arrest by warrant. Both statutes and common law protect governmental employees involved in these activities, as legal process enforcement is necessary to implement the judicial system. Normally, law enforcement officers, such as sheriffs, participate in these processes.

5.9. Law enforcement officials are authorized by statutes and common law to make warrantless arrests, usually when a felony is committed or suspected in their presence. Under the defense of citizen's arrest, private persons may restrain suspected felons without liability for assault, battery, false imprisonment, infliction of emotional distress, trespass to land, or other intentional torts.

5.10. Parents are permitted to use reasonable force to punish or correct their children. Persons standing in place of parents, such as educators, are said to be *in loco parentis* and may also employ reasonable force to penalize students or maintain order. Modern cases and statutes have become more sensitive to child abuse problems, and so this defense has been substantially narrowed in recent years.

5.11. Most state statutes of limitations restrict the time period within which a plaintiff may file his or her intentional tort causes of action against a defendant. In most states, these are two-year statutes, meaning that a plaintiff has two years from the date that the intentional tort was committed within which to file his or her lawsuit against the tortfeasor. It is vital to research specific statutes of limitations for each particular tort.

REVIEW QUESTIONS

1. What are defenses? How are they applied against intentional torts? In what type of situation would a defense most likely be raised?
2. Explain self-defense. Against which intentional torts might this defense be used? What is reasonable force? How is it defined? How is it similar to necessary force?
3. Discuss defense of persons or property. How is it similar to self-defense? Different? How is defense of persons different from defense of property? Similar? How is reasonable force defined for this defense?
4. What is rightful repossession? What type of property is involved? Against which intentional torts might this defense be applied? How is

reasonable force defined? What is the role of wrongful dispossession or denial of possession? Must the property owner's efforts to repossess be taken within a certain time frame? What is this called?

5. Describe consent. Is the defense widely applicable to the intentional torts? What is informed consent? Implied consent?

6. Explain mistake. What is the role of the good faith conviction? Why must the information believed be inaccurate? How broad is the defense?

7. Does privilege include all defenses to intentional torts? Why? Against which intentional torts would the defense be utilized? What are its characteristics? What is the role of motive? Of socially acceptable goals? Of less injurious alternatives?

8. What are the elements of necessity? How is it used as an intentional tort defense? What is the significance of external forces? Why must the action be reasonably necessary?

9. Discuss the various types of public official immunity for legal process enforcement. What intentional torts might apply to these cases? How does the defense operate in each such instance?

10. What is warrantless arrest? Citizen's arrest? How are these protected from intentional tort liability?

11. Who may use reasonable discipline? Against whom may it be employed? What are the elements of the defense? What is the modern status of the defense in courts and legislatures?

12. What are statutes of limitations? What is the time period most commonly used for tort causes of action? How can statutes of limitations be used as a defense to intentional torts?

PROBLEMS

In the following hypotheticals, identify the intentional torts and available defenses involved, if any, and support your answers.

1. Kimberly Bach drives a delivery truck for The Dough Boy, a local bakery. One day, while making a delivery, Kimberly saw an automobile parked along the side of the street begin to move. There was no one inside the car, and it appeared to have slipped out of gear. The car rolled with increasing speed down a hill toward a crowded sidewalk along which several businesses were having outdoor sales. None of the shoppers saw the runaway vehicle approaching. Kimberly rammed her truck into the rear right side of the car, causing it to spin sideways. This stopped it from rolling into the pedestrians. The auto owner sued Kimberly for damaging the car, and the owner of The Dough Boy also sued Kimberly for injuring the delivery truck.

2. Memphis Safeway, a student at the city college, visited the school bookstore to purchase some notebooks. Outside the bookstore were a series of locking boxes within which students placed their backpacks, briefcases, or other belongings that the bookstore forbade customers to bring into the store. Memphis placed his backpack into one of the lockers and entered the bookstore. However, he forgot to take the key from the box. Harper Ridgewell, another student, opened the box and thought the backpack was his, as he owned a pack almost identical to Memphis's. Harper had placed his own pack in one of the boxes but had also forgotten to take the key. Later, Memphis discovered the pack missing, and a bookstore cashier described Harper as the culprit. Harper had not examined the pack closely but had thrown it into his car trunk and forgotten about it. Memphis sued Harper.

3. Leroy McPhillen frequented a pub called Bottom's Up!. Late one Saturday night, an intoxicated man began shouting obscenities at a woman sitting at the table next to Leroy's. The woman ignored the man and continued to drink her beer. The man approached the lady, looking ominous. Leroy stood and asked the fellow over to the bar for a drink. The man grumbled that Leroy should mind his own business. The man reached out and grabbed the woman's wrist, and Leroy neatly twisted the man's other arm behind his back while restraining him with a neck hold. The man protested vehemently, but Leroy did not let go. Leroy placed the man firmly into a chair and told him not to move or else Leroy would have to punch him. The woman told Leroy that the man was her husband and asked him to leave them both alone. Leroy left the bar. The man sued Leroy.

4. Peter Delaney works as an assistant manager at a local clothing store. One evening, while emptying trash outside the back of the store, Peter saw someone toying with a lock on the back door of another store. He could not see who the person was. Peter telephoned the police from inside his store and returned to the alley. He yelled out to the mysterious person not to move, because he was armed, and the police were coming. In fact, Peter did not possess any weapons, but bluffed to scare the culprit. The suspicious character turned out to be a new employee at the neighboring store who was trying to determine which key opened the rear door lock. Peter did not know this individual. The person sued Peter.

5. Maybelle Startler was purchasing some merchandise on layaway at a local department store. She had made her final payment and had requested that the items be delivered to her house. After a few days, she telephoned the store manager to complain that the goods had not been delivered. The manager explained that she would first have to pay the entire purchase price before delivery would be possible. She protested that she had, in fact, paid in full. She went to the store and showed the layaway clerk her payment receipts. The clerk refused to

produce the merchandise. Maybelle walked behind the counter, went up the stairs to the layaway storage area, and retrieved her items. The clerk notified store security, who took Maybelle into custody and locked her in an empty storeroom next to the rest rooms. The room was unlit and not heated. The police arrived after an hour to question Maybelle, and after a few minutes she was released. Maybelle sued the store and the store counterclaimed against Maybelle.

PROBLEM ANSWERS

1. Kimberly Bach would have a successful necessity defense against both the automobile owner and her boss, the truck owner, for damaging the vehicles. Kimberly committed trespass to chattel by damaging the vehicles. However, she was legally justified, because her actions were reasonably necessary to avert the more serious harm of having the runaway car crash into the pedestrian crowd at the bottom of the hill. The car became runaway by external forces (slipping out of gear, with no parking brake on), through no fault of Kimberly's. The threat to lives posed by the runaway car far exceeded the value of the damaged chattels, so Kimberly's actions were reasonable.

   You could also apply the privilege defense to these facts. Kimberly was justified in damaging the runaway vehicle to achieve the socially desirable goal of saving lives. Kimberly could not have taken any less damaging action to stop the runaway car, since she had little time to act before the car crashed into the crowd.

2. Memphis Safeway sued Harper Ridgewell for trespass to chattel and conversion, but Harper could use the mistake defense. Harper had a good faith belief that his taking Memphis's backpack was justified, because Harper reasonably thought that the backpack belonged to him (incorrect information upon which belief was based).

   Did Harper act reasonably by not carefully examining the backpack's contents to determine his error? One might ask whether, under similar circumstances, the average person would check the contents of a backpack which he or she presumes to be his or hers. How easy it would be for someone to grab what appears to be the right backpack and, without another thought, toss it into the back seat of his or her car.

3. The man sued Leroy McPhillen for battery and probably assault and, perhaps, even false imprisonment (because of the "don't get out of that chair, or else" threat). Leroy would apply the defenses of defense of persons and mistake.

   For defense of persons, Leroy used reasonable force to defend and protect the woman from injury when the man threatened her with physical injury by grabbing her wrist. Leroy reasonably believed that his actions (grabbing the man's arm, twisting it behind his back, using the neck hold, and forcing him to sit in a chair) were necessary to prevent the man from injuring the woman. A reasonable person would have acted similarly under these circumstances. Thus, Leroy used necessary force to counter the attacking force.

For mistake, Leroy had a good faith belief that his actions were justified to prevent the man from injuring the woman. This belief turned out to be mistaken, since the man and woman were spouses and, apparently, the husband did not intend to hurt his wife. Still, Leroy could not have known this, especially since husbands have been known to strike wives (and vice versa) in bars. Thus, Leroy's belief was reasonable and his actions were legally justified.

Accordingly, Leroy would not be liable to the man for any of the intentional torts mentioned, because of these two defenses.

4. The person sued Peter Delaney for false imprisonment and probably, if she had good counsel, intentional infliction of emotional distress. Both torts would be based upon Peter's bluff with the nonexistent weapon to intimidate the captive.

   Peter would attempt to use the defense of citizen's arrest. Peter reasonably believed that an unknown person, seen late at night toying with a store lock in an alley, might be a burglar. He could not see clearly what the person was doing with the lock, because it was dark. He could not have identified the person as a store employee, because he did not know the individual. Peter's actions were reasonably necessary to detain the suspected felon. The defense should protect Peter from liability.

   There is some question as to whether Peter's weapon threat was excessive and unreasonable. However, if Peter reasonably believed (as he did) that he was dealing with a felon, it seems reasonable for him to have used the weapon ruse to protect himself and immobilize the culprit. A reasonable person would have acted similarly. (Actually, a reasonable person probably would have watched the suspect until police arrived, rather than endangering himself or herself as Peter did.)

5. Maybelle Startler sued the store for false imprisonment, assault, battery, infliction of emotional distress, and trespass to chattel (this last because the store wrongfully denied her possession of her chattels). The store counterclaimed against Maybelle for trespass to land, trespass to chattel, and conversion, the latter two because she took what the store perceived to be its personal property.

PROJECTS

1. Does the common law of your state recognize all the defenses discussed in this chapter? Is any of the terminology different? Are any defenses defined under statutes?

2. Brief *Ashcraft v. King,* 228 Cal. App. 3d 604, 278 Cal. Rptr. 900 (1991). Which intentional tort(s) did the California Court of Appeal find in this case? How did the court rule on the defense(s)? What was the significance of the conditional aspect of one defense?

3. Brief *Hogenson v. Williams,* 542 S.W.2d 456 (Tex. Civ. App. 1976). Analyze the defense(s) and intentional tort(s) discussed in the court's opinion. What precedents did the court use to define each defense? What elements were included in each defense? How are these different from the definitions provided in this textbook? How are they similar?

4. Brief *Fridovich v. Fridovich,* 598 So. 2d 65 (Fla. 1992). Did the court consider the defendants' communications with the police or prosecutor to be absolutely privileged? What is the effect of a qualified privilege? Why did the dissent cringe from the majority's ruling?

CHAPTER 6
Negligence

OUTLINE

DATA-GRAPHIC TORTS

Victoria v. Guest

Deborah Guest was driving her compact sports car along Riverview Drive downtown. She came upon a gently curving part of the road, which sloped slowly along the perimeter of a city park. She was driving at 45 m.p.h., which was the posted speed limit. Behind her approached Dale Sanders, a teenager who was driving a large pickup truck. Dale was driving at approximately 75 m.p.h. As Sanders roared past Guest, the truck sideswiped Guest's car, sending it careening from the right side of the road and tumbling into the park. The car rolled over and seriously injured several people (Victoria and others) who were walking in the park at the time. These people sued Guest and Sanders.

Both Guest and Sanders owed duties of care to adjacent pedestrians. Arguably, both breached these duties, because Sanders was driving at excessive speed and Guest's vehicle hit the pedestrians. But what was the cause-in-fact of the pedestrians' injuries? But for Sanders's high-speed sideswiping of Guest's car, Guest would not have caromed off the road into the pedestrians nearby. Sanders is plainly the cause of the harm. Therefore, Sanders, not Guest, caused the bystanders' injuries.

On the issue of proximate cause, was it reasonably foreseeable that Guest's car would have rolled upon the injured persons in the park? Vehicles sideswiped at high speeds often will roll off roads, as did Guest's automobile. Further, it was reasonably foreseeable that people would be walking in the adjacent park and would be harmed by a tumbling vehicle. Thus, it can also be said that Sanders proximately caused the pedestrians' injuries.

INTRODUCTION

The field of negligence comprises the most complex pieces of the torts puzzle. What makes negligence enigmatic is its conceptual ambiguity. The elements of negligence appear to be so broadly defined that it is difficult to discern clear lines for negligent behavior. But negligence is not a mathematical equation. Instead, negligence resembles probability theory, in which specific conduct is more likely than not to be considered negligent under a particular set of circumstances. In this chapter, the following negligence puzzle pieces are sorted and assembled:

- The elements of negligence.
- The tortfeasor's duty of reasonable care.
- The scope of duty, reasonable care, and the reasonable person standard.
- Cause-in-fact, but-for causation, substantial factor analysis, and joint and several liability.
- Proximate cause and reasonable foreseeability.
- Damages available in negligence actions.
- Burdens of proof and rejoinder in negligence cases.
- Res ipsa loquitur.

6.1 NEGLIGENCE

Most people equate negligence with carelessness. The phrase conjures up images of actions that are slovenly, haphazard, heedless, or foolhardy. As a legal concept, negligence is much more precise, but it embodies all of these characteristics.

Negligence Defined: Reasonable Care

Negligence may be broadly defined as the failure to exercise reasonable care to avoid injuring others or their property. Reasonable care depends upon the exact circumstances of each case. This is the "shifting sands" aspect of negligence with which legal students—and the legal system—struggle. The key term is *reasonableness*. In any tort case in

LEGAL TERMS

negligence
Broadly defined, the failure to exercise reasonable care to avoid injuring others or their property. This includes both actions and failures to act (omissions). Its elements include a duty of reasonable care and scope of duty, breach of duty by the tortfeasor, causation of injury, proximate cause, and damages.

which negligence might exist, ask the threshold question: Did the tortfeasor act unreasonably under the circumstances? This is essentially all that negligence entails.

Acts or Omissions

The tortfeasor can be negligent either by doing or not doing something. When courts speak of **negligent acts or omissions** by the tortfeasor, they mean that the tortfeasor behaved unreasonably either by doing a specific careless activity or by failing to do something that the tortfeasor should have done.

Negligent actions are positive events; something is done. For instance, if Roger lit a fire in high winds that carried sparks onto a neighbor's roof and set the house ablaze, Roger's action (heedless burning) would be deemed unreasonable. Negligent omissions are usually phrased negatively; the tortfeasor failed to do a reasonable act. For example, suppose Marie's front porch had a rotten step that she failed to repair. A salesperson visiting her home falls through the step and breaks a leg. Marie's omission (failure to repair the step) would be considered unreasonable.

Like all areas of law, negligence has developed discernible elements that may be enumerated and outlined more clearly. Section 6.2 outlines the elements of negligence.

6.2 ELEMENTS OF NEGLIGENCE

Negligence may be specifically defined as the tortfeasor's failure to exercise reasonable care which causes a foreseeable injury to another person or that person's property. Negligence includes the following elements:

1. Duty of reasonable care and scope of duty (foreseeability of victim)
2. Breach of the duty by the tortfeasor
3. Causation of injury to the victim (cause-in-fact or substantial factor)
4. Proximate cause (foreseeability of injury)
5. Damages to the victim (recovery).

Each of these elements is required for negligence to exist, so each element is a threshold question. These questions resemble the nested analytical boxes analogy discussed in chapter 2. If "no" answers any single element, negligence does not exist. For example, the first question (largest box) is: Did the tortfeasor owe a duty of reasonable care to the injured party? If not, then the analysis stops, with the conclusion that no negligence has occurred. If yes, then the next box is opened: Did the tortfeasor breach the duty of reasonable care? If not, the inquiry is finished, and once again the analyst surmises that there was no negligence. If yes, then one continues opening nested boxes through causation, proximate cause, and injury. Each element must be satisfied for negligence to arise.

Each of the elements of negligence receives detailed treatment in the following sections.

6.3 SCOPE OF DUTY AND STANDARDS OF REASONABLE CARE

Negligence analysis begins with the duty of reasonable care. First, the scope of the duty must be determined. This focuses on the foreseeability of the victim.

Duty Defined

Duty in tort law is the obligation either to do or not to do something. In negligence, the duty of **reasonable care** is the responsibility to act reasonably so as to avoid injuring others. This may also be stated negatively: the duty of reasonable care is the obligation *not* to behave *un*reasonably so as to avoid injuring others.

For example, motor vehicle operators owe a duty of reasonable care to drive carefully and avoid injuring other drivers, their vehicles, or pedestrians. Suppose Parker is driving on a four-lane highway and chooses to pass the truck in front of him. He fails to look in the rear-view mirror before pulling into the left lane. Unbeknownst to Parker, another vehicle was attempting to pass him, and he pulled directly in front of that driver. This action forced that driver to swerve and collide with a telephone pole. Did Parker violate any duty of reasonable care?

In analyzing this duty hypothetical, the first question is: Did Parker owe the other driver a duty of reasonable care? Parker owed anyone driving or walking upon the street a duty to drive safely. By failing to check his rear-view mirror to see if any traffic was approaching from behind in the left lane, Parker breached his duty to the other driver. He acted imprudently by not looking for other traffic before he switched lanes.

Scope of Duty

Clearly, one does not owe a duty of reasonable care to everyone else in the universe. **Scope of duty** is a limitation on the persons to whom one owes the duty.

For example, while driving on the four-lane highway in her city, Janet owes no duty of reasonable care to someone driving in another city hundreds of miles away. Janet's actions (i.e., driving her car) could not possibly have any effect on such a person. Janet's scope of duty does not extend to individuals who cannot be affected by her carelessness. Scope of duty is often described in terms of reasonable foreseeability.

LEGAL TERMS

negligent acts or omissions
    When a tortfeasor behaves unreasonably either by doing specific careless actions or failing to do what should have been done to safeguard the victim.

duty
    In negligence law, the obligation to use reasonable care to avoid injuring others or their property. In tort law, duty is the obligation either to do or not to do something.

reasonable care
    The standard of care in negligence cases; the duty to act reasonably so as to avoid harming others. Defined in terms of the reasonable person standard. Sometimes called *ordinary care.*

scope of duty
    In negligence law, defined in terms of those individuals who might foreseeably be injured as a result of the tortfeasor's actions. This is called *reasonable foreseeability.* The scope of duty includes all those foreseeable plaintiffs who could have been hurt because of the tortfeasor's conduct. This is called *foreseeability of the victim.*

Foreseeability

Foreseeability in tort law is the notion that a specific action, under particular circumstances, would produce an anticipated result. If an injury were foreseeable, then one could take precautions to avoid the behavior that might be expected to cause harm. If a tortfeasor failed to take such precautions, he or she breached the duty of reasonable care.

For instance, in our preceding driving example, Parker did not check his rear-view mirror before attempting to pass on a four-lane highway. Is it foreseeable that another vehicle might be passing Parker in the lane he was trying to enter, and that the failure to look behind him could result in a collision? This consequence is clearly foreseeable. Suppose, however, that it is late at night, and that the other driver trying to pass Parker did not have headlights on. Thus, Parker could not see the car approaching as he moved into the left lane to pass the truck. Was it reasonably foreseeable that another driver would come up from behind without headlights? No. So the result (the other driver swerving to avoid hitting Parker's car) was not foreseeable under these facts. A slight difference in the circumstances changes the answer.

Foreseeable Plaintiffs Theory

Foreseeability limits the scope, or extent, of the duty owed to others. One asks the threshold question: Was it reasonably foreseeable that the person injured would be harmed as a consequence of the tortfeasor's actions? If so, the scope of the duty of reasonable care includes the individual hurt. This is sometimes called the **foreseeable plaintiffs theory**, because it was reasonably foreseeable that the plaintiff (who is suing the tortfeasor for negligence) would be damaged because of the tortious conduct.

Persons outside this range of duty are considered **unforeseeable plaintiffs**, because the tortfeasor could not reasonably have anticipated that they would be harmed by the tortfeasor's actions. People driving several hundred feet in front of Parker would not likely be influenced by either Parker or the swerving other driver. They would be beyond Parker's scope of duty, and so his would not be required to exercise reasonable care toward them. However, persons driving close behind Parker and the swerving driver could reasonably be expected to become involved in the accident. These individuals would be within Parker's scope of duty. His failure to use reasonable care (by not looking in the rear-view mirror, which caused him to cut off the swerving driver) violated his duty to them as well as to the swerving driver.

Figure 6-1 outlines scope of duty and the foreseeable plaintiffs theory.

Scope of Duty	Foreseeable Plaintiffs Theory
The tortfeasor owes a duty of reasonable care to avoid injuring others or their property.	The plaintiff may recover from the defendant only if it were reasonably foreseeable that the defendant's actions would injure the plaintiff.
Duty includes persons for whom it is reasonably foreseeable that injury will occur as a result of the tortfeasor's actions.	Persons outside the defendant's scope of duty are considered unforeseeable plaintiffs.

FIGURE 6-1
Scope of Duty of Reasonable Care and Foreseeable Plaintiffs Theory

THE CASE OF DRUNKEN DUTY

In negligence litigation, an injured plaintiff always argues that the defendant's scope of duty extends to the injured party. The contention sometimes reaches absurdity. Plaintiffs may attempt to avoid personal responsibility for their own injuries by claiming that a defendant breached some supposed duty of care. In the following case, an intoxicated driver injured himself and then sought damages against the tavern owner for having served alcohol to the plaintiff when he was already visibly drunk. As the Oklahoma Supreme Court observed, negligence law will not assist careless persons in avoiding personal responsibility for their apparent stupidity.

Ohio Casualty Insurance Co.
v. Todd
813 P.2d 508 (Okla. 1991)
(Supreme Court of Oklahoma)
June 11, 1991

SUMMERS, Justice.
The question certified for our resolution calls upon us to decide whether *Brigance v. Velvet Dove Restaurant, Inc.* [citation omitted], should be extended to create a common law cause of action against a tavern owner for an adult who voluntarily becomes intoxicated and is injured as a result of his own inability to drive a vehicle properly. We decline to extend *Brigance* to this situation, following the reasoning used by a majority of jurisdictions.
[. . .]

On November 6, 1986, Rick Robertson was injured in a one-car accident after having been served alcohol in Todd's Tavern. [. . .]
Robertson [. . .] [alleged] that the employees of Todd's Tavern served him alcoholic beverages when he was noticeably intoxicated in violation of [Okla. Stat. tit. 37,] § 537 [1981], and that for this reason Todd is liable for [Robertson's] injuries. Todd moved to dismiss [. . .].
All agree that the pertinent case is *Brigance* [. . .]. Robertson urges that *Brigance* should be extended to cover the situation at bar. Todd, however, asserts that *Brigance* creates a cause of action for innocent third parties, and should not be stretched to include a situation wherein the inebriate sues for his own injuries.

In *Brigance* we recognized for the first time a common law "dram shop" action; a third party who was injured in an intoxicated driver's auto accident may now state a cause of action against the restaurant that served liquor to the driver. At common law, such an action was not possible. [. . .]

In changing the common law rule and creating this cause of action, we acknowledged that legal duty and liability are matters of public policy and are therefore subject to the changing attitudes and needs of society. [Citation omitted.] We pointed out that protection must be afforded to the innocent bystander [. . .].

The creation of this cause of action, therein limited to third parties, served to protect the innocent by allowing liability to be placed not only on the intoxicate drivers but concurrently on those parties who continued to serve alcohol to their customers already noticeably intoxicated. [Citation omitted.]

Left open by *Brigance* was the question of whether the consumer-inebriate would have a cause of action against the vendor for on-premises consumption. [. . .]

The elements of negligence are "(1) the existence of a duty on [the] part of defendant to protect plaintiff from injury; (2) a violation of that duty; and (3) injury proximately resulting therefrom." [Citations omitted.] All three of these elements must exist before the plaintiff has a valid cause of action. Robertson, relying on [Okla. Stat. tit. 37,] § 537(A)(2) [Supp. 1985], urges that a duty exists on the part of a tavern keeper to refrain from serving alcoholic beverages to an adult customer who is noticeably intoxicated. Section 537(A)(2) states in relevant part that no person shall "[s]ell, deliver or knowingly furnish alcoholic beverages to an intoxicated person."

[. . .] Because we find that the duty of the tavern owner does not extend to an adult customer who voluntarily consumes intoxicants and is injured, we need not address the question of proximate cause.

[. . .]

Several states have considered the question. See Annot., 98 A.L.R.3d 1230 (1980). A majority of them have refused to create a cause of action for an adult who voluntarily drinks to the point of intoxication and is thereby injured. These jurisdictions have generally concluded that as a matter of public policy drunken persons who harm themselves are responsible for their condition, and should not prevail either under a common law or statutory basis. [Citations omitted.] Focusing on the "duty" concept, these courts hold the view that no duty should be imposed "upon the tavernkeeper, and protection should not be extended, because the adult voluntarily created the vulnerability that is the problem." [Citation omitted.]

[. . .]

If this Court were to create a cause of action against the tavern owner, the inebriate could be rewarded for his own immoderation. Such was not the intent of *Brigance,* nor will we allow such a reward. [. . .]

Then there are the practical consequences of recognizing such suits. "Pause, if you will and contemplate the vast number of claims that may be urged by drunks, if they were entitled to every expense and injury that are natural concomitants of their intoxication." [Citation omitted.] In a world where alcohol is readily available for consumption by adults the ultimate accountability should rest on the adult consumer, absent unusual circumstances or injury to an innocent third party. [. . .]

Here, the question is simply whether the intoxicated adult must bear the responsibility for his own injury which occurred due to his voluntary consumption of an excessive amount of alcohol. [. . .]

Accordingly, under the facts as presented to us we find that the tavern owner has no liability to the intoxicated adult who voluntarily consumes alcoholic beverages to excess and sustains injuries as a result of his intoxication.

CASE QUESTIONS

1. What was the court's public policy justification for its decision? Do you agree or disagree? Explain.
2. Suppose a passenger in Robertson's vehicle had been injured. Would the passenger have a cause of action against the tavern owner under the common law and statute? Explain.

Standards of Reasonable Care

Reasonable care is a most elusive concept in negligence law. It depends upon the particular facts of each problem. Still, tort law has developed an abstract measure of reasonable care, called the **reasonable person standard**.

The Reasonable Person Standard

The *reasonable person* is an imaginary individual who is expected to behave reasonably under a given set of circumstances to avoid harming others. The tortfeasor is alleged to have done something, or have failed to do something, that was unreasonable and that caused the victim's injuries. The tortfeasor's conduct is measured under the reasonable person standard in this fashion: In the same or similar circumstances, would the reasonable person have acted as the tortfeasor behaved? If so, then the tortfeasor did not violate his or her duty of reasonable care. If not, then the tortfeasor breached the duty.

In our previous driving hypothetical, would the reasonable person have looked in his or her rear-view mirror before entering the left lane to pass a truck on a four-lane highway, when it was reasonably foreseeable that another vehicle might already be occupying that lane while attempting to pass the reasonable person's car? Checking the rear-view mirror when changing lanes seems reasonable, and so the reasonable person could be expected to do so under these conditions. Parker did not, however. Therefore, Parker acted unreasonably in this case. He violated his duty of care to the swerving driver because he did not act as the reasonable person would have behaved in the same situation.

The mythical reasonable person may seem too intangible to compare to real-life persons. Nevertheless, American and English courts have relied on the concept in over 200 years of court decisions (though older opinions refer to the *reasonable man*).

LEGAL TERMS

reasonable person standard
Measurement by an imaginary individual, used to define reasonable care in negligence cases. The reasonable person is expected to behave reasonably under a given set of circumstances to avoid harming others. The tortfeasor's conduct is compared to the reasonable person's to determine if the tortfeasor violated the duty of reasonable care. The trier-of-fact decides the reasonable person standard in a particular case.

Who Decides How the Reasonable Person Would Have Acted

The trier-of-fact in a negligence lawsuit determines whether the defendant did not act as the reasonable person would have behaved in a specific case. This is usually a jury, but it could be the judge in a bench trial. In effect, the jurors decide what was reasonable by investigating how they, and others they know, would have behaved. Suddenly, the reasonable person standard becomes clear: it is what the jurors conclude was reasonable under the circumstances. This settles the question of whether the defendant breached the duty of reasonable care to the plaintiff.

At first glance, the reasonable person standard seems arbitrary, since each juror determines the defendant's negligence based upon his or her own personal, gut-level response. However, sociologists would remind us that this is precisely how each individual views the world—through the eyes of his or her own experience. The judicial system safeguards against one capricious definition of reasonableness by offering the option of a jury trial, which forces several persons to agree upon an appropriate measure of due care. Although a judge in a bench trial is the sole trier-of-fact, the judge's legal training is presumed to compensate for any bias in defining reasonableness.

Matching Skills and Handicaps

The reasonable person is supposed to resemble the defendant as closely as possible in terms of special abilities. This enables the trier-of-fact to assess reasonableness more precisely in a specific case. For example, if the defendant were a plumber and was alleged to have negligently installed a leaking water line, the reasonable person would also possess the same training and knowledge as plumbers employed in the defendant's geographical area. This is sometimes called the **professional community standard of care**, which is based on the custom and practice among professionals working in the defendant's community. This measure is determined through expert testimony from members of the defendant's profession. Physicians, attorneys, accountants, veterinarians, electricians, beauticians—those in virtually every professional activity—are evaluated in negligence lawsuits by this standard of care.

The defendant's limitations also are important in shaping the reasonable person standard. For instance, if the defendant were physically handicapped, then the reasonable person would likewise share identical handicaps. One could hardly decide how a blind defendant should have behaved by comparison with a reasonable person who has normal vision. This forces the trier-of-fact to empathize with the defendant's situation to understand more clearly how the defendant acted. The jury, in effect, must conceptualize how the reasonable person would have behaved in a wheelchair, with impaired hearing, or without certain limbs. The outcome of this

LEGAL TERMS

professional community standard of care
　The standard of reasonable care used in negligence cases involving defendants with special skills and knowledge.

empathy should be a more accurate reasonableness definition that best fits the defendant and the circumstances of the case. The result, ideally, is a just and equitable outcome in the litigation.

Figure 6-2 summarizes the reasonable person standard.

1.	Ask: Would the reasonable person have acted as the defendant did, under the same or similar circumstances?
2.	Match the skills or abilities of the reasonable person to those of the defendant (e.g., physician, attorney, plumber, rodeo rider) if these abilities were involved in the alleged negligent actions (professional community standard).
3.	Trier-of-fact decides how the reasonable person would have acted in a particular situation.

FIGURE 6-2
Reasonable Person
Standard

THE CASE OF THE MISDIAGNOSED DOG

In medical malpractice actions, the reasonable person assumes the professional qualifications of physicians in the defendant's field. The professional community standard of care defines whether the defendant's conduct was negligent. Veterinarians, like most professionals, are subject to malpractice actions. In the following case, the Ohio Court of Appeals was satisfied that the defendant veterinarian had violated the professional standard of care.

Turner v. Sinha
65 Ohio App. 3d 30,
582 N.E.2d 1018 (1989)
(Court of Appeal of Ohio)
October 10, 1989

PER CURIAM.

This is an appeal by defendant-appellant, Kapildeo N. Sinha, D.V.M., from a judgment rendered in favor of plaintiff-appellee, Terri Turner, by the Small Claims Division of the Hamilton Municipal Court.

On August 11, 1988, Turner filed a complaint against Sinha alleging malpractice and requesting judgment in the amount of $500 plus interest. A hearing was held on September 16, 1988. Turner testified that on March 28, 1988, between 8:30 and 9:00 p.m., her pedigreed Old English Sheepdog, Cadbury, was hit by a car. She was not able to contact her family veterinarian so she took Cadbury to the Hamilton Avenue Animal Hospital where Sinha was on duty. Sinha indicated that X-rays could not be taken of the dog immediately and that until the X-rays were taken, he could not give a diagnosis of the dog's condition. Sinha produced a statement showing a price list for services of $258 and insisted that Turner and her husband sign the paper and pay a deposit before treatment could continue.

Sinha took two sets of X-rays but stated he could not tell if the dog's back was broken and that he needed more X-rays which would cost an additional $15. Later, Sinha stated that the third set of X-rays were inconclusive and the dog would have to be left there overnight.

The next morning, Turner called the animal hospital and received a report that her dog was in a lot of pain. However, Sinha was not yet in the office. She called her family veterinarian, who was also not in the office. After a recommendation from a friend, she called another veterinarian, one Dr. Tscheiller, who asked her if the dog could get up and if its paws were stiff. When Turner replied that it could not sit up and that its paws were stiff, Tscheiller told her that the dog's back was broken. He also told her to get Cadbury out of the Hamilton Avenue Animal Hospital and to take it to her regular veterinarian.

Sinha called shortly afterwards and told her that Cadbury's back was not broken. Turner informed him that she would be coming to get her dog and take it to her veterinarian. She then called her regular veterinarian who told her to bring the dog and the X-rays with her. She called the animal hospital and was told she would have to put down a $20 deposit on the X-rays before they could be taken out of the office.

When she arrived at the animal hospital, she was told that since there was some dispute about the bill she could not take the dog until she paid $258 in cash. She talked with Sinha and his associate, one Dr. Cable, who stated that the dog's back was not broken. They insisted on payment before she could take it home.

Turner went home to collect the cash and waited approximately one and one-half hours to get the X-rays. By the time she got to her veterinarian's office, he had left for the day. She called Tscheiller who told her to bring Cadbury in the next morning.

Tscheiller and his associate, one Dr. Rothenbush, examined Cadbury and studied the X-rays taken by Sinha. They found that the dog's entire pelvis had been crushed and that there was a fracture further up in the spine. They charged $40 to put the dog to sleep and dispose of the body.

Turner claimed at the hearing that the dog should have been put to sleep immediately and that the charges by Sinha were needless and excessive.

[. . .]

The trial court [. . .] found in favor of Turner, awarding her $400 plus court costs. This appeal followed.

[. . .]

In his first assignment of error, Sinha states that the judgment in favor of Turner was against the manifest weight of the evidence. He argues that the dispute between the parties is about the correct reading of the X-rays. He claims that there was no evidence before the court that he could determine without X-rays that the injuries to the dog's spine were so extensive as to make it necessary to put the dog to sleep immediately. [. . .] We find this assignment of error is not well taken.

[. . .]

"Liability for negligence is predicated upon injury caused by the failure to discharge a duty owed to the injured party." [Citation omitted.] The amount of care required of a person to establish whether he or she has discharged a duty to another is the degree of care which an ordinarily careful and prudent person would exercise under the same or similar circumstances. [Citation omitted.]

As applied to professionals, the standard of care has been stated:

"'Unless he represents that he has greater or less skill or knowledge, one who undertakes to render services in the practice of a profession or trade is required to exercise the skill and knowledge normally possessed by members of that profession or trade in good standing in similar communities.'" [Citations omitted.]

Thus, in order to establish negligence by a veterinarian, it must be shown that the injury complained of was caused by the doing of a particular thing that a veterinarian of ordinary skill, care and diligence would not have done under like or similar circumstances, or by the failure or omission to do some particular thing that such a veterinarian would have done under like or similar circumstances. [Citations omitted.]

[. . .] Turner presented evidence that Tscheiller had told her that if a dog cannot get up on its hips or if its paws are stiff, then its back is broken, implying that X-rays are unnecessary. When she told him about the treatment given her dog at the animal hospital, he said that "he had never heard such a story and to get [the dog] out of there * * *."
[. . .] Tscheiller and Rothenbush examined the X-rays taken by Sinha and discovered that the dog had a crushed pelvis and a spinal fracture, yet Sinha had told her that the dog's back was not broken. Tscheiller and Rothenbush also told her that they could not believe that Sinha had not seen the fractures, which were very clear.

Thus, there was sufficient evidence from which the trier of fact could determine that Sinha had incorrectly interpreted the X-rays and had failed to diagnose the dog's injuries. These were things which a veterinarian of ordinary skill and diligence would not have done under similar circumstances. [. . .]

Judgment affirmed.

CASE QUESTIONS

1. To counter the plaintiff's evidence, could the defendant have offered testimony from other veterinarians to establish that he had not violated the professional standard of care? Explain.
2. What is your emotional reaction to the parties in this case? Do you detect a similar response from the Ohio Court of Appeals? Explain.

The next hypothetical examines another situation in which the standard of care is at issue. Note how scope of duty, foreseeability and the reasonable person standard are established.

HYPOTHETICAL

Edward crafts jewelry that he sells in his novelty shop. He uses adhesive to hold stones in settings. This glue melts when exposed to temperatures above 140 degrees Fahrenheit and is corrosive in liquid form. Jewelers in Edward's part of the country routinely use the adhesive because it is inexpensive and durable, and its qualities are common knowledge in the trade. One of Edward's customers, Deedra, bought a necklace with a sapphire setting held in place by the glue. Deedra wore the necklace while visiting her health club's spa, in which the temperature rose above the glue's melting point. Deedra suffered severe burns from the adhesive. Did Edward owe Deedra a duty of reasonable care, and if so, did he breach the duty?

Edward owed a duty to exercise reasonable care in constructing jewelry that his patrons could safely wear. The scope of duty included Deedra, who was a foreseeable plaintiff (as she was one of his customers). It was reasonably foreseeable that Deedra would wear the necklace under conditions in which the glue might melt, because persons often use spas without first removing jewelry. Thus, Deedra's injury was reasonably foreseeable. A reasonable jeweler would have known of the relatively low melting temperature and corrosive nature of the adhesive and have anticipated the meltdown risk. Other substances with higher melting points, such as solder, could have been used instead, and the reasonable jeweler would know this as well. Edward, however, did not follow these professional practices. By failing to comply with the reasonable standard of care, Edward breached his duty of care to Deedra.

One might disagree with the reasoning in this hypothetical, however, particularly in terms of foreseeability of injury. Arguably, Edward could not have reasonably predicted that a customer would wear the necklace in a spa, which is unusually hot and encourages users to remove metal objects from their bodies. Thus, one might conclude that Edward did not breach his duty of care to Deedra, because the harm could not have been reasonably anticipated. This is an equally correct interpretation of this hypothetical! It illustrates how different people define foreseeability and, thus, the scope of duty owed. Consider jurors deciding this aspect of negligence, who might easily develop different opinions given the same facts. This is the "shifting sands" element of negligence in action.

6.4 CAUSATION OF INJURY

Even if the defendant breaches his or her duty of care owed to the plaintiff, the defendant will not be legally negligent, nor liable for the plaintiff's injuries, unless the defendant's actions caused the harm.

Cause-in-Fact

Causation is a critical component of negligence. To be liable, the tortfeasor must have caused the victim's injuries. *Causation of injury* relates to the tortfeasor's actions that result in harm to the injured party. Courts frequently refer to this as **cause-in-fact**, meaning that, in negligence litigation, the defendant's misconduct produced the plaintiff's injuries.

Causation may be direct or indirect. **Direct causation** is often called **but-for causation**, a term often applied in the common law. The formula is straightforward: but for the tortfeasor's (defendant's) actions, the victim (plaintiff) would not have been harmed. But-for, or direct, causation is straight-lined, that is, the tortfeasor's behavior is usually the immediate cause of the victim's misfortune. For example, if Samantha spills a beverage on a stairway and does not clean it up, and Daniel slips on the slick spot and falls down the stairs, Samantha has caused Daniel's injuries. The causation is direct: but for Samantha's failure to clean the drink spill on the stairs, Daniel would not have slipped and fallen.

Consider another illustration. Suppose an automobile mechanic changes the tires on Quinn's car but neglects to tighten the lug nuts properly. While the vehicle is moving, the left rear tire comes loose and flies off. The car skids out of control and crashes into a telephone pole, hurting Quinn. Again, there is direct causation: but for the mechanic's failure to tighten the nuts sufficiently, the tire would not have come off and Quinn would not have collided with the pole.

Indirect causation occurs when several forces combine to produce injuries. For example, in the loose tire example, suppose the tire had not come completely off the automobile but was wobbling loosely. However, as Quinn was driving, he encountered broken glass on the highway, which punctured his left rear tire. Because of the flat tire and the looseness of all the tires, Quinn lost control of the car and crashed. Here, two factors resulted in Quinn's injuries: the glass that ruptured his tire and the loose nuts that lessened his control of the vehicle. In this version of the facts, the but-for test does not provide a clear-cut answer. Could one now say that, but for the mechanic's failure to tighten the nuts, Quinn would not have driven into the pole? Did not the flat tire also cause him to lose control of the car? Would the punctured tire alone have caused him to lose control and crash? To resolve this causation dilemma, the but-for test serves poorly. Instead, one needs a formula that satisfactorily accounts for the multiple factors that produced the injuries. For indirect causation, there is substantial factor analysis.

Substantial Factor Analysis

Substantial factor analysis states that the tortfeasor is liable for injuries to the victim when the tortfeasor's misconduct was a *substantial factor* in producing the harm. In the preceding tire illustration, the broken glass flattened Quinn's tire and made the car difficult to handle. However, had the lug nuts not also been loose, the tires would not have been wobbling. Quinn probably would have been able to control the vehicle better and might not have crashed at all. The mechanic's failure to tighten the nuts was a substantial factor in Quinn's losing control and colliding with the

LEGAL TERMS

cause-in-fact
Cause of injury in negligence cases. If the tortfeasor's actions resulted in the victim's injuries, then the tortfeasor was the cause-in-fact of the victim's harm. Cause-in-fact includes direct, or but-for, causation as well as indirect causation.

but-for (direct) causation
A form of causation of injury in negligence cases. The formula is applied as a question: But for the defendant's actions, would the plaintiff have been harmed? If yes, then the defendant directly caused the plaintiff's injuries.

indirect causation
A form of causation of injury in negligence cases. The most common type is substantial factor analysis.

substantial factor analysis
A form of indirect causation in negligence cases. The tortfeasor is liable for injuries to the victim when the tortfeasor's conduct was a substantial factor in producing the harm.

pole. Thus, the mechanic would be liable, even though the broken glass and punctured tire also influenced the accident.

The classic substantial factor analysis case is *Summers v. Tice,* 33 Cal. 2d 80, 199 P.2d 1 (1948). In this case, the plaintiff was hunting quail with two defendants. When the birds were flushed out, the defendants aimed and fired their shotguns in the plaintiff's direction, striking the plaintiff and causing severe physical injuries. It was unclear which defendant's shot hit the plaintiff, because both defendants used the same gauge shotgun and size of shot. The California Supreme Court applied the substantial factor test in determining causation and liability. Although it could not be conclusively established which defendant's weapon caused the plaintiff's injuries, either defendant's action was sufficient to produce the resulting harm. Quoting a Mississippi Supreme Court case, Justice Carter stated: "We think that . . . each is liable for the resulting injury . . ., although no one can say definitely who actually shot [the plaintiff]. To hold otherwise would be to exonerate both from liability, although each was negligent, and the injury resulted from such negligence."

Summers v. Tice resembles another type of case in which multiple forces combine to produce harm. When two or more defendants act together to produce the plaintiff's injury, the courts consider them to have *acted in concert.* All defendants are held liable for their combined conduct in such cases. This is called **joint and several liability**, another form of causation.

Joint and Several Liability

Multiple tortfeasors are each held individually accountable to the victim for the combined negligent behavior of all the tortfeasors. For instance, suppose that a surgical team, composed of two surgeons, three nurses, and an anesthesiologist, loses count of surgical sponges and leaves one in the patient's abdomen. The patient contracts peritonitis as a consequence. Because all of the medical personnel acted together in the operation, they are said to have functioned in concert. Their collective conduct produced harm to the patient. Thus, each individual would be personally liable for the patient's injuries. In other words, all of the personnel would be jointly and severally liable.

Multiple tortfeasors may injure a victim by acting in sequence, rather than simultaneously as in the medical malpractice example. The sequence of combined events produces the harmful results. For example, assume that a shipping company does not refrigerate a shipment of perishable food. As a result, the items spoil in transit. The shipment arrives at a supermarket, which fails to notice the spoiled condition of the products and stocks them on its shelves. Carla's roommate buys some of the goods but does not check them for freshness, despite obvious odors and discoloration. After her roommate cooks dinner, Carla eats the bad food and becomes seriously ill.

Who does Carla sue? Several tortfeasors combined negligent behavior to produce her injury. First the shipper failed to refrigerate the food, and it turned rotten. Next the grocery store failed to notice the spoiled food and stocked it. Then Carla's roommate failed to notice the spoilage and prepared the food for her to eat. All these tortfeasors—the shipping company, the supermarket, and Carla's roommate—contributed to a sequence of events that resulted in her illness. Carla would not have become sick had any of these tortfeasors identified the threat (spoiled food) and taken reasonable precautions to avoid injuring customers. But for the concerted conduct of these tortfeasors, Carla would not have been hurt. Therefore, they are all jointly and severally liable to her for the harm caused.

Figure 6-3 outlines the three types of causation-of-injury theories.

Cause-in-Fact (Direct) (But-For Causation)	Cause-in-Fact (Indirect) Substantial Factor Analysis	Joint and Several Liability
But for the defendant's actions, the plaintiff's injury would not have happened.	When multiple defendants combine to injure the plaintiff, a single defendant is liable if his or her actions were a substantial factor in producing the harm.	When multiple defendants act together to injure the plaintiff, all defendants are liable for the harm.

FIGURE 6-3
Causation of Injury Theories

Courts Blur the Distinctions

American Jurisprudence 2d, a legal encyclopedia, provides an excellent and accurate summary of legal principles gleaned from multitudes of court opinions. As the quoted discussion hints, courts blur the distinctions between direct and indirect causation, but-for and substantial factor causation, and proximate cause. There is an almost endless variety of definitions of these terms in the common law. Despite the confusion, concepts surface that are essentially identical to those discussed in this chapter. The excerpt is included here to reflect the different analytical approaches to the causation query.

57A AMERICAN JURISPRUDENCE 2D *Negligence*
§§ 431, 434, 436, 464, 471, 474-75, 478
(1989)

[All Footnotes Omitted.]

[§ 431] Cause in fact as an element of proximate cause means that the wrongful act was a substantial factor in bringing about the injury and without which no harm would been incurred. [. . .]

[§ 434] There are two steps in analyzing a defendant's tort liability. The first is determining whether he breached his duty of care, the second whether the breach was at least a cause of the accident. Liability for negligence is predicated upon a causal connection between the

LEGAL TERMS

joint and several liability
A form of causation of injury in negligence cases. The theory applies in cases in which two or more tortfeasors combine, or act in concert, to produce the victim's injuries, even though it may be impossible to determine which tortfeasor caused which specific injuries.

negligence alleged as the wrong and the injury of which complaint is made, and the common law refers the injury to the proximate, not the remote, cause, and establishes as an essential element of liability for negligence what has traditionally been referred to as proximate cause, or, as it is now frequently denominated, legal cause. [. . .]

[§ 436] The Restatement of Torts 2d says that, in order for a negligent actor to be found liable for another's harm, it is necessary not only that the actor's conduct be negligent toward the other, but also that the negligence of the actor be a legal cause of the other's harm. The Restatement further points out that the conduct of a negligent actor need not be the predominant cause of the harm. The wrongful conduct of a number of third persons may also be a cause of the harm, so that such third persons may be liable for it, concurrently with the actor. [. . .]

[§ 464] It has been recognized that the issue of "causation in fact" is regarded as an aspect of "proximate cause" [. . .]. Traditionally, courts have used the term "proximate cause" as descriptive of the actual "cause in fact" relation which must exist between a defendant's conduct and a plaintiff's injury before there may be liability. Additionally, the courts have used the same term as a shorthand description of various complex legal concepts and principles which have nothing to do with the fact of actual causation, but which define and control the existence and extent of liability [. . .].

In all cases where proximate cause is in issue, the first step is to determine whether the defendant's conduct, in point of fact, was a factor in causing plaintiff's damage. [. . .] If the inquiry as to cause in fact shows that the defendant's conduct, in point of fact, was not a factor in causing plaintiff's damage, the matter ends there, but if it shows that his conduct was a factor in causing such damage, then the further question is whether his conduct played such a part in causing the damage as makes him the author of such damage and liable therefor in the eyes of the law. [. . .]

[§ 471] Most jurisdictions have historically followed this so-called "but-for" causation-in-fact test. It has proven to be a fair, easily understood and serviceable test of actual causation in negligence actions [. . . .]. Where the "but for["] test is recognized, it has been said to be useful and generally adequate for the purpose of determining whether specific conduct actually caused the harmful result in question, but that it cannot be indiscriminately used as an unqualified measure of the defendant's liability [. . . .].

[§ 474] The "but-for" test, while it explains the greater number of cases, does not in all instances serve as an adequate test. If two causes concur to bring about an event, and either one of them, operating alone, would have been sufficient to cause the identical result, some other test is needed. [. . .] The response of many courts to this problem has been to apply the "substantial factor" test, either in addition to or in place of the "but for" test. [. . .]

[§ 475] The substantial factor test [. . .] makes the question of proximate or legal cause depend upon the answer to the question, "was defendant's conduct a substantial factor in producing plaintiff's injuries?"

As pronounced in the Restatement, Torts 2d, the test is as follows: The actor's negligent conduct is a legal cause of harm to another if (a) his conduct is a substantial factor in bringing about the harm, and (b) there is no rule of law relieving the actor from liability because of the manner in which his negligence has resulted in the harm. [. . .]
[§ 478] Many courts lump the "but for" and the "substantial factor" tests together and apply them both, with some taking the view that the "but for" standard is only one element of the "substantial factor" standard, and a few holding that in the great majority of cases the two tests amount to the same thing [. . .]

Causation becomes clearer through an example. The following illustration should lend substance to the analytical formula.

HYPOTHETICAL

Cindy runs a beauty salon. Aspen is one of her regular customers. Cindy received a shipment of hair coloring products in unlabeled bottles. Rather than return the shipment, Cindy placed the bottles in a storeroom for future use. She applied one bottle to Aspen's hair without carefully checking its contents beforehand. Because of unusually high pH levels in Aspen's hair, the product turned Aspen's hair bright blue. Did Cindy cause Aspen's injury?

But for Cindy's failure to inspect the bottle's contents prior to treating Aspen's hair, Aspen would not have suffered hair discoloration. Direct causation functions easily and clearly to conclude that Cindy caused Aspen's injury.

Suppose instead that Angie, one of Cindy's employees, had taken the bottle from the storeroom and applied it to Aspen. Would both Cindy and Angie be liable for Aspen's harm and damage? Cindy failed to identify the unlabeled bottles before storing them. Angie failed to check the bottle's contents before applying them to Aspen's hair. Both combined in their unreasonable actions to produce the harmful result. Accordingly, Cindy and Angie are jointly and severally liable to Aspen.

Suppose the bottles had been mislabeled by the manufacturer. Cindy unknowingly stocked the bottles, assuming the labels to be correct. Angie then applied the contents of one bottle to Aspen's hair without observing that the contents were the wrong color and texture (a point that an experienced beautician should reasonably have known). The but-for test does not produce clear results in this case. One cannot say that, but for the manufacturer's mislabeling, Aspen would not have been hurt, because Angie actually misapplied the product to Aspen's hair. Neither may one contend that, but for Angie's use of the improperly labelled product, Aspen would not have been harmed, because Angie was not responsible for the mislabeling. Substantial factor analysis, however, helps to reach an acceptable answer. Angie's failure to inspect the bottle's contents and determine the error before applying the mixture to Aspen's hair was a substantial factor in producing Aspen's injury. Accordingly, Angie would be liable to Aspen.

6.5 PROXIMATE CAUSE

Joint and several liability is simple to discern when the chain of negligent events is relatively short and direct, such as in the preceding bad food or hair discoloration hypotheticals. However, when the sequence of activity is long, drawn-out, and complicated by peculiar twists and unexpected occurrences, then the three types of causation analysis (cause-in-fact, substantial factor analysis, and joint and several liability) become unreliable for determining whether the tortfeasor is liable to the victim. Another analytical tool must be applied to establish negligence in such circumstances. This approach is called proximate cause.

Foreseeability of Injury

Proximate cause, or *legal cause* as it is sometimes called, exists when the tortfeasor's actions cause a foreseeable injury to the victim. Court opinions often refer to the plaintiff's injuries as the natural and probable consequence of the defendant's misconduct. The key to proximate cause is foreseeable injury. Was the victim's injury the reasonably foreseeable result of what the tortfeasor did? If so, then the tortfeasor's actions proximately caused the plaintiff's harm. If not, then proximate cause did not exist, and the defendant will not be liable to the plaintiff under negligence theory.

Proximate cause is distinguishable from causation. The term *proximate cause* is unfortunate because it is a constant source of confusion with causation. *Causation* is the chain of events linking the tortfeasor's conduct to the victim's injury. *Proximate cause* is the zone within which the plaintiff's injury was reasonably foreseeable as a consequence of the defendant's behavior. Think of proximate cause as a circle. Actions inside the circle cause foreseeable injuries to victims. Actions outside the circle are beyond the **zone of foreseeability**. Figure 6-4 illustrates this concept.

Consider a hypothetical. Patrick is building an additional garage and workshop in his backyard. As he is excavating to install the foundation, he hits an underground natural gas pipeline that services his neighborhood. The pipe ruptures and disrupts gas supplies to the other houses in the area. As a result, those houses with gas heat cannot use their furnaces. It is January, and outside temperatures fall well below freezing at night. With no heat, the water pipes in the neighbors' homes freeze and burst, causing

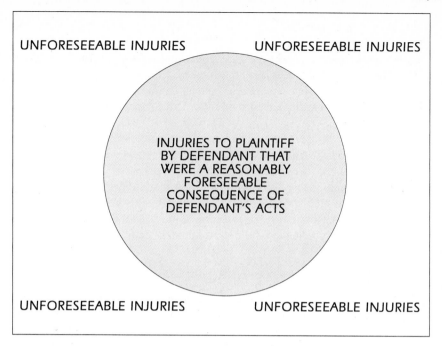

UNFORESEEABLE INJURIES   UNFORESEEABLE INJURIES

INJURIES TO PLAINTIFF
BY DEFENDANT THAT
WERE A REASONABLY
FORESEEABLE
CONSEQUENCE OF
DEFENDANT'S ACTS

UNFORESEEABLE INJURIES   UNFORESEEABLE INJURIES

FIGURE 6-4
Proximate Cause Zone
of Foreseeability

substantial water damage to the structures and furnishings. Did Patrick proximately cause the harm to the neighbors' houses?

It was reasonably foreseeable that an underground utility line might be severed. If this line were carrying a heating source, such as natural gas, it would likewise be reasonably foreseeable that neighboring homes would lose their heat service. Because it was winter, it was also reasonably foreseeable that temperatures could go below freezing and cause water pipes in unheated buildings to freeze and burst. Water damage to structures and furnishings is a natural and inevitable consequence of broken pipes. Clearly, Patrick's actions proximately caused the injury to his neighbors' homes, because the harm was reasonably foreseeable as a result of Patrick's breaking the natural gas pipeline.

Proximate Cause and Scope of Duty Combined

Some legal scholars have included scope of duty as an aspect of proximate cause. This seems logical, as both include the element of foreseeability, but there is a subtle distinction. Scope of duty examines whether it was reasonably foreseeable that the plaintiff would be injured as a result of the defendant's actions. Proximate cause focuses upon whether the injury itself was reasonably foreseeable.

Thus, it is possible for the tortfeasor to owe a duty of reasonable care to the victim but not proximately cause the injury if the harm was unforeseeable. For instance, suppose that Shannon, who manages a shoe store,

LEGAL TERMS

proximate cause
  Legal cause in negligence (and some absolute liability) cases. Proximate cause exists when the tortfeasor's actions cause a reasonably foreseeable injury to the victim. Courts often refer to the plaintiff's injuries as being the natural and probable consequence of the defendant's misconduct.

zone of foreseeability
  An aspect of proximate cause in negligence cases. If it were reasonably foreseeable that the tortfeasor's actions would produce the victim's injuries, then the tortfeasor proximately caused the harm.

gave away free helium balloons to families as a promotional gimmick. One of her customers, Addison, suffered from a rare allergy to helium, but was unaware of this condition. Addison inhaled some helium from the balloon to make himself talk in a high-pitched, funny voice, which is a common side effect of helium inhalation. Instead, Addison went into anaphylactic shock, suffered cardiac arrest, and died. Did Shannon proximately cause Addison's death?

Definitely, Shannon owed a duty of reasonable care to all of her patrons to maintain reasonably safe premises. But Addison's uncommon sensitivity to helium (of which even he was unaware) was not something that Shannon could reasonably have been expected to anticipate. The injury simply was not reasonably foreseeable. The vast majority of the population (say, 98 percent) would not possess this allergy and would suffer no ill effects. Accordingly, Shannon did not proximately cause Addison's injury.

"Taking the Victim as You Find Him"

Nonetheless, many appellate courts decide this issue differently. These opinions speak of a tortfeasor's **"taking the victim as you find him."** This means that peculiar health conditions are considered to be reasonably foreseeable, as one must always assume that a victim could suffer from an odd affliction such as helium allergy. Most of these cases, however, involve more deliberate actions (such as striking the head of a person with an "eggshell skull" and killing him or her). Such cases involve more intentional torts than negligence (battery, in the eggshell-skull cases), as is typical with the taking-the-victim cases. Still, taking-the-victim analysis surfaces in pure negligence cases as well.

Taking-the-victim cases make almost any physical injury reasonably foreseeable. This raises proximate cause to the point at which the tortfeasor becomes an insurer of the victim's safety. Such reasoning removes the cases from the realm of negligence and deposits them in the field of strict liability, which is discussed later in this text.

THE CASE OF THE PARKING LOT KILLER

Proximate cause poses potent analytical challenges for the courts. Whether injuries are reasonably foreseeable is often a matter of personal preference among individual jurors. Gut feelings play a significant part in gauging this aspect of negligence. As the following case suggests, proximate cause does not always include the injured party, although one might wish otherwise.

Lewis v. Razzberries, Inc.
222 Ill. App. 3d 843,
584 N.E.2d 437 (1991)
(Appellate Court of Illinois)
December 6, 1991

Justice McNAMARA delivered the opinion of the court:

Plaintiff, Allan B. Lewis, special administrator of the estate of Shara B. Lewis, filed a complaint sounding in negligence against defendant Razzberries, Inc. [...]. In this alleged wrongful death action, plaintiff's decedent [Shara Lewis] was shot to death by a patron, Edward Siegelman, in a parking area adjacent to Razzberries. Plaintiff appeals the trial court's grant of summary judgment in favor of Razzberries, alleging that it owed a duty of care to protect against reasonably foreseeable criminal acts; [...] and that the tavern owner had sufficient notice of the potential risk of danger to [Shara Lewis]. (Siegelman was later convicted of involuntary manslaughter and sentenced to a term of imprisonment.) (Judgment was entered in favor of Razzberries [...]).

Josephine Jardine testified [...] that on December 11, 1984, she met with [Shara Lewis] around [...] midnight, they drove Jardine's car to Razzberries, [... and] Jardine parked her car in an area which was neither paved nor improved with lines designated for the parking of vehicles. [...] Jardine's car was parked 23 feet off the southwest corner of the property and within the public right-of-way [...]. There were no signs delineating the property owned by Razzberries, nor were there any signs posted indicating the areas where it was permissible for patrons to park.

As she parked, Jardine noticed a familiar car owned by Siegelman, whom she had previously dated. Siegelman arrived at Razzberries at approximately 9:00 p.m. [...]

Upon entering the tavern, Jardine stated that she and [Lewis] were approached by Siegelman, and that he began to make threatening remarks to her. Jardine asked Siegelman to leave them alone. At one point, Siegelman grabbed Jardine's arm and told her that, "I'm going to shoot you when you leave here." Jardine was not afraid of Siegelman; rather, she became aggravated and annoyed at him. Jardine did not inform any of the tavern employees or the police about Siegelman's threats because she did not believe that Siegelman would harm her.

At approximately 1:00 a.m., Jardine and [Lewis] decided to leave the tavern. [...] Norman Richko, the bartender on duty, wanted to have an employee escort the women to their car. Jardine saw that Richko was busy [...], and she waited approximately 20 minutes. While she was waiting for the escort, Siegelman again approached her, grabbed her arm and told her that he wanted her one more time. After Jardine rebuffed Siegelman's advances, he angrily walked back toward a corner of the bar. Jardine decided to wait no longer because she believed she had enough time to get into her car as she was parked near the building. The two women walked quickly to the car.

Jardine unlocked the car, and entered the driver's seat while [Lewis] walked around to the passenger's side. At that point, Siegelman began pounding very hard on the driver's window with both fists. Siegelman then walked away [...].

As Jardine attempted to put the key into the ignition, Siegelman again returned and began pounding on the car window. At that point, Jardine opened the car door. Siegelman suddenly pulled out a gun and leaned into the car. Jardine attempted to push the gun away from her. [...] During the course of the struggle the gun went off once, fatally wounding [Lewis].

[. . .]

The trial court granted summary judgment in defendant's favor [. . .], finding that the tavern owner did not owe a duty of care beyond the premises owned or controlled by it. [. . .]

Sidebar: The court's discussion of duty is omitted. The court agreed with the trial court that the tavern owed the plaintiff no duty, since Jardine's car was parked 23 feet beyond the tavern's property boundaries. You may wish to read the full text of the opinion to see the court's reasoning. What possible difference could 23 feet make in terms of the scope of duty, when no property lines were marked, no parking spaces were indicated, and people routinely parked adjacent to the tavern in the area that Jardine used?

Plaintiff finally asserts that defendant had sufficient notice of the potential risk of danger to place defendant on notice of the reasonable foreseeability of a criminal attack upon Jardine and [Lewis]. [. . .] [R]easonable foreseeability must be judged by what was apparent to defendant at the time of the complained of conduct, and not by what may appear through hindsight.

Upon review of the record, we do not find that defendant could have reasonably foreseen that Siegelman would have resorted to the drastic behavior that resulted in the death of [Lewis]. We first take note of the failure of Jardine or [Lewis] to alert the tavern employees that Siegelman had made threats to Jardine. While Siegelman voiced threats to Jardine, she stated in her deposition that she was not afraid that he would harm her; rather, she became aggravated and annoyed by him. Jardine also testified that Siegelman did not tell her that he had a gun, nor did she have reason to believe that he carried one.

Although Richko, the bartender, was aware that Siegelman approached Jardine on several occasions, and that the verbal exchanges became increasingly heated, we do not find that conduct sufficient for him to conclude that Siegelman was likely to become violent. Indeed, Richko stated that Siegelman never presented a problem prior to that night, and described him as a gentleman.

[. . .]

Judgment affirmed.

CASE QUESTIONS

1. Do you agree with the court that Siegelman's actions were not reasonably foreseeable? Explain your analysis.
2. Would the outcome of this case have been different if Jardine or Lewis had reported Siegelman's threats to the bartender or police? Why or why not?

THE CASE OF THE FIRE-BREATHING ELECTRIC POLE

The zone of foreseeability has to end somewhere. In the following case, the North Carolina Court of Appeals ruled that the plaintiff was not a foreseeable plaintiff.

Westbrook v. Cobb
105 N.C. App. 64,
411 S.E.2d 651 (1992)
(Court of Appeals of North Carolina)
January 17, 1992

On the morning of 28 January 1985, defendant was driving an automobile in an easterly direction along R.P. 1757 near Grifton when he struck a utility pole across from the Westbrook house. Trooper J.R. Letchworth was called to investigate the accident. When he arrived he found defendant's car against a utility pole, which was partially broken and pushed over. A transformer was attached to the utility pole and wires ran across the road from it to service plaintiff's house. The utility pole was located off the paved portion of the highway.

At the time of the accident, Donald Johnson, Chief of the Grifton County Fire Department, lived down the road across an open field from plaintiff's house. His mother told him of the accident and approximately ten to fifteen minutes later he arrived at the scene. He was standing against defendant's car when he turned to discover the Westbrook home on fire. After ascertaining the house was empty, Johnson drove into Grifton to set off the fire alarm. Johnson got the fire truck, returned to the scene and began fighting the fire. During this time, plaintiff was at some stables approximately one and one-half miles from his home but his brother had alerted him to the fire. Almost simultaneously with the arrival of the fire truck, plaintiff arrived with his brother.

Plaintiff assisted in bringing the fire under control. With the fire seemingly under control, but water still being applied to the house, plaintiff and his brother entered the house to retrieve a metal box with titles, deeds and birth certificates. While inside, plaintiff and his brother decided to attempt to retrieve additional items. Plaintiff was in the process of getting some clothes off a rack when he apparently injured himself. He believed the injury to be only a pulled muscle but when the condition did not improve, plaintiff's doctor referred him to an orthopaedic surgeon who eventually performed surgery on plaintiff's back for an acutely herniated disc.

After the fire was extinguished, Mr. Johnson conducted an investigation of the fire, during which time he discovered a gas line underneath the kitchen with an electric line across it. Evidence at trial tended to establish the blow to the utility pole and transformer caused a surge of electricity to run through the wires into the house. The electrical wire sparked, thereby igniting the gas line next to it and causing a blow torch effect on the kitchen floor. While the evidence was conflicting as to the precise cause of the fire, all of the experts agreed that the fire was related in some way to the impact to the utility pole.

This case was tried before a jury. At the close of plaintiff's evidence, defendant moved for a directed verdict pursuant to Rule 50(a), N.C. Rules of Civil Procedure, which was granted. Plaintiff thereby appeals that judgment.

[. . .]

WALKER, Judge.

Plaintiff sets forth five assignments of error in his brief. Of these we need only to consider the first assignment, which is whether the trial court erred in entering a directed verdict at the close of plaintiff's evidence in favor of the defendant on the grounds plaintiff did not establish the requisite elements of a negligence action. Specifically, we find plaintiff failed to prove the essential element of proximate cause, and the trial court did not err in directing a verdict for defendant.

[. . .]

In order to sustain a claim of actionable negligence, plaintiff must prove (1) defendant owed a duty to plaintiff, (2) defendant failed to exercise proper care in the performance of that duty, and (3) the breach of that duty was the proximate cause of plaintiff's injury, which a person of ordinary prudence should have foreseen as probable under the conditions as they existed. [Citations omitted.] Since the absence of any one of these elements will defeat a negligence action, we need only address the question of proximate cause. The North Carolina Supreme Court has stated:

> Proximate cause is a cause which in natural and continuous sequence, unbroken by any new and independent cause, produced the plaintiff's injuries, and without which the injuries would not have occurred, and one from which a person of ordinary prudence could have reasonably foreseen that such a result, or consequences of a generally injurious nature, was probable under all the facts as they existed. Foreseeability is thus a requisite of proximate cause, which is, in turn, a requisite for actionable negligence (citations omitted).

[Citation omitted.] The test of foreseeability as an element of proximate cause does not require that defendant should have been able to foresee the injury in the precise form in which it occurred. Thus, where the defendant could have reasonably foreseen the consequences of his actions and his actions produced a result in continuous sequence, without which the injury would not have occurred, the defendant's actions will be deemed to have proximately caused the plaintiff's injury. [Citation omitted.]

A steadfast definition of "reasonable foreseeability" has not yet been promulgated, leaving the courts to analyze the facts and ascertain whether an ordinarily prudent man could have foreseen his actions would lead to this result.

[. . .] Foreseeability is not construed, however, to require the defendant to anticipate events which are merely possible. [Citation omitted.]

Here, we do not believe the chain of events resulting in plaintiff's injury to be reasonably foreseeable and within the contemplation of an ordinarily prudent individual. A defendant could not reasonably expect that as a result of his vehicle striking a utility pole with a transformer attached, with wires extending to the house across the street, that such wires would be pulled causing sparks which would then ignite a fire in the house. A defendant could not further reasonably expect that as a result of this house fire a resident of said house would arrive on the scene from a different location, would voluntarily proceed to enter the house while water was still being applied to it, and injure his back in the process of retrieving personal property. Although we are not prepared to promulgate a bright line test for the doctrine of foreseeability and application thereof, we are also not prepared to extend the concept to encompass the facts in this case.

[. . .] "[I]t is 'inconceivable that any defendant should be held liable to infinity for all the consequences which flow from his act,' some boundary must be set." [Citations omitted.] Consequently, we cannot find plaintiff's injury to have been the natural result of a continuous sequence of actions set into motion by defendant's initial act of striking the utility pole. In this case, plaintiff's intentional and purposeful entry into the house interrupted the causal chain of events between defendant's act and plaintiff's injury, so that the occurrence was not one which naturally flowed from defendant's negligence.

[. . .]

Affirmed.

CASE QUESTIONS

1. Do you agree with the court in *Westbrook* that the plaintiff's physical injuries were not reasonably foreseeable? Explain.
2. Do you agree that the house fire was not reasonably foreseeable? Explain.
3. Apply cause-in-fact analysis to *Westbrook*. What result do you achieve?

The range of the zone of foreseeability is further explored in the next example.

HYPOTHETICAL

Colleen operates a laundromat. Geoffrey often washes and dries his clothes there. One day, while Geoffrey was loading his laundry into the washer, the machine unexpectedly began agitating and injured his arms and hands. Did Colleen proximately cause Geoffrey's injuries?

Foreseeability of injury is the starting point. Was it reasonably foreseeable that the washer Geoffrey used would short-circuit and suddenly begin operating while Geoffrey was loading his clothes? It is not uncommon for electrical, mechanical devices to jump to life by themselves unexpectedly. This often occurs when electrical wiring short-circuits after the wires' insulation has frayed. Because people must insert their hands and arms inside the washing machine drum to load clothing, it is reasonably foreseeable that a shorted machine might start itself while a patron's arms were inside. Thus, Geoffrey's injuries were reasonably foreseeable and Colleen proximately caused the harm suffered.

Suppose, however, that Geoffrey's arms and hands were not trapped inside the machine when it suddenly began agitating. Suppose, instead, that the surprise simply frightened Geoffrey, who was unusually susceptible to sudden, loud noises and suffered a heart attack as a consequence of the shock. Could Colleen have reasonably anticipated this tragedy? Most courts would reverse the reasonable person standard (applying it to the plaintiff) and say that a reasonable person would not be so easily alarmed (to the point of heart failure) by an upstart washing machine. However, a few courts would employ taking-the-victim analysis and say that even this remote and unexpected injury was foreseeable.

Figure 6-5 summarizes the elements of proximate cause.

6.6 DAMAGES

Damages are the injury that the plaintiff suffered as a result of the defendant's tortious conduct. As in all torts, damages must be proven for negligence. Courts will not compensate a victim unless some documentable harm has been done.

Recall that, with certain intentional torts such as battery, assault, or trespass, no physical harm is required. With a technical trespass, it is sufficient that the tortfeasor engaged in the unauthorized act. Battery can be achieved merely by unconsented touching. In negligence law, however, some determinable injury must be proven for the tortfeasor to be held liable to the injured party. Normally, this involves monetary losses as a result of harm to a person or the person's property. For instance, if someone loses muscular control in the legs after an automobile accident with a careless driver, then the injured party could demonstrate economic loss as a consequence of the harm. The plaintiff could quantify the losses sustained through lost wages, inability to continue an occupation, loss of bodily function, emotional impairment, and related damages.

This vital element of the negligence puzzle is often glossed over by legal scholars and courts. Following such reasoning, damage is often assumed from the fact that the plaintiff sued the defendant for negligence. Of course, it is always a mistake to assume anything in legal study. The plaintiff must prove actual injury to recover. This harm may be physical or emotional, but it must exist.

1. Was the plaintiff's injury a reasonably foreseeable result of the defendant's actions?
2. Did the defendant's duty of reasonable care include the plaintiff?
3. Does the case involve special circumstances, in which the plaintiff has peculiar physical or emotional characteristics (such as brittle bones, mental illness, or sensitivity to noise) so that the defendant must take the victim as he finds him?

FIGURE 6-5
Proximate Cause
Elements

Compensatory Damages

Compensatory damages are most common in negligence cases. As the name suggests, *compensatory damages* are designed to compensate the victim for the tortfeasor's negligence. Normally, the plaintiff proves monetary losses, such as out-of-pocket expenses (e.g., medical, property repair), lost income, pain and suffering, loss of property value, or loss of bodily function.

Punitive Damages

Punitive or *exemplary damages,* which are often awarded for intentional torts such as fraud or intentional infliction of emotional distress, are almost nonexistent in negligence cases, because negligence involves carelessness rather than wanton or intentionally tortious behavior. The punishment component of punitive damages would be excessive in most negligence cases, although exemplary damages are occasionally used in gross negligence cases. **Gross negligence** involves carelessness that exceeds ordinary, reasonable care standards and approaches willful and wanton misconduct. If the negligence is sufficiently excessive, the court might allow punitive damages for the injured party. For instance, if a surgeon left a scalpel inside a patient during an operation, this might be considered gross negligence by the medical community. Such misconduct exceeds that degree of reasonable care ordinarily expected of doctors. Physicians simply are expected to avoid such slipshod surgical efforts.

Figure 6-6 summarizes damages in negligence actions.

Plaintiff must suffer actual loss as a result of injury.
Loss is usually gauged in monetary terms.
Compensatory damages provide the plaintiff with recovery for losses that resulted from the defendant's actions (out-of-pocket expenses, pain and suffering, lost income, lost property value, loss of bodily function).

FIGURE 6-6
Damages in Negligence Cases

LEGAL TERMS

damages
The injury that the plaintiff suffered as a result of the defendant's actions. The most common types of damages involve loss of money or value. In most tort cases, compensatory damages are awarded, although punitive, or exemplary, damages are sometimes given, particularly in cases involving intentional torts or gross negligence.

gross negligence
When a tortfeasor's actions or omissions approach willful and wanton misconduct. Gross negligence violates the ordinary, reasonable care standard to extremes.

6.7 PROVING NEGLIGENCE

Proof is an essential aspect of all litigation. A cynic might suggest that what is true or false is irrelevant; rather, what can be proven during a lawsuit is all that matters. Negligence claims are normally proven through the typical evidentiary processes. These include oral testimony, depositions, documentary evidence, and demonstrative evidence (such as photographs or computer simulations).

Burdens of Proof and Rejoinder

The plaintiff has the burden of proving that the defendant was negligent. This forces the plaintiff to prove by a preponderance of the evidence that all negligence elements existed (duty, breach, causation, proximate cause, and injury). The evidence must establish that the defendant's actions were negligent and caused the plaintiff's injuries.

Once the plaintiff has made a **prima facie case** (meaning that proof has been established by or beyond a preponderance), the burden shifts to the defendant, who must then counter the plaintiff's evidence with proof of his or her own. This is sometimes called the defendant's **burden of rejoinder** or **rebuttal**. The defendant must disprove the plaintiff's case against him or her.

In some cases, however, the burden of proof is different. What if the plaintiff cannot prove the defendant's negligence? Consider an example. Suppose a patient were unconscious during an operation. Suppose the surgical nurse failed to remove all the sponges from the patient, and later the patient contracted peritonitis. How could the plaintiff prove that the defendants (nurse, surgeon, and hospital) were negligent in leaving the sponge inside the plaintiff? What witnesses could the plaintiff call to testify, other than the surgical team? The plaintiff was unconscious and unaware of the entire procedure. How could the plaintiff meet the burden of proof in such circumstances? Such unusual cases require a special burden of proof, which is called *res ipsa loquitur.*

Res Ipsa Loquitur

Res ipsa loquitur is Latin meaning "the thing [*res*] speaks [*loquitur*] for itself [*ipsa*]." It is used in negligence cases in which the plaintiff is in a disadvantaged position for proving the defendant's negligence. Under the doctrine of res ipsa loquitur, the defendant's negligence is presumed as a result of his or her actions. This shifts the burden of proof to the defendant. In other words, the defendant must disprove his or her negligence from the outset of litigation. The plaintiff's burden of proof is converted into the defendant's burden of rejoinder.

Elements of Res Ipsa Loquitur

The plaintiff must prove only certain essential facts, such as what injury occurred, what the defendant was doing, and how the defendant's action (or inaction) related to the plaintiff's harm. To use res ipsa loquitur, the circumstances of the case must strongly imply negligence by someone. Court opinions often quote the following elements:

1. The defendant (or his or her employee[s]) must have been in exclusive control of the object or action that produced the plaintiff's injury.

2. The plaintiff's injury must be of a type that ordinarily would not have happened unless negligence were involved.

3. The defendant must be in a better position to prove his or her lack of negligence than the plaintiff is to prove the defendant's negligence.

Certain courts and legal scholars add a fourth element, which states that the plaintiff cannot have contributed to his or her own injuries. This, however, simply states contributory and comparative negligence, which are two similar defenses to negligence and are discussed in chapter 8.

Defendant's Exclusive Control

For res ipsa loquitur to apply, the events that led to the plaintiff's injury must have been under the defendant's exclusive control. This includes the defendant's employees. For example, suppose the plaintiff were walking through the defendant's warehouse. Suppose the defendant's employees had stacked many crates of merchandise, and the stacks rose 30 feet high. If a top crate fell upon and injured the plaintiff, but nobody except the plaintiff was present in that part of the building, who could the plaintiff point the finger toward as having been negligent? Using res ipsa loquitur, the plaintiff would shift the burden of proof to the defendant (warehouse owner) to show that the crates had been safely stowed. Because the crates were under the defendant's exclusive control, and one crate fell and hurt the plaintiff, the first element of res ipsa loquitur would be satisfied.

Presumption of Negligence

Res ipsa loquitur also insists that the plaintiff's injury be one that normally would not have happened unless negligence were involved. Consider the preceding illustration. Crates usually do not fall over in warehouses unless they are improperly stacked. Negligence may be presumed in this case because the box indeed fell. This would not normally occur if ordinary, reasonable care were used to store the crates. Because the box did fall on the plaintiff, then the defendant must not have exercised reasonable care in stacking the crates. At least the court will make this presumption and allow the defendant to refute it by proving that reasonable care was used when storing the boxes.

Defendant's Superior Proof Position

Under res ipsa loquitur, the defendant must be in a better position to prove that he or she was not negligent than the plaintiff is to establish the defendant's negligence. In the warehouse example, the plaintiff did not see how the crate fell. None of the defendant's employees were present or nearby when the accident occurred. No witnesses actually saw why the crate fell. But the defendant originally stacked the crates. This makes it easier for

LEGAL TERMS

prima facie case
The plaintiff's burden of proof in civil cases. Normally this is equivalent to the preponderance of the evidence.

burden of rejoinder (or rebuttal)
The defendant's burden of proof to disprove the plaintiff's evidence in a lawsuit.

res ipsa loquitur
Latin meaning "the thing speaks for itself." A burden of proof used in negligence cases. Under this doctrine, the defendant's negligence is presumed as a result of his or her actions. This shifts the burden of proof to the defendant. The doctrine applies in cases in which the defendant had exclusive control over the object or activity causing the victim's injuries. The plaintiff's injuries must be of a type that ordinarily would not have happened unless negligence were involved. The defendant must have been in a better position to prove his or her lack of negligence than the plaintiff was to prove such negligence. Some courts state that the plaintiff cannot have contributed to his or her injuries if the doctrine is to apply.

the defendant to prove that reasonable care was used in stacking the boxes. The plaintiff is at a disadvantage to prove the defendant's negligence. However, the defendant can more easily show that safeguards were used in stacking the crates (such as ropes tied to support beams and crates, or walls and doors surrounding the stacked boxes). In this fashion, the defendant could prove that reasonable care was used when stacking the crates, and therefore no negligence happened.

THE CASE OF THE UNKIND CUT

Res ipsa loquitur is a favorite theory in medical malpractice litigation. However, it is not an automatic trump card through which plaintiffs can avoid proving breach of the professional standard of care. As the following case illustrates, not every careless medical act is presumed negligent.

Wendenburg v. Williams
784 S.W.2d 705 (Tex. Ct. App. 1990)
(Court of Appeals of Texas)
January 11, 1990

OPINION

MURPHY, Justice.

Hans Wendenburg, M.D. appeals an adverse judgment in a medical malpractice action brought by Suzanne and Rickie Williams. Appellant, in eight points of error, alleges the trial court erred in submitting an instruction on res ipsa loquitur to the jury and that the evidence was legally and factually insufficient to support the jury's findings of negligence and proximate cause. We reverse and remand to the trial court.

Suzanne Williams' iliac artery and iliac vein were perforated by appellant during a lumbar laminectomy. Appellant does not deny perforating Mrs. Williams' blood vessels, but contends the injury did not result from his negligence. The jury found that appellant was negligent in perforating Mrs. Williams' blood vessels and that his negligence was a proximate cause of her injuries.

[. . .] In a medical malpractice case based on negligence, the plaintiff must prove breach of duty and proximate cause by medical testimony. [. . .]

Thus, if a plaintiff cannot present expert testimony that a violation of the proper medical standard proximately caused his injury, then he has not presented legally sufficient evidence to prove his cause of action. [Citation omitted.] An exception to this rule is recognized where the nature of the alleged malpractice and injuries are plainly within the common knowledge of laymen. [Citation omitted.]

The doctrine of res ipsa loquitur will imply negligence in those cases where (1) the character of the accident and the circumstances surrounding it lead to the conclusion that it would not occur in the absence of negligence, and (2) the injury is caused by some instrumentality or agency within the defendant's exclusive control. [Citation omitted.]

[. . .]

Texas courts have allowed application of this doctrine in malpractice actions in those circumstances where the negligence is obvious to a layman. Examples of such situations include the use of certain mechanical instruments, operating on the wrong portion of the body, or leaving surgical instruments or sponges in the body. [Citation omitted.]

[. . .]

Appellant performed Mrs. Williams' operation with a microscope and used several small, specialized surgical tools [. . .]. Appellant, to reach the disc, had to cut through several layers of tissue and perform the operation through a hole one-eighth of an inch wide. To remove the tissue, appellant used a pituitary rongeur, a sophisticated instrument used to grip and "bite" the tissue between the vertebrae of the spine. Testimony at trial revealed that extensive training is required for the proper use of such an instrument. We conclude that the proper use of a pituitary rongeur is not a matter within the common knowledge of laymen; therefore, the doctrine of res ipsa loquitur does not apply. The trial court erred in submitting the negligence issue with a res ipsa loquitur instruction. [. . .]

[. . .] We reverse the trial court's judgment and remand for a new trial consistent with this opinion.

CASE QUESTIONS

1. When discussing the "common knowledge of laypersons" element of res ipsa loquitur, the court focuses upon the complexity of the medical instrument used in the operation. Would it not be more appropriate to ask whether the defendant's cutting of the iliac artery and vein while operating on the vertebrae was within a layperson's common knowledge? Why or why not?
2. Aside from the res ipsa loquitur issue, do you believe the defendant breached his professional standard of care? Explain your reasoning.

Res ipsa loquitur cases often involve medical malpractice, particularly surgery. The doctrine is not restricted to such negligence cases, however, as the following hypothetical illustrates.

HYPOTHETICAL

Eugene supervises a road repair crew employed by Pavement Plus, Inc. The county contracts road construction and renovation to Pavement Plus. Eugene's crew was filling potholes on Elm Avenue one spring day. One of Eugene's employees, Everest, improperly mixed the asphalt so that it would not harden adequately. This bad asphalt was used to fill the Elm Avenue holes. Rutherford, who lives on Elm Avenue, drove over the patched potholes a few days later. The asphalt collapsed and the front right tire of Rutherford's automobile wedged in a hole, bending the front axle.

Rutherford discovered that Pavement Plus had repaired the street, but had kept no record of the asphalt mixtures used.

Could Rutherford use res ipsa loquitur to shift the burden of proof? Evaluate the elements under these facts. Pavement Plus's foreman, Eugene, and an employee were under exclusive control of the weak asphalt used to fix the street. Asphalt does not normally collapse under vehicular weight unless it is improperly prepared or applied. The defendant is in the best position to prove that the mixture was suitable, as its employees prepared and applied the asphalt. Thus, res ipsa loquitur applies in this case, and the plaintiff need only prove what happened (i.e., his car was damaged when he fell through an asphalted hole that the defendant repaired). The defendant must now establish that its employees used reasonable care in preparing and applying the asphalt. As an aside, this problem also illustrates the value of retaining written records (in this case, of asphalt mixture) to document reasonable care.

Figure 6-7 summarizes proof of negligence and res ipsa loquitur.

SUMMARY

6.1. Negligence is the failure to use reasonable care to avoid injuring others or their property. Reasonable care is dependent upon the particular facts of each case. The key is the reasonableness or unreasonableness of the tortfeasor's actions under the circumstances.

6.2. There are five elements of negligence: duty of reasonable care, breach of duty, causation, proximate cause, and injury. The elements are considered sequentially. If any one is missing, then no negligence occurred.

Burdens of Proof and Rejoinder (Rebuttal)	Res Ipsa Loquitur
Plaintiff must generally prove the efendant's negligence beyond a preponderance of the evidence.	"The thing speaks for itself." This doctrine shifts the burden of proof to the defendant, who must disprove the presumed negligence.
	Elements: (1) the defendant's exclusive control over acts or objects that injured the plaintiff; (2) the plaintiff's injury must be one that ordinarily does not occur without negligence; and (3) the defendant is in best position to prove that he or she was not negligent.

FIGURE 6-7
Burden of Proof,
Burden of Rejoinder
(Rebuttal), and Res
Ipsa Loquitur

6.3. The duty of reasonable care is the tortfeasor's obligation to act reasonably to avoid injuring others. The tortfeasor does not owe this duty to everyone in the world, however; the injured party must fall within the scope of the tortfeasor's duty. This means that it must have been reasonably foreseeable that the plaintiff would be harmed as a consequence of the defendant's actions. This is called the reasonable plaintiffs theory. Only foreseeable plaintiffs (who were actually injured as a result of the defendant's conduct) may recover damages in a negligence lawsuit. Reasonable care is defined by the standard of the mythical reasonable person. Would a reasonable person have acted in the same way the defendant did, under the same or similar circumstances? The trier-of-fact decides how the reasonable person would have behaved. The reasonable person standard is adjusted to reflect the defendant's special skills or limitations.

6.4. The tortfeasor's actions must cause the victim's injuries. Causation under negligence is usually shown through cause-in-fact. Cause-in-fact states that but for the defendant's misconduct, the plaintiff would not have been harmed. When multiple tortfeasors are involved in producing the victim's injuries, however, but-for causation does not function well. An alternative causation theory, substantial factor analysis, states that each defendant is liable for the plaintiff's injuries if that defendant was a substantial factor in producing the harm. Joint and several liability holds multiple defendants liable for a plaintiff's injuries when those defendants combine to create the harm.

6.5. Proximate cause is different from causation. Proximate cause declares the line at which injuries are reasonably foreseeable. Inside the boundary are tortfeasors' actions that could reasonably have been anticipated to produce the victim's harm. Outside the perimeter are injuries that were not reasonably foreseeable as a consequence of the tortfeasor's behavior. This circle is sometimes called the zone of foreseeability. Some courts speak of proximate cause in terms of foreseeability and scope of duty. Other courts state that tortfeasors take their victims as they find them, which means that the particular injury the plaintiff suffered (usually due to some peculiar physical condition) is always considered foreseeable.

6.6. Damages must be proven in every negligence case. The plaintiff must prove that he or she suffered some actual loss as a result of the defendant's actions, whether physical injury, emotional injury, or harm to property. This loss is normally quantified in monetary terms as consequential damages.

6.7. The plaintiff most often must prove that the defendant was negligent in causing the plaintiff's injuries. This burden of proof calls for a preponderance of the evidence. Once established, the defendant has the burden of rejoinder, or rebuttal, to counter the plaintiff's prima facie case. In certain cases, however, the plaintiff is at a disadvantage in proving the defendant's negligence. Res ipsa loquitur allows the plaintiff to shift the burden of proof to the defendant. Thus, the defendant must disprove the plaintiff's allegations of negligence. Res ipsa loquitur applies in cases in which the defendant exclusively controlled the object or action that hurt the plaintiff; that the plaintiff's injury was one that ordinarily would not happen without negligence; and the defendant is in the better position to prove that he or she was not negligent.

REVIEW QUESTIONS

1. Provide a broad definition of negligence. What key factors are involved in analyzing negligence problems?

2. List the elements of negligence. How do they fit together? How do you apply each part to a particular problem?

3. What is duty? How does it relate to reasonable care? How do you define the scope of duty? What role does foreseeability play in scope of duty? What is the foreseeable plaintiffs theory? What is reasonable care? Who is the reasonable person, and why is he or she important in negligence analysis? Who defines this standard and how? How does the standard vary in different cases?

4. Define causation. What is cause-in-fact? But-for causation? How do direct and indirect causation differ? What is substantial factor analysis, and when is it used? How does it differ from joint and several liability? How is it similar?

5. Define proximate cause. What role does foreseeability play? What is the zone of foreseeability? How is scope of duty involved? What is taking the victim as you find him? How is it applied?

6. How are damages determined in negligence cases? What are consequential damages?

7. How is negligence normally proven? Who generally bears the burden of proof? The burden of rejoinder or rebuttal? When is negligence presumed? What Latin phrase is used to describe this presumption? What are this doctrine's elements, and how are they used?

PROBLEMS

In the following hypotheticals, determine if negligence exists and if the tortfeasor will be liable to the injured party. Identify the plaintiff(s) and the defendant(s).

1. Carlson Pledsoe operates a tanning salon. Meg McKinley is one of his customers. The salon uses tanning beds which are equipped with ultraviolet lights above and below the customer. These lights are

automatically regulated to control radiation exposure. Meg visited the salon and, while lying upon one of the tanning beds, fell asleep. The automatic regulator became stuck at maximum intensity. Meg was severely burned by the radiation.

2. Daniel Miller operates a backhoe for a construction company. Douglas Treefell hired the company to excavate a swimming pool in his back-yard. Daniel dug the hole using the backhoe. Unbeknownst to Douglas, Daniel, or the neighbors, the United States Army had used the area during World War II as an undercover training facility for minesweep-ers and several unexploded land mines remained buried in the ground. Daniel hit one with the backhoe shovel, which detonated the explosive. The shovel was blasted away from the machine, flew several feet into the air, and crashed into Douglas's new truck. The impact pushed the truck into the street, causing Debbie Wiley, a neighbor who was driv-ing a van down the street, to swerve into Douglas's front yard, hitting and felling an oak tree (that had been weakened by termites), which crashed into Robert Farlow's house next door to Douglas's home.

3. Bud Askew is a professional painter. He bought exterior latex paint to apply to Joe Barley's barn. The paint store incorrectly labelled the paint as oil-based when in fact it was water-based. Bud painted the barn without noticing the difference. After several severe summer thun-derstorms, the paint wore off.

4. Samantha Jacobs is a chemical dependency counsellor. One of her cli-ents, Happy Trevor, has been addicted to alcohol and tobacco for years. He has suffered severe liver damage. Samantha recommended hypnotherapy as a possible cure. Hypnosis is frequently used to treat chemical addiction, and Samantha is a state-certified hypnotherapist. After hypnotizing Happy, she discovered through regression that he had had a traumatic experience involving alcohol at age seven. She felt certain that this memory was the key to his current addiction. When Samantha attempted to bring Happy out of his hypnotized state, how-ever, she discovered, much to her dismay, that he had fixated and would not return to consciousness. As a result, Happy remained regressed at seven years of age. Psychiatrists indicated that this condi-tion occurs in only 1 in every 10,000 hypnosis cases.

5. Nellie Stevens plays guitar and sings in a rock-and-roll band at a local tavern, The Whiskey Slick. One of her songs, "Death to Phone Solicitors," contains certain explicit and graphically descriptive de-tails. Josie Aztway, a bartender at the Slick, suffers from paranoid delusions. She found Nellie's lyrics overwhelmingly absorbing, and she took them literally. After hearing Nellie's "Death" song at work one night, Josie returned to her apartment, loaded her revolver, drove downtown to a local telephone solicitation business, entered, and shot six operators.

PROBLEM ANSWERS

1. Carlson Pledsoe was negligent in maintaining a faulty tanning bed regulator that injured Meg McKinley (however, *see* the later discussion of factual gaps, which could reverse this conclusion).

   Proceed through the negligence elements sequentially. First, did Carlson owe Meg a duty of reasonable care? Because Meg was one of Carlson's customers, Carlson owed her a duty to provide reasonably safe tanning equipment. Did the scope of duty include Meg? Yes. It was reasonably foreseeable that Meg would be injured by radiation overdose if the tanning bed's regulator failed to function properly. Thus, Meg was a reasonably foreseeable plaintiff.

   Second, did Carlson breach his duty to Meg? Yes. By failing to maintain a properly operating tanning bed, Carlson failed to exercise reasonable care to avoid injuring Meg.

   Apply the reasonable person test: Would a reasonable person have operated a tanning bed with a defective regulator that could produce serious burns upon customers like Meg? The simple answer is no. Reasonable persons would have inspected the equipment to determine faults such as the broken regulator. Further, the reasonable person standard should be adjusted to reflect Carlson's expertise in tanning services. Expert testimony could be used to establish the professional community standard for inspecting tanning equipment amongst tanning salon businesspersons.

   Factual Gaps: This case raises certain "factual gaps" purposely omitted from the text summary. Namely, one needs to know how often Carlson inspected the tanning beds to determine if they were functioning correctly. If Carlson made inspections reasonably often (such as daily, or three times weekly, etc.), then, arguably, Carlson satisfied his duty of care to Meg by maintaining reasonably safe tanning equipment. The regulator may have gotten stuck by itself, with no indications of problems. Carlson could have inspected the bed immediately before Meg used it, and he might not have been able to detect any regulator problems.

   Assuming that you decide that Carlson failed to conduct timely or sufficiently thorough inspections, proceed to causation. Was Carlson's breach of duty the cause-in-fact of Meg's injuries? Yes. But for Carlson's failure to maintain a properly functioning tanning bed, Meg would not have been injured.

   Next consider proximate cause. Were Meg's injuries the natural and probable consequences of Carlson's providing a tanning bed with a defective regulator? Were Meg's injuries (severe burns from radiation overdose) reasonably foreseeable results, when the regulator stuck on maximum power? Yes. It was also reasonably foreseeable that Meg would fall asleep under the lights' warming and soothing effect.

Finally, Meg suffered significant physical injuries, so her damages are easily proven.

Res ipsa loquitur does not apply to this case, although Meg is in a disadvantaged position to prove that Carlson was negligent in maintaining the defective regulator. Some of the elements are satisfied. Carlson had exclusive control over the object producing Meg's injuries (the tanning bed). Carlson is in a better position to prove his lack of negligence than Meg is to prove his negligence. Carlson could prove that he (or his employees) routinely inspected the equipment, and that malfunctions could occur at any moment in a normally operating regulator.

However, Meg's injuries were *not* of the type that ordinarily would not happen without negligence. As previously noted, routine inspections might not locate a properly functioning regulator that suddenly and unexpectedly stuck during Meg's use.

Accordingly, the doctrine does not apply. Meg would have to prove that Carlson breached his duty by failing to conduct timely inspections, a question that, for purposes of this problem, has been left open for you to decide (as a trier-of-fact).

2. The key to this hypothetical is proximate cause (reasonable foreseeability of the injuries).

   This is one of those problems in which foreseeability of injury and scope of duty combine. Was it reasonably foreseeable that the injured parties' property would have been harmed as a result of the backhoe's detonation of buried, unknown Army land mines?

   There are several possible plaintiffs here (Douglas Treefell, Debbie Wiley, and Robert Farlow), and so, ordinarily, there would be many duties of reasonable care, and foreseeabilities of injuries, to define. But the zone of foreseeability stops the negligence analysis for all the plaintiffs at the same point.

   A single inquiry disposes of the case: Was it reasonably foreseeable that Miller's backhoe would detonate unknown, buried land mines, which would explode and produce its destructive sequence of events? No. Nobody involved in this case knew (or reasonably could have known) about the Army testing facility, which presumably had been secretly used nearly 50 years ago. Therefore, nobody involved in the case could have reasonably anticipated the presence of buried land mines and the resulting catastrophic events. Thus, all the plaintiffs were unforeseeable plaintiffs. Miller did not breach any duty to them vis-à-vis the land mines and his excavating. (There is a factual improbability in this hypothetical, though: namely, how could the houses in this subdivision have been built without somebody coming across these land mines sooner?)

3. The key to this hypothetical is Bud Askew's professional standard of care. Clearly, Bud owed his customer, Joe Barley, a duty of reasonable care to properly apply paint to Barley's barn. Obviously, the scope of duty included Barley's barn, as it was the direct object associated with Bud's negligence.

Did Bud breach his duty by failing to notice that the paint was water-based instead of oil-based? Yes. Expert testimony would establish painters' professional community standard. Any reasonable professional painter can immediately distinguish between water- and oil-based paints. Water-based paints are thinner and do not have the same texture or smell as oil-based paints, which, not surprisingly, have an oily, pungent, petroleum-like odor. By failing to notice this difference, Bud plainly breached his professional duty of care.

All the remaining negligence elements fall neatly into place. But for Bud's application of the wrong paint, the paint would not have worn off the barn after the thunderstorms; thus, cause-in-fact is established. Furthermore, proximate cause exists: it was reasonably foreseeable that water-based paints could not withstand severe summer rains, as expert testimony would confirm. Joe's barn was damaged, so compensable injury exists. Bud was negligent and hence is liable for Joe's damages.

4. This hypothetical concentrates upon professional standard of care and proximate cause's foreseeability of injury. Did Samantha Jacobs violate her professional duty of reasonable care in hypnotizing Happy Trevor, who remained in a fixated regression state? Expert testimony would probably indicate that Samantha had *not* breached the duty, since fixation occurs in only 1 out of every 10,000 hypnosis cases. Thus, the injury (fixation) was not reasonably foreseeable as a result of routine regression hypnotherapy. Accordingly, Samantha's treatment did not proximately cause Happy's injuries, and so no negligence liability would exist.

If one works sequentially through the negligence formula, the proximate cause question would not be reached. The analysis would end with the "no breach of duty" conclusion. However, for purposes of understanding the concepts, it is worth discussing proximate cause and foreseeability of injury.

5. The six telephone solicitation operators (or their estates) might try to sue Nellie Stevens for negligence, but they would lose. The key here is scope of duty—specifically, foreseeable plaintiffs theory. Was it reasonably foreseeable that Nellie's song would prompt a mentally ill individual (Josie Aztway) to gun down these six plaintiffs? No. These operators are unforeseeable plaintiffs. A reasonable person would not anticipate that a mentally unbalanced listener would act out song lyrics in this manner. Thus, Nellie did not owe the operators a duty of reasonable care in singing her songs publicly, and, accordingly, Nellie is not liable to these plaintiffs for negligence.

PROJECTS

1. Find a recent court opinion in your state that defines the elements of negligence. Do these elements differ from those discussed in this chapter? If so, in what ways?

2. In class or study groups, create your own hypotheticals using the negligence formula in this chapter. Then change the facts to alter the outcomes of the cases.

3. Brief *Banks v. City of Richmond,* 232 Va. 130, 348 S.E.2d 280 (1986). Did the Supreme Court of Virginia rule the defendant's omission to be the proximate cause of the explosion? Was there an intervening cause? Explain.

4. Brief *Bogovich v. Nalco Chemical Co.,* 213 Ill. App. 3d 439, 572 N.E.2d 1043 (1991). How did the Appellate Court of Illinois define proximate cause? What was the outcome of this case?

5. Brief *Adams Township v. Sturdevant,* 570 N.E.2d 87 (Ind. Ct. App. 1991). What was the Indiana Court of Appeals' definition of proximate cause and foreseeability? How did it decide this appeal?

CHAPTER 7
Special Negligence Actions

DATA-GRAPHIC TORTS

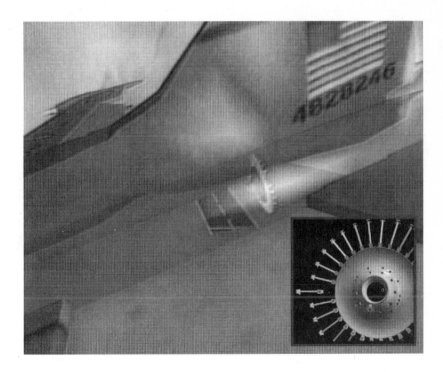

Tobias v. Jetstream Corp.

Jetstream Corporation operates a jet engine maintenance division. One of its primary customers is the United States Air Force. Jetstream has a rigid policy requiring all its employees to use only new parts to repair engines. However, the corporation was lax in enforcing this policy, as it did not control the source of engine parts. The common practice was for the repair crews themselves to order all parts. Nick Unstead, a chief mechanic, had been a Jetstream employee for 15 years and had repaired thousands of jet plane engines without any subsequent problems. One day,

Unstead worked with the crew repairing an engine fan on an Air Force F-190 jet. The job was highest priority, and the crew was working under extreme pressure to complete the job as soon as possible. Unstead knew that a replacement fan blade was needed, but that it might take over a week to receive it from the overseas parts manufacturer. Unstead knew that he could quickly obtain a used blade from a mechanic friend who worked for a national airline maintenance company. Unstead telephoned the friend and ordered the used part, which he installed two days later in the F-190. One month later, the used blade broke loose from the fan, because of metal fatigue, while the jet was conducting low-level, simulated bombing runs across an interstate highway. This mishap caused the plane's engine to shut down, and the plane crashed into a trailer park adjacent to the highway, killing several residents whose families (Tobias and others) sued Jetstream Corporation under vicarious liability theory (for its employee's negligence). Expert witnesses testified that, had the used blade not been installed, the engine would not have malfunctioned and the plane would not have crashed.

Is Jetstream vicariously liable for the negligence of its employee, Unstead? Under respondeat superior, the employer is liable only for an employee's torts committed within the scope of employment. Jetstream's policies established that employees could not install used parts to repair jet engines. However, this policy would not insulate Jetstream from vicarious liability, because Unstead was acting within the scope of his employment by repairing the engine, although he used improper parts. Jetstream did not properly enforce its rule and, thus, implicitly consented to its employees installing used parts. Thus, the corporation would be vicariously liable for Unstead's negligence in installing a defective fan part that proximately caused the plane crash and deaths.

DATA-GRAPHIC TORTS

Brewery v. West Militia Tile Co.

Arthur Brewery is a frequent customer of the West Militia Tile Company, a distributor of bath and floor tile. One evening, when Brewery was walking through the company warehouse to assist in filling a tile order, a light fixture attached to the ceiling suddenly broke loose and fell on Brewery's head. Brewery, as well as countless other customers, had often walked unhindered through the warehouse, with no suggestions from company employees that the premises were off-limits. Brewery sued West Militia for negligently maintaining its warehouse in an unsafe condition.

Brewery was an invitee, even in the warehouse. The company readily accepted customers' presence in the warehouse; accordingly, Brewery was implicitly invited to remain on these premises while his order was being filled. West Militia owed Brewery a duty of care to discover and correct hidden defects, such as the broken light. By failing to do this, West Militia breached its duty to Brewery and would be liable under negligence theory.

INTRODUCTION

In certain circumstances, negligence theory has evolved special legal concepts to apply to particular types of activities. These pieces of the torts puzzle have distinctive shapes and sizes.

Special negligence actions are cases involving certain well-defined activities. Special rules of negligence apply in these instances. The most common special negligence actions involve property ownership, employer/employee activities, and motor vehicle use. Theories of vicarious liability, in which someone is held accountable for the negligence of another person, and negligent infliction of emotional distress add unique and recognizable shapes to the puzzle.

The basic negligence formula discussed in chapter 6 applies to all special actions discussed in this chapter. Always keep this approach in mind when examining any negligence problem. However, each special action has its own peculiar analytical twists and turns that distinguish these from the other torts puzzle pieces. This chapter identifies and assembles the following pieces:

- Premises liability.
- Distinctions between trespassers, licensees, and invitees.
- Attractive nuisance.
- Bailment liability.
- Vicarious liability and respondeat superior.
- Negligent infliction of emotional distress.

7.1 PREMISES LIABILITY

Special negligence rules apply to owners and occupiers of land. **Occupiers** include individuals who do not own but use real estate, including tenants (lessees). For simplicity's sake, we will speak in terms of the owner.

LEGAL TERMS

occupiers
Individuals who do not own but use real estate, including tenants (lessees).

The term *occupier* may always be substituted for *owner,* because negligence theories apply to both.

Land Owner's Different Duties of Reasonable Care

As negligence law developed in the late nineteenth and early twentieth centuries, American courts devised different standards of reasonable care for land owners or land users. The distinctions depended upon who the injured party (plaintiff) was, in terms of the victim's purpose for being on the land where the owner's negligence was alleged to have occurred.

Victim's Status on Land Defines Scope of Duty

For example, under old common law, the land owner owed a different duty of reasonable care to the injured party depending upon whether the victim was a trespasser, a licensee, or an invitee. (These terms are explained later in this section.) Thus, the plaintiff's status as a trespasser, licensee, or invitee determined the scope of duty that the owner owed.

Modern Judicial Trends

Courts and legal scholars for decades have complained that this three-tier analytical approach is arbitrary and unnecessary. After all, ordinary negligence theory appears adequately equipped to establish the land owner's duty of reasonable care. If an owner acted unreasonably in maintaining his or her realty, and as a result a victim was harmed, then the owner should be liable. Regular negligence theory works well to produce a just result, say these critics.

Many courts have in fact abolished the three-tier land owner standards of care. The landmark case was *Rowland v. Christian,* 69 Cal. 2d 108, 443 P.2d 561, 70 Cal. Rptr. 97 (1968) (superseded by statute, as explained in *Perez v. Southern Pacific Transport Co.,* 218 Cal. App. 3d 462, 267 Cal. Rptr. 100 (1990)), in which the distinctions were ousted in favor of traditional negligence theory. Many states have followed the California Supreme Court's lead. Still, many courts continue to apply the three-tier system.

Land Owner's "Zero Duty" Toward Trespassers

Land owners owe no duty of reasonable care toward trespassers. Owners may not intentionally injure trespassers upon their real estate, but they need not search their realty and safeguard it for trespassers' unauthorized uses. Courts favoring this policy reason that a land owner should not be required to exercise ordinary reasonable care to protect a tortfeasor (i.e., trespasser) from harm. Because the trespasser is committing an intentional tort, negligence law insists only that real estate owners avoid intentionally injuring trespassers. Otherwise, the trespasser *assumes the risk* of entering someone else's land without permission.

Special Rule for Trespassing Children: Attractive Nuisance

Land owners owe a higher duty of reasonable care to trespassing children, however. The reasoning behind this special rule states that children, especially when young, are so inexperienced and naive that they may not fully appreciate dangers lurking upon the land. Therefore, owners must exercise ordinary, reasonable care to safeguard their realty for trespassing children who are enticed onto the land to investigate the dangerous condition that injured them. Young children are often attracted out of curiosity to investigate dangerous conditions on realty, such as abandoned wells, railroad tracks, swimming pools, or unused machinery. These alluring items are often hazardous, a fact that the trespassing child may not understand. The attraction element has given this special rule its name of **attraction theory** or, more commonly, **attractive nuisance**. If a trespassing child is injured as a result of having been enticed onto the land to investigate some dangerous condition, then the landowner is liable for such harm.

Restatement (Second) of Torts § 339

Many courts now follow § 339 of the *Restatement (Second) of Torts* and hence have discarded the attraction element to the theory. For these courts, it is sufficient that (1) the injury to the trespassing child was reasonably foreseeable; (2) the danger on the land presented an unreasonable risk of harm to trespassing children; (3) the danger on the land was artificial, meaning manmade rather than natural; (4) because of the child's youth, he or she could not appreciate the risks involved or did not discover (and understand) the threat; (5) the threatening condition was located at a place across which children were likely to trespass; and (6) the land owner failed to exercise reasonable care to protect trespassing children from the danger that caused the harm. Under this version of attractive nuisance, the danger did not have to entice the child onto the land. It is adequate that the child encountered and was hurt by a danger that he or she did not fully discern.

Beneath all its trimmings, *Restatement* § 339 is simply negligence theory applied to trespassing children. The basic negligence elements are there, and the reasoning is identical.

A number of jurisdictions depart from the *Restatement*'s artificial condition element. These courts would include natural dangers, such as streams, quicksand, or rock formations, as risks against which the land owner must take precautions to protect trespassing children.

LEGAL TERMS

attractive nuisance (attraction theory)
In the negligence law of many states, owners and occupiers of land owe a duty of ordinary, reasonable care to safeguard their realty for children who might trespass onto the property, having been enticed or attracted there out of curiosity.

HYPOTHETICAL

Maybelline is a student attending the local community college. She occasionally trespasses across Farmer Bob's cattle pasture when she walks from her apartment to campus. One day, while cutting across the land, Maybelline encountered Bob's prize bull, which was in a particularly agitated frame of mind. The bull charged and knocked Maybelline to the ground, injuring her. Is Bob liable?

Because Maybelline was a trespasser, Bob owed her no duty of reasonable care. Accordingly, she took her chances by walking across the pasture without permission. Bob would not be liable for her injuries.

Suppose that Maybelline were five years old and came upon Bob's farm to pet the "nice moo-moo." Attractive nuisance theory would hold Bob liable. Maybelline was enticed onto the realty by the animal which, due to her youth, she did not realize was dangerous. Bob failed to exercise reasonable care to protect trespassing children such as Maybelline from the risk of a free-roaming bull. The threat from the bull was unreasonable, as a child of Maybelline's age could not be expected to escape a charging bull. Young children are likely to be lured onto land to approach livestock. The dangerous condition was artificial, because Bob had placed the bull in the pasture to graze. Any of the attractive nuisance theories discussed previously would hold Bob accountable under these facts.

Suppose, instead, that Maybelline were a cat burglar who was breaking into Bob's barn late one night. Unbeknownst to Maybelline, Bob had wired a shotgun to the windows inside the barn; anyone raising the window frame would instantly be shot. Maybelline tried to enter through the window and was seriously hurt by the gun blast. Would Bob be liable?

Although Bob owed Maybelline (who was trespassing) no duty of reasonable care, he could not set a lethal trap for would-be burglars. Land owners cannot create an unreasonable danger to injure trespassers. Bob would be liable for Maybelline's injuries in this factual scenario.

Licensees Defined

Licensees are persons who have permission to be upon another's land. They are distinguishable from trespassers in that the land owner has consented to their presence upon his or her realty. This consent may be expressed or implied. Examples of licensees include social guests, such as friends who gather at a person's house to study or neighbors coming over to borrow tools; door-to-door salespersons or charitable solicitors (when the land owner has not prohibited their entry by posting warning signs); and frequent trespassers to whose incursions the land owner implicitly consents (such as when trespassers frequently use shortcuts that the land owner does not discourage through fencing or sign-posting).

Land Owner's Duty of Reasonable Care Toward Licensees

Owners owe licensees a duty of reasonable care in using the real estate. This includes the owner's obligation to correct known dangers (both artificial and natural) on the land. In other words, if the owner knows (or reasonably should know) that a hazardous condition exists on the realty, then he or she must exercise reasonable care in safeguarding licensees from these risks. For example, if an abandoned well has not been covered, and a travelling salesperson visits and falls into the well (which cannot be seen because of overgrown grass), then the land owner has breached his or her duty of reasonable care to the salesperson, assuming that the owner knew (or should have known) that the well was there and could not be detected.

For licensees, the owner is not required to discover and correct unknown threats on the land. For invitees, however, the owner is obligated to do this, as we shall see later.

HYPOTHETICAL

Irving owns an apartment building. Fundraisers for a local charity frequently solicit contributions from his tenants. Irving does not object to this solicitation, although he does not encourage it. Sterling is one of the charity's fundraisers. While visiting Irving's apartment complex, Sterling broke his leg when he fell through a rotten wooden stairway. Sterling could not see the rotting from the top of the steps, but the damage was evident if one looked up from below the stairway. Is Irving liable to Sterling?

Sterling is a licensee, since Irving permitted him to come onto the apartment premises. The key in this case is whether the rotten steps were a known hazard. Perhaps Irving did not know that the steps were rotten. However, Irving reasonably should have known that his apartment steps were dangerous. A building owner is expected to be aware of such easily discoverable risks, as it is easily foreseeable that a stairway user would be hurt if rotten steps collapsed. Thus, Irving would be liable for Sterling's injuries.

Suppose, instead, that Irving had posted signs clearly warning, "NO SOLICITORS ALLOWED! ALL TRESPASSERS WILL BE PROSE-CUTED!" Would he be liable for Sterling's injuries? In this version of the facts, Sterling would be a trespasser, and so Irving would not owe a duty of reasonable care to Sterling. Accordingly, Irving would not be liable for the harm to Sterling.

Suppose that Irving had posted such signs, but did nothing further to discourage solicitors from coming onto his premises. Suppose that

LEGAL TERMS

licensee
    Persons having permission to be upon another's land. This permission may be expressed or implied. In the negligence law of many states, owners and occupiers of land owe licensees a duty of reasonable care to correct known dangers on the real estate.

door-to-door salespersons and charitable solicitors, including Sterling, regularly visited the apartments with impunity. Under this set of facts, Irving has implicitly consented to the solicitors' presence, including Sterling's. Thus, Sterling would be a licensee.

Invitees Defined

Invitees, or *business invitees* as older court opinions call them, are persons invited upon the land owner's premises. Originally, the common law restricted the term to individuals invited onto premises for business purposes, such as customers to a grocery, clothing store, amusement park, or tavern. Modern cases, however, state that an invitee need not be seeking any business-related purposes when he or she enters another's real estate. It is sufficient that the land owner encourage the invitee to visit.

Usually, invitees are persons coming onto the land for some purpose that the owner wishes to serve. Commonly, this includes any business, but could also include nonprofit organizations, such as churches, soup kitchens, charitable hospitals, or even colleges.

Land Owner's Duty of Reasonable Care Toward Invitees

Land owners owe the highest duty of reasonable care to invitees. Owners must not only repair known dangers on the property but also must discover and correct unknown risks. This is a broader standard, requiring the land owner to take extra efforts to render his or her premises reasonably safe for invitees.

The logic underlying this stiffer standard of care suggests that an owner who invites someone onto his realty should be expected to exercise greater caution to insure that the premises are reasonably danger-free. After all, the invitee would not be on the land to begin with had it not been for the owner's invitation.

Invitees and Licensees Distinguished

Invitee is a subcategory of *licensee*, yet the terms are distinguishable. All licensees have the owner's implied or expressed permission to be on the land, but the land owner does not have to invite or encourage licensees to visit; rather, the owner may just passively tolerate the licensees' presence. With invitees, however, the owner impliedly or expressly invites them onto the real estate. This reflects the owner's active role in getting the invitees onto his or her land. Usually, the owner seeks customers for business; hence, courts often speak of business invitees.

Implicit or Express Invitation

The land owner's invitation to others to enter the premises may be expressed (e.g., a welcome sign outside a church, or a business posting its hours on its door) or implied (e.g., a business leaving its doors open during business hours).

Limited Areas of Invitation

Obviously, most land owners do not invite people into every nook and cranny of his or her property. Certain regions are off-limits. For example, most businesses have storage rooms, manager's offices, or machinery rooms that patrons are specifically discouraged from entering. Virtually any business has door signs warning "private," "authorized personnel only," "keep out," and similar prohibitions. The owner's invitation to invitees does not include such areas. If an individual were injured while visiting an off-limits zone, then that person would be considered merely a licensee, or perhaps even a trespasser (depending upon how sternly the warning was phrased— such as "no trespassing—keep out!"), rather than an invitee.

LEGAL TERMS

invitee
A person who has been invited onto the premises by the land-owner or occupier. This invitation may be expressed or implied. Owners and occupiers owe invitees a duty of reasonable care to discover and correct defects on the real estate. Invitees are sometimes called *business invitees* in older cases.

THE CASE OF THE FREE-FALLING FLIGHT ATTENDANT

The outcomes of premises liability cases often hinge upon subtle factual distinctions that place participants within one of the three familiar categories. Courts adhering to the three-tier approach are hesitant to discard the formula, despite the difficulties in its application, as the following case demonstrates.

Egede-Nissen v.
Crystal Mountain, Inc.
A93 Wash. 2d 127,
606 P.2d 1214 (1980)
(Supreme Court of Washington,
En Banc)
February 14, 1980

HICKS, Justice.
This is an action for personal injuries sustained by petitioner A. E. Egede-Nissen, a Norwegian national, when she fell from a chairlift at Crystal Mountain ski area. A Pierce County Superior Court jury found Crystal Mountain, Inc., negligent, assessed total

damages of $150,000, and found Egede-Nissen "contributorily negligent" to the extent of 55 percent.

Sidebar: Contributory negligence is one defense to negligence and is discussed in chapter 8. The jury probably intended to find the petitioner *comparatively negligent* to the extent of 55 percent. Contributory negligence would completely bar the plaintiff's recovery. Presumably, Justice Hicks placed "contributorily negligent" in quotation marks to imply this misstatement.

Crystal Mountain appealed and the Court of Appeals, Division Two, reversed and remanded for a new trial. [Citation omitted.] We agree with the Court of Appeals, although we base our conclusion on somewhat different grounds.

[. . .] Crystal Mountain, Inc., operates recreational ski facilities on public-owned land open to the public for recreational purposes. [On] April 25, 1973, plaintiff Egede-Nissen, a stewardess, and several members of her Scandinavian Airlines System (SAS) flight crew traveled to Crystal Mountain to picnic and sightsee. The ski lodge and chairlifts were not open for business, although the C-4 chairlift was running as an accommodation for three employees of a ski manufacturing company. No lift attendants were present.

From the loading area of the C-4 lift, the SAS group noted two or three skiers on the slopes above. Captain Hartvedt decided to ride the lift up to the skiers and look for and inquire about a picnic site. He boarded a moving chair and Egede-Nissen impulsively decided to accompany him. In her haste to board, she slipped and landed in a precarious position facing and grasping the chair with her lower torso and legs dangling below. Captain Hartvedt, occupying the same chair, attempted to stabilize her without himself falling from the chair.

Crystal Mountain employees working in the C-1 lift area had observed the foregoing situation develop and two of them immediately hastened to the C-4 lift, intending to assist Egede-Nissen. In the course of their efforts, one of the employees stopped the lift, restarted it and then stopped it a second time. The chairs on the lift swayed markedly at each stop. Following the second stop, Egede-Nissen's hold on the chair became insecure and she fell 30 feet to the ground, sustaining injuries.

Petitioner commenced this negligence action against Crystal Mountain in Pierce County Superior Court in June 1973. The case was not tried until November 1976, at which time it was vigorously, often heatedly, contested. A verdict was returned in favor of the plaintiff in the amount of $67,500.

A major legal question at trial was Egede-Nissen's status (invitee, licensee or trespasser) aboard the chairlift. Her status depended upon a factual determination whether Crystal Mountain had given adequate notice, by signs or barricades, that the C-4 lift was not in public operation. On that issue, the evidence was sharply in conflict.

[. . .]

We granted Egede-Nissen's petition for discretionary review to consider, *inter alia,* whether we should abandon the traditional common-law categories of entrants upon land and adopt a unified standard of reasonable care under the circumstances. [The court cited *Rowland v. Christian* in a footnote.]

Petitioner Egede-Nissen and amicus curiae urge this court to discard the categorical approach to landowner liability. Although we have questioned the common-law classification scheme in the past, we are not ready at this time to totally abandon the traditional categories and adopt a unified standard. [. . .]

[. . .] There is no serious dispute that [. . .] Egede-Nissen's status upon *entering* the Crystal Mountain area was that of a public invitee. [Citation omitted.] Accordingly, as to her, Crystal Mountain's duty was to maintain its premises in a reasonably safe condition. This duty, however, extends only to the "area of invitation"—that portion of the premises arranged so as to lead an invitee to reasonably believe it is open to her. [Citation omitted.]

Petitioner's status aboard the chairlift turned on the resolution of a factual dispute—whether Crystal Mountain had given adequate notice that the C-4 lift was closed to the public. Initially, Egede-Nissen's status was that of a public invitee, which status she would retain until adequately warned of limits to the area of her invitation. [Citations omitted.] If, however, petitioner unreasonably strayed beyond the area of invitation, her status would change from that of invitee to a licensee or trespasser, with a corresponding change in the duty owed to her by Crystal Mountain.

[. . .]

In the instant case, it was Crystal Mountain's theory that Egede-Nissen was at best a licensee and more properly a trespasser aboard the C-4 lift, to whom it owed a duty only to refrain from willful or wanton misconduct. While there was substantial evidence to support the trespasser theory, as pointed out by the Court of Appeals, [. . .] [a]s previously noted, her [Egede-Nissen's] status was dependent upon factual resolution.

The Court of Appeals also found [trial court jury] instruction No. 18 to be erroneous because it assumed petitioner to be an invitee as a matter of law. [. . .]

Egede-Nissen's status aboard the lift was dependent upon the scope of the invitation extended to her by Crystal Mountain. [Citation omitted.] The scope of the invitation was a contested matter to be resolved by the jury. As pointed out by the Court of Appeals, [citation omitted], the trial court erred in giving instruction No. 18, which assumed that Egede-Nissen had the status of an "invitee." The resolution of that question was dependent upon facts to be found by the jury. We hold that the trial court was sufficiently apprised of the defect in instruction No. 18 and that the giving of the instruction constituted reversible error for which a new trial is required.

[. . .]

As modified herein, the Court of Appeals is affirmed.

CASE QUESTIONS

1. In the Washington Court of Appeals' *Egede-Nissen* opinion, the lower court gave a detailed discussion of the "notice of lift closure" issue. As Acting Chief Judge Reed stated the majority opinion:

> The major factual dispute in the case revolves around the extent of defendant's efforts to cordon off the loading area of the C-4 lift or warn away visitors. Plaintiff's witnesses, the other SAS crew members, testified that the loading area was not blocked and that there were no warning signs present. In fact, Tollef Bakke, the SAS copilot, testified that the only writing he noticed were two phrases written on a blackboard: "400 yards to go" and "You see what you get." Captain Hartvedt also stated that he read the phrase "You see what you get" on the blackboard. In contrast, defendant's witnesses, all employees of Crystal Mountain, stated that the area was surrounded by metal rope and fencing, and that a "Sorry Lift Closed" sign had been posted.

Egede-Nissen v. Crystal Mountain, Inc., 21 Wash. App. 130, 584 P.2d 432 (1978). You can see how sharply the parties' witnesses disagree on this issue. Suppose you were a juror in the case. If you believed the plaintiff's witnesses over the defendant's, what would be the outcome of the liability issue? What if you believed the defendant's witnesses instead? Would the outcome change? Explain.

2. What reversible error did the trial court commit in this case? How did it influence the jury's decision?

3. As you can see from the reprinted opinion, the Washington Supreme Court affirmed the court of appeals' decision to reverse and remand the case for a new trial. Given the facts as presented in the preceding excerpts, how would you decide the plaintiff's status issue? Do you think that Egede-Nissen was a trespasser, licensee, or invitee with regard to the lift chair? Support your conclusion using the legal elements discussed in the opinion and the concepts discussed in this chapter.

4. What does *En Banc* mean, in the heading at the beginning of the *Egede-Nissen* opinion?

From a plaintiff's standpoint, being included as an invitee spells maximum tort relief—at least in terms of monetary damages. The following examples explore invitee cases.

HYPOTHETICALS

Elvis operates a shelter for homeless persons. Anyone forced to live on the streets is welcome at the facility. Jo Ellen frequently visits the shelter for free meals and a bed for the night. While sleeping one evening, Jo Ellen was stabbed by a loose, rusty wire through the mattress upon which she was lying. She had to undergo precautionary medical treatment for tetanus. Would Elvis be liable for Jo Ellen's injury?

Jo Ellen was an invitee, because she was homeless and Elvis expressly encouraged persons such as her to use his premises. Jo Ellen was injured as a result of a hidden danger (the loose wire) that could have been discovered if Elvis had inspected the mattresses for wear and tear. Thus, Elvis failed to exercise reasonable care to make the shelter reasonably safe for his patrons. As a result, one of his customers, Jo Ellen, was harmed, so Elvis is liable to her.

Danielle manages a local appliance store. Wayne came in one day to look for a new washer and dryer. Danielle showed Wayne a popular model. Wayne wished to see the units operate, but there were no electrical outlets nearby. Danielle went to her office to get an extension cord. Meanwhile, Wayne wandered through a set of swinging doors labeled "warehouse—employees only," hoping that he might find another salesperson who could locate an extension cord. Instead, he found a fork-loading truck that swerved around a wall and knocked Wayne to the ground, severely injuring him. The truck driver did not expect anyone to be in the area. Is Danielle liable to Wayne?

Wayne was an invitee when he visited the store to look for new appliances. However, he ceased to be an invitee when he entered the restricted area (the warehouse) without permission. Because he had been invited into the store originally, most courts would say that Wayne became a licensee once he entered the storeroom, as it is reasonably foreseeable that customers might mistakenly trespass into such a limited-access area. Danielle owed Wayne a duty of reasonable care to discover and correct known dangers on the premises. In this case, the fork truck was not threatening in and of itself, as a rotten stairway or improperly stacked boxes would be. The danger would be considered unknown, as it was not reasonably foreseeable that a patron would be hurt by a truck moving around a restricted-access warehouse. Accordingly, Danielle would not be liable for Wayne's injury.

Arguably, though, the threat of the fork truck harming a wayward customer *was* foreseeable, because the truck driver reasonably should have anticipated that patrons might enter the warehouse from time to time, looking for salespersons or restrooms. This would make the risk known, and arguably, Danielle breached her duty of reasonable care when her employee failed to watch for patrons while driving the truck through the warehouse. This reasoning is equally sound and persuasive. Once again, the shifting sands of negligence slip underfoot.

Using Traditional Negligence Theory in Land Owner Cases

As noted earlier, many courts have eliminated the trespasser/licensee/invitee approach in favor of regular negligence theory. Instead of forcing the injured party into one of these three categories, many courts simply ask the routine negligence questions: Was the injury reasonably foreseeable? Did the land owner's scope of duty include the victim? Did the owner cause the victim's injury? and so forth. Many courts, however, cling tenaciously to the older three-tier analysis. This demonstrates how entrenched precedent becomes; once a rule of law becomes settled, it is difficult to raze the monolith and renovate its concepts. The law changes at a snail's pace. More often than not, this provides valuable stability and predictability in legal problem solving. Nonetheless, it also makes legal principles slow to adapt to the rapid changes of our dynamic society.

Figure 7-1 summarizes the special negligence analysis for land owners and occupiers.

Another type of property may be the object of negligence. This is personal property, or chattels, which are the subject of bailments, discussed in § 7.2.

Duty to Trespasser	Land owner/occupier owes no duty of reasonable care; is required only to avoid intentional (or willful and wanton) injury.
Duty to Licensee	Land owner/occupier owes duty of reasonable care to correct known dangers on premises.
Duty to Invitee	Land owner/occupier owes duty of reasonable care to discover and correct unknown dangers on premises.
Traditional Negligence Theory	Applies regular negligence standards to determine land owner/occupier liability.
Duty to Trespassing Children (Attractive Nuisance Theory)	Land owner/occupier owes duty of reasonable care to protect trespassing children from artificial dangers on premises, when (1) injury to child is reasonably foreseeable, (2) danger presented unreasonable risk of harm, (3) child could not appreciate dangerous condition, and (4) danger existed at place at which children are likely to trespass.

FIGURE 7-1
Land Owners'/
Occupiers'
Negligence Liability

7.2 BAILMENTS

A **chattel** is personal property. Personal property includes everything that is not land, which is real property. Chattels include this textbook, an automobile, a cat, a bicycle, and the chewing gum a classmate just borrowed from another student.

A **bailment** exists when the personal property owner, called the **bailor**, delivers possession of his or her chattel to someone else, called the **bailee**, who keeps it until the bailor requests that the item be returned or delivered to someone else. Examples of bailments include attended pay parking garages, lockers at the college bookstore, dry cleaners, and commercial shippers. Any business in which the chattel owner transfers possession of the personal property to the bailee, who keeps it on the owner's behalf, creates a bailment relationship between owner and holder.

Bailee's Negligence Liability: Three-Tier Benefit Scheme

Historically, courts developed a three-tier approach to bailments, just as with land owners' negligence. First of all, the bailee must exercise reasonable care to safeguard the owner's personal property while the bailee possesses it. However, the standard of care differs depending upon who benefits from the bailment relationship.

Bailment Benefit Analysis

The bailor and the bailee often do not benefit equally in a bailment relationship. In some cases, only the bailor benefits. This is called a *bailment for the bailor's sole benefit*. For instance, suppose Ann asks Eleanor, her neighbor, to store Ann's automobile in Eleanor's garage while Ann is away on vacation. Ann is the bailor, because she owns the property. Eleanor is the bailee, because Ann delivered possession of the car to her. No payment is exchanged for this bailment; it is simply a friendly arrangement between neighbors. Eleanor gets nothing from the deal. Ann, as bailor, derives all the benefits, since her car is being protected from weather and theft in her neighbor's garage.

What if only the bailee benefits? For example, suppose Eleanor borrows Ann's lawn mower to cut her grass. Eleanor does not offer to pay for borrowing the mower, and Ann does not ask for anything in return. Ann, the bailor, receives no benefit. Eleanor, as bailee, gets to use the mower. This is *bailment for the bailee's sole benefit*.

Bailments that benefit only the bailor or bailee are often *gratuitous bailments*. This is because the nonbenefiting party does not receive any payment or compensation for his or her role in the bailment relationship. The foregoing illustrations are gratuitous bailments.

Most often, both bailor and bailee benefit. For instance, suppose Charles takes his overcoat to the dry cleaners. Charles, the bailor, owns the coat but delivers possession to the dry cleaners, the bailee, to clean the chattel. Charles will pay the bailee for dry cleaning, and in return he receives a clean overcoat. Both Charles and the dry cleaners profit from the bailment relationship. This is called a *mutual benefit bailment* and is typical of *bailments for hire,* in which the bailee is in the bailment business. Examples include pawn shops, attended pay parking lots, pay storage lockers, and commercial shippers.

Bailees' Different Standards of Care for Each Type of Bailment

When a bailment is for the sole benefit of the bailor, the bailee owes only a duty of slight care to safeguard the personal property from harm. **Slight care** is that degree of caution one uses when involved in relatively unimportant activities in which damage is not a concern.

With a mutual benefit bailment, the bailee owes a duty of ordinary, reasonable care to safeguard the chattel from damage. This is the standard defined in chapter 6.

LEGAL TERMS

chattel
Personal property, such as an automobile, a pet, clothing, appliances, this textbook, or a bicycle.

bailment
An arrangement in which the personal property owner (the bailor) delivers possession of the chattel to someone else (the bailee), who keeps it until the owner requests the item's return or delivery to a third party. In negligence law, different standards of care apply, depending upon who benefits from the bailment. For a bailment for the bailor's sole benefit, the bailee owes a duty of slight care to safeguard the chattel from harm. For a bailment for mutual benefit, the bailee owes a duty of reasonable care. For a bailment for the bailee's sole benefit, the bailee owes a duty of great care.

bailor
Personal property owner.

bailee
Person in possession of personal property that he or she does not own.

slight care
That degree of caution one uses when involved in unimportant activities in which damage is not a concern. This is the standard of care used in bailments for the bailor's sole benefit.

When a bailment benefits only the bailee, the bailee owes a duty of great care to safeguard the personal property from injury. **Great care** is an extraordinary degree of caution one uses when involved in exceedingly important activities in which extreme care should be used to avoid injury.

Modern Judicial Trends

In recent years, courts have begun to abandon the three-tier analysis for bailments, just as many have done for land owners' negligence liability. Instead, these modern courts apply regular negligence theory to decide if the bailee failed to exercise reasonable care in protecting the bailor's chattel from harm. This approach is easier to apply, because benefits analysis often is difficult to conceptualize. It is easier simply to ask whether the bailee used reasonable care in safeguarding the personal property.

LEGAL TERMS

great care
An extraordinary degree of caution one uses when involved in exceedingly important activities in which extreme care should be used to avoid injury. This is the standard of care applied in bailments for the bailee's sole benefit.

THE CASE OF THE STRIPPED CAR

Every bailee's nightmare is to have a chattel in his or her possession damaged or stolen. As the case excerpted here illustrates, sometimes a bailee can escape liability when the bailor fails to prove that the appropriate standard of care was violated. One wonders why this issue was not proven at trial.

Hobart v. P.J.'s Auto Village, Inc.
136 Vt. 287, 388 A.2d 419 (1978)
(Supreme Court of Vermont)
June 6, 1978

DALEY, Justice.

The plaintiff brought his vehicle to the defendant's place of business for certain repairs which the defendant undertook to perform. One night while the car was in a lot used by the defendant as a storage area for used cars and vehicles undergoing repair, some unknown person or persons jacked up the car and stole two wheels and tires. Damage occurred to the exhaust, suspension and brake systems when the car was lowered or fell to the ground unsupported by the missing wheels. The plaintiff brought suit claiming that his damages were proximately caused by the negligence of the defendant in failing to protect the vehicle from

vandals. In a trial by court, the defendant was found liable. He now appeals claiming the judgment is not supported by the trial court's findings of fact and conclusions. We agree.

[. . .] In the case of a bailment for hire the bailee is liable for injury to the property bailed that results from his failure to exercise due car and diligence in its preservation. The burden was upon the plaintiff to prove that the defendant did not exercise such care and was negligent.

It is also the well-established law that negligence, to be actionable, must be the proximate cause of the injury for which compensation is sought. [Citation omitted.]

The trial court found (1) that some automobiles awaiting service were stored outdoors overnight adjacent to that portion of the building containing the service department, (2) that the storage area was not enclosed by a fence or other structure, (3) that while the storage area was illuminated, it was not illuminated as brightly as another portion of the premises where other automobiles were stored, (4) that the business premises were unguarded at night except for routine police patrols at management's request, (5) that an L-shaped storage canopy effectively screened the storage area from the most likely direction of public view, [. . .] because the canopy was more brightly illuminated and the dealer had a policy of always filling the canopy at the close of business with a row of closely parked automobiles, and (6) at least one car dealer in the Burlington area maintains a fenced area for cars parked outside awaiting repairs.

Apart from the isolated instance of fencing by one other dealer in the locality, the trial court did not address the question of what precautions a reasonable garagekeeper would have taken under circumstances where he had knowledge of occasional vandalism to automobiles stored on his premises overnight.

In short, the plaintiff's evidence and the trial court's findings do not support its apparent conclusion, not specifically stated, that the defendant failed to exercise the care required of it and that such failure constituted negligence. Even if we were to assume that it did, there is no finding that such negligence was the proximate cause of the plaintiff's loss. Our reading of the record convinces us that the plaintiff's evidence would not support a finding of proximate cause even if one had been made.

Under these circumstances, since there is no basis for the judgment as rendered, we will enter judgment for the defendant.

Reversed; judgment for the defendant.

CASE QUESTIONS

1. Do you agree with the court that the plaintiff failed to prove a standard of care for garagekeepers? What about the one car dealer in the area who used fencing? Is that not sufficient proof, presuming the defendant did not counter with more persuasive evidence? Explain.

2. Do you agree with the court that the plaintiff failed to prove that the defendant's acts or omissions proximately caused the plaintiff's injuries? If you had been a juror at trial, how would you have decided this issue? Explain.

Both bailment benefit analysis and regular negligence theory can be applied to the following hypotheticals.

HYPOTHETICALS

Amelia owns several airplane hangers at the local airport. Many pilots store their single- and double-engine airplanes in the hangers for a monthly fee. Theresa owns a single-engine Piper aircraft that she uses for commercial aerial photography. In December, Amelia decided to cut costs by disconnecting electrical service to the hangers. Consequently, none of the stored planes could use their engine block heaters (which plug into electrical outlets for power). Theresa came to fly her plane during this time and found the engine damaged because the heater had no electricity to function. Is Amelia liable to Theresa?

This is a bailment relationship, because Theresa (owner/bailor) delivered possession of her chattel (airplane) to Amelia (storer/bailee) to store in the hanger. It is a mutual benefit bailment, as Amelia received a monthly payment from Theresa for storage fees, and Theresa's plane was protected from weather and theft.

Did Amelia breach her duty of reasonable care in safeguarding the bailment property? Because airplane owners commonly use block heaters to keep engines warm during cold winter months, and because Amelia provided electrical outlets for plane owners to use for precisely that purpose, then it was reasonably foreseeable that engine damage would result if the electricity were discontinued. Amelia failed to use ordinary, reasonable care in protecting Theresa's plane's engine from such harm. Accordingly, Amelia breached her duty and would be liable to Theresa for damages.

Melvin borrowed Janet's lawn mower to mow his grass. Janet loaned the mower for free. While using the mower, Melvin ran over a large rock in his yard and broke the mower's blade. Melvin could not see the rock because of the tall grass. Would Melvin be liable to Janet for the loss?

Janet is the bailor (owner) who delivered possession of her personal property (lawn mower) to Melvin, who is the bailee (possessor). This is a bailment solely for the bailee's benefit, since Janet received nothing from the relationship, and Melvin derived all the benefit from using the mower free of charge. Accordingly, Melvin owed Janet a duty of great care to safeguard her lawn mower from damage. Accordingly, Melvin should have closely examined the tall grass to find any hidden threats, such as large rocks that could break the blade if mowed over. Ordinary, reasonable care requires such a search. Thus, Melvin breached his duty of great care and would be liable to Janet for damaging the mower blade.

Mark asked Nye to keep his pet parrot while he was out of town. No payment was discussed, but Nye agreed. Nye did not know exactly what type of food the bird ate, so he telephoned a veterinarian, who recommended a particular brand of parrot food available at local pet stores. Nye fed the parrot for several days. One morning, Nye discovered that the bird was seriously ill. He rushed it to the veterinarian, who diagnosed that the bird had had an allergic reaction to the feed. Would Nye be liable to Mark for the veterinary expenses and injury to the parrot?

Nye (bailee/possessor) owed Mark (owner/bailor) a duty of slight care. This is because the bailment relationship was solely for Mark's benefit. Nye was not paid for his efforts. Mark benefited, though, since Nye watched over the bird in Mark's absence.

Did Nye fail to exercise slight care in feeding the bird? Nye telephoned a veterinarian to discover which type of food to use. A reasonable person, using slight care, would have done the same thing. Nye had every reason to believe the veterinarian's judgment, as veterinarians are professionals experienced in the care of animals such as parrots. Nye used slight care in feeding Mark's parrot, and accordingly Nye would not be liable to Mark for the bird's unfortunate injuries.

Figure 7-2 lists the special negligence analysis for bailments.

7.3 VICARIOUS LIABILITY

Previous chapters have presented hypotheticals in which someone acting on behalf of the defendant actually caused harm to the plaintiff. These have been employees of defendant businesses, in most problems. This illustrates one aspect of vicarious liability.

Vicarious Liability Defined

Vicarious liability is the liability of one person, called the *principal,* for the tortious conduct of another, subordinate individual, called the *agent,* who was acting on the principal's behalf. In negligence law, principal/agent relationships most often involve employers and employees. The situation is simple. The principal is the employer, who hires the agent (employee) to work on the employer's behalf.

Employment Not Essential Element

The principal/agent relationship, however, does not have to be that of employer and employee. Nineteenth- and early twentieth-century cases

LEGAL TERMS

vicarious liability
  The liability of one person (the principal) for the tortious conduct of another, subordinate individual (the agent) who was acting on the principal's behalf. In tort law, the main vicarious liability theory is respondeat superior.

Bailment for Bailor's Sole Benefit	Bailee owes duty of slight care to safeguard chattel from harm.
Bailment for Mutual Benefit	Bailee owes duty of ordinary, reasonable care to protect chattel from injury.
Bailment for Bailee's Sole Benefit	Bailee owes duty of great care to guard personal property from damage.
Traditional Negligence Theory	Applies regular negligence elements to determine bailee's liability.

FIGURE 7-2
Bailee's Negligence Liability in Bailment Cases

spoke of *master and servant*. This older classification suggested that the servant could work for the master without being paid. Thus, whether the agent is compensated for acting upon the principal's behalf is largely irrelevant to the issue of vicarious liability. Instead, focus upon this inquiry: Was one person acting on behalf of another? If so, a principal/agent relationship is present, and vicarious liability could exist.

Respondeat Superior

The employer is responsible for the negligence (or, for that matter, any torts) that his or her employees commit while working. This doctrine of vicarious liability is called **respondeat superior**, a Latin phrase meaning, "Let the superior answer."

Liability Within Scope of Employment

Not every employee activity gives rise to the respondeat superior doctrine, however. An employer is responsible for an employee's actions that fall within the scope of employment. **Scope of employment** can be described as the range of conduct that the employer expects the employee toperform as part of his or her job. For example, a truck driver is expected to make deliveries and pick-ups for her employer; these actions fall within the scope of employment. But the driver is not expected to rob a liquor store while driving the company truck; this action falls outside the scope of employment.

Outside Scope of Employment: Examples

Employers are not liable for torts committed by employees that fall outside the scope of employment. Thus, in the preceding example, the employer would be responsible if the truck driver negligently crashed into another vehicle while making deliveries. However, the employer would not be accountable for the robbery (which actually involves criminal behavior but illustrates the scope concept).

Suppose the driver used the truck for personal purposes while not working, thereby going against company policy. Assume that the driver then negligently collided with another vehicle. Would the employer be responsible? No. The driver was acting outside the scope of her employment. She was using the truck not for the employer's business, but for unauthorized personal use.

Coming and Going Rule

Employers are usually not vicariously liable for the negligence of their employees while the employees are coming to or going from work. This is called the **coming and going rule**. The only situation in which an

LEGAL TERMS

respondeat superior
Latin meaning "let the superior answer." A theory of vicarious liability in which the principal is responsible for torts committed by the agent. It is often used in employer/employee situations in negligence cases.

employer would be liable in such circumstances is if the employee were performing work-related activities while on the way to or from the job.

Frolic and Detour Rule

Employers are not vicariously liable for the negligence of their employees when employees go off on their own to handle personal matters, even though they might be performing work otherwise. For instance, suppose that, while making deliveries for her employer, the truck driver decided to stop by the local tavern for a quick drink. The employer probably did not authorize this sidetrack from the employee's assigned duties. Visits to the pub fall outside the employee's scope of employment. Thus, if the driver were negligent while pursuing activities unrelated to employment during ordinary working hours, this would be considered **frolic and detour**, and the employer would not be vicariously liable.

Independent Contractors

An **independent contractor** is someone who has entered into a contract with another person to perform a specific task. The independent contractor controls how he or she accomplishes the job. The individual hiring the independent contractor simply agrees to pay him or her for doing the chore. Independent contractors are distinguishable from employees in that the employer does not control how an independent contractor does the job. On the other hand, employers do control how their employees perform their tasks.

No Vicarious Liability for Independent Contractors

Persons hiring independent contractors are not vicariously liable for the independent contractors' negligence. The reasoning is that the independent contractor is engaging in his or her own work and should be responsible for his or her own negligence. The hirer is simply buying the independent contractor's finished service, and has nothing to do with how the independent contractor achieves the desired results.

For example, suppose Tom hires a plumber to install a new shower in his house. Tom has nothing to do with the actual job; in fact, he only lets the plumber in to go to work. The plumber negligently installs the water lines, so that the hot faucet is connected to the cold water line and vice versa. After the shower is completed, Tom's visiting friend is the first to use it and shockingly discovers the mistake, suffering severe burns. Is Tom vicariously liable to his friend for the plumber's negligence? No. The plumber was an independent contractor. Tom had no say in how the plumber completed the job. Tom merely paid the final price after the

scope of employment
The range of conduct that the employer expects the employee to perform as part of his or her job. Under respondeat superior theory, the employer is liable for the torts of an employee when the employee was acting within the scope of his or her employment.

coming and going rule
Rule used when employees commit torts while coming to, or going from, work. In respondeat superior cases, this rule helps decide whether an employee's actions fall outside the scope of employment.

frolic and detour rule
Rule used when employees commit torts while sidetracking from regular work activities. In respondeat superior cases, this rule helps decide whether an employee's actions fall outside the scope of employment.

independent contractor
A person who has entered into a contract with another to perform a specific task. Persons hiring independent contractors are not liable for the independent contractors' torts under vicarious liability.

plumber did the work. Thus, Tom cannot be vicariously liable for the plumber's negligence. Instead of suing Tom, his friend should sue the plumber.

THE CASE OF THE UNYIELDING POSTAL CARRIER

Scope of employment can be a fuzzy line in some cases. Courts sometimes struggle to apply the coming and going rule, as this case reveals. Although the concurring opinion suggests that the rule can be effortlessly applied, the majority, in its reading of the facts, discerned more subtle employment-related activities for which vicarious liability could exist.

Konradi v. United States
919 F.2d 1207 (7th Cir. 1990)
(U.S. Court of Appeals,
Seventh Circuit)
November 29, 1990

POSNER, Circuit Judge.
While driving to work early one morning, Robert Farringer, a rural mailman, struck a car driven by the plaintiff's decedent, Glenn Konradi, killing him. The suit is against the United States under the Federal Tort Claims Act, 28 U.S.C. §§ 1346(b), 2671 *et seq.* [. . .] The basis of [plaintiff's] claims is that Farringer's negligence in failing to yield the right of way to Konradi at an intersection was the cause of the accident. The district judge dismissed the suit on the government's motion for summary judgment. He ruled that the accident had not occurred within the scope of Farringer's employment by the Postal Service, which let off the Service [. . .].

The parties agree that the question whether the accident occurred within the scope of Farringer's employment is governed by Indiana law, [citations omitted], that under Indiana law it is a question of fact [citation omitted], and therefore that the judge was right to dismiss the case on summary judgment only if no reasonable jury, presented with the evidence that was

before the judge when he ruled, could have answered the question in the plaintiff's favor. [. . .]

The general rule is that an employee is not within the scope of his employment when commuting to or from his job. As the Supreme Court of Indiana put it the last time it addressed the issue, more than three decades ago, "an employee on his way to work is normally not in the employment of the corporation." [Citation omitted.] The rub is "normally" [. . .]. In *State v. Gibbs,* 166 Ind. App. 387, 336 N.E.2d 703 (1975), the employer furnished the employee with a car for use on the job but also allowed him to take it home at night. The accident occurred while he was driving home, and the employer was held liable. In *Gibbs v. Miller,* [152 Ind. App. 326, 283 N.E.2d 592 (1972)], the employer was held liable for an accident that occurred when its traveling salesman, who used his own car to make his rounds, was driving home for lunch from an appointment with a customer; he had other appointments scheduled for that afternoon. On the other hand, in *City of Elkhart v. Jackson,* 104 Ind. App. 136, 10 N.E.2d 418 (1937), which also involved an employee driving the company car at lunch time—this time he was returning to work after lunch when the accident occurred—the accident was held to be outside the scope of employment. [. . .] In *City of Crawfordsville v. Michael,* 479 N.E.2d 102 (Ind. Ct. App. 1985), the employee was using the company car (actually truck) for personal business on his day off when the accident occurred; he too was held not to have been acting within the scope of his employment.

It is impossible to find the pattern in this carpet without a conception of what the law is trying to accomplish by making an employer liable for the torts of his employees committed within the scope of their employment and by excluding commuting from that scope—"normally." The Indiana decisions are few and not articulate on these issues [. . .].

[. . .] The liability of an employer for torts committed by its employees [. . .] when they are acting within the scope of their employment [is] the liability that the law calls "respondeat superior." [. . .]

[. . .] But the law has to draw some lines for ease of administration, and a rough-and-ready one is between accidents on the job and accidents off the job—including accidents while commuting—in recognition of the fact that the employer's ability to prevent accidents by employees is normally much less when the employees are not at work. Indiana recognizes, however, that the line is indeed a rough one [. . .].

The Postal Service, Farringer's employer, requires its rural postal carriers to furnish their own vehicle (Farringer's was a pick-up truck) in making their rounds. [Citation omitted.] The alternative would be for the Service to buy or lease mail trucks for these carriers to use. [. . .] The Postal Service's rule pretty much guarantees that its mailmen will drive to and from work, and by doing this it increases the amount of driving [. . .]. One cost of more driving is more accidents, and this cost can be made a cost to the Postal Service [. . .]. Farringer's postmaster required the postal carriers to take the most direct route in driving to and from work, and hence not to divagate for personal business. Nor was the carrier to stop for such business, or give anyone a ride. [. . .]

The rules of commuting that the postmaster has imposed upon his carriers may [. . .] reflect a belief that the work of a rural deliveryman begins when he gets into his car in the morning and ends when he gets out of it in the evening. [. . .] Of course the two *Gibbs* cases are factually different from our case—every case is factually different from every other case—but that is no warrant for refusing to follow them in this case unless the factual differences between them and this case are connected with a difference in principle.

[. . .] [T]he imposition of liability on the Postal Service [may] be consistent with most of the Indiana cases [. . .]. By driving to and from work Farringer conferred a *benefit* on his employer because he was bringing an essential instrumentality of the employer's business. [. . .] The employer exerted substantial *control* over the employee's commuting, as shown by the regulations discussed earlier. And finally the employee while commuting was in the *service* of the employer [. . .].

[. . .] [T]he district court acted prematurely in granting summary judgment. [. . .] [T]he dismissal of the United States is reversed and the case remanded for further proceedings consistent with this opinion. [. . .]

MANION, Circuit Judge, concurring.

[. . .]

Indiana law is clear that, with very limited exceptions, an employee is not within the scope of his employment while driving to and from work. [. . .] Unless we have some exceptional circumstance, a rural postal worker driving to work is on his own and not within the scope of his employment. [. . .] [T]here is virtually no evidence that Farringer was in the scope of his employment. Farringer was driving his own car to work, not the government's. He was not providing any benefit to the government while en route; his job did not begin until he reached the post office to sort and pick up his mail for delivery. He was not, as in *Gibbs v. Miller,* going home for lunch and to do some paperwork in between business appointments, while receiving payment for mileage incurred on the trip. He was not, as in *State v. Gibbs,* properly driving a state-owned vehicle home from work following the day's activities, while on call 24 hours a day. Rather, he was simply travelling to work. Until he is at work, Indiana does not impose his misdeeds on the employer.

[. . .] I do not agree with this court that the "employer exerted substantial control over the employee's commuting, as shown by the regulations discussed [. . .]."

CASE QUESTIONS

1. Do you agree with the majority or the concurring opinion on the question of whether the employee was acting within the scope of his employment? Explain.
2. Do you believe the majority's decision would have satisfied Judge Manion if Farringer had been driving a postal truck instead of his own vehicle? Why or why not?
3. Suppose Farringer had already sorted his mail the previous night and had it with him the day of the accident. Would his driving to work then have been within the scope of employment, according to Judge Manion's approach? Explain.

Motor Vehicle Vicarious Liability

Since the first half of the twentieth century, courts ruled that passengers in automobiles could be held vicariously liable for the driver's negligence. Using this analysis, if the automobile occupants were involved in a joint enterprise, such as a family travelling to a single destination, then the driver's negligence could be imputed to the passengers. This outcome may seem unfair, because a passenger has no actual control over how the driver operates the vehicle. Legal commentators have long criticized this type of vicarious liability. The better principle, long employed by the courts, holds the vehicle owner vicariously liable for the negligence of a driver other than the owner. For instance, suppose Linda's younger brother is driving her car negligently. He crashes into a motorcyclist, injuring her. Under vicarious liability, Linda would be accountable for her brother's negligence, because he was carelessly using her vehicle and injured another person as a result.

This concept is based upon public policy. Automobile owners are more likely to have insurance to cover injuries produced by a driver's negligence.

Many state legislatures have enacted statutes imposing vicarious liability on owners for the negligence of others who drive their vehicles. These are sometimes called *motor vehicle consent statutes.*

HYPOTHETICALS

Sarah is a physician. Her nurse's aide, Gladys, draws blood from patients as part of her responsibilities on the job. One day, Gladys used a contaminated needle and thus infected a patient when she drew blood for testing. Would Sarah be vicariously liable for Gladys's negligence?

Gladys was performing a specific job assignment on Sarah's behalf. Drawing blood falls within Gladys's scope of employment. Under respondeat superior, Sarah would be accountable for Gladys's negligent act of using a contaminated needle and infecting a patient.

Suppose Gladys worked for a blood bank that routinely did blood draws and tests for area physicians. Under this scenario, Sarah would not have control over how Gladys acted. Gladys's employer is the blood bank, which would be an independent contractor in relation to Sarah. Accordingly, Sarah would not be accountable for Gladys's negligence.

Fargo is a fast-food restaurant manager. Mitchell is one of his employees. Fargo asked Mitchell to drive across town to a soft drink supplier and pick up additional carbonated water. While on this errand, Mitchell stopped by the post office to check his mail. As he was leaving the post office parking lot, he failed to look both ways and collided with another vehicle. Would Fargo be vicariously liable for Mitchell's negligent driving?

Although Mitchell was running a business-related errand on Fargo's behalf, stopping by the post office to check personal mail falls outside Mitchell's scope of employment. This is frolic and detour. Thus, Fargo would not be responsible for Mitchell's negligent conduct.

Suppose Fargo had been a passenger in Mitchell's car during this incident. By driving together to get the soft drink items, Fargo and Mitchell would have been involved in a joint enterprise. Furthermore, Fargo (as the boss) could have controlled his employee, Mitchell, and instructed him not to stop at the post office. By permitting Mitchell to check his mail, Fargo implicitly consented to Mitchell's detour. This would place the detour within the scope of Mitchell's employment. Assuming that no statutes stated differently, Fargo would be vicariously liable.

Figure 7-3 outlines vicarious liability.

Vicarious Liability	Liability of principal for negligent actions of agent serving on principal's behalf. Commonly involves employer/employee relationships.
Respondeat Superior	"Let the superior answer": Doctrine through which employers may be held vicariously liable for employees' negligent actions committed within the scope of employment.
Scope of Employment	Range of conduct that employer expects of employee during performance of assigned employment responsibilities.
Coming and Going Rule	Employers are not vicariously liable for employees' negligence while employees are coming to and going from work, unless employer has specifically requested employee to carry out a specific work-related task during such times.
Frolic and Detour Rule	Employers are not vicariously liable for employees' negligence when employees deviate from assigned tasks within scope of employment. Usually involves employees going off on their own to pursue personal needs.
Independent Contractors	Employers are not liable for independent contractors' negligence, because I.C.'s act independently and are responsible for their own conduct.
Motor Vehicle Vicarious Liability	Motor vehicle owners and passengers may be held vicariously liable for the driver's negligence if they are involved in joint enterprise. Liability may also be established in motor vehicle consent statutes.

FIGURE 7-3
Vicarious Liability

7.4 NEGLIGENT INFLICTION OF EMOTIONAL DISTRESS

As discussed in chapter 3, **emotional distress** consists of mental anguish caused by a tortfeasor. This condition includes fright, anxiety, shock, grief, mental suffering, shame, embarrassment, and emotional disturbance. The tort exists when the tortfeasor inflicts psychological injury on the victim. Chapter 3 discussed intentional and reckless infliction of emotional distress. The elements of negligent infliction of emotional distress are similar, except that the tortfeasor acted negligently to produce the psychological harm. **Negligent infliction of emotional distress** consists of: (1) Outrageous conduct by the tortfeasor, which (2) the tortfeasor reasonably should have anticipated would produce (3) significant and reasonably foreseeable emotional injury to the victim; when (4) the tortfeasor breached his or her duty of reasonable care to avoid causing such emotional harm to the victim; and (5) the victim was a reasonably foreseeable plaintiff. Here, ordinary negligence theory is superimposed over the basic emotional distress infliction formula discussed in chapter 3.

Extra Elements in the Common Law

These generalized elements of negligent infliction of emotional distress are synthesized from those of many jurisdictions. Different courts apply various special requirements to negligent infliction cases, and it is always wise to check the rules and formulations of the particular jurisdiction in which your case lies.

Impact Rule

A minority of courts insist that some physical impact accompany the emotional injury. Thus, the tortfeasor must negligently do something that physically touches the victim if the victim is to recover damages for negligent infliction of emotional distress. This is often called the **impact rule**, and it has been severely criticized in the legal literature and judicial decisions.

The purpose of the impact requirement is to protect against false claims of emotional distress. Because mental anguish is largely invisible, courts at the turn of the century felt that the defendant had to make contact with the plaintiff to justify compensating something as easy to fake as mental harm. Modern courts utilizing the impact rule have seen impact in almost any physical touching. Something as casual as putting one's hand on a classmate's shoulder would be considered sufficient contact to satisfy the impact rule. Hence, it would seem that, as a safeguard against faked claims of emotional distress, the physical impact requirement does little or nothing to ensure honesty and sincerity for allegations of mental hurt.

Physical Manifestations Rule

The majority of courts have abandoned the impact rule in favor of the **physical manifestations rule**. This requires that, in addition to mental suffering, the plaintiff must experience physical symptoms as a result of the emotional distress. This rule is also thought to protect against bogus claims of emotional injury. After all, if a victim experiences some physical malady associated with an emotional harm, such as an ulcer, hives, sleeplessness,

LEGAL TERMS

emotional distress
Mental anguish. In the intentional torts called intentional and reckless infliction of emotional distress, the mental anguish is caused by the tortfeasor's outrageous conduct.

negligent infliction of emotional distress
Outrageous conduct by the tortfeasor which the tortfeasor reasonably should have anticipated would produce significant and reasonably foreseeable emotional injury to the victim. By his or her actions, the tortfeasor must breach the duty of reasonable care, and the victim must be a reasonably foreseeable plaintiff.

impact rule
Rule used by a minority of courts in negligent infliction of emotional distress cases. For the victim to recover under this rule, the victim must have suffered some physical contact from the tortfeasor's actions.

physical manifestations rule
Doctrine applied in negligent infliction of emotional distress cases. Under the rule, the plaintiff may recover damages if he or she suffered physical symptoms accompanying the mental anguish.

weight loss, or bowel dysfunction, then the probability is that the emotional harm is genuine.

Zone of Danger Rule

What happens when the negligent action occurs to someone else, and the plaintiff is a bystander who witnesses a negligent injury to another person? Could the tortfeasor be liable to the bystander for negligent infliction of emotional distress? Consider an example. Suppose parents witnessed their child being struck by a negligent driver. Would the parents have a cause of action against the driver for negligent infliction of emotional distress?

No impact occurred to the parents, although they may suffer physical manifestations as a result of witnessing their child's injury. The proper question, however, may be phrased in ordinary negligence terms: Did the driver owe (and breach) a duty of reasonable care to the parents by injuring their child? Did the driver's actions cause the parents' emotional suffering? Does proximate cause exist? Were the parents injured?

Certainly, the driver could not reasonably anticipate that any bystander would suffer emotional distress as a result of the driver's negligent act of hitting a pedestrian. There must be some way to limit the scope of duty (and, hence, the range of foreseeable plaintiffs). Courts have attempted to establish such limits by creating the **zone of danger rule**. Under this rule, only bystanders who fall within the zone of danger can recover for negligent infliction of emotional distress. In other words, these individuals must have been threatened by the original negligent action (e.g., negligent driving of a vehicle) and have reasonably feared for their own safety.

Family Relationships Rule

Other courts have restricted recovery in negligent infliction cases to bystander plaintiffs who are related to the victim who they witnessed being injured. This may be called the **family relationships rule.**

Sensory Perception Rule

Still other courts have insisted that the bystander perceive the traumatic, negligent event directly through the senses (e.g., seeing the collision; hearing the child's screams; feeling the heat of the car exploding; smelling the burning clothing). This may be labelled the **sensory perception rule**.

California Approach

The California courts were first to produce a further evolutionary development in negligent infliction law. In *Dillon v. Legg,* 68 Cal. 2d 728,

441 P.2d 912, 69 Cal. Rptr. 72 (1968), the California Supreme Court jettisoned the zone of danger rule and focused upon pure foreseeability. The straightforward question was, simply: Was the emotional injury reasonably foreseeable, given the tortfeasor's actions? This analysis neatly handled bystanders as well as immediate victims of negligent conduct. The court produced the following guidelines to decide the foreseeability issue:

1. The bystander's closeness to the emotionally disturbing incident *(physical proximity)*

2. The bystander's relationship to the injured party *(family relationships rule)*

3. The bystander's personal perception of the emotionally distressing occurrence *(sensory perception rule)*

4. Physical manifestations arising from the emotional distress.

The *Dillon* approach has been both praised and debunked by other courts and legal scholars. It presents another twist in negligent infliction cases, in a continuing attempt to clarify the circumstances in which a plaintiff may hold a defendant liable for this type of negligent tort.

sensory perception rule
Doctrine used in negligent infliction of emotional distress cases. Under the rule, a bystander may recover damages if he or she witnesses a tortfeasor injuring another person, so long as the bystander perceives the event directly through his or her own senses.

THE CASE OF THE RETURN OF THE LIVING DEAD

In *Decker v. The Princeton Packet, Inc.,* partially reprinted in chapter 3, the New Jersey Supreme Court held that a false obituary was not defamatory per se, when published without malicious intent or additional defamatory information. The opinion also discussed intentional and negligent infliction of emotional distress. Review chapter 3's reprint (in § 3.8) for the relevant facts.

Decker v. The Princeton Packet, Inc.
9116 N.J. 418, 561 A.2d 1122,
85 A.L.R.4th 797 (1989)
(Supreme Court of New Jersey)
August 8, 1989

[. . .]

Finally, the [trial] court concluded that plaintiffs were not entitled to any recovery based on any claims for negligent or intentional infliction of emotional distress. It rejected plaintiffs' negligent-infliction-of-emotional-distress claim because New Jersey case law does not allow recovery for the negligent infliction of emotional distress outside the zone-of-risk and family-observation theories.

Plaintiffs appealed to the Appellate Division, which upheld the trial court's ruling [. . .].

[. . .] [P]laintiff alleged that the publication of the false obituary based on an unsigned death notice left at defendant's office without any attempt to ascertain its truth or falsity constituted negligence that caused her emotional distress. These injuries included the loss of her job in part due to the obituary [. . .] and the aggravation of emotional distress.

The tort involving the negligent infliction of emotional distress can be understood as negligent conduct that is the proximate cause of emotional distress in a person to whom the actor owes a legal duty to exercise reasonable care. [Citation omitted.] Thus, to establish liability for such a tort, a plaintiff must prove that defendant's conduct was negligent and proximately caused plaintiff's injuries. The negligence of defendant, however, depends on whether defendant owes a duty of care to the plaintiff, which is analyzed in terms of foreseeability. "[L]iability should depend on the defendant's foreseeing fright or shock severe enough to cause substantial injury in a person normally constituted." [Citation omitted.]

While the foreseeability of injurious consequences is a constituent element in a tort action, foreseeability of injury is particularly important in the tort of negligent infliction of emotional harm. This reflects the concern over the genuineness of an injury consisting of emotional distress without consequent physical injury. In these situations, there must be "an especial likelihood of genuine and serious mental distress, arising from special circumstances, which serves as a guarantee that the claim is not spurious." [Citation omitted.] In emotional distress cases, there has been "a constant concern about the genuineness of the claim."

The progression has been from denying recovery unless the emotional distress is accompanied by physical impact [citation omitted], to permitting recovery if the emotional distress results in physical injury, [citation omitted]. More recently, we have found a sufficient guarantee of genuineness, even in the absence of physical injury, if the plaintiff perceives an injury to another at the scene of the accident, the plaintiff and the victim are members of the same family, and the emotional distress is severe. [Citations omitted.] Thus, recovery for negligent infliction of emotional harm requires that it must be reasonably foreseeable that the tortious conduct will cause genuine and substantial emotional distress or mental harm to average persons. [Citations omitted.]

Unless a plaintiff's alleged distress is truly genuine and substantial, the tort of negligent infliction should not be broadened to permit recovery of damages. [. . .] Thus, in the *Buckley* case, the Court observed that plaintiff's emotional distress "complaints amount to nothing more than aggravation, embarrassment, an unspecified number of headaches, and loss of sleep," and, as a matter of law, could not constitute severe mental distress sufficient to impose liability. [Citation omitted.]

[. . .]

In this case, the emotional distress alleged by Marcy Decker resulting from the false report of her death, and, derivatively, the emotional distress assertedly experienced by Ms. Decker's son and mother, are not materially different from that described in cases like *Buckley* [citation omitted], in which the injury is not sufficiently palpable, severe, or enduring to justify the imposition of liability and the award of compensatory damages. Rather the alleged emotional distress approximates the subjective reactions of ordinary persons who feel victimized by the false report of death, namely, annoyance, embarrassment, and irritation. [. . .] [T]here is no suggestion in the record that any serious or substantial distress on the part of Ms. Decker and her family would be particularly foreseeable. These considerations dictate rejection of the claim for the negligent infliction of emotional distress under these circumstances as a matter of law.

CASE QUESTIONS

1. Do you agree with the court that the plaintiff and family's emotional distress was not reasonably foreseeable? How would a newspaper reasonably expect a person and family to react to reading an erroneous obituary for which no attempt at verification was made?
2. How does the court's discussion of the elements of negligent infliction of emotional distress compare with this chapter's presentation?

The diversity of negligent infliction of emotional distress formulas used in different jurisdictions makes analysis dependent upon a specific state's version. The following hypothetical considers the varieties discussed in this section.

HYPOTHETICAL

Heddison owns an apartment building. Skyler and Melville are brothers who share an apartment. One day, while barbecuing on their apartment balcony, Skyler stepped upon rotten floorboards, which collapsed. Heddison had known about this dangerous condition for months but did not correct it. Skyler fell through the balcony floor and hung upside down by one leg 30 feet above the ground. Meanwhile, Melville, who was waxing his car in the parking lot below, became very upset upon seeing this situation develop. As he ran upstairs to assist his brother, Skyler fell and suffered debilitating injuries. Subsequently, Melville began having horrible nightmares involving endless falling. He would awaken nightly in cold sweats. He lost weight, had little appetite, and developed a phobia about heights. This phobia made it extremely difficult for Melville to continue his occupation as a roofing installer. Heddison's liability to Skyler is an issue of land owner liability, which we discussed at the beginning of this chapter. Would Heddison be liable to Melville for negligent infliction of emotional distress?

Clearly, Melville suffered no physical impact as a result of Heddison's negligence. Melville did not come into contact with the rotten balcony when it gave way. In states following the impact rule, Melville could not recover damages against Heddison for negligent infliction.

In states following the zone of danger rule, Melville was not sufficiently close to the dangerous balcony to be threatened by its condition. He was not even below the point at which Skyler fell, which would have placed him at risk. Under the zone of danger test, Melville could not recover.

In jurisdictions following California's approach, it was reasonably foreseeable that Melville would be emotionally harmed by witnessing Skyler's life-threatening situation, which Skyler became involved in because of Heddison's negligent maintenance of the balcony. Melville is Skyler's brother, so the family relationship test is met. Melville saw Skyler dangling from the balcony and knew that he could fall and be killed. This satisfies the sensory perception rule. Melville was standing close to the accident site, and thus met the physical proximity standard. He also displayed physical symptoms resulting from his mental anguish. All of the *Dillon* criteria have been satisfied. Accordingly, Heddison would be liable to Melville for negligent infliction of emotional distress, under the California theory.

Figure 7-4 illustrates the various analytical approaches to negligent infliction of emotional distress.

Common Elements *(applying standard negligence theory to emotionally distressing conduct)*	(1) outrageous conduct by tortfeasor, when (2) tortfeasor reasonably should have anticipated that behavior would produce (3) significant and reasonably foreseeable injury in plaintiff, (4) tortfeasor breached duty of reasonable care, and (5) victim was foreseeable plaintiff.
Impact Rule	Plaintiff must experience physical impact from defendant's actions to recover for negligent infliction of emotional distress.
Physical Manifestations Rule	No physical impact is required, but plaintiff must experience physical symptoms associated with mental anguish that defendant caused.
Zone of Danger Rule	Bystander witnessing negligent injury to third party must have been immediately threatened by the negligent activity.
Family Relationships Rule	Bystander must be a family relative of the person injured by the tortfeasor's negligent act.
Sensory Perception Rule	Bystander must perceive with his or her senses (sight, hearing, smell, touch, taste) the injury to another person as a result of the tortfeasor's negligent act.

FIGURE 7-4
Elements of
Negligent Infliction
of Emotional Distress

SUMMARY

7.1. In premises liability, owners and occupiers of land owe special duties of reasonable care to individuals who are injured while visiting the premises. Traditionally, courts have defined these duties differently, depending upon the injured party's status on the realty. There are three such distinctions: trespasser, licensee, and invitee. Land owners owe no duty of reasonable care to trespassers; they must simply refrain from intentionally injuring trespassers. Special rules, called attractive nuisance theory, apply to trespassing children. Licensees are persons that the owners permit to come onto their real estate. To licensees, land owners owe a duty to correct known dangers on the premises. Land owners owe a duty to discover and correct unknown risks on the premises for invitees, who have come onto the premises at the owners' expressed or implied invitation. The owner may limit the places on the land to which such invitation extends. Many courts have abandoned this three-tier analysis in favor of regular negligence theory.

7.2. Chattels are personal property. They are the subject of bailments. In a bailment relationship, the chattel owner (bailor) delivers possession of the property to another person (bailee) who keeps the object until the bailor asks for its return or delivery to someone else. The bailee owes the bailor a duty of care to safeguard the bailment property from harm. This duty depends upon which party benefits from the bailment. This is called bailment benefits analysis. If the bailor alone benefits, then the bailee owes only a duty of slight care with regard to the chattel. If both bailor and bailee benefit, then the bailee owes a duty of ordinary, reasonable care. If only the bailee benefits, then the bailee owes a duty of great care. Recent court decisions have moved away from these distinctions toward regular negligence theory in bailment cases.

7.3. Vicarious liability is the liability of one person (principal) for the negligent actions of another (agent). Many vicarious liability situations involve employer/employee relationships. Under the doctrine of respondeat superior, the employer must answer to the injured party for the employee's negligence when the employee has acted within the scope of his or her employment. This normally involves assigned tasks during normal working hours. Special rules apply for employees coming to and going from work, and for employees who frolic and detour from assigned tasks to pursue personal pleasures. A person hiring independent contractors is not vicariously liable for their negligence. Many states have motor vehicle consent statutes holding a vehicle owner liable for another driver's negligence.

7.4. Negligent infliction of emotional distress occurs when the tortfeasor engages in outrageous conduct that produces a reasonably foreseeable mental injury in a reasonably foreseeable victim. Many states have different rules to decide negligent infliction cases. A few courts require that the tortfeasor cause some physical impact to the emotionally distressed victim. Many courts hold that mental anguish is recoverable when accompanied by physical manifestations or symptoms. Others allow bystanders to recover when they witness negligent injuries to other people when the bystanders fall within the zone of danger. Courts that follow California's reasoning base liability upon foreseeability, using physical manifestations, physical proximity, family connection, and whether the bystander witnessed the injury to determine the outcome of negligent infliction litigation.

REVIEW QUESTIONS

1. Define the three classes of plaintiffs to whom land owners and occupiers owe duties of reasonable care.

2. Describe the land owner/occupier's duty of reasonable care to trespassers. Does the rule apply to all trespassers?

3. What is attractive nuisance? To which type of plaintiffs would the doctrine apply? Why is the land owner/occupier's duty of reasonable care different for these plaintiffs?

4. Discuss the land owner/occupier's duty of reasonable care to licensees. How do licensees differ from trespassers? From invitees?

5. What duty of reasonable care does the land owner/occupier owe to invitees? Why and how are invitees distinguishable from licensees and trespassers?

6. Explain how you might use traditional negligence theory to determine land owners'/occupiers' liability to persons injured on the real estate. Do you find this approach easier than the three-tier analysis discussed in problem 1? Why or why not?

7. What are bailments? Who is the bailor and the bailee? Which one owes the other a duty of reasonable care? Why?

8. What is bailment benefits analysis? How is it used to determine the standards of reasonable care? Would traditional negligence theory be easier to apply? Why or why not?

9. Define vicarious liability. What types of relationships involve this theory? What is respondeat superior? Explain scope of employment, the coming and going rule, and the frolic and detour rule. Why are these important to your analysis? How does vicarious liability relate to independent contractors? To motor vehicle owners or passengers?

10. Explain negligent infliction of emotional distress. What are its elements? In what types of factual situations would the tort apply? Describe the different analytical approaches to this tort. Define the impact rule, the physical manifestations rule, the zone of danger rule, the family relationships rule, and the sensory perception rule. How

have the California courts combined these concepts in negligent infliction cases?

━━━━━━

PROBLEMS

In the following hypotheticals, determine which type of special
negligence action applies, if any. For sake of convenience, use the three-
tier analysis for landowner/occupier liability, as well as bailment benefit
analysis.

1. "Softy" Clydesdale rents an apartment from Whisperwood Property
   Management, Inc. His next-door neighbor, Leslie Steymore, frequently
   visits to watch basketball on Softy's big-screen television. Softy had a
   can of aerosol cleaner in his utility closet. He set the can too close to
   the gas furnace, and the can slowly became overheated. One evening
   while watching the game, Leslie dropped and broke a glass. She
   opened the utility closet to fetch a broom to clean up the mess. Unfortunately, the cleaner can exploded just as she opened the closet door,
   injuring her severely.

2. Emily Walters owns a pasture outside of town upon which she grazes
   cattle and horses. Ted Virtue sometimes crosses the pasture as a short-
   cut to work. All around the property are posted signs stating in clear,
   red-and-black letters, "NO TRESPASSING! YES, *YOU!*" One day
   Emily saw Ted cutting across her land and warned him not to continue
   doing so in the future. Ted ignored the warning. Weeks later, Ted fell
   into a mud bog (which he could not see, because it was covered by
   fallen leaves). He sank to his chest and could not escape. He remained
   there for three days until a passing postal carrier stumbled upon his
   predicament. Ted suffered from severe malnutrition and exposure from
   the incident. As a result, he contracted pneumonia and was hospitalized
   for two weeks.

3. Davis Marlowe operates a beauty shop. Margaret Vestibule comes in
   regularly for perms and haircuts. One of Davis's employees, Flower
   Wilson, absent-mindedly left her electric shears on the seat of one of
   the hair dryers. Davis did not notice the shears when he had Margaret
   sit in that chair to dry her newly permed hair. Unknown to everybody,
   the shears had an electrical short. When Davis turned on the hair dryer,
   the shears shorted out and electrocuted Margaret, who was unknowingly sitting against the shears.

4. Susan Rayfield hired Grass Goddess, a lawn care company, to fertilize
   and water her yard. One of the company's employees, Sylvester Pell,
   incorrectly mixed the fertilizer so that it contained 12 times too much
   potassium. Pell applied this mixture to Susan's grass. Honey Kinfinch,
   Susan's neighbor, came to Susan's party that night and played volley-
   ball in the backyard. She frequently fell and rolled on the grass while

diving to return the ball over the net. The next day, Honey developed a painful rash all over her body. She usually noticed these symptoms, although less severely, when she ate bananas, which are high in potassium.

5. John Stokely is a sales executive for a local automobile dealership. He often drives to the manufacturing facility 150 miles from the dealership to check on new orders. John's employer reimburses him for gasoline, food, and lodging, and provides John with a dealer car to drive. While driving to the manufacturing plant, John decided to stop by his cousin's house for dinner. His boss accompanied him on the visit "to get a decent meal for a change." While on the way there, John collided with and injured a motorcyclist.

6. Tilford Matthews has a five-year-old son with whom he often plays catch in the front yard. Sometimes the wind catches their ball and blows it into the street. Tilford has warned his son never to chase the ball into the road, but one day, when the ball blew into the street, Tilford's son ran after it. A truck driver swerved and struck the boy with the edge of the vehicle's bumper. The child suffered only a few bruises and scrapes. Tilford, however, developed a nervous twitch, ulcers, and an extreme sensitivity to sudden movements. He lost weight and experienced terrible nightmares about the incident.

PROBLEM ANSWERS

1. Leslie Steymore was an invitee, as she was a social guest of Softy Clydesdale. In other words, Softy expressly consented to Leslie's presence in his apartment, by allowing her to visit to watch television. Softy had a duty of reasonable care to correct known dangers on the premises. Since Softy originally set the aerosol can next to the furnace, he reasonably should have anticipated that the can could overheat and explode, causing injuries such as Leslie's. Accordingly, Softy would be liable to Leslie for negligence.

2. In this premises liability hypothetical, it is unclear whether Ted Virtue was an adult or a minor. This ambiguity was intentional, to see if the reader noted its importance.

   For purposes of discussion, assume, as seems probable, that Ted was an adult trespasser. The facts announced that Ted crossed Emily Walters's land on his way to work. Because children under age 12 are not usually employed, we may safely assume that Ted was at least a teenager and, more likely, an adult.

   Emily Walters had posted many "no trespassing" signs; furthermore, she plainly warned Ted against further trespassing. Accordingly, Emily owed no duty of care to Ted. He assumed whatever risks he encountered while trespassing upon Emily's land, including the mud bog within which he became trapped. Emily did not intentionally injure Ted. Thus, Emily would not be liable for negligence for Ted's injuries.

What if Ted had been between ages 12 and 18? Would the outcome of the case have been different, under attractive nuisance theory? No. As a teenager, Ted reasonably should have observed Emily's warning and "no trespassing" signs. He could have exercised greater caution while continuing to trespass. Attractive nuisance generally applies for younger children who cannot readily appreciate the dangers posed by trespassing. Ted clearly could have recognized the risks. Thus, attractive nuisance theory would not apply.

3. This hypothetical poses negligence issues for premises liability and vicarious liability.

    Margaret Vestibule was an invitee, because she was one of Davis Marlowe's regular customers invited to patronize his business. Accordingly, Davis owed Margaret a duty of reasonable care to inspect the premises to discover and correct known and unknown dangers. Clearly, Davis should have been aware of the electric shears left on the dryer seat. Further, through reasonable inspection of the shears, Davis could have discovered the electrical short. Thus, Davis breached his duty of care to Margaret and would be liable for negligently causing her injuries.

    The second issue is vicarious liability. Is Davis responsible for Flower Wilson's negligent actions? Flower breached the duty of care by leaving the dangerous shears where someone would sit. Further, Flower should have recognized the electric short, simply by using the shears. Thus, Flower was negligent. Under respondeat superior, Flower's negligence may be imputed to Davis, her employer. Davis is responsible for Flower's negligent acts that fall within the scope of her employment. Flower's careless placement of the defective shears clearly falls within this scope. Thus, Davis would be vicariously liable to Margaret for Flower's negligence.

4. This hypothetical involves issues of vicarious liability and premises liability. The analysis should focus upon Susan Rayfield's liability to Honey Kinfinch for the latter's severe allergic reaction to potassium.

    Under vicarious liability, the issue may be phrased as follows: Is Susan liable for the negligence of Grass Goddess's employee, Sylvester Pell, under respondeat superior? Or is the company an independent contractor?

    The company (and its employee) are independent contractors. Although Susan hired the firm, it controlled how Susan's lawn was fertilized. Susan had no say in how the company performed its tasks. Thus, under vicarious liability, Susan would not be liable to Honey for the latter's injuries.

Would Susan be liable to Honey under premises liability? Honey was a social guest, as Susan expressly consented to Honey's presence at the party. Moreover, Susan invited Honey onto the premises for a specific purpose that Susan wished to serve (namely, to hold a party). Arguably, then, Honey was more than a mere licensee—she was an invitee.

This distinction is critical to the hypothetical's outcome. If Honey were a licensee, then Susan's duty of reasonable care only required her to correct known dangers on the premises. However, if Honey were an invitee, then Susan's duty required her to discover and correct unknown dangers, such as the excessive potassium treatment. If the invitee standard applies, then Susan would be liable for Honey's injuries. If the licensee standard applies, Susan would not be liable.

Most courts would hold that Honey was a licensee, because the common law routinely defined social guests in this category. But a persuasive argument may be made that the invitee standard applies. Arguably, Honey's injuries were not reasonably foreseeable, as an acute allergic reaction to potassium is medically unusual. However, under "taking the victim as you find him" analysis, Susan would still be liable, provided that Honey were defined as an invitee.

5. There are two issues involved in this hypothetical. First, assuming that John Stokely was negligent in colliding with the motorcyclist, is John's employer liable under respondeat superior for the cyclist's injuries? Second, again assuming John's negligence, is John's boss vicariously liable, as a passenger pursuing a joint enterprise?

Under respondeat superior, John's employer is liable for John's negligence committed within the scope of employment. John's actions fall within this scope because he was driving to the manufacturing facility on business. John was not engaged in frolic and detour by going to his cousin's for dinner, because the company anticipated John's stopping for meals while travelling to the manufacturing plant. The fact that John's boss accompanied him to his cousin's validates the business-related nature of the meal stop. If John were negligent in hitting the cyclist, then his employer must answer for the negligence through vicarious liability.

What about John's boss's liability as a passenger, under the old common law rule? Because John and his boss were engaged in a joint enterprise (i.e., driving to the plant), the boss could be held vicariously liable for John's negligence. However, there is almost certainly a relevant state statute that would affect this issue.

6. This hypothetical involves negligent infliction of emotional distress. There is a threshold consideration—namely, was the truck driver negligent toward Tilford Matthews's son? This is intentionally ambiguous in the facts, again to see if the reader spotted the issue.

Presume, for the sake of argument, that the driver was negligent toward Tilford's son. Say the driver was speeding when he struck the child and, applying the elements, negligence can be easily demonstrated vis-à-vis the driver and child.

Now proceed to the negligent infliction question. Here, the liability would be the driver's toward Tilford. First, consider whether the elements have been satisfied. Was the truck driver's conduct outrageous? Recall from chapter 3 that outrageousness is defined according to the reasonable person standard: would a reasonable person have suffered substantial emotional anguish as a result of the tortfeasor's actions? It is reasonable that, as a parent, Tilford would suffer mental trauma from observing his son being struck by a speeding trucker. The driver reasonably should have anticipated that, if he struck a child, an onlooking parent would be emotionally distraught. Thus, Tilford's mental anguish was reasonably foreseeable. The driver breached his duty of reasonable care to avoid causing such emotional harm to Tilford, by striking his son while speeding. As the injured child's parent, Tilford is clearly a reasonably foreseeable plaintiff, for emotional distress purposes.

This case would be determined by the so-called extra elements. In those few states adhering to the impact rule, Tilford could not recover, as he was not physically impacted by the driver's negligent action. Nor was Tilford within the zone of danger, since he was several feet safely removed from the collision site. However, Tilford suffered physical symptoms caused by the emotional distress, which satisfies the physical manifestations test. As the child's father, Tilford also satisfies the family relationships test. Further, Tilford saw and heard the collision; accordingly, he satisfies the sensory perception test. In states following the impact rule and zone of danger rule, Tilford could not recover against the driver for negligent infliction of emotional distress. However, in states following the physical manifestations, family relationships, or sensory perception rules, Tilford could recover. Under *Dillon v. Legg,* Tilford could recover, because his mental anguish was reasonably foreseeable, given the driver's actions, and the court's four guidelines have been met.

PROJECTS

1. Which special negligence actions discussed in this chapter are included in your state's common law? Are any controlled by statute? Has your state legislature enacted a motor vehicle consent statute?

2. Brief *Boyles v. Kerr,* 806 S.W.2d 255 (Tex. Ct. App. 1991). You may wish to review the court's discussion of invasion of privacy as a refresher for chapter 3. For purposes of this project, however, focus on the negligent infliction of emotional distress issue. How did the court rule on this point?

3. Brief *Sussman v. Florida East Coast Properties, Inc.*, 557 So. 2d 74 (Fla. Dist. Ct. App.), *review denied*, 574 So. 2d 143 (Fla. 1990). How did the Florida Court of Appeals define "scope of employment"? Do the coming and going rule or the frolic and detour rule apply in this case? Why or why not?

4. Brief *Biggs v. Brannon Square Associates*, 174 Ga. App. 13, 329 S.E.2d 239 (1985). Did the court find attractive nuisance theory applicable in this case? What approach to premises liability did the court use?

CHAPTER 8
Defenses to Negligence

DATA-GRAPHIC TORTS

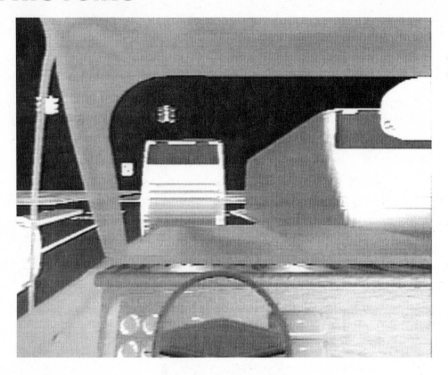

Calloway v. Dunne

Dennis Calloway was driving on State Road 31, a paved two-lane highway, during a sunny March afternoon. The weather was clear and dry. Directly ahead of Calloway was an 18-wheel semi-truck driven by Howard Longford. Ahead of Longford's truck was a large delivery van driven by Agnes Dunne. Calloway could not see Dunne's truck ahead of Longford's. All three vehicles were driving northbound, and all were driving at approximately the same speed (40 m.p.h.). Calloway was "hugging" Longford's bumper, with only five feet of distance separating the two vehicles. Suddenly, without signalling, Longford's truck pulled off the road. Before Calloway could apply his brakes, he collided with the rear end of Dunne's truck. Longford later stated to police that he had swerved to avoid colliding with Dunne's truck, which had stopped without warning. Dunne later stated that she had stopped suddenly to avoid a large pothole in the road. The police later noted that the pothole could easily have been avoided without stopping. Calloway told the police that he could not possibly have stopped or avoided crashing into Dunne, who "had no business stopping in the middle of the highway in the first place." Calloway sued Dunne.

This problem illustrates comparative negligence. Calloway was contributorily negligent in driving so close to Longford. A reasonable person would not tailgate another vehicle at 40 m.p.h. on a two-lane highway, where sudden speed changes occur frequently. It was reasonably foreseeable that Calloway would rear-end Dunne's vehicle in such a situation. However, Dunne was more negligent in stopping on the highway with two vehicles closely following. Applying comparative negligence, the jury might determine a 60/40 percent negligence split (Dunne 60 percent, Calloway 40 percent).

DATA-GRAPHIC TORTS

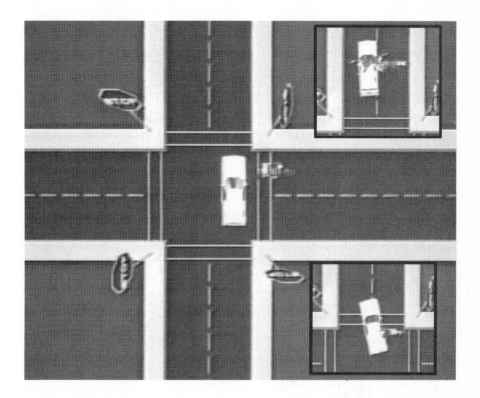

Danners v. Wilson

First Street is an east-west street intersecting Main Street, a north-south road. Buddy Wilson approached the intersection driving his automobile north on Main Street. Driving west on First was Toni Danners, riding a motorcycle. Neither Danners nor Wilson was speeding, but both also ran stop signs. Danners struck the side of Wilson's car and was hurled over the top, suffering serious injuries. Danners sued Wilson for negligently running the stop sign. Wilson countered that Danners was contributorily negligent.

It is easy to conclude that Wilson negligently ran his stop sign and contributed to causing the collision. But, by also running her stop sign, Danners contributed to her own injuries. Under traditional contributory negligence theory, Danners could recover nothing from Wilson, even if Wilson were mostly responsible for the accident.

The unfairness of this outcome suggests that comparative negligence would be a more equitable approach. Using comparative negligence, the jury could apportion the liability of both Wilson and Danners. Given the fact that both ran stop signs, the jury might split the negligence percentages at roughly 50/50.

DATA-GRAPHIC TORTS

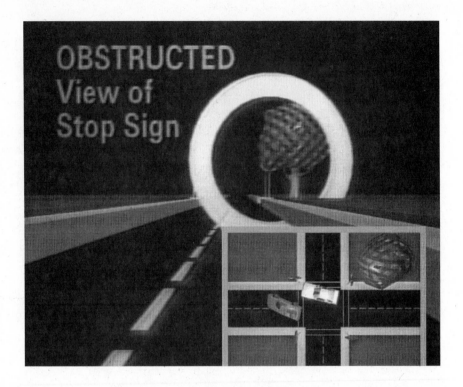

Tomey v. Davies

At Baker Street and Elm Avenue is a four-way-stop intersection. Baker is a north-south street; Elm runs east-west. Heading east on Elm, Sylvia Davies drove up to and stopped at the intersection. Approaching at 40 m.p.h. (the posted speed limit), heading north on Baker, was Jill Tomey. Tomey could not see the posted stop sign facing her direction, which was obscured by a tree's foliage. Out of the left front of her windshield, Tomey saw Davies's vehicle stopped and, assuming that she (Tomey) had the right-of-way, continued toward the intersection without braking. Tomey glanced out her right window when she heard a sudden loud noise in the distance. Meanwhile, Davies had proceeded into the

intersection, anticipating that the approaching Tomey would stop. Tomey did not stop but, instead, collided directly with the side of Davies's automobile, severely injuring Tomey.

Tomey sued Davies for negligence. Davies replied that Tomey ran the stop sign and thus was contributorily negligent in causing all of her injuries. Tomey responded, first, that she could not see the stop sign because of the tree leaves blocking it from view. Therefore, Tomey could not have anticipated that she had to stop, and thus did not breach her duty of care to herself or Davies. Further, Tomey replied that Davies saw Tomey fast approaching the intersection and had the last clear chance to avoid the collision by remaining stopped until Tomey had passed.

INTRODUCTION

Tort defenses are an important protection for defendants. They provide legal justification for the defendants' actions. These defenses introduce new, colorful pieces to the torts puzzle, which is now two-thirds complete.

Defendants' defenses excuse negligent behavior. In effect, defenses provide defendants with a blame-shifting weapon. Negligence defenses examine any plaintiff misconduct that was involved in causing the plaintiff's injuries. Even though the tortfeasor was negligent toward the victim, the tortfeasor's mischief is forgiven (totally or partially) because of the victim's participation in producing his or her injuries.

The pieces to be located and assembled in this chapter include:

- How negligence defenses are used.
- Contributory negligence.
- Last clear chance.
- Comparative negligence.
- Assumption of risk.
- Statutes of limitations.

8.1 HOW NEGLIGENCE DEFENSES ARE USED

Negligence defenses are peculiarly shaped pieces of the torts puzzle. It is easy to confuse them with other pieces. Always remember these basic analytical rules:

1. *Negligence defenses are used only by the defendant against the plaintiff.*
   Put more generally, these defenses are responses to negligence allegations. The party alleged to have been negligent can use defenses against the party alleging negligence. In cases involving counterclaims, in which the defendant counter-sues the plaintiff, remember that the defendant becomes a counter-plaintiff against the original plaintiff, who becomes a counter-defendant, at least as far as the counterclaim is concerned. The same holds true for third-party complaints and answers.

2. *Negligence defenses are applied only in response to the plaintiff's allegations that the defendant acted negligently.*
   Again, in counterclaims and third-party claims, remember who is the alleging party and who is the alleged wrongdoer. In a counterclaim, the defendant might allege that the plaintiff acted negligently toward the defendant. Re-title the parties to reflect their new roles toward each other with respect to the counterclaim. The counter-defendant (i.e., the plaintiff) would be entitled to use negligence defenses against the counter-plaintiff (i.e., the defendant).
   The same is true for third-party claims. Recall that defendants may become third-party plaintiffs, bringing third-party defendants into the

litigation through cross-complaint. The scenario is this: A plaintiff sues a defendant, alleging that a tort has been committed. The defendant cross-sues a third-party defendant for that third party's participation in committing the tort. Negligence defenses are available to the third-party defendant against the third-party plaintiff's negligence claims.

3. *Ask who is alleging negligence and who is alleged to have been negligent.*

The alleged tortfeasor is the person who may utilize defenses. A simple analogy might assist in remembering how negligence defenses are applied. Suppose Kelly throws a snowball at Mel. Mel blocks the snowball with a garbage can lid as a shield. Kelly (throwing the snowball) is the plaintiff, and the snowball itself is the accusation that Mel was negligent. Mel is the defendant, who allegedly committed the tort. Mel's shield is the negligence defenses discussed in this chapter. Mel avoids liability (i.e., being struck by the snowball) by using his shield to deflect the plaintiff's negligence allegations. Kelly, the snowball (accusation) thrower, does not use the shield, since she is doing the throwing. Only the intended recipient of the snowball (Mel, the defendant) needs to block the attack with the shield.

8.2   CONTRIBUTORY NEGLIGENCE AND LAST CLEAR CHANCE

With this fundamental approach in mind, it is time to begin piecing together these tort puzzle pieces. We begin with contributory negligence.

Contributory Negligence Defined

Contributory negligence is the plaintiff's negligence that contributed to his or her injuries. The elements of contributory negligence include:

1. The plaintiff's duty of reasonable care to himself or herself
2. The plaintiff's breach of that duty
3. The plaintiff's actions (or failures to act) that contributed to his or her injuries (causation, proximate cause)
4. Resulting injuries to the plaintiff.

Duty of Care to Oneself

One has a duty of reasonable care to protect oneself from injury. If a person breaches this duty by causing injury to himself, then he has been negligent toward himself. Suppose a tortfeasor (defendant) also participated in causing the harm. Nonetheless, the victim (plaintiff) contributed to the resulting injury. This is contributory negligence.

Consider this illustration. Suppose that Zelda is speeding while driving to school. Suppose that another driver runs a stop sign, and the vehicles collide with one another. By failing to stop at the sign, the other driver breached the duty of reasonable care to other vehicle users such as Zelda. The other driver's negligence proximately caused injuries to Zelda and her vehicle. However, because Zelda was speeding, she contributed to her own injuries. Apply the contributory negligence formula: (1) Zelda breached her duty of reasonable care to herself by exceeding the speed limit; (2) but for Zelda's excessive speed, she would not have reached the intersection at precisely the time the other driver ran the stop sign; (3) Zelda's high speed proximately contributed to the collision with the other driver. Accordingly, Zelda was contributorily negligent.

Common Law Rule

At common law, contributory negligence barred the plaintiff from recovering any damages from the defendant. Even if the defendant were negligent in causing 99 percent of the plaintiff's harm, and the plaintiff were only 1 percent contributorily negligent, the courts ruled that the plaintiff could collect nothing against the defendant.

Last Clear Chance

When a defendant uses the contributory negligence defense against a plaintiff, the plaintiff has a defensive weapon with which to respond. This is called **last clear chance** and is a rebuttal to a contributory negligence defense. Last clear chance theory states that, although the plaintiff was contributorily negligent in causing his or her own injuries, the defendant had the last opportunity to avert harm but, because of the defendant's negligence, the defendant failed to take advantage of this "last clear chance" to avoid hurting the plaintiff.

Effect of Last Clear Chance

Last clear chance nullifies the contributory negligence defense. In other words, the defendant cannot escape liability for his or her negligence (by invoking the contributory negligence defense) if the defendant had the last clear chance to avoid the injury.

An example should clarify the concept. Consider the preceding speeding/stop sign hypothetical. Recall that the defendant (the other driver) was negligent in running the stop sign. However, Zelda (the plaintiff) was contributorily negligent in speeding. Nevertheless, the defendant had the last clear chance to avoid crashing into Zelda's vehicle—a reasonable person would have slowed while approaching the stop sign and seen Zelda's rapidly approaching vehicle. Since Zelda had the right-of-way, she was not as likely to anticipate oncoming traffic as was the other driver, as he or she

LEGAL TERMS

contributory negligence
A defense to negligence, which points out the plaintiff's negligence that contributed to his or her injuries. Its elements include the plaintiff's duty of reasonable care to himself or herself and the plaintiff's breach of that duty which contributed to his or her injuries. Causation and proximate cause are relevant in this analysis. Contributory negligence absolutely bars the plaintiff's recovery against the defendant.

last clear chance
A plaintiff's response to the defendant's defense of contributory negligence, which states that, although the plaintiff contributed to his or her injuries, the defendant had the last opportunity to avoid injuring the plaintiff. Last clear chance nullifies the contributory negligence defense.

approached the stop sign. The defendant should have been going slower than Zelda and should have been able to stop more quickly and easily than Zelda. This was the defendant's last clear chance to avert the collision.

HYPOTHETICAL

Alfred Peddlemore owns the Peddlemore Moving Company. Midge Hargrade packed several boxes of books. The boxes were marked "garden supplies" in clear, black block letters. Alfred arrived to load the boxes into the company van. Because of an estimation error, there was insufficient room in the van for all of Midge's furniture. Alfred decided to haul the remaining boxes in an open pickup truck. He selected items that would not be harmed if they got wet, including the boxes marked "garden supplies." He did not know that they actually contained books. While Alfred drove across town, a thunderstorm flooded the back of the pickup, destroying the texts.

Alfred was negligent in failing to safeguard all of Midge's property by moving it in an enclosed vehicle. He breached his duty of reasonable care to move the property safely. All of the elements of negligence appear to be satisfied. Alfred can use contributory negligence as a defense, because Midge mismarked the boxes, and this mistake misled Alfred into loading the books into an open truck exposed to the elements. Midge was contributorily negligent by using the mislabelled boxes, which resulted in rain damage to her books. However, Alfred had the last clear chance to avoid disaster. As a professional mover, he should have double-checked the contents of each box that Midge had loaded. The reasonable person, as a professional mover, would have assumed that customers often do not correctly mark boxes they pack themselves. This last opportunity to identify the labelling error would have prevented the book damage. Because he failed to avail himself of this last clear chance, Alfred cannot successfully plead the contributory negligence defense. Accordingly, Alfred's negligence would render him liable to Midge for the book damage.

Figure 8-1 summarizes the elements of contributory negligence and last clear chance.

Unfairness of Contributory Negligence

Is the common law theory of contributory negligence fair and just? Even if the defendant was 99 percent responsible for the plaintiff's injury, the plaintiff's 1 percent of contributory negligence completely barred the

Contributory Negligence	Last Clear Chance
Plaintiff's duty of reasonable care to himself or herself	Although plaintiff was contributorily negligent, defendant had the last reasonable opportunity to avoid harming plaintiff (as a consequence of defendant's negligence)
Plaintiff breaches duty	Nullifies contributory negligence defense
Plaintiff acts, or fails to act, which contributes to his or her injuries (causation and proximate cause)	Plaintiff uses last clear chance to respond to defendant's use of contributory negligence defense
Plaintiff is injured	

FIGURE 8-1
Contributory Negligence and Last Clear Chance

plaintiff's claim. Would it not be more logical for the defendant's liability to reflect his or her share of responsibility for the injury?

Many legal scholars and judges criticized the common law rule for much of the twentieth century. It seemed unduly harsh to the plaintiff, who might have been only marginally involved in injuring himself or herself. Also, it allowed the defendant, who might have been significantly responsible for the plaintiff's harm, to completely avoid liability.

THE CASE OF THE UN-EASY RIDER

Negligence is contagious. Those around a careless person sometimes find themselves infected by carefree, irresponsible attitudes. As a result, it is occasionally difficult to determine the degree to which each party is at fault.

The old contributory negligence defense made no effort to apportion fault. It simply and arbitrarily torpedoed the plaintiff's action if he or she were the least bit at fault for his or her injuries. As § 8.3 discusses, comparative negligence attempts to resolve this unfairness. The following case discusses last clear chance and contributory and comparative negligence, as modified by Arizona statute.

Dykeman v. Englebrecht
166 Ariz. 398, 803 P.2d 119 (1990)
(Court of Appeals of Arizona)
August 16, 1990

VOSS, Presiding Judge.
Appellant/Plaintiff Heidi Leigh Dykeman appeals from a jury verdict finding her 60 percent at fault and apportioning damages accordingly. She raises the following issues of appeal:

1. Did the trial court err by refusing to instruct the jury on the last clear chance doctrine?
[. . .]

Plaintiff, a passenger on a motorcycle driven by defendant, was injured when the motorcycle hit a curb during a turn. Defendant contended that plaintiff jerked and improperly shifted her weight during the turn, causing the accident. Both plaintiff and defendant had been drinking alcoholic beverages. It is undisputed that plaintiff was very intoxicated at the time of the accident, and that defendant had a blood alcohol content of .128 two hours after the accident.

[. . .]

Plaintiff contends that the trial court erred by refusing to give the jury an instruction regarding the last clear chance doctrine. She argues that defendant had the last clear chance to avoid the accident when he allowed her to get on the motorcycle in an inebriated condition. Defendant asserts that last clear chance is not applicable, and, in any event the doctrine was effectively abolished by the enactment of [Ariz. Rev. Stat.] § 12-2505, the comparative negligence statute in Arizona.

Prior to the enactment of Arizona's comparative negligence statute, a contributory negligence defense could preclude a plaintiff, whose own negligence contributed in any degree to his injury, from recovering from a negligent defendant. [Citations omitted.] The last clear chance doctrine was judicially created to alleviate the harshness of the contributory negligence rule. [Citations omitted.] Arizona recognized this doctrine. [Citation omitted]. The doctrine provides that a contributorily negligent plaintiff may recover from a negligent defendant if:

1) The plaintiff could not have avoided the injury after he negligently subjected himself to risk of harm;
2) The defendant knew or should have known of the plaintiff's perilous situation; and,
3) The defendant had the last clear chance to avoid the harm by the exercise of reasonable care and failed to do so.

[Citation omitted.] The doctrine has been criticized because of the confusion it creates in the law of torts. [Citation omitted.]

In 1984 our state legislature enacted the Uniform Contribution Among Tortfeasors Act [citation omitted]. This legislation established comparative negligence in Arizona. The statute provides:

[Ariz. Rev. Stat.] § 12-2505

The defense of contributory negligence or of assumption of risk is in all cases a question of fact and shall at all times be left to the jury. If the jury applies either defense, the claimant's action is not barred, but the full damages shall be reduced in proportion to the relative degree of the claimant's fault which is a proximate cause of the injury or death, if any.

Under this statute a negligent plaintiff is not prohibited from recovering from a negligent defendant; instead his award is reduced by the percentage of his own fault.

Plaintiff asserts that last clear chance remains a viable doctrine despite Arizona's adoption of comparative negligence. We disagree and agree with the jurisdictions that have found that the last clear chance doctrine is superfluous in a comparative negligence system. [Citations omitted.]

The last clear chance doctrine was specifically created to enable a negligent plaintiff to recover from a negligent defendant in a contributory negligence system. However, its application in a comparative negligence system would directly contravene the intent of the statute because [last clear chance] provides complete recovery to a negligent plaintiff rather than apportioning recovery based upon degrees of fault. [Citation omitted.] An instruction on the doctrine, then, would misstate the law and confuse the jury. [. . .]

Additionally, the doctrine is unnecessary in a comparative negligence system. By definition, comparative negligence avoids the harshness inherent in an all-or-nothing contributory negligence system because it "distribute[s] responsibility, in proportion to the degree of fault attributable to the parties who have negligently caused an injury." [Citation omitted.] A comparative negligence system, then,

accomplishes the same result as the last clear chance doctrine as it enables a negligent plaintiff to recover from a negligent defendant. The trial court correctly refused the instruction.

[. . .]

Affirmed.

CASE QUESTIONS

1. Which do you consider the more just doctrines: (a) contributory negligence and last clear chance, or (b) comparative negligence? Do you agree with this court's opinion? Explain.

2. Has your state adopted a statute similar to the Arizona statute discussed here?

Courts and legislatures have modified the common law rule by adopting comparative negligence theory, which is discussed in § 8.3. This defense avoids the unjust outcome in contributory negligence cases.

8.3 COMPARATIVE NEGLIGENCE

The comparative negligence defense has replaced contributory negligence in most states' common law or statutes. Primarily since the 1960s, courts and legislatures have adopted the defense as an alternative to the rigid, unfair results that contributory negligence often produced. The defense of comparative negligence enables the defendant's liability to be adjusted according to the extent of the plaintiff's contribution to his or her own injuries. **Comparative negligence** may be defined as a measurement and comparison of the plaintiff's and the defendant's negligence in causing the plaintiff's injuries.

Elements

The comparative negligence defense has three elements:

1. The plaintiff was negligent in contributing to his or her own injuries.

2. Calculation of the percentage of the plaintiff's negligence that contributed to his or her injuries.

3. Calculation of the percentage of the defendant's negligence that produced the plaintiff's injuries.

LEGAL TERMS

comparative negligence (culpability factoring, liability apportionment)
A defense to negligence. When the plaintiff's negligence contributed to his or her injuries, comparative negligence calculates the percentages of the defendant's and the plaintiff's negligence and adjusts the plaintiff's damages according to the numbers. This is sometimes called *culpability factoring* or *liability apportionment.* The trier-of-fact decides the percentages.

In some jurisdictions, a fourth element is included: the defendant must have been more negligent than the plaintiff.

The Balancing Act

Comparative negligence balances the degrees of each party's negligence that produced the plaintiff's harm. In effect, the plaintiff's and defendant's negligence are compared to see which was more responsible for causing injury. This comparative negligence balancing is typically measured in percentages of negligence. This is sometimes called **culpability factoring** or **liability apportionment**.

For instance, consider the speeding/stop sign example discussed earlier in this chapter. The defendant ran a stop sign. This is more negligent than merely speeding, as the plaintiff's speeding alone would not have produced the accident. It took the greater negligence of the defendant (i.e., failing to stop at the sign) to cause the damage. The defendant was more negligent than the plaintiff in that example. But what percentages of negligence would be assigned to the plaintiff (for contributing to the injuries) and the defendant (for negligently causing the harm)? Well, the defendant was more than half responsible, so the defendant's percentage must be higher than 50 percent. What percentages would be used? Defendant 75 percent, plaintiff 25 percent? 60/40? 90/10?

Readers may find this approach frustrating. What are the correct percentages? There is no exact formula. It depends upon the facts of each case. Whatever percentages are selected, readers and triers-of-fact probably rely on intuition and gut feeling as much as anything.

Who Decides the Percentages

The trier-of-fact decides the percentages in comparative negligence. Thus, the jury (or judge, in a bench trial) must closely examine the facts and assign negligence percentages to the plaintiff and the defendant.

Why Calculate Percentages

Comparative negligence is used to calculate the amount of the defendant's liability to the plaintiff. Assume that the following percentages were selected for the speeding/stop sign problem: Defendant 75 percent negligent, plaintiff 25 percent negligent. What would be the outcome of the case? The defendant would be liable to the plaintiff for 75 percent of the amount plaintiff received in damages. If the plaintiff recovered judgment against the defendant, receiving a $100,000 damages award, under this percentage the defendant would be liable for $75,000.

The advantages of comparative negligence are immediately apparent. Instead of completely barring the plaintiff's recovery (as common law contributory negligence would have done), culpability factoring enables the plaintiff to recover damages for the defendant's share of responsibility in causing the injuries. Liability apportionment also protects the defendant from paying for the plaintiff's share in harming himself or herself. The result is a just and equitable outcome to the litigation.

Criticism of Comparative Negligence

Comparative negligence has been criticized for its arbitrary and capricious approach to assigning percentages of negligence. Critics complain that liability apportionment is imprecise and based entirely upon the emotional attitudes of the jury or judge. Think back to the speeding/stop sign illustration. If one disapproved of running stop signs more than speeding, would one not be more likely to hike the defendant's percentage of liability? Of course, juries are composed of several people, a fact that is intended to balance out such personal biases. Still, disapproval of comparative negligence continues in the legal literature and court opinions.

This attack on the defense is simplistic. Juries always decide the facts of each case based on their personal feelings and attitudes. Which witness does the jury believe? Which exhibit is most persuasive? Which attorney makes the best case presentation? Which party seems the most honest? Has the plaintiff proven the case by a preponderance of the evidence (which, as discussed in chapter 1, is sometimes called the "51 percent line")? These are all intuitive, subjective decisions with which triers-of-fact have wrestled for centuries. Using percentages in culpability factoring is no more arbitrary than any other fact-finding process that juries and judges use everyday. Further, comparative negligence decides the lawsuit more fairly than contributory negligence ever could. The plaintiff recovers the extent of damages that the defendant was responsible for causing. It makes sense to one's sense of fair play.

HYPOTHETICAL

Ikeda Osaka manages and owns a hotel. Frances Borgioni is a guest. The smoke detector in Frances's room has a dead battery and will not function. None of Ikeda's employees has checked the detector recently, despite a management protocol instructing maintenance to check batteries every month. The customer staying in the room next to Frances's smoked in bed and started a fire. Smoke poured under the door adjoining the two rooms, but the malfunctioning detector did not awaken Frances before the room became filled with smoke. Frances awoke, coughing, and stumbled to the hallway door. He could not get the door open, however, because he had placed his own safety lock on the door, and that lock jammed as he was trying to escape. Frances passed out from smoke inhalation and suffered severe burns. Fortunately, the fire department rescued him.

Frances sued Ikeda for negligently failing to maintain an operative smoke detector in the room. Ikeda responded that Frances had contributed to his own injuries by placing his own lock on the door, so that he could not escape. May Ikeda invoke the defense of comparative negligence?

Was Ikeda negligent in failing to maintain a functioning smoke detector in Frances's room? Analyze the facts and apply the elements of negligence. If one decides that Ikeda was negligent (which is arguably the correct answer), then the comparative negligence defense should next be considered. Apply its elements. Was Frances negligent in contributing to his own injuries? Frances breached his duty of reasonable care to himself by placing a defective lock on the door, which prevented his escape during the fire. But for this act, Frances could have escaped before passing out from the smoke. Frances was negligent in harming himself. Next, decide if Ikeda's negligence exceeded Frances's. Would Frances have been endangered by the smoke at all if his smoke detector had activated? This would have given Frances more time to escape the room before the smoke thickened and knocked him unconscious. Ikeda's negligence exceeded Frances. Now use liability apportionment. What percentages would be assigned? Ikeda's must be at least 51 percent. 60/40? 70/30? 80/20? There is no single correct answer here. A juror must use his or her best judgment based upon the facts.

Figure 8-2 lists the elements of comparative negligence.

8.4 ASSUMPTION OF RISK

Assumption of risk is another defense to negligence. **Assumption of risk** means that the plaintiff assumed the risk of doing (or not doing) something that resulted in his or her injuries. Assumption of risk involves (1) the plaintiff's voluntary assumption of a known risk (2) with a full appreciation of the dangers involved in facing that risk.

Elements of Comparative Negligence
Plaintiff was negligent in contributing to his or her own injuries (defendant was also negligent in causing plaintiff's injuries)
Culpability factoring (liability apportionment): Calculate each party's percentage of negligence [How much did plaintiff contribute to his or her own injuries?] [How much was defendant responsible for plaintiff's harm?]
In some jurisdictions, defendant's percentage of negligence must be greater than plaintiff's percentage negligence

FIGURE 8-2
Comparative
Negligence

Voluntary Assumption of Known Risk

For the assumption of risk defense to insulate the defendant from negligence liability, the plaintiff must have voluntarily decided to engage in an activity that the plaintiff knew (or reasonably should have known) was dangerous. In other words, the plaintiff must willfully face a known risk.

For instance, suppose Gilda's employer orders her to carry stacked boxes down a long flight of stairs. Her employer specifically instructs her to carry all the boxes in a single trip. To do this, however, Gilda must hold the boxes in front of her, blocking her forward vision. She knows that it is dangerous to descend stairs when she cannot see where she is going. Gilda slips and falls because her right foot missed a step. She sues her employer for negligence. The employer alleges that Gilda assumed the risk. Did she? No. Gilda did not voluntarily assume the dangerous activity. In fact, she was coerced into carrying all the boxes in one trip. She would not have done so but for her employer's command. Thus, Gilda did not voluntarily assume the risk of falling down the stairway.

Suppose that Brian slipped on some liquid somebody had spilled on the stairway. Brian thought the stairs were clean and dry, since he had walked up them just a few minutes earlier. He was unaware of the new danger that had appeared to threaten his safety. Brian did not assume a known risk.

Suppose that Gilda was carrying the boxes into a storeroom instead of down a stairway. The room was pitch black, and she knew that the ceiling light bulb was burned out. Nevertheless, she carried the boxes into the room in which she could not clearly see. Gilda stumbled over a mop and broom on the floor, and the boxes fell upon and injured her. Again, she sues her employer for negligence in failing to replace the burned-out bulb. Her employer replies that Gilda voluntarily assumed a known risk—she knew the bulb was burned out. Further, she knew that the room was so dark that it would take her eyes several minutes to adjust. Still, she entered the room despite the obvious danger that she could fall over invisible objects. Gilda assumed the risk in this version of the facts.

Full Appreciation of Danger

The plaintiff must fully understand the dangerous nature of the activity that he or she voluntarily undertakes. Suppose that Brett was visiting a friend's woods. He came across a cavern and decided to explore it. He had no way of knowing that, higher above him, on a nearby hill, a highway construction crew was preparing to detonate dynamite. They exploded a powerful charge, which sent a shock wave through the ground and caused part of the cavern walls to collapse, trapping Brett inside the cave. He sues the highway company for negligence in detonating excessively powerful explosives. Run through the negligence formula to determine if the company was negligent toward Brett, closely examining foreseeability of

LEGAL TERMS

assumption of risk
A complete defense to negligence. The plaintiff assumes the risk of doing (or not doing) something that resulted in his or her injuries. The plaintiff voluntarily assumes a known risk with a full appreciation of the dangers involved in facing the risk.

the injury and foreseeable plaintiffs theory. Presuming that the company acted negligently, it responds with the defense of assumption of risk.

Did Brett voluntarily assume a known risk with a full appreciation of the dangers involved? He willfully entered the cave. He knew (or reasonably should have known) that cavern walls sometimes fall in. That risk was known, but he had no way to anticipate the additional danger created by a forceful explosion. He did not fully appreciate this aspect of the risk in entering the cave. Arguably, the dynamite was also an unknown risk to him. Thus, the company's defense would fail.

The Complete Defense

Assumption of risk is a complete defense to negligence. Like common law contributory negligence, it totally bars the plaintiff's recovery. If the plaintiff assumed the risk, the defendant cannot be liable for negligence.

THE CASE OF TREADING ON THIN ICE

When plaintiffs and defendants share a negligent experience, it is inevitable that the defendants will argue assumption of risk. Because the plaintiff volunteered to share the dangers, he or she should not recover, says the defendant. As the following case illustrates, this argument, like the litigants, sometimes treads upon thin ice.

Thompson v. Hill
366 N.W.2d 628 (Minn. Ct. App. 1985)
(Minnesota Court of Appeals)
April 23, 1985

HIERENGARTEN, J.
Respondent Juli-Ann Thompson commenced suit against appellant Douglas Hill under Minn. Stat. § 573.02 for the wrongful death of her husband, Dennis Ray Thompson. The case was bifurcated with the issues of liability and damages tried separately. The jury first returned a verdict finding Hill 60% negligent and [Dennis Ray] Thompson (decedent) 40% negligent. The jury subsequently returned a verdict assessing Juli-Ann's damages at $318,000. As a surviving spouse, Juli-Ann received no-fault benefits totalling $27,500.

The trial court deducted this sum from Thompson's recovery after reducing the jury award by the 40% [comparative] negligence attributed to decedent.

The trial court denied Hill's motion for judgment N.O.V., or, in the alternative, for a new trial. Judgment was entered on August 6, 1984. We affirm.

FACTS
Dennis Thompson drowned when the vehicle in which he and Douglas Hill were riding broke through the ice of the Mississippi River near Winona, Minnesota. Hill, a close friend and employee of the Thompsons, was driving an automobile owned by Thompson at the time of the accident.

Thompson and Hill had been friends for nearly three years prior to the accident. They had spent a lot of time together, including fishing on the Mississippi River.

During the morning of February 2, Hill and Thompson ran several errands when Thompson asked Hill to drive. The two then ran a few more errands before they headed back to the Thompson home.

As they passed Lake Winona, Hill spotted several fish houses and suggested that they take a closer look. There were several other vehicles on the lake so they proceeded to drive onto the ice. They spent no more than 15 minutes driving around before exiting the lake at the point at which they had entered.

Sometime later, Thompson commented that he wanted to go look at the boathouse located on the Mississippi. He told Hill to head towards the river and Hill selected the route. They proceeded onto the ice, which appeared the same as Lake Winona. Neither Hill nor Thompson made an effort to determine the thickness of the ice nor did they make a complete stop before proceeding.

They then headed diagonally upstream when they noticed steam rising from the river. Thompson commented that steam meant open water and told Hill to turn around. Hill turned around and headed downstream. After travelling a short distance, Hill noticed that there were no other tracks on the river and that he "didn't like that" and "felt uncomfortable" so he suggested that they "should turn around." Before he could head towards shore, there was "a loud cracking or crumbling sound" and the front of the auto began to sink.

Hill escaped through the back tailgate of the jeepster and heard Thompson splashing behind him. Hill attempted to grab Thompson but he lost his hold and Thompson went under the ice.

ISSUES

1. Was there a primary assumption of the risk which would preclude a finding of negligence on the part of Hill?

2. Were Thompson and Hill engaged in a joint enterprise, thereby imputing Hill's negligence to Thompson?

3. Did the trial court err when it denied Hill's request for an instruction on the doctrine of secondary assumption of risk?

4. Did the trial court err when it deducted the no-fault benefits paid to Juli-Ann after it reduced the verdict by the percentage of negligence attributed to Thompson?

ANALYSIS

I.

Hill argues he was entitled to judgment notwithstanding the verdict because the doctrine of primary assumption of risk precludes a finding of negligence on his part. Primary assumption of risk is an absolute bar to the plaintiff's recovery. "Primary assumption of the risk * * * indicates that the defendant did not even owe the plaintiff any duty of care." [Citation omitted.] If Hill owed no duty to Thompson, there was no negligence.

The doctrine does not apply because Hill, as the driver, owed Thompson certain duties of reasonable care while driving on the river ice. Hill owed his passenger "the duty to operate the car with reasonable care so that the danger of riding in it is not increased or a new danger added to those assumed when the guest entered the car." [Citation omitted.]

Although Thompson assumed certain risks when he and Hill proceeded onto the ice, Hill was not relieved of his duties as the driver to use reasonable care, including proper lookout for dangers incident to driving on river ice. The jury could reasonably have found Hill breached his duty. First, after they spotted the steam rising from the river, Hill was negligent in not immediately driving off of the ice towards shore. Second, the area in which they were travelling did not contain any tracks which, in itself, should warn a driver that the ice might be thin or unsafe.

The law is well settled in this jurisdiction that in examining a verdict on appeal the evidence must be considered in the light most favorable to the prevailing party and the verdict must be sustained if it is possible to do so on any reasonable theory of evidence. The verdict should not be disturbed unless it is manifestly and palpably contrary to the evidence. [Citation omitted.] Based on all of the evidence, the jury could find that it was negligent for Hill to continue driving on the ice.

[. . .]

A passenger in a motor vehicle has a duty to use that care which a reasonable person riding as a passenger would use under like circumstances. It is the duty of the passenger to exercise reasonable care for his own safety. A passenger has a duty to take active measures to protect himself from danger only when it is apparent to him that he can no longer rely upon the driver for protection, as when the driver by his conduct shows that he is incompetent to drive or the driver is unmindful of or does not know of a danger known to the passenger, and then only if the passenger becomes aware of the danger at the time and under circumstances when he could have prevented the harm.

[. . .]

[. . .] [S]econdary assumption of risk [is] defined [. . .] as follows:

> Assumption of risk is voluntarily placing (oneself) (one's property) in a position to chance known hazards. To find that a person assumed the risk you must find:
>
> 1. That he had knowledge of the risk.
> 2. That he appreciated the risk.
> 3. That he had a choice to avoid the risk or chance it and voluntarily chose to chance it.

[Citation omitted.] In light of our comparative negligence statute, Minn. Stat. § 604.01, secondary assumption of risk is no longer a complete bar to the plaintiff's recovery. Instead, it is an aspect of contributory negligence. [Citation omitted.] [. . .] [C]ontributory negligence and secondary assumption of risk were merged.

> [W]here a defendant has a duty to exercise ordinary care, that plaintiff's "secondary, express or implied" assumption of risk, as distinguished from "primary" assumption of risk, becomes part of the defense of contributory negligence and is to be measured under the comparative negligence statute, Minn. St[at.§] 604.01.

[Citation omitted.] "Fault," as used in our comparative fault statute, "includes breach of warranty, unreasonable assumption of risk not constituting an express consent, misuse of a product and unreasonable failure to avoid an injury or to mitigate damages." Minn. Stat. § 604.01, subd. 1a (1982).

An instruction on assumption of risk would have focused the jury's attention on Thompson's comparative negligence and prejudiced plaintiff. The instruction would have also forced the jury to apportion fault to Thompson under both the general fault instruction and under the assumption of risk instruction. The jury would have been needlessly confused. Improper submission of secondary assumption of risk to the jury is reversible error. [Citation omitted.] Based on the facts of this case, it would have been improper to submit the issue of assumption of risk to the jury.

[. . .]

DECISION

The doctrine of primary assumption of risk does not apply because the driver owed his passenger certain duties of reasonable care while driving on the ice of the Mississippi River.

[. . .]

A separate instruction on secondary assumption of risk would have needlessly confused the jury.

[. . .]

Affirmed.

CASE QUESTIONS

1. In *Thompson,* the Minnesota Court of Appeals distinguished between primary and secondary assumption of risk. Notice how primary assumption of risk focuses upon whether the defendant owed a duty of reasonable care to the plaintiff. Does this simply return to the original question of the defendant's negligence? Is this actually a defense at all?

2. How is the *Thompson* court's definition of secondary assumption of risk similar to the assumption of risk definition discussed in this chapter? How has this defense been changed by the Minnesota comparative negligence statute? Does the statute merely merge the defense into culpability factoring? Explain.

3. Review the *Thompson* jury's comparative negligence percentages, as noted at the beginning of the opinion. Do you agree with the figures, based upon the facts given in the case? Why or why not? What percentages would you have assigned? Explain.

Assumption of risk is somewhat more difficult to establish than contributory or comparative negligence. The following example demonstrates how the elements must be carefully considered.

HYPOTHETICAL

Erving Tanford owns East of Tansmania, a tanning salon. Elizabeth Bundy is one of Tanford's customers. She had been visiting the salon twice a week for 10 years. She always used the same tanning bed. Because of faulty equipment, Elizabeth was exposed during each session to five times more ultraviolet radiation than is normally emitted by tanning equipment. Elizabeth was diagnosed with skin cancer. She sued Tanford for subjecting her to excessively intense ultraviolet light, which is a powerful carcinogen. Tanford was negligent in exposing Elizabeth to such extremely high doses of ultraviolet radiation. Can he offer assumption of risk as a defense?

Did Elizabeth voluntarily assume a known risk with a full appreciation of the dangerous consequences? Clearly, she willfully visited the salon twice weekly for 10 years. She chose to use the same bed each time. She knew (or reasonably should have known) that ultraviolet radiation is carcinogenic. But did she fully understand the danger? Did she realize that the equipment emitted five times more radiation than normal? Could she have known about this aspect of the threat? Not likely. Accordingly, she did not assume the risk, and the defense would not protect Tanford from liability.

Suppose a warning were posted above the tanning bed that Elizabeth used, declaring, "DANGER! EMITS EXCESSIVE ULTRAVIOLET LIGHT. USE AT YOUR OWN RISK." Now Elizabeth would have been alerted to the threatening condition. She would have a full appreciation of the dangers involved in using the equipment. Under this version of the facts, Elizabeth would have assumed the risk, and Tanford would not be liable for negligence.

Figure 8-3 outlines the elements of assumption of risk.

8.5 STATUTES OF LIMITATIONS

Statutes of limitations are statutes restricting the time within which a plaintiff may file a lawsuit for particular causes of action against a defendant. Chapter 5 discussed statutes of limitations as applied to intentional torts. There are also such statutes for negligence actions. Many of these statutes specify that various negligence lawsuits must be filed within two years of the negligent acts giving rise to the plaintiff's claims.

States' statutes of limitations vary in numbers of years and among the different types of negligence. The period for medical malpractice claims, for instance, may be two years in one state and three years in another. Similarly, lawsuits involving premises liability may have one-year statutes of limitations in one state and three-year statutes in another. One should become familiar with the specific statutes of limitations in one's own state for the various types of negligence causes of action.

Figure 8-4 shows two typical statutes of limitations for negligence actions.

FIGURE 8-3
Assumption of Risk

Elements of Assumption of Risk
Plaintiff voluntarily assumes a known risk
Plaintiff fully appreciates the dangers involved in facing the risk

Two-Year Statute of Limitations (with three-year absolute limit for injuries not discovered within two years)	Three-Year Statute of Limitations
Connecticut General Statutes Annotated § 52-581 (West 1991): No action to recover damages for injury to the person, or to real or personal property, caused by negligence, or by reckless or wanton misconduct, or by malpractice of a physician, surgeon, dentist, podiatrist, chiropractor, hospital or sanatorium, shall be brought but within two years from the date when the injury is first sustained or discovered or in the exercise of reasonable care should have been discovered, and except that no such action may be brought more than three years from the date of the act or omission complained of, except [for counterclaims].	New York Civil Practice Law & Rules § 214 (McKinney 1992): The following actions must be commenced within three years: [. . .] 5. an action to recover damages for a personal injury except as provided in sections 214-b, 214-c and 215; [. . .] [providing special rules concerning specific torts and time injury was detected]

FIGURE 8-4
Examples of Negligence
Statutes of Limitations

SUMMARY

8.1 Negligence defenses are used only by the defendant against the plaintiff. The defenses are applied only in response to the plaintiff's allegations that the defendant acted negligently. To determine which party uses negligence defenses, one should ask who is alleging negligence and who is alleged to have been negligent.

8.2 Contributory negligence is the plaintiff's negligence that contributed to his or her own injuries. The plaintiff was negligent toward himself or herself and caused (in whole or in part) the harm. This defense exonerates the defendant whose negligence harmed the plaintiff. At common law, any amount of contributory negligence by the plaintiff, however small, would bar the plaintiff's recovery against the negligent defendant. Critics have argued that this defense is unreasonably harsh, in that a defendant who was overwhelming responsible for hurting the plaintiff might still avoid liability because of the plaintiff's minuscule contributory negligence. Last clear chance is the plaintiff's response to the contributory negligence defense. Last clear chance means that, although the plaintiff was contributorily negligent, the defendant still had the last opportunity to avoid harming the plaintiff. Last clear chance nullifies the contributory negligence defense.

8.3. Comparative negligence is an alternative defense that has largely replaced contributory negligence in both the common law and statute.

Comparative negligence measures and compares the negligence of both the plaintiff and the defendant. This allows the trier-of-fact to adjust the plaintiff's recovery to reflect more accurately each party's degree of negligence in causing the harm. The calculation is often in percentages of negligence. This is sometimes called culpability factoring or liability apportionment. These percentages are based entirely upon the trier-of-fact's subjective opinion regarding the specific facts of each case. Critics have criticized the defense for this uncertainty.

8.4. Assumption of risk is another negligence defense. It states that the plaintiff voluntarily assumed a known risk with full appreciation of the dangers involved. Like contributory negligence, assumption of risk is a complete defense to negligence. In other words, it totally excuses the defendant's negligence and erases the defendant's liability to the plaintiff.

8.5. Most state statutes of limitations restrict the time period within which a plaintiff may file a negligence cause of action against a defendant. In most states, these are two-year statutes, meaning that a plaintiff has two years from the date that the negligent act was committed within which to file a lawsuit against the tortfeasor. It is vital to research the specific statutes of limitations for each particular tort.

REVIEW QUESTIONS

1. How are negligence defenses used? Which party uses them? Against whom are the defenses used? What is the purpose of negligence defenses?

2. Define contributory negligence. What are its elements? What is the common law rule? Why is it a particularly effective defense?

3. Explain last clear chance. How is it used? Who uses it against whom? What is its importance to contributory negligence?

4. Why is the contributory negligence defense unfair? What changes have courts and legislatures made to create a more equitable defense? What is this defense called?

5. Define comparative negligence. What are its elements? What is culpability factoring? Liability apportionment? Why are percentages used? Who decides these percentages? Is this defense more fair than contributory negligence? Why or why not?

6. What is assumption of risk? List its elements. Who uses the defense against whom? Must the risk be voluntarily assumed? What is "full appreciation of danger" and why is it significant? How effective is this defense in avoiding the defendant's liability?

7. What are statutes of limitations? What time period is most commonly allowed for negligence causes of action? How can limitations statutes be used as a defense to negligence?

PROBLEMS

In the following hypotheticals, determine which negligence defense applies, if any.

1. The Tapajós Inn, owned by Guillermo Estaben, has a swimming pool with no lifeguards on duty. The pool is surrounded by a high wire fence, and access to the pool is restricted to guests, who must use their room keys to reach the facility. Signs posted in several places on the fencing read, in bold, black lettering: "NO LIFEGUARD ON DUTY. SWIM AT YOUR OWN RISK! NO DIVING, RUNNING, OR HORSE PLAY. ADULTS MUST SUPERVISE CHILDREN. BE CAREFUL!" Tony Harmon, a 16-year-old, and his family are staying at the Inn. Tony and his 17-year-old girlfriend, Tanya Martin, went swimming in the pool after midnight. There were no signs indicating times when the pool was open or closed. At 1:45 a.m., hotel maintenance activated the automatic pumps to drain the pool for cleaning. None of the Inn staff checked to see if the pool was being used. While swimming underwater, Tanya got her left foot caught in a pool drain, as a result of the powerful suction of the pumps. She would have drowned had Tony not rescued her. She suffered torn tendons in her foot and ankle, and she developed an extreme phobia toward water. She experienced nightmares and acute nervousness after the incident. There were no signs indicating that the pool could be drained remotely nor that the drains were dangerous when the pumps were running.

2. Farabee St. Claire owns an ice-skating rink. Charles and Martha Samuelson visited the rink on their 10th wedding anniversary. Charles had not skated since high school (15 years earlier), but Martha often went skating at the rink. Because of a broken thermostat, one corner of the ice thawed and a small puddle formed. As Charles skated through the water, he slipped and fell to the ice, breaking his right arm. Martha, who was skating close behind, collided with Charles and also fell to the ice, suffering a concussion. Martha was a talented skater and could have avoided Charles by leaping over his body, but she did not think to do so in her surprise and confusion under the circumstances.

3. The Happy Hollow Mental Hospital houses many emotionally disturbed individuals. One patient, Marjorie Magpie, a convicted arsonist, escaped from her maximum security room. No guards were on duty in that part of the hospital, and an attendant had left Marjorie's door unlocked. As Marjorie wandered out of a wooded area onto a highway, she hitchhiked a ride from Pamela Sweetbird, who was driving back to the university at which she worked. Pamela noticed that Marjorie was dressed in a hospital gown and blue jeans, but Marjorie explained that she was a medical student at the university and often wore these gowns, because they were comfortable. Pamela dropped

Marjorie off at a bus stop located only a few hundred yards from Pamela's home. Marjorie saw Pamela stop at the house and then drive away again. Later that day, Pamela's house burned down. Police arrested Marjorie for having set the fire.

4. Beth Sageveil is an accountant. Pavel Rubenstein is one of her clients. Beth completed Pavel's federal and state tax returns for 1991. Beth made a critical addition error, however, and as a result, Pavel underpaid his taxes. Both the Internal Revenue Service and the State Department of Revenue assessed hefty penalties against Pavel for the underpayment. Pavel had signed the returns without reading them, although the instructions on each return clearly advised the taxpayer to read carefully through the returns to verify their accuracy, even if a professional tax preparer had been used.

5. Malt Finchley owns a sporting-goods store. Abraham Waite came in to buy a new shotgun. One of Malt's employees, Saul Demure, handed Abraham a shotgun which, unbeknownst to Saul or Abraham, was loaded. Neither Saul nor Abraham checked the gun to see if it was loaded. The trigger, however, had a keyed lock that prevented it from being pulled. Abraham asked that the lock be removed so that he could feel the trigger's sensitivity. Saul opened the lock and Abraham tested the trigger. The gun discharged, shooting another customer, Toby Benchsmith, in the stomach. Toby saw Abraham aim the gun in his general direction. Instead of stepping aside, Toby jokingly shouted, "Hey, don't shoot me, I'm on your side!"

PROBLEM ANSWERS

1. Tanya Martin would sue The Tapajós Inn's owner, Guillermo Estaben, for negligently operating the automatic pumps without first determining if the swimming pool was vacant. The hotel maintenance crew committed the negligent actions, for which Estaben would be liable under respondeat superior. Further, because Tanya was an invitee on the premises, Estaben owed her a duty of reasonable care to protect her from known (and unknown) dangers, such as the powerful pumps (a known risk), which foreseeably could trap a swimmer's limb as a result of the strong suction. Tanya could state a prima facie case for negligence. She would also claim negligent infliction of emotional distress, because of her resulting water phobia.

Estaben could plead the defense of assumption of risk. The pool's signs clearly stated that no lifeguards were present and that swimmers used the facility at their own risk.

The key to this defense, however, is whether Tanya voluntarily assumed a known risk with full appreciation of the dangers involved. Certainly, Tanya was aware of the ordinary risks of swimming—getting cramps, hitting one's head against the side or bottom while diving, etc. But Tanya could not have anticipated the danger that caused her injuries. There were no signs warning patrons that the pool would be automatically drained at night. No open or closed hours were posted for the area. Tanya could not have reasonably anticipated the risk of powerful pumps trapping her underwater. Thus, Tanya did not voluntarily assume a known risk with complete comprehension of the danger. Accordingly, Estaben's assumption of risk defense would fail.

Estaben might also plead the defenses of contributory and comparative negligence, but both would likewise fail. Tanya did not breach her duty of reasonable care toward herself by swimming in the pool late at night. There was no reason for her to know that swimming at 1:45 a.m. was any more dangerous than swimming during daylight, as no open/closed or maintenance schedule signs were posted. Because the drain danger was not reasonably foreseeable, she was not contributorily (or comparatively) negligent in swimming.

2. Charles and Martha Samuelson were invitees at the ice-skating rink. Accordingly, the owner, Farabee St. Claire, owed them a duty of reasonable care to discover and correct known and unknown dangers on the premises. This includes thawing areas of ice. Farabee breached this duty, and the remaining negligence elements can also be demonstrated. Charles and Martha would have stated successful causes of action against Farabee.

Farabee has no negligence defenses against Charles. Charles did not assume a known risk, as he was unaware of the melted ice, so no assumption of risk existed. Further, Charles did not breach his duty of reasonable care to himself. As a novice skater, he could not reasonably have been expected to avoid the slick spot. In fact, his injuries, caused by falling, were not only reasonably foreseeable but practically inevitable, as any beginning skater/juror could imagine. Thus, neither contributory nor comparative negligence applies to Charles's case. Farabee would be liable to Charles for negligently causing his injuries.

However, Farabee would claim that Martha committed contributory negligence by failing to avoid striking her fallen spouse. Martha was a talented skater and, according to the facts, could have avoided Charles's sprawled body by leaping over him. By failing to react in this reasonable fashion, Martha breached her duty of care to herself, which contributed to her injuries. Thus, contributory negligence would bar Martha's negligence claim against Farabee.

This outcome seems unduly harsh for Martha. One could argue on her behalf that her failure to avoid Charles (i.e., freezing up) was perfectly reasonable. She was taken by surprise and would have been concerned for Charles's well-being, even in the instant before hitting him. So, arguably, Martha was not contributorily negligent.

Assume, however, that contributory negligence is established. Applying comparative negligence, the outcome for Martha's case would be different. The melted ice created the initial risk, which caused Charles to fall. But for this added danger (Charles lying on the ice), Martha would not have been at risk herself. Thus, Farabee's negligence was greater in permitting the ice to thaw than Martha's in failing to jump across her prone husband. What negligence percentages should be applied? Consider the following: Farabee's liability—95 percent; Martha's contribution— 5 percent.

3. One may become immersed in the threshold question, namely, was the Happy Hollow Mental Hospital negligent in permitting an arsonist/ patient to escape and burn down Pamela Sweetbird's home? Certainly, the issue of proximate cause is indefinite. Was it reasonably foreseeable that Marjorie Magpie would escape, hitch a ride with an unsuspecting passerby (Pamela), and conclude by torching Pamela's house? Marjorie was a convicted arsonist. Thus, the hospital was fully aware that, if free, she might be inclined to set fire to property, perhaps that of the first person she encountered on the "outside" (which, in this hypothetical, was Pamela). Thus, jurors could be persuaded that the events in this problem were reasonably foreseeable, and thus the hospital could be liable to Pamela for negligently allowing Marjorie to escape and commit arson.

First, the hospital would argue that Pamela was contributorily or comparatively negligent by picking up Marjorie as a hitchhiker. Pamela knew, or reasonably should have known, that the hospital was located nearby. She recognized that Marjorie was wearing a hospital gown and blue jeans. Would a reasonable person have recognized that Marjorie was most likely an escaped patient? Yes. Would a reasonable person have avoided picking up such a hitchhiker? Yes. So it would seem that Pamela breached her duty of reasonable care to herself by picking up Marjorie.

But that would be an incorrect analysis. There remains another, fundamental inquiry; namely, would a reasonable person have anticipated that picking up a hitchhiker, even an escaped patient from a mental hospital, would result in the burning of the reasonable person's house? No. Pamela might reasonably have anticipated being attacked while Marjorie was inside the vehicle, but Pamela could not reasonably have expected that Marjorie would return later to set Pamela's house ablaze. Because the fire was not a reasonably foreseeable consequence of Pamela's self-negligence, Pamela was not contributorily (or comparatively) negligent. The hospital's defense would be unsuccessful.

Nor could the hospital claim assumption of risk as a defense. Pamela did not assume a known risk with full appreciation of the danger involved, because she could not have anticipated that Marjorie would burn down the house, which was the particular risk that Pamela would have had to assume for this defense to protect the hospital from liability.

4. Pavel Rubenstein would sue Beth Sageveil for negligence in the form of professional malpractice. Clearly, Beth violated her professional community's standard of care by making an elementary addition

mistake (the accountant's equivalent of a surgeon's leaving a scalpel inside a patient's abdomen). The negligence elements may be easily demonstrated in this hypothetical.

Beth would argue that Pavel assumed the risk of mathematical mistakes by failing to review the returns before signing them. Did Pavel voluntarily assume a known risk with full appreciation of the dangers involved? A reasonable person would know that addition mistakes can occur on complex mathematical documents such as tax returns. By signing the forms without reading them, Pavel willfully assumed this known risk. He also should have known that addition errors could result in governmental tax penalties, as reasonable persons are presumed to know that tax authorities levy such penalties under law. This satisfies the full appreciation of danger requirement. Thus, Pavel assumed the risk of incurring fines for inaccurate tax returns and, accordingly, Beth would not be liable for malpractice.

One might argue that Pavel justifiably relied upon Beth's expertise in computing his tax liability on the forms. However, this does not excuse Pavel's failure to read the returns before signing them. Even experts, such as accountants, make the occasional mathematical mistake.

Beth could also successfully plead contributory and comparative negligence against Pavel, since, by signing without reading, he violated his duty of reasonable care to himself. Pavel's contributory negligence would absolutely bar his recovery, as would assumption of risk. However, his comparative negligence would only reduce Beth's liability. The probable percentages would be: Beth—60 percent; Pavel—40 percent (based primarily upon the expectation that most jurors would be more sympathetic to Pavel, unless the voir dire happened to select an unusually high number of professionals).

5. Initially, this hypothetical involves issues of vicarious liability and joint and several liability. Under respondeat superior, Malt Finchley would be responsible for the negligence of his employees, such as Saul Demure. So vicarious liability would exist, if Saul had been negligent.

Toby Benchsmith, the innocent bystander in this hypothetical, would sue Malt and Saul, as well as Abraham Waite, the other customer. Herein lies the joint and several liability issue. Both Abraham and Saul were negligent by not first checking to see if the shotgun was loaded. The duo acted together to cause Toby's injuries. Thus, all three defendants would be liable under negligence.

The defendants would respond with the defenses of contributory or comparative negligence. The critical question is whether Toby breached his duty of reasonable care to himself by standing in the shotgun's direct line of fire instead of standing clear. Would a reasonable person have anticipated that the gun might be loaded and prudently step clear? Yes. So Toby breached his self-duty, which contributed to his injuries. Contributory negligence would totally bar Toby's recovery; comparative negligence would require culpability factoring (liability apportionment). What percentages should be applied? One could pick Saul (vicariously, Malt)—40 percent (supplying loaded gun); Abraham—40 percent (firing loaded gun); Toby—20 percent (failing to avoid line of fire).

One may argue vehemently that Toby was not contributorily or comparatively negligent. Why, one might say, would Toby have reasonably anticipated that Saul would hand Abraham a loaded weapon inside the store to test its trigger? Arguably, this situation would not be reasonably foreseeable, and so Toby would not have proximately caused his own injuries. Thus, neither defense would apply.

PROJECTS

1. Reread the *Egede-Nissen* opinion reprinted in § 7-1. Do you agree with the jury's determination that the plaintiff was 55 percent "contributorially negligent"? When the plaintiff's negligence exceeds the defendants', should this bar the plaintiff's recovery? What does this verdict suggest about the Washington rule for comparative negligence?

2. Brief *Knight v. Jewett*, 225 Cal. App. 3d 759, 275 Cal. Rptr. 292 (1991), *review granted,* ___, Cal. 3d ___, 804 P.2d 1300, 278 Cal. Rptr. 203 (1991), which was reprinted in part in chapter 5. Which defense did the California Court of Appeal address? Was the defense successful in protecting the defendant from negligence liability?

3. Brief *Li v. Yellow Cab Co.,* 13 Cal. 3d 804, 532 P.2d 1226, 119 Cal. Rptr. 858 (1975). What are the different approaches various states have used in developing comparative negligence? How did the California Supreme Court justify adopting its comparative negligence rule?

4. Does your state have one (or more) comparative negligence statutes? Have the courts in your state modified the common law contributory negligence or assumption of risk defenses?

5. In class or study groups, create your own hypotheticals using the negligence defenses discussed in this chapter. Then change the facts to alter the outcomes of the problems.

CHAPTER 9
Strict, or Absolute, Liability

OUTLINE

DATA-GRAPHIC TORTS

Mentor v. Kelley

Jonathan Kelley cleared several trees on his farmland. After cutting them into various lengths, he hauled them away in the back of his pickup truck. He did not tie the logs down, and one log rolled to the side of the pile, sticking out over the left side of the truck. Kelley could easily have seen this protruding log by looking into his rear-view mirror, but he did nothing to correct the condition. Heading east on Center Avenue, Kelley approached the intersection of Center and Daniel Drive. Center was an east-west road and Daniel a north-south street. Stopped at the intersection, facing north on Daniel Drive, was a school bus from the Nine Hills Elementary School, filled with second-graders who were taking a field trip to the Museum of Natural History at the university. As Kelley turned right onto Daniel Drive, the askew log crashed through the left side windows of the school bus. Several students were cut by flying glass and four suffered concussions as the log clobbered them in the head. The injured children's parents (James and

Mildred Mentor, among others) sued Kelley, alleging that his hauling unsecured lumber constituted an abnormally dangerous activity. Would the parents succeed on this theory, and, thus, be able to hold Kelley absolutely liable for the children's injuries?

No, although most elements of the *Restatement (Second) of Torts* § 520 are satisfied in this hypothetical. The log sticking out from the driver's side of Kelley's truck posed a high risk of substantial harm to oncoming vehicles. This risk could easily have been removed through the exercise of reasonable care (here, by strapping down the logs). By driving with the logs unsecured, Kelley acted inappropriately by imperiling other vehicles with the loose log. The hazards of the askew log clearly outweigh the benefits of hauling.

However, under § 520's common usage principle, an abnormally dangerous activity is one that is not commonly undertaken. Trucks routinely haul a variety of items, including cut timber, even if the items are not securely fastened down. Thus, Kelley was not engaged in an abnormally dangerous activity.

In this scenario, the children's parents should have sued under negligence theory. Kelley's negligence can easily be established in this case.

INTRODUCTION

Intentional torts and negligence comprise the bulk of the torts puzzle. Having assembled these pieces, the big torts picture is largely complete. However, there remain several important torts to piece together before the puzzle is whole. The remainder of the puzzle mostly consists of strict, or absolute, liability. Products liability is one form of strict liability. The terms *strict liability* and *absolute liability* are interchangeable. Strict liability differs from intentional torts and negligence in that fault is unnecessary to establish liability. From the defendant's standpoint, absolute liability can be serious trouble indeed.

This chapter assembles the following pieces of the tort puzzle:

- Wild animal owner absolute liability.
- Distinctions between wild and domestic animals.
- Absolute liability for abnormally dangerous activities.
- Toxic tort strict liability.
- Proximate cause in strict liability cases.

9.1 STRICT LIABILITY GENERALLY

Under intentional torts and negligence, tortfeasors are held accountable for their wrongful actions. Fault is an essential part of the reasoning. What was the defendant's misconduct that hurt the plaintiff? Was it intentional, willful, and wanton, or was it negligent action? Placing the blame is second nature in negligence or intentional torts analysis.

Fault Is Irrelevant

Absolute or strict **liability** holds the tortfeasor responsible for his or her behavior regardless of fault. In other words, the tortfeasor could have used every possible degree of care to protect against injuring the victim, but this would not prevent liability. Fault is irrelevant to absolute liability. The tortfeasor would be strictly liable just because he or she did something specific that hurt the plaintiff.

Limitations to Absolute Liability

One's sense of fair play may rebel against strict liability. One might think that it is unfair to hold a defendant accountable even if he or she did not intentionally or negligently misbehave. This fault concept extends throughout every area of law. This is why absolute liability is restricted to certain types of activities, such as abnormally dangerous tasks and defectively manufactured products.

Public Policy Objectives Behind Strict Liability

Under strict liability, society (through its courts and legislatures) has decided that the person engaged in certain ventures should bear the risk of liability to individuals innocently injured as a consequence of the dangerous or defective item or action. It is society's decision that persons owning wild animals, using fire or explosives, or manufacturing products are in the best economic position to pay for plaintiffs' injuries arising from these activities.

Insurance Analogy

Absolute liability resembles insurance. Defendants are insuring, or guaranteeing, the safety of plaintiffs who come into contact with what tort law calls **abnormally dangerous** or **ultrahazardous instrumentalities**. These activities or objects are just plainly dangerous by their very nature.

Historical Development

Ancient English common law held the owners of animals, slaves, or objects absolutely liable for causing the death of another person. For instance, suppose a boat broke its mooring and floated downstream, colliding with and drowning a swimmer. In medieval England, the boat would be considered a *deodand,* because it killed someone. The term originated from the Latin *Deo dandum,* which translates as "a thing to be given to God." The ecclesiastical courts insisted that the offending, sinful property be seized and placed into God's service. Deodands had to be forfeited to the church or the crown, or sometimes to the injured party's surviving family, to be used in pious pursuits. It was seen as a charitable redemption: the owner

LEGAL TERMS

absolute liability
  Also called *strict liability.* Under absolute liability, the defendant is liable to the plaintiff regardless of fault. Absolute liability applies in cases involving abnormally dangerous activities, wild animal attacks, and products liability.

abnormally dangerous instrumentalities (activities)
  Activities or objects that are, by their very nature, extremely hazardous to persons or property. These are relevant to strict, or absolute, liability cases.

would pay for his or her sinful chattel by giving it up. It did not matter that the chattel killed accidentally. This was probably one of the earliest forms of strict liability.

9.2 ANIMAL OWNERS' LIABILITY

Modern absolute liability first arose in the common law involving private ownership of wild animals and the use of fire or explosives. This section discusses owners' liability for injuries inflicted by their wild animals.

Wild Animals Defined

The ancient common law cases use the Latin term *ferae naturae*, meaning "wild nature," to refer to wild animals. These are animals that have naturally wild dispositions, as opposed to tame animals, which are called *domitae naturae*, meaning "domesticated nature." Examples of *ferae naturae* include deer, bison, elk, bear, snakes, bees, stream or ocean fish, coyotes, foxes, wild birds, lions, tigers, gophers, raccoons, opossums, or prairie dogs.

Ownership of Wildlife

Under ancient English common law, the king owned all wildlife in the realm. This is why poachers were often hanged or beheaded for taking the crown's property during medieval times. As English law evolved, an average person could claim ownership of a wild animal—the trick was to catch the beast. Once someone had control over a wild animal, it was considered to be his or her property until it escaped to its natural, free state. The common law cases call this ownership the exercise of **dominion and control** over the wild animal. American common law holds that the state (or the federal government), under its police power, owns wildlife in trust for the benefit of all citizens. This is why one must obtain state or federal hunting or fishing licenses to take wildlife.

For example, suppose Kathleen has an apiary—in other words, she is a beekeeper. The bees are wildlife, *ferae naturae*. However, if Kathleen catches and places them in her apiary hives, they may stay and produce honey for her. Now Kathleen owns the bees. As long as she exercises dominion and control over the insects, they are hers. But once the bees fly away, they are *ferae naturae* again, and Kathleen does not own them (that is, unless she catches them again).

Importance of Wildlife Ownership

Wildlife ownership is important for purposes of absolute liability. If a wild animal injures someone, the victim cannot sue the beast (or, at the very least, cannot easily collect judgment). Instead, the plaintiff looks to

---

ultrahazardous instrumentalities (activities)
Activities or objects that are, by their very nature, extremely dangerous to persons or property. These are relevant to strict, or absolute, liability cases.

ferae naturae
Latin meaning "wild nature" and referring to wild animals. Owners whose wild animals injure others are absolutely liable for the harm.

domitae naturae
Latin meaning "domesticated nature" and referring to tame, domestic animals. Owners are absolutely liable for injuries caused by their domestic animals only if the animals displayed vicious propensities. Otherwise, the owners would be liable only if their negligence in handling the animals caused the injuries.

dominion and control
The power that an owner exercises over his or her wild animals. This control is the way in which a person comes to own a wild animal and is relevant to absolute liability cases involving injuries caused by wildlife.

the animal's owner for compensation. Owners are strictly liable for the injuries their wildlife inflicts. It does not matter that the owner exercised every precaution to safeguard others from being hurt by the wild animals. If the beast attacks and hurts someone, the owner must compensate the victim for the injuries. Because the common law presumes that wild animals are dangerous by nature, strict liability applies to any injuries they cause.

Suppose Kathleen's bees sting a visitor to the apiary. The victim will sue Kathleen under strict liability. One might argue that premises liability, using negligence theory, should apply instead, because Kathleen owns the land and the chattels that harmed the plaintiff, but this argument would lose. Because the bees are wildlife, Kathleen is absolutely liable for their mischief.

Comparison with Domesticated Animals

Domitae naturae are animals that the law presumes to be harmless. Examples of domestic animals include dogs, cats, pet birds, or livestock such as pigs, horses, cows, or sheep. When domesticated animals hurt someone, the common law states that the owner is liable if he or she were negligent in handling the animals. Liability would also arise if an owner intentionally used domestic animals to hurt someone. For example, suppose an attack dog's owner ordered the animal to attack a victim. This is a form of battery, as the animal would be considered an extension of the tortfeasor's body.

Vicious Propensity Rule

Owners may be held absolutely liable for injuries caused by their domestic animals if the animals exhibit vicious tendencies. When a dog growls or snarls, when a bull paws the ground and snorts, or when a cat arches its back and hisses, these are all demonstrations of vicious propensities. When a domestic animal routinely displays these characteristics, so that it gets a reputation for viciousness, it is said to have *vicious propensities*. An owner of such an animal will be held strictly liable for any injuries the beast inflicts, under the so-called **vicious propensity rule**. All states except Indiana have adopted this common law principle. Indiana has a hybrid vicious propensity rule, peculiar to its common law heritage, under which an owner's negligence in handling the animal must be proven, whether or not the animal displays a vicious propensity.

Defenses in Animal Absolute Liability Cases

Normally, negligence or intentional tort defenses are ineffective against strict liability. However, certain exceptions have arisen in the common law for particular types of absolute liability, such as cases involving animals. The following defenses can protect an animal owner from strict liability:

1. Assumption of risk

2. Contributory and comparative negligence

3. Consent

4. Self-defense and defense of others.

Assumption of Risk

If the individual injured by a wild (or vicious-propensity domestic) animal voluntarily assumed a known risk, with full appreciation of the dangers involved, then the owner is not strictly liable for the inflicted injuries. Courts justify this defense on equitable grounds. It would be unfair to hold owners absolutely liable for harm their animals caused if the victims chose to subject themselves to the danger. This may colloquially be phrased as the "you got what you asked for" theory.

Contributory and Comparative Negligence

Courts often rule that the plaintiff's contributory or comparative negligence in an animal attack will prevent the owner's absolute liability. Some courts state that a plaintiff's contributory negligence bars strict liability altogether. This means that the plaintiff would have to prove that the defendant (owner) was negligent in keeping the animal that attacked and hurt the plaintiff. Other courts simply ignore absolute liability theory and reshape the case in a negligence mold, in which the plaintiff's and defendant's respective degrees of negligence are compared.

Consent

An injured plaintiff might have consented to exposure to a dangerous animal. Consent is usually based upon a person's employment responsibilities while working around animals. For example, suppose Gordon works for a police-dog-training facility, where he serves as an attack victim. He knows from observation and experience that the dogs will attack when given certain command words. Even if a command were given while Gordon was not wearing his protective padding, and he was bitten by one of the dogs, he has implicitly consented to this danger as part of his job. Basically, this is assumption of risk couched in consent terms. The same reasoning would apply for keepers, trainers, or feeders of wild animals for zoos or circuses.

LEGAL TERMS

vicious propensity rule
Doctrine in absolute liability cases involving domestic animals. Normally, owners are not strictly liable for injuries caused by their domestic animals. However, if the animals display vicious propensities and hurt someone or some property, then the owner is absolutely liable. Vicious propensities are proven by past episodes of the animal's nasty behavior.

Self-Defense and Defense of Others

Recall the intentional tort defenses of self-defense and defense of others from chapter 5. When a wild or vicious domestic animal attacks a victim, but the owner used the animal as a means of self-defense or defense of other persons, then the owner would not be strictly liable for the inflicted injuries. For instance, suppose someone attacks Arthur while he is out walking his dog, which has a vicious reputation around the neighborhood. To repel the danger, Arthur commands his dog to attack. His assailant is knocked to the ground, chewed up a bit, and scared away. Arthur would not be absolutely liable for his dog's injuries. The same scenario would arise if Arthur saw someone attacking a member of his family or a friend and he used the dog to protect that person. However, remember the limitations to these defenses. One may not become the aggressor and still use them to escape liability. Hence, if Arthur's dog had chased the fleeing attacker down the street, Arthur could not use these defenses to avoid liability.

Dog-Bite Statutes

Most jurisdictions have statutes that have changed the common law owner liability (and the available defenses) in dog-bite cases. These statutes can substantially affect a dog owner's liability and defenses.

THE CASE OF BITE-WORSE-THAN-BARK

Postal carriers have an endless series of anecdotes about nasty dogs. Fortunately, most such encounters end without serious harm to either person or pet. However, in hapless cases, one or the other suffers serious injury. In the case here, the plaintiff was faced with an extremely vicious canine breed, as the expert testimony established. But a dog is a dog, and dogs are presumed harmless, according to the traditional common law, which the Texas Court of Appeals vapidly recites. One wonders if stare decisis leads to cognitive atrophy.

Powers v. Palacios
794 S.W.2d 493 (Tex. Ct. App. 1990),
rev'd on other grounds,
813 S.W.2d 489 (Tex. 1991)
(Court of Appeals of Texas)
June 29, 1990

OPINION

SEERDEN, Justice.

Brenda Powers sued Paul Palacios, seeking damages for injuries, including loss of a finger, sustained when a pit bull dog kept at his residence attacked her while she was delivering mail. Following a jury trial, the trial court rendered a take-nothing judgment. We affirm the judgment of the trial court. [. . .]

Appellant's point of error number four complains of the refusal of the trial court to submit her proposed Question 4 to the jury.

The evidence showed that appellant was attacked by a dog which was kept at appellee's residence. The dog was of a breed commonly known as a pit bull.

Appellant presented expert testimony that these dogs have a savage and vicious nature and are dangerous to humans.

Appellant's requested Special Issue 4 would have inquired of the jury:

Did Defendant Paul Palacios allow, either by express consent or implied consent, Jessie Palacios (the dog's owner) to have on Paul Palacios's premises a vicious animal on Feb. 23, 1987, the day of the attack?

Appellant correctly cites *Marshall v. Ranne,* [citation omitted] which is the leading Texas case relating to the law of wild and vicious animals. It holds that suits for damages caused by vicious animals should be governed by the law of strict liability. It also expressly adopts as the correct rule the *Restatement (Second) of Torts* §§ 507, 509 (1938).

These sections provide a distinction between the strict liability of a possessor of a "wild animal" (§ 507) and an "abnormally dangerous domestic animal" (§ 509) by providing that the possessor of the latter must have "reason to know" that the animal has dangerous propensities abnormal to its class, while the only condition for imposing liability on the possessor of a "wild animal" is that the damage result from a dangerous propensity characteristic of wild animals of its class.

Appellant's proposed Question 4, and her argument in support thereof, presupposes that the pit bull is a wild animal. The court refused to submit the request, but submitted Question 5, which inquired whether appellee had reason to know that the dog had dangerous propensities abnormal to its class. This question is consistent with the *Marshall* rule on abnormally dangerous domestic animals. The jury answered Question 5 "No."

We have been cited no cases differentiating between wild and domestic animals. *Black's Law Dictionary* contains these definitions:

> Domestic animals. Such as are habituated to live in or about the habitations of men, or such as contribute to the support of a family.

> Wild animals. Animals of an untamable disposition; animals in a state of nature. [Citation omitted.]

We hold that the trial court was correct in refusing to submit to the jury the question based on appellant's theory that the dog in question was a wild animal. [. . .]

The judgment of the trial court is affirmed.

CASE QUESTIONS

1. The plaintiff's expert testimony established that the defendant's pit bull had "a savage and vicious nature" that is "dangerous to humans." Would this not satisfy the *Black's Law Dictionary* definition of *wild animal* as one with "an untamable disposition"? Explain.
2. Does the expert testimony that pit bulls, as a breed, are "dangerous to humans" contradict Black's definition of *domestic animals* as those "habituated to live in or about the habitations of men, or such as contribute to the support of family"? Why or why not?
3. Why do you think the jury did not apply the strict liability rule applicable in vicious propensity cases? How could the defendant not have reason to know of the pit bull's viciousness, given the plaintiff's expert testimony about their inherent malevolence?

Dog-bite hypotheticals present interesting applications of absolute liability. In the following example, consider the vicious propensity rule and its effects on the canine owner's liability.

HYPOTHETICAL

Toby Jones owns a towing service. He uses Doberman pinscher dogs to guard the parking lot in which he keeps towed vehicles. The area is surrounded by large, barbed-wire fences with "no trespassing" signs attached every few feet. The guard dogs would bark, snarl, bite, and lunge at anyone who came near the fencing. Early one morning, Chet Paisley stopped by to claim an automobile that had been towed for illegal parking. After paying the storage fees, Chet walked back to the holding area. Toby had forgotten to chain the dogs from the night before, and they were running loose in the parking lot. When they saw Chet, they attacked and severely injured him.

The common law presumes that dogs are harmless, domestic creatures. However, there is considerable evidence that Toby's Dobermans displayed vicious propensities. Accordingly, the harmlessness presumption falls aside, and the dogs are viewed as potentially dangerous, like wild animals. Under absolute liability, Toby would be responsible for Chet's injuries. Toby's negligence or intent are irrelevant here. It only matters that the dogs were abnormally dangerous instrumentalities, because of their vicious propensities. Once strict liability applies, the result is easy: the animal owner must compensate the victim for his or her injuries.

Would the result have been different if Toby had posted signs stating, "WARNING! DANGEROUS ATTACK DOGS! DO NOT ENTER WITHOUT AUTHORIZED PERSONNEL TO ACCOMPANY YOU"? If Chet had seen such signs but entered regardless, he would have assumed the risk. Chet would have voluntarily assumed a known risk (the dangerous dogs) with full appreciation of the threat involved (being bitten or mauled). Chet would also have been contributorily negligent in entering the enclosed parking lot without Toby or another employee accompanying him.

Figure 9-1 summarizes animal owner strict liability and the available defenses.

9.3 ABNORMALLY DANGEROUS ACTIVITIES

Abnormally dangerous activities are inherently perilous because of the actions and the devices involved. Common examples include the use of explosives, flammable substances, noxious gases, poisons, hazardous wastes

Wildlife (ferae naturae)	Domestic Animals (domitae naturae)	Defenses
Owner strictly liable for injuries caused by wild animals	Owner absolutely liable for injuries caused by domestic animals *only* if such animals display vicious propensities	1. Assumption of risk 2. Contributory negligence 3. Comparative negligence 4. Consent 5. Self-defense 6. Defense of others

FIGURE 9-1
Animal Owners' Absolute Liability and Defenses

(the so-called **toxic torts**), or (in some jurisdictions) electricity, natural gas, and water supplied through unprotected utility lines. Many early twentieth-century cases refer to *ultrahazardous activities*. This is the term used by the original Restatement of Torts § 520 (the oft-called First Restatement). Although some courts split hairs distinguishing ultrahazardous from abnormally dangerous, the expressions are essentially interchangeable.

Restatement (Second) Rule

The *Restatement (Second) of Torts* § 520 declares that persons engaged in abnormally dangerous activities shall be strictly liable for injuries caused by their actions. The *Restatement* lists several criteria for absolute liability:

1. The abnormally dangerous activity created a high risk of substantial injury to an individual or his or her property.
2. This risk could not be removed through the use of reasonable care.
3. The activity is not commonly undertaken (the common usage principle).
4. The activity was inappropriately undertaken in the place in which the victim was harmed.
5. The hazards that the activity creates outweigh the benefits that the activity brings to the community.

High Risk of Substantial Injury

To be abnormally dangerous, the defendant's activity must create a great threat of seriously injuring the plaintiff or the plaintiff's property. For instance, consider a highway construction company that uses dynamite to excavate rock and earth. Dynamite is dangerous stuff. It presents an enormous risk of injuring others nearby if it is not used properly. The threat of harm is significant, as people could be killed or their property destroyed if the dynamite were not used correctly.

LEGAL TERMS

toxic tort actions
Involve toxic chemicals, pollution, hazardous waste disposal and transportation, and other environmentally sensitive issues. Toxic tort actions apply many tort theories, including trespass to land, negligence, absolute liability for ultrahazardous substances, products liability, and nuisance.

Reasonable Care

If the tortfeasor could have eliminated the risk of harm through the use of reasonable care, then the activity is not abnormally dangerous, and absolute liability does not apply. For example, a utility company could exercise reasonable care and protect citizens from the great threat posed by electricity or natural gas simply by using insulated wires or double-sealed underground pipelines. Reasonable care could easily eliminate the risks of electrocution or explosion. If the utility company actually used these (or other) reasonable precautions, but a victim nonetheless was somehow injured, then the activity (supplying electricity or natural gas) would not be ultrahazardous.

Note the hidden implication in this element, though. Failure to use reasonable care to safeguard others from the risks involved in the activity could make it abnormally dangerous. For instance, suppose a utility ran electricity through uninsulated wires. Many courts have held that this would make the activity ultrahazardous, so the utility company would be strictly liable for injuries. However, not all courts interpret the *Second Restatement*'s reasonable care standard in this way.

Common Usage Principle

Abnormally dangerous activities and substances are those not commonly undertaken or used in everyday life. This is sometimes called the **common usage principle**. For instance, consider explosives, toxic chemicals, or poisonous gases. How often does the average person use them? Does anyone in the reader's neighborhood? What about the manufacturing plant across town? But, it could be said, that is only one facility, and the vast majority of the public in the community does not use such substances. These, then, would be examples of abnormally dangerous substances, because they are not commonly used.

What about flammable substances? Many courts have included these as ultrahazardous items. But virtually everyone uses gasoline every day. Would gasoline not fall within common usage? Whether gasoline is abnormally dangerous depends upon how it is being used. Suppose SludgeCo Oil Company operates a gasoline refinery, with several massive fuel tanks storing hundreds of thousands of gallons. Few people in the community probably have such facilities in their backyards. Gasoline may be commonly used, but not in the way this storage facility uses it. The gas one keeps in his or her garage for the lawn mower would not be ultrahazardous; however, the huge storage tanks would be abnormally dangerous.

Inappropriate Use in Certain Place

To be ultrahazardous, the activity or substance must have been inappropriately performed or used in the place in which the victim was harmed.

For example, suppose a chemical manufacturer opened a plant adjacent to a housing subdivision that uses well water. Suppose that the plant dumped toxic chemicals into holding ponds on its premises. Harmful chemicals could seep into the ground and contaminate the water supplies of nearby residents. Perhaps several of these homeowners became ill as a consequence. The activity (using toxic chemical retention ponds) is abnormally dangerous because it created a serious risk of substantial harm, was not of common usage, and was inappropriately undertaken at the location in which the plaintiffs were harmed (adjacent to residences).

Hazards Outweigh Benefits: Balancing Test

Courts often apply a balancing test to decide if an activity is abnormally dangerous. Such an analysis compares the dangers created by the activity with the benefits that the community derives from the activity. This is similar to the benefits analysis used in many nuisance cases, which is discussed in chapter 11.

For example, suppose the state government is building a new highway to improve access between hospitals and an isolated rural town. The construction crew uses dynamite to clear the area for the road. A nearby homeowner suffers structural damage to her house as a result of the blasting and sues the government under strict liability theory. Courts following the *Second Restatement* would balance the benefits derived against the risks involved. The highway would improve the community's access to hospital facilities. The dangers created by dynamite use, which in this case involved structural damage, are probably outweighed by these benefits.

Many courts have applied the *Second Restatement*'s approach throughout this century. Several jurisdictions, however, have rejected the rule, either in whole or in part. Still, the *Second Restatement* provides a comprehensive, general formula for analyzing abnormally dangerous activities and absolute liability.

Defenses

Many state legislatures have enacted statutes protecting certain abnormally dangerous activities from strict liability. These statutes usually shield public utilities distributing electricity and natural gas, private contractors performing construction (particularly highway) work for the government, and municipal zoos or parks that maintain wild animals. Under these statutes, the protected entities cannot be held absolutely liable for injuries caused by wild animals or ultrahazardous activities. Instead, plaintiffs must prove that the protected defendants were negligent or committed intentional torts.

LEGAL TERMS

common usage principle
Doctrine in strict liability cases that defines abnormally dangerous activities and substances as those not commonly undertaken or used in everyday life.

Public Policy Objectives Behind Statutory Immunity

Legislatures often justify such immunity statutes on the grounds that government (and the private companies that often work under governmental contracts) must be protected from the harshness of strict liability if certain essential activities are to be performed. How, the argument goes, can governments build roads, operate zoos or parks, supply utilities, or enable private industry to satisfy energy demands, if these activities carry the burden of strict liability whenever someone inadvertently gets hurt? This reasoning is similar to the benefits balancing act that courts often apply under the *Second Restatement* approach. Because legislatures enact statutes, and the public can change the legislature (through voting) and thus change the statutes, citizens who disagree with the immunity laws can elect new legislators to modify these provisions.

THE CASE OF THE SATURDAY NIGHT SPECIAL

Most Americans recall the 1981 assassination attempt on President Ronald Reagan. Several bystanders were seriously injured when John Hinckley fired his fateful shots. Searching for a deeper pocket than Hinckley's, one injured person sued the manufacturer of Hinckley's gun, commonly called a "Saturday Night Special," under ultrahazardous activity and products liability theories. The D.C. Court of Appeals shot down the appellants' attempt to hold the manufacturer absolutely liable.

Delahanty v. Hinckley
564 A.2d 758 (D.C. 1989)
(District of Columbia
Court of Appeals)
October 11, 1989

FERREN, Associate Judge:
Thomas and Jean Delahanty, appellants, filed suit in the United States District Court for the District of Columbia against John Hinckley for injuries Thomas suffered when Hinckley attempted to assassinate President Ronald Reagan. The Delahantys also sued the manufacturer of the gun, R.G. Industries, Inc., its foreign parent company, Roehm, and individual officers of Roehm.

Appellants advanced three legal theories for holding the gun manufacturers liable in these circumstances: negligence, strict products liability [. . .], and a "social utility" claim apparently based on strict liability for abnormally dangerous activities under *Restatement (Second) of Torts* §§ 519, 520 (1977) [. . .].

The District Court dismissed appellants' complaint against the gun manufacturers and their officers for failure to state a claim upon which relief could be granted. [Citation omitted.] On appeal, the United States Court of Appeals for the District of Columbia Circuit *sua sponte* asked this court [. . .] to decide whether, in the District of Columbia, "manufacturers and distributors of Saturday Night Specials may be strictly liable for injuries arising from these guns' criminal use." [Citation omitted.] On consideration of this question, we conclude that traditional tort theories—negligence and strict liability under the *Restatement (Second) of Torts*—provide no basis for holding the gun manufacturer liable. [. . .]

We reject each of the theories appellants have advanced in the federal courts and in this court. [. . .]

Appellants also present what they call a "social utility claim," arguing that the manufacturer should be held strictly liable because the type of gun in this case is "inherently and abnormally dangerous with no social value." Appellants appear to base this claim [. . .] on liability for abnormally dangerous activities, *Restatement (Second) of Torts* §§ 519, 520, a doctrine not yet explicitly adopted in the District of Columbia [. . .].

Like other courts that have considered the issue [. . .] we reject application of the "abnormally dangerous activity" doctrine to gun manufacture and sale. [Citations omitted.]

Appellants argue that the marketing of the guns is the abnormally dangerous activity for which the manufacturers should be held liable. We cannot agree. The cause of action under *Restatement* § 519 applies only to activities that are dangerous in themselves and to injuries that result directly from the dangerous activity. [Citation omitted.] "The marketing of a handgun is not dangerous in and of itself, and when injury occurs, it is not the direct result of the sale itself, but rather the result of actions taken by a third party." [Citation omitted.] Furthermore, handgun marketing cannot be classified as abnormally dangerous by applying the factors of *Restatement* § 520 [. . .]. For example, any high degree of risk of harm, or any likelihood that such harm will be great, would result from the use, not the marketing as such, of handguns. [. . .]

In sum, given appellants' proffered theories, we perceive no basis under the facts alleged for holding the gun manufacturers and their officers liable under the law of the District of Columbia for Hinckley's criminal use of the gun.

CASE QUESTIONS

1. Apart from negligence or strict liability, is there another avenue by which manufacturers and sellers of "Saturday Night Specials" could be held absolutely liable for resulting injuries when the weapons are used in crimes? What governmental agency would have to be involved in this process?
2. What does *sua sponte* mean, as used in the court's opinion?

Cases involving toxic substances (discussed further in chapters 4 and 11) often revolve around absolute liability theory, applying the abnormally dangerous activity analysis. Of all the causes of action usually associated with toxic torts (including trespass to land, negligence, nuisance, and strict liability), absolute liability offers the best common law avenue for plaintiffs to recover.

HYPOTHETICALS

Gordon Jamison owns a photography business. Developing film involves using several corrosive chemicals not ordinarily used by most people. Elmer Treble visited the store one day to get his pictures developed. He asked Gordon if he could use the restroom. Gordon, who was busy with another customer, nodded toward the rear of the shop. The restroom was in the back storeroom, to the left, while the darkroom, in which the chemicals were kept, was to the right. Neither door was marked. Elmer walked into the darkroom and, fumbling for a light switch, knocked over several vats of acid onto himself, suffering severe burns.

Elmer wishes to sue Gordon under strict liability for maintaining an ultrahazardous activity. Was the darkroom abnormally dangerous? Apply the *Second Restatement*'s formula. Did the keeping of acids in open vats in the darkroom create a high risk of substantial injury to Elmer, who was wandering in search of the restroom? Acids are perilous, particularly in pitch-black rooms that innocent bystanders like Elmer might encounter without realizing the threat. There was great risk of significant harm. Could the risk have been removed through the exercise of reasonable care? Yes. If Gordon had posted signs on the doors, or if he had locked the darkroom door, then Elmer would never have spilled the acids. Reasonable care could have eliminated the danger; therefore, the activity was not abnormally dangerous, and so strict liability cannot apply. Recall, however, that Elmer could also sue Gordon under negligence theory instead of absolute liability, so perhaps Elmer could still recover damages for his injuries.

□ □ □

Consider another hypothetical. Suppose local businesses operated a Fourth of July fireworks celebration, which involved shooting the fireworks into the air high above town. Suppose excessive explosives were used in the fireworks. When they were detonated, flaming debris fell onto nearby houses, causing many fires. Could the homeowners succeed in a strict liability lawsuit against the companies responsible for the fireworks display?

Were the fireworks abnormally dangerous activities? Apply the *Second Restatement*'s criteria for absolute liability. Fireworks exploding in mid-air create a tremendous risk that flaming debris could fall onto buildings' roofs, setting fires. The threat and the harm are substantial. Could reasonable care have avoided the risk? Fireworks that explode in the air are going to fall somewhere, perhaps in flaming pieces. No degree of reasonable care could prevent the danger of resulting fires. Aerial fireworks of the types described in this example are not commonly used by the public. The fireworks were inappropriately used in the area in which the fires occurred, because the power used was excessive and the fireworks detonated above the houses, subjecting them to the severe fire risk. The threat of harm outweighs the benefits to the community, as fireworks displays are conducted only once or twice per year and the benefits are purely aesthetic and momentary. The fireworks promoters will be strictly liable to the homeowners. This conclusion assumes, of course, that there are no state statutes or local ordinances granting the fireworks promoters immunity from absolute liability.

Figure 9-2 summarizes absolute liability for abnormally dangerous activities. All absolute liability cases, as discussed in this chapter, must satisfy the requirements of proximate cause, which is discussed in § 9.4.

Definitions and Examples	Restatement (2d) of Torts § 520	Defenses
Abnormally dangerous = Ultrahazardous	Activity creates high risk of substantial harm	Statutory immunities for certain types of ultrahazardous activities
These activities are, by their very nature, perilous	Risk could not be eliminated through exercise of reasonable care	Most often include governmental activities involving uses of explosives, chemicals, or energy service
Examples: use of explosives, flammable substances, noxious gases, or poisons	Activity is not commonly undertaken (common usage principle)	Immunities reflect public policy objectives to balance necessary public services against individual right to compensation for injury
Some courts include unprotected use of utilities (electricity, natural gas, water)	Activity is inappropriate in place where injury happened	
	Hazards created outweigh community benefits from activity	

FIGURE 9-2
Absolute Liability for Abnormally Dangerous Activities and Defenses

9.4 SCOPE OF LIABILITY: PROXIMATE CAUSE

Proximate cause in absolute liability cases is defined similarly to cause in negligence cases. (Review the definition of proximate cause discussed in chapter 6.) Animals or abnormally dangerous activities must proximately cause the victim's injuries if the tortfeasor is to be held strictly liable. For absolute liability purposes, proximate cause has the following elements:

LEGAL TERMS

proximate cause
  Legal cause in some absolute liability cases. Proximate cause exists when the tortfeasor's actions cause a reasonably foreseeable injury to the victim. Courts often refer to the plaintiff's injuries as being the natural and probable consequence of the defendant's misconduct.

1. The plaintiff's injuries must have been a reasonably foreseeable consequence of the defendant's actions; and
2. The victim must have been a foreseeable plaintiff (meaning that it must have been reasonably foreseeable that the plaintiff would be injured as a result of the defendant's activities).

These elements are defined the same as in negligence theory, as discussed in chapter 6.

No Duty of Reasonable Care

When applied to strict liability cases, proximate cause does not include the duty of reasonable care, which is an element of negligence theory. Nevertheless, some courts insist on including the duty while discussing proximate cause in absolute liability cases. But negligence is irrelevant to strict liability; therefore, the duty of reasonable care (as used in negligence's proximate cause analysis) is also irrelevant.

In the hypotheticals discussed throughout this chapter, apply the proximate cause standard to each example. Did the tortfeasor's actions proximately cause the victim's injuries? A variety of answers are possible. As with negligence, proximate cause in absolute liability cases can be a poser, but at least these puzzle pieces fit together to further complete the pattern.

SUMMARY

9.1. Fault is irrelevant to strict liability. If the tortfeasor is found to be absolutely liable, his or her negligence or intent does not affect the liability. This may seem harsh and unfair, because a tortfeasor might exercise every degree of care to avoid injuring others and still be held responsible under absolute liability. Strict liability is limited to cases involving abnormally dangerous instrumentalities, such as wild animals, vicious domestic animals, ultrahazardous activities, and products liability. Through its courts and legislatures, the public has established absolute liability as an insurance measure to protect innocent victims from harm caused by particularly perilous pursuits.

9.2. The common law calls wild animals *ferae naturae* ("wild nature") and domestic animals *domitae naturae* ("domesticated nature"). At common law wild animals are presumed to be naturally dangerous, while domestic animals are assumed to be harmless and docile creatures. Wild animals may be owned by individuals who capture and restrain the beasts. This is called exercising dominion and control. Owners are absolutely liable for injuries their wild animals inflict. However, owners are strictly liable only for injuries caused by their domestic animals if these animals exhibited vicious propensities. The defenses of assumption of risk, contributory and comparative negligence, consent, and self-defense or defense of others apply to animal liability cases.

9.3. Abnormally dangerous, or ultrahazardous, activities are inherently perilous. Use of explosives, flammable substances, noxious gases, poisons, hazardous wastes, and sometimes electricity, natural gas, or water utilities are examples. The *Restatement (Second) of Torts* § 520 states that persons engaged in abnormally dangerous activities are strictly liable for injuries caused by these activities. The activity must create a high risk of substantial harm, which risk could not have been eliminated through the exercise of reasonable care; the activity or substance must not be commonly undertaken or used; the activity must have been inappropriately used in the place in which the injury happened; and the activity's hazards must outweigh the activity's benefits to the community. As a defense to strict liability, many legislatures have enacted statutes protecting certain activities from absolute liability.

9.4. Absolute liability in animal and abnormally dangerous activity cases is limited by proximate cause. For strict liability to apply, the defendant's actions must have proximately caused the plaintiff's injuries. This means that the plaintiff's injuries must have been reasonably foreseeable as a consequence of the defendant's conduct, and it must have been foreseeable that the plaintiff could be injured as a result of the defendant's actions. This is called foreseeable plaintiffs theory. There is no duty of reasonable care when proximate cause is applied to strict liability cases, because the duty involves negligence theory, which is irrelevant to absolute liability.

REVIEW QUESTIONS

1. How is strict, or absolute, liability different from negligence and intentional torts? What role does fault play in absolute liability? What are the limitations to strict liability? What are the public policy objectives behind absolute liability? How is strict liability like insurance?

2. How does the common law define wild animals? Domestic animals? What does the common law presume about each type of animal? How can wildlife be owned? Why is this important to the question of liability? When does strict liability apply to injuries inflicted by wild animals? By domestic animals? What is the vicious propensity rule? What defenses apply to animal owner absolute liability cases?

3. What are abnormally dangerous activities? Ultrahazardous activities? How does the *Restatement (Second) of Torts* define the term? What elements are required for absolute liability to apply? What is the function of reasonable care? What is the common usage principle? What balancing test do courts apply in abnormally dangerous activity cases?

4. How is proximate cause defined in strict liability cases? Why is it important? How is it different from proximate cause in negligence theory?

PROBLEMS

In the following hypotheticals, determine if absolute liability applies and if the tortfeasor will be strictly liable to the injured party. Are any defenses relevant? If so, how would they be applied?

1. Heather Muffin works at the municipal zoo. She feeds and cleans the cages for the various species of monkey on exhibition. One day, Heather received a telephone call from "Spider" Tomey, exhibits supervisor, who instructed her to report to the exotic bird building to substitute for another employee who was ill. Heather had never worked with these birds before and was unfamiliar with their habits, although she received feeding and watering instructions from Spider. As she was cleaning one of the walk-in cages, a toucan landed on the back of her neck, scratching and biting at her ears. The scratches required stitches. There were no municipal ordinances discussing the zoo or its operation, apart from the enabling act that established the zoo and its supervision by the city's department of parks and recreation.

2. Miller Thurber owns a bulldog, which he kept chained in his backyard. The dog often barked and growled at anyone passing by the house on the sidewalk. One morning, Josie Taylor, an employee of the electric company, visited Thurber's house to read the meter, which was located in the backyard. Josie had read Thurber's meter before and knew about the dog. She peeked around the house but could not see the dog. She assumed it was inside the house, because the chain was lying on the ground. As she walked over to the meter, the dog leaped from the bushes, knocked Josie down, and chewed on her arms and hands. Josie was hospitalized as a result of these injuries.

3. Olaf Nurdoff owns a gas station. While a tanker truck was filling his underground fuel tanks, Olaf was using a welding torch inside his garage area to repair a customer's car. He inadvertently knocked over the torch, still lit, which fell into a puddle of gasoline from the tanker. The puddle ignited and burned across the ground to the tanker pipe connected to the underground tanks. Both the tanker truck and the fuel in the underground tanks then ignited and exploded. Several patrons and their vehicles were severely injured.

4. The Belladonna Pharmaceutical Company manufactures medicines. It uses certain chemical solutions that turn bad and must be destroyed. These solutions are kept in steel barrels in the firm's back lot, awaiting pickup from a local waste disposal company. Bud Marvelle works for the trash company. He had never collected trash from Belladonna

before, as he normally rode the residential trash routes. Bud's supervisor failed to instruct him to take a special sealed tank truck to get Belladonna's chemicals. Instead, Bud drove an open-top trash truck used to haul dry garbage. Bud tossed the barrels into the truck, and several of them ruptured and leaked. As Bud drove down the highway to the dump, chemical sludge spilled out the back of the truck onto an automobile driven by Madison Ventura. Madison stopped and touched the sludge caked across the front of his car. It made his hands burn. Frightened, Madison drove to a local hospital emergency room. His skin had absorbed much of the chemical waste, and he became severely ill and had to be hospitalized for several weeks.

PROBLEM ANSWERS

1. Heather Muffin would sue the city, naming either (or both) the city and the municipal zoo as defendants, depending upon her state's civil procedure statutes regarding filing lawsuits against governmental units. No municipal ordinances immunize the city (zoo) from wild animal owner liability.

   The city (zoo), as owner of the wild animals in the zoo, ordinarily would be absolutely liable for injuries inflicted by these animals. Proximate cause is satisfied, because Heather's injuries were reasonably foreseeable and she was a foreseeable plaintiff. However, the defendant(s) would employ the defenses of consent, assumption of risk, and contributory (or comparative) negligence.

   Consent would be a successful defense against Heather's claim. As a zoo employee, Heather impliedly consented to the dangers associated with working with wild animals there, including the risk of injury in handling the animals.

   Assumption of risk would similarly protect the city (zoo) from liability. As a zoo employee, Heather voluntarily assumed a known risk (possible injury while handling wild animals) with full appreciation of the dangers involved (large, wild birds can claw, peck, etc.). Heather's unfamiliarity with the specific habits of toucan birds would not affect this defense. She reasonably should have anticipated that frightened toucans might scratch and bite her if she (a stranger to the birds) entered their cages.

   Heather also committed contributory or comparative negligence. She breached her duty of reasonable care to herself by not taking precautions to prevent the birds from injuring her. For instance, she could have worn a heavy overcoat and hat, which exotic bird handlers often wear while cleaning cages. The reasonable person standard applied to Heather would be modified to reflect the experience and expertise of a reasonable zoo employee accustomed to handling wildlife. Accordingly, Heather's failure to take reasonable precautions contributed to her injuries.

Contributory negligence would totally preclude Heather's claims. Comparative negligence would have the effect of removing strict liability from consideration and replacing it with assigned negligence percentages. This, in effect, converts the case from absolute liability to negligence.

2. Miller Thurber's bulldog exhibited vicious propensities through its past behavior of barking and growling at passersby. Josie Taylor was aware of the dog's viciousness. As a reasonable person would have done, Josie inspected the yard carefully for the dog before entering. She was reasonably convinced that the dog was inside Miller's house, since the chain was lying on the ground, and presumably Josie had seen the dog chained up during past visits to read the meter. Josie did not see the dog hiding in the bushes (this can be presumed from the facts). Under the vicious propensity rule, Miller would be absolutely liable for Josie's injuries inflicted by the bulldog. Proximate cause is also satisfied, as the dog's attack was reasonably foreseeable and Josie was a foreseeable plaintiff.

No defenses apply in this hypothetical. Josie did not consent to the attack. She was not contributorily or comparatively negligent, nor did she assume the risk. Although she knew about the dog's viciousness, she did not know that the dog was lurking in the bushes, waiting to attack. To Josie, this was an unknown danger that she did not voluntarily assume.

3. The patrons would sue Olaf Nurdoff under strict liability for their physical injuries and damage to their vehicles.

By using a welding torch while a gasoline tanker truck was unloading fuel, Olaf was engaged in an abnormally dangerous activity. Under *Restatement (Second) of Torts* § 520, Olaf's torch use created a high risk of substantial injury to his patrons and their vehicles, in the event that the torch ignited the gasoline, as it did. Further, Olaf could not have removed the risk through the exercise of reasonable care, because using a torch at all in the proximity of gasoline vapors or fuel puddles is inherently dangerous—an explosion could occur at any instant. People do not commonly use torches around large quantities of gasoline. This is especially true of individuals experienced with fuels, such as gas-station owners. Using a torch in a gasoline station was inappropriate. Clearly, the hazards created outweighed the benefit to the community (i.e., Olaf's welding for a customer's benefit versus the risk of massive explosion).

Olaf would be absolutely liable under the *Second Restatement* rule. Proximate cause is satisfied because the injuries were reasonably foreseeable and the victims were all foreseeable plaintiffs.

No defenses apply to this hypothetical.

4. Madison Ventura would probably sue both the local waste disposal company (Bud Marvelle's employer, under respondeat superior) and the Belladonna Pharmaceutical Company.

    Belladonna is a red herring in this hypothetical. Belladonna did not proximately cause Madison's injuries. In fact, it did nothing to injure Madison. Although it did supply the chemicals, Belladonna did not cause them to come into contact with Madison. Direct causation links Bud as the sole cause-in-fact of Madison's injuries. Thus, Belladonna would not be liable to Madison under any tort theory.

    Bud's employer, however, would not be so fortunate. By picking up the hazardous chemicals, the trash company was engaged in an abnormally dangerous activity. Again, *Restatement (Second)* § 520 applies.

    The second element is the key to this hypothetical. Could Bud have removed the risk posed by the chemicals through the exercise of reasonable care? Yes. The company had a special sealed tank truck to collect Belladonna's chemicals. This precaution constitutes reasonable care.

    However, the company failed to use reasonable care when the supervisor failed to instruct Bud to use the special truck. Failure to use reasonable care converts Bud's activities into ultrahazardous behavior.

    The *Second Restatement*'s other elements are satisfied. By using an ordinary trash truck, Bud created a high risk of substantial injury to Madison. Hauling dangerous chemicals is not a common activity. Driving a trash truck with leaking toxic chemicals along a public highway was inappropriate. Definitely, the hazards to other drivers, such as Madison, outweighed the benefits that toxic trash removal provided to the community.

    Proximate cause is satisfied, as it was reasonably foreseeable that the chemicals could leak from an unsealed truck onto adjacent vehicles and injure their occupants. As an adjacent driver, Madison was a foreseeable plaintiff.

    This case also illustrates another toxic tort situation. The federal Hazardous Materials Transportation Act, discussed in chapter 4, would apply to this problem.

PROJECTS

1. Brief *Pulley v. Malek,* 25 Ohio St. 3d 95, 495 N.E.2d 402 (1986). How did the Ohio Supreme Court rule on the applicability of the common law assumption-of-risk defense in this dog-bite case?

2. Does your state have any statutes concerning dog-bite liability? If so, what defenses are included in the statutes?

3. Does your state have any statutes that limit absolute liability for abnormally dangerous activities? Are there any state statutes pertaining to hazardous waste disposal or transportation?

4. Do your state courts follow the *Second Restatement* approach to strict liability in abnormally dangerous activities?

5. In class or study groups, create your own hypotheticals using the strict liability theories and defenses discussed in this chapter. Then change the facts to affect the outcomes of the problems.

CHAPTER 10
Products Liability

10.5 COMPARISON TO CONTRACT LAW WARRANTIES
Similarities Between Products Liability and Breach of Warranty
Difference Between Products Liability and Breach of Warranty
SUMMARY

DATA-GRAPHIC TORTS

Langtree v. Summer Breeze Corp.

Veronica Langtree bought an oscillating table fan at the local hardware store. The fan was manufactured by the Summer Breeze Corporation. The fan contained a screw which, when tightened, held the fan in a fixed position. Unbeknownst to Langtree, the screw on her fan did not contain a retaining washer, which weakened the screw's ability to hold the fan in place as it operated. Langtree used the fan for several weeks without any problems. Then, one day, while she was running an errand, the screw broke, causing the fan to fall forward. This caused the engine to overheat and a fire ensued, burning Langtree's apartment furnishings.

Langtree's products liability lawsuit would surely be settled quickly. Tests could easily demonstrate this assembly defect. Summer Breeze, with insurance funds in hand, would pay Langtree's claims for the lost belongings destroyed because of the defective fan.

DATA-GRAPHIC TORTS

Kenmore v. Surefire Shot Corp.

Surefire Shot Corporation manufactures rifles. One of its popular .22-caliber models, the "West Virginian," has a safety catch that prevents the firing pin from striking the cartridge in the firing chamber. The safety used on this rifle model was originally designed for another Surefire Shot rifle, the "Montanan," which had a microscopically shorter span between the safety lever and the firing pin. Thus, on the West Virginian models, the safety pin was microscopically too short and, when the safety lever was pressed, the safety pin might not reach the firing pin area sufficiently to block the firing pin from striking the cartridge. Thus, the safety might not prevent the gun from firing. Kim Kenmore bought one of

the West Virginian rifles from a Surefire Shot dealer. On several hunting trips, the safety functioned properly. During one expedition, however, Kenmore raised the gun to sight a distant animal target. The safety was engaged and Kenmore squeezed the trigger, assured that the gun would not discharge. Surprisingly, the safety failed, and Kenmore was thrown backwards, unprepared for the rifle's recoil. She struck her head on a rock and had to be hospitalized.

This hypothetical illustrates a design defect in a defective product. The safety used on Kenmore's rifle model was insufficiently long to consistently prevent the gun from firing. Surefire Shot would be liable for Kenmore's injuries as a result of the defective safety and misfiring incident.

DATA-GRAPHIC TORTS

Uptown Apartment Complex, Inc. v. Boilermaker Corp.

The Uptown Apartment Complex, Inc., operates a steam heating system in its apartment building, powered by a basement boiler that it purchased from the Boilermaker Corporation in 1982. After 10 years, the insides of the steam heating pipes began to deteriorate as a result of lime deposits from the steam. Metal shavings from these copper pipes began flaking off and were carried through the pipe system to the boiler's primary pressure tank. The copper flakes in this tank gradually created a static electricity charge which, over a period of several months, gradually increased until the boiler exploded, substantially damaging the premises. Boilermaker provided all its customers with routine maintenance manuals that alerted users to check the boiler filters once every six months for metal residue. Uptown had never checked the filters. Uptown sued Boilermaker under products liability theory. Who would prevail?

Boilermaker. Uptown failed to maintain the boiler according to the manufacturer's maintenance instructions; thus, Uptown's misuse of the boiler proximately caused the damage to its building. The defective condition, in fact, was alien to Boilermaker's boiler—copper shavings from Uptown's pipes caused the static electricity problem. Thus, the boiler was in a substantially changed condition (when it exploded) than when it left the manufacturer, since it was contaminated by an outside agent. Boilermaker would not be liable to Uptown under products liability theory.

INTRODUCTION

Products liability is another type of strict liability. Generally, under products liability, the manufacturer or seller of a product is absolutely liable for any injuries caused by a defect in the product. Products liability occupies a prominent position in the torts puzzle, as it is involved in a sizeable portion of tort litigation. It is probably the most significant development in tort law since the courts accepted negligence theory as a separate tort. The puzzle pieces to be sorted and assembled in this chapter include:

- The parties in products liability cases.
- The elements of products liability.
- *Restatement (Second) of Torts* § 402A.
- The defenses to products liability.
- Comparing products liability with contract law warranties.

10.1 PRODUCTS LIABILITY THEORY AND HISTORY

Products liability was established as a distinct tort theory in the landmark case of *Greenman v. Yuba Power Products, Inc.,* 59 Cal. 2d 57, 377 P.2d 897, 27 Cal. Rptr. 697 (1962). In this case, the California Supreme Court completed over 100 years of legal evolution that culminated in strict products liability.

Public Policy Objectives Behind Products Liability

Products liability is society's decision, through its courts and legislatures, that businesses manufacturing and selling defective products are in the best economic position to bear the expenses incurred when a faulty product injures an innocent user. The theory may be simply put: Why should the hapless victim shoulder the burdens (medical costs, permanent injuries, etc.) produced by a defectively made product? Instead, should not the manufacturer or seller of that product be liable for the resulting harms? Does that not seem reasonable and ethical? If one has ever been hurt by a defective product, one might answer affirmatively. If one were a manufacturer or seller, however, he or she might feel differently.

Historical Development of Products Liability

In the early nineteenth century, English and American common law held that persons injured by defective products had to sue under contract law rather than tort law. These courts felt that the appropriate cause of action was breach of contract or, more precisely, breach of warranty. A **warranty** is a guarantee that a product or service meets certain quality standards. If a product fails to meet such standards, as is the case when a product is defective, then the warranty has been breached.

LEGAL TERMS

products liability
A type of strict, or absolute, liability, in which the manufacturer or seller is strictly liable for injuries caused by defective products. Its elements include: the defect must render the product unreasonably dangerous; the seller or manufacturer must be in the business of selling such products; the product cannot have substantially changed between the time it left the seller/ manufacturer's hands and the time it reached the ultimate user; the defect must have proximately caused the ultimate user's injuries; and the ultimate user must have used the product properly. Some states add that the ultimate user must have been reasonably foreseeable, and the seller/manufacturer must have been responsible for the condition in which the defective product was maintained. A few states require a product sale.

warranty
A guarantee from the seller or manufacturer that a product complies with certain quality standards. Warranties also may be used for services. If a product or service fails to comply with a warranty's standards, breach of warranty has occurred and the buyer may successfully sue the seller for damages incurred.

Under early nineteenth-century English and American common law, only persons who had made contracts with the manufacturer or seller of a defective product could recover damages for breach of warranty or breach of contract. This contractual relationship is called **privity of contract**. Privity exists when parties are directly engaged in an agreement between them. If Joseph contracts with Harris, in which Joseph agrees to sell Harris a product for a certain price, then there is privity of contract between them. The landmark case that announced the privity rule was *Winterbottom v. Wright,* 10 Meeson & Welsby 109, 152 Eng. Rep. 402 (1842). In this case, the plaintiff drove a horse-drawn coach for the Postmaster-General. This coach was manufactured especially for the Postmaster-General by the defendant. The plaintiff was maimed when the vehicle's axle broke and threw him from the carriage seat. The plaintiff sued the defendant for failing to properly maintain the coach under a service contract. The court held that the plaintiff was not a party to either the service agreement or the manufacturing agreement. Thus, the plaintiff lacked privity of contract, and therefore could not recover for the injuries caused by a defectively assembled coach. The only party that could sue under such circumstances would be the Postmaster-General, with whom the defendant contracted to make the carriage. But in this case the Postmaster-General was not harmed. The injured plaintiff was left without compensation.

Almost immediately, American courts began to carve out exceptions to the privity-of-contract rule. In *Thomas v. Winchester,* 6 N.Y. 397 (1852), the New York Court of Appeals ruled that a mislabelled medicine (which actually contained poison) was inherently dangerous, and accordingly the injured party did not have to have privity of contract with the manufacturer or seller to recover damages. In this case, the plaintiff's husband had purchased a bottle, labelled "dandelion extract," that in actuality contained belladonna, a deadly poison. The defendant manufacturer who mislabelled the product sold it to a druggist, who resold it to a physician, who prescribed it to the plaintiff. There was no privity of contract between the plaintiff and the defendant. Nonetheless, the court permitted the plaintiff to recover damages for injuries caused when she took the poison from the mislabelled bottle. The court reasoned that poisons are imminently dangerous by their very nature. Accordingly, remote users of a mislabelled drug could be seriously injured. Thus, privity of contract is unnecessary if the defective product (such as a mislabelled poison) is imminently dangerous. Later courts characterized this as the **imminent danger exception** to the privity-of-contract rule.

Throughout the nineteenth century, the New York Court of Appeals, and many courts following its lead, expanded the imminent danger rule to include spoiled food, explosives, improperly assembled scaffolding, an exploding coffee urn, and defectively made automobile wheels. Many courts found liability in contract warranty law, but this still required privity of contract. The landmark case in this century, which is often said to have sparked modern products liability law, is *MacPherson v. Buick Motor Co.,*

LEGAL TERMS

privity of contract
A contractual relationship between buyer and seller of a product or service. In tort law, privity was required between the plaintiff and the defendant in nineteenth- and some early twentieth-century defective product cases.

217 N.Y. 382, 111 N.E. 1050 (1916). Writing for the majority, Justice Cardozo declared that privity of contract was obsolete. If a product, because of its defective manufacture, became unreasonably dangerous, then the manufacturer or seller would be liable for injuries caused by the defective product. Cardozo applied negligence theory to determine whether the defective product was unreasonably dangerous. The manufacturer had to be negligent in making the faulty product.

MacPherson ushered in a cascade of court opinions following and expanding its precedent. In *Escola v. Coca Cola Bottling Co.,* 24 Cal. 2d 453, 150 P.2d 436 (1944), Justice Traynor of the California Supreme Court, in his concurring opinion, opined that negligence was no longer necessary for defective product manufacturers to be liable. Instead, he proposed strict liability. It took 18 years before the California Supreme Court adopted this view in *Greenman v. Yuba Power Products.* Many other state courts quickly joined the new common law theory.

The American Law Institute followed *Greenman* with its famous *Restatement (Second) of Torts* § 402A, which virtually every American jurisdiction has adopted (in some form or another) as the definitive rule for strict products liability. The *Restatement*'s position is discussed in greater detail in § 10-3.

10.2 PARTIES

Three classes of parties are involved in products liability cases: the product manufacturer, the seller, and the ultimate user.

Manufacturers and Sellers

The **product manufacturer** makes the defective product that gives rise to the entire products liability lawsuit. **Seller** includes anyone who is in the business of selling goods such as the one that is faulty. This includes the manufacturer as well as wholesalers and retailers. **Wholesalers** are businesses that buy and sell goods to **retailers**, which in turn sell the products to customers, usually individual persons.

The Ultimate User

When we buy a product, we are **purchasers**. In products liability law, however, the party injured by flawed merchandise need not be the original buyer. Instead, a member of the purchaser's family, or a friend of the buyer, could recover damages if hurt by a defective product. The key is whether it is reasonably foreseeable that the user would have utilized the product. This individual is called the **ultimate user**, because that person eventually used the product that caused an injury.

In products liability litigation, the ultimate user becomes the plaintiff who sues various defendants: the retailer, the wholesaler(s), and the

imminent danger exception
A nineteenth- and early twentieth-century exception to the privity of contract requirement in defective product cases.

product manufacturer
The maker of a product which, if defective, gives rise to products liability.

seller (wholesaler, retailer)
Anyone who is in the business of selling goods which, if defective, would incur strict liability to the injured ultimate product user. The term includes manufacturers, wholesalers, and retailers.

purchaser
An individual who buys a product. If injured because of a product defect, the purchaser may recover under products liability theory from the seller or manufacturer.

ultimate user
In products liability law, a person who is injured by a defective product. It must have been reasonably foreseeable that the injured party would use the defective product.

manufacturer. The plaintiff uses a shotgun approach to products liability—namely, sue all the sellers. This may seem excessive, but the plaintiff has a logical explanation. The plaintiff sues all the sellers along the product distribution chain to ensure that one of them (probably the manufacturer) will have sufficient monies to pay a judgment. In tort law, this is called **"going for the deep pocket."** In other words, the plaintiff tries to sue defendants that have money and could satisfy a damages award. Figure 10-1 shows the product distribution chain between manufacturers, sellers, purchasers, and ultimate users. The deficient product passes through many hands before reaching its unfortunate victim.

Now that we have met the parties to products liability actions, it is time to investigate the elements of products liability.

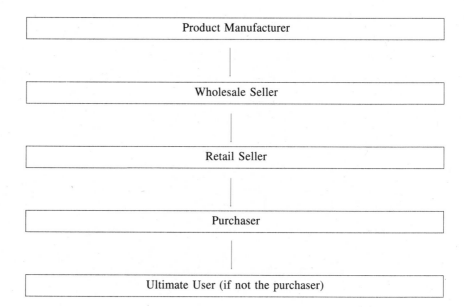

FIGURE 10-1
Product Distribution Chain

10.3 ELEMENTS

Products liability is defined as strict, or absolute, liability for the seller or manufacturer of a defectively made product that injures a user of the item.

No Privity of Contract Requirement

Privity of contract is not required in products liability. The ultimate user need not have purchased the merchandise directly from the seller or manufacturer, although some states require that a sale of the product have

occurred somewhere between the manufacturer and the ultimate user. However, it need not be a direct transaction between the two.

Negligence Is Irrelevant

Remember that the seller or manufacturer's negligence is irrelevant to strict liability. It does not matter how much care the seller or manufacturer used in making or maintaining the product. Every possible precaution could have been utilized, but that simply makes no difference. If the product was defective, and a user was harmed as a result, absolute liability applies—period.

A Typical Products Liability Formula

There are five elements of products liability, as defined by most state courts or statutes:

1. The defect must render the product unreasonably dangerous to use.
2. The seller or manufacturer must be in the business of selling products such as the flawed one(s).
3. The product cannot have been substantially changed between the time it left the seller or manufacturer's hands and the time it reached the ultimate user.
4. The defect must have proximately caused the ultimate user's injuries.
5. The ultimate user must have used the product properly, i.e., in a way that the product was designed to be used.

In some jurisdictions, several additional elements are required:

6. The ultimate user must have been foreseeable (foreseeable plaintiffs theory).
7. The seller or manufacturer must have been responsible for the condition in which the product was maintained.
8. In a few states a sale of the product must have occurred. This could be a sale between the manufacturer and a wholesaler, or a wholesaler to a retailer, or a retailer to a customer. Basically, someone at some point had to buy the defective thing.

Restatement (Second) Rule

Section 402A of the *Restatement (Second) of Torts* contains fewer elements than those just discussed. It states:

> (1) One who sells any product in a defective condition unreasonably dangerous to the user or consumer or to his property is subject to liability for physical harm thereby caused to the ultimate user or consumer, or to his property, if

(a)   the seller is engaged in the business of selling such a product, and

(b)   it is expected to and does reach the user or consumer without substantial change in the condition in which it is sold.

(2)   The rule stated in Subsection (1) applies though

(a)   the seller has exercised all possible care in the preparation and sale of this product, and

(b)   the user or consumer has not bought the product from or entered into any contractual relation with the seller.

Subsection (2)(a) of § 402A indicates that the seller is liable regardless of the degree of care used to safeguard the public from injury by the defective product. Subsection (2)(b) states that privity of contract is unnecessary for strict liability to apply.

Unreasonably Dangerous Products

The product must be unreasonably dangerous as a result of its defect. Courts look to see if the product has become unreasonably threatening because of its defect. There are four types of unreasonably dangerous defects: (1) fault in product design; (2) error in product manufacturer or assembly; (3) improper product maintenance; and (4) manufacturer/seller's failure to warn.

Faulty Product Design

Products can be unreasonably dangerous if they have a defective design. Courts look to see whether the product is inherently dangerous because of a poor design but for which (that is, if such a defect did not exist) the product would have been safe to use. For instance, suppose a manufacturer assembles a toy with small, removable parts that can be swallowed by an infant, and thereby cause serious injury or death. The toy would be inherently dangerous, because the removable parts design would expose small children to the dangers of choking. This design defect makes the product unreasonably dangerous.

Courts decide faulty design (which make products unreasonably dangerous) in terms of three tests: the consumer contemplation test, the danger/utility test, and the state-of-the-art discoverability test.

Consumer Contemplation Test   In its Comments, *Restatement* § 402A states that a product is unreasonably dangerous if the consumer ordinarily would not appreciate the threat inherent in its design. This assumes that the ultimate user, like most people, understands that some products have dangers built in to their uses. The defect becomes unreasonably hazardous because the reasonable person would not be expected to anticipate the danger created by the faulty design. Legal commentators and courts have labelled this the **consumer contemplation test**.

For example, suppose that Nicholas bought a top-loading washing machine. He had to lean across the control panel to load his clothing inside. In doing so, he might accidentally press the start button with his body. This might start the machine while his hands were inside the washing drum. Nicholas could get his fingers caught, which would probably produce some nasty injuries.

Under the consumer contemplation test, would a reasonable person have anticipated this situation? Nicholas should have seen where the start button was located as he began loading his laundry into the machine. He knew that the machine could begin operating once this button was pushed. He should have known that his body could press against the switch and start the washer. In other words, he should have contemplated the risk inherent in the product's poor design. Thus, the product was not unreasonably dangerous under the consumer contemplation test.

Danger/Utility Test Many courts and legal scholars have formulated another test to determine if a product is unreasonably dangerous by its design. This is called the **danger/utility test**. Under this standard, a product is unreasonably hazardous if the danger created by its design outweighs the benefits derived from its use. Consider the previous washing machine example. The danger created by the poorly located button arises only if Nicholas happens inadvertently to press it with his body while his arms are inside the machine. Normally, he derives tremendous benefits from the device—he gets clean clothes. If he is cautious where he stands while loading, Nicholas should be able to avoid the accidental start risk. Using the danger/utility test, the washer is not unreasonably dangerous.

State-of-the-Art Discoverability Test If manufacturers could have discovered hazards created by defective product designs, using current, state-of-the-art technologies, then failure to do so makes a design-flawed product unreasonably dangerous. For example, suppose an automobile manufacturer installed ordinary glass in the small vent windows in a vehicle's doors. State-of-the-art crash testing would quickly indicate that this glass shatters into sharp, pointed fragments during a collision. This glass could seriously harm a driver or passenger. If the car maker did not discover this defect through modern testing procedures, then it would be strictly liable for any injuries caused by the fragile windows.

Error in Product Manufacture or Assembly

Safely designed products may become unreasonably dangerous as a result of improper assembly or manufacture. For instance, suppose a lawnmower manufacturer failed to tighten the bolt holding the blade with sufficient torque. This could result in the blade flying off during use. Suppose this happened to a purchaser, who was severely cut by the blade. The

LEGAL TERMS

consumer contemplation test
A theory in products liability concerning faulty product design that makes a product unreasonably dangerous. If a reasonable person would not have anticipated the danger created by the fault in the product, then the product is unreasonably dangerous.

danger/utility test
A theory in products liability concerning faulty product design that makes a product unreasonably dangerous. Under the test, a product is unreasonably hazardous if the danger created by its design outweighs the benefits derived from its use.

lawn mower, although designed properly, became unreasonably dangerous because it was not suitably assembled. This is sometimes called an **assembly defect**.

Improper Product Maintenance

Sellers occasionally fail to maintain merchandise properly. When a buyer purchases the product, it might not function correctly because of a **maintenance defect**. For example, suppose a lawn and garden shop sells chain saws. The chain on such a saw must be oiled frequently to operate appropriately. Oil is stored inside the saw in a special reservoir. Suppose the seller forgot to keep oil in its chain saws. While displaying one model to a customer, one of the seller's employees started a saw. Without oil, the saw froze up and the chain snapped, sailing through the air into the face of the surprised patron. The product was unreasonably dangerous because the seller did not properly maintain it.

The seller was negligent in forgetting to keep oil in the saw. Using the negligence formula, the seller would also be liable under negligence theory, as well as products liability.

Seller or Manufacturer's Failure to Warn

Sometimes products are unreasonably dangerous by their very nature. Lawn mowers, chain saws, poisons, and chemicals can be lethal if not cautiously used. However, purchasers may not always spot the obvious dangers in a product. Accordingly, manufacturers and sellers have an obligation to warn the ultimate user about inherent product dangers. Failure to warn could result in strict liability. For instance, look at almost any household appliance. Each one warns not to place hands or feet here or there, because of rotating knives, extremely hot surfaces, or the presence of scalding waters. If one uses rat poison or insect sprays, the containers warn not to ingest the contents or get them in one's eyes. These are common examples of warnings that manufacturers and sellers use to avoid absolute liability. If the user is warned, then the user knows the risks.

Business Requirement

Section 402A and most common law and statutory versions of products liability insist that the manufacturer or seller be engaged in the business of selling products such as the defective item(s) that injured the ultimate user. This requirement is easily met in most cases involving manufacturers, wholesalers, or retailers. Its purpose is to exclude products liability for people who are not in the business of selling such goods. For example, suppose Laurie sold Micron a vacuum cleaner, which she had bought from a department store. Because of a design defect, it exploded and injured Micron. Products liability is not intended to hold Laurie liable for this mishap, because she neither manufactured nor was in the business of selling such merchandise. Laurie, like Micron, is essentially an innocent bystander. Under products liability theory, she would not be liable for the defective product. Instead, Micron would sue the department store and manufacturer.

Substantially Unchanged Condition Requirement

For products liability to apply, the product must reach the ultimate user without any substantial changes in its condition from the time it left the manufacturer or seller. This is a crucial requirement. If something happened along the product distribution chain to alter the product (perhaps creating the unreasonably dangerous condition), then it would be unfair to hold manufacturers or sellers accountable for something they did not cause.

For instance, suppose Rachel purchased milk at a nearby grocery. The milk was fresh when she bought it. However, during the drive home, Rachel gets caught in traffic tangled because of an automobile accident. As a result, it takes her over an hour to arrive home. The temperature outside was 100 degrees, and her vehicle had no air conditioning. During this period, the milk spoiled. A visiting relative later drank the milk and suffered food poisoning. The relative wishes to sue the grocery. However, products liability would not apply, because the milk did not reach the ultimate user (Rachel's relative) in a substantially unchanged condition.

In some states, products liability common law or statutes require that, for strict liability to exist, the manufacturer or seller must be responsible for how the defective product was maintained. This seems logical. If the seller were not in any way responsible for how the product was assembled or stored (until it was sold or used), then that seller would have no control over the products it distributes. Products liability attempts to place the blame on the party responsible for the defect, so this requirement seems sensible to protect innocent sellers from absolute liability for product defects caused by someone else.

Proximate Cause

Recall chapter 9's discussion of proximate cause in strict liability cases. That analysis also applies in products liability cases: the defective product must have been the proximate cause of the plaintiff's injury if liability is to attach.

Proper Use Requirement

The ultimate user must use the defective product properly in order for products liability to apply. In other words, the user must use the product for some function for which it was designed or intended to be used. For example, if Cliff wanted to climb onto his roof, he would probably use a ladder. If one of the ladder's rungs broke (because of the manufacturer's

LEGAL TERMS

assembly defect
A theory in products liability concerning whether a defective product is unreasonably dangerous. Errors in product manufacture or assembly may render a product unreasonably hazardous despite a safe design.

maintenance defect
A theory in products liability concerning whether a defective product is unreasonably dangerous. If a seller fails to maintain a product properly, and the product later causes injury to the product's ultimate user, then the product was unreasonably dangerous.

failure to use proper glues), and Cliff fell to the ground and broke various bones, he would be entitled to sue the manufacturer and seller under products liability. However, if he had used stacked vegetable crates to climb upon instead of a ladder, and these collapsed under his weight, Cliff could not sue under products liability. Vegetable crates are neither designed nor intended for people to climb on. They are supposed to be used to store produce.

Foreseeable Plaintiffs Theory

In some jurisdictions, it must have been reasonably foreseeable that the ultimate user would use the defective product. This is called **foreseeable plaintiffs theory** in negligence. Some ultimate users are not reasonably foreseeable. For example, it is highly improbable that a one-year-old infant would come into contact with industrial cleaners used in manufacturing processes. Such a person could not be a reasonably foreseeable ultimate user of such a product. However, members of a product purchaser's family, or the buyer's neighbors, could be foreseeable users of defective goods. How many times in one's family has more than one individual used an appliance or tool? Have you ever borrowed products from your neighbors?

Consider Diana, who borrowed a pen from a classmate with which to take notes during the lecture. The pen had a manufacturing defect that made the plastic casing unusually brittle. While writing, the pen shatters in Diana's hand, and she is cut by the many tiny fragments. Was Diana a reasonably foreseeable ultimate user? Yes. Classmates often share pens, pencils, notebooks, and many other products during classes. It was reasonably foreseeable that someone might borrow a pen to take notes in class. Diana could sue the pen manufacturer under products liability as a foreseeable plaintiff.

LEGAL TERMS

foreseeable plaintiffs theory
A theory used in analyzing products liability cases in some jurisdictions. Under this theory, if it were reasonably foreseeable that the injured victim would be an ultimate user of a defective product, then the seller or manufacturer would be strictly liable for injuries caused by the product defect.

THE CASE OF THE SATURDAY NIGHT SPECIAL (THE SEQUEL)

In the last discussion of this case, the D.C. Court of Appeals ruled that the sale of a "Saturday Night Special" handgun was not an ultrahazardous activity for purposes of absolute liability. The Appellants also argued products liability theory, but as in the first round, the court once again guns down this proposition, exempting the manufacturer from strict liability. Reread the earlier excerpt (§ 9.3) for the facts and procedural history.

Delahanty v. Hinckley
564 A.2d 758 (D.C. 1989)
(District of Columbia
Court of Appeals)
October 11, 1989

FERREN, Associate Judge:
[. . .]
Appellants advanced three legal theories for holding the gun manufacturers liable in these circumstances: negligence, strict products

liability under the *Restatement (Second) of Torts* § 402A (1965), and a "social utility" claim apparently based on strict liability for abnormally dangerous activities [. . .]. Appellants alleged in their complaint that: Hinckley needed an easily concealable weapon for his assassination attempt; the gun manufactured by [the defendant] is an easily concealable, inexpensive handgun; the gun is poorly constructed, unreliable, and therefore not useful for legitimate purposes such as military use, target practice, or self-defense; as a result of the gun's low price, it is used for criminal purposes; and the manufacturers knew of the gun's criminal uses.

[. . .]

Appellants first claim the manufacturers of the gun used by Hinckley are strictly liable for sale of a defective product. They rely on *Restatement (Second) of Torts* § 402A, which imposes liability for the sale of "any product in a defective condition unreasonably dangerous to the user or consumer . . . ". We join the other courts which have rejected the application of this theory in circumstances such as these. [Citations omitted.] Appellants point to no malfunction of the gun caused by improper design or manufacture that led to Thomas Delahanty's injuries. Instead, appellants argue that the manufacturers had a duty to warn of the dangers of criminal misuse of the gun. There is no duty to warn, however, "when the danger, or potentiality of danger, is generally known and recognized." *Restatement (Second) of Torts,* § 402A comment j. Because hazards of firearms are obvious, the manufacturer had no duty to warn. [Citation omitted.]

CASE QUESTIONS

1. Suppose that, when Hinckley fired at the president, the handgun had exploded because of a defective firing pin. Suppose also that Delahanty had been injured by the flying shrapnel. Would Delahanty's products liability claim against the manufacturer have succeeded under these facts? Would Delahanty have been the ultimate user under these facts? Explain.
2. What if the bullets that struck Delahanty had been defectively manufactured, so that they exploded upon impact. Would Delahanty then have had a products liability claim against the bullet manufacturer? Would Delahanty have been the ultimate user under these facts? Explain.

Having analyzed the various elements of products liability, we may now proceed to apply the theory to hypotheticals.

HYPOTHETICALS

Burgess Primer Corporation manufactures paint. Eleanor bought Burgess's "Supreme Ease" paint at Painter Place, a local retailer that carried Burgess products. Eleanor selected various colors, which store employees mixed together. While applying the paint indoors, Eleanor noticed that the paint stung her skin as it splattered from her roller. Apparently, Eleanor was allergic to certain oils that had been mixed into the paint. When she showered later that day, she noticed that the paint had left her arms and face mottled with burn marks. Many of these became infected. Medical tests indicated that a significant percentage of the population suffered this allergic reaction to the paint mix.

Are Burgess Primer Corporation (as manufacturer) and Painter Place (as seller) strictly liable for an unreasonably dangerous product? Applying the generic formula, first ask if the defect made the product unreasonably dangerous. The fault here is product assembly (i.e., how the paint was mixed). Using the consumer contemplation test, would a reasonable person anticipate that he or she might be allergic to paint oils? This is not an obvious hazard that an ordinary person would detect from a can of paint. Thus, the product's dangerous condition rendered it unreasonably dangerous to the ultimate user, Eleanor. Under the danger/utility test, the hazard in using the product outweighed the benefits, as many people were allergic to the particular mix.

Both Burgess and Painter Place were engaged in the business of selling paint. The product reached the ultimate user, Eleanor, in the same condition as it left the retailer. Eleanor also used the paint properly, in a way in which paint is intended to be used. It was reasonably foreseeable that Eleanor would use the paint she bought at a retail store, so she is a foreseeable plaintiff. Both Burgess and the retailer were responsible for how the paint was maintained. Further, a sale occurred (for those jurisdictions requiring it). So far, even with the extra elements, it seems as though strict liability will favor Eleanor.

But who was the proximate cause of Eleanor's injuries? Burgess manufactured the paint base and the various colors. However, the paint did not become unreasonably dangerous until Painter Place's employees mixed it. Therefore, Burgess, as manufacturer, did not proximately cause Eleanor's injuries. Painter Place was clearly the proximate cause of the harm. Proximate cause is a crucial determination, because it absolves Burgess from strict products liability. Painter Place is absolutely liable for Eleanor's injuries under products liability theory.

□ □ □

Consider another hypothetical. Fairfield Seed Company sold sweet corn seeds to retail variety stores. Fairfield had erroneously treated the seeds with a toxic insecticide used for field corn seeds. As the corn grew, this chemical was absorbed into the ears of sweet corn. When the gardeners (who had bought the seed from the retailers) ate the corn, they became ill.

Would the retail variety stores and Fairfield be strictly liable for the gardeners' injuries from an unreasonably dangerous product? Apply either the consumer contemplation test or the danger/utility test. The reasonable gardener would not expect sweet corn seeds to be treated with a poison harmful to humans. The risks far outweigh the benefits. Both Fairfield and the retailers were in the business of selling garden seeds. Fairfield improperly prepared the seeds, which would be a manufacturing defect. The dangerous seeds reached the ultimate users in the same condition as when they left the manufacturer. Fairfield was responsible for the condition of the product. Fairfield's insecticide coating proximately caused the gardeners' injuries, because the ultimate users ate the contaminated ears of corn grown from the poisoned seed. The gardeners used the product as it was designed (i.e., to grow corn to eat) and were foreseeable plaintiffs. All the elements of products liability have been met; thus, Fairfield is strictly liable for the gardeners' injuries caused by the poison corn.

What about the retailers' liability, however? There are two critical queries here. First, did the retailers proximately cause the ultimate users' injuries? Second, were the retailers responsible for the condition in which the defective product was maintained?

The retailers did not contaminate the seeds. The seeds came in sealed packages, which the retailers simply stocked on shelves for customers to pick up and purchase. Thus, the retailers did nothing to proximately cause the gardeners' injuries. Furthermore, the retailers had no control over the manufacturing processes that contaminated the seeds. They were not responsible for how the seeds were prepared. The retailers maintained the condition of the seeds just as they were supposed to, namely, by stocking their shelves with sealed packages. Under this analysis, the retailers would not be strictly liable for the harm to the gardeners.

Figure 10-2 summarizes the elements of products liability, under both the generic, common law formula and the *Second Restatement* § 402A.

10.4 DEFENSES

Equipped with the elements pieces, the products liability portion of the torts puzzle assembles quite easily. But there are a few missing pieces. As shown in chapter 9, there are several defenses to absolute liability. Some of those defenses also apply to products liability.

Contributory Negligence Not a Defense

Courts have generally held that contributory negligence is not a defense in products liability cases. This seems logical, because contributory negligence is a defense to negligence and negligence has no place in strict liability cases. Allowing the ultimate user's contributory negligence to bar absolute liability for a defective product would be the legal equivalent of mixing apples and oranges.

Typical Common Law or Statutory Formula	Comparison with Restatement (2d) of Torts § 402A	Additional Elements (in Some States)
Defect makes product unreasonably dangerous	Same	Ultimate user must be reasonably foreseeable (foreseeable plaintiffs theory)
Manufacturer or seller must be in business of selling products such as the defective one(s)	Same	Manufacturer or seller must be responsible for condition in which defective product was maintained
Defective product cannot have been substantially changed from time it left manufacturer or seller until it was used by ultimate user	Same	A sale of the defective product must have occured
Defect must have proximately caused the ultimate user's injuries	Not included	
Ultimate user must have used the product properly (in a way in which it was designed or intended to be used)	Not included	
Implicit	Degree of care that manufacturer or seller used in making or maintaining the defective product is immaterial; also, no contractual relationship or sale is required	Some states, by statute or common law, require a sale

FIGURE 10-2
Elements of
Products Liability

Ultimate User's Misuse of Product

This is not to say, however, that the plaintiff (the ultimate user) can use a defective product irresponsibly or wantonly. The ultimate user is expected to use the product properly, as it was intended to be used. This is an element of products liability, although some courts consider product misuse to be a defense. If the ultimate user misuses a defective product and is injured as a consequence, his or her products liability claim against the manufacturer or seller will be denied, because the harm resulted from the plaintiff's misuse of the product. This defense is effective even though the misused product was defective.

Some product uses may be unusual, but are not actually misuses. For example, chairs are designed to be sat on. Yet how often has the reader used a chair as a stepping stool to reach something stored on a high shelf? Using a chair as a ladder is not a misuse of the product, because it is reasonably foreseeable that one might use a chair for such a purpose. In other words, reasonably foreseeable uses, even though the product may not originally have been intended or designed for such functions, are acceptable uses. A products liability claim would not be barred if the ultimate user used the product in a reasonably foreseeable fashion.

Assumption of Risk

Assumption of risk, on the other hand, is usually accepted as a defense. The ultimate user assumes the risk of being injured by a hazardous product in three ways: (1) by discovering the defect but disregarding it and using the product anyway; (2) by failing to properly maintain the product; and (3) by failing to follow instructions or heed warnings for safe product use.

Ignoring a Discovered Defect

Recall the basic definition of assumption of risk from chapter 8. **Assumption of risk** is the plaintiff's voluntary assumption of a known risk with a full appreciation of the dangers involved in facing that risk. In products liability cases, the plaintiff is the ultimate user. The ultimate user assumes the risk by discovering a product defect and then ignoring the risks involved and using the product anyway. For example, suppose Steve discovers that his circular saw blade is bent. The warp would cause the blade to rub against the saw's protective sheathing when it rotated. This would create sparks, which could burn him. Steve decides that the risk is worth taking and he uses the saw. Sparks fly into his eyes (because he was not wearing protective eyewear). Steve assumed a known risk with a full comprehension of the possible hazardous consequences.

Failure to Properly Maintain Product

Ultimate users cannot recover in products liability if they failed to properly maintain the product for safe uses. Courts often characterize this as an assumption-of-risk defense. The circular saw example illustrates this type of assumption of risk. Steve did not maintain the saw so that it could be safely used. The blade was bent. Before using it, he should have replaced the damaged blade with a new blade, or at least had the bad blade repaired. It is the ultimate user's responsibility to maintain the merchandise for safe uses.

Consider another illustration. Suppose Gil failed to put motor oil in his automobile. If he proceeded to drive for hundreds of miles, his motor

LEGAL TERMS

assumption of risk
A defense to negligence. The plaintiff takes on the risk of doing (or not doing) something that resulted in his or her injuries. The plaintiff voluntarily assumes a known risk with a full appreciation of the dangers involved in facing that risk. Assumption of risk is a complete defense to negligence claims.

would undoubtedly burn out. He failed to properly maintain the vehicle by putting in the suitable amount of lubrication. Gil could not recover under products liability from the manufacturer or seller. He assumed the risk of ruining his car by not properly maintaining it.

Failure to Follow Instructions or Heed Warnings

How often have you used a product without first reading the instructions? Surely everyone has done this. Most of the time the products we use are sufficiently simple that we can use them properly after a quick glance. With a complex product, however, following instructions could prevent injuries. Products liability plaintiffs often argue that defectively designed products are unreasonably dangerous. However, sometimes these plaintiffs did not follow the manufacturer's instructions for product use and as a consequence were hurt. Also, an ultimate user occasionally disregards manufacturer's warnings that specifically point out the dangers inherent in the product design. Both of these actions are types of assumption of risk.

Assume, in the saw example, that the manufacturer printed on the side of the saw, "WARNING! DO NOT USE IF BLADE IS BENT!" If Steve disregarded this warning and were hurt from the bent saw, he could not recover damages for a defectively designed product. Steve assumed the risk by ignoring the warning.

Suppose, instead of a bent blade, that the blade was merely loose. The instructions included directions for blade tightening. If Steve did not read or follow these directions, and he was hurt because the blade flew off while he was using the saw, he could not recover damages under products liability. Steve assumed the risk by failing to follow instructions to properly maintain the product. Note that once again product maintenance appears in the puzzle.

THE CASE OF THE TOXIC FIRE PAINT

Product misuse does not always require an unusual use of an item. Sometimes the product may be applied to achieve the results for which it was intended, but the actual operation of the item is inappropriate and causes the user's injuries. As the following case illustrates, the paint was used as paint is ordinarily intended. However, the way in which the paint was applied was the misuse. Nor were the firefighters reasonably foreseeable plaintiffs. Although one cannot help but sympathize with the plaintiffs, the Fourth Circuit's analysis of products liability theory reaches the correct result.

Higgins v.
E.I. DuPont de Nemours & Co.
863 F.2d 1162 (4th Cir. 1988)
(U.S. Court of Appeals, Fourth Circuit)
December 23, 1988

MURNAGHAN, Circuit Judge:
Plaintiffs Higgins and Jones appeal from the district court's order granting summary judgment in favor of defendant, E.I. DuPont de Nemours & Co., Inc. ("DuPont"), regarding

their survival actions. Plaintiffs also appeal the dismissal of their wrongful death actions [. . .]

Plaintiffs brought the actions to recover for the deaths of their children and fetuses who allegedly died from the teratogenic effect of chemicals contained in Imron paint. Each of the husbands had worked for the Baltimore City Fire Department in the same fire house, where they used Imron paint to "touch up" the fire engines. Plaintiffs claimed that the deaths were caused by glycol ether acetates and lead supplied by Dow and contained in Imron paint which was developed, manufactured and distributed by DuPont. DuPont advertised Imron paint for sale through distributors for use by industrial professionals, such as fleet truck and transit systems, body shops, marinas, car dealers and manufacturers of aircraft, fire engines, heavy duty construction equipment, and utility vans. Imron was sold and delivered by DuPont to C & R Paint Supply, Inc. ("C & R"), which in turn, sold and delivered the product to the Key Highway repair yard of the Baltimore City Fire Department, where fire apparatus was regularly painted and repainted. C & R never sold or delivered Imron paint directly to the City firehouses nor did it directly solicit business from the Fire Department through sales representatives. Furthermore, it is undisputed that C & R understood that the City's fire vehicles were repaired and painted only at the Key Highway repair shop. Nothing suggests that C & R even suspected that Imron paint was sent out to the individual fire houses until 1985 when it received an unusual request from the City Fire Department for some empty quart containers.

However, from 1979 to 1985, the City Fire Department's Key Highway facility redistributed quantities of Imron in both marked (i.e., with DuPont's labels affixed) and unmarked one-gallon paint cans, coffee cans, or glass jars to the plaintiffs for their use in touching up fire apparatus in the firehouse. The city did not provide the plaintiffs with separate instructions or warnings as to the use of Imron, or with protective clothes to wear while applying the Imron paint.

Each of the labels affixed to the Imron paint products which C & R sold to the City Fire Department stated in clear lettering on the front of the cans:

FOR INDUSTRIAL USE ONLY by professional, trained personnel. Not for sale to or use by the general public.

This warning was accompanied by instruction on the back of the label which required the use of a supplied-air respirator, eye protection, gloves, protective clothing and adequate ventilation. Furthermore, C & R supplied material Safety Data Sheets ("MSDS") to the City Fire Department which repeated the safety precautions [. . .]. However, none of the information constituting a warning specifically warned of the possible teratogenic effects of the product.

[. . .]

The district court found that the firefighters were not "professional, trained personnel" for the obvious use of Imron products, i.e., painting. That they were professional firefighters and not professional painters was evidence from the manner in which they mixed and applied the paint. The evidence shows that the firefighters painted in their fire department work uniforms, mixed the paint in cups and sometimes with their fingers and did not heed any of the label precautions which a professional painter would have taken seriously. We agree with the district court that the labels were adequate enough to warn plaintiffs that they were not sufficiently well-trained to use Imron paint. Therefore, DuPont did not distribute a product which was unreasonably dangerous when used for a purpose and in a manner that is reasonably foreseeable, i.e., for industrial use by trained painters. Imron paint was not defective. [Citations omitted.]

Because plaintiffs did not fall into the class of foreseeable users of Imron paint which DuPont had specifically circumscribed to limit its potential liability, the district court held that had the City heeded the warning and not redistributed Imron paint in unlabeled cans to the firehouse, plaintiffs would not have been injured. Likewise, plaintiffs could not complain when they failed to observe the warnings on the Imron paint cans which the City redistributed to them in the original, labeled cans. The district court held that such a misuse of the product barred recovery as a matter of law. Although our sympathy rests with the plaintiffs who have suffered unspeakable losses, we must agree with the district court that plaintiffs' real complaint lies with the City Fire Department and not DuPont. [. . .]

Misuse of a product may bar recovery against the manufacturer where the misuse is the sole proximate cause of damage, or where it is the intervening or superseding cause. [Citation omitted.] Product misuse is defined as use of a product in a manner that could not reasonably be foreseen by the defendant. [Citations omitted.] Reasonably foreseeable uses include "'the incidental and attendant consequences that accompany normal use.'" [Citations omitted.] The district court found that the normal use of Imron paint was restricted to industrial purposes for which professional painters, who appreciated the attendant risks, were required. The district court held that DuPont could not reasonably foresee that either the City would redistribute Imron paint in either labeled or unlabeled containers or that plaintiffs, who were amateur painters, would use Imron paint after reading the various conspicuous warnings contained on the labeled cannisters [*sic*] which did reach them. [. . .] [W]e still agree with the basic reasoning of the district court, [. . .] that the firefighters were not professional, trained personnel. Plaintiffs failed to provide any contradictory evidence. DuPont had a right to rely on its warning to cut off the chain of causation and to insulate it from becoming a virtual insurer against all injuries arising from its product. [Citation omitted.]

Affirmed.

CASE QUESTIONS

1. Was it not reasonably foreseeable that Imron paint might be shifted into unmarked containers for easier use? Why or why not? What is the significance of DuPont's labeling for this issue?

2. Two of the multiple defendants in this case were the mayor and city council of Baltimore, Maryland. Do you believe the plaintiffs would succeed against them, under respondeat superior, for the torts of the Baltimore City Fire Department? Explain the tort theories that the plaintiffs could successfully apply.

Defenses are a defective product manufacturer's best friend. Even if every products liability element is satisfied, defenses can spare the seller from the wrath of strict liability, as the following hypotheticals illustrate.

HYPOTHETICALS

Douglas owns a tire repair shop. He sells new tires from all the national brands and repairs old tires. Marjorie came into the shop one day with a punctured tire. Douglas agreed that it could be patched and repaired, but he instructed Marjorie to use the tire only as a spare for emergencies. He recommended that she purchase a reconditioned tire for regular use. Marjorie insisted that Douglas put her patched tire back onto her car. Douglas warned that the patch might not hold up over long-term, constant use. Nevertheless, he had the repaired tire re-mounted on her car. Later the following month, while Marjorie was driving to work, the patch failed and the tire blew out. Marjorie's car ran off the road, collided with a telephone pole, and injured her.

Marjorie's products liability claim against Douglas would fail. Marjorie assumed the risk of using the patched tire contrary to Douglas's specific instructions and warnings. She voluntarily assumed a known risk with a full appreciation of the hazards involved. The defense of assumption of risk would protect Douglas from strict products liability.

□ □ □

The Oasis Sprinkler Company manufactures underground lawn sprinkler systems. Oasis offers a do-it-yourself kit for handy customers. Josephine purchased one of these kits. The detailed assembly instructions directed her to attach the sprinkler heads to the underground pipe using a special copper clamp. "Be certain to crimp the clamp with pliers to ensure a snug connection," read the instructions. Josephine did not crimp the clamps, although she did put them in place. Later, while the sprinkler system was in use, one of the sprinkler heads flew into the air under the force of the water pressure. It struck Josephine's daughter, Janice, in the forehead, causing a wound that required several stitches to close the cut.

Could Janice and Josephine win a products liability lawsuit against Oasis? Not if the assumption-of-risk defense can be successfully applied. Josephine disregarded the manufacturer's specific instructions for assembling the product. However, Oasis failed to warn about the possible dangers that could occur if the clamps were not crimped. So we have a manufacturer's failure to warn situation versus a user's failure to follow instructions defense. Which wins? Is the manufacturer's failure to warn sufficient to hold Oasis liable for an unreasonably dangerous product? Or is Josephine's failure to obey instructions a complete defense under assumption of risk?

The key to this problem is whether a reasonable ultimate user (i.e., a reasonable person) would have anticipated that the sprinkler heads might fly off under high water pressure if the clamps were not crimped. Most people know that water carried through pipes is under great pressure, which makes the water a powerful, focused force. A loose connection could easily give way and send a sprinkler head flying in any direction. Reasonable persons know this from everyday experience with garden hoses or plumbing. Josephine should have anticipated this risk; therefore, it is considered a known risk that she voluntarily assumed, despite a full appreciation of the dangers involved. Assumption of risk will overpower the manufacturer's failure to warn of this particular hazard. Accordingly, the defense of assumption of risk will protect Oasis from strict products liability.

□ □ □

One last hypothetical reveals the misuse puzzle piece. The Comfort King Corporation manufactures recliner chairs. When Herbert visited a friend, who owned such a recliner, Herbert noticed that a light bulb was burned out in his friend's hallway. He used the recliner as a ladder to reach the light fixture. As he stood on the chair, it reclined, sending him sprawling across the hall, and smashing his head into a closet doorknob. Herbert thought the chair was unreasonably dangerous, so he sued Comfort King under products liability.

Comfort King, however, shrugged off the lawsuit. The product misuse defense was there to protect the company from strict liability. Recliner chairs are not designed or intended to be used as ladders or stoops. After all, recliners *recline*. They cannot be safely stood upon for that reason. Herbert should have reasonably anticipated the danger created by misusing the chair in this fashion. Herbert's misuse of the product is a solid products liability defense for Comfort King.

Figure 10-3 lists the defenses to products liability.

10.5 COMPARISON TO CONTRACT LAW WARRANTIES

Products liability has roots in contract law warranties. A *warranty* is a guarantee that a product seller gives a buyer. The guarantee states that the product will perform to certain standards or will not break down over a period of time. This warranty is part of the contract between the buyer and the seller.

If the products fails to comply with the guarantee, the warranty is *breached*. This **breach of warranty** is also a violation of the parties' agreement that the product shall remain in a particular condition while used.

Similarities Between Products Liability and Breach of Warranty

Breach of warranty is similar to products liability in that both involve strict liability. For some reason, many contract law textbooks fail to notice

Contributory Negligence	Assumption of Risk	Product Misuse by Ultimate User
Not considered a defense in products liability cases	Ultimate user's voluntary assumption of known risk with full appreciation of dangers involved	If ultimate user misuses the product, then he or she cannot recover under products liability
	Occurs when ultimate user ignores a discovered defect and uses the product while knowing of its dangerous condition	Reasonably foreseeable uses are *not* misuses of products
	Occurs when ultimate user fails to properly maintain product	
	Occurs when ultimate user fails to follow instructions or heed warnings for safe product use	

FIGURE 10-3
Defenses to Products Liability

this. If the product fails to comply with the seller's warranty, then that is breach of warranty. The seller is liable for this breach—period . . . just like absolute liability. If the seller breaches the warranty, then the seller is liable to the buyer for damages for breach of warranty (i.e., breach of contract). It is that simple.

Products liability and breach of warranty are also similar in that both typically involve defective and unreasonably dangerous products. In almost every products liability lawsuit, the plaintiff's complaint will plead both causes of action, assuming that the defendant warranted the product to the plaintiff.

Like products liability, many product warranty statutes or modern common law cases permit the reasonably foreseeable ultimate user (other than the purchaser) to recover damages for breach of warranty. In contract law, this is intended to extend the agreement to include (most often) the buyer's family. So, even under contract law, the ancient privity-of-contract requirement has been loosened.

Difference Between Products Liability and Breach of Warranty

The obvious difference between breach of warranty and products liability is the *contract requirement*. For breach of warranty, there must be an agreement between the seller and the buyer which includes the guarantee, either explicitly or implicitly. Under products liability, no contract is

LEGAL TERMS

breach of warranty
When a product fails to comply with the seller or manufacturer's guarantee under the sales contract.

required. This is clearly stated in *Restatement (Second) of Torts* § 402A. Without a contract requirement, products liability can apply in many more cases than can breach of warranty, which is usually limited to litigation between product buyers and sellers.

A detailed discussion of warranty law is beyond the scope of this text, but the reader will probably study breach of warranty in business law courses. It is an important part of the contract law puzzle and deserves close attention.

SUMMARY

10.1. Products liability became a distinct tort theory in the early 1960s. For over 100 years, American and English courts combined contract law and negligence to hold manufacturers and sellers liable for injuries caused by defective products. Finally, in 1962, strict liability was applied to such cases. As a matter of public policy, products liability places the risk of harm created by unreasonably dangerous products upon those who make and sell them. The law presumes that the innocent user should not be forced to bear the costs associated with harmful products.

10.2. The parties in products liability cases include the manufacturer, other sellers (such as retailers or wholesalers), and the consumers, or ultimate users, of the product. Often the ultimate user is a member of the product buyer's family or a neighbor or friend. By looking at a product's distribution chain, it becomes clear how the product leaves the manufacturer and reaches the ultimate user.

10.3. Products liability is strict, or absolute, liability. No privity of contract is required between the manufacturer or seller and the ultimate user. The manufacturer or seller's negligence is irrelevant. The product must contain a defect rendering it unreasonably dangerous to use. This fault may arise in a design defect, by improper product maintenance, or by the manufacturer or seller's failure to warn the buyer of hazards in using the product. The manufacturer or seller must be engaged in the business of selling products like the defective one. The product cannot be substantially changed from the time it left the manufacturer or seller and reached the ultimate user. The defect must proximately cause the ultimate user's injuries. The ultimate user must use the product in a way in which it was designed or intended.

10.4. Contributory negligence is not a defense to products liability. Product misuse is a defense, although it is often included as an element in the products liability formula. If the ultimate user misuses the product, even though the product is defective, the manufacturer and seller will not be strictly liable for the harm. Assumption of risk is another defense to products liability. If the ultimate user ignores a discovered defect and, by using the product, is hurt, the user has assumed the risk, and the manufacturer or seller would not be strictly liable. The same is true if the ultimate user fails to properly maintain a product, follow instructions, or heed warnings for safe use.

10.5. Products liability is similar to contract law warranties. First, both involve absolute liability. Second, both involve defective or unreasonably dangerous products. Third, under many warranty statutes and common law, the ultimate user is protected even if he or she was not the original product purchaser. Products liability is different from warranty law because, for breach of warranty, there must be a contract between the manufacturer or seller and the buyer.

REVIEW QUESTIONS

1. What are the public policy objectives behind products liability? How are they similar to the public policy objectives mentioned in chapter 9 for "regular" strict liability?

2. How did modern products liability evolve? What were some of the landmark cases during the nineteenth and early twentieth centuries that led these developments? What was the imminent danger exception? It was an exception to what rule?

3. How is negligence relevant to products liability? Is privity of contract required? Who are the parties in products liability cases? Who is the ultimate user?

4. Discuss the elements of a typical products liability formula. How are these different from the elements in *Restatement (Second) of Torts* § 402A? How are they similar?

5. How would you define an unreasonably dangerous product? What is faulty product design? Explain the consumer contemplation test, the danger/utility test, and the state-of-the-art discoverability test. Why are these tests important?

6. Explain how errors in product manufacture or assembly make a product unreasonably dangerous for products liability purposes.

7. In products liability, what role does improper product maintenance play? Manufacturer or seller's failure to warn of product hazards?

8. Define (a) the business requirement, (b) the substantially unchanged condition requirement, and (c) the proper use requirement. Why are they relevant to products liability? Does proximate cause play any role? What about foreseeable plaintiffs theory?

9. Is contributory negligence a defense to products liability? Why or why not? What about product misuse?

10. Explain how assumption of risk operates as a defense to products liability. Identify the three ways in which the ultimate user assumes the risk of using a defective product.

PROBLEMS

1. WedgeCorp manufactures golf clubs. The clubs have rubberized grips that golfers hold onto to swing them. Waldo Maillor bought his wife a set of clubs for her birthday. Cindy Maillor is a avid golfer and uses the clubs three times weekly at the local country club. When WedgeCorp manufactured the clubs, they used an improperly mixed glue that did not tightly bond the grips to the end of the clubs. While Cindy was swinging a five iron, the grip came loose and the club sailed through the air, striking Cindy's golfing partner, Betty Payless, in the forehead.

2. Better Bovine, Inc. (BB) sells dairy cattle to farmers. These livestock are raised on one of BB's pasturing farms outside of town. To control weeds, BB's employees sprayed pasture land with herbicides. The cattle ate this grass and absorbed the chemicals into their systems. These chemicals reduced the cows' milk production. Several farmers who purchased BB cows suffered substantial economic losses when the animals' milk productivity plummeted.

3. Whopper Toys Corporation manufactures "Mr. Killjoy," a combat doll. Mr. Killjoy comes equipped with sharp plastic swords that you can fit into his hands for mock battles. Whopper indicated on its packaging that this toy was not suitable for children under the age of six years. This was the only warning printed on the package. Franco Delgado bought a Mr. Killjoy figure for his four-year-old son, Francisco. While playing with Charlotte, a three-year-old neighbor girl, Francisco had the doll "attack" her. Its sword stabbed Charlotte through her nose, leaving a permanent scar.

4. Omar Muhammad is an accountant who lives in an apartment next to Joyce Madison. Omar sold his electric stove to Joyce for $200. Omar had never kept the electric heating elements on top of the stove particularly clean. In fact, they were caked with grease and dirt. The first time Joyce turned on the stove, the heating elements caught fire and set Joyce's long hair ablaze.

5. The Steak Out restaurant has a reputation for excellent steaks. One day it received a meat shipment from the Midwestern Meat Packing Company, a national meat distributor. When the shipment left Midwestern, it was shipped in a refrigerated truck. However, en route to The Steak Out, the truck's refrigeration system broke down, but the driver never noticed. The meat spoiled. When the Steak Out's employees unloaded the truck, they did not notice that the meat smelled bad. In fact, the meat did not smell much, if at all. Nevertheless, customers served from this shipment of beef became seriously ill from food poisoning.

6. Peter Breezeway bought a large screwdriver, made by the Hand Tool Manufacturing Company, from his local hardware store. Unknown to anyone, the screwdriver had a microscopic crack in its shaft. If

excessive pressure were exerted on the screwdriver, it would snap. Peter used the screwdriver to pry open sealed crates that he received at work. One day, while prying open a crate, the screwdriver broke, severely cutting the tendons in Peter's left hand.

7. Bartholomew Benton works for the United States Department of Defense. One day he noticed that his paper-shredding machine made a loud grinding noise while operating. He opened the maintenance door, but could see nothing wrong with the parts inside. Bart continued using the machine, despite the horrible noise. Several co-workers complained to him about it. The grinding occurred because the machine was out of lubricating oil, which, according to the machine's instruction manual, should have been checked at least monthly. No one had checked the oil level since the machine was purchased over a year ago. While Bart was using the machine, its gears froze up, and broke loose the paper-shredding blades. These lodged in Bart's thighs, cutting him deeply.

PROBLEM ANSWERS

1. Is WedgeCorp strictly liable, under products liability law, for Betty's injuries? Using the "typical products liability formula" discussed in this chapter, the basic elements are satisfied:

> (1) The defectively glued grip (an assembly defect) rendered the club unreasonably dangerous to use, as the grip would most likely give way while a golfer was swinging the club, which could render it an extremely dangerous projectile, just as in this problem.
> (2) WedgeCorp was engaged in the business of manufacturing and selling golf clubs such as the defective one in this case.
> (3) According to the facts in this problem, the clubs' condition was not substantially changed from the time they left WedgeCorp until they reached Cindy Maillor, the ultimate user.
> (4) It was reasonably foreseeable that a defectively glued grip would come loose while Cindy was swinging the club, causing the club to fly through the air, striking Betty Payless, who was standing nearby. Thus, the defect proximately caused Betty's injuries.
> (5) Cindy was using the golf club properly, i.e., swinging to hit a golf ball, an activity for which the product was obviously designed.

Applying the elements from the *Second Restatement's* § 402A, one should reach these same conclusions.

The key to this hypothetical, however, is whether the injured party, Betty, was an ultimate user. Betty was not using the defective golf club at the time of her injury. Instead, Cindy, the owner of the club, was using it when the defectively glued rubberized grip came loose. Thus, Cindy, not Betty, would be considered the ultimate user. WedgeCorp is not absolutely liable under products liability theory.

However, Betty should prevail in her products liability lawsuit against WedgeCorp. Under foreseeable plaintiffs theory, it was reasonably foreseeable that Betty, Cindy's companion, would be injured while Cindy was using the club. This would place Betty within the zone of foreseeability for purposes of proximate cause (which, under products liability, is the range in which reasonable plaintiffs theory is considered). WedgeCorp is strictly liable to Betty for her injuries caused by the defective club.

No defenses apply to this hypothetical, because there was no assumption of risk or product misuse.

2. Is Better Bovine strictly liable, under products liability theory, for the farmers' economic losses incurred when their cattle, purchased from BB's stock, experienced diminished milk production as a result of ingesting BB's herbicides? First of all, cattle are goods and, accordingly, are covered by products liability statutes. Some states have specific provisions pertaining to livestock, in addition to commercial warranty statutes under states' versions of the Uniform Commercial Code. Applying the typical products liability elements discussed in this chapter, the elements are satisfied.

(1) The cattle suffered an "assembly defect," in that they were injured by absorbing harmful chemicals while eating grass sprayed with BB's herbicides.

(a) Did this absorption render the cattle unreasonably dangerous to the ultimate user or to the user's property? Yes. By absorbing these chemicals, the cattle's milk production significantly declined. Although this presented no direct physical danger to the farmers (the ultimate users of the products), it did clearly harm the farmers' property (the cattle themselves). Under *Restatement (Second)* § 402A and most state statutory versions, products liability includes harms to the ultimate user's property as well as personal injuries. Thus, the chemically tainted cattle were unreasonably dangerous.

(b) The chemicals would probably contaminate the cattle's milk, which could directly threaten the farmers (if they drank the milk) or, for that matter, any subsequent purchasers of the milk. But that goes beyond the scope of this problem, which involves only the farmers' economic losses from declining milk production.

(2) BB is in the business of selling cattle such as the ones hurt in this problem.

(3) The cattle's condition was not substantially changed from the time they were contaminated with the herbicides to the time they reached the farmers.

(4) The chemical absorption proximately caused the farmers' economic losses. It was reasonably foreseeable that these chemicals would diminish the cattle's milk productivity, from which the farmers' economic hardships reasonably would, and did, follow.

(5) The farmers used the cattle properly, in a manner in which they were intended, which was, obviously, milk production.

No defenses apply in this hypothetical, because there was no assumption of risk and no product misuse. BB shall be strictly liable to the farmers for their economic losses for the tainted cattle, under products liability theory.

3. This hypothetical focuses upon the product misuse and assumption-of-risk defenses. First, review the products liability elements to determine if a prima facie case has been stated. Decide whether Mr. Killjoy was unreasonably dangerous, with his sharp plastic swords that could, and did, injure children such as Charlotte. This is a design defect, which, under the consumer contemplation test, makes the toy unreasonably dangerous. Although a reasonable adult would plainly anticipate the dangers created by sharp plastic swords, reasonable young children, even at age six or beyond, might overlook or forget the risks when playing. Thus, the product includes an unreasonably dangerous design for the ultimate users (who are young children).

   Charlotte was a reasonably foreseeable ultimate user, because children often share toys with playmates and frequently engage in mock battles with warlike toys such as Mr. Killjoy. Charlotte's injuries were reasonably foreseeable for purposes of proximate cause.

   The text's so-called typical formula includes lack of product misuse as an element of products liability. Some states' statutes or common law include this as an element, while others (and *Restatement (Second)* § 402A) leave it as a defense. For purposes of convenience, we may consider it defensively for this problem.

   Although it was reasonably foreseeable that young children would use the toy to pretend-attack each other, the toy contained clear warnings to adults that the toy was inappropriate for children under age six. Franco Delgado bought the toy for his four-year-old son, Francisco, who used it to hurt his neighbor and friend, three-year-old Charlotte. Both children were clearly too young to be using this toy, as the manufacturer plainly warned the purchaser. Had he been acting reasonably, Mr. Delgado would not have purchased this toy for his son. This represents product misuse, a defense that would insulate Whopper Toys Corporation from strict products liability. Assumption of risk would likewise protect the corporation, as Mr. Delgado reasonably should have anticipated that his son and friend could be hurt by, and would not understand the dangers inherent in, those sharp plastic swords. By giving the toy to his son and failing to heed the manufacturer's age warnings for safe product use, Mr. Delgado assumed a known risk with full appreciation of the dangers involved.

4. Joyce Madison's products liability lawsuit against Omar would fail, because Omar is not engaged in the business of selling electric stoves such as the one he sold to Joyce. Thus, products liability would not apply.

   One might erroneously jump immediately to defenses, looking to Joyce's use of the obviously dirty stove as assumption of risk or product misuse (because stoves are not intended to be used when so filthy).

Although these are interesting defenses, they are wasted ammunition in this hypothetical.

5. The customers would likely sue the Steak Out restaurant (seller) and the Midwestern Meat Packing Company (manufacturer) under products liability.

The customers' cause of action against the manufacturer would fail under this theory, because the defective products (spoiled meat) reached the customers in a substantially changed condition from the state in which it left the manufacturer. Accordingly, the manufacturer would not be strictly liable.

The customers' cause of action against the restaurant, however, would be successful. The meat was spoiled when the restaurant received it from the shipper. It was still spoiled when the restaurant served it to its customers, who became seriously ill as a result. No substantial change in product condition occurred from the time it left the restaurant's (seller's) hands until it reached the ultimate users. The spoiled meat was unreasonably dangerous as a major health risk, the restaurant was in the business of selling this type of food, the defect (spoilage) proximately caused the customers' injuries, and the customers used the products properly (human consumption). Thus, this chapter's typical products liability elements were satisfied and, accordingly, the restaurant would be strictly liable for the customers' injuries.

One might be outraged at the outcome of this hypothetical. It may be argued that the shipper was the proximate cause of the customers' injuries. They will be on the right track for the restaurant's joinder of the shipper as a third-party defendant. The restaurant will successfully allege that the shipper's negligence, or, more likely, gross negligence or negligence per se (discussed in chapter 11), proximately caused the customers' injuries. The shipper plainly violated its duty of care to properly ship refrigerated foods. All the elements can be checked off easily.

Negligence per se (see chapter 11) would apply if the shipper violated a state health statute pertaining to the proper shipment of refrigerated food, which it almost certainly did. Gross negligence would exist here, because the driver's failure to discover the broken refrigeration system on the truck is carelessness beyond that of ordinary, reasonable care. It approaches wanton misconduct. Thus, gross negligence would apply, which could afford the plaintiffs punitive damages under some state statutes.

6. Peter Breezeway would successfully recover from his local hardware store and the Hand Tool Manufacturing Company under products liability. Both defendants were engaged in the business of selling goods such as the defective screwdriver. The screwdriver's defective condition had not substantially changed from the time it left the manufacturer until it reached the ultimate user, Peter. The defect proximately caused Peter's injuries, as it was reasonably foreseeable that Peter would hurt his hand—as he did—if the screwdriver broke under pressure.

A tough threshold question is whether the defect rendered the screwdriver unreasonably dangerous. Many courts would rule that this was a defective design case, although actually it is a defective assembly or manufacture case. Under the design analysis, such courts would apply the state-of-the-art discoverability test to determine the question of unreasonable dangerousness. It is likely that the manufacturer had technological equipment or testing procedures capable of detecting the microscopic flaw in the screwdriver shaft. Regardless, this test is misapplied to this hypothetical. The proper analysis focuses on whether the product became unreasonably dangerous because of its assembly defect. Because of the microscopic crack, the screwdriver shaft was likely to break when used under pressure, just as Peter used it. Given the reasonable foreseeability of the injuries (i.e., the high probabilities that (1) users exert significant torque when using screwdrivers, and (2) a broken shaft could severely cut a user's hand), the defect rendered the screwdriver unreasonably dangerous.

The key issue in this hypothetical is whether Peter properly used the screwdriver. Product misuse, as previously noted, may be invoked as an element or a defense, depending upon a particular state's products liability statutes or common law. Was Peter's use of the screwdriver as a prying tool to open sealed crates a reasonably foreseeable use? Yes. Screwdriver shafts are thick metal rods ideally suited for prying open many sealed containers. Small prying bars closely resemble large screwdrivers in this regard. Assuming that this case involved a large screwdriver, then Peter's use would be considered reasonably foreseeable and, therefore, not a misuse.

No other defenses apply in this case, because Peter could not reasonably have discovered the microscopic defect. The Hand Tool Manufacturing Company would be strictly liable to Peter under products liability theory.

7. The keys to this hypothetical would be product misuse and assumption of risk. Bartholomew Benton improperly used the paper-shredding machine by failing to follow the manufacturer's maintenance instructions and by continuing to use the machine although it was obviously functioning under some disability, as evidenced by the annoying grinding noise.

Bart assumed the risk of the machine's shredding blades breaking and injuring him when he ignored a discovered defect and continued using the machine. A reasonable person would have anticipated that the grinding noise might be caused by lubrication deficiency and, accordingly, that the mechanism could break apart if the stresses of ordinary use continued. Furthermore, Bart (and his co-workers) failed to properly maintain the machine through routine lubrication checks as prescribed by the manufacturer's instruction manual. This also illustrates the user's failure to follow the manufacturer's instructions for safe product use. All point to these conclusions: (1) Bart voluntarily assumed a known risk with full appreciation of the dangers involved; and (2) Bart misused the product, because it was not designed or intended to be used when its lubricant was absent. The machine manufacturer would not be liable to Bart for his injuries under products liability theory.

PROJECTS

1. Which version of products liability do your state courts follow? Is it different from, or identical to, the *Second Restatement's* § 402A?

2. Has your state legislature enacted any products liability statutes? If so, how are they similar to the elements discussed in this chapter? How are they different?

3. Brief *Hardy v. Chemetron Corp.*, 870 F.2d 1007 (5th Cir. 1989). Did the Fifth Circuit Court of Appeals rule that the product was unreasonably dangerous when it left the manufacturer? How did the court justify its conclusion?

4. Brief *Amatulli v. Delhi Construction Corp.*, 77 N.Y.2d 525, 571 N.E. 2d 645, 569 N.Y.S.2d 337 (1991). This is a swimming pool case. Compare the court of appeals' analysis with that in the *Winant* case in project 5.

5. Brief *Winant v. Carefree Pools,* 709 F. Supp. 57 (E.D.N.Y.), *aff'd,* 891 F.2d 278 (2d Cir. 1989). This is another swimming pool case. Compare the U.S. District Court's analysis of New York law with that in the *Amatulli* case from project 4.

CHAPTER 11
Special Tort Actions

OUTLINE

DATA-GRAPHIC TORTS

Marie v. Pillsbury

Bill Pillsbury was driving a flatbed semi-truck along a two-lane portion of Route 66 (a famous United States highway). His truck was carrying a cargo of roofing shingles, stacked in six-foot-high bundles. Bill had failed to securely fasten straps along the rear end of the shingle stacks.

After the truck hit a bump, part of the end stack tumbled onto the highway. Joanne Marie, who was driving behind Pillsbury, saw the shingles fall and swerved into oncoming traffic to avoid hitting them. In doing so, Marie collided head on with another vehicle.

In this hypothetical, a state statute required all flatbed truck operators to securely fasten down all cargo. Violations were punishable by a $500 fine assessed as a traffic offense by the state police. In its committee reports, the state legislature declared that the statute was intended to protect other vehicles from loose cargo falling onto the roads at high speeds.

Marie sued Pillsbury, claiming negligence per se. Because Pillsbury violated the statute, which was intended to protect drivers such as Marie, Pillsbury's failure to comply with the safety requirements of the statute constituted negligence as a matter of law, and thus Pillsbury's negligence would be presumed.

DATA-GRAPHIC TORTS

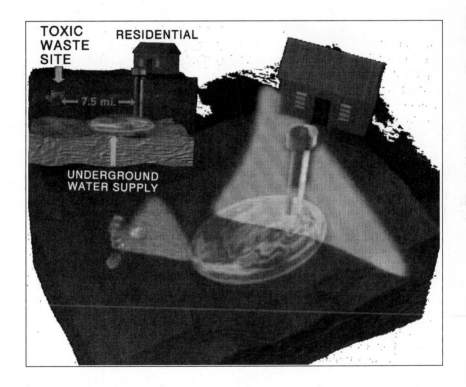

Harrison v. Cascade Chemical Corp.

The Cascade Chemical Corporation (CCC) manufactures a variety of chemicals used in manufacturing telephone and electric pole insulators. Waste chemicals were stored in barrels but remained highly toxic for over 100 years. In the 1930s, prior to the enactment of federal and state statutory and regulatory requirements for toxic waste disposal, CCC simply buried several hundred barrels on vacant farmland. The barrels were buried 150 feet underground in an abandoned well shaft that was then sealed and filled with dirt and rock. Over time, the barrels slowly leaked into the surrounding ground, contaminating adjacent underground water supplies. Tests indicated that the contamination reached toxic levels within 10 years of initial barrel seepage. The Harrison family lived seven-and-one-half miles from one of CCC's burial sites. The Harrisons built their home in 1975 and drank water from a well 175 feet deep. Unbeknownst to anyone, the well water was contaminated with CCC's toxic runoff. In 1991, the eldest Harrisons, Bob and Ann, both mysteriously suffered liver dysfunction. Tests showed that toxic chemicals in their water supply had gradually destroyed certain liver cell functions and caused liver failure. The chemicals were directly linked to CCC's buried barrels. The Harrisons sued CCC under absolute liability theory (for an abnormally dangerous activity), as well as for negligent storage of hazardous waste.

CCC's toxic barrels also constitute trespass to land and nuisance.

INTRODUCTION

The reader has now reached a part of the torts puzzle that is often overlooked in paralegal education. These forgotten torts are just as important as the major torts of negligence and strict liability. The torts puzzle cannot be completed without them.

Special tort actions include nuisance, which involves issues of both tort and property law, and negligence per se, which is often a statutory tort. Tort litigation also often includes wrongful death actions, which are usually associated with negligence claims. Within the past 25 years, a new, related tort, wrongful life, has emerged in the appellate courts. Another rapidly developing area of modern tort law is so-called toxic torts, which involve hazardous substances, toxic waste disposal, and other environmental issues.

This chapter investigates these special tort actions. Much of our discussion will incorporate negligence and absolute liability theories. These concepts give the special torts puzzle pieces peculiar shapes and colors. Specifically, the following pieces will be located and assembled:

- Private nuisances.
- "Coming to the nuisance" defense.
- Public nuisances.
- Nuisances per se.
- Nuisance remedies: abatement, damages, and injunctions.
- Negligence per se.
- Wrongful death statutes.
- Wrongful life actions.

11.1 PRIVATE NUISANCES

A **nuisance** is an unreasonable or unlawful use of one's real property that injures another person or interferes with another person's use of his or her real property. Nuisances are defined by common law and by statute.

There are two types of nuisances: private and public. Occasionally, the same activity constitutes both a private and a public nuisance. These are sometimes called *mixed nuisances.*

Private Nuisance Defined

A **private nuisance** occurs when someone (1) uses his or her land in such a way as to (2) unreasonably and substantially interfere with (3) another person's use and enjoyment of his or her land. The tortfeasor (defendant) is the land user whose activities offend his or her neighbors. The neighboring land user(s) (plaintiff[s]) sue the tortfeasor for engaging in a private nuisance. The second element in commission of a private nuisance, unreasonable and substantial interference, is the most susceptible of interpretation.

Unreasonable and Substantial Defined

Whether the tortfeasor's use of real estate is unreasonable and substantially interferes with another's land use is usually defined in terms of offensiveness. The critical question is: How offensive is the tortfeasor's land use? Offensiveness is determined by applying the reasonable person standard. Would a reasonable person with ordinary sensitivities find the tortfeasor's land use unreasonably offensive? If so, then the tortfeasor has unreasonably and substantially interfered with the plaintiff's use and enjoyment of his or her land. Therefore, the tortfeasor has committed a private nuisance.

Community Standard

The reasonable person standard is normally a community standard. In other words, it asks how people living in the community in which the alleged nuisance is taking place would react to the activity. This *reasonable community* reaction supposedly evaluates whether the tortfeasor's land use is unreasonable and a substantial interference with neighboring land uses.

Use and Enjoyment

Use and enjoyment is a term of art in nuisance law. The two are always used together. The term use would be sufficient, but enjoyment imparts an emotional aspect to nuisance law. The alleged nuisance activity ruins the pleasure neighbors gain through the ways in which they use their real estate. This seems to make the tortfeasor's activities more blameworthy.

LEGAL TERMS

nuisance
An unreasonable or unlawful use of one's real estate that injures another person or interferes with another person's use of his or her real property. There are two types: private and public. When the same activity constitutes both a public and a private nuisance, it may be called a *mixed* nuisance.

private nuisance
The use of one's land so as to unreasonably and substantially interfere with another person's use and enjoyment of his or her land.

Classic Examples

There are many common examples of private nuisances to which to apply the elements just explained. These situations can be classified in broad categories: (1) physical effects on land; (2) health hazards or offending sensibilities; and (3) unwanted associations with neighboring uses.

Physical Effects on Land

Neighboring land users often complain if a tortfeasor's use of realty creates constant vibrations, pollution of water or soil, destruction of crops, flooding, excessive clutter, or unwanted excavations.

Ground Vibrations   For example, suppose a manufacturing plant next door to Jenny's house operates 24 hours a day. This plant uses heavy machinery that produces powerful vibrations. These vibrations can be felt for hundreds of feet in all directions. The ground actually shakes slightly from the effect. Over several years, this phenomenon has caused Jenny's house foundation to crack. She would argue that these constant vibrations were an unreasonable and substantial interference with her use and enjoyment of her home. In short, the manufacturing plant would be creating a private nuisance.

Pollution of Water or Soil   Consider another example. Suppose a chemical processing plant dumped its waste waters onto vacant land behind its buildings. These wastes seeped into the soil and polluted underground water supplies. The chemicals also spread across the soil surface onto neighboring lands, making them sterile. These are unreasonable and substantial interferences with the neighboring landowners' use and enjoyment of their realty. The chemical plant has produced a private nuisance.

Crop Destruction   Take another hypothetical. The Blackout Power Company burns coal to produce electricity. Thick, black smoke belches from its tall smokestacks. As the wind disperses the smoke, coal dust settles on the neighbors' land, upon which grow corn and soybeans. The neighbors' crops grow poorly because of the coal dust on their leaves. Blackout's activity is an unreasonable and substantial interference with the neighboring farmers' use and enjoyment of their crop land. A private nuisance exists.

Flooding   Flooding can also be a private nuisance. Suppose Deatra lives along a small creek. Several miles downstream, another landowner erects a dam to create a small lake for fishermen. However, the lake extends beyond the downstream user's land and floods Deatra's property, including her home. Although this case could involve issues of *riparian* (water) law, in terms of nuisance law, the downstream landowner has unreasonably and substantially interfered with Deatra's use and enjoyment of her real estate by flooding her out.

Excessive Clutter Few individuals would ever want to live adjacent to a junkyard or trash dump. Most people find such land uses to be offensive to many senses, one of which is sight. Having to look at junk or trash piled high next door can be aesthetically depressing. Many courts have found such uses to be private nuisances for this reason, although, more commonly, neighbors are also offended by refuse odors.

Unwanted Excavations Excavation companies sometimes purchase soil from vacant lot owners to haul away and use in construction projects. These excavations leave deep and, for some people, unsightly holes in the vacant lots. Suppose Andy's house is next to several vacant lots that have been excavated in this fashion. A quick search of the case law reveals that several courts would find this to be a private nuisance.

Health Hazards or Offending Sensibilities

People's **sensibilities** are ways in which their physical senses (sight, hearing, smell, taste, and touch) and their emotional senses (what they find disgusting, repulsive, threatening, etc.) are affected. Private nuisances offend a person's sensibilities. They can also create health hazards.

Noxious Odors Land uses that produce harmful, obnoxious odors are frequent candidates as private nuisances, as in the previous trash dump example. Suppose Nicki lives next to a livestock farm, a chemical processing plant, or a paper mill. These may not create any bad smells at all, but sometimes they emit a powerful and dreadful stink. Much nuisance litigation has involved offensive odors produced by activities such as these.

Smoke and Dust Smoke and dust emissions can produce serious health hazards for neighbors. Consider the Blackout Power Company example. Neighbors who breathe the coal-dust-laden air could suffer severe respiratory injury. If this happened, the courts would probably rule that Blackout was involved in creating a private nuisance.

Excessive Noise and Temperatures Land uses that produce excessive noise can harm neighbors' health. In nuisance litigation, many plaintiffs have complained of sleep loss, nervousness, and associated physical and emotional symptoms because of a neighbor's excessive noise. Imagine how Eric might be affected if he lived next to a motor vehicle race track that ran late-night races on week nights.

LEGAL TERMS

sensibilities
In nuisance law, ways in which people's physical and emotional senses are affected.

Factories producing extreme heat might also pose health problems for neighbors. Persons living adjacent to steel mills have sued for nuisance because of the high temperatures produced by the blast furnaces. The heat from these operations can raise air temperatures to uncomfortable levels. When the heat becomes unreasonable, the courts may find private nuisances.

Toxic Tort Nuisances   The disposal or transportation of hazardous wastes or toxic chemicals are frequently the ground for private nuisance actions. Underground or surface water supplies that are contaminated by leaking toxic chemical dumps, or air that is filled with poisonous dusts (such as uranium dust vented from a nuclear power plant) are excellent examples of private nuisances. Much of the toxic tort litigation brought today involves nuisance actions.

Incessant Telephone Calls   Creditors occasionally use intimidation tactics to coerce customers to pay delinquent accounts. A favorite technique is the late-night telephone call. The creditor might telephone a delinquent customer several times late at night, every day for weeks or even months, to try to persuade the patron to pay the overdue amounts. Customers subjected to such harassment often suffer emotional distress and related physical manifestations.

Courts routinely determine that such activity constitutes a private nuisance. It is an unreasonable interference with the customer's use and enjoyment of the privacy of his or her home life. In fact, plaintiffs besieged with incessant phone calling often sue the culprit under several causes of action—namely, the intentional torts of invasion of privacy or intentional infliction of emotional distress—along with nuisance.

Unwanted Associations with Neighboring Uses

For decades, landowners have rushed to the courthouse to file private nuisance actions against the owners of houses of ill repute, X-rated movie theatres, adult bookstores, and liquor or gambling establishments. These cases illustrate clearly the personal nature of offensiveness. Some persons simply cannot abide living in the vicinity of these types of activities. They do not wish to be associated with these land uses. These persons typically become plaintiffs in nuisance lawsuits in an attempt to drive out activities that they find repugnant.

In cases such as these, courts often struggle with community standards to decide if the activities are private nuisances. Are the plaintiffs overreacting, or are their objections reasonable? Would reasonable persons agree that having to live adjacent to establishments engaged in these pursuits is an unreasonable and substantial interference with the use and enjoyment of the realty? This is not an easy question to answer, as can be seen by reading some of the hundreds of appellate court opinions discussing the subject.

"Coming to the Nuisance" Defense

Often, a person will move into a neighborhood in which one of the activities previously described is already situated. In many cases, the manufacturer, trash dump, junkyard, or adult bookstore has been doing business in the same location for years. The plaintiff came to the area after the alleged nuisance was already there. When this happens, and the plaintiff then sues for private nuisance, the defendant may plead the "coming to the nuisance" defense. The **coming to the nuisance defense** involves the plaintiff who owns or uses land at a location in which the alleged nuisance activity was already occurring. If the plaintiff came to the nuisance, then he or she cannot recover against the defendant. The defense is similar to the defense of assumption of risk, in that the plaintiff knew (or reasonably should have known) that the preexisting activity would offend him or her. Consequently, a reasonable person would not have chosen to buy or use land adjacent to a known, present, and distasteful land use next door. In essence, the plaintiff assumes the risk of obnoxiousness from the nuisance activity by coming to the place while knowing that the nuisance is already there, waiting to offend the plaintiff.

LEGAL TERMS

"coming to the nuisance" defense
A defense to private nuisance lawsuits that may be used successfully when the plaintiff owns or uses land at a location in which the alleged nuisance activity was previously occurring. The plaintiff is said to have "come to the nuisance" and thus cannot recover against the defendant.

THE CASE OF INTRUSION ON HOG HEAVEN

Incompatible land uses often make unhappy neighbors. Unfortunately, it is not always apparent that such incompatibilities will exist until after the activities have cohabitated for some time. Then one of the landowners usually is harmed by the other, and a nuisance action enters the picture. As the case here illustrates, a business can create a nuisance through its own actions or those of its customers.

Sherk v. Indiana Waste Systems, Inc.
495 N.E.2d 815 (Ind. Ct. App. 1986)
(Court of Appeals of Indiana)
July 31, 1986

CONOVER, Judge.
Plaintiff-Appellant Dale J. Sherk (Sherk) appeals a negative judgment in his nuisance action against Defendants-Appellees Indiana Waste Systems, Inc. (IWS) and Prairie View Farms, Inc.

We reverse.

ISSUES

Sherk presents three issues for review. Because we reverse we consider only two issues. Restated, they are

1. whether the trial court erred in finding IWS and Prairie View were not responsible for noise generated by others, and

2. whether the trial court erred in finding IWS's use of the land was reasonable and thus a good defense to this action.

FACTS

Sherk raises hogs. IWS operates a landfill on land adjacent to Sherk's former hog breeding facility. IWS leases its land from Prairie View. Sherk's hogs suffered a 50% reduction in conception rates from the time IWS started its operation there. Eventually, Sherk had to close down his hog breeding facility at that location because of such losses.

Sherk, attributing that reduction to noise from the landfill operation, sued IWS and Prairie View Farms, Inc. (hereinafter collectively IWS). Sherk alleged IWS operated its landfill in such a noisy manner it constituted a nuisance and damaged him.

The case was tried by the court. [. . .]

The trial court found *inter alia* (1) noise generated by IWS's operation of its landfill did not cause Sherk's problem, (2) truck traffic increased as a result of the opening of the landfill, (3) noise emanating from the increased truck traffic caused the reduction in conception rates, and (4) IWS's operation of the landfill was reasonable. The trial court entered judgment against Sherk. He appeals.

[. . .]

Sherk contends the trial court erred when it concluded IWS was not responsible for the noise and vibration generated by the trash hauling trucks entering and leaving its landfill. Sherk also contends the trial court erred when it decided reasonableness of use is a defense to an action for a nuisance and IWS's use of its land is reasonable. [. . .]

When deciding whether one's use of his property is a nuisance to his neighbors it is necessary to balance the competing interests of the landowners. In so doing we use a common sense approach. Mere annoyance or inconvenience will not support an action for a nuisance because the damages resulting therefrom are deemed *damnum absque injuria* in recognition of the fact life is not perfect. [Citations omitted.] Thus, "reasonable use" of one's property may be a defense to a nuisance action where the use merely causes *incidental* injury to another. [Citation omitted.] Where, however, one uses his property for his profit so as to practically confiscate or destroy his neighbor's property he should be compelled to respond in damages, for it can hardly be said such use is reasonable. [Citation omitted.] Whether one's use of property is reasonable is determined by the effect such use has on neighboring property. Liability is imposed in those cases where the harm or risk thereto is greater than the owner of such property should be required to bear under the circumstances. [Citations omitted.]

Sherk argues but for the landfill operation there would have been no noise obstructing the free use of his property as a hog breeding facility. Thus, he opines, IWS should be liable for the noise generated by the trash hauling trucks. IWS in turn argues because the trial court found its use of its property was reasonable IWS is absolved of any responsibility for its customers' noisy trucks.

[. . .] [A] business may be liable for the acts of its customers or others if acts by them upon the business property or in going to or leaving it obstruct a neighbor's use of his property. [Citations omitted.]

The facts found by the trial court here show (1) the conception rate of Sherk's pigs ranged between 70% and 90% before the landfill began its operations; (2) the rate was reduced to 30% following the opening of the landfill; (3) the reduction in rate of conception was due to the noise generated by the trash hauling trucks traveling to and from the landfill.

It is apparent but for the landfill there substantially would have been no noisy truck traffic in the vicinity of Sherk's pigs, and they would have continued breeding successfully in the peace and tranquility which they apparently require. The interference here is more than a mere annoyance or incidental harm. The use of IWS's property has destroyed the usefulness of Sherk's property as a hog breeding facility. The evidence and all reasonable inferences from it leads inescapably to the conclusion IWS's use of its property was unreasonable in relation to Sherk's use of his property as a hog breeding facility.

Because the trial court found no liability, it made no findings as to damages. While a proper remedy for nuisance may consist of damages or injunction or some combination of the two [. . .], Sherk seeks no injunction, only damages.

Reversed, and remanded for hearing and determination as to Sherk's damages only.

CASE QUESTIONS

1. Do you agree with the Court that IWS's use of its property was unreasonable? Why or why not?
2. Suppose that IWS had begun operating its landfill before Sherk established his hog breeding facility. Would the outcome of the case be different? Explain.

Private nuisance hypotheticals provide the reader with some of the earthiest factual situations in tort law. Students can easily relate to intrusions upon their senses or values. However, one must guard against identifying too strongly with the offended individual over the business allegedly creating the nuisance. As the following examples illustrate, each party in the nuisance story has its side to tell.

HYPOTHETICALS

Harvey Foreman bought a house in a residential subdivision in 1989. His real estate is adjacent to 70 acres of pasture land. In 1990, the pasture was sold to the Waste Away Company, which erected a trash processing plant and landfill in 1991. This plant began compacting trash for landfill use as well as incinerating trash. Early in 1992 Harvey began smelling unpleasant odors and smoke from the trash piles and smokestacks. In warm weather, the smell was extremely nasty. Fumes seemed to hover all around the neighborhood. Does Harvey have a cause of action for private nuisance?

When Harvey bought his home in 1989, he assumed that he would be living next door to pasture land, which is free from odors and has a clear, natural view. He probably anticipated that wildlife or livestock would graze the realty next door. This rustic expectation was shattered in 1990 when Waste Away transformed the land into a trash processing facility and landfill.

Using the private nuisance formula, first ask whether Waste Away's use of its real estate unreasonably and substantially interfered with Harvey's use and enjoyment of his property. Every day, odors and smoke floated across Harvey's land from the trash facility. The neighborhood became inundated with the foul smell of piled or burning trash. Reasonable persons with ordinary sensibilities (or, as it is sometimes called, sensitivities) would find such odors and smoke to be offensive. Most subdivision residents in Harvey's community could reasonably be expected to react adversely to the invading stench. Waste Away has created a private nuisance.

□ □ □

Consider another hypothetical. The Sanctified Brethren Church purchased a building site for a new cathedral in July 1991. Across the street, one block away, were several taverns, an X-rated movie theatre, and an adult bookstore. Once construction began, members of the church filed suit against the owners of these businesses, claiming private nuisance. Would the church's lawsuit be successful?

No. Assuming that the church could first prove that these businesses constituted a private nuisance, the businesses could avail themselves of the coming to the nuisance defense. The church knew that these businesses were already located in the neighborhood when it purchased its building site. The church voluntarily decided to situate its cathedral within close proximity of activities that church members found offensive. Therefore, the church would fail in its lawsuit.

There are literally thousands of different factual patterns involving private nuisance to be found in the court reporters. This tort can be quite interesting to study, given the variety and peculiarity of the fact scenarios that allegedly produce nuisances. One might wish to consult the index to the *American Law Reports* series, published by The Lawyers' Cooperative Publishing Company. (These are abbreviated as A.L.R., A.L.R.2d, A.L.R.3d, A.L.R.4th, A.L.R.5th, and A.L.R. Fed.) Each series contains many annotations involving different examples of nuisances. These are often entertaining as well as enlightening—one reason that nuisance is frequently regarded as a "fun" tort subject in law study. Figure 11-1 lists the elements to private nuisance.

11.2 PUBLIC NUISANCES

Private nuisances are only part of the nuisance portion of the torts puzzle. Public nuisances are distinguishable. A **public nuisance** is a land

Elements	Examples	Defense
Activity that unreasonably and substantially interferes with use and enjoyment of another's land	Physical effects on land (vibrations, pollution, crop destruction, flooding, junk clutter, or excavations)	Coming to the nuisance
Unreasonable and *substantial* defined by community standard (reasonable person standard) regarding offensiveness of activity	Health hazards and offending sensibilities (noxious odors, smoke, dust, extreme noise or temperature, incessant telephone calling)	Plaintiff arrives to use land after nuisance activity already exists
Defendant's activity must proximately cause plaintiff's injuries	Unwanted associations with neighboring uses (prostitution houses, distributors of explicit sexual material, gambling institutions)	

FIGURE 11-1
Elements of Private Nuisance

use that injures the public at large rather than just a single individual. A public nuisance unreasonably interferes with the public's enjoyment of legal rights common to the public. The elements of public nuisance may be broken down as: (1) The tortfeasor's use of land that (2) unreasonably and substantially interferes with (3) the public's use and enjoyment of legal rights common to the public.

Unlike private nuisances, which can adversely affect a single person, a public nuisance must harm the general public. More than one person must always be affected (or, at least, potentially affected) by the alleged nuisance activity. This does not require a multitude of angry citizens. Residents of a single neighborhood would suffice.

The standard of unreasonable and substantial interference is identical to that used in private nuisances, except that the interference must be to the public rather than a sole plaintiff.

Use and Enjoyment of Common Legal Rights

The use and enjoyment element in public nuisance is significantly different from the one discussed in private nuisances. With public nuisances, he tortfeasor's obnoxious land use interferes with the public's common legal rights, such as the right to peaceably assemble in public places, the right to use public streets and sidewalks without being subjected to offensive activities, or the right to safe and healthy conditions in one's neighborhood.

LEGAL TERMS

public nuisance
A land use that injures the public at large rather than a single individual. Its elements include the tortfeasor's use of land that unreasonably and substantially interferes with the public's use and enjoyment of legal rights common to the public. The government acts as plaintiff against the defendant. Coming to the nuisance is not a defense in public nuisance cases.

Governments as Plaintiffs

Although citizens often file public nuisance complaints with their local governmental agencies, it is the government, through its municipal governing bodies (e.g., city council, county commissioners) or its prosecuting attorneys, that sues defendants alleged to be committing public nuisances. This is because the government represents the public at large and must enforce its citizens' legal rights against tortfeasors. At common law, or by statute or, in some states, by state constitutional provision, state and local governments have the authority to protect their citizens from public nuisances. The source of this power is the states' **police powers**, which give governments authority to file lawsuits or enact legislation to protect the public's health, welfare, safety, or morals. These are usually very broad powers that give governments considerable flexibility to forbid certain so-called offensive activities.

Types of Public Nuisances

Almost all public nuisances are defined by statute or ordinance. Many such laws focus on land uses *which legislators believe* a majority of the population would find offensive, unhealthy, or immoral. The reader may know from personal experience that this belief may be unfounded or exaggerated. That, of course, depends upon whether one agrees or disagrees with what the government has labelled a public nuisance. Common targets of public nuisance laws include institutions devoted to (1) gambling, (2) prostitution, (3) distribution of sexually explicit materials, (4) sale of alcohol, or (5) toxic waste management. Other typical public nuisances include (1) allowing certain weeds or poisonous plants to grow on one's land; (2) failing to comply with health code provisions by keeping one's residence clean and vermin-free; and (3) keeping unrestrained wild or vicious animals on one's property. However, public nuisances may also include many of the same activities discussed in the private nuisances section.

Mixed Nuisances

Often, the same activity can constitute both a private and a public nuisance. These are sometimes called **mixed nuisances.** Apply this rule of thumb in such cases: The greater the number of persons adversely affected by an allegedly offensive land use, the more likely it will be considered a public, as well as a private, nuisance.

Nuisances Per Se

Courts often consider activities violating public nuisance statutes to be **nuisances per se.** *Per se* is Latin, meaning "by itself." In tort law, it usually means that some behavior has violated a statute, and therefore the

LEGAL TERMS

police powers
  The state's authority to file lawsuits or enact legislation to protect the public's health, welfare, safety, or morals.

defendant is automatically liable. Sometimes courts, in the common law, decree that certain conduct is per se tortious. Negligence per se is an example. Per se nuisances have also been established by common law court decisions.

A public nuisance per se is an activity that violates the statute and is automatically considered a public nuisance. The tortfeasor thus loses from the start of litigation, simply by violating the statute. Statutes (and, rarely, common law) may also declare certain private nuisances to be per se nuisances.

"Coming to the Nuisance" Not a Defense

Generally, courts do not recognize the coming to the nuisance defense in public nuisance cases. This defense focuses on the individual plaintiff who purchases or uses land next to a preexisting, private nuisance activity. Public nuisances, by definition, affect the public at large, and the very existence or continuation of the public nuisance activity is considered harmful, whether it was preexisting or not.

mixed nuisance
An activity that constitutes both a public and a private nuisance.

nuisance per se
A nuisance activity that violates a specific statute, and thus is considered a nuisance "by itself." No further proof is needed to establish nuisance. Most often applied in public nuisance cases involving statutes or ordinances.

THE CASE OF THE DOOR-TO-DOOR SOLICITATION

Many people commonly think of door-to-door salespersons as nuisances, but the law does not automatically define them as such. As the following case suggests, not all forms of solicitation are included in public nuisance ordinances, such as the Florida example in this case.

Jacobs v. City of Jacksonville
762 F. Supp. 327 (M.D. Fla. 1991)
(U.S. District Court,
Middle District of Florida)
April 8, 1991

ORDER

JOHN H. MOORE, II, District Judge.

This cause was tried before the Court on March 11, 1990. [. . .] [T]he Court now issues the following findings of fact and conclusions of law.

[. . .]

Plaintiff, Jerry L. Jacobs, does business under the fictitious name of Youth Opportunities Unlimited (hereinafter "Y.O.U."), and is a person who, personally and through his employees, sells or offers for sale merchandise by traveling from door-to-door, while carrying such merchandise. Y.O.U. is a for-profit organization which derives income through the sale of cookies, candy, and other items. These sales are conducted primarily by teenagers who are Y.O.U. members. Plaintiff holds a city permit to operate as a peddler of merchandise.

[. . .]

Plaintiff and the Y.O.U. salespersons conduct the door-to-door activities in various neighborhoods in Jacksonville on a rotating basis; as a result, sales in any particular neighborhood are made no more than a few times per year. Each individual Y.O.U. product item is sold to the consumer for $4.00. [. . .] No evidence was introduced to show that a large number of the residences solicited found Y.O.U.'s sales activities to be annoying or injurious, although the evidence did show that Y.O.U. salespersons are occasionally unwelcome at a few residences.

[. . .]

The City of Jacksonville, through Officer J.P. Baptist of the Jacksonville Sheriff's Office, has threatened Plaintiff with arrest under [Jacksonville ordinance] § 250.303, for engaging in residential door-to-door peddling activities without invitation. [. . .]

In most instances, Plaintiff has not been expressly "requested or invited" by the owner or occupant of the private residence before engaging in door-to-door sales activity. [Citation omitted.] Plaintiff does not solicit at any private residence where a "No Solicitation" sign is visible.

[. . .] The Court finds that Plaintiff is a "peddler" as defined in the Code, [. . .] subject to the prohibition on door-to-door peddling set forth in J.O.C. § 250.303.

[. . .]

Under Florida law, unless a homeowner manifests externally in some manner his or her wish to remain unmolested by the visits of solicitors or peddlers, a solicitor or peddler may take [. . .] an implied invitation to call upon residences [. . .]. *Prior v. White,* 132 Fla. 1, 180 So. 347, 355 (1938). In *Prior,* the Florida Supreme Court invalidated an anti-peddling ordinance of New Smyrna Beach, Florida, as applied to the door-to-door sales activities of a Fuller Brush Company salesman. The New Smyrna ordinance was virtually identical to the Jacksonville ordinance now at issue. The court held that peddling and soliciting in New Smyrna was not a public nuisance because custom and usage established an implied invitation to solicit sales at private residences, and therefore could not be punished as a crime or misdemeanor. [Citation omitted.] The court further held that a municipality cannot, through an attempted exercise of its police powers, declare by ordinance or otherwise that an activity

is a public nuisance, when in fact such activity is not proved to be a public nuisance. [Citation omitted.]

Prior v. White is still good law in Florida, never having been overruled by the Florida Supreme Court. Recent cases also have held that a municipality may not declare an activity to be a public nuisance unless that activity does in fact constitute a public nuisance. [Citations omitted.] In addition, Florida courts continue to recognize the implied invitation theory. [Citation omitted.] Since the principles set forth in *Prior* remain part of the law of Florida, *Prior* is binding upon this Court in its interpretation of Florida law. [. . .] Thus, the facts of each case must be examined carefully to determine whether the type of door-to-door peddling engaged in by the parties in that case constitutes a public nuisance. [Citation omitted.]

A public nuisance is defined as an activity that "violates public rights, subverts public order, decency or morals, or causes inconvenience or damage to the public generally." [Citations omitted.] It is not completely clear under *Prior* which party bears the burden of proving that peddling is or is not a public nuisance. [. . .]

In this case, door-to-door peddling in Jacksonville, Florida has not been proved to be a public nuisance. The Defendants have introduced virtually no evidence that proves peddling in Jacksonville by Y.O.U. or by others is a public nuisance, and have made little attempt to make such a showing. [. . .]

Even assuming the Plaintiff bears the burden of proving that door-to-door peddling [. . .] is not a public nuisance, the Court finds that Plaintiff has met this burden. The evidence introduced at trial showed that Y.O.U. sold 90,000 items in Jacksonville in 1990, an average of roughly one item per residence solicited. The evidence showed that a sizeable number, approximately one-half, of the residences solicited made a purchase from Y.O.U. Thus, thousands of customers in Jacksonville evidently did not find Plaintiff's organization materially annoying to them personally, which demonstrates that Y.O.U.'s activities do not materially inconvenience the public at large or subvert public order. [...] Thus, Plaintiff has affirmatively proved, in the absence of any effective rebuttal evidence by the Defendants, that Y.O.U.'s activities do not inconvenience the public in a manner that amounts to a public nuisance. Accordingly, under the authority of *Prior v. White,* the ordinance is unreasonable and an invalid exercise of the police power as applied to the Plaintiff and the Y.O.U. organization.

[...]

ORDERED AND ADJUDGED:

[...] Defendants are permanently enjoined from arresting or prosecuting Plaintiff or any members of Youth Opportunities Unlimited under color of Jacksonville Ordinance Code § 250.303. [...]

CASE QUESTIONS

1. How does the court's definition of a public nuisance differ from that discussed in this chapter?
2. Do you agree with the court that the plaintiff's activities did not violate the ordinance? Explain.

As *Jacobs* demonstrates, what constitutes a public nuisance or a nuisance per se is generally a question of common law interpretation and statutory construction. But underlying questions of substance and form are the value judgments implicit in all nuisance per se or public nuisance cases. The following examples present such choices. Despite the temptation to become caught up in "good" versus "bad," one must concentrate on the legal elements and their application to the facts.

HYPOTHETICALS

Armstrong McCarter has an apiary in his backyard. He lives in a suburban neighborhood. Several hundred honeybees congregate in Armstrong's hives. The bees produce honey which Armstrong sells at local groceries. Frequently, children in the area have been stung by honeybees. Parents complained to Armstrong, but he simply shrugged off each incident, stating that there was no proof that his bees were responsible. However, there were no other honeybee colonies in the neighborhood. A town ordinance prohibits the keeping of wildlife within the city limits. Has Armstrong committed a public nuisance or a nuisance per se?

Armstrong's use of his land (maintaining an apiary) substantially and unreasonably interfered with his neighbors' use and enjoyment of the public streets and sidewalks in the area, as well as their own realty. Children were often stung by honeybees, and the only large honeybee colony in the neighborhood was Armstrong's. A trier-of-fact could reasonably infer that Armstrong's bees were responsible for the attacks. Of course, a local governmental agency would first have to sue Armstrong for public nuisance, and the case would have to go to trial. Reasonable persons would find these bee encounters to be offensive and dangerous. The public at large was threatened by Armstrong's *ferae naturae*. The bees unreasonably and substantially interfered with citizens' use of public streets and sidewalks. Under its police power, the local government would have authority to sue Armstrong for public nuisance.

Armstrong also violated the local ordinance prohibiting the keeping of wildlife within the city limits. This constitutes a nuisance per se, giving the town government another cause of action against Armstrong.

□ □ □

Consider another hypothetical. Darling Davis operates a massage parlor across from the local public high school. Although there is no evidence of prostitution at the establishment, Davis offers nude massages, during which both customers and masseurs disrobe. From across the street, high-school students can see clearly through the windows of Davis's building. Is Davis engaged in a public nuisance?

Davis's use of her land could adversely affect the students. The erotic views could disrupt school activities as children (and adults) cluster around windows to catch the revealing sights next door. Arguably, this is an unreasonable and substantial interference with a public right—namely, the right to use the public school for educational pursuits. Under its police powers, the municipal government could sue Davis for public nuisance.

Admittedly, cases such as Davis's involve value judgments and presume a threat to the public morals. One may agree or disagree with the alleged public threat produced by a massage parlor next to a school. However, many cases have involved exactly these fact situations, and courts promptly conclude that public nuisances have occurred.

Figure 11-2 lists the elements of public nuisances and nuisances per se.

11.3 REMEDIES FOR NUISANCES

When one has identified a private or public nuisance, what does one do about it? In other words, what remedies are available to plaintiffs against

Elements	Examples	Defense
Activity that unreasonably and substantially interferes with public's use and enjoyment of legal rights common to public at large	Prostitution establishments Pornography distributors	Coming to the nuisance *not* a defense to public nuisances
Plaintiff is governmental agency responsible for protecting public interest harmed by public nuisance activity	Historically, gambling and alcohol establishments were often considered public nuisances, although not normally at the present time	
State and local governments have authority to litigate public nuisances under general police powers to protect public health, safety, morals, and welfare	Allowing noxious weeds to grow on one's land Failing to comply with public health statutes Keeping unrestrained wild animals on one's land	
Mixed nuisances include public and private nuisances		Coming to the nuisance defense effective against private nuisance portion of mixed nuisance actions
Nuisances per se are nuisance activities that violate statutes or ordinances		Coming to the nuisance defense not usually effective against nuisance per se actions

FIGURE 11-2
Elements of
Public Nuisances,
Mixed Nuisances, and
Nuisances Per Se

defendants? **Remedies** are the relief that plaintiffs receive against defendants in lawsuits. The most common remedy in tort actions is *money* **damages**, in which the defendant must pay the plaintiff a sum of money to satisfy the judgment. The trier-of-fact sets the amount owed after a trial has been held.

Other, nonmonetary remedies are also available for torts such as nuisance. These are called equitable remedies. **Equitable remedies** do not involve money damages; instead, the court orders the defendant to do (or, more commonly, *not* to do) something. When the court orders a defendant to do something, it is called a **mandamus order**. When the court orders a defendant not to do something, it is called an **injunction** or *restraining order.*

For centuries, money damages were considered inappropriate in nuisance cases. Courts would apply only equitable remedies. In nuisance law, the most common equitable remedies include (1) abatement and

injunctions
Equitable remedies
frequently used in
nuisance cases; court
orders to defendants to
cease and desist from
engaging in nuisance
activities. Injunctions
include temporary
restraining orders
(T.R.O.s), temporary
injunctions, and
permanent injunctions.

(2) injunction, although now money damages are occasionally permitted in nuisance cases.

Abatement

In nuisance cases, abatement is the most common remedy plaintiffs seek. With **abatement**, the defendant is ordered to cease, or *abate,* the nuisance activity. Abatement is often permanent. The defendant must desist from conducting the nuisance activity after a judgment for abatement is entered. This provides complete relief for the plaintiff, because the nuisance activity will be discontinued. Abatement can create harsh economic consequences for defendants, but the public policy behind abatement is clear: Nuisance tortfeasors have injured someone (or, if the public, many people). As long as the nuisance continues, the plaintiff(s) will continue to be hurt. The only certain solution is to stop the nuisance altogether.

Money Damages

When abatement could impose an unreasonably severe economic burden upon the nuisance tortfeasor, courts have broken with the ancient common law tradition and awarded plaintiffs money damages instead of abatement. This way, the plaintiffs can be compensated for their injuries produced by the nuisance activities, and the defendant can survive (economically) by staying in business, even though the nuisance also continues. Courts using this alternative are usually attempting to balance interests between conflicting land uses.

Injunctions

Courts enforce abatement through injunctive relief. *Injunctions* are court orders to defendants to cease and desist from engaging in nuisance activities. There are two types of injunctions: (1) temporary injunctions, including temporary restraining orders (T.R.O.s); and (2) permanent injunctions.

Temporary Injunctions

Temporary injunctions are often used from the time a plaintiff files suit until the first court hearing. The plaintiff, in his or her complaint, asks the court to issue a **temporary restraining order (T.R.O.)**, forbidding the defendant from conducting an alleged nuisance activity until a court hearing can be held to determine if the activity constitutes a nuisance. Under most rules of civil procedure, T.R.O.s may be issued for up to 10 days, while the court convenes a hearing to decide if a nuisance has occurred. After the hearing, if the evidence convinces the judge that a nuisance is happening, the court may order further temporary injunctive relief, banning the defendant's nuisance activity until a trial on the merits may be held.

The purpose of temporary injunctions is to protect the plaintiff from further harm if a nuisance is in fact occurring. Plaintiffs often must post bonds to compensate the defendant if the court or jury later decides that the defendant did not engage in a nuisance. This is to protect the defendant from economic losses suffered while the injunctions were in effect and the defendant was not permitted to conduct the nuisance activity (which could mean lost profits or extra expenses).

temporary restraining order (T.R.O.)
A type of injunction, which is an equitable remedy. Frequently used in nuisance cases.

permanent injunctions
Abatement orders instructing the defendant to permanently stop doing the nuisance activity.

contempt
A judicial remedy used if a defendant fails to comply with the trial court's injunctive orders. Used in nuisance cases.

Permanent Injunctions

Permanent injunctions are abatement orders instructing the defendant to permanently stop doing the nuisance activity. They are usually issued after a trial on the merits, once the trier-of-fact has concluded that a nuisance exists. If the defendant fails to obey a permanent injunction by continuing the nuisance, the court can punish the defendant by holding him or her in **contempt**. This punishment may involve monetary fines or even imprisonment.

THE CASE OF THE GREAT TEXAS DUST-OFF

State statutes often provide private citizens and public agencies with authority to litigate against private or public nuisances. As the following case indicates, private citizens may enforce nuisance actions against tortfeasors under the Texas Clean Air Act. The Texas Court of Appeals, in an excellently reasoned and articulate opinion, explains the applicable nuisance remedies.

Manchester Terminal Corp. v. Texas TX TX Marine Transportation., Inc.
781 S.W.2d 646 (Tex. Ct. App. 1989)
(Court of Appeals of Texas)
October 26, 1989

OPINION

EVANS, Chief Justice.

Manchester Terminal Corporation (Manchester) appeals from an order of the trial court granting a plea of abatement and dismissing Manchester's cause of action for lack of subject matter jurisdiction. Manchester, the owner and operator of a marine terminal storage facility on the Houston Ship Channel, initiated this action against appellees, Texas TX TX Marine Transportation, Inc. (Texas Marine), the operator of a petroleum coke facility, Atlantic Richfield Company d/b/a [doing business as] Lyondell Petrochemical Company (Lyondell), the owner and operator of a petroleum coke refinery, and the Port of Houston Authority (Port of Houston), the owner of the land on which the petroleum coke facility is located.

Manchester alleged that the activities of Texas Marine and Lyondell in transporting and storing petroleum coke on the Port of Houston property generated large amounts of petroleum coke dust, which settled on Manchester's property and contaminated its facilities and stored goods. Manchester alleged that this pollution significantly impaired its ability to solicit and accept goods for storage, resulting in substantial economic injury and posing a significant health hazard to its employees and the employees of other companies working at its terminal. Manchester characterized these actions as constituting trespass and nuisance, and asserted that they violated Tex. Const. art. I, sec. 17. Manchester sought a permanent injunction to prevent the transportation and storage of petroleum coke at the Texas Marine facility, as well as more than $12.5 million in damages.

Texas Marine and Lyondell filed a plea to the jurisdiction and a plea in abatement, in which they asserted that Manchester's cause of action was already the subject of proceedings before the Texas Air Control Board (TACB) [. . .].

In Manchester's first three points of error, it asserts that the trial court erred in [. . .] dismissing its cause of action because (1) the Texas Clean Air Act explicitly recognizes the right of private persons to bring common-law actions to abate or recover for nuisances or conditions of pollution [citation omitted]; [other two points of error omitted.] [. . .]

We sustain these points of error.

[. . .]

["]The Texas Clean Air Act (the Act) was enacted to safeguard the air resources of the State from pollution by controlling or abating air pollution or emissions of air contaminants, consistent with the protection of health, general welfare and physical property of the people, including the aesthetic enjoyment of the air resources by the people and the maintenance of adequate visibility." [Citation omitted.] The Act provides that its provisions are to be vigorously enforced. [Citation omitted.]

[. . .] [S]ection 1.06 [of the Act] expressly provides:

Sec. 1.06. Nothing in this Act affects the right of any private person to pursue all common law remedies available to abate a condition of pollution or other nuisance or recover damages therefor, or both.

Section 1.06, which has been a part of the Act since its inception, clearly and directly expresses the legislature's intent to preserve *the right of any private person to pursue all common-law remedies available to abate a condition of pollution or other nuisance, or to recover damages therefor or both.* Manchester's pleadings allege both trespass and nuisance, which are well-recognized common-law remedies to abate or recover damages for pollution.

[. . .]

Texas Marine and Lyondell also argue that a court decree granting injunctive relief to Manchester would, in effect, nullify and set aside the statutory permits issued by the TACB. We disagree. Although Texas Marine may hold a valid permit from the TACB authorizing the emission of specified amounts of pollutants into the air, neither the permit nor the underlying legislation gives Texas Marine the right to conduct its business in a manner which, under the law, constitutes a trespass or a nuisance. [Citation omitted.]

It has long been the law in this state that proof of negligence is not essential to imposition of liability for creation or maintenance of a nuisance. A nuisance does not rest on the degree of care used, but on the degree of danger or annoyance existing even with the best of care. [Citation omitted.] When a commercial enterprise causes or permits the escape of noxious things such as smoke, soot, or odor, so as to substantially impair the comfort or enjoyment of those occupying neighboring property, such activity may be judicially declared a nuisance, justifying equitable relief or an award of damages. [Citations omitted.]

Unless a particular commercial enterprise constitutes a nuisance per se, courts are reluctant to enter an injunctive order that will absolutely prohibit the operation of a lawful business. [Citation omitted.] The courts will intervene, however, if a business is being conducted in such a manner as to constitute a nuisance to particular individuals. In such a case, a court, in the exercise of its equitable powers, may frame its decree to permit the continuation of the enterprise, and also protect the aggrieved individual against further loss. [Citations omitted.]

Under the pleading in this case, it would be possible for the trial court to fashion a decree that would allow Texas Marine to continue its business operations under the TACB permit, and at the same time, require that Texas Marine refrain from operating its business in a manner that would cause further loss or damage to Manchester. The trial court could also award damages to Manchester without adversely affecting Texas Marine's ability to conduct its lawful business operations pursuant to the TACB permit. We therefore overrule the contentions that any relief granted to Manchester under its pleadings would have the effect of nullifying the permit issued by the TACB. [. . .]

[. . .]

The order of the trial court is reversed and the cause remanded for further proceedings.

CASE QUESTIONS

1. How did the Texas Court of Appeals define nuisance in *Manchester?*
2. What remedies did the court of appeals consider appropriate in this case?
3. Given the facts reported in the court's opinion, could the defendant's petroleum coke dust emissions have been considered a public nuisance or a nuisance per se, discussed in § 11.2? Explain your analysis. Did the *Manchester* court think that a nuisance per se occurred in this case?

Review of Hypotheticals

Review the hypotheticals from the previous sections of this chapter. Consider which remedies are suitable. In class or study groups, one may wish to discuss whether money damages is an appropriate alternative to abatement. Figure 11-3 restates the remedies available in nuisance lawsuits.

Having assembled the nuisance portion of the torts puzzle, it is time to investigate another special tort action, negligence per se, which is examined in § 11.4.

Equitable Remedies	Money Damages
Abatement (permanent prohibition against nuisance activity)	Money damages may be awarded if abatement would put unreasonable economic burdens on the defendant
Temporary injunctions (forbidding nuisance activity during litigation process)	
Permanent injunctions (used for abatement)	

FIGURE 11-3
Remedies for
Nuisances

11.4 NEGLIGENCE PER SE

Negligence per se is behavior that is automatically negligent as a matter of law. When a statute defines certain conduct as negligent, and a tortfeasor violates the statute by engaging in that activity, then the tortfeasor is presumed to have been negligent by violating the statute. To meet the burden of proof, a plaintiff need only show that the defendant's actions violated the negligence statute. The defendant is then presumed negligent. This shifts the proof burden to the defendant, who must then present effective negligence defenses to avoid liability. A per se negligent defendant might also avoid liability by showing that he or she was not the proximate cause of the plaintiff's injuries. In other words, the defendant would have to prove that his or her violation of the statute did not proximately cause the plaintiff's harm.

Defenses to Negligence Per Se

The negligence defenses of contributory negligence, comparative negligence, and assumption of risk also apply to negligence per se cases.

Plaintiff Within Class of Persons Protected by Statute

Not every statutory violation constitutes negligence per se. To recover under negligence per se theory, the plaintiff must be within the class of persons protected by the statute or ordinance. For example, suppose a restaurant serves maggot-infested meat to its customers. This violates several state and local health statutes. Suppose Kent ate at the restaurant and became ill. He would fall within the class of persons protected by the health statutes that require restaurants to serve wholesome food to patrons. The restaurant's violation of the statutes would be considered negligence per se, and Kent would have an excellent cause of action against the establishment.

Absolute Liability Mislabelled as Negligence Per Se

Courts occasionally equate negligence per se with strict, or absolute, liability. However, the two tort theories are distinct. Negligence per se simply presumes negligence because of the tortfeasor's violation of a statute. Negligence is based upon the tortfeasor's failure to exercise reasonable care. Absolute liability holds the tortfeasor accountable, regardless of fault, for doing an abnormally dangerous activity. No degree of care is sufficient to avoid strict liability.

This confusion between absolute liability and negligence per se occurs because of the outcomes in each type of case. If the defendant violates a negligence statute, he or she is presumed automatically negligent. Liability is almost as certain as in strict liability cases. Thus, the two concepts are often equated, although they are substantially different.

Toxic Torts as Negligence Per Se

Statutes sometimes declare that violations of regulations regarding the transportation, disposal, or management of hazardous or toxic substances create a presumption of negligence as a matter of law. These statutory provisions boost plaintiffs' causes of action against tortfeasors who carelessly control abnormally dangerous materials.

LEGAL TERMS

negligence per se
  Automatic negligence "by itself," or as a matter of law. When a defendant's actions violate a negligence statute, then negligence is presumed to exist without further proof.

THE CASE OF THE STATUTORY HANGOVER

In *Ohio Casualty,* partially reprinted in chapter 6, the reader faced an intriguing negligence issue: Did a tavern owner violate a duty of care by serving alcohol to an intoxicated customer who subsequently injured himself? The Oklahoma Supreme Court said no. Review the earlier reprint for the relevant facts. In the portion of its opinion reprinted here, the court rules on the negligence per se issue. After the court's decision, the inebriated driver must have felt a severe case of statutory hangover.

Ohio Casualty Insurance Co.
v. Todd
813 P.2d 508 (Okla. 1991)
(Supreme Court of Oklahoma)
June 11, 1991

SUMMERS, Justice:
[. . .] Section 537(A)(2) [Oklahoma Statutes] states in relevant part that no person shall

"[s]ell, deliver or knowingly furnish alcoholic beverages to an intoxicated person."

A. NEGLIGENCE PER SE

Robertson [the intoxicated driver/customer] urges that Todd [the tavern owner] violated Section 537(A)(2) and that the violation amounted to negligence per se. In *Hampton v. Hammons* [citation omitted], we explained the elements which must be found before the violation of a statute is negligence per se. [. . .] [W]e pointed out that (1) the injury must have been caused by the violation, (2) the injury must be of a type intended to be prevented by the ordinance, and (3) the injured party must be one of the class intended to be protected by the statute.

Because we find the third element to be missing, we do not address the first two. In *Brigance,* we stated that the purpose behind Section 537(A)(2) was to protect innocent third parties who were injured by intoxicated persons. In *Cuevas v. Royal D'Iberville Hotel* [citation omitted], the Mississippi Supreme Court construed a statute similar to Section 537(A)(2), and found that the intoxicated person was excluded from the class of persons meant to be protected by the statute. In making this determination, the court pointed out the class to be protected was the general public, and that this class, while broad in range, could not be said to include "an adult individual . . . who voluntarily consumes intoxicants and then, by reason of his inebriated condition, injures himself." [Citation omitted.] We agree.

We find nothing in Section 537(A)(2), or in any of the statutes regulating the sale of alcohol, which indicate[s] that the legislature intended to protect the intoxicated adult who, by his own actions, causes injury to himself. Instead, it appears that the legislature intended to protect the "unsuspecting public"—in effect all of the populace except the willing imbiber. [Citations omitted.] Thus, a violation of Section 537(A)(2) does not amount to negligence per se under the facts of this case.

CASE QUESTIONS

1. What if a passenger riding in Robertson's vehicle had been injured? Would the passenger then have a cause of action against the tavern owner for violating § 537(A)(2), under negligence per se theory? Explain.
2. Do you agree with the court that Robertson does not fall within the scope of the class protected by § 537(A)(2)? Explain.

As *Ohio Casualty* illustrates, not every statutory violation is negligence per se. All elements must be satisfied for the doctrine to apply. The following hypotheticals further demonstrate this principle.

HYPOTHETICALS

Woodrow Smelter was driving his automobile at night along the Old River Road. Although it was pitch black, he did not have his headlights on. This violated a local county ordinance and state statute requiring headlight use at all times beginning an hour before sundown and ending an hour after sunrise. Woodrow collided with Bertha Godfrey, a pedestrian walking along the side of the road. Bertha sues Woodrow for negligence per se. Was he?

By driving without headlights, Woodrow violated an ordinance and statute that required motor vehicles to use lights at night. This was intended to protect other drivers and pedestrians from "invisible" vehicles hitting them in the dark. Bertha falls within the classification of persons protected by the statute and ordinance. Therefore, she could successfully sue Woodrow for negligence per se.

□ □ □

Consider another hypothetical. Barfly Beer Company sells "Brewster's Choice," a "light" beer low in calories. One of its distributors, the Barley Brothers Emporium, sells the product in town. A state health statute requires any manufacturer or seller of items for human consumption to distribute them in containers free from foreign substances. Barley collected empty bottles to send back to Barfly to be cleaned and reused. Sometimes, drinkers would put cigarette butts into the bottles. Neither Barley nor Barfly checked the bottles for foreign substances; they were simply sent back to the Barfly plant, refilled, and redistributed. Leigh Ann drank one of the beers from a bottle with a cigarette butt floating in the bottom. As one might imagine, Leigh Ann became physically ill as a result. Aside from the clear products liability issue, has Barfly or Barley been negligent per se?

The health statute was intended to protect consumers like Leigh Ann from injuries caused by foreign objects floating inside beverage bottles. Barfly and Barley each violated the statute. Their negligence may be presumed.

Figure 11-4 summarizes negligence per se.

11.5 WRONGFUL DEATH

Wrongful death statutes give the surviving family members of a deceased tort victim a cause of action against the tortfeasor whose negligence or intentional torts resulted in the victim's death.

LEGAL TERMS

wrongful death statutes
  Statutes giving surviving family members of a deceased tort victim a cause of action against the tortfeasor whose negligence or intentional torts caused the victim's death.

Defendant's actions are automatically considered negligent because they violated a negligence statute or ordinance
Plaintiff must fall within class of persons protected by statute
Defendant's statutory violation must proximately cause plaintiff's injuries
Negligence defenses apply to negligence per se

FIGURE 11-4
Elements of Negligence Per Se

Typical Facts in Wrongful Death Cases

The factual pattern in wrongful death actions may be summarized as follows: (1) a tortfeasor commits a tort against the victim; (2) the victim dies as a result of the tortfeasor's actions; (3) the victim's spouse or children, or both, sue the tortfeasor for wrongfully causing the victim's death.

Plaintiffs in Wrongful Death Actions

Under wrongful death statutes, the surviving family members, usually the victim's spouse or children, become the plaintiffs. However, some statutes allow the victim's parents or siblings to become plaintiffs. The victim's estate may also be permitted to sue the defendant for wrongful death damages under some statutes.

Damages

Wrongful death statutes usually define the types of damages that plaintiffs may recover against defendants. These damages include lost lifetime earnings potential and loss of consortium.

Lost Lifetime Earnings Potential

A tort victim's surviving family members may recover damages for the lost income that the victim would likely have earned had he or she not been killed by the tortfeasor. Wrongful death statutes usually define these damages in terms of the decedent's lost earnings potential based upon income at the time of death. This income base is projected over time. The future time period used is normally the victim's life expectancy, which is calculated from insurance actuarial tables. The projected earnings potential is usually adjusted for the victim's projected living expenses, had he or she survived.

Loss of Consortium

Wrongful death statutes (or the common law) often permit a tort victim's surviving family to recover damages for the lost love and companionship of the decedent. This is similar to pain and suffering damages. However, many statutes do not allow recovery of such damages. Wrongful death statutes (or courts interpreting them) often label this type of damages **loss of consortium**. Many statutes define *consortium* as both economic and intangible benefits lost to a victim's surviving family because of the victim's death. The intangible element could include lost love, companionship, and even the survivors' mental anguish upon losing a loved one.

Defenses

In wrongful death actions, the tortfeasor may use any defense applicable to the specific tort that produced the victim's injury. For example, suppose the victim had been contributorily or comparatively negligent, or assumed the risk, of the defendant's actions that killed the victim. Suppose the tortfeasor killed the victim while acting in self-defense or defense of others. The tortfeasor may escape liability for wrongfully causing the victim's death if any of the suitable tort defenses apply in the case. Defenses are available in a wrongful death action just as if the victim were still alive and, as plaintiff, were suing the defendant.

LEGAL TERMS

loss of consortium
Damages in a wrongful death lawsuit that compensate the surviving family members of a deceased tort victim for lost love or companionship, as well as mental anguish.

A CASE OF "DEATH-BEFORE-LITIGATION"

Some issues that come before appellate courts seem to have obvious answers. Some are so obvious, in fact, that one wonders why an appeal was necessary to answer them. The Montana Supreme Court may have been thinking this very question as it wrote the following straightfaced opinion, in response to a perfectly serious Ninth Circuit Court of Appeals query. Note Justice Gray's remarkable judicial restraint in avoiding humorous gibes that a lesser jurist might have felt compelled to include in the opinion. (Case questions are omitted following the case, as there is nothing left to ask.)

Carroll v. W.R. Grace & Co.
830 P.2d 1253 (Mont. 1992)
(Supreme Court of Montana)
January 14, 1992

GRAY, Justice.

This case is before us on certified questions from the Ninth Circuit Court of Appeals concerning the point at which a Montana wrongful death action accrues. [. . .]

Appellant (and defendant), W.R. Grace and Company, claims that the action accrues at the date of injury. Respondent (and plaintiff), Edith Carroll, claims that a wrongful death action accrues at the death of the injured person. We conclude that a wrongful death action does not accrue until the death of the injured person.

Charles Carroll (decedent) was employed by W.R. Grace and Company (Grace) at its vermiculite mine located in Libby, Montana, from 1958 until 1976; he underwent yearly chest x-rays provided by Grace from 1967 until 1976. Decedent retired in 1976, but continued to seek medical help regarding shortness of breath and a heart condition.

Mr. Carroll died in 1989, thirteen years after retirement. His autopsy report listed the cause of death as "severe interstitial fibrosis with pulmonary failure, apparently due to 'asbestosis.'" Decedent's medical records show that he had been diagnosed as suffering from asbestosis as early as 1972.

Edith Carroll, wife of decedent, filed a survival claim and a wrongful death claim against Grace, her husband's former employer, asserting that her husband's asbestosis was related to his employment at Grace's mine. She contends that she did not know his death was related to his employment until she read the autopsy report. She filed her suit as a diversity action in the United States District Court within two months of her husband's death.

Grace moved for summary judgment based on the running of the statutes of limitations for both survival and wrongful death claims. The U.S. District Court granted summary judgment, holding that the statute of limitations had run on both claims. Edith Carroll appealed to the United States Court of Appeals for the Ninth Circuit. The Ninth Circuit affirmed the District Court's holding that the survival claim was barred by the applicable three-year statute of limitations, but stated that Montana law was not definitive on the issue of when a wrongful death action accrues. [. . .]

Wrongful death claims are creatures of statute in Montana. As such, the question of when a wrongful death claim accrues requires an analysis of the general accrual statute and the wrongful death statute itself.

The general accrual statute for all actions in Montana provides:

[A] claim or cause of action accrues when all elements of the claim or cause exist or have occurred, [and] the right to maintain an action on the claim or cause is complete [. . .] .

The wrongful death statute reads:

Action for wrongful death. When injuries to and the death of one person are caused by the wrongful act or neglect of another, the personal representative of the decedent's estate may maintain an action for damages against the person causing the death [. . .] .

The language of Montana's general accrual statute is plain and straightforward: "all elements" of a claim must exist before the claim can accrue. [Citation omitted.] The meaning is equally clear and not susceptible to differing interpretations: only when all elements exist is a claim complete. [The general accrual statute] applies, by its terms, to all claims and causes of action. Thus, a wrongful death claim, like any other cause of action, accrues only when all elements of the claim have occurred; the claim simply does not exist until that time. The question, then, is whether death is an element of a wrongful death claim.

The wrongful death statute references ". . . injuries to *and the death* of one person . . . ". [Citation omitted.] (Emphasis added.) When these occurrences are caused by the "wrongful act or neglect of another," a wrongful death action may be maintained against the person who caused the death of the injured person. [Citation omitted.] It is clear from the legislature's use of the conjunctive "and" that the death of the injured person is an element of a wrongful death claim.

The wrongful death statute contains additional language mandating the conclusion that death is an element of the claim. "[T]he personal representative of the decedent's estate . . ." files a wrongful death action. [Citation omitted.] A "decedent" is indisputably a person who has died and a personal representative of an estate cannot be appointed until there is a decedent. Thus, the death itself is a critical element in a wrongful death action.

To summarize, no claim exists until all elements of a cause of action occur pursuant to [the general accrual statute], and death is an element of a wrongful death claim under [. . .] Montana's wrongful death statute. Therefore, we hold that a wrongful death action in Montana accrues at the time of decedent's death.

The following example illustrates how a wrongful death action might arise under a hypothetical statute.

HYPOTHETICAL

Jordan Vic Orthmell owns a cement manufacturing plant. One of his employees, Toby Noogle, drives a cement truck. One of Jordan's customers is Sally Sinchim, who was installing a swimming pool at her home. Toby came to pour cement for the pool. Sally's husband, Abraham, stood beneath the truck inside the excavated pool area. Without first checking to see if anyone was in the way, Toby dumped the entire truckload of cement on top of Abraham, who suffocated and died. Assume that this jurisdiction's wrongful death statute permits family survivors to sue tortfeasors for "negligently, wantonly, or intentionally" causing a victim's death. What is the likely result?

Sally could sue Toby (and, by respondeat superior, Toby's employer, Jordan) for causing the wrongful death of her husband, Abraham. Toby was negligent in pouring the cement without first seeing if anyone was inside the dangerous dumping area. Because Abraham died, Sally has a cause of action for wrongful death.

The family survivors' specific legal rights are entirely dependent upon the language of each wrongful death statute. It is important to become familiar with the wrongful death statutes in one's state, if one intends to work with plaintiffs for this special tort action. Figure 11-5 summarizes the standard ingredients of wrongful death statutes.

11.6 WRONGFUL LIFE

Wrongful life actions are lawsuits for the wrongful birth of a child. These are also called *wrongful birth* or *wrongful pregnancy* actions. The plaintiffs are usually the surprised parents, and the defendant is normally the

LEGAL TERMS

wrongful life actions
Lawsuits for the wrongful birth of a child. Sometimes called *wrongful pregnancy* actions. Most cases involve ineffective sterilization operations, which is basically a form of medical malpractice.

Tortfeasor commits tort against victim, causing victim's death
Victim's surviving spouse and children (or victim's estate) may sue tortfeasor to recover damages under wrongful death statute
Most statutes or courts allow damages for victim's lost lifetime earnings potential and for loss of consortium
Same tort defenses apply in wrongful death actions, depending upon the specific tort tortfeasor committed against deceased victim

FIGURE 11-5
Elements of Wrongful Death Statutes

physician who performed ineffective sterilization surgery upon either the mother or the father. Wrongful life, then, can be considered another form of medical malpractice, which is negligence.

Typical Fact Pattern: Unwanted Pregnancy

The typical situation involving unwanted pregnancy is as follows: A couple visit a physician, wishing a vasectomy or tubal ligation to prevent future conceptions. The doctor performs the surgery. However, because of the surgeon's negligence, the operation fails. The couple end up conceiving a child and then end up litigating against the physician whose negligence "caused" the unexpected (or unwanted) birth of a child.

Birth Defects

In certain cases, the plaintiffs (parents) sue the physician for the unwanted birth of a child born with birth defects or other congenital problems. This may occur when a doctor assures a couple that an unborn child will not be harmed by a disease the mother contracted during pregnancy, but when born, the child does in fact have substantial birth defects caused by the mother's infection. Another such situation involves a child who is born with genetic defects that a doctor assured the parents were not present or inheritable.

Wrongful Life: The New Tort

Wrongful life actions are a recent tort invention, having arisen within the last 25 years. This new tort has received mixed reviews from appellate courts across the United States. Some jurisdictions reject the tort altogether; others permit it in circumstances involving birth deformities; and still others allow the action even for healthy but unwanted children when sterilization has failed. Wrongful life litigation demonstrates the ingenuity of attorneys and legal scholars searching for new sources of recovery for harmed plaintiffs. Depending upon one's point of view, one may consider this tort just another form of "chiseling" against the medical profession, or one may find it a perfectly acceptable compensation for innocent parents who might be unprepared (or unable to afford) family additions. Certainly, the cases have involved much emotion and moral judgment.

Damages

In addition to the expenses incurred during pregnancy and delivery of the "wrongful life" child, plaintiffs seek (and sometimes recover) damages from the responsible physician(s) for the cost of raising the child until he or she reaches the age of majority, most often defined by modern statutes as 18 years of age. One can imagine the enormous judgments such plaintiffs might receive under these circumstances.

THE CASE OF THE BOTCHED BABYSTOPPER

Many wrongful birth cases involve unsuccessful sterilization operations. As the case here demonstrates, the potential liability for negligent physicians can be staggering, if they are required to compensate the parents for the costs of rearing the unexpected child through adulthood. Note the New Mexico Supreme Court's focus upon the actual issue, as well as its well-reasoned policy analysis. As to the outcome of the case, one can only speculate on the resulting effects on medical malpractice insurance premiums.

Lovelace Medical Center v. Mendez
111 N.M. 336, 805 P.2d 603 (1991)
(Supreme Court of New Mexico)
January 7, 1991

OPINION

MONTGOMERY, Justice.

We granted certiorari to consider the following two questions of substantial public interest: [jurisdictional issue omitted] (2) On the merits, may the parents of a normal, healthy baby conceived as a result of a negligently performed, unsuccessful sterilization operation recover the costs of raising the child from birth to adulthood?

The court of appeals held that the answer [. . .] is yes and reversed the district court's partial summary judgment in favor of the defendant hospital. We agree with the court of appeals, [. . .] and remand the case to the district court for trial. [. . .]

Joseph Mendez was conceived after his mother, Maria Mendez, underwent a tubal ligation, which allegedly was negligently performed by a physician employee of the defendant, Lovelace Medical Center. The physician found and ligated only one of Maria's two fallopian tubes and then failed to inform her of the unsuccessful outcome of the operation. She thus remained fertile, took no birth-control precautions, and conceived Joseph in due course. He was born as a normal, healthy baby.

[. . .] [T]he district court in Mr. and Mrs. Mendez's medical malpractice action against Lovelace granted its motion for partial summary judgment, holding as a matter of law that the costs of raising Joseph to majority were not recoverable. [. . .]

[. . .] [T]he fundamental question on the merits issue in this appeal is a question as to measure of damages. Given that a tort has occurred (the doctor's negligence in performing the sterilization operation and failing to inform the mother of the unsuccessful outcome) and given that an injury has resulted from this tort (the mother's continued fertility, despite her desire and effort to be sterilized), what is the measure of damages to compensate her for the injury she has suffered? [. . .] [I]t is virtually undisputed that some elements of damages are compensable for this tort—e.g., Mrs. Mendez's pain and suffering associated with her pregnancy and Joseph's birth; the cost of a subsequent sterilization; and her expenses, including lost wages, associated with the pregnancy and the birth. To be sure, the most controversial item of claimed damage—the cost of raising Joseph to adulthood—is the critical issue in this case; but it is an issue primarily involving quantification of the plaintiff's loss.

Thus, when the trial court, in entering partial summary judgment in favor of Lovelace, held that the birth of a child was not a "compensable legal harm," it was addressing the wrong issue. The question is not whether the birth of the baby is a legal harm, or an injury; it is whether the damages that may be awarded for the harm that indisputably was inflicted on Mrs. Mendez extend to the reasonable costs of raising the baby to adulthood. [. . .] [I]t is not the birth of the child that is the harm; it is, as we explain below, the invasion of the parents' interest in the financial security of their family—an invasion clearly foreseeable (or at least reasonably to be foreseen, as a jury might determine) by the doctor as the probable consequence of his negligence in performing the procedure in question.

[. . .] In this case, the wrongful act was Lovelace's negligent performance of the sterilization operation and subsequent failure to inform Mrs. Mendez that she was still fertile. [. . .]

[. . .] [W]e believe the couple suffered at least two forms of harm. First, as indicated previously, Mrs. Mendez remained fertile despite her desire to be infertile. From the standpoint of the couple, their desire to limit the size of their family—to procreate no further—was frustrated. Within the Restatement's [(Second) of Torts] definition of harm, this was a loss or detriment to them.

Second, their interest in financial security—in the economic stability of their family—was impaired. The undesired costs of raising another child to adulthood—costs which they had striven to avoid and had engaged Lovelace to help them avert—were suddenly thrust upon them. This was a detriment [. . .]. Was it legally compensable—i.e., an injury, an invasion of a legally protected interest?

[. . .]

In holding that Mr. and Mrs. Mendez could not recover the costs of rearing Joseph to majority, the district court was declaring, in effect, that their interests in financial security and in limiting the size of their family were not worthy of legal protection.

We agree with the court of appeals that the district court was mistaken in so holding. The interest in one's economic stability is clearly an example of an interest that receives legal protection in a wide variety of contexts. [Citations omitted.] In the context of a negligently performed, unsuccessful sterilization operation, the Supreme Court of Wisconsin has very recently held that the costs of raising the child to majority may be recovered because, among other things:

> Individuals often seek sterilization precisely because the burdens of raising a child are substantial and they are not in a position to incur them . . . .
>
> [T]he love, affection, and emotional support they [the parents] are prepared to give do not bring with them the economic means that are also necessary to feed, clothe, educate and otherwise raise the child. That is what this suit is about [. . .]. [Citation omitted.]

Other courts have allowed recovery of child-rearing costs based at least in part on the recognition that an interest to be protected in this setting is the parents' desire to safeguard the financial security of their family. [Citations omitted.] [. . .]

We hold, therefore, that the Mendezes' interest in the financial security of their family was a legally protected interest which was invaded by Lovelace's negligent failure properly to perform Maria's sterilization operation (if proved at trial), and that this invasion was an injury entitling them to recover damages in the form of the reasonable expenses to raise Joseph to majority.

[. . .]

We affirm the decision of the court of appeals and reverse the judgment of the district court, remanding the cause to that court for further proceedings consistent with this opinion [. . .].

CASE QUESTIONS

1. In a portion of its opinion, omitted from the preceding excerpt, the court rejected the "off-setting benefits" principle used by some courts. This principle balances child-rearing costs with the noneconomic benefits that parents derive from a child. Do you believe that this balancing approach is appropriate? Why or why not? Is it not similar to comparative negligence's liability apportionment?

2. Does the court correctly focus upon the actual harm? Can you present an argument supporting the trial court's formulation of the issue?

Wrongful life cases often carry powerful emotional implications. Even a casual reading of cases such as *Lovelace* is likely to stir sentiments. But the temptation to become lost in value judgments must be resisted. Once again, focusing upon the legal elements carries the reader to the appropriate conclusions, as the following example demonstrates.

HYPOTHETICAL

Paul and Vicky Jonson visited Dr. Fritz Halpner, M.D., to see if Paul could get a vasectomy. Paul was concerned that he could transmit a genetic disease to his unborn child. Several members of Paul's family had been afflicted with the congenital disease. Dr. Halpner performed the sterilization surgery. A few months later, Vicky discovered that she was pregnant. Paul's operation did not "take." The Jonsons refused abortion on religious grounds. The Jonsons' baby daughter was born deformed as a result of the genetic disease transmitted from Paul. The Jonsons sued Dr. Halpner for medical malpractice, specifically alleging wrongful life.

Dr. Halpner's vasectomy operation did not prevent Vicky from becoming pregnant. Worse yet, the Jonson child was afflicted with congenital deformities because of Paul's genetically defective sperm. This child would not have been born in this unfortunate condition but for the doctor's negligence is performing the faulty operation. The Jonsons would appear to have a valid claim against Dr. Halpner for the tort of wrongful life.

Figure 11-6 lists the elements of wrongful life.

Also called *wrongful birth* or *wrongful pregnancy* actions
Usually a form of medical malpractice. in which physician has negligently performed an ineffective sterilization operation
May include cases involving children born with birth defects
Damages include parents' medical expenses for unwanted birth and, in some jurisdictions, the costs of raising the child

FIGURE 11-6
Elements of
Wrongful Life
Actions

SUMMARY

11.1. A private nuisance is an unreasonable and substantial interference with another person's use and enjoyment of his or her land. Whether a nuisance activity is unreasonable and substantial depends upon its degree of offensiveness. The reasonable person standard is applied to test offensiveness and is based upon the community standard for persons living in the vicinity of the nuisance activity. Private nuisances often involve physical effects on the land, such as vibrations, pollution, and flooding. Private nuisance may also produce health hazards, such as poison gases, hazardous wastes, smoke, or dust, or effects offending the plaintiffs' sensibilities, such as odors or even incessant telephone calling. Private nuisances also include unwanted associations with neighboring uses, such as prostitution houses or gambling emporiums. "Coming to the nuisance" is the primary defense in private nuisance actions.

11.2. Public nuisances are activities that harm the public at large rather than a single individual. These nuisances unreasonably and substantially interfere with the public's use and enjoyment of legal rights common to the public. Governmental agencies litigate against public nuisance tortfeasors to enforce the general public's legal rights. State and local governments have the authority to litigate public nuisances under the police powers of the states. Public nuisances often involve so-called immoral activities, such as gambling, prostitution, distribution of sexually explicit materials, or sale of alcohol. Others include permitting noxious weeds to grow on one's property, carelessly disposing of toxic substances, or violating public health laws. Often, nuisances may be both private and public. These are called mixed nuisances. Nuisances per se are activities that violate statutes or ordinances. Public nuisances are often per se nuisances. "Coming to the nuisance" is usually not a defense in public nuisance cases.

11.3. Equitable remedies are usually awarded in nuisance litigation instead of money damages. Money damages are sometimes given when equitable remedies would be excessively harsh to the defendant. The relief most often granted involves abatement and injunctions. In abatement, the court orders the defendant to cease and desist the nuisance activity. Normally, the activity must be permanently discontinued. Courts enforce abatement by injunctions. Permanent injunctions forbid the activity forever. Temporary injunctions, such as temporary restraining orders (T.R.O.s), merely halt the defendant's nuisance activity until the court can conduct hearings or a trial on the merits. Defendants who disregard injunctions may find themselves in contempt of court, for which they can be fined or imprisoned.

11.4. Negligence per se is any activity that violates a negligence statute. It is considered automatic negligence simply because the defendant's conduct violated the statutory provisions. To recover damages, the plaintiff must fall within the class of persons that the statute was intended to protect. The same defenses apply to negligence per se that apply to ordinary negligence cases. Furthermore, the defendant's statutory violation must have proximately caused the plaintiff's injuries.

11.5. Wrongful death statutes provide surviving family members of a deceased tort victim with the right to sue the tortfeasor for wrongfully causing the victim's death. The statutes often grant the deceased victim's estate the right to pursue this cause of action. The tortfeasor's wrong may include negligence or intentional torts. Wrongful death damages usually consist of the victim's lost lifetime earnings potential and loss of consortium. Consortium includes the lost love and companionship between the dead victim and his or her family. The tortfeasor may use any defenses applicable for the alleged tort that caused the wrongful death. If the tortfeasor were accused of negligently causing the victim's death, then negligence defenses would apply. If the tortfeasor's intentional tort killed the victim, then intentional tort defenses would apply.

11.6. Wrongful life actions are lawsuits for the wrongful birth of a child. Usually, parents sue a physician for malpractice for negligently performing a sterilization operation. These cases often involve children born with birth defects. The tort has developed within the past quarter-century. Damages include the medical costs associated with pregnancy and birth, as well as the costs of raising the unwanted child. Court reactions to the tort have been mixed. Some jurisdictions reject the tort altogether, while others embrace it in whole or in part.

REVIEW QUESTIONS

1. Define private nuisance. Who are the parties to this litigation? What is unreasonable and substantial interference? How is it determined? What is the role of the community standard? What is use and enjoyment?

2. Name the common types of private nuisance. Can you provide hypotheticals to illustrate each? What is "coming to the nuisance"?

3. What is a public nuisance? How is it distinguishable from a private nuisance? Who is affected by a public nuisance? Who acts as plaintiff? What are some common examples of public nuisance? Does "coming

to the nuisance" apply? What are common legal rights? What are mixed nuisances? What is a nuisance per se?

4. What remedies are used in nuisance cases? What about money damages? What is abatement? What are injunctions? Explain the difference between temporary and permanent injunctions. When is a T.R.O. used? What is contempt?

5. Explain negligence per se. When does it occur? What role do statutes play in this special tort? What defenses apply?

6. What are wrongful death statutes? Who are the plaintiffs in wrongful death litigation? What types of torts can be involved? What damages are awarded? What defenses apply?

7. What is wrongful life? What are the usual fact situations involving this special tort? What damages may be awarded?

PROBLEMS

In the following hypotheticals, identify the relevant cause(s) of action, suitable defense(s) (if any), and appropriate remedies.

1. Pestro Chemical Corporation manufactures *Dredroxiphine,* a poison used in insect sprays. A railway line delivers tanker cars full of the chemical to be unloaded into the plant. On breezy days, the fumes from the unloading stations drift across the highway onto Elmer Parsley's farm. The odors are pungent and are especially irritating to the sinuses. When Elmer and his family work outside on windy days, they are constantly besieged by the poison's smell. Their eyes water excessively, their noses run, and they are gripped by sneezing fits. Other farmers in the area have complained of similar symptoms. Visits to the family physician revealed that Elmer has absorbed minute amounts of the chemical in his lungs and through his skin. Medical studies link exposure to the chemical with several forms of cancer. Elmer has farmed on his property since 1947. Pestro constructed its plant in 1972.

2. Wowser's Video Palace rents X-rated videotaped movies. A local ordinance restricts rental of such materials to persons over the age of 18 years. Wowser's employees never check customer identifications, however, and often rent X-rated movies to underage individuals. Citizens Rallying Against Pornography, a local citizens' group, has asked the county prosecutor to take action against Wowser's. The prosecutor has asked you to summarize the appropriate cause(s) of action in a short paragraph.

3. O'Brien Halloway is a plumber. According to a state statute, all plumbers must be licensed by the state's professional licensing agency. O'Brien failed to make his annual licensing payment to the agency.

The statute provides that, if annual payments are not made on time, then the plumber's license is automatically revoked. The statute also goes on to say that plumbing without a license is considered an actionable tort. O'Brien later installed kitchen plumbing in Nina Larfort's home. Several pipes began leaking water almost immediately, damaging Nina's kitchen cabinets and floor tile. O'Brien's failure to tighten the pipe fixtures sufficiently produced the leaks. Nina had to spend $6,500 for repairs.

4. Quintin and Ursella Xenopher were driving along Interstate 928 on the beltway around the city. Terri May Nordmeier was driving while intoxicated. Her blood alcohol level was .214, and a state criminal statute provides that .10 is legally drunk. A related state civil statute provides injured parties with a tort cause of action against a tortfeasor who causes injuries while violating criminal statutes. Terri's automobile collided with the Xenophers' vehicle, killing Quintin. Ursella suffered permanent disability in her left leg.

5. Dr. Sarah Davis Strongfelt, M.D., performed a tubal ligation upon Jennifer Colfield to prevent impregnation. Jennifer was a single, 24-year-old woman who had a sexual relationship with her boyfriend, Miles Vieman. Six months after her operation, Jennifer discovered that she was pregnant. She could not afford the costs of raising a child, but she did not want to get an abortion. Miles refused to subsidize Jennifer's medical expenses or contribute to the child's upbringing. The local adoption agencies (managed by rigid-thinking administrators) refused to speak with Jennifer, because she had a history of narcotic abuse. She did not consult with out-of-town adoption agencies, which would have been happy to assist her in placing the child in a foster home.

PROBLEM ANSWERS

1. Pestro Chemical Corporation is engaged in a private nuisance as a toxic tort, and Elmer Parsley would sue to abate Pestro's chemical production. Pestro's method for unloading the tanker cars allowed airborne toxic chemical vapors to be carried onto Elmer's farm. Whenever Elmer and his family worked outdoors on windy days, they suffered severe physical reactions from breathing the chemical-tainted air. This constitutes an unreasonable and substantial interference with Elmer's use and enjoyment of his real estate. Reasonable persons in the community, such as other neighboring farmers, would find Pestro's activities highly offensive, because it would significantly interfere with their farming activities, most of which necessarily are conducted outdoors in the open air. Pestro's actions proximately caused Elmer's

(and his family's) injuries. In particular, Elmer has been exposed to a powerful carcinogen. Thus, Elmer's private nuisance action against Pestro would be successful.

Pestro could not successfully invoke the coming to the nuisance defense, since Elmer has lived on his farm since 1947 and Pestro built its plant in 1972.

Elmer would petition the trial court for abatement, requesting a permanent injunction against Pestro's Dredroxiphine production. Pestro would argue excessive economic hardship from abatement and would insist that money damages would be more appropriate in this case. However, because Pestro's poison is a carcinogen, its production presents a substantial health hazard. In its balancing test, the trier-of-fact would weigh this health threat against the economic hardship to the corporation. (In certain cases, the court might rule on this issue as a matter of law, depending upon statutory regulation for poison production, health codes, etc.) As a hypothetical juror, assess this balancing of land uses. You may conclude that the health risk is more important than the economic injuries to the defendant.

There is a possible abatement solution that would minimize the defendant's economic hardships while protecting the neighboring landowners from exposure to the toxic chemicals. The court could order Pestro to cease open-air unloading of its tanker cars. Pestro could construct buildings within which the chemicals could be unloaded from trains. This would virtually eliminate any open-air contamination, and thus Elmer (and his family and neighbors) would not be exposed to the airborne contaminants. Pestro could continue producing the poison in safer confines. This *targeted use abatement* would accommodate both parties and resolve the nuisance problem equitably.

Elmer could also sue under a theory of strict liability, because Pestro was engaged in an abnormally dangerous activity. Under this cause of action, Elmer could recover monetary damages for his (and his family's) personal injuries caused by Pestro's activities. You may recall that, in chapter 4, Elmer sued Pestro under the theory of trespass to land.

2. In this hypothetical, your summaries (for the county prosecutor) should conclude that Wowser's Video Palace was engaged in a public nuisance. Citizens Rallying Against Pornography filed its complaint with the proper governmental authority, the prosecutor, who is empowered to enforce the local ordinance restricting X-rated video rentals to persons under age 18. Because Wowser's routinely rented such materials to underage customers, it violated the ordinance. This constitutes a public nuisance per se.

Wowser's activity satisfies the elements for public nuisance. By renting its sexually explicit videos to underage youth, Wowser's unreasonably and substantially interfered with the public's use and enjoyment of a legal right common to the public, which is the right to protect children from exposure to pornographic materials. The ordinance establishing age restrictions for video rentals is a valid exercise of the state's police power to protect public welfare and morals.

The appropriate remedy in this case depends upon the penalties prescribed by the ordinance. The hypothetical facts are silent on this point. Probably, the ordinance prescribes monetary fines for first violations. Abatement through permanent injunction would probably be authorized for subsequent violations. The ordinance might also include imprisonment penalties for violations.

3. Nina Larfort would successfully sue O'Brien Halloway for negligence per se. O'Brien violated the state statutory plumbing licensing requirements. The statute specifically indicated that violations were actionable torts, which would include O'Brien's negligence in acting as a plumber without a license. O'Brien was negligent in installing Nina's kitchen plumbing, as Nina could prove through expert testimony to establish that O'Brien violated the professional community standard. However, Nina need not prove this initially, because O'Brien's negligence is presumed as a matter of law.

O'Brien could counter this negligence presumption by proving that his efforts did not proximately cause Nina's property damage. However, the facts indicate that his plumbing resulted in substantial leakage. The facts offer no other explanations, so you may safely conclude that O'Brien will be unable to defeat the presumption and Nina will recover damages under negligence per se.

4. Terri May Nordmeier would be liable to Ursella Xenopher under two tort theories: negligence per se, as applied to Ursella's injuries, and wrongful death, as applied to the late Quintin Xenopher.

Terri violated the state criminal statute by driving while intoxicated. According to a related state civil statute, persons who are injured as a result of a tortfeasor's criminal conduct may sue the tortfeasor under applicable tort law. Terri's conduct is at least negligent, although it actually rose to the level of willful and wanton misconduct. In any event, Terri's violation of the criminal statute means that she is presumed negligent under the civil statute and thus provides Ursella with a per se negligence cause of action. Ursella could recover damages for her personal injuries caused in the collision.

Further, pursuant to the civil statute, Ursella could recover damages against Terri for the wrongful death of Ursella's husband, Quintin. Depending upon the state's wrongful death statute, Ursella could probably recover loss of consortium and lost lifetime earnings potential.

5. Jennifer Colfield's cause of action against Dr. Sarah Davis Strongfelt would be wrongful life. Jennifer would have to prove that Dr. Strongfelt was negligent in performing an ineffective sterilization operation. To establish medical malpractice, Jennifer would need expert testimony to establish the professional medical community standard of care. Jennifer could also invoke res ipsa loquitur to shift the burden

of proof to the defendant, as such operations do not usually fail in the absence of negligence.

Jennifer's damages would include all medical expenses associated with her pregnancy and her child's birth. Some states would permit recovery of child-rearing expenses, although others specifically exclude this type of damages.

PROJECTS

1. Brief *Nowlon v. Koram Insurance Center, Inc.*, 1 Cal. App. 4th 1437, 2 Cal. Rptr. 2d 683 (1991). According to the California Court of Appeal, when can a defendant's statutory violation constitute negligence per se? What was the court's rationale?

2. Brief *City of Lincoln v. ABC Books, Inc.*, 238 Neb. 378, 470 N.W.2d 760 (1991). For the purposes of tort study, you may overlook the First Amendment constitutional law issues presented in the opinion. What type of nuisance did the court find in the case, if any? What remedies did it consider suitable?

3. Brief *Cygan v. City of New York,* 165 A.D.2d 58, 566 N.Y.S.2d 232 (1991), *appeal denied,* 78 N.Y.2d 855, 578 N.E.2d 443, 573 N.Y.S.2d 645 (1991). In the plaintiff's wrongful death action, did the appellate division consider the city's actions to be the proximate cause of the plaintiff's husband's suicide? What was the court's reasoning, particularly on the foreseeability issue?

4. Brief *Walker v. Mart,* 164 Ariz. 37, 790 P.2d 735 (1990). Did the court recognize the plaintiff's claims for wrongful birth? Explain the court's analysis.

5. Brief *Town of Georgetown v. DeRiemer,* 1990 Westlaw 80463 (Del. Ch. 1990), not published in A.2d. In his humorous opinion, the vice chancellor ruled on the existence of a public nuisance. What was the reasoning behind the court's decision? Do you agree or disagree? Explain. (Note that Delaware still utilizes separate equity courts, called Courts of Chancery.)

6. Brief *Rollins Environmental Services, Inc. v. Parish of St. James,* 775 F.2d 627 (5th Cir. 1985). How did the Fifth Circuit Court of Appeals resolve the conflict between an ordinance and the Federal Toxic Substances Control Act? What was the basis for the court's decision?

CHAPTER 12
Tort Immunities

DATA-GRAPHIC TORTS

Littner v. State Department of Transportation

Midas Zephyr, an employee of Boanco Farms, Inc., was driving to work one morning. As he approached the freeway on a merging entrance ramp, he failed to yield to oncoming traffic. There was, however, no posted yield sign, because the state highway department had failed to place one at that location. Zephyr merged at 55 m.p.h. and collided with an approaching truck (going 65 m.p.h.) on the freeway. The truck driver, Marge Littner, became a paraplegic as a result of the accident. She sued the state, through its Department of Transportation, alleging negligence in failing to post a yield sign. The state countered with sovereign immunity, citing state court decisions observing the governmental/proprietary distinction.

Assume that the state was negligent in failing to post a yield sign, and also assume that this state does not have a governmental tort liability statute.

Posting traffic signs is a function of a state's police power, which is designed to protect the public health, safety, welfare, and morals. American courts generally characterize this as a governmental function. Absent a statute declaring a governmental unit liable for negligent placement of traffic signals, Marge could not recover from the state, which would succeed with its sovereign immunity defense. Fortunately for Marge, most state statutes would permit tort lawsuits against the state for negligence of this type.

INTRODUCTION

Up to now, there have been a few pieces, here and there, missing in the torts puzzle. The reader may have been working around them, knowing that the scattered holes would be easier to fill when the number of loose pieces was reduced. The missing pieces are tort immunities, and they almost complete the torts puzzle, filling in these gaps.

Tort immunities are absolute defenses against a plaintiff's tort claims. If the defendant successfully invokes an immunity defense, he or she cannot be held liable for any torts committed. It is the reverse of absolute liability. Tort immunities absolutely protect the defendant from tort liability. There are many types of tort immunity, but the most common include sovereign (governmental) immunity and legal infirmities such as infancy or insanity.

The puzzle pieces to be sorted and assembled in this chapter include:

- Sovereign (governmental) immunity.
- Public officials' immunity.
- Young children's immunity.
- Statutes of limitation.

12.1 GOVERNMENTAL, OR SOVEREIGN, IMMUNITY

Sovereign (governmental) immunity has a long and storied history throughout the annals of tort law. To understand modern applications of this doctrine, one must trace its roots and development.

History

In the history of tort law, governments have held an enviable position. Until the twentieth century, governments were immune from liability for torts committed by their employees. This immunity was called **sovereign immunity**, or (in modern times) **governmental immunity**. It stemmed from the ancient English (and Western European) legal tradition that the king could not be sued by his subjects unless he consented. Official tortfeasors thus enjoyed an enviable immunity from liability unless they agreed to be sued, which one would naturally not if one had committed any torts.

Courts applied the legal maxim *The king can do no wrong*. This maxim traces its origins to pre-Roman times when the emperor was considered divine and, thus, incapable of errors that the law could remedy.

Modern Applications

For centuries, sovereign immunity protected the Crown and all its subordinates. Later, English and American common law spoke of governmental bodies (and their employees) as enjoying sovereign immunity. The term *king* was replaced with *government* in the American system, because our sovereigns are elected officials serving as presidents, governors, mayors, legislators, or (at the state and local level) judges.

Beginning in the early twentieth century, American courts began to whittle away at the governmental immunity doctrine. Many state courts have abolished sovereign immunity as an absolute defense to governmental liability. Legislatures have enacted statutes, such as the Federal Tort Claims Act, that specifically authorize lawsuits against torts committed by governmental employees (for which governmental agencies could be responsible under respondeat superior).

Early Twentieth-Century Cases

Many courts found the absolute defense of sovereign immunity to be unreasonably harsh on the plaintiffs. To avoid the full force of the immunity, early in the century American courts began distinguishing the different types of governmental activities that were or were not exempt from tort liability. There were two categories: governmental and proprietary. This is sometimes called the **governmental/proprietary distinction**.

Governmental Actions

When governmental bodies perform certain public protection activities, such as providing fire, police, or ambulance services, they are considered to be undertaking *governmental functions*. Persons performing governmental functions are immune from tort liability, under the early twentieth-century court decisions. Even if the fire, police, or ambulance departments committed torts against a citizen while performing their duties, the old case law would define these as governmental actions immune from liability.

Proprietary Actions

Governmental bodies also perform certain business-like activities (usually associated with the private sector). These are defined as *proprietary actions* and do not carry immunity from tort liability. For example, a municipality may provide utility services to its residents, such as water, sewer, electric, or natural gas, but this activity more closely resembles a private business enterprise than a public, governmental function. If the governmental agency providing such services committed torts, the government would be liable, and the immunity defense would not prevent liability.

Difficulty with the Governmental/Proprietary Distinction

Courts have struggled with the governmental/proprietary distinction for decades. What about cities that provide garbage collection? What about public parks? Are these governmental or proprietary functions? Courts often decide based upon whether a fee is assessed to users of these services. If a fee is charged, then the activity is considered proprietary. If not, then it is governmental. This may be called the **fee standard**.

Similar to the fee standard is the *pecuniary benefit test.* When governments provide services for profit, then the activities are proprietary. If governments offer services for the common public good, without economic benefit to the governmental units themselves, then the activities are governmental.

Modern Steps to Eliminate the Distinction

Within the past 20 years, many state courts have abolished the governmental/proprietary distinction and with it the defense of sovereign immunity. These courts now focus upon whether the governments committed any torts—just as courts would handle any other tort lawsuit. Many state legislatures and Congress have enacted statutes eliminating or restricting sovereign immunity to particular types of services, such as public parks or utilities.

Encyclopedia Illustrations

57 AMERICAN JURISPRUDENCE 2D *Municipal, County, School, and State Tort Liability* §§ 1-2, 5, 19, 61-62, 71, 87, 92, 94-97 (1988)

[All footnotes omitted.]

Generally, where there is tortious injury there is liability. Sovereign or governmental tort immunity is an exception to the rule [. . .].

Sovereign or governmental tort immunity avoids tort liability to the extent of the immunity conferred. Often described as a bar to liability, immunity creates freedom from tort liability in the form of an exemption based on the nature or status of the defendant and denies the courts' jurisdiction to consider the plaintiff's claim. Its effect is not to deny the tort, only the resulting liability.

The roots of sovereign immunity from tort liability extend to medieval England. The doctrine flows from the concept that one could not sue the king in his own courts, hence the phrase "the king can do no wrong." The doctrine, as it developed at common law, had its origins in the English feudal system, and is firmly set in traditional concepts of state sovereignty, as is evident from the fact that the Eleventh Amendment to the United States Constitution broadly grants states immunity from suit in federal courts.

The early English case of *Russell v. The Men of Devon* is credited as initially applying the doctrine of sovereign tort immunity to local governments [. . .].

Most jurisdictions generally adhere to the view that municipal corporations, counties, and other political subdivisions of the state are only generally subject to liability in tort under the express provisions of a state tort claims act or other statute, or a judicial limitation or abrogation of immunity, and hold that they specifically retain immunity from

LEGAL TERMS

governmental/ proprietary distinction
In governmental, or sovereign, immunity cases, courts historically have separated governmental actions into two categories: governmental and proprietary. Governmental actions include public protection functions such as fire, police, or ambulance services. In the older common law, these activities were immune from tort liability. Proprietary actions were governmental endeavors that were more business-like, such as supplying utility service to the public. In the older common law, these activities were not immune from tort liability.

fee standard
A test courts use in applying the governmental/ proprietary distinction. If a governmental agency assesses a fee for an activity, it is considered proprietary. If not, it is considered governmental.

liability for certain functions and activities, based on distinctions as to the nature of particular acts or functions as governmental or proprietary and discretionary or ministerial. In these jurisdictions, municipalities and counties may be held liable in tort as any private person or corporation, subject to exceptions whereby immunity is retained to the extent expressly provided by statute or determined by judicial decision and subject to limitations on the amount and nature of damages recoverable. For this purpose, a local public entity would generally include counties, municipalities, and all other local governmental bodies. [. . .]

In many jurisdictions, the courts have deemed the doctrine of governmental tort immunity for municipal corporations, counties, and political subdivisions of the state a court-made rule, subject to judicial abrogation or abolition without legislative action, and have expressly declared that the doctrine would no longer be recognized [. . .]. In most jurisdictions, judicial abrogation or limitation of local governmental immunity has been quickly followed by legislative reinstatement of the doctrine in varying degrees and subject to similar limitations for particular functions, causes of action, and recoverable damages.

[. . .]

The state, as sovereign, is generally regarded as immune from liability and suit in its own courts or in any other court without its consent and permission. Accordingly, when the state's acts or omissions, or those of its officers, agents, employees, departments, agencies, and other instrumentalities, give rise to potential tort liability, a tort action may not be maintained against the state in its own courts, whether the action is brought by its own citizens, the citizens of another state, or the citizens or subjects of a foreign state, unless the state by statute has consented to be sued in tort, has otherwise waived its immunity or been estopped to raise the defense, has lost its immunity by judicial abrogation of the doctrine, or has engaged in activities or functions beyond the scope of its tort immunity. [. . .] However, the doctrine of sovereign immunity from suit for torts is disfavored, and subject to a steady movement away from immunity.

[. . .]

Traditionally, sovereign immunity from tort liability was viewed as a rule of social policy serving to protect the state from burdensome interference in the performance of its governmental functions and to protect the state's control over its funds, property, and instrumentalities. Among the multitude of purposes purportedly served were those of protecting the public purse, providing for smooth operation of government, eliminating public inconvenience and danger that might spring from officials being fearful to act, assuring that citizens would be willing to take public jobs, and preventing citizens from improperly influencing the conduct of government through the threat or use of vexatious litigation. It served to protect and preserve public funds and to ensure that the state provided its citizenry appropriate services while holding taxes at reasonable levels.

[. . .]

The courts of some states have abrogated or limited the otherwise applicable common-law doctrine of state sovereign immunity from tort liability, finding the doctrine to have been originally a court-made rule and therefore subject to judicial repudiation or modification, although such judicial action is usually followed by quick legislative action to reinstate immunity, at least in part, and may be accompanied by limitations based on the nature of the particular act or function alleged as giving rise to liability.

[. . . .]

A common test for the applicability of governmental tort immunity is whether the act or function giving rise to potential liability can be characterized as governmental or proprietary in nature. Immunity is retained for governmental or public acts or functions but liability may be imposed if the act or function is deemed merely proprietary or private in nature. The basis of the governmental/proprietary distinction in the law of governmental tort immunity and liability has been described as difficult to state. It originated with the courts [. . .]. However, the application of the rule is fraught with difficulties, inconsistencies, uncertainties, and illogical results to the extent that there is a clear trend away from the rule by judicial abrogation or legislative action.

[. . .]

The governmental/proprietary distinction often applicable in determining the tort immunity or liability of municipalities, counties, and schools, whereby liability may be imposed for proprietary acts or functions while immunity is retained for governmental ones, is not as widely applied in actions against the state or its agencies. [. . .]

Under the rule distinguishing between governmental and proprietary acts or functions [. . .], there is no clear line between acts or functions that are proprietary, [. . .] and those that are governmental [. . .]. Powers and functions considered governmental or public in one jurisdiction are often viewed as proprietary or private in another, making it impossible to state a rule sufficiently exact to be of much practical value in applying the test, as courts have noted frequently in their decisions abandoning or abrogating the governmental/proprietary test as a measure of state or local tort immunity or liability.

[. . .]

The underlying test for distinguishing between governmental and proprietary acts or functions, and thereby determining whether a state or local governmental entity is immune from or subject to tort liability, is whether the act performed is for the common good of all, as for the use and benefit of the general public, or whether it is for the special benefit or profit of the [governmental] corporate entity. [. . .]

[L]ocal governmental entities are not immune from tort liability for proprietary functions exercised in an enterprise of a commercial character or usually carried on by private individuals or for the profit, benefit, or the advantage of the governmental unit conducting it, or conducted primarily for pecuniary benefit [. . .]. Thus when a municipal corporation undertakes to furnish a service of a commercial character to individuals for a price, or engages in an undertaking the object of which is profit to itself, liability attaches for negligence in the performance of such compensated service, although such enterprises may ultimately subserve a public need. [. . .]

12.2 PUBLIC OFFICERS

Somewhat different from sovereign immunity is the individual tort immunity granted to certain public employees engaged in their official capacities. Certain governmental officials are immune from personal liability for any torts committed while they were performing their public duties.

Who Is Protected

Legislators and judges enjoy an absolute immunity from tort liability for acts in their official governmental capacities. In performing legislative or judicial functions, it is possible that these public officials might commit torts against individual citizens. The common law protects judges and legislators from any liability whatsoever for having committed such torts. Executive branch officials, however, do not receive this blanket immunity, although administrative officers serving judicial or legislative functions do receive absolute immunity. For example, an agency adjudication officer, prosecutor, or county council legislator would be protected completely from tort liability.

Rationale for Immunity

Governmental official immunity is intended to ensure that legislators and judges may pursue their public duties without the chilling effect that fear of tort liability might have. Imagine how cautious legislators or judges would have to be in decision making if, with each sensitive topic, they had to worry about tort liability. These officials might become paralyzed by second-guessing, and the liability spectre could influence their public policy decisions. This rationale for the immunity is often repeated in the common law. To encourage maximum public benefit from the services of the public's judges and legislators, the law must totally protect these officials from tort liability.

THE CASE OF THE REALLY BAD COFFEE

Judicial immunity is an ancient English and American legal principle. It is a common law norm. However, it is not applied mindlessly by the appellate courts. In appropriate circumstances, the immunity is ineffective. One expects judges to act in a professional, dignified, restrained, and impartial fashion. Ninety-nine percent of the time, judges are somber, firm, stately, formal, and equitable. The other 1 percent act like the trial judge in the following case.

Zarcone v. Perry
572 F.2d 52 (2d Cir. 1978)
(U.S. Circuit Court of Appeals,
Second Circuit)
March 3, 1978

FEINBERG, Circuit Judge:

In this unusual civil rights case, William M. Perry, a former judge of the District Court of Suffolk County, appeals from a verdict in favor of plaintiff Thomas Zarcone, after a jury trial in the United States District Court for the Eastern District of New York [. . .]. The basis of Zarcone's suit was that Perry and other defendants had deprived plaintiff of his constitutional rights in violation of 42 U.S.C. § 1983. The jury awarded plaintiff $80,000 compensatory damages [. . .] [and] $60,000 punitive damages against Perry [. . .]. Only Perry appeals, and on the sole ground that the punitive damages award against him was excessive. We affirm. [. . .]

The incident that gave rise to the lawsuit occurred on April 30, 1975. On that night, then Judge Perry was in his chambers during a break in an evening session of traffic court in Suffolk County, Long Island. Zarcone was operating a mobile food vending truck outside the courthouse. Perry asked Deputy Sheriff Windsor to get some coffee, which he did. Both Perry and Windsor thought the coffee tasted "putrid," and Perry told Windsor to get the coffee vendor and bring him "in front of me in cuffs." Perry directed two plainclothes officers, who happened to be nearby, to accompany Windsor. Wearing his sheriff's uniform equipped with badge, gun and handcuffs, Windsor went to Zarcone and told him that the judge said the coffee was terrible and that Zarcone had to go inside to see the judge. Windsor handcuffed Zarcone, despite the vendor's protestations that it was not necessary. When Zarcone said he was too embarrassed to go into the courthouse that way, one of the officers suggested that Zarcone walk between them with Zarcone's jacket over his hands.

The group then marched through the hallway of the courthouse, in full view of dozens of people. Zarcone heard someone yell that they were locking up the frankfurter man. When they arrived at Perry's chambers, the judge asked if the Sheriff had "the coffee vending man there in handcuffs." Upon entering the chambers, Perry ordered Zarcone to be left "in handcuffs until I get finished with him." A pseudoofficial inquisition then began. Zarcone stood in front of the judge's desk, behind which the judge sat. A court reporter was present, along with Windsor and the two police officers. Perry told Zarcone that "I have the two cups of coffee here for evidence." According to Zarcone, whom the jury must have believed, Perry then started screaming at him, threatening him and his "livelihood" for about 20 minutes, and thoroughly scaring him. Just before Zarcone was allowed to leave, Perry commanded Windsor to note Zarcone's vehicle and vending license numbers and told Zarcone, "Mister, you are going to be sorrier before I get through with you."

After Zarcone left, he resumed his mobile truck route and came back to the night traffic courthouse about 45 minutes later. Shortly thereafter, Windsor returned and told Zarcone they were to go back to the judge. Zarcone asked if he had to be handcuffed again, but Windsor said no. When they reappeared before Perry, he told Zarcone that he was going to have the two cups of coffee analyzed. Perry also said that if Zarcone would admit he did something wrong, then Perry would drop the charges. Zarcone consistently denied that anything was amiss with the coffee, and no charges were filed.

We have described the night's events in such detail to impart some of the flavor that must have so impressed the jury. The unfortunate occurrence was publicized at the time, and ultimately let to the removal of Judge Perry from the bench. There were unpleasant consequences for Zarcone, as well: He testified that he was very upset by the incident, that he could not sleep, and that he started to stutter and get headaches. Zarcone also required treatment at the Coney Island Hospital, he could not work, and his wife asked him to move out of the house. We need not dwell on this any further, except to note that Perry does not complain here about the jury's award to Zarcone of $80,000 compensatory damages. However, Perry does challenge the amount of punitive damages, and we now turn to this issue.

[. . .] [G]iven Perry's position, his relationship of power and authority to plaintiff, who was a simple coffee vendor, the handcuffing, threats and intimidation inflicted upon plaintiff, and Perry's outrageous conduct, we are not compelled to conclude that the jury acted out of "passion and prejudice." [Citation omitted.] In short, we do not find that the verdict of $60,000 shocks our conscience. Perhaps to some the award might seem high and the incident exaggerated out of proportion. But the abuse of official power here was intolerable, and when a jury has dealt with it severely, as it should, we will not draw fine lines to restrain its dispensation of justice.

Judgment affirmed.

CASE QUESTIONS

1. What do you suppose Judge Perry would have done to Zarcone if he had also sold Perry a frankfurter?
2. Under traditional common law, judges are absolutely immune from tort liability for all judicial actions, regardless of malice or extremity. Why did the Second Circuit deviate from this long-standing rule, repeatedly espoused by the United States Supreme Court? Was Judge Perry's action a judicial act? You might wish to read *Stump v. Sparkman* (see Project 1 at the end of this chapter) for an applicable definition.

12.3 CHILDREN OF TENDER YEARS

For centuries, the common law has held that young children, often referred to as "children of tender years" in the court opinions, may be immune, or are subject to limited, tort liability.

Definition

Children of tender years are usually defined as young children under the age of seven years. Under traditional common law, any person under the age of 21 (and in the past 20 years, 18) is classed as a **minor**. However, only very young children normally enjoy the tender-years immunity. Although many opinions, particularly older cases, have granted immunity to teenagers, most cases limit tender years to below age seven. A significant number of cases, however, include the eight-to-twelve age group within the immunity.

Absolute Immunity for Intentional Torts

Most states still follow the ancient common law rule that children of tender years are incapable of committing intentional torts. They are immune from intentional tort liability. This immunity is based upon the concept that young children are mentally and emotionally incapable of having the proper intent to commit an intentional tort. Because they are so young, they lack the experience and development to appreciate fully the significance of their actions, which sometimes are tortious in nature.

For instance, suppose a four-year-old child tosses a sharpened pencil to get another child's attention. This pencil strikes the other child in the eye, causing injury. Had adults been involved, this would be a clear case of battery. However, most states would rule that the pencil-thrower was immune from liability for this intentional tort. Children of tender years are presumed to be incapable of the intent element in intentional torts.

Immunity from Negligence

Most courts do not grant absolute negligence immunity to young children. Instead, the child tortfeasor's age is merely one factor to be considered in determining the standard of reasonable care which the reasonable child of tender years would have used in a particular case. A minority of states have held that children below a certain age (usually seven years) cannot commit negligence and are therefore immune from liability. Most states, however, would agree that only extremely young children, often less than three or four years of age, are incapable of negligence and would be immune.

LEGAL TERMS

children of tender years
    Young children, often under the age of seven years, who are generally immune from, or subject to limited, tort liability. The majority of states still follow the ancient common law that granted absolute immunity for young children committing intentional torts. Most states do not grant total immunity to young children in negligence cases. Instead, the age and knowledge of the child tortfeasor is considered to determine whether negligence occurred.

minors
    Under traditional common law, persons under 21 (under modern common and statutory law, 18) years of age.

THE CASE OF THE ALL-TOO-REAL SHOOT-'EM-UP

All children play games. Some include pretend combat or other imitation conflicts. No one intends to hurt anyone else. However, when real weapons are used, the results can be frightening, as in the case here. Note the dissent's perspective as well as the majority's.

DeLuca v. Bowden
42 Ohio St. 2d 392, 329 N.E.2d 109
(1975)
(Supreme Court of Ohio)
June 4, 1975

[Footnotes omitted.]

PRIOR HISTORY: APPEAL from the Court of Appeals for Lucas County.

This is an action to recover damages for personal injuries sustained by plaintiff, Joseph DeLuca, Jr., a minor, brought by his father as next friend. On May 15, 1971, the plaintiff was struck in the eye and seriously injured by a BB or some other substance shot from the barrel of a BB-gun. Defendants Doyle Wayne Ayers and Thomas Jeffrey Coffman were playing with the BB-gun when it was fired. Both are minors who at the time were under seven years old.

The BB-gun was owned by Don Wayne Bowden, a minor aged 17. The Ayers and Coffman boys had played with the gun at Bowden's home on other occasions, and, on the date of the injury, the boys took the gun from the basement and were playing with it "down the street."

Action was brought in the Court of Common Pleas against Bowden, Coffman and Ayers, and against the parents of all three boys. Upon motion, the court dismissed the actions against the parents of Bowden and Ayers for failure to state a claim, and granted summary judgment on behalf of Coffman, Coffman's parents, and Ayers. At that point, the only remaining defendant was Don Wayne Bowden, the owner of the gun.

The Court of Appeals affirmed the action of the trial court with respect to all the parents, but reversed the granting of summary judgment for Ayers and Coffman. The court stated that although a minor under the age of seven is not responsible for damages resulting from his negligence, citing this court's decision in *Holbrock v. Hamilton Distributing, Inc.*

(1967), 11 Ohio St. 2d 185, 228 N.E.2d 628, such minor could be liable for an intentional tort, and the question of his capacity to commit an intentional tort was a matter of fact for the jury.

Depositions submitted in the Court of Appeals indicated that Doyle Wayne Ayers actually fired the BB-gun, and that Thomas Jeffrey Coffman may have cocked the gun, but did not hold or fire it at the time of the injury. Upon motion for reconsideration, the court modified its decision and affirmed the granting of summary judgment on behalf of Coffman.

Defendant Ayers appealed and the plaintiffs cross-appealed. No appeal was taken as to the parents' actions.

The cause is before this court pursuant to our allowance of a motion to certify the record.

[. . .]

STERN, J.

In *Holbrock v. Hamilton Distributing, supra,* this court held that a child under the age of seven is conclusively presumed to be incapable of contributory negligence. Our goal in that case, stated at page 189, was "a clear and simple rule which we believe will reach just and accurate results while also achieving a desirable judicial economy."

The instant case presents the question of whether a child under the age of seven is liable for primary negligence or for an intentional tort. Appellees suggest that our decision in *Holbrock* does not necessarily require that children of tender years be considered free of liability for primary negligence. They argue first that a child may more easily comprehend his own acts than the acts of others, and second, that incapacity for contributory negligence is grounded in a policy of imposing a higher standard of care for the protection of injured children. The former argument is wholly speculative, and the distinction it suggests between primary and contributory negligence is simplistic. The acts which constitute negligence are the same, whether that negligence is primary or contributory, and so too is the level of capacity and understanding necessary to a finding of negligence.

Appellees argue that lack of capacity for contributory negligence, as found in *Holbrock,* is grounded in a policy of imposing a higher standard of care for the protection of children. That argument has some merit. However, this is because we recognize that children, especially children of tender years, gradually acquire the capacity to understand and appreciate the consequences of their acts as they acquire age and experience. Only with some maturity does a child begin to realize that his choice of acts may injure himself or others, and only then can it be said that he possesses the capacity to act "reasonably." The practical need for some simple and just rule is the same in this case as in *Holbrock,* and we adhere to the rule stated therein.

The issue presented in *Holbrock* was whether a child under the age of seven was capable of contributory negligence as a matter of law. As this court pointed out, three choices of law were presented by the decisions from other jurisdictions. A similar choice among three rules of law is presented in fashioning a rule for determining the liability of a child under the age of seven for an intentional tort. The first is that a child under seven years of age is conclusively presumed to be incapable of harmful intent. [Citations omitted.] The second is that a child of any age may be liable for an intentional tort, and that the age of the child is relevant only insofar as determining whether the child knew with substantial certainty that his intentional act would bring about a harmful or offensive contact. [Citations omitted.] The third is that the child is strictly liable for trespass if he actually intended the physical act which caused the injury. [Citation omitted.]

The basic dilemma of all these cases is that a child of tender years has only some dim and imponderable responsibility for his acts—and yet those acts, as those of an adult, may cause injury to others. It is probably inevitable as a part of growing up that in rare cases a child will cause severe injuries to others. Yet it is most difficult to attach blame to a child of tender years for those injuries in any sense comparable to the blame attachable to an adult, whom we hold responsible for his acts. Our laws and our moral concepts assume actors capable of legal and moral choices, of which a young child is incapable. [Citation omitted.] For that reason, a child under seven years of age was at common law considered incapable of criminal responsibility. For the same reason, we cannot accept those rules which hold a child strictly liable, or which permit a jury to find liability, in cases of intentional tort. Our choice is between rules which permit the imposition of a legal judgment upon a young child for his intentional acts, and a rule which holds that members of society must accept the damage done by very young children to be no more subject to legal action than some force of nature or act of God. Our choice is the latter rule. The same public policy considerations which led this court in *Holbrock* to hold that children under the age of seven are not liable for contributory negligence, convince us that children under the age of seven also should not be held liable for intentional torts.

Judgment accordingly.

WILLIAM B. BROWN, J., Concurring.

Although I concur in the syllabus and judgment, I do so on policy grounds only, and not for the reasons stated in the majority opinion.

That opinion, in effect, grants absolution to all persons under seven, after proposing that young children should not be blamed for their misdeeds.

That premise is based upon the comparison of infant mischief with harm caused by an act of God, *vis major,* and other natural phenomena. I suggest that such comparison is faulty inasmuch as in the first instance there is a source for recovery, a person, and in the latter, [there is] no such source or available defendant. [Citation omitted.]

CELEBREZZE, J., dissenting.

The majority today determines that a child under the age of seven years is not legally responsible for his intentional or negligent conduct. We are to look upon this conduct as akin to the forces of nature or acts of God. If I read the rationale adopted by the majority correctly, we make this policy decision because it would be unfair to attach the degree of blame leveled at an adult to an infant, since his capacity to understand and appreciate the consequences of his acts is in the early stages of development and is only gradually acquired with age and experience.

First, there is no discussion directly to the question of who must bear the loss. When, as here, the choice is between an innocent, minor victim and the infant who fired the BB-gun which injured him, I choose to lay the responsibility on the doorstep of the infant-perpetrator, or those who should be held to answer for him. (In this case actions against the parents were dismissed.)

Second, and related to the first point, this is not an area easily separated into well-defined categories. There is a well-recognized line of case law supporting the position that age is only of consequence in determining what an infant knows, and thus whether the requisite intent is present. If the child does not have some awareness of the natural consequences of his intentional acts, liability will not attach. [Citations omitted.]

The jury system should not be presumed to be unable to handle a question such as this. The rationale offered in *Holbrock v. Hamilton Distributing* (1967), 11 Ohio St. 2d 185, 189,

that "* * * the conclusive presumption approach * * * provides a clear and simple rule which we believe will reach just and accurate results while also achieving a desirable judicial economy," seems to me to ignore obvious, and recurring problems.

Finally, the problems I refer to seem clear from an examination of the facts before us. Here, we have two infants with a BB-gun, injuring a third minor. As Douglas, J., said in *Peak v. United States* (1957), 353 U.S. 43, 46, "common sense often makes good law." Common sense tells me that these two six-year-olds, probably first-graders, have been exposed to guns and what guns do since they began to notice television. To say that they are conclusively presumed to have no awareness of the natural consequences of pointing and firing a rifle is to ignore common sense as well as common experience.

In the same vein, while admittedly conjectural, I would find it difficult to vote for a rule which leaves society prey to the precocious or malicious among our infant society. We admit to, and protect against, the malicious and dangerous in the adult population, and yet we would dismiss the same conduct in their progeny under the age of seven years as acceptable conduct because of the lack of experience and capacity natural to infancy. Also, those same parents could be expected to effectively inculcate this idea in their young, with possible ominous results. In my opinion, there are to many exceptions inherent in differing degrees of [children's] development for the conclusive presumption rule to be equitable, and we must recognize all aspects of this problem.

For those reasons, I respectfully submit that our jury system is adequate, and should determine the effect of infancy on liability for intentional acts.

CASE QUESTIONS

1. Do you agree with the majority opinion in *DeLuca*? Or do you find the concurring or dissenting opinions more persuasive? Explain your conclusions.

2. Do you agree with dissenting Justice Celebrezze that the majority's absolute intentional tort immunity rule for children younger than seven years of age ignores the differences in children's growth and understanding under various sets of circumstances? Do you believe that the jury should be allowed to examine the facts of each case to decide if children younger than seven years could comprehend the probable consequences of their intentional torts? Explain your reasoning.

3. Do you agree with Justice Stern, writing for the majority, that an absolute immunity rule reaches "just and accurate results"? When Justice Stern states that the immunity rule achieves "a desirable judicial economy," is this just another way of saying that the rule is easier for courts to apply? Could you characterize the rule as being a "judicial reflex," meaning that the rule can be applied without thinking (or justifying) the outcome? Or would you consider that too harsh and cynical a viewpoint? Explain.

4. In the next-to-last paragraph of the dissent, Justice Celebrezze mentions a "conjectural" problem with the majority's immunity rule. The dissent conjures the horrors of malicious young children inflicting vicious intentional torts upon society with impunity, protected absolutely by the immunity defense. Did you find this argument persuasive or merely exaggerated? Explain.

Children's immunity is never easy to determine. For example, suppose a five-year-old child swings a golf club backwards, planning to reverse the stroke and hit a golf ball. While doing the backswing, the club accidentally hits another child in the forehead, opening a nasty gash. Was the golfer negligent? Most states would apply a reasonable five-year-old child standard to gauge negligence. Some others follow the under-seven absolute immunity rule. This immunity varies widely among, or even within, jurisdictions, as shown in *DeLuca* and in the project cases.

12.4 STATUTES OF LIMITATIONS

Statutes of limitations are statutes establishing time limits within which plaintiffs may file tort actions against defendants. As shown in chapters 5 and 8, these time frames vary for different torts and between states.

There are statutes of limitations for tort lawsuits against governmental units. These often establish an elaborate written notification procedure that the plaintiff must follow to notify all the relevant governmental agencies

LEGAL TERMS

statute of limitations
The time period within which a plaintiff must file his or her tort action against a defendant. Time periods vary for different types of torts and between various state statutes.

(and their directors) that a lawsuit has been filed against them. Two examples of such statutes are reproduced in Figure 12-1.

SUMMARY

12.1. Tort immunities are absolute defenses against a plaintiff's tort claims. Sovereign, or governmental, immunity is an ancient common law defense that protected governments from tort liability. The doctrine was based on the presumption that "the king could do no wrong," which, in America, translated that the government could not be sued without its

Florida Statutes Annotated § 768.28 (West 1991) (including waiver of sovereign immunity)	Montana Code Annotated §§ 2-9-301, -302 (1991)
(1) In accordance with s. 13, Art. X, State Constitution, the state, for itself and for its agencies or subdivisions, hereby waives sovereign immunity for liability for torts, but only to the extent specified in this act. [. . .] (6)(a) An action may not be instituted on a claim against the state or one of its agencies or subdivisions unless the claimant presents the claim in writing to the appropriate agency, and also [. . .] presents such claim in writing to the Department of Insurance, within 3 years after such claim accrues and the Department of Insurance or the appropriate agency denies the claim in writing; [. . .] (12) Every claim against the state or one of its agencies or subdivisions for damages for a negligent or wrongful act or omission pursuant to this section shall be forever barred unless the civil action is commenced by filing a complaint in the court of appropriate jurisdiction within 4 years after such claim accrues; except [for contribution and medical malpractice actions, which have separate statutes of limitations].	§ 301: (1) All claims against the state arising under the provisions of parts 1 through 3 of this chapter [i.e., liability exposure and insurance coverage, title 2—government structure and administration] must be presented in writing to the department of administration. (2) A complaint based on a claim subject to the provisions of subsection (1) may not be filed in district court unless the claimant has first presented the claim to the department of administration and the department has finally denied the claim. [. . .] § 302: A claim against the state or a political subdivision is subject to the limitation of actions [i.e., statutes of limitations] provided by law [i.e., as specified by statute for specific tort actions].

FIGURE 12-1
Examples of Statutes of Limitations for Governmental Tort Claims

consent. American courts have drastically reduced or eliminated sovereign immunity during the twentieth century. In the early decades of this century, courts avoided the immunity by distinguishing between governmental and proprietary actions in which government agencies were engaged. Many states have abolished sovereign immunity altogether as an absolute defense.

12.2.   Public officers, such as judges or legislators, are immune from personal liability for any torts committed while they are performing their official duties. This ensures that governmental officials may act independently and freely to perform their civil responsibilities, without fear of constant tort liability for their every public action that might tortiously affect individual citizens in some way.

12.3.   "Children of tender years" are very young children, often under the age of seven years, although many courts have defined the term as including children to age twelve or even through the teenage years. Children of tender years are immune from intentional tort liability in most jurisdictions. Often, a specific age boundary is used. Many courts state that children under seven years are absolutely immune. Others do not rigidly follow any age barrier. For negligence, most courts apply a reasonable-child-of-tender-years standard to decide whether negligence has occurred. A minority of states use definite age limits, such as the seven-year-old rule, for negligence cases.

12.4.   Statutes of limitations restrict the time period within which a plaintiff may file tort causes of action against a defendant. There are statutes of limitations for tort lawsuits against governmental units. These often establish written notification procedures that the plaintiff must follow to notify all the relevant governmental agencies (and their directors) that a lawsuit has been filed against them.

REVIEW QUESTIONS

1.   What are tort immunities? What is their function in tort litigation? Who do they protect?

2.   Define sovereign, or governmental, immunity. What is the historical rationale behind the defense? How have modern American courts applied the doctrine?

3.   What is the governmental/proprietary distinction? How it is used? How are governmental actions defined? Proprietary actions? What is the significance of these distinctions?

4.   What is the modern trend among American courts toward sovereign immunity? How has the defense changed during this century?

5. What are public officers' immunities? Who do they protect? Why are these governmental officials granted immunity?

6. Define children of tender years. Who is protected by this defense? How does the immunity differ for intentional torts and negligence?

7. What are statutes of limitations? How do they apply to governmental tort liability?

PROBLEMS

1. Superior Court Judge Emily Doud McKinnley granted summary judgment to the defendant in a negligence lawsuit. The plaintiff had sued the defendant for negligently causing personal injuries. The plaintiff suffered extensive injuries and was unable to work for the remainder of his life. Upon appeal, the state court of appeals reversed Judge McKinnley's summary judgment order. The appellate court admonished the trial judge for refusing to accept certain key evidence that the plaintiff offered at hearing. The appellate court stated that there was no legal basis for granting summary judgment in the case. The trial transcript clearly indicated that the judge had become angry at plaintiff's counsel's attempts to admit the evidence despite warnings to desist. After the appeal, the plaintiff wished to sue Judge McKinnley for judicial malpractice.

2. Shelby Sarville drives a garbage truck for the City of New Ventura. The city charges its customers a monthly trash-hauling fee, which is based upon the size of the trash container used. Citizens may use the city's service, although many people hire private trash companies instead. One day, while backing up to empty a trash dumpster, Shelby failed to look in his rear-view mirrors. A five-year-old girl tried to squeeze between the truck and dumpster on her bicycle. She mistimed the squeeze, and the truck crushed her against the dumpster, causing severe internal injuries. (Be sure to address the contributory negligence issue in this case.)

3. Daphne Torque is an eight-year-old girl who often plays with her neighborhood friends. While hiking through the woods on Saturday afternoon, two of Daphne's neighbors, Paul (age seven) and Anne (age ten) Heifer, decided to "ditch" Daphne, that is, the duo would abandon Daphne in the woods and flee the scene. The sun had just gone down, and it was becoming quite dark when Paul and Anne ditched Daphne. Once Daphne realized that she was alone in the forest, she became frightened and ran toward home. She twisted her ankle and fell, striking her head against a tree root. She was knocked unconscious. Several hours later, a police search party located her body. She suffered a concussion and dehydration.

PROBLEM ANSWERS

1. The plaintiff's "judicial malpractice" lawsuit against Superior Court Judge Emily Doud McKinnley would fail. Judge McKinnley would successfully invoke the absolute tort immunity defense. Judge McKinnley was performing her official capacities as a judge, albeit rather badly, if one accepts the court of appeals' admonitions. Nonetheless, the judge would be immune from tort liability, regardless of how incompetently she performed her duties.

   The plaintiff's appropriate avenue of relief would be to file with the state supreme court judicial misconduct charges against the judge under the state's Code of Judicial Conduct.

2. Shelby Sarville's negligence in backing up the garbage truck may be imputed to his employer, the City of New Ventura, under respondeat superior. The city would argue sovereign immunity, assuming the defense was still available in this hypothetical jurisdiction. The city would characterize its trash collection service as a governmental function, because it provides a public health service to the general public. However, this characterization is faulty. The city's trash collection is a proprietary function, clearly comparable to services available from private trash haulers in the area. Further, the city assessed users' fees for its service, which, under the fee standard, indicates a proprietary function. Because proprietary functions carry no immunity from tort liability, the city would be liable to the five-year-old victim injured as a result of Shelby's negligence.

   Contributory negligence would be another possible defense in this hypothetical. The five-year-old girl tried to squeeze between the truck and dumpster as the truck was backing up. This suggests that the girl violated her duty of reasonable care to herself and contributed to her own injuries through her own negligence. However, this victim is a child of tender years. Just as extremely young children are immune from negligence liability, so are they immune from contributory negligence. The facts do not address whether the courts in this hypothetical's jurisdiction consider five-year-old children absolutely immune. Assuming not, the reasonable five-year-old person standard would be applied to determine if the girl acted unreasonably under the circumstances. Preschool children frequently misjudge speed and distances of approaching vehicles, thinking that they can avoid harm through a speedy burst. The girl here may have acted as a reasonable five-year-old, who might not fully appreciate the dangers involved. If this were the court's decision, then the girl would not have been contributorily negligent, and so this defense would fail.

3. Daphne Torque (through her parents or guardian) would sue Paul and Anne Heifer (through their parents or guardian) for negligently causing Daphne's injuries, and for intentional or reckless infliction of emotional distress.

The intentional/reckless infliction cause of action would be dismissed under the common law child's absolute immunity for intentional torts. Thus, the Heifers would not be liable to Daphne under these tort theories.

Under negligence, however, the children of tender years immunity is not available, at least for Anne. Anne, at age ten, should reasonably have anticipated that Daphne, age eight, would become frightened when she discovered herself alone in the darkened woods. A reasonable ten-year-old person would have foreseen that, frightened and panicky, Daphne would run to escape the forest and, in doing so in the darkness, could trip, fall, and severely injure herself. Daphne's injuries were reasonably foreseeable. Thus, Anne's behavior fell below the reasonable standard of care among child playmates under the circumstances. Anne's ditching maneuver would be a breach of duty, which proximately caused Daphne's injuries.

At age seven, Paul Heifer would probably escape liability, even if absolute child immunity were not available. Younger siblings often mimic elder siblings' behavior without considering the potentially adverse consequences. Paul's behavior, then, could be viewed as acceptable for a reasonable seven-year-old playing with his older ten-year-old sister and the plaintiff.

The defendants would argue that Daphne assumed the risk and was contributorily negligent in causing her own injuries. These defenses would probably be available, because Daphne, at age eight, is above the typical tender-years age ceilings of seven or below. Thus, Daphne would not be immune from these defenses.

But the defenses would fail. A reasonable eight-year-old person often plays in the woods with friends during daylight and would not anticipate being abandoned after dark. Finding oneself alone in the forest, a reasonable eight-year-old might become extremely frightened and react, just as Daphne did, by fleeing rapidly from the scene. Because of Daphne's youth, she could be excused from anticipating the dangers involved in running through the dark woods. Accordingly, she could not have knowingly assumed this risk. Further, her behavior complied with the reasonable person standard, and so she was not contributorily negligent.

PROJECTS

1. Brief *Stump v. Sparkman,* 435 U.S. 349, 98 S. Ct. 1099, 55 L. Ed. 2d 331 (1978). Did the Supreme Court grant the trial judge absolute immunity in this case? What was its rationale? What were the dissents' rationales in response?

2. Brief *Camerlinck v. Thomas,* 209 Neb. 843, 312 N.W.2d 260, 27 A.L.R.4th 1 (1981). What immunity did the Nebraska Supreme Court grant to the six-year-old child in this negligence case? How does this standard compare with the one in *DeLuca?* Notice the *Camerlinck*

court's review of the tender-years immunity defense in Nebraska. This case exemplifies the evolutionary process of common law issues.

3. Brief *Gymnastics USA v. McDougal,* 92 Or. App. 453, 758 P.2d 881, *review denied,* 307 Or. 77, 763 P.2d 731 (1988). To what extent did the Oregon Court of Appeals consider relevant the age of the tortfeasor in intentional tort cases?

4. Brief *Powell v. District of Columbia,* 602 A.2d 1123 (D.C. 1992). Did the D.C. Court of Appeals apply the governmental/proprietary distinction, or another test? Explain the court's reasoning.

5. Brief *Larouche v. Doe,* 594 A.2d 1297 (N.H. 1991). Did the New Hampshire Supreme Court rule that the state had waived its sovereign immunity? What was the court's rationale?

CHAPTER 13
Paralegal Ethics

DATA-GRAPHIC TORTS

The torts puzzle is complete! All of the pieces are in place. The straight pieces representing the American legal system and legal analysis surround the entire subject. The intentional tort pieces stand out clearly, as opposed to the multi-detailed negligence pieces. The uniformity in the strict and products liability pieces is in striking contrast to the special negligence actions, which vary in shape and form. Special tort actions and tort immunities complete the variety of shapes and images.

Now that the puzzle is assembled, the big picture of tort law comes sharply into focus. The entire subject—the puzzle itself—has common, interconnecting lines, making the image integrated and whole. And what is the picture? It is an analytical process, a way of thinking about tort problems. This is the end result of all the work assembling the tort puzzle.

No longer is there confusion about the individual torts and how they interrelate. As Professor Harry Pratter, of the Indiana University School of Law-Bloomington, often instructed, "[In legal studies], all things become clear [in the end] at final exam time!" Truly, the big picture has appeared, and the reader may wonder that once he or she did not know how to perform the complicated legal analysis that has now become second nature.

INTRODUCTION

Cynics say that legal ethics is a contradiction in terms. They scoff that lawyers and their staffs, like used car dealers or politicians, are universally suspect as underhanded manipulators vying for innocent victims' money. Honest attorneys, legal assistants, and legal secretaries rankle at this false, misleading stereotype. Ethical and unethical behavior exists in every profession. There are always rotten apples whose odor taints the wholesomeness of the whole bushel. But, conversely, there are lots of good-quality apples ready for market amongst the handful of rancid produce. The bad apples can easily be identified and removed from the lot.

This is the role of legal ethics: to identify and remove inappropriate conduct from the legal profession. Honest legal practitioners strive to avoid ethical dilemmas—to keep the fruit from spoiling, so to speak. Unscrupulous persons are culled and expelled through disciplinary sanction from state supreme courts or disciplinary agencies.

This final chapter discusses this extremely important aspect of paralegal work, namely, the real-world ethical concerns one encounters daily as a legal assistant. It is no exaggeration to say that legal ethics may be the most important area of study in the legal assistance field. The last puzzle pieces to be assembled include:

- NALA's ethics rules applicable to legal assistants.
- The ABA's ethics standards applicable to paralegals.

13.1 NALA ETHICS CODES

The National Association of Legal Assistants, Inc. (NALA) has promulgated two sets of ethics codes designed specifically for paralegals. The Code of Ethics and Professional Responsibility was issued in 1977. NALA updated and improved this code in 1984 with its Model Standards and Guidelines for Utilization of Legal Assistants. For purposes of comparison, the first will be called the *Code* and the latter the *Model Standards*.

Restricted Duties

Canon I of the Code states that legal assistants shall not perform any duties that only lawyers may fulfill, nor shall paralegals perform activities that attorneys are prohibited from doing. For instance, legal assistants may not engage in the unauthorized practice of law. This is expressly forbidden in Code Canons III and VI. Only attorneys licensed and in good standing with a state's bar licensing authority (usually the state bar or the state supreme court) may practice law. As explained in the Model Standards, this includes providing legal advice to clients, representing clients in court proceedings, contacting adverse parties on a client's behalf, establishing legal fees, accepting clients' cases on behalf of attorneys or the law firm, and preparing legal documents without attorney supervision.

Paralegal Representation Before Administrative Agencies

Many state and federal administrative agencies permit nonlawyers, including legal assistants, to represent parties appearing before the agencies in adjudicatory or rule-making hearings. Such representation is not the unauthorized practice of law, because it is expressly permitted by administrative rules and regulations.

Some state courts refuse to recognize such administrative authorization, and there are common law decisions declaring nonlawyer client representation before administrative agencies to constitute unauthorized legal practice. These courts argue that only the judicial branch has authority to regulate the practice of law. State constitutions or, more often, state statutes vest this regulatory power most frequently in the state supreme court, which might delegate supervisory authority to a state bar agency. In the case of legislative declarations, the state legislature may simply amend its statutes excluding administrative agency party representation regulations from the courts' authority. However, when a state constitution plainly roots regulatory power over law practice in the courts, the legislature must pursue constitutional amendment procedures. This is a cumbersome process.

In most instances, however, the courts simply look the other way, allowing nonattorneys to represent clients before administrative agencies that have expressed a willingness to accept such circumstances.

Lay Representation in Justice or Small Claims Courts

Many state statutes permit nonlawyers to represent litigants before justices of the peace (commonly called justice courts) or small claims courts. The common law in most states narrowly construes such statutes, indicating that such lay representation is intended for (1) "one-time" appearances, (2) family or business employee representation, or (3) civil cases only. Thus, legal assistants who attempt to carve a niche by representing clients in justice or small claims courts on a regular basis would, under these courts' interpretations, engage in unauthorized law practice.

Supervised Duties

Canon II of the Code declares that legal assistants may perform any delegated tasks supervised by a licensed attorney. The supervising lawyer must remain directly responsible to the client, maintaining or establishing the attorney-client relationship and assuming full accountability for the legal services supplied. This provision permits paralegals to conduct initial consultations with clients, in which they gather factual information from the client. It also allows legal assistants to complete legal research and writing tasks, investigate cases, compile evidence, arrange (but not conduct) discovery, and prepare materials for trial. However, at each phase, the attorney must guide and direct the paralegal's efforts.

The Model Standards reiterate Code Canon II, adding that a legal assistant should disclose his or her status as a paralegal (rather than a lawyer) at the outset of any professional relationship with clients, or when dealing with other attorneys, courts, administrative agencies, or the general public. The Model Standards also emphasize the supervising attorneys' duty to monitor and train legal assistants.

No Independent Legal Judgment

Code Canon IV forbids legal assistants from exercising independent, professional legal judgment in place of an attorney's. The Model Standards are comparable, stating that a legal assistant may perform services for a lawyer, provided that they do not require the exercise of independent legal judgment, and provided that the attorney supervises the paralegal's efforts. Canon V also reminds legal assistants to act prudently so that they can determine the extent to which they may assist a client without an attorney's presence. This is especially important during fact-gathering client consultations or when discussing details with clients on the telephone.

Protecting Client Confidences

Legal assistants must protect client confidences under Code Canon VII and the Model Standards. It is unethical for a paralegal to violate any statute controlling privileged communications. Examples of privileged communications include discussions between attorney and client, physician and patient, husband and wife, clergy and parishioner, and counsellor and patient.

Clearly, when clients speak with attorneys and their staff, there is an expectation that confidences and disclosures shall remain inside the office. The rule of thumb for legal assistants, like all law office staff, is simply not to discuss sensitive client information with anyone. One should always consult with the supervising attorney to see if particular client information is privileged.

Avoiding the Appearance of Impropriety

Code Canon VIII warns legal assistants to avoid conduct that would be considered, or even simply appear to be, unethical.

Integrity and Competency

Similarly, Code Canon IX states that paralegals shall maintain their integrity and a high degree of competency. This may require legal assistants to complete continuing legal education, as most states now require of attorneys. In fact, Code Canon X encourages paralegals to "strive for perfection through education" to better assist the legal profession and the public.

Catchall Provision

The Code includes a catchall provision declaring that legal assistants shall do everything "incidental, necessary, or expedient" to maintain the ethics and responsibility required by statutes or court rules of legal professionals.

Lawyer Ethics Rule Application

Code Canon XII and the Model Standards includes legal assistants within the coverage of the American Bar Association's ethics codes. The current version of the ABA regulations is the Model Rules of Professional Conduct, which replaced the Code of Professional Responsibility. All states have their own versions of these attorney ethics provisions, many of which are modeled directly upon the ABA versions.

Model Standards' List of Permissible Activities

To clarify ambiguities in the Code, NALA's Model Standards list permissible activities for legal assistants to perform, provided that such items do not conflict with or contradict statutes, court rules, administrative rules and regulations, or the attorneys' ethics codes. Under this list of permissible activities, legal assistants may do the following, under the attorney's supervision and guidance:

1. Conduct client interviews and maintain general contact with clients.
2. Locate and interview witnesses.
3. Conduct investigations and legal research for an attorney's review.
4. Draft legal documents for a lawyer's review.
5. Draft correspondence and pleadings for an attorney's review and signature.
6. Summarize depositions, interrogatories, and testimony for a lawyer's review.
7. Attend will executions, real estate closings, depositions, court or administrative hearings, and trials, along with an attorney.
8. Write and sign letters, provided that the legal assistant's status is plainly indicated and the correspondence does not contain independent legal opinions or advice.

Legal Effect of NALA Rules

It is important for the reader to note that NALA's ethics provisions have no force of law, in and of themselves. NALA is a private organization, and accordingly its promulgations are advisory. However, courts are likely to give considerable credence to NALA's rules, as historically courts have accepted the ABA's ethics codes as definitive statements of the law.

AN EXAMPLE OF COURT-ORDERED ETHICS

Some courts have promulgated rules addressing the ethical use of legal assistants, as the following illustration shows. Note the similarities and distinctions between the Rhode Island regulations and NALA's Code.

Provisional Order No. 18
454 A.2d 1222 (R.I. 1983)
(Supreme Court of Rhode Island)
February 1, 1983

GUIDELINES FOR USE OF LEGAL ASSISTANTS

These guidelines shall apply to the use of legal assistants by members of the Rhode Island Bar Association. A legal assistant is one who under the supervision of a lawyer, shall apply knowledge of law and legal procedures in rendering direct assistance to lawyers, clients and courts; design, develop and modify procedures, techniques, services and processes; prepare and interpret legal documents; detail procedures for practicing in certain fields of law; research, select, assess, compile and use information from the law library and other references; and analyze and handle procedural problems that involve independent decisions. More specifically, a Legal Assistant is one who engages in the functions set forth in Guideline II. Nothing contained in these guidelines shall be construed as a determination of the competence of any person performing the function of a legal assistant, or as conferring status upon any such person serving as a legal assistant.

GUIDELINE I

A lawyer shall not permit a legal assistant to engage in the unauthorized practice of law. Pursuant to Canon 3 of the Rhode Island Supreme Court Code of Professional Responsibility, the lawyer shares in the ultimate accountability for a violation of this guideline. The legal assistant remains individually accountable for engaging in the unauthorized practice of law.

GUIDELINE II

A legal assistant may perform the following functions, together with other related duties, to assist lawyers in their representation of clients: attend client conferences; correspond with and obtain information from clients; draft legal documents; assist at closings and similar meetings between parties and lawyers; witness execution of documents; prepare transmittal letters; maintain estate/guardianship trust accounts; transfer securities and other assets; assist in the day-to-day administration of trusts and estates; index and organize documents; conduct research; check citations in briefs and memoranda; draft interrogatories and answers thereto, deposition notices and requests for production; prepare summaries of depositions and trial transcripts; interview witnesses; obtain records from doctors, hospitals, police departments, other agencies and institutions; and obtain information from courts. Legal documents, including but not limited to, contract deeds, leases, mortgages, wills, trusts, probate forms, pleadings, pension plans and tax returns, shall be reviewed by a lawyer before being submitted to a client or another party.

In addition, except where otherwise prohibited by statute, court rule or decision, administrative rule or regulation, or by the Code of Professional Responsibility, a lawyer may permit a legal assistant to perform specific services in representation of a client. Thus, a legal assistant may represent clients before administrative agencies or courts where such representation is permitted by statute or agency or court rules.

Notwitding any other part of this Guideline,

1) Services requiring the exercise of independent professional legal judgment shall be performed by lawyers and shall not be performed by legal assistants.

2) Legal assistants shall work under the direction and supervision of a lawyer, who shall be ultimately responsible for services and duties performed by legal assistants.

3) The lawyer maintains direct responsibility for all aspects of the lawyer-client relationship, including responsibility for all actions taken by and errors of omission by the legal assistant.

GUIDELINE III

A lawyer shall direct a legal assistant to avoid any conduct which if engaged in by a lawyer would violate the Code of Professional Responsibility. In particular, the lawyer shall instruct the legal assistant regarding the confidential nature of the attorney/client relationship, and shall direct the legal assistant to refrain from disclosing any confidential information obtained from a client or in connection with representation of a client.

GUIDELINE IV

A lawyer shall direct a legal assistant to disclose that he or she is not a lawyer at the outset in contacts with clients, courts, administrative agencies, attorneys, or, when acting in a professional capacity, the public.

GUIDELINE V

A lawyer may permit a legal assistant to sign correspondence relating to the legal assistant's work, provided the legal assistant's non-lawyer status is clear and the contents of the letter do not constitute legal advice.

Correspondence containing substantive instructions or legal advice to a client shall be signed by an attorney.

GUIDELINE VI

Except where permitted by statute, court rule or decision, a lawyer shall not permit a legal assistant to appear in court as a legal advocate on behalf of a client. Nothing in this Guideline shall be construed to bar or limit a legal assistant's right or obligation to appear in any forum as a witness on behalf of a client.

GUIDELINE VII

A lawyer may permit a legal assistant to use a business card, with the employer's name indicated, provided the card is approved by the employer and the legal assistant's non-lawyer status is clearly indicated.

GUIDELINE VIII

A lawyer shall not form a partnership with a legal assistant if any part of the partnership's activity involves the practice of law.

GUIDELINE IX

Compensation of legal assistants shall not be in the manner of sharing legal fees, nor shall the legal assistant receive any remuneration for referring legal matters to a lawyer.

GUIDELINE X

A lawyer shall not use or employ as a legal assistant any attorney who has been suspended or disbarred pursuant to an order of this court, or an attorney who has resigned in this or any other jurisdiction for reasons related to a breach of ethical conduct.

Entered as an order of this court this 1st day of February, 1983.

[Signatures of the Justices.]

QUESTIONS

1. Under the Rhode Island Rules, paralegals are liable for engaging in the unauthorized practice of law. Assume that these rules applied in your state. What sanctions could be imposed under your state statutes or court rules?
2. Has your state supreme court enacted paralegal ethics rules? If so, how are they different from Rhode Island's? The NALA rules?

13.2 NFPA ETHICS RULES

The National Federation of Paralegal Associations (NFPA) has also established ethical rules for appropriate legal assistant conduct. NFPA's Affirmation of Responsibility lists six categories, which are outlined in Figure 13-1. Like NALA's codes, these rules alone have no legal effect upon paralegals. However, courts and bar authorities may incorporate them in their decisions, thus incorporating them into the common law or administrative law.

The ABA's ethics rules also apply to legal assistants. These standards are discussed in § 13.3.

13.3 ABA ETHICS STANDARDS

The American Bar Association (ABA) has promulgated its own sets of ethical regulations for attorneys. Currently it follows the Model Rules of Professional Conduct (Model Rules), which replaced its older Code of Professional Responsibility (CPR). Many state bars and courts have adopted the ABA's Model Rules and Code as legally binding and enforceable regulations against attorneys and their employees. Courts have ruled that the ABA's standards apply to legal assistants. Thus, paralegals should become familiar with the provisions of the ABA Model Rules and the CPR.

FIGURE 13-1
NFPA Affirmation of Responsibility

1. A paralegal shall take initiative in the expansion of the paralegal's role in the legal profession within the parameters of the unauthorized practice of law statutes.
2. A paralegal shall maintain the highest level of ethical conduct.
3. A paralegal shall maintain a high level of competence and shall contribute to the integrity of the paralegal profession.
4. A paralegal shall preserve client confidences and privileged communications.
5. A paralegal shall serve the public interests by contributing to the availability and delivery of quality legal services.
6. A paralegal shall promote the development of the paralegal profession.

ABA Code of Professional Responsibility

The CPR is divided into nine Canons, all of which broadly prescribe ethical conduct for lawyers. Figure 13-2 summarizes the Canons. Within the Canons are Disciplinary Rules (DRs) and Ethical Considerations (ECs) which provide more detailed guidance on ethical issues. The DRs and ECs carefully discuss permissible attorney conduct in advertising; soliciting clients; contacting clients, adverse parties, or the public; protecting client confidences; establishing and sharing legal fees; withdrawing from representation; undertaking unauthorized practice of law; maintaining prohibited interactions with client's interests; providing competent and zealous representation; and other ethical questions. The ABA Model Rules, although they use different phraseology, address identical concerns.

Ethics codes tend to be cut-and-dried when presented abstractly. It is more helpful to explore their application in real-world settings.

CANON 1: A Lawyer Should Assist in Maintaining the Integrity and Competence of the Legal Profession.
CANON 2: A Lawyer Should Assist the Legal Profession in Fulfilling Its Duty to Make Legal Counsel Available.
CANON 3: A Lawyer Should Assist in Preventing the Unauthorized Practice of Law.
CANON 4: A Lawyer Should Preserve the Confidences and Secrets of a Client.
CANON 5: A Lawyer Should Exercise Independent Professional Judgment On Behalf of a Client.
CANON 6: A Lawyer Should Represent a Client Competently.
CANON 7: A Lawyer Should Represent a Client Zealously Within the Bounds of the Law.
CANON 8: A Lawyer Should Assist in Improving the Legal System.
CANON 9: A Lawyer Should Avoid Even the Appearance of Professional Impropriety.

FIGURE 13-2
ABA Code of Professional Responsibility Canons

A CASE OF UNAUTHORIZED PRACTICE

Several states have statutes permitting nonattorneys to represent clients in certain specialized courts (e.g., justice-of-the-peace, small claims, city, traffic). These statutes are often written plainly and clearly. The legislature's intentions should be sufficiently obvious, even to the courts. But as the following case illustrates, courts may be unwilling to permit uninitiated "outsiders" into the client representation arena. After reading the Montana Supreme Court's opinion, one might wonder if this is just another boost to the lawyers' practice monopoly.

Sparks v. Johnson
___ Mont. ___,
826 P.2d 928 (1992)
(Supreme Court of Montana)
February 6, 1992

OPINION AND ORDER

[PER CURIAM]

This is an original proceeding arising out of a criminal theft prosecution in the City Court of Whitefish, Montana. Petitioners Karen Sparks, the defendant in that proceeding, and Jerry O'Neil, seek declaratory and injunctive relief, including a writ of mandamus. They request this Court's declaration that O'Neil and other non-attorneys similarly situated have the right, pursuant to §§ 25-31-601 and 37-61-210, MCA [Montana Code Annotated], to act as attorneys in Montana courts of limited jurisdiction on a regular and recurring basis. The Office of the Attorney General responded, as did Whitefish City Judge Brad Johnson.

The petition before us raises the question of lay representation in Montana's courts of limited jurisdiction. While it is clear that Article VII, § 2(3) of the 1972 Montana Constitution vests exclusive jurisdiction in this Court to make rules governing practice in all Montana courts, we have not heretofore comprehensively addressed this issue which now is arising with increasing frequency. Because of the statewide importance and implications of the issue, we accept original jurisdiction of this petition [. . .] in order to provide guidance on the question of lay representation to the courts of limited jurisdiction throughout the state.

The underlying facts upon which this proceeding is based are not in dispute. The Whitefish City Attorney filed a complaint against Karen Sparks in Whitefish City Court for misdemeanor theft pursuant to § 45-6-301, MCA. At her initial appearance on September 18, 1991, Sparks appeared and acknowledged that she possessed a copy of the complaint and that she was aware an arrest warrant had been issued. Sparks was informed of her right to counsel and her right to a continuance so she could obtain counsel. Sparks pled not guilty and requested a court-appointed attorney. The court explained that it was not seeking confinement for Sparks and, therefore, would not provide her with a court-appointed attorney. Sparks persisted, prompting the court to provide defendant with an Affidavit/Request for Court Appointed Counsel form.

After Sparks' repeated attempts to secure court-appointed counsel, the court issued a Memorandum on Oct. 17, 1991, concluding again that she was not entitled to court-appointed counsel but could obtain private counsel. On or about Oct. 21, 1991, Jerry O'Neil filed a notice of appearance in the Whitefish City Court indicating that he would appear on behalf of defendant Sparks. The court subsequently denied O'Neil the right to represent Sparks in City Court and a jury trial was set for Nov. 7, 1991.

The present petition was filed with this Court on Nov. 8, 1991, seeking a stay of pending proceedings in the Whitefish City Court, a declaratory judgment that O'Neil has the right under §§ 25-31-601, MCA, and 37-61-210, MCA, to act as an attorney in the justice and city courts of Montana, and related injunctive and mandamus relief. This Court stayed the underlying proceedings. [. . .]

Standing is a threshold issue. [Citation omitted.] Thus, we must determine at the outset whether Jerry O'Neil has standing in the action before us. We conclude that he does not.

Although included as a "petitioner" in the caption of the petition to this Court, O'Neil essentially seeks to come before us as a legal representative of Sparks. O'Neil, an acknowledged lay person and not an attorney of record, possesses no legally recognized relationship to

Sparks; therefore, he will not be recognized by this Court in the conduct or disposition of the case. [Citation omitted.] We construe this action to be a pro se action by Karen Sparks seeking representation by the person of her choice in the city court criminal proceeding in which she is a defendant.

Sparks contends that § 25-31-601, MCA, authorizes lay representation in criminal cases in Montana justices' courts. She argues further that § 37-61-210, MCA, extends that right to lay representation in criminal cases to city courts. We disagree.

Section 25-31-601, MCA, provides that "[p]arties in justice's court may appear and act in person or by attorney; and any person, except the constable by whom the summons or jury process was served, may act as attorney." The statute is found in Title 25 of the Montana Code Annotated, entitled "Civil Procedure." Chapter 31 of that Title is "Procedure in Justices' Courts."

Section 25-31-601, MCA, is limited, by its plain language and placement in the Montana codes, to civil litigation in justices' courts. It does not apply to criminal proceedings in those courts or in other courts of limited jurisdiction. The criminal procedure statutes applicable to courts of limited jurisdiction, set forth in title 46, Chapter 17, parts 1 through 4, do not contain language permitting representation by "any person."

Sparks' further contention that lay representation in criminal proceedings is extended to city courts by virtue of § 37-61-210, MCA, is also incorrect, even aside from our conclusion above that Montana law does not authorize lay representation in criminal proceedings in justices' courts.

Section 37-61-210, MCA, is entitled "penalty for practicing without license" and provides that "[i]f any person practices law in any court, except a justice's court or a city court, without having received a license as attorney

and counselor, he is guilty of a contempt of court." Sparks' reliance on § 37-61-210, MCA, as authority for legal representation by "any person" in a criminal proceeding in city court, is erroneous. Both the plain language and the placement of § 37-61-210, MCA, in the Licensing part of Title 37 (entitled "Professions and Occupations"), Chapter 61 (entitled "Attorneys at Law") of the Montana Code Annotated make it clear that it is a licensing and penalty statute. It does not, by its terms, authorize practice in either justices' or city courts; it merely alludes to, and exempts from penalty, such practice as may be authorized by other statutes. Therefore, we conclude that only such practice before courts of limited jurisdiction as is specifically authorized by existing statute or Court rule can be undertaken by lay people.

Sparks' reliance on a past Order of this Court in a case to which she was not a party is also to no avail. Orders without accompanying opinions have no precedential value from case to case, but pertain only to the circumstances of the action involved. [Citation omitted.]

Sparks' final contention is that § 25-31-601, MCA, authorizes lay representation of parties in courts of limited jurisdiction on a regular and recurring basis. While this is a case of first impression in Montana, statutes similar to § 25-31-601, MCA, have been addressed in other states and held applicable only to a "one time" representation of a party in a justice or magistrate court.

State ex rel. Freison v. Isner (W.Va. 1981), 285 S.E.2d 641, involved a collection agency appearing in magistrate court on behalf of petitioner's creditors through its nonlawyer manager. The court found that the statute authorizing appearances by lay persons in civil litigation did not permit the unauthorized practice of law, but anticipated the representation of a party by a nonlawyer on a "casual, non-recurring, non-pay basis as a means of assisting the party pro se." [Citation omitted.] The *Freison* court concluded that the West Virginia law, similar to Montana's, provides only for "an isolated or casual appearance by a non-lawyer friend or relative of a party to proceedings in magistrate court . . . ." [Citation omitted.]

Similarly, the Supreme Court of Iowa held that a bill collector who attempted to bring suit in justice court as an assignee of his various clients was prohibited from doing so. *Bump v. Barnett* (Iowa 1944), 16 N.W.2d 579. The Iowa court, in referring to a statute much like § 25-31-601, MCA, stated that:

> "The salutary purpose of the statute may not thus be perverted to encourage the growth of a class of 'justice court lawyers,' unfettered by the rules that bind licensed attorneys and without training in law and ethics."

[Citation omitted.] The Iowa court concluded that the bill collector was engaged in the illegal practice of law by his repeated representations in justice court.

We agree with the reasoning of the West Virginia and Iowa courts. Section 25-31-601, MCA, was not intended to permit the unauthorized practice of law; the intent is to enable a friend or relative to assist and speak on behalf of a party at one proceeding. We hold that the statute is a "one-time only" grant of a privilege in justices' court civil proceedings. Further, we extend this specific privilege to civil proceedings in city courts pursuant to our constitutional authority to make rules governing practice for all Montana courts.

Finally, even if the underlying proceeding in Whitefish City Court were a civil one, it is clear that O'Neil's representation of Sparks would not be permissible. We take judicial notice that O'Neil attempted to represent at least one other person in a criminal action in a court of limited jurisdiction. [Citation omitted.] We also note that petitioner's brief herein provides a list of O'Neil's "clients." Neither O'Neil nor any other lay person has authority to represent "clients" on a recurring basis in courts of limited jurisdiction. Such recurring representation constitutes the unauthorized practice of law.

Nothing herein impacts on the "student practice rule" at the University of Montana School of Law. Under this rule, students who have completed two years of law school are supervised by a licensed attorney and perform legal activities in Montana courts.

IT IS THEREFORE ORDERED that the Petition herein, and all relief requested therein, is denied and dismissed.

IT IS FURTHER ORDERED that the stay of further proceedings in *City of Whitefish v. Karen Sparks* is hereby lifted.

DATED this 6th day of February, 1992.

Chief Justice Turnage and Justices Harrison, Gray, Trieweiler, McDonough, Hunt, and Weber concur.

CASE QUESTIONS

1. Under the Montana statute, "any person" other than the constable who delivered service of process is permitted to act as attorney for a litigant in justice court. How did the Montana Supreme Court discover, in this plain, unambiguous language, that the rule only applies to a litigant's "friend or relative to assist and speak on behalf of a party at one proceeding" on a "one-time only" basis? Do you agree with the court's interpretation?

2. Legal assistants would be considered lay persons under *Sparks*. Thus, despite the Montana legislature's broad statutory authorization, paralegals would be engaging in the unauthorized practice of law by appearing in justice court to represent a litigant in more than a single case. Do you believe that this is simply the court's attempt to protect the state bar from nonattorney competition? Or do you believe the Court was primarily motivated to protect the public from inexperienced lay legal representation? Explain.

3. The *Sparks* court notes that the Montana Constitution vests it with exclusive authority to regulate law practice before the state's courts. Why, then, did the court not rule Mont. Code Ann. §§ 25-31-601 and 37-61-210 unconstitutional, as an impermissible legislative encroachment upon judicial functions?

13.4 HYPOTHETICAL PROBLEMS

Consider the following hypotheticals, which illustrate the various ethical precepts discussed in the first section. For convenience, assume that the courts would accept the NALA provisions as part of the common law pertaining to unethical conduct by legal professionals. Although these problems are hypothetical, they are captioned according to the format used in attorney disciplinary complaints or court contempt proceedings.

 HYPOTHETICALS

In re Piper

Leslie Piper is a legal assistant in the law firm of Hawker, Hillary, Iscoff, & Prill. The firm represents Carl "Bump" Ostrem in a matter involving fraud and misrepresentation. Ulysses Masterdam had sold Ostrem a hot tub, indicating that it was brand new when, in fact, it had been previously used and repossessed. Piper telephoned Masterdam, requesting a complete refund of Ostrem's payment as well as "damages" for misrepresentation. When Masterdam became angry and offensive, Piper threatened criminal prosecution against Masterdam under the criminal fraud statute. Under the ABA's Model Rules and CPR, it is impermissible for lawyers to coerce payment of civil obligations by threatening criminal action.

Has Piper acted unethically? Yes. Piper engaged in behavior prohibited by the ABA CPR and Model Rules by threatening criminal prosecution to settle Ostrem's civil claims. An attorney could not have ethically made such statements; neither could Piper.

In re Nover

Bradley Nover is a paralegal working for the mortgage department of First National City State Bank. One of Nover's duties is to file liens and mortgages at the county recorder's office. The department employs one attorney who is supposed to supervise its six legal assistants, including Nover. However, because of the heavy workload, Nover often finds himself working solo. Nover left a draft of a mortgage release on the lawyer's desk for review. It was returned the next day with no changes. Nover notified Lester Arnold, against whose land the mortgage had been filed. Arnold had just paid the full balance due on the mortgage. Nover told Arnold that the mortgage release would be mailed within the next few days. However, Nover failed to follow through, and the release was never filed. Several months later, when Arnold attempted to sell his realty, he discovered Nover's error. Arnold sued the bank for slander of title.

Has Nover acted unethically? Yes. Nover should have filed the mortgage release after consulting with his supervising attorney and communicating with Arnold. Nover's failure to do so resulted in tortious injury to Arnold. This demonstrates incompetent and improper professional conduct.

In re Quentlen

Sandra Quentlen is a legal assistant employed at the law firm of Bingham, Dingham, & Clingham. She works for three personal injury (P.I.) attorneys in the firm. During the first few months of her training, Quentlen spent much time discussing procedural and substantive legal questions with her supervising attorneys, particularly when she had questions concerning the appropriate discovery forms to use in different circumstances. After six months, however, Quentlen became sufficiently adept at handling discovery that the attorneys simply turned over the client files to her after the initial consultation. Quentlen then proceeded to handle each P.I. file herself, with the attorneys simply signing the appropriate documents. Quentlen met with clients and witnesses; she drafted and filed all interrogatories and motions for discovery; and she handled all witness interviews.

Has Quentlen acted unethically? Yes. Without her lawyers' active supervision, Quentlen has engaged in the unauthorized practice of law by single-handedly coordinating discovery. She has exercised independent legal judgment in preparing and filing discovery documents. She may also have used independent legal judgment in advising clients or discussing legal questions with witnesses. She met with litigants without disclosing her status as a legal assistant.

In re Madisson

Oscar Madisson is a paralegal in the insurance department of Indemnicorp, a large insurance corporation. His duties consist of researching recent developments in tort law pertaining to insurance. He has been employed by Indemnicorp for five years performing these tasks. However, he has not enrolled in any paralegal courses at the local university (which has a legal administration program) since he graduated from the institution six years ago. Unknown to Madisson, the state legislature enacted new legislation substantially revising tort liability for municipal employees. Madisson advised one of the corporation's officers to settle an insurance claim, based upon the old municipal tort liability statute. As a consequence, the insured sued the company for negligence.

Has Madisson committed an ethical faux pas? Clearly. Madisson failed to remain abreast of current developments in the law. His carelessness would also render Indemnicorp liable, under respondeat superior, for his negligence.

In re Walkinski

Donna Walkinski is a legal assistant working at the law firm of Cedar, Pine, Maple & Elm. One of her tasks is to handle initial client consultations. Walkinski met with John and Beverly Parker, both of whom wished to file an action against Michael Denton for cutting down several trees on the Parkers' land without permission. The following conversation excerpts transpired between Walkinski and the Parkers:

WALKINSKI: "Hello, my name is Donna Walkinski. I'll be meeting with you today to discuss that lawsuit you want to file against Denton."

[Walkinski then took the Parkers to the conference room.]

WALKINSKI: "Now let me explain what we'll be doing today. I need to obtain some factual information to use when I prepare your court complaint."

[Walkinski then proceeds to ask various factual questions.]

J. PARKER: "After we complained to Denton about cutting down the trees, he offered to give us the wood for our fireplace. We took it. Does that affect our legal rights?"

WALKINSKI: "No. Denton committed trespass to land by cutting the trees. You can still recover damages for the value of the trees."

B. PARKER: "We sold the cut wood. Would we have to deduct that from what we ask for in court?"

WALKINSKI: "No. Getting the wood doesn't matter at all, as a matter of law."

[At the end of the meeting, Walkinski mentioned the following.]

WALKINSKI: "Now it will take me several days to prepare these pleadings. I will give you a call when they're ready, so you can come back and we will review them and sign them."

PARKERS: "Thank you. We'll make an appointment for next week as we leave."

Walkinski engaged in the unauthorized practice of law. She made no mention of her status as a legal assistant to the Parkers. In fact, the Parkers may easily have believed Walkinski to be a licensed attorney, given her conduct during the consultation. Furthermore, Walkinski provided the clients with independent legal advice which, incidentally, was incorrect.

In re Larken

Edith Larken is a paralegal employed at the law firm of Tried, True, Tested & Tempered. One day she telephoned Simms O'Connor, a dishwasher employed at The Living End, a restaurant against which one of Tried's clients, Amanda Marcia, had several tort claims, including negligence, negligent infliction of emotional distress, and battery. Marcia had contracted food poisoning after eating at the restaurant. Larken telephoned O'Connor to see if he would be willing to make a statement in the case. The following conversation ensued:

LARKEN: "Do you remember anything about the food they were serving that night?"

O'CONNOR: "Yeah, well, the boss wouldn't like me saying this, but there was an awful stench back there [in the kitchen] when they were cooking something."

LARKEN: "Was it the pork? Did anyone say anything to the manager or the cook about it?"

O'CONNOR: "I don't rightly know if it was pork or not. I don't remember anyone talking about it. But the smell was pretty bad. Everybody back there must have noticed it."

LARKEN: "The doctors weren't sure whether the pork made our client sick or something else, so it's important that we know for sure whether the smell came from spoiled pork."

O'CONNOR: "I really don't know for sure. I'm the dishwasher, so I don't work much with the food before it's cooked and eaten. After some folks get done with a meal, it's hard to tell what was on the plate."

LARKEN: "Thanks for your help. I'll be in touch if I need any more information."

O'CONNOR: "Sure, glad to help out."

Larken disclosed client confidences when she told O'Connor about the physicians' uncertainty as to the cause of Marcia's ailment. This admission could be fatal to Marcia's case, in the event O'Connor related the statement to the restaurant management.

In re Dennison

Paul Dennison is a legal assistant employed by Bartram J. Hollingsworth III, attorney at law. One of Hollingsworth's clients is Aslo, Simon & Conley, an investment firm. Hollingsworth instructed Dennison to telephone Doubleday Savings Bank to discuss a computer inaccuracy on one of Aslo's commercial investment accounts. Hollingsworth feared that Aslo might possibly be liable for defamation by computer. Dennison spoke with Ernest Duley, commercial investment coordinator, who himself was a paralegal with whom Dennison attended college. Dennison mentioned the error to Duley. Duley inquired about the high frequency of withdrawals and deposits in the account. Dennison replied that Aslo had to cover "unexpected exigencies." Duley asked Dennison to elaborate. Dennison mentioned that Aslo's had been the primary financing partner in the recent Southside Mall fiasco, in which both Aslo and several of their investment clients "lost a bundle." Dennison told Duley that, as a result, funds from Aslo's client investment accounts had had to be temporarily diverted. Duley warned that this "revenue dunking" was illegal commingling of client and nonclient funds. Dennison laughed, saying, "I guess we can't slip things past you, can we?" Later, Duley recommended to the bank's executive vice president to report Aslo's conduct to the attorney general's office.

Dennison acted unethically. Like Larken in the previous hypothetical, Dennison disclosed confidential client information (i.e., the Southside Mall losses, the commingling of funds). Furthermore, Dennison's involvement in illegal commingling violated the NALA and ABA rules precluding legal professionals from engaging in unlawful or inappropriate activities.

13.5 FURTHER ETHICS INFORMATION

The American Bar Association, as well as some state bars, issues ethics opinions to attorneys advising them of appropriate or inappropriate conduct under certain factual circumstances. State courts also report opinions involving attorney discipline which discuss ethical considerations. Although these cases involve attorneys, many also address legal ethics involving paralegals or legal secretaries. NALA and NFPA have also collected ethics opinions and court cases directly involving legal assistant ethics problems. State paralegal associations may also have researched such cases. One is encouraged to contact these sources for additional ethics information pertinent to one's jurisdiction.

SUMMARY

13.1. NALA has issued two ethics codes applicable to legal assistants. These rules broadly summarize the activities in which paralegals may ethically engage. NALA's Code and Model Standards declare that legal assistants may not engage in the unauthorized practice of law, shall perform delegated duties under attorneys' supervision, shall not apply independent legal judgment, shall protect client confidences, shall maintain professional integrity and educational competence, and shall comply with the various rules and statutes regulating attorneys' conduct.

13.2. The NFPA, another national legal assistant organization, has also issued ethical rules applying to paralegals. They emphasize the paralegal's role in working to provide legal services to the highest standards of ethics and professional integrity.

13.3. The ABA's Code of Professional Responsibility and Model Rules of Professional Conduct apply to legal assistants. These rules provide both broad and particular guidance to attorneys and their staff regarding unethical behavior.

13.4, 13.5. Hypothetical problems provide the best illustrations of unethical versus ethical conduct among legal assistants. One should consult the state bar, the ABA, and paralegal associations, as well as NALA, for further information concerning paralegal ethics practices.

REVIEW QUESTIONS

1. Who has designed ethics provisions specifically addressing legal assistants?
2. In such ethics codes, what activities are specifically authorized? Under which ethics code are these listed?
3. What is the unauthorized practice of law? What types of actions can it include?
4. Under what circumstances are legal assistants permitted to represent clients? What are some courts' reactions?
5. When can legal assistants perform legal tasks? What restrictions apply under the ethics codes?
6. What must legal assistants recall when dealing with clients, adverse parties, witnesses, or the general public?

PROJECTS

1. Brief *Committee on Professional Ethics & Conduct of the Iowa State Bar Association v. Lawler,* 342 N.W.2d 486 (Iowa 1984). What ethical violations did the Iowa Supreme Court determine occurred as a result of the attorney's and paralegal's actions?
2. How is "unauthorized practice of law" defined in your state statutes? What are the penalties for violations?
3. Does your state have a statute that permits lay representation of clients in certain courts? If so, how does it compare to the Montana statute discussed in the *Sparks* case, reprinted earlier in the chapter?

GLOSSARY

abatement An equitable remedy used in nuisance cases; a court order compelling the defendant to cease conducting a nuisance activity.

abnormally dangerous instrumentalities (activities) Activities or objects that are, by their very nature, extremely hazardous to persons or property. These are relevant to strict, or absolute, liability cases.

absolute liability Also called *strict liability*. Under absolute liability, the defendant is liable to the plaintiff regardless of fault. Absolute liability applies in cases involving abnormally dangerous activities, wild animal attacks, and products liability.

abuse of process An intentional tort that occurs when the tortfeasor misuses a civil legal proceeding against another person to achieve an unlawful objective, and the victim is harmed as a result. Misuse can include the threat to misuse legal process.

administrative rules and regulations Rules issued or promulgated by administrative agencies to enforce or interpret statutes and ordinances. These agencies are granted authority to make regulations by enabling acts passed by legislatures.

appellant The party that lost at trial is called the appellant or *petitioner* on an appeal. The appellant argues that the trial court erred in its decisions in the case and that the appellate court should reverse the trial court's decisions.

appellate courts Courts that review the decisions of trial courts to determine if the trial judge made the correct rulings to apply the law to the facts of the case. Appellate courts examine the trial transcripts to determine if the trial judge committed any legal errors that prejudiced the outcome of the case. Examples of appellate courts include the United States Supreme Court, United States Circuit Courts of Appeals, and state supreme courts.

appellate jurisdiction An appellate court's authority to hear appeals from trial or lower appellate court decisions. Examples include the United States Supreme Court, the United States Circuit Courts of Appeals, and the state supreme and intermediate appellate courts.

appellee The party that won at trial is called the appellee or *respondent* on an appeal. The appellee argues that the trial court was correct in its decisions in the case and that the appellate court should affirm the trial court's decisions.

apprehension An element of assault. An assault occurs if the intended victim reasonably fears for his or her physical safety as a consequence of the tortfeasor's actions. This fear is called *apprehension*.

appropriation One type of the intentional tort of invasion of privacy. Occurs when the tortfeasor uses a person's name or likeness, without permission, to gain some benefit.

arbiter-of-law The role of the judge in a trial. As arbiter-of-law, the judge decides all issues of law in the lawsuit, including admissibility of evidence and granting or denial of the litigants' motions.

assault The tortfeasor's attempt to make harmful or offensive contact with another person

429

without consent. Assault is an attempted battery and is an intentional tort. Its elements include the tortfeasor's placing the intended victim in reasonable apprehension for his or her physical safety, and an imminent threat of contact as a result of the tortfeasor's conduct.

assembly defect A theory in products liability concerning whether a defective product is unreasonably dangerous. Errors in product manufacture or assembly may render a product unreasonably hazardous despite a safe design.

assumption of risk A complete defense to negligence. The plaintiff assumes the risk of doing (or not doing) something that resulted in his or her injuries. The plaintiff voluntarily assumes a known risk with a full appreciation of the dangers involved in facing the risk.

attachment A court-ordered remedy in a civil lawsuit, in which the court orders the sheriff to seize the defendant's property on the plaintiff's behalf to prevent the defendant from disposing of the property to avoid paying the plaintiff's judgment. Governmental officials engaged in attachment proceedings are generally immune from intentional tort liability.

attractive nuisance (attraction theory) In the negligence law of many states, owners and occupiers of land owe a duty of ordinary, reasonable care to safeguard their realty for children who might trespass onto the property, having been enticed or attracted there out of curiosity.

bailee Person in possession of personal property that he or she does not own.

bailment An arrangement in which the personal property owner (the bailor) delivers possession of the chattel to someone else (the bailee), who keeps it until the owner requests the item's return or delivery to a third party. In negligence law, different standards of care apply, depending upon who benefits from the bailment. For a bailment for the bailor's sole benefit, the bailee owes a duty of slight care to safeguard the chattel from harm. For a bailment for mutual benefit, the bailee owes a duty of reasonable care. For a bailment for the bailee's sole benefit, the bailee owes a duty of great care.

bailor Personal property owner.

battery The tortfeasor's intentional, unconsented touching of another person in an offensive or harmful manner. Battery is a completed assault and is an intentional tort.

bench trial A trial in which the judge determines the facts of the case and decides issues of law. The judge serves as both trier-of-fact and arbiter-of-law. There is no jury in a bench trial.

beyond a reasonable doubt The prosecutor's burden of proof in a criminal case. The defendant must be proven guilty of having violated the criminal law beyond a reasonable doubt by the judge or jury. This is the most difficult burden of proof to meet.

breach of warranty When a product fails to comply with the seller or manufacturer's guarantee under the sales contract.

burden of rejoinder (or rebuttal) The defendant's burden of proof to disprove the plaintiff's evidence in a lawsuit.

but-for (direct) causation A form of causation of injury in negligence cases. The formula is applied as a question: But for the defendant's actions, would the plaintiff have been harmed? If yes, then the defendant directly caused the plaintiff's injuries.

castle rule Applies in cases of self-defense or defense of others. This rule permits dwellers to use any amount of force, including deadly force, to repel an intruder.

cause-in-fact Cause of injury in negligence cases. If the tortfeasor's actions resulted in the victim's injuries, then the tortfeasor was the cause-in-fact of the victim's harm. Cause-in-fact includes direct, or but-for, causation as well as indirect causation.

cause of action The plaintiff's legal claim(s) against the defendant. Frequently, the plaintiff has more than one cause of action in a lawsuit.

chattel Personal property, such as an automobile, a pet, clothing, appliances, this textbook, or a bicycle.

children of tender years Young children, often under the age of seven years, who are generally immune from, or subject to limited, tort liability. The majority of states still follow the ancient common law that granted absolute immunity for young children committing intentional torts. Most states do not grant total immunity to young children in negligence cases. Instead, the age and knowledge of the child tortfeasor is considered to determine whether negligence occurred.

civil law Law that pertains to disputes between private parties and defines legal rights and obligations between parties. Tort law is an example.

clear and convincing evidence In particular civil cases, usually involving certain intentional torts, the plaintiff's burden of proof to convince the judge or jury to award judgment in his or her favor.

coming and going rule Rule used when employees commit torts while coming to, or going from, work. In respondeat superior cases, this rule helps decide whether an employee's actions fall outside the scope of employment.

coming to the nuisance defense A defense to private nuisance lawsuits that may be used successfully when the plaintiff owns or uses land at a location in which the alleged nuisance activity was previously occurring. The plaintiff is said to have "come to the nuisance" and thus cannot recover against the defendant.

commercial disparagement An intentional tort that happens when a tortfeasor communicates false or misleading statements to third parties about a person's goods, services, or business enterprise. The tortfeasor must intend to harm the victim's ability to use goods, furnish services, or conduct business. There are three categories: disparagement of goods, disparagement of services, and disparagement of business.

common law Judge-made law. Common law is composed of court decisions issued primarily by state appellate courts. Each state has its own common law, which may vary considerably among states. American common law is based upon English common law and is centuries old.

common usage principle Doctrine in strict liability cases that defines abnormally dangerous activities and substances as those not commonly undertaken or used in everyday life.

community In defamation cases, a significant number of persons acquainted or familiar with the victim who see or hear defamatory statements about the victim.

comparative negligence (culpability factoring/ liability apportionment) A defense to negligence. When the plaintiff's negligence contributed to his or her injuries, comparative negligence calculates the percentages of the defendant's and the plaintiff's negligence and adjusts the plaintiff's damages according to the numbers. This is sometimes called *culpability factoring* or *liability apportionment*. The trier-of-fact decides the percentages.

complainant Person filing a criminal complaint with the police or prosecutor.

concurrent jurisdiction Several courts that have the authority to try the same types of cases. For instance, a county small claims court often may hear the same civil cases as a municipal court. Justices of the peace and state district courts often hear the same types of criminal cases.

consent A victim's voluntary acceptance of the tortfeasor's actions, provided that the victim understood (or reasonably should have understood) the consequences of the tortfeasor's behavior. Consent is a defense to every intentional tort.

constitutions The highest form of law in the United States. The United States Constitution is the supreme law of the land. Each state has its own constitution which is the supreme law of that state, subordinate only to the federal Constitution.

consumer contemplation test A theory in products liability concerning faulty product design that makes a product unreasonably dangerous. If a reasonable person would not have anticipated the danger created by the fault in the product, then the product is unreasonably dangerous.

contempt A judicial remedy used if a defendant fails to comply with the trial court's injunctive orders. Used in nuisance cases.

contributory negligence A defense to negligence, which points out that the plaintiff's negligence contributed to his or her injuries. Its elements include the plaintiff's duty of reasonable care to himself or herself and the plaintiff's breach of duty that contributed to his or her injuries. Causation and proximate cause are relevant in this analysis. Contributory negligence absolutely bars the plaintiff's recovery against the defendant.

conversion An intentional tort that occurs when a tortfeasor, without consent, intentionally deprives an owner of possession of his or her chattel, either permanently or for an indefinite period of time. The tortfeasor then *converts* the personal property to his or her own use.

criminal law Law that defines conduct prohibited by legislative bodies, for which penalties, including fines and imprisonment, are prescribed.

damages The injury that the plaintiff suffered as a result of the defendant's actions. The most common types of damages involve loss of money or value. In most tort cases, compensatory damages are awarded, although punitive, or exemplary, damages are sometimes given, particularly in cases involving intentional torts or gross negligence. In nuisance cases, money damages are less common, because courts usually order equitable remedies for nuisance. Courts may issue money damages as an alternative to abatement if injunctive relief would create extreme economic hardship for the defendant.

danger/utility test A theory in products liability concerning faulty product design that makes a product unreasonably dangerous. Under the test, a product is unreasonably hazardous if the danger created by its design outweighs the benefits derived from its use.

defamation Injury to one's reputation in the community; includes *libel* (written defamation) and *slander* (oral defamation).

defamation by computer An intentional tort that occurs when the tortfeasor includes false personal information or false information about a person's credit rating in a computer database. This false information must be communicated to third parties, and it must injure the victim's ability to obtain credit.

defendant The party against whom a lawsuit is filed. The defendant allegedly infringed upon the legal rights of the plaintiff, who filed the lawsuit. In tort law, the *tortfeasor* is normally the defendant. In criminal proceedings, the defendant is alleged to have violated the criminal law.

defense of persons A defense to the intentional torts of assault, battery, and false imprisonment. Its elements include the use of reasonable force to defend or protect a third party from injury when the third party is threatened by an attacking force.

defense of property A defense to the intentional torts of assault and battery. Its elements include the use of reasonable force to protect property from damage or dispossession when another person, called the invader, attempts to injure or wrongfully take possession of the property.

dispossession Occurs when a tortfeasor deprives a chattel owner of possession of his or her property without consent. An important element in the intentional torts of trespass to chattel and conversion.

dominion and control The power that an owner exercises over his or her wild animals. This control is the way in which a person comes to own a wild animal and is relevant to absolute liability cases involving injuries caused by wildlife.

domitae naturae Latin meaning "domesticated nature" and referring to tame, domestic animals. Owners are absolutely liable for injuries caused by their domestic animals only if the animals displayed vicious propensities. Otherwise, the owners would be liable only if their negligence in handling the animals caused the injuries.

duty In negligence law, the obligation to use reasonable care to avoid injuring others or their property. In tort law, duty is the obligation either to do or not to do something.

ejectment Use of reasonable force to expel a trespasser to land.

emotional distress Mental anguish. In the intentional torts called intentional and reckless infliction of emotional distress, the mental anguish is caused by the tortfeasor's outrageous conduct.

entry Occurs when a tortfeasor interferes with a landowner's exclusive right to use the land. There are two types: personal and physical.

equitable remedies Remedies that do not include money damages. Examples include injunctions, restraining orders, and mandamus orders.

exclusive jurisdiction The only court in which certain types of lawsuits may be filed. For example, all bankruptcy cases must be filed in United States Bankruptcy Court.

exclusive right of possession A landowner's right to use his or her property without interference from other persons.

execution (sheriff's) sales Governmental sales of a defendant's property to satisfy a plaintiff's judgment. Governmental officials engaged in execution sales are generally exempt from intentional tort liability.

executive branch One of three branches of government at the federal, state, and local levels. The executive branch enforces and administers statutes enacted by the legislative branch. Examples include the president and the cabinet, governors, mayors, and administrative agencies.

false imprisonment Occurs when a tortfeasor intentionally confines a victim without the victim's consent. Elements of this intentional tort are: confinement without captive's consent, tortfeasor's intent to confine victim, confinement for an appreciable (meaning unreasonable) length of time, and no reasonable means of escape available to the captive.

false light in the public eye One type of the intentional tort of invasion of privacy. Occurs when the tortfeasor publicly attributes to another individual spurious opinions, statements, or actions.

family relationships rule Doctrine used in negligent infliction of emotional distress cases. Under the rule, a bystander may recover damages if he or she witnesses a tortfeasor injuring a relative of the bystander.

fee standard A test courts use in applying the governmental/proprietary distinction. If a governmental agency assesses a fee for an activity, it is considered proprietary. If not, it is considered governmental.

ferae naturae Latin meaning "wild nature" and referring to wild animals. Owners whose wild animals injure others are absolutely liable for the harm.

foreseeability The notion that a specific action, under particular circumstances, would produce an anticipated result. In negligence law, if it were reasonably foreseeable that the plaintiff would be harmed by the defendant's actions, then the scope of duty includes the plaintiff. Foreseeability of injury is another aspect of negligence theory, which falls within proximate cause. Foreseeability is defined in terms of reasonableness.

foreseeable plaintiffs theory A theory used in analyzing negligence cases and, in some jurisdictions, products liability cases. Under this theory, if it were reasonably foreseeable that the injured victim would be harmed as a consequence of the tortfeasor's actions, then the tortfeasor's scope of duty includes the victim. The victim is said to be a *foreseeable plaintiff.* Unforeseeable plaintiffs fall outside the defendant's scope of duty, because their injuries could not have been reasonably anticipated as a result of the defendant's conduct. The theory is also used in products liability analysis: if it were reasonably foreseeable that the injured victim would be an ultimate user of a defective product, then the seller or manufacturer would be strictly liable for injuries caused by the product defect.

fraud An intentional tort that occurs when the tortfeasor intentionally makes false statements to entice the victim to give up something of value to the tortfeasor. Similar to the intentional tort of misrepresentation.

frolic and detour rule Rule used when employees commit torts while sidetracking from regular work activities. In respondeat superior cases, this rule helps decide whether an employee's actions fall outside the scope of employment.

general jurisdiction A court having the right to try a lawsuit involving any type of law. In the state systems, most counties have courts that may try all civil or criminal cases. These are often called district, superior, or circuit courts.

"going for the deep pocket" A phrase commonly used among attorneys and judges in tort cases, meaning that the plaintiff has sued a defendant with sufficient assets to satisfy a tort judgment.

governmental/proprietary distinction In governmental, or sovereign, immunity cases, courts historically have separated governmental actions into two categories: governmental and proprietary. Governmental actions include public protection functions such as fire, police, or ambulance services. In the older common law, these activities were immune from tort liability. Proprietary actions were governmental endeavors that were more business-like, such as supplying utility service to the public. In the older common law, these activities were not immune from tort liability. Courts sometimes applied a fee standard to decide into which category the government conduct fell. If the government charged a fee for the activity, then it was considered proprietary. The distinction is less important today, since many state legislatures have abolished or curtailed sovereign immunity.

governmental (sovereign) immunity Governments' immunity from tort liability for the torts of their employees. In recent years, legislatures have abolished or substantially limited this immunity.

great care An extraordinary degree of caution one uses when involved in exceedingly important activities in which extreme care should be used to avoid injury. This is the standard of care applied in bailments for the bailee's sole benefit.

gross negligence When a tortfeasor's actions or omissions approach willful and wanton misconduct. Gross negligence violates the ordinary, reasonable care standard to extremes.

hot pursuit In the intentional tort defense of rightful repossession, the property owner's prompt pursuit of the person who wrongfully took the property. The term is also commonly used in criminal law for police pursuit of criminal suspects.

imminent danger exception A nineteenth- and early twentieth-century exception to the privity of contract requirement in defective product cases.

impact rule Rule used by a minority of courts in negligent infliction of emotional distress cases. For the victim to recover under this rule, the victim must have suffered some physical contact from the tortfeasor's actions.

in loco parentis Latin for "in place of the parent." It is used with the intentional tort defense of reasonable discipline. Parents may authorize other persons, such as teachers or day care personnel, to supervise their children; supervision includes reasonable disciplinary measures.

in personam jurisdiction Personal jurisdiction. The trial court's authority to make binding decisions over the actual persons involved in the lawsuit. For example, state courts have in personam jurisdiction over state residents.

in rem jurisdiction Object jurisdiction. The trial court's authority to make binding decisions over the object, or thing, in dispute in a lawsuit. This usually involves disputed property rights. *Rem* is Latin for "thing."

independent contractor A person who has entered into a contract with another to perform a specific task. Persons hiring independent contractors are not liable for the independent contractors' torts under vicarious liability.

indirect causation A form of causation of injury in negligence cases. The most common type is substantial factor analysis.

infliction of emotional distress Results from someone's outrageous conduct which is designed to cause another to suffer anxiety, fright, or anguish.

informed consent Occurs when the victim of an intentional tort voluntarily agrees to the tortfeasor's actions, provided that the victim understands (or reasonably should understand) the consequences of the tortfeasor's conduct. This is the knowledge factor of the defense of consent.

injunctions Equitable remedies frequently used in nuisance cases; court orders to defendants to cease and desist from engaging in nuisance activities. Injunctions include temporary restraining orders (T.R.O.s), temporary injunctions, and permanent injunctions.

intent In tort law, the desire to achieve a harmful result that the law defines as tortious.

intentional infliction of emotional distress
An intentional tort that occurs when the tortfeasor's outrageous conduct, which is intended to cause severe mental anguish in the victim, actually causes the victim such emotional suffering as a result of the tortfeasor's actions.

intentional torts Torts in which the conduct is intended to harm another person or a person's property. All intentional torts include two elements: intent and injurious behavior.

invasion of privacy An intentional tort that occurs when someone publicly exploits another's private affairs in an unreasonably intrusive manner. The tort includes four separate versions: appropriation, unreasonable intrusion, public disclosure of private facts, and false light in the public eye.

invitee A person who has been invited onto the premises by the landowner or occupier. This invitation may be expressed or implied. Owners and occupiers owe invitees a duty of reasonable care to discover and correct defects on the real estate. Invitees are sometimes called *business invitees* in older cases.

joinder The process of bringing third parties into a lawsuit. Most often, a third-party defendant is joined into a lawsuit because of his or her liability to the plaintiff.

joint and several liability A form of causation of injury in negligence cases. The theory applies in cases in which two or more tortfeasors combine, or act in concert, to produce the victim's injuries, even though it may be impossible to determine which tortfeasor caused which specific injuries.

judgment A court's decision in favor of one of the litigants. At the trial court level, judgment is given either to the plaintiff or the defendant.

judicial branch One of three branches of government at the federal, state, and local levels.

The judicial branch conducts civil and criminal trials and resolves legal disputes between litigants. It also interprets legislation and examines the actions of the executive and legislative branches to determine if they are constitutional. Examples include the federal courts, state appellate courts, and local trial courts.

jurisdiction The court's authority to try or hear certain types of cases and to bind the parties involved in the lawsuit by its decisions. The two basic categories of jurisdiction are *subject matter jurisdiction* and *jurisdiction over the parties.*

jury trial Trials conducted with a jury. The jury is called the *trier-of-fact* because it decides issues of fact. The judge serves as *arbiter-of-law* to decide questions of law.

last clear chance A plaintiff's response to the defendant's defense of contributory negligence, which states that, although the plaintiff contributed to his or her injuries, the defendant had the last opportunity to avoid injuring the plaintiff. Last clear chance nullifies the contributory negligence defense.

legislative branch One of three branches of government at the federal, state, and local levels. The legislative branch enacts statutes or ordinances that are subordinate only to constitutions in the hierarchy of law. Examples include Congress, state legislatures, city councils, and county commissions.

libel One type of the intentional tort of defamation. Occurs when the tortfeasor communicates to a third person a false and disparaging written statement about the victim. The communication is called *publication.* The victim's reputation in the community must suffer as a result of the tortfeasor's actions.

licensee Persons having permission to be upon another's land. This permission may be expressed or implied. In the negligence law of many states, owners and occupiers of land owe licensees a duty of reasonable care to correct known dangers on the real estate.

limited jurisdiction A court's authority to try only certain types of lawsuits. For example, small claims courts often hear only civil cases involving claims under a certain dollar amount, such as $5,000 or less.

litigation Another term for lawsuit. A dispute between two parties regarding civil or criminal law, in which the parties ask the courts to resolve legal conflicts.

loss of consortium Damages in a wrongful death lawsuit that compensate the surviving family members of a deceased tort victim for lost love or companionship, as well as mental anguish.

maintenance defect A theory in products liability concerning whether a defective product is unreasonably dangerous. If a seller fails to maintain a product properly, and the product later causes injury to the product's ultimate user, then the product was unreasonably dangerous.

malice In malicious prosecution cases, the complainant's intent to file spurious criminal charges against the victim.

malicious prosecution An intentional tort that happens when a private citizen purposely and in bad faith files with the prosecutor a groundless criminal complaint against another person who is acquitted from, or has dismissed, the criminal charges against him or her. The victim must prove some injury as a result of the malicious prosecution, and this is often shown by harm to the victim's reputation. Also occurs when a prosecutor purposely and in bad faith files groundless criminal charges against a defendant.

mandamus order Often called a *writ of mandamus;* a court order compelling a party to a lawsuit to do something related to the litigation. It is one type of equitable remedy.

minors Under traditional common law, persons under 21 (or, under modern common and statutory law, 18) years of age.

misrepresentation An intentional tort that occurs when the tortfeasor knowingly makes false statements or purposefully behaves in such a way as to deceive the victim. Comparable to the intentional tort of fraud.

mistake An intentional tort defense. It is a good faith belief, based upon incorrect information, that one is justified in committing an intentional tort under the circumstances.

mixed nuisance An activity that constitutes both a public and a private nuisance.

motive The goal that a person wishes to accomplish by taking a particular action. In tort law, motive is similar to intent. It is a factor in the intentional tort defense of privilege.

necessary force That degree of force reasonably perceived as required to repel an attack or resist confinement. It is an aspect of self-defense.

necessity An intentional tort defense. Its elements include committing an intentional tort to avert more serious injury caused by some force (other than the tortfeasor) when the tortfeasor's actions were reasonably necessary to avert the greater harm. It is similar to the defense of privilege.

negligence Broadly defined as the failure to exercise reasonable care to avoid injuring others or their property. This includes both actions and failures to act (omissions). Its elements include a duty of reasonable care and scope of duty, breach of duty by the tortfeasor, causation of injury, proximate cause, and damages.

negligence per se Automatic negligence "by itself," or as a matter of law. When a defendant's actions violate a negligence statute, then negligence is presumed to exist without further proof.

negligent acts or omissions When a tortfeasor behaves unreasonably either by doing specific careless actions or failing to do what should have been done to safeguard the victim.

negligent infliction of emotional distress Outrageous conduct by the tortfeasor which the tortfeasor reasonably should have anticipated would produce significant and reasonably foreseeable emotional injury to the victim. By his or her actions, the tortfeasor must breach the duty of reasonable care, and the victim must be a reasonably foreseeable plaintiff.

nuisance An unreasonable or unlawful use of one's real estate that injures another person or interferes with another person's use of his or her real property. There are two types: private and public. When the same activity constitutes both a public and a private nuisance, it may be called a *mixed nuisance.*

nuisance per se A nuisance activity that violates a specific statute, and thus is considered a nuisance "by itself." No further proof is needed to establish nuisance. Most often applied in public nuisance cases involving statutes or ordinances.

occupiers Individuals who do not own but use real estate, including tenants (lessees).

original jurisdiction A court's authority to decide the outcomes of trials. This is the court in which a lawsuit is first filed.

permanent injunctions Abatement orders instructing the defendants to permanently stop doing the nuisance activities.

petitioner The party that lost at trial is called the petitioner or *appellant* on an appeal. The petitioner argues that the trial court erred in its decisions in the case and that the appellate court should reverse the trial court's decisions.

physical manifestations rule Doctrine applied in negligent infliction of emotional distress cases. Under the rule, the plaintiff may recover damages if he or she suffered physical symptoms accompanying the mental anguish.

plaintiff The party filing a lawsuit. The plaintiff is the party whose legal rights have allegedly been infringed by the defendant.

police powers The state's authority to file lawsuits or enact legislation to protect the public's health, welfare, safety, or morals.

precedent Common law decisions made by courts in the past, which direct today's courts in deciding legal issues in litigation. There are two types of precedent: mandatory and persuasive. *Mandatory precedents* must be followed by the courts of a particular system. *Persuasive precedents* are nonbinding decisions originating from outside a particular court system. Precedents may be changed by the courts that issued them

or by higher appellate courts within the same system.

preponderance of the evidence In civil litigation, the burden of proof that the plaintiff must satisfy to convince the judge or jury that he or she is entitled to judgment. This is sometimes called "crossing the 51 percent line," because the plaintiff must "out-prove" the defendant by over half the evidence. More often, it is referred to as making a prima facie case.

prima facie case The plaintiff's burden of proof in civil cases. Normally this is equivalent to the preponderance of the evidence.

private nuisance The use of one's land so as to unreasonably and substantially interfere with another person's use and enjoyment of his or her land.

privilege An intentional tort defense. It is the legal justification to engage in otherwise tortious conduct to accomplish a compelling social goal. For example, the defense could apply in a case in which trespass to land was committed to save a drowning person. Similar to the defense of necessity.

privity of contract A contractual relationship between buyer and seller of a product or service. In tort law, privity was required between the plaintiff and the defendant in nineteenth- and some early twentieth-century defective product cases.

probable cause In malicious prosecution cases, the reasonable belief that the accused is guilty of the alleged crime.

process serving The method by which a defendant in a lawsuit is notified that a plaintiff has filed suit against the defendant. Also called *service of process.* Governmental officials engaged in process serving are generally immune from intentional tort liability.

product manufacturer The maker of a product which, if defective, gives rise to products liability.

products liability A type of strict, or absolute, liability, in which the manufacturer or seller is strictly liable for injuries caused by defective products. Its elements include: the defect must render the product unreasonably dangerous; the seller or manufacturer must be in the business of selling such products; the product cannot have substantially changed between the time it left the seller/manufacturer's hands and the time it reached the ultimate user; the defect must have proximately caused the ultimate user's injuries; and the ultimate user must have used the product properly. Some states add that the ultimate user must have been reasonably foreseeable, and that the seller/manufacturer must have been responsible for the condition in which the defective product was maintained. A few states require a product sale.

professional community standard of care The standard of reasonable care used in negligence cases involving defendants with special skills and knowledge.

proximate cause Legal cause in negligence (and some absolute liability) cases. Proximate cause exists when the tortfeasor's actions cause a reasonably foreseeable injury to the victim. Courts often refer to the plaintiff's injuries as the natural and probable consequence of the defendant's misconduct.

public disclosure of private facts One type of the intentional tort of invasion of privacy. Occurs when the tortfeasor communicates purely private information about a person to the public without permission, and a reasonable person would find this disclosure extremely objectionable.

public nuisance A land use that injures the public at large rather than a single individual. Its elements include the tortfeasor's use of land that unreasonably and substantially interferes with the public's use and enjoyment of legal rights common to the public. The government acts as plaintiff against the defendant. Coming to the nuisance is not a defense in public nuisance cases.

publication A tortfeasor's communication to third parties. Publication is an element of defamation (libel and slander), commercial disparagement, slander of title, and defamation by computer.

purchaser An individual who buys a product. If injured because of a product defect, the purchaser may recover under products liability theory from the seller or manufacturer.

quasi in rem jurisdiction Exists when courts must decide the ownership rights to a specific piece of property between litigants. Occurs most often when the rights to property located in one state are disputed in a lawsuit in that state's courts.

reasonable care The standard of care in negligence cases; the duty to act reasonably so as to avoid harming others. Defined in terms of the reasonable person standard. Sometimes called *ordinary care*.

reasonable discipline An intentional tort defense. Its elements include the use of reasonable force by a parent, guardian, or authorized individual against a child to maintain order or punish unacceptable misconduct.

reasonable force That degree of force reasonably necessary to dispel an attacking force. It is an element of self-defense and defense of persons or property.

reasonable person standard Measurement by an imaginary individual, used to define reasonable care in negligence cases. The reasonable person is expected to behave reasonably under a given set of circumstances to avoid harming others. The tortfeasor's conduct is compared to the reasonable person's to determine if the tortfeasor violated the duty of reasonable care. The trier-of-fact decides the reasonable person standard in a particular case.

reckless infliction of emotional distress An intentional tort that occurs when the tortfeasor's outrageous conduct causes the victim to suffer severe mental anguish. Intent to produce the emotional suffering is not necessary. Instead, it is sufficient that the tortfeasor knew, or reasonably should have known, that his or her misbehavior would produce emotional distress. Often with this tort, the tortfeasor's conduct is wanton, with no apparent regard for the victim's suffering.

remand The decision of an appellate court to send a case back to the trial court with instructions as to how certain legal issues should be correctly decided. This term is often used with *reversed,* which means that the appellate court overturned the trial court's decision in a case.

remedies Relief that the plaintiff receives against the defendant in a lawsuit; commonly include money damages or equitable relief, such as an injunction or mandamus.

replevin A court-ordered remedy in which the court orders the sheriff to seize property that the defendant has wrongfully taken or withheld from the plaintiff. Governmental officials engaged in replevin proceedings are generally immune from intentional tort liability.

res ipsa loquitur Latin meaning "the thing speaks for itself." A burden of proof used in negligence cases. Under this doctrine, the defendant's negligence is presumed as a result of his or her actions. This shifts the burden of proof to the defendant. The doctrine applies in cases in which the defendant had exclusive control over the object or activity causing the victim's injuries. The plaintiff's injuries must be of a type that ordinarily would not have happened unless negligence were involved. The defendant must have been in a better position to prove his or her lack of negligence than the plaintiff was to prove such negligence. Some courts state that the plaintiff cannot have contributed to his or her injuries if the doctrine is to apply.

respondeat superior Latin meaning "let the superior answer." A theory of vicarious liability in which the principal is responsible for torts committed by the agent. It is often used in employer/employee situations in negligence cases.

respondent The party that won at trial is called the respondent or *appellee* on an appeal. The respondent argues that the trial court was correct in its decisions in the case and that the appellate court should affirm the trial court's decisions.

rightful repossession A defense to trespass to land, trespass to chattel, conversion, assault, and battery. Its elements include the use of reasonable force to retake possession of personal property of which the owner has been wrongfully dispossessed, or to which the owner has been wrongfully denied possession. Efforts to retake the chattel must be made promptly after the original dispossession (or denial of possession) occurs.

scope of duty In negligence law, defined in terms of those individuals who might foreseeably be injured as a result of the tortfeasor's actions. This is called *reasonable foreseeability.* The scope of duty includes all those foreseeable plaintiffs who could have been hurt because of the tortfeasor's conduct. This is called *foreseeability of the victim.*

scope of employment The range of conduct that the employer expects the employee to perform as part of his or her job. Under respondeat superior theory, the employer is liable for the torts of an employee when the employee was acting within the scope of his or her employment.

self-defense The exercise of reasonable force to repel an attack upon one's person or to avoid confinement. It is a defense to the intentional torts of assault, battery, and false imprisonment. The reasonable force used to counter an attacking force must be necessary to prevent bodily injury, offensive contact, or confinement.

seller (wholesaler, retailer) Anyone who is in the business of selling goods would incur strict liability to the injured ultimate product user if those goods were defective. The term includes manufacturers, wholesalers, and retailers.

sensibilities In nuisance law, ways in which people's physical and emotional senses are affected.

sensory perception rule Doctrine used in negligent infliction of emotional distress cases. Under the rule, a bystander may recover damages if he or she witnesses a tortfeasor injuring another person, so long as the bystander perceives the event directly through his or her own senses.

slander One type of the intentional tort of defamation. Occurs when the tortfeasor communicates to a third person a false and disparaging oral statement about the victim. The communication is called *publication.* The victim's reputation in the community must suffer as a result of the tortfeasor's actions.

slander of title An intentional tort that results when the tortfeasor falsely and maliciously disparages the ownership rights that an individual has in property. The tortfeasor must intend to hinder or damage the owner's use of the property, and the false statements must be communicated to third parties.

slight care   That degree of caution one uses when involved in unimportant activities in which damage is not a concern. This is the standard of care used in bailments for the bailor's sole benefit.

stare decisis   Latin for "Let the decision stand." A legal doctrine that restricts appellate courts from changing common law precedents frequently. The concept adds stability to the law by honoring long-standing, accepted legal concepts affirmed through generations of court decisions.

statute of limitations   The time period within which a plaintiff must file his or her tort action against a defendant. Time periods vary for different types of torts and among various state statutes.

statutory law   Statutes and ordinances enacted by legislatures. Statutory law is subordinate only to constitutions in the hierarchy of law.

strict (absolute) liability   When the defendant is liable to the plaintiff regardless of fault.

subject matter jurisdiction   The power of a court to try or hear certain types of cases. This authority arises from constitutions or statutes. There are six varieties: original, exclusive, concurrent, general, limited, and appellate.

substantial factor analysis   Form of indirect causation in negligence cases. The tortfeasor is liable for injuries to the victim when the tortfeasor's conduct was a substantial factor in producing the harm.

"taking the victim as you find him"   A theory of negligence cases which states that the victim's injuries were reasonably foreseeable even if the tortfeasor were unaware of the victim's peculiar physical, health, or other preexisting conditions. In effect, the tortfeasor takes the victim as the tortfeasor finds him, and thus proximately causes the harm.

temporary restraining order (T.R.O.)   A type of injunction, which is an equitable remedy. Frequently used in nuisance cases.

tort   A wrongful injury to a person or a person's property. There are three broad categories of torts: intentional torts, negligence, and strict (absolute) liability. Other torts include nuisance and wrongful death.

tort immunities   Absolute defenses against a plaintiff's tort claims. The defendant invokes an immunity defense with which to avoid liability.

tortfeasor   The person who commits a tort. Translated from the Latin, the tortfeasor is the "doer" of the tort.

toxic tort actions   Actions involving toxic chemicals, pollution, hazardous waste disposal and transportation, and other environmentally sensitive issues. This litigation applies many tort theories, including trespass to land, negligence, absolute liability for ultrahazardous substances, products liability, and nuisance.

transferred intent   In battery cases, the tortfeasor's intention to strike another person through some object, such as a thrown stone. Also occurs when the tortfeasor intends to strike one victim but inadvertently hits another individual instead.

trespass   Unlawful or unreasonable interference with the use of someone's property.

trespass to chattel   Occurs when the tortfeasor intentionally deprives or interferes with the chattel owner's possession or exclusive use of personal property. The tortfeasor's possession or interference must be unauthorized, which means that the owner cannot have consented.

trespass to land   An intentional tort that occurs when the tortfeasor intentionally enters upon a landowner's real estate without consent. This trespass interferes with the landowner's exclusive right of possession.

trial courts   One of two types of courts. Trial courts decide particular lawsuits between litigants. They hear testimony, take evidence, and determine who wins or loses at trial. Examples include United States District Courts and local trial courts such as district courts, circuit courts, superior courts, municipal courts, city courts, county courts, magistrate courts, small claims courts, courts of common pleas, or justices of the peace.

trier-of-fact   The role of the jury in jury trials, or of the judge in bench trials. The trier-of-fact weighs the evidence during trial and decides factual issues.

ultimate user   In products liability law, a person who is injured by a defective product. It must have been reasonably foreseeable that the injured party would use the defective product.

ultrahazardous instrumentalities   Activities or objects that are, by their very nature, extremely dangerous to persons or property. These are relevant to strict, or absolute, liability cases.

unforeseeable plaintiffs   Persons whose injuries the tortfeasor could not reasonably have anticipated as a result of the tortfeasor's actions.

unreasonable intrusion   One type of the intentional tort of invasion of privacy. Occurs when the tortfeasor engages in an excessive and highly offensive invasion upon another person's seclusion or solitude.

vicarious liability   The liability of one person (the principal) for the tortious conduct of another, subordinate individual (the agent) who was acting on the principal's behalf. In tort law, the main vicarious liability theory is respondeat superior.

vicious propensity rule   Doctrine in absolute liability cases involving domestic animals. Normally, owners are not strictly liable for injuries caused by their domestic animals. However, if the animals display vicious propensities and hurt someone or some property, then the owner is absolutely liable. Vicious propensities are proven by past episodes of the animal's nasty behavior.

warranty   A guarantee from the seller or manufacturer that a product complies with certain quality standards. Warranties also may be used for services. If a product or service fails to comply with a warranty's standards, breach of warranty has occurred and the buyer may successfully sue the seller for damages incurred.

wrongful death statutes   Statutes giving surviving family members of a deceased tort victim a cause of action against the tortfeasor whose negligence or intentional torts caused the victim's death.

wrongful life actions   Lawsuits for the wrongful birth of a child. Sometimes called *wrongful pregnancy actions*. Most cases involve ineffective sterilization operations, which is basically a form of medical malpractice.

zone of danger rule   Doctrine used in negligent infliction of emotional distress cases. Under the rule, if a bystander witnesses substantial injury to another person, often a relative, then the bystander may recover damages for negligent infliction of emotional distress if he or she fell within the zone of danger created by the tortfeasor's conduct that hurt the other person.

zone of foreseeability   An aspect of proximate cause in negligence cases. If it were reasonably foreseeable that the tortfeasor's actions would produce the victim's injuries, then the tortfeasor proximately caused the harm.

INDEX

NOTE: Italicized page numbers refer to non-text material. Italicized page numbers following the word "defined" refer to definitions in the margins of the referenced pages.